The Poetics and Politics of Place
Ottoman Istanbul and British Orientalism

edited by Zeynep İnankur, Reina Lewis and Mary Roberts

PERA
MÜZESİ

The Poetics and Politics of Place
Ottoman Istanbul and British Orientalism

Edited by
Zeynep İnankur, Reina Lewis and Mary Roberts

Pera Museum Publication 46
Symposium Series 1
İstanbul, 2011

ISBN: 978-0-295-99110-8

Graphic Design
TUT Ajans, www.tutajans.com

Color Separation and Printing
Mas Matbaacılık A.Ş.
Hamidiye Mah., Soğuksu Cad. No:3
34408, Kağıthane, İstanbul
Tel: (0212) 294 10 00 E-mail:info@masmat.com.tr

This book arises from papers presented at the syposium *Ottoman Istanbul and British Orientalism* held at Suna and İnan Kıraç Foundation Pera Museum between 27-28 November 2008.

Distributed throughout the world
(excluding Turkey) by
University of Washington Press
P.O. Box 50096
Seattle, WA 98145-5096 USA
www.washington.edu/uwpress

The editors dedicate this book to
Zeynep İnankur's beloved mother, Türkan İnankur,
who passed away during its preparation.

Contents

Acknowledgments 7

Preface
Suna, İnan & İpek Kıraç 9

List of Illustrations 11

Introduction: Disruptive Geographies
Mary Roberts, Reina Lewis and Zeynep İnankur 19

PART I: Institutions, Collections, Exhibitions

I - Staging *The Lure of the East:*
Exhibition Making and Orientalism
Christine Riding 33

II - Cultural Exchange and the Politics of Pleasure
Reina Lewis 49

III - Bringing It Home?
Orientalist Painting and the Art Market
Nicholas Tromans 65

IV - The Searight Collection
Sarah Searight 77

V - Cultural Consignment and Cultural (Ex)Change
Donald Preziosi 89

VI - Orientalism and Photography
Nancy Micklewright 99

PART II: Constructing History and the Politics of Place

VII - Between the Sublime and the Picturesque:
Mourning Modernization and the Production of
Orientalist Landscape in Thomas Allom and Reverend
Robert Walsh's *Constantinople and the Scenery of the
Seven Churches of Asia Minor* (c. 1839)
Wendy M. K. Shaw 115

VIII - Genealogies of Display: Cross-Cultural Networks
at the 1880s Istanbul Exhibitions
Mary Roberts 127

IX - Osman Hamdi Bey and the Historiophile Mood:
Orientalist Vision and the Romantic Sense of the Past
in Late Ottoman Culture
Ahmet Ersoy 145

X - Traveling East: Veiling, Race, and Nations
Teresa Heffernan 157

XI - "Solitary Eagle"?: The Public and Private Personas
of John Frederick Lewis (1804-1876)
Briony Llewellyn 167

XII - An Ottoman Traveler to the Orient: Osman Hamdi Bey
Edhem Eldem 183

PART III: Cultural Mediators, Boundaries, Exchanges

XIII - Mary Adelaide Walker
Zeynep İnankur 199

XIV - The Dragoman Who Commissioned His
Own Portrait
Aykut Gürçağlar 211

XV - European Artists at the Ottoman Court:
Propagating a New Dynastic Image in the
Nineteenth Century
Günsel Renda 221

XVI - The Interpretation of Pictoral Space in
Nineteenth-Century Ottoman Landscape Painting
Semra Germaner 233

XVII - Orientalism and Aestheticism
Tim Barringer 243

XVIII - The Reception of John Frederick Lewis at the
Exposition Universelle in 1855
Peter Benson Miller 259

Notes on Contributors 273

Index 277

Acknowledgments

The editors would like to thank the Suna and İnan Kıraç Foundation for their generous support of both the symposium *Ottoman Istanbul and British Orientalism* held at the Pera Museum, Istanbul, in November 2008, and the completion of this book. Our personal thanks go to Özalp Birol, General Manager of the Suna and İnan Kıraç Foundation Culture and Art Enterprises, who has been visionary and determined in pursuing the potential he saw in our initial proposal. We also gratefully acknowledge the enthusiastic support for this project from Pat Soden, Director, and Jacqueline Ettinger, Acquisitions Editor at the University of Washington Press. This book owes much to the essential work carried out at the Foundation by Barış Kıbrıs, Fatma Çolakoğlu and Zeynep Ögel whom we also thank very much. Our gratitude also goes to all of those who were involved in production and design of this book, including the copy-editor Kris Wischenkämper, translators to Turkish Melis Şeyhun and Cem Akaş, Turkish editor Nihal Boztekin, layout advisor Ian Whiteling, cover designer Timuçin Unan, his team Selen Baycan Patır and Füsun Dokuz. The editors would like to thank all the owners of paintings and artworks who have so generously given permission for material to be reproduced in this volume.

Preface

Suna, İnan and İpek Kıraç

The first large-scale international exhibition project of the Suna and İnan Kıraç Foundation Pera Museum was *The Lure of the East*, initiated by the Yale Center for British Art and Tate Britain. The seeds of this project were sown in 2005, and the exhibition was held at Pera Museum between September 26, 2008 and January 11, 2009. The exhibition itself, along with the special events and film screenings that accompanied it, received great interest from the public, the media and art circles.

The symposium entitled *Ottoman Istanbul and British Orientalism*, that took place on November 27–28, 2008 at the Pera Museum Auditorium with the participation of local and international scholars, was the most comprehensive oral event of this package.

Organized by a committee made up of Professor Zeynep İnankur from Mimar Sinan Fine Arts University, Professor Reina Lewis from London College of Fashion, University of the Arts London, Professor Mary Roberts from University of Sydney and M. Özalp Birol, General Manager of the Suna and İnan Kıraç Foundation Culture and Art Enterprises, this two-day international symposium hosted twenty-five select scholars and researchers from all over the world as speakers, who discussed Istanbul as a destination for British painters of the nineteenth century and examined the greater ramifications of the cultural exchanges between the Ottoman Empire and Europe during the same period. The speakers also analyzed the relationship between the exhibited works that focused on British art and the Ottoman and Orientalist works in the Suna and İnan Kıraç Foundation collection; other topics included Ottoman patronage of the arts, art training in the Ottoman capital and museum exhibits.

This significant book is comprised of a large portion of the papers delivered at the symposium. We would like to extend our heartfelt thanks especially to Professor Zeynep İnankur, Professor Reina Lewis and Professor Mary Roberts, who have selflessly taken part for over two years in the preparation process, as well as to the management and staff of the Suna and İnan Kıraç Foundation Pera Museum and to all individuals and institutions who have contributed to the making of the book.

List of Illustrations

Figure 1.1 Draft poster design for *The Lure of the East: British Orientalist Painting* exhibition at Tate Britain showing a detail of *Hhareem Life, Constantinople*, John Frederick Lewis (1804–1876), 1857, watercolor, 61.2 x 48.1 cm, Laing Art Gallery, Newcastle-upon-Tyne (Tyne and Wear Museums). (Design by Rose, London UK.)

Figure 1.2 Advertisement design for *The Lure of the East: British Orientalist Painting* exhibition at Tate Britain showing a detail of *Leila*, Frank Dicksee (1853–1928), 1892, oil on canvas, 100 x 126 cm, Private Collection. (Design by Rose, London UK.)

Figure 1.3 Poster design for *The Lure of the East: British Orientalist Painting* exhibition at Tate Britain showing a detail of *The Arab Interior*, Arthur Melville (1855–1904), 1881, oil on canvas, 95 x 72.8 cm, National Gallery of Scotland, Edinburgh. (Design by Rose, London UK.)

Figure 1.4 Front cover of *The Lure of the East: British Orientalist Painting* exhibition catalog showing a detail from *The Arab Interior*, Arthur Melville (1855–1904), 1881, oil on canvas, 95 x 72.8 cm, National Gallery of Scotland, Edinburgh. (Catalog cover designed by Atelier Works.)

Figure. 1.5 Installation photograph taken at the entrance of *The Lure of the East: British Orientalist Painting* exhibition at Tate Britain. (Exhibition designed by Atelier Works. Photography © ChrisGascoigne.)

Figure 1.6 Installation photograph taken within the "Harem and Home" gallery of *The Lure of the East: British Orientalist Painting* exhibition at Tate Britain. (Exhibition designed by Atelier Works. Photography © ChrisGascoigne.)

Figure 2.1 *A Visit: Harem Interior, Constantinople, 1860*, Henriette Browne (1829–1901), 1861, oil on canvas, 89 x 114 cm, Private Collection. Courtesy of Marco Frignati Art Advisory, London.

Figure 2.2 *The Lure of the East*, installation shot showing *A Visit: Harem Interior, Constantinople, 1860*, Henriette Browne, at Tate Britain, June 2008. © Tate, London, 2010.

Figure 2.3 *The Lure of the East* placemats from Pera Museum café, 2008, showing (top to bottom): Frank Dicksee, *Leila* (with Augustus John, *Colonel T. E. Lawrence* detail); John Frederick Lewis *The Courtyard of the Coptic Partiarch's House in Cairo* (with John Frederick Lewis *Hhareem Life, Constantinople* detail); John Frederick Lewis *Hhareem Life, Constantinople* (with Augustus John, *Colonel T. E. Lawrence* detail). Courtesy of Suna and İnan Kıraç Foundation.

Figure 2.4 Location shot, Pera Museum café, Istanbul, showing *Leila* placemat in use. Courtesy of Suna and İnan Kıraç Foundation.

Figure 2.5 *The Lure of the East* poster featuring Augustus John, *Colonel T. E. Lawrence*, with graffiti reading "English spy," and detail, Istanbul 2008. Photograph by Nicholas Tromans.

Figure 3.1 Poster for *The Lure of the East* outside the Pera Museum, September 2008. (Photo: author.)

Figure 3.2 Poster for *The Lure of the East* near the Sharjah Art Museum, February 2009. (Photo: author.)

Figure 4.1 *Mountain Villages in Lebanon*, Rodney Searight (1909–1991), 1935, pencil, 26 x 35.5 cm. Trustees of the Victoria and Albert Museum.

Figure 4.2 *Mount Sinai,* Edward Lear (1818–1888), 1849, pen and brown ink and pencil, 33.1 x 51.1 cm. Trustees of the Victoria and Albert Museum.

Figure 4.3 *Excavation of the Great Temple of Ramesses II at Abu Simbel*, Louis Maurice Adolphe Linant de Bellefonds (1799–1883), probably 1818–19, watercolor over pencil 17.1 x 23.9 cm. Photo © Victoria and Albert Museum, London.

Figure 4.4 *Summer Houses and the Castle of Europe on the Bosphorus*, Thomas Allom (1804–1872), 1846, watercolor heightened with white, over pencil, 19.4 x 30.7 cm. Photo © Victoria and Albert Museum, London.

Figure 4.5 *A Turkish Coffee House*, by Amadeo Preziosi, 5th Count (1816–1882), 1854, pencil and watercolor heightened with white, 40.7 x 58.8 cm. Photo © Victoria and Albert Museum, London.

Figure 5.1 *Woman Dressed in Yasmak in Istanbul*, Amadeo Preziosi, 5th Count (1816–1882), 1841, engraving on paper, 51.5 x 61.7 cm. Collection of the Jewish Museum of Greece.

Figure 6.1 Photograph, photographer unknown, c. 1881–1910, gelatin silver print, 40 x 33 cm, Pierre de Gigord Collection. The Research Library, Getty Research Institute, Los Angeles, California (96.R.14).

Figure 6.2 Album page from album belonging to an officer of 1st BN King's Shropshire Light Infantry, photographer unknown, c. 1882–85, albumen print, album page dimensions 31 x 37 cm, Album 7612-112, no. 3. Courtesy of the Council of the National Army Museum, London.

Figure 6.3 Album page from album belonging to an officer of 1st Dorset Regiment, Zangaki (upper image), lower image photographer unknown, c. 1885–86, albumen print, album page dimensions 55 x 37.5 cm, Album 8408-98, nos 15 and 16. Courtesy of the Council of the National Army Museum, London.

Figure 6.4 Photograph, Abdullah Frères, c. 1860s, albumen print. Courtesy of the Getty Research Institute, Los Angeles, California.

Figure 7.1 *Constantinople viewed from the Golden Horn*, Frontispiece of Allom and Walsh, *Constantinople and the Scenery of the Seven Churches of Asia Minor*, c. 1839. Universitätsbibliothek Basel.

Figure 7.2 *Market Place of Tophane*, Title page illustration, Allom and Walsh, *Constantinople and the Scenery of the Seven Churches of Asia Minor*, c. 1839. Universitätsbibliothek Basel.

Figure 7.3 *Reception Room of the Seraglio*, Allom and Walsh, *Constantinople and the Scenery of the Seven Churches of Asia Minor*, c. 1839. Universitätsbibliothek Basel.

Figure 7.4 *Entrance to the Divan, Constantinople*, Allom and Walsh, *Constantinople and the Scenery of the Seven Churches of Asia Minor*, c. 1839. Universitätsbibliothek Basel.

Figure 7.5 *Baluk Hana and Method of Fishing for the Red Mullet*, Allom and Walsh, *Constantinople and the Scenery of the Seven Churches of Asia Minor*, c. 1839. Universitätsbibliothek Basel.

Figure 8.1 *Tombeau du Sul. Mahmoud*, and detail, Vassilaki Kargopoulo (1826–1886). Research Library, Getty Research Institute, Los Angeles, (96.R.14).

Figure 8.2 *Le Dr Serviçen, Membres du Comité central du Croissant Rouge*, in *Album de la Société ottomane de secours aux blessés militaires: Guerre 1877–1878*, folio 01, Research Library, Getty Research Institute, Los Angeles (96.R.14).

Figure 8.3 *İki Müzisyen Kız,* (Two Musician Girls), Osman Hamdi Bey (1842–1910), 1880, oil on canvas, 58 x 39 cm, Suna and İnan Kıraç Foundation Orientalist Paintings Collection, Istanbul.

Figure 8.4 *Yeşil Türbe'de Dua* (Prayer in the Green Tomb), Osman Hamdi Bey (1842–1910), 1881. © Christie's Images Limited 2011.

Figure 8.5 *The Commentator on the Koran: Interior of a Royal Tomb, Bursa, Asia Minor*, John Frederick Lewis (1804–1876), 1869, oil on wood, 62.5 x 75.5 cm, Elton Hall Collection.

Figure 8.6 *Vazo Yerleştiren Kız*, (Young Girl Placing a Vase) Osman Hamdi Bey (1842–1910), 1881, oil on canvas, 55 x 37 cm, Feryal and Kemal Gülman Collection.

Figure 8.7 *Roumeli Hissar*, Mary Adelaide Walker, From Mary Adelaide Walker, *Old Tracks and New Landmarks. Wayside Sketches in Crete, Macedonia, Mitylene, etc*, (London: Richard Bentley, 1897), illustration facing page 356.

Figure 9.1 *Aksaray Pertevniyal Valide Mosque* (1871), Sarkis and Agob Balyan (architects). Photograph by the author.

Figure 9.2 *In the Tomb of the Princes*, Osman Hamdi Bey (1842–1910), 1908, oil on canvas, 122 x 92 cm. Reproduced by permission of the MSGSÜ İstanbul Resim ve Heykel Müzesi.

Figure 9.3 *Burhaneddin Bey in the Role of Tarık*, after the cover page of *Musavver Muhit* 1, no. 3 (6 Teşrin-i Sani 1324 [November 19, 1908]).

Figure 9.4 *Inhabitants of the Province of Syria*, in Osman Hamdi Bey and Marie de Launay, *Elbise-i 'Osmaniyye/Les Costumes populaires de la Turquie en 1873* (Istanbul: Levant Times and Shipping Gazette, 1873) Part 12, Plate 32.

Figure 9.5 *The Miraculous Fountain*, Osman Hamdi Bey (1842–1910), 1904, oil on canvas. After Adolphe Thalasso, *L'Art Ottoman: Les peintres de Turquie* (Paris: Librairie artistique internationale, 1911).

Figure 11.1 *John Frederick Lewis*, John Watkins (1823–1874), 1864, albumen print mounted on card as a carte-de-visite, 8.8 x 5.9 cm, Royal Academy of Arts, London.

Figure 11.2 *John Frederick Lewis*, "SEM", 1868–74, pencil and watercolor on grey-green paper, 22.2 x 14.2 cm, signed with monogram SEM (or CSM, or CMS), inscribed J. F. Lewis R.A. © Ashmolean Museum, Oxford.

Figure 11.3 *Interior of a Mosque at Cairo—Afternoon Prayer (The 'Asr)*, John Frederick Lewis (1804–1876), 1847, oil on panel, 31 x 21 cm, signed and dated JFL/1857, Private Collection. © Mathaf Gallery, London.

Figure 11.4 *Self-Portrait of the Artist as a Boy*, John Frederick Lewis (1804–1876), 1816–18, pencil on brown wove paper, 16.5 x 11.2 cm, inscribed J. Lewis, Royal Academy of Arts, London.

Figure 11.5 *Self-Portrait as a Young Man*, John Frederick Lewis (1804–1876), early 1820s, pencil and chalk on wove paper, 8.8 x 6.3 cm, inscribed JF Lewis by himself, Royal Academy of Arts, London.

Figure 11.6 *An Arab, Seated in a Cairo Bazaar*, John Frederick Lewis (1804–1876), 1857, oil on board, 31.2 x 20.2 cm, signed and dated JFL/1857, Private Collection. © Christie's Images Limited 2010.

Figure 11.7 *An Arab of the Desert of Sinai*, John Frederick Lewis (1804–1876), 1858, oil on panel, 43.5 x 30.5 cm, signed and dated JFL/1858, Shafik Gabr Collection, Cairo. Reproduced by kind permission of Mr. Shafik Gabr, Chairman and Managing Director of ARTOC Group for Investment and Development, Egypt.

Figure 11.8 *Portrait Sketch of John Frederick Lewis*, Sir Francis Grant PRA (1803–1878), 1865–68, pen and ink wash on a sheet of Royal Academy stationery of the 1860s, 17.6 x 11 cm (sheet size), inscribed on the backing sheet JF. Lewis R.A, Private Collection. Courtesy of Lowell Libson Ltd, London.

Figure 12.1 Kurdish worker standing by a plaque decorated with a low relief of [...] danes, son of Aroandes II, paternal ancestor of Antiochus I of Commagene, on the western terrace of the tumulus of Antiochus on Nemrut Dağı, Osman Hamdi Bey (1842–1910) or Osgan Efendi (1855–1914), May 1883, glass plate negative, 13 x 18 cm, Istanbul Archaeological Museums, photograph collection, negative 11201.

Figure 12.2 Kurdish worker and the monumental head of Apollo-Mithras on the eastern terrace of the tumulus of Antiochus on Nemrut Dağı, Osman Hamdi Bey (1842–1910) or Osgan Efendi (1855–1914), May 1883, glass plate negative, 18 x 13 cm, Istanbul Archaeological Museums, photograph collection, negative 11183.

Figure 12.3 Osman Hamdi Bey reclining on Antiochus' monumental head on the western terrace of the tumulus of Antiochus on Nemrut Dağı, Osgan Efendi (1855–1914), May 1883, glass plate negative, 13 x 18 cm, Istanbul Archaeological Museums, photograph collection, negative 11190.

Figure 12.4 Osgan Efendi next to a monumental eagle head on the western terrace of the tumulus of Antiochus on Nemrut Dağı, Osman Hamdi Bey (1842–1910), May 1883, glass plate negative, 13 x 18 cm, Istanbul Archaeological Museums, photograph collection, negative 11203.

Figure 12.5 Osman Hamdi Bey preparing a cast of a plaque representing the dexioxis (handshake) between Antiochus and Hercules, on the western terrace of the tumulus of Antiochus on Nemrut Dağı, Osgan Efendi (1855–1914), May 25, 1883, glass plate negative, 13 x 18 cm, Istanbul Archaeological Museums, photograph collection, negative 11216.

Figure 12.6 Osgan Efendi preparing a cast of a plaque representing the dexioxis (handshake) between Antiochus and Hercules, on the western terrace of the tumulus of Antiochus on Nemrut Dağı, Osman Hamdi Bey (1842–1910), May 25, 1883, glass plate negative, 18 x 13 cm, Istanbul Archaeological Museums, photograph collection, negative 11173.

Figure 12.7 Group of Kurds at the tumulus of Karakuş. Osman Hamdi Bey (1842–1910) or Osgan Efendi (1855–1914), 18 May 1883, glass plate negative, 13 x 18 cm, Istanbul Archaeological Museums, photograph collection, negative 11175.

Figure 12.8 Group of Kurds in front of the north-western column of the tumulus of Karakuş, Osman Hamdi Bey (1842–1910) or Osgan Efendi (1855–1914), May 18, 1883, glass plate negative, 18 x 13 cm, Istanbul Archaeological Museums, photograph collection, negative 11193.

Figure 12.9 Local figure on horseback, Osman Hamdi Bey (1842–1910) or Osgan Efendi (1855–1914), May or June 1883, glass plate negative, 13 x 18 cm, Istanbul Archaeological Museums, photograph collection, negative 11247. One is tempted to imagine that the man on horseback is no other than Osman Hamdi Bey in local garb. However, the quality of the photograph does not allow for proper verification.

Figure 12.10 Two local figures, Osman Hamdi Bey (1842–1910) or Osgan Efendi (1855–1914), May or June 1883, glass plate negative, 18 x 13 cm, Istanbul Archaeological Museums, photograph collection, negative 11248.

Figure 12.11 Group of armed Kurds, Osman Hamdi Bey (1842–1910) or Osgan Efendi (1855–1914), May or June 1883, glass plate negative, 13 x 18 cm, Istanbul Archaeological Museums, photograph collection, negative 11254.

Figure 13.1 Photograph taken midway through the construction of the Crimean Memorial Church, 1864–65, Crimean Memorial Church's Inventory.

Figure 13.2 Title page of *Broken Bits of Byzantium* by C. G. Curtis and M. Walker (London, 1861), dedicated to Fanny Montrose Curtis by Mary Walker.

Figure 13.3 Illustration by Mary Walker, signed MW. In *Broken Bits of Byzantium* by C. G. Curtis and M. Walker (London, 1861).

Figure 13.4 *Princess Fatma, Daughter of Sultan Abdülmecid, Ruben 1266*, Engraving, Topkapı Palace Museum Library.

Figure 13.5 Illustration facing page 321 by Mary Adelaide Walker from Lady Hornby, *Constantinople during the Crimean War* (London: Richard Bentley, 1863).

Figure 13.6 Illustration facing page 38 by Mary Adelaide Walker from Lady Hornby, *Constantinople during the Crimean War* (London: Richard Bentley, 1863).

Figure 14.1 *The Interpreter of the French Ambassador*, Fenerci Mehmet Efendi, 1811, gouache on paper, 23 x 17 cm, from the Fenerci Mehmed Album, Private Collection of Rahmi M. Koç.

Figure 14.2 *Interprète de la Porte/Dragoman*, unknown Ottoman artist, c. 1779–80, gouache on paper, 20.8 x 14.8 cm, from an album taken from the print collection of the King of Poland Stanisław August Poniatowski to the Library of Warsaw University in 1818. Courtesy of the University of Warsaw Library.

Figure 14.3 *Portrait of Jacobus Tarsia*, unknown painter, second half of the seventeenth century, oil on canvas, 148 x 94.5 cm, Koper Regional Museum.

Figure 14.4 *Portrait of Antoni Łukasz Crutta*, Jean-François Duchateau, (1750–1796), 1775, oil on canvas, 28.7 x 20.9 cm, Warsaw Royal Castle. Photographed by Andrzej Ring.

Figure 15.1 *Genealogical Tree of the Ottoman Sultans*, anonymous, 1866–67, oil on canvas, Topkapı Palace Museum 17/135.

Figure 15.2 *Sultan Selim III*, Jean-François Duchateau, 1792, oil, 33 x 24 cm, Topkapı Palace Museum 17/32.

Figure 15.3 *Sultan Mahmud II*, Marras, 1832, oil on ivory, 6 cm in diameter, Topkapı Palace Museum 17/208.

Figure 15.4 *Sultan Mahmud II*, Henri-Guillaume Schlesinger, 1839, oil, 2.56 x 1.93 cm, Musée de Versailles, 4842.

Figure 15.5 *Sultan Abdülmecid*, David Wilkie, 1840, oil on wood, 70 x 54 cm, Topkapı Palace Museum 17/120

Figure 15.6 *Sultan Abdülaziz*, Pierre Desiré Guillemet, 1873, oil, 140 x 93 cm, Topkapı Palace Museum 17/943.

Figure 15.7 *Sultan Abdülaziz*, Charles Fuller, c. 1872, bronze, Beylerbeyi Palace, Istanbul.

Figure 16.1 *Mosque of Mihrimah Sultan in Üsküdar*, Ahmet Ziya Akbulut, (1869–1938), oil on canvas, 100 x 80.5 cm, Mimar Sinan Fine Arts University Museum of Painting and Sculpture.

Figure 16.2 *Mosque of Mihrimah Sultan in Üsküdar*, Abdullah Frères, end of nineteenth century, photograph, II. Abdülhamid Yıldız Palace Album no. 90819. İ.Ü. Kütüphane ve Dokümantasyon Daire Başkanlığı.

Figure 16.3 *Çadır Pavilion in the Yıldız Palace Gardens*, Abdullah Frères, end of nineteenth century, photograph, II. Abdülhamid Yıldız Palace Album no. 90815. İ.Ü. Kütüphane ve Dokümantasyon Daire Başkanlığı

Figure 16.4 *Çadır Pavilion in the Yıldız Palace Gardens*, Şevki, 1891, oil on canvas, 73 x 92 cm, Mimar Sinan Fine Arts University Museum of Painting and Sculpture.

Figure 16.5 *Impressions from Şehzadebaşı*, Ahmet, end of nineteenth century, oil on canvas, 75 x 101 cm, Mimar Sinan Fine Arts University Museum of Painting and Sculpture.

Figure 16.6 *Street at Şehzadebaşı*, Abdullah Frères, end of nineteenth century, photograph, II. Abdülhamid Yıldız Palace Album no. 90819. İ.Ü. Kütüphane ve Dokümantasyon Daire Başkanlığı

Figure 16.7 *Marmara Bosphorus*, (detail), Mıgırdıç Melkonyan, 1844, oil on wood, silk and canvas, 60 x 90 cm, Naval Museum Istanbul.

Figure 17.1 *A Corfiot Warrior Reclining*, John Frederick Lewis (1804–1876), 1840, watercolor, Private Collection.

Figure 17.2 *In the Bezestein, El Khan Kalil, Cairo (The Carpet Seller)*, John Frederick Lewis (1804–1876), 1860, watercolor and bodycolor on paper, Blackburn Museum and Art Gallery, Blackburn.

Figure 17.3 *Cimabue*, Frederic Leighton (1830–1896), 1868, oil on canvas, 264.8 x 87.6 cm. Photo © Victoria and Albert Museum, London.

Figure 17.4 *A Lady Receiving Visitors: The Apartment is the Mandarah, the Lower Floor of the House, Cairo*, John Frederick Lewis (1804–1876), 1873, oil on panel, Yale Center for British Art, New Haven CT.

Figure 17.5 View of the Arab Hall with tiles by William de Morgan (1839–1917) and frieze by Walter Crane (1845–1915). Leighton House Museum, Kensington & Chelsea, London, UK.

Figure 17.6 *A Frank Encampment in the Desert of Mount Sinai, 1842*, John Frederick Lewis (1804–1876), 1856, watercolor and body color on paper, Yale Center for British Art, New Haven CT.

Figure 18.1 *The Hhareem*, John Frederick Lewis (1804–1876), 1853, watercolor, 88.6 x 133 cm, Private Collection.

Figure 18.2 *The Arab Scribe, Cairo*, John Frederick Lewis (1804–1876), 1852, watercolor, 47.1 x 60 cm, Private Collection. Courtesy of Christie's.

Figure 18.3 *Frieze for a Vase Commemorating the London Exposition in 1851*, Jean-Léon Gérôme (1824–1904), 1852, oil on canvas, 55 x 310 cm, Musée d'Orsay, Paris.

Figure 18.4 *Dancing Dervishes of Constantinople*, After Constantin Guys, from the *Illustrated London News* 23, no. 649 (October 15, 1853): 321. Wood engraving, Bibliothèque Nationale de France, Paris.

Figure 18.5 *Fumeurs en Orient (Smokers in the Orient)*, Constantin Guys (1802–1892), c. 1853–55, watercolor, brown ink and pencil, 21 x 30.5 cm, Musée du Louvre, Département des arts graphiques, Paris.

Figure 18.6 *Prayer in the House of an Arnaut Chieftain*, Jean-Léon Gérôme (1824–1904), 1857, oil on canvas, 66 x 95.25 cm, Najd Collection. Courtesy of Mathaf Gallery, London.

Introduction: Disruptive Geographies

Mary Roberts, Reina Lewis and Zeynep İnankur

This book sets into dialog histories of nineteenth-century British Orientalist and late Ottoman visual cultures by drawing together the distinctive perspectives of specialists in these often separated fields. As the range of material contained in these pages makes clear, these are both issues for art historical deliberation and for curatorial practice which often become embedded in debates about contemporary cultural politics. Prompted by the installation of *The Lure of the East* in Istanbul, our volume takes the movement of these British Orientalist paintings as the exhibition relocated from New Haven, to London, Istanbul and Sharjah as an opportunity to consider the diverse spatial and social relations that underlie historical and contemporary interpretations of Orientalist visual cultures. Thinking through these issues from the perspective of Istanbul, the former capital of the Ottoman Empire, enables a potentially disruptive reframing of debates about Orientalism in terms of Ottoman culture.

Prioritizing the Ottoman capital as a central site of cultural encounter between British artists and Ottoman elites, this volume challenges the often unexamined Western metropolitan bias in the study of Orientalist art. In doing so this volume contributes to the recent emphasis within the fields of art history and post-colonial studies on rethinking Orientalism's "imaginative geographies" through a focus on indigenous engagements and on the uneven and contested cultural politics of regional Orientalisms. The Ottoman Empire and most especially Ottoman Istanbul provides examples of how a non-Western imperial center was engaged in the selective adaptation of Western cultural forms (including Orientalism) in the construction of its own imperially inflected visual culture. In foregrounding this different geography and related processes of exchange, our project extends the more familiar intra-European comparative rubric that often structures the interdisciplinary study of comparative empires. Such an approach reveals multi-directional patterns of influence, encompassing multiple imperial centers as sites where distinctive center–periphery relationships are constructed thereby disrupting a binary formulation of the East/West divide. This approach is exemplified by Zeynep Çelik's recent study of the ways the French and Ottoman Empires constructed, imagined and administered their imperial peripheries through architecture and urban planning.[1] Our book contributes to this rethinking of the role of visual culture in terms of these new geographic vectors, through a focus not on the dominant model of Ottoman–French relations but that between Britain and the Ottoman Empire. This oblique angle offers new perspectives on the study of Ottoman visual culture and insights into both its historical and contemporary resonances. Rethinking the constitutive geographic vectors of imperial cultures has also been a major imperative in recent debates about British art, with which many chapters here are also engaged. The recent volume *Art and the British Empire*, challenges the occlusion of empire from the heartland of British art studies by focusing on diverse British colonial contexts in order to reassert empire as a fundamental category in British art historiography.[2] While sharing this disruptive geographic aspiration, our book shifts the focus outside British colonial territory thereby contributing to such historiographic revisions by resituating British Orientalism within a "connected world of empires."[3]

Where *The Lure of the East* featured only paintings, this book situates painting in the context of other visual and material cultural forms from photographs and other reprographic technologies, to archeology and contemporary café culture. Authors also explore relationships between literary and visual representation in travel accounts by Western and Ottoman travelers to and within the region. This book is structured in three sections with the first section focusing on contemporary practices of collecting and displaying Orientalist and Ottoman visual culture. Highlighting the international mobility of these works, chapters in this section analyze the shifting cultural politics of its diverse recontextualizations. Parts II and III of this book shift attention to the nineteenth-century. British and Ottoman Orientalisms are brought into dialog in Part II as authors examine diverse ways esthetic languages were configured and reconfigured in response to the particularities of place in the cosmopolitan capital of the Ottoman Empire. Chapters in Part III focus on figures and forms of cultural mediation and challenge the ways in which British Orientalism is too narrowly circumscribed when undue emphasis is placed on its distinctiveness as a national tradition.

Part I: Institutions, Collections, Exhibitions

Western Orientalist painting is inherently about movement and places—real and imagined—and the movement of the paintings in *The Lure of the East* from their permanent locations to participate in the exhibition forms one significant set of journeys. But, once assembled into this temporary alliance, the exhibitions' transition to each of its venues provides an opportunity to think afresh about the materiality of the art object, regarding the paintings as mediated cultural artifacts within whose histories of movement and reception this exhibition is but one chapter. Attending to *The Lure of the East* in Istanbul prompts us to think not just about the content of the pictures—the images of the Orient—but of the diverse processes of their physical production, distribution, circulation, exchange, and consumption.

The location of the exhibition in Istanbul brought British Orientalist art into a direct physical relationship with the spaces of the former Ottoman capital that had inspired many of those artists in the nineteenth century. But more than this return to "source," the exhibition's arrival was facilitated by and seen in the context of particular developments in collecting and public display in contemporary Istanbul. Here, the works were viewed in conjunction with the Pera Museum's permanent collections of Ottoman and Orientalist painting, in particular through the accompanying exhibition *Istanbul: The City of Dreams* curated by Zeynep İnankur, Barış Kıbrıs and Günsel Renda. This context immediately inserted British Orientalism within a framework of comparative cultures and artistic exchange, telling a story of new audiences for Orientalist art and of new and multiple Orientalisms.

The Pera Museum is the only museum in Turkey to specialize in Orientalist painting. Established in 2005 the museum is based on the collections of the Kıraç and Gönül families, notably the Orientalist paintings collected since the 1970s by the museum's patrons, Suna and İnan Kıraç, and augmented by Suna's sister Sevgi and her spouse Erdoğan Gönül. The development of this collection and the decision to create a public museum is emblematic of the political and cultural power of the Turkish Republican secular commercial elite in the last quarter of the twentieth century. Families like the Koç, as well as the Sabancı and Eczacıbaşı have played a significant role in the development of public cultural and intellectual life through the endowment and management of museums, universities, and research centres.

That *The Lure of the East* could be seen in the context of the Kıraç collection of Western Orientalist paintings and Ottoman material culture, paintings, and decorative arts, is the result of a more recent instalment in the longstanding movement of Western art into the domain of the erstwhile Ottoman empire and demonstrates the importance of historical and contemporary commercial contexts. Yet the acquisition in the twentieth century of Western Orientalist painting marks a new and distinct phase in the exchange of Orientalist images. As is well documented, and discussed in this volume, it is common today to acknowledge that the largest market for Orientalist art is the Gulf, but initially the most marked revitalization of commercial interest lay more with North Africa and the Middle East, notably Turkey. Changing regional economies mean that Turkish buyers are now often outstripped by Gulf collectors, in a shift towards different markets with a concomitant shift of preferences for different types of Orientalist art.

Nicholas Tromans, the curator of *The Lure of the East*, provides a fascinating account of recent developments in the market for Orientalist art. This supports his compelling argument that art history should more often include within its analysis the mechanisms of the art market rather than studying only its commodities. Putting Orientalist paintings into a material studies frame, Tromans incorporates into critical practice auction house and dealer marketing materials identifying them as a crucial mode by which meaning is made. In this way, he suggests, the significance of Middle East/North African buyers is not simply that they keep prices buoyant, but that their geographically specific consumption activities are mobilized by the market in the creation of new forms of value for Orientalist art. In the promotional discourse of the commercial art sector, the apparent abilities of Middle Eastern buyers to adjudicate which paintings are "authentic" in their representation of regional life is validated as a new form of cultural capital that can rescue paintings from criticisms of imperialistic misrepresentation of Eastern cultures: "The market likes to talk about pictures being allowed, courtesy of the salesroom, to regain a lost homeland."

The different reasons why collectors might favor particular artists, scenes, or geographical references, become a crucial element of a wider discussion of the pleasures available in the consumption of Orientalist imagery, attending to the distinct temporalities and spatialities in which art objects are encountered and to the different gazes that rest on them. One of the key arguments of this book concerns precisely how these networks of economic, social, and personal relations, differently constituted in particular places and times, have an impact on the movement of art objects and the ways in which we are able to view them.

The three chapters in this volume about *The Lure of the East*, by Nicholas Tromans, Christine Riding, and Reina Lewis, together provide a sustained critical analysis of the contextually specific resonances of this exhibition in its various iterations. Each offers the "behind the scenes" information that is rarely brought into the public domain. Christine Riding, the Tate's curator and project leader for *The Lure of the East*, provides an insider account of the processes of curating and marketing that explores how and why generic curatorial and institutional procedures took on particular valencies in relation to the theme of this exhibition. Whereas most gallery visitors experience an exhibition as a fully finished, self-contained entity, her account makes visible the might-have-beens and what-ifs that lie behind the apparently securely bounded exhibition and accompanying catalog.

As Riding's frank account demonstrates, unlike other historical exhibitions at Tate Britain, this exhibition posed pressingly contemporary political dilemmas for the gallery when it was installed in 2008. As the first Orientalist exhibition in a major public gallery after the 9/11 attacks of 2001, and seen in the UK after the London bombs of 7/7 in 2005, *The Lure of the East* emerged at a time when museums and galleries in the UK were charged by government policy not only to represent and respond to the diversity of the population but also through their activities to contribute to "social cohesion." As British concepts of multiculturalism shifted from a focus on ethnicity to one concerned with faith, the potential religious sensitivities of the exhibition were not surprisingly seen as acute. As Lewis and Riding both discuss, the Tate's extended interpretation strategy was designed to bring alternative voices and perspectives into the space of the gallery. External communications were similarly loaded. Riding's fascinating revelations about the debates between the marketing and curatorial teams over the poster for *The Lure of the East* brings into critical awareness the full range of institutional discourses that mediate the public interaction with the images.

The desire at Tate Britain to provide an interpretive frame that could accommodate both the "conventional" museum visitor and reach out to/avoid offending viewers of Muslim or Middle Eastern origin resonates with Donald Preziosi's argument about the always ideological role of the object in the museum. He argues that the primary concern of the public museum—national, regional, or ethnic, and privately or publicly funded—is the "social management of memory and desire," through the organization of objects/relics. Identifying museums as central institutions for the construction of collective histories that serve to legitimate the preferred version of the present, Preziosi emphasizes the temporal and locational contingency of our interaction with objects. Reflecting on his own melancholic encounter in the Jewish Museum in Athens with his ancestor Count Amadeo Preziosi's painting of the Jewish cemetery in Istanbul, Donald explores how our personal response to individual objects is inevitably linked to modes of accumulation and "dramaturgic" display. Seen as always in process, the apparently "closed" collection must inevitably, he argues, invoke the extraneous or expelled objects outside the gallery doors. The point for Preziosi is "that collection always co-exists, and is co-defined and co-determined by, re-collecting and de-collecting or deaccessioning." Processes of deaccessioning can extend from epistemic and actual violence in the excision of images to apparently uncontentious alterations to the archive whose implications like all modes of collection formation are never solely esthetic.

Nancy Micklewright is also concerned with the implications of archiving and collecting in her exploration of Orientalist photography. Her chapter issues a challenge to what has emerged as the canon of Orientalist photography that has, she argues, given disproportionate importance to ethnographic scenes of local people and the notoriously sexualized depictions of Oriental women. This narrow focus, she asserts, seriously "distorts the historical record." As an antidote, Micklewright emphasizes the vast cache of photographs of and from the region available for study. Looking initially at albums compiled by British soldiers serving in the Middle East in the 1880s, Micklewright points to the total absence of this type of imagery in the military albums. Illustrating the often unseen diversity of photographic collections, she evaluates how the dissemination of more celebrated private collections can impact on scholarly and popular understandings. Comparing the Jacobson Collection acquired by the Getty Research Institute with one of the several recently compiled popular large format books on Orientalist photography, Micklewright analyzes the persistence of the (often eroticized) exotic as the organizing principal of these compilation activities. For historians of photography faced with a vast quantity of photographs from which to select, the significance of these or other current collections lies not just in particular images, but in their potential popular or crossover appeal. The popularity of collecting Orientalist photographs, due in part to their relative financial accessibility as compared with paintings, provides evidence of visual Orientalism's ongoing lure, demonstrating that for many "amateur" collectors, including those whose personal access to acquisition is restricted to reproductions online, or in books, posters and postcards, the familiar Orientalist pleasures of the exotic still hold their appeal.

Precisely to whom, how, and in what ways Orientalist pleasures can be recuperated is explored by Reina Lewis in her analysis of *The Lure of the East* in its first three locations. Reporting that this exhibition provided her first chance to view Henriette Browne's *The Visit*, Lewis reflects on how scholarship in the area has developed since her initial studies of Western women Orientalists. It is not simply, she points out, that new primary research has "unearthed" further instances of women's contributions to Orientalist and imperial cultures. This archival activity has gone hand in hand with and contributed to the development of new critical approaches in theories of the female gaze and feminist postcolonial studies. Mounting a combined challenge to the masculinist presumptions of early postmodern theories of pleasure, it becomes possible to recognize diverse forms of Orientalism and the multiple modes of pleasure they permit. Emphasizing that visual pleasure is always historically contingent and located, Lewis addresses how *The Lure of the East* became a flashpoint for pleasure or panic in its different moments of production and display. Her nuanced account of post 9/11 and post 7/7 British multicultural politics sensitively evaluates the Tate's interpretation strategy. Emphasizing the materiality of cultural artifacts, Lewis attends to the different patterns of purchasing and lending that characterize the new patrons of Orientalist art, relating generational changes in the Middle East and Gulf art market to the development of regional Orientalist nostalgias in which the local past can be recuperated variously as exotic, ironic or authentic by both tourists and mass consumers as well as local new and established elites. Situating the exhibition at the Pera Museum as part of the revitalization of the old European quarter for contemporary consumer culture, Lewis explores how both the secular liberal elite and the emergent Islamic commercial bourgeoisie are able to utilize the late Ottoman past to create new forms of, often surprisingly linked, cultural capital as both groups seek to develop Istanbul as a global city and centre for regional capital.

On a related vein, as Tromans makes clear, the shift in regional wealth that initially moved the centers of consumption of Orientalist painting from Turkey and North Africa to the Gulf is now also accompanied by an investment in the generation of local and international prestige through the endowment of public exhibition spaces and museums, such as the project in the Emirates to which the Sharjah exhibition was linked. But in most cases, the development of a private collection precedes the museum that might, like the Pera Musuem, subsequently house it. Once constituted as a museum collection subsequent purchases will likely fall under a mix of private and professional purview, but the foundational role of the private collector in the genesis of the subsequently public collection requires recognition and analysis.

One of the key players in the revaluation of Orientalism in Britain was the private collector, Rodney Searight, whose daughter Sarah Searight's account here of how he built his collection starting in the 1950s demonstrates the impact of collectors on both the popular, commercial and academic reception of Orientalist art. She explains that when he first began collecting Orientalist representations he was one of the very few buyers and even into the 1960s the work was as she puts it, "disgracefully cheap." Rodney Searight did not limit himself to paintings, he collected topographic drawings, sketches, and books, nor did he privilege professional practice over the work of amateurs, which is one of the reasons why his collection, housed at the Victoria and Albert Museum since 1987, remains such a valuable scholarly resource. Like the Orientalist artists whose work he collected, Searight's interest was directly linked to his experiences working in the region, in his case for the oil industry. The collection rapidly expanded after his retirement in the mid-1960s and the first of several important public exhibitions of the work was held at London's Leighton House in 1971. Searight became increasingly determined that his collection should remain intact and available as a public resource. In his lifetime, Rodney Searight was himself such a resource: often indispensible in matters of attribution and provenance when consulted by scholars, dealers, and collectors. Paradoxically, his contribution to the successful re-evaluation of Orientalist art in combination with the rise of oil wealth in the region raised interest in Orientalism to the extent that he was by the 1980s often priced out of the market that he had helped to create.

The varying spending power of different regional elites is a key factor in the shift in buying patterns for Orientalist art, but so too are generationally driven changes in taste. In the 1980s the primacy of the Turkish market was recognized by Sotheby's. Today, with Orientalist paintings realizing higher prices, these sales may have shifted in focus to Gulf buyers, but the development by London dealers of Turkish collectors as a niche market continues with the sale of contemporary Turkish art—often previewed to collectors in Istanbul only to be sold in London, to predominantly Turkish buyers. As art works accrue value through their movement from Turkey to London—still recognized as the prestige generating center for art sales—and then with many of them coming back to Turkey for private collection and display, the ways in which different modes of moving art objects can confer distinction on artists and owners are yet again demonstrated. In the Turkish context, such practices of collection, display and patronage of European art have a longstanding history that had an impact upon contemporary engagements with this art. Chapters in Part II shift focus to this nineteenth-century context thus forging links between contemporary and historical interpretations of Ottoman and British visual cultures. This book brings the two into view of each other in order to historicize the present without presentizing the past.

Part II: Constructing History and the Politics of Place

The challenge that many authors in this volume address is how to conceptualize cultural encounter and exchange in the context of nineteenth-century Istanbul. The cosmopolitanism of the multi-ethnic, multi-religious Ottoman Empire was, as Teresa Heffernan argues, profoundly threatening to some nineteenth- and early twentieth-century British travelers to the city who sought to impose legibility premised upon racial and ethnic categories derived from contemporary European racial sciences. Heffernan's attention to the complex structures of racial thinking in British travel literature provides crucial insights about the broader context for British Orientalist visual culture. The oft-repeated assumption in these texts about the enslavement of Muslim women was, Heffernan argues, an expression of a British Imperialist "desire to police race, class, and national boundaries." For other British visitors and long-term residents, however, particularly expatriate painters, the cosmopolitan Ottoman capital provided professional opportunities unlikely to have been available to them in Britain as they initiated art exhibitions and capitalized upon elite Ottoman patronage which included elite Ottoman women. Staff and associates of the British embassy were important conduits for visiting professional British artists but were also major players in Istanbul's local art scene. The primary patrons of the arts in this city were, however, the Ottoman Sultans who sponsored and collected the work of Ottoman, Levantine and foreign artists. Painting was primarily an elite preoccupation within nineteenth-century Ottoman society and was forged through an engagement with European artists and art institutions.[4] Analyzing British art in this complex site of cultural contact and exchange prompts a reconsideration of the cultural politics of nineteenth-century British Orientalism.

One of the unexamined assumptions about British Orientalism is the focus on Europe, particularly Britain, as the site for display and critical reception of this art in the nineteenth century. To date the focus within art historical studies has primarily been on Orientalist works by professional British artists exhibited at London's major institutions such as the Royal Academy and the Old Watercolour Society. Shifting the focus to Istanbul, Mary Roberts analyzes two British-initiated exhibitions held there in the early 1880s and the concomitant questions this raises about the politics of display. The contested critical reception of the 1880 exhibition, Roberts argues, reveals how Istanbul as an artistic "contact zone" was contested and differentially construed by nineteenth-century Ottoman and British art critics. So too, the paintings produced in this context reveal, Roberts argues, different ways cultural identities were constructed through an esthetics of place—from the British expatriate Mary Walker's "mobile panorama" of Istanbul to Osman Hamdi's representation of cultural patrimony in the Empire's former capital. As cultural events involving Istanbul's Ottoman and European painters, these exhibitions are on the margins of British art, but by placing them within this rubric as part of the exhibiting genealogy of *The Lure of the East*, Roberts challenges the study of British Orientalism as a hermetic national category. Indeed this geographic shift disrupts the very framing of British Orientalism as circumscribed by national parameters. Roberts proposes instead that we understand these British-initiated art exhibitions not in binary terms of Britain's representation of its "others," but instead in terms of intersecting networks forged through shifting national, pedagogic, gender-based and local alliances between Istanbul's Ottoman Muslim and non-Muslim elites, visiting and resident Europeans.

This shift to Ottoman Istanbul as a focus for a study of British Orientalism also raises questions about how other British artists who represented the city inscribed a particular esthetics of place. What happens to familiar Orientalist and colonial visual conventions when they are deployed by British artists to represent the capital of the Ottoman Empire? Some of the visual tropes that function to bolster imperial claims when representing British colonial territories, such as India or Australia, are disabled or reconfigured in the context of Istanbul as these imported conventions intersect with the geopolitics of this particular place.

Wendy Shaw addresses this issue in her chapter by examining the ways in which the conventions of the sublime and the picturesque operate in Thomas Allom's now iconic representations of the capital in his *Constantinople and the Scenery of the Seven Churches of Asia Minor.* Shaw invokes a notion of the "itinerant imperialist" to characterize the operations of the picturesque in this context, a counterpoint to British colonial representations of India. The challenge was to assimilate Ottoman rather than British imperial modernization via the vocabulary of the picturesque. Shaw identifies a range of strategies by which British ambivalence towards Ottoman modernization is contained through image and text, including: selective representation that favors an overdetermined exoticism; misrecognition where prior modernization in the capital was construed as traditional Ottoman urban forms; and a focus on the Ottoman Christian subject as avatar of modernization thereby preserving the Muslim other of Europe. The picturesque is thus posited in these British representations of Ottoman Istanbul as a framing device that "foreclosed a relationship between the future and its past." In this and other chapters in this volume new terms and categories are coined to characterize the way familiar esthetic devices are reconfigured to encapsulate the particular forms of spectatorial experience derived through an encounter with the city of Istanbul.

How are such British Orientalist representations of Ottoman Istanbul to be distinguished from those by contemporaneous Ottoman artists? What kinds of esthetic choices were made by Ottoman painters working in their capital? For the authors in this book who are analyzing nineteenth-century Ottoman painting, answers to these questions pivot around an examination of the complex ways in which Ottoman painters inhabit European esthetics and how they reiterate and redeploy Orientalist tropes. Such an approach resists an anachronistic or binary logic that has often structured previous discussion. In using the categories of Ottoman, Orientalism, and Ottoman Orientalism, authors in this volume resist assuming that these are either mutual exclusive terms or that they can be deployed ahistorically as categories. Instead the particular and at times contradictory histories of Ottoman forms of engagement with European Orientalist esthetics and tropes is rigorously investigated. These chapters make clear the limitations of any overarching simplification that forces a choice between determining categorically that nineteenth-century Ottoman artists are either figures of resistance to European Orientalism *tout court* or simply acquiescent to Orientalist conventions and politics. Instead there is an insistence on historicity, not in order to evade the issue of the politics of this art, but rather to register its myriad complexities.

Ahmet Ersoy, for example, argues that the esthetic language of academic Orientalism was particularly felicitous for the articulation of an Ottoman historical imaginary in Osman Hamdi Bey's art. The Tanzimat period of modernization initiated by the Ottoman State in 1839 brought with it a profound sense of rupture from Ottoman history. Ersoy makes the case that in this context Orientalist painting provided an esthetic language by which Osman Hamdi was able to create the pictorial fiction of access to that past. For Ersoy, Osman Hamdi Bey's historical genre paintings use the visual language of academic realism to invoke the Ottoman past as a fantasy space, but do so, he proposes, by referencing a local milieu in which to imagine a contemporary relationship to the past. Osman Hamdi's persistent use of embedded self-portraiture in his historical genre paintings reinforced such associations. This antiquarian urge was coterminous with a traditional craft revival and both are invoked through the visual pleasures in Ottoman artifacts that suffuse so many of Osman Hamdi Bey's canvases.

The status of the Ottoman elite in relation to debates about Orientalism and Empire has been of particular interest to historians, political theorists, cultural, architectural and art historians in recent years. Responding to Edward Said's early formulation in his now seminal book *Orientalism*[5], about the various ways that imperial power relations structured Western representations of Middle Eastern cultures, scholars have developed new understandings of the terrain as characterized by uneven and shifting relations of cultural, political and commercial exchange. These relationships impacted on both the Western imperial centers and those territories and cultures discursively produced as its peripheries. In this light, the Ottoman Empire emerges as a prime exemplar by which to disrupt the previously dominant binary model of Western imperial center and colonial margin. The fact that the Ottoman elite were representatives of an imperial power that was non-Western and Muslim complicates neat divisions of power relations along religious and geopolitical lines in the age of European imperial ascendancy. Ussama Makdisi, for example, has extended and particularized Said's initial formulation by "looking at how Ottomans represented their own Arab periphery as an integral part of their engagement with, explicit resistance to, but also implicit acceptance of, Western representations of the indolent Ottoman East." Attending to "Ottoman Orientalism" in this way, Makdisi argues, complicates "the simple dichotomy of Western imperialism/non-Western resistance that has characterized so much recent historiography of the Ottoman and non-Western world."[6] Osman Hamdi Bey is a central figure for the articulation of this concept in relation to visual culture. For Makdisi,

Osman Hamdi Bey's role in articulating Ottoman Orientalism is typified by his archeological interests in Baalbek and Sidon, and Istanbul's Imperial Museum, along with his role in the costume book project that the Ottoman State presented as part of its contribution to the Vienna Universal Exposition of 1873. So too in recent years art historians have debated the cultural politics of Osman Hamdi Bey's paintings complicating existing formulations about visual culture in terms of early Saidean Orientalism.[7]

Edhem Eldem intervenes in this debate in his chapter for this volume, nuancing the analysis by rejecting the either/or designation of Orientalist or Ottoman Orientalist, embracing both categories and asserting their applicability at different points in Osman Hamdi Bey's career. Eldem analyzes the shifting perspectives on the Empire's peripheries inscribed in various writings about Osman Hamdi's travels between Istanbul, Paris, Baghdad and Eastern Anatolia. This approach registers the shifting designation of centers and peripheries in these texts, bringing into focus three distinct moments. Hamdi Bey's early letters from Baghdad reveal the harsh edge of Ottoman Orientalism in his demeaning characterization of local residents. This approach contrasts with the detached colonial/Orientalist tone in the 1883 account of his trip to South Eastern Anatolia and Kurdistan, a text which registers an ethnographic approach to the local Kurds tinged with exoticism. Such an approach is imbued with a nostalgic inflection in the 1896 fictional accounts of his Baghdad years that were written by Lindau but based on conversations with Osman Hamdi Bey. Osman Hamdi's approach to the Empire's peripheries across these texts, Eldem argues, shift from more locally engaged Ottoman Orientalism to Orientalism as his role mutates from passive observer to active participant. Such a shift parallels Osman Hamdi's physical and professional mobility; from a junior Ottoman bureaucrat immersed in local political concerns to a more nostalgic romanticized view of the Empire's peripheries, the reflections of an older man back in the Empire's capital.

Edhem Eldem's argument against a single and consistent characterization of Osman Hamdi's contribution to nineteenth-century culture is borne out in the complex picture of the artist's cultural practice that emerges across the various chapters in this book. This can simultaneously accommodate Ahmet Ersoy's argument about Osman Hamdi's paintings as articulating an Ottoman historical imaginary, and Mary Roberts's revelation of the historical and contemporary political resonances of Osman Hamdi's painting of the Bursa tomb of Sultan Mehmed I for the Ottoman critic in 1880 (from which she derives the concept of a "devotional effect," an affective spectatorship fusing political patriotism with religious devotion), as well as Edhem Eldem's complex picture of Osman Hamdi Bey's shifting construction of the Empire's peripheries and the concomitant changes in his self-fashioning.

The discussion about Ottoman art in this period is most often contextualized in relation to contemporary French painting because it was in Paris that a number of these artists were trained. The focus, in this volume on British and Ottoman painters therefore offers the possibility of some novel conjunctions and comparisons. Just as authors in this book emphasize a more complex account of Osman Hamdi Bey, Briony Llewellyn argues for a similarly nuanced understanding of John Frederick Lewis's self-fashioning through her analysis of the complex range of self-portraits that he produced across his career. Lewis spent a year in the Ottoman capital in 1840–41 and yet he is most readily associated (and associated himself) with the subsequent decade he spent in Cairo. As Llewellyn argues it was the Ottoman-Egyptian elite who became the point of identification for his "Oriental" persona as he selectively adopted elements of traditional Ottoman dress in his Eastern self-portraits. Analyzing Lewis in the context of a study of Ottoman Istanbul is a reminder of the close cultural ties between the Ottoman and Ottoman-Egyptian elites, even in these years when such relations were politically strained. Just as Osman Hamdi Bey's journeying produced a range of complex constructions of self and other, so too Lewis, Llewellyn argues, produced a contrasting, sometimes conflicting range of self-representations. Lewis produced most of his Eastern self-portraits once he had returned to Britain, many of them embedded within his Orientalist genre paintings. These portraits, Llewellyn agues, are to be understood alongside his other self-representations as a respectable Victorian gentleman. Analyzed together they reveal Lewis's ambivalent relationship to his professional context in Britain. He was, Llewellyn argues, a distinguished member of the British art establishment who ricocheted between public display and reticence, a recluse with an ongoing concern about his public persona.

Part III: Cultural Mediators, Boundaries, Exchanges

Analyzing nineteenth-century British Orientalism in Ottoman Istanbul brings into focus figures who to date have been marginalized or occluded from histories of British art. This encompasses local Ottoman patrons for visiting British artists and figures of cultural mediation such as translators and the long-term British residents of Istanbul. Authors in this volume offer both new archival findings about these individuals as well as critical reassessments of their contribution to visual culture. In doing so these scholars are expanding the canon of Orientalism and refashioning the parameters by which it is understand.

While John Frederick Lewis's visit to Istanbul was a notable, but relatively minor part of his career as an artist, and his identity as an Orientalist painter was founded primarily on his Cairo decade, his professional reputation was consolidated through his subsequent career as an Orientalist painter back in England. His current sanctioning as the major British Orientalist of his generation is due in part to his professional successes in the capital of the British Empire. The artistic career of his countrywoman, Mary Adelaide Walker, is the antithesis of this narrative and a comparison between the two is illuminating. Her marginality in British art histories is attributable to her position as both a woman and a foreign resident.

Yet as Zeynep İnankur demonstrates Mary Walker was a well-known figure in the Istanbul art scene in the nineteenth century, with an artistic career that spanned fifty years in the Ottoman capital. She received numerous prestigious art commissions through the highest levels of Ottoman patronage, was one of the capital's important art teachers for Ottoman, Levantine and foreign women in both private and State-funded educational institutions and was also a major contributor as both exhibitor and member of the organizing committee for the art exhibitions held in the Ottoman capital in the 1880s. Through her painstaking research, İnankur has brought Walker into greater visibility and the figure that emerges through this is intriguing. Walker's is not the more familiar narrative of the colonial amateur woman artist, but instead that of a professional painter who received prestigious art commissions at the highest levels of Ottoman society despite never exhibiting at the Royal Academy or any of the other major British art institutions. Well connected within British diplomatic and Ottoman circles Walker was, İnankur argues, an important figure of cultural mediation in nineteenth-century Istanbul.

In the multi-lingual environment of Ottoman Istanbul the translator, like the expatriate, was a crucial figure of cultural transmission. Translators played an important role at the highest levels of Ottoman society, facilitating diplomatic negotiations, trade missions and political relations between the Sublime Porte and foreign powers. The professional class of translators, the dragomans, who worked for the Ottoman court came from among the Ottoman-Greek community of Istanbul based in the district of Phanar (Fener). Known as Phanariots, they had a professionally sanctioned position within Ottoman court culture until the Greek war of independence in 1821. Aykut Gürçağlar examines selected representations and self-representations of the dragoman from the seventeenth to the nineteenth century. Gürçağlar emphasizes the dual role of the translators as "trans-imperial subjects," both maintaining boundaries and building bridges between cultures.

In this chapter, translation operates not just as a professional category it also functions as an exemplar of and a multivalent metaphor for the processes involved in cultural mediation. Portraiture is examined as a form of visual translation and when the dragoman himself was the patron, Gürçağlar argues, it became a means of inscribing identity and status particularly through their distinctive, flamboyant costume that read simultaneously as Oriental exotica to the foreign viewer and yet was not really part of the Ottoman dress code either. In his chapter, Gürçağlar explores the way the image of the dragoman is translated between different categories of representation: from audience scenes commissioned by foreign ambassadors inscribing the dragoman's professional status within court culture, to the typological representation of the dragoman in costume books, to honorific portraiture which foregrounds the dragoman's agency. As with any form of translation there are both losses and gains in the movement between one visual language and another. David Wilkie's engraved sketch of the British consul's Albanian dragoman is positioned by Gürçağlar within this lineage and in this context the difference between this and the earlier dragoman representations are remarkable. The symbols of the interpreter's profession are absent in a period when Ottoman dress reform ensured the homogenization of elite male dress. This coincided with the diminution of the professional status of dragoman culture within the Ottoman Empire in the nineteenth century.

Analyzing art works by British Orientalists within the context of Ottoman cultural history relocates them within a different nexus of meaning than when they are interpreted within the heartland of British art; unfamiliar interpretive valences emerge. Just as Gürçağlar's chapter provides an Ottoman context for reading Wilkie's dragoman imagery, so too Günsel Renda locates Wilkie's portrait of Sultan Abdülmecid within the longstanding tradition of portraits commissioned by the Ottoman sultans. As Renda demonstrates, iconographic innovation within this tradition was often leveraged via commissions from foreign artists. With its leisurely pose, Wilkie's portrait introduces a greater informality to the representation of the Ottoman ruler, reflecting, Renda argues, his lifestyle in a European manner, thus propagating an image he sought to project to his British allies. One of these two portraits by Wilkie was for Queen Victoria, part of a continuing tradition of Ottoman engagement with European conventions of gifting and exchanging royal portraits. Even more radically it was British sculptor Charles Fuller who was commissioned to produce the first equestrian statue of the Sultan Abdülaziz in 1871. But this was by no means a particularly British service rendered to the Ottoman sultans. As Renda demonstrates, artists of many European nationalities as well as local painters worked at the behest of the sultans to produce these portraits whose function was both for foreign diplomatic purposes and local elite audiences. In Renda's chapter, the observations of British travel writers are read critically in relation to contemporaneous Ottoman sources and provide important supplementary evidence for understanding the life of these images within Ottoman culture. As Renda demonstrates, the observations of foreigners such as Julia Pardoe and Robert Walsh among others provide rare insights into the social function of the new Ottoman portrait medals and the public ceremonies for hanging the sultan's portraits in public offices within the Empire's capital.

As Wendy Shaw investigates the adaptations of Western pictorial conventions in British representations of the cityscapes of Ottoman Istanbul, Semra Germaner analyzes their counterpoint in the first Ottoman paintings on canvas of Istanbul that deploy the rules of Western perspectivalism. These Ottoman cityscapes, Germaner argues, occupy a crucial place in the development of modern Ottoman painting and yet they emerge from a pedagogic context where perspectivalism was deployed less for esthetic than military purposes. This generation of painters were trained in the military schools and did not subsequently pursue professional artistic careers. As part of the modernization process that took place within the Ottoman army from the late eighteenth century onwards, painting and studies of perspectivalism were taught alongside topography and mapping, skills that were crucial for the successful conduct of a modern army; this was art in the service of Empire. Despite the fact that esthetic criteria were not the main emphasis in these works, they create an intriguing esthetic effect. The perspectival articulation in the landscapes of the Darüşşafaka and military school graduates convey an impression of real space but the complete absence of figures creates, Germaner notes, "a silent and unreal world." Often carefully crafted through a painstaking process of copying from photographs, Germaner observes that "it is always the eye of the camera that dominates in these paintings." With their rendition of this compelling "silent and unreal world," these landscapes bear witness, Germaner argues, to a process of restructuring Ottoman visual memory situated as they are "at the intersection between modernity and tradition."

Like other authors in this volume, Peter Benson Miller holds up to challenge and critical scrutiny the unquestioned assumptions and occlusions that can result from Orientalism being uncritically compartmentalized into national tendencies. Benson Miller's chapter carefully excavates the artistic context in the mid-1850s in which as he puts it "the English channel was more of a conduit than a boundary." The focal point for the cross-channel transactions in Benson Miller's chapter is the critical reception of Lewis's watercolors at the Exposition Universelle of 1855 and their impact on Jean-Léon Gérôme as he gradually shifted away from Academic tenets towards Orientalist ethnographic genre painting. Despite the abundant rhetoric of cultural competition between Britain and France in this period, the French critics were nonetheless fascinated by Lewis and other British artists in 1855 partly because of the perceived documentary capacity of British watercolor. Exploring this moment when ethnographic criteria was at the forefront of the French critical response to Lewis's *The Hhareem*, both by those who were champions and dissenters, Benson Miller challenges unquestioned assumptions in the current literature on British Orientalism that asserts any simple distinctions between a British preoccupation with "truthfulness" and a French predilection for heightened eroticism. Benson Miller's challenge to this doxa is particularly compelling because he embeds the work of these two major figures of British and French Orientalism back within a moment of cross-channel artistic influence, exploring affinities between their respective work.

Benson Miller further complicates this picture by drawing into his analysis the historically coterminous channel crossing of Constantin Guys whose watercolor sketches of events from the various theatres of the Crimean war were being printed in the *Illustrated London News* in the same year that Lewis's watercolors were on display in Paris. In doing so Benson Miller draws attention to the largely overlooked role of Guys's Oriental motifs in Baudelaire's later definition of this artist as avant-garde hero in his famous essay "The Painter of Modern Life."

Like Benson Miller, Tim Barringer addresses a web of links that art historians have tended to occlude, but these are not intra-European connections rather they are within the study of British art. Within British art histories, Aestheticism is often addressed as a tendency that stands apart from "the world of politics and ideology" while British Orientalism is assumed to be inextricably enmeshed within this domain. In their crudest characterization, there is a tendency to associate the British Orientalist with a realist sensibility derived from adventures in the Middle East while the domain of the British Aestheticist is assumed to be the rarefied world of esthetic experimentation and the pursuit of "art for art's sake" in the artist's metropolitan studio. Barringer's chapter both rhetorically posits such distinctions and undoes them through a carefully woven analysis that brings together the art and biographical mythology attending two key figures of each tendency—John Frederick Lewis and Frederic Leighton. Drawing on recent analyses that stress performativity in Lewis's dandyish "Oriental" self-fashioning, Barringer stresses an analogy with Leighton's embedded early self-representations where "the past was [his] Orient, his space of fantasy." Barringer emphasizes conjunctions of Aestheticism and Orientalism (poetics and politics) in the work of both painters. He argues that despite its Aestheticist posture of withdrawal from the world, Leighton's art, like Lewis's, was inextricably linked to contemporary Orientalist ideologies. Yet he finds in Lewis's work a criticality that is absent from Leighton's Orientalism. In Lewis's painting, *The Frank Encampment*, an image of the decadent Aesthete and Orientalist, "Leighton's true double" as Barringer puts it, is to be found in the supine figure of Lord Castlereagh. By contrasting the British aristocrat with the dignified and monumental presence of the Sheikh in this painting, according to Barringer, in this instance "Lewis offered up Orientalist art as a possible site of resistance against empire and its cultural assumptions."

Reframings

Understanding the cross-cultural dynamism of contemporary impulses for collecting and exhibiting Orientalist art and recognizing the particular ways in which these consumption patterns, (their diverse pleasures and politics), are both geographically located and marked by different national and transnational cultural flows is germaine to the chapters in the first part of this volume. The critical scrutiny of this recent international phenomenon is brought into dialog with an historical understanding of the global and interactive dimensions of East/West relations as forged through visual culture in the second and third parts of this book. The fact that the Ottoman Empire was long involved in the selective patronage of Western art and adaptation of Western esthetic forms provides a corrective to any tendencies to regard the development of current regional art markets as a unique or unprecedented phenomenon. Attention to the history of transculturation within the Ottoman Empire and the reciprocal impact on European art practice, provides particular instances of hybridity that reframe the binary structure of previous postcolonial analyses.

Although the frame for this volume is British-Ottoman cultural exchanges and the primary geographic focus is Istanbul, the diversity of chapters contained here indicate the book's more complex geographical reach. Examining the cultural patterns of the sultans' art patronage, pedagogic influence or art exhibitions in nineteenth-century Istanbul, for example, reveals the impossibility of containing the topic within a single paradigm of cultural exchange. So too, an emphasis on the multiplicity of center/periphery relations as they are constructed through both Ottoman and British visual cultures contributes to a geographic decentering that has motivated other recent studies in the field. While this alternative imperial focus contributes to developments in transnational studies and global historiographies, the examples in this book also caution against reductive generalizations. Chapters in this volume demonstrate through detailed historicized cultural analyses the need for nuanced renderings of time and place in order to map the complex and particular relations of Ottoman and Orientalist poetics and politics.

Notes

1 Zeynep Çelik, *Empire, Architecture and the City. French-Ottoman Encounters, 1830–1914* (Seattle and Washington: University of Washington Press, 2008), 5.

2 Tim Barringer, Geoff Quilley and Douglas Fordham, eds., *Art and the British Empire* (Manchester and New York: Manchester University Press, 2007), 3.

3 C. A. Bailey and L. T. Fawaz, eds., *Modernity and Culture: From the Mediterranean to the Indian Ocean* (New York: Columbia University Press, 2002), 1. See also Çelik, *Empire, Architecture and the City*.

4 Semra Germaner and Zeynep İnankur, *Constantinople and the Orientalists* (Istanbul: Türkiye İş Bankası Kültür Yayınları, 2002) and Günsel Renda, ed., *A History of Turkish Painting*, (Geneva/Istanbul: Palasar 1988).

5 Edward Said, *Orientalism* (New York: Random House, Harmondsworth: Penguin, 1978).

6 Ussama Makdisi, "Ottoman Orientalism," *The American Historical Review* 107, no. 3 (2002): 768. See also Selim Deringil, *The Well-Protected Domains. Ideology and the Legitimation of Power in the Ottoman Empire, 1876–1909* (London and New York: I. B. Tauris, 1998).

7 See for example, Zeynep Çelik, "Speaking Back to Orientalist Discourse," in *Orientalism's Interlocutors. Painting, Architecture,*

Photography, ed. Jill Beaulieu and Mary Roberts (Durham and London: Duke University Press, 2002), 19–41; and for a summary of the various positions see Edhem Eldem, "Osman Hamdi Bey ve Oryantalizm." *Dipnot* 2, (Winter/Spring 2004): 39–67.

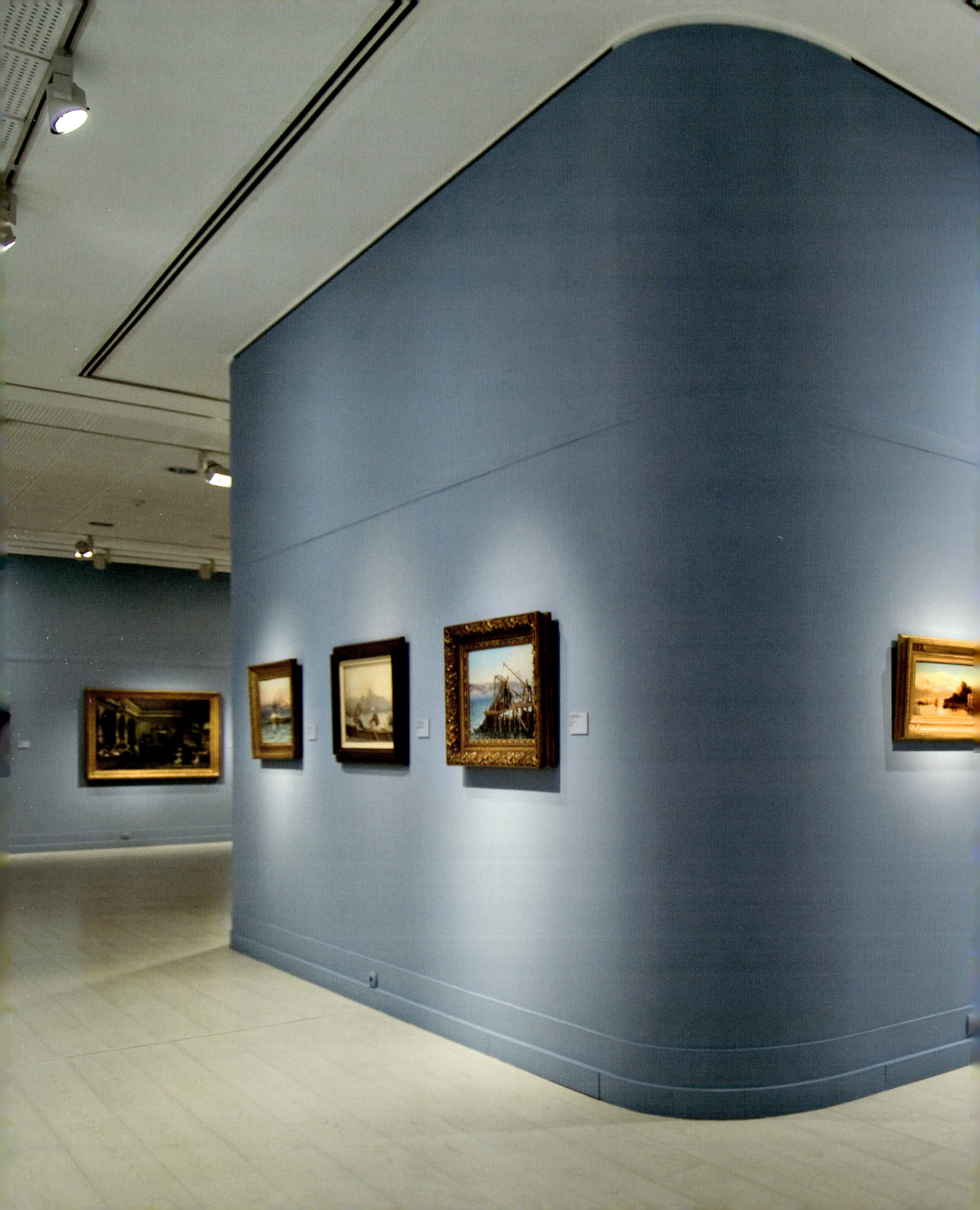

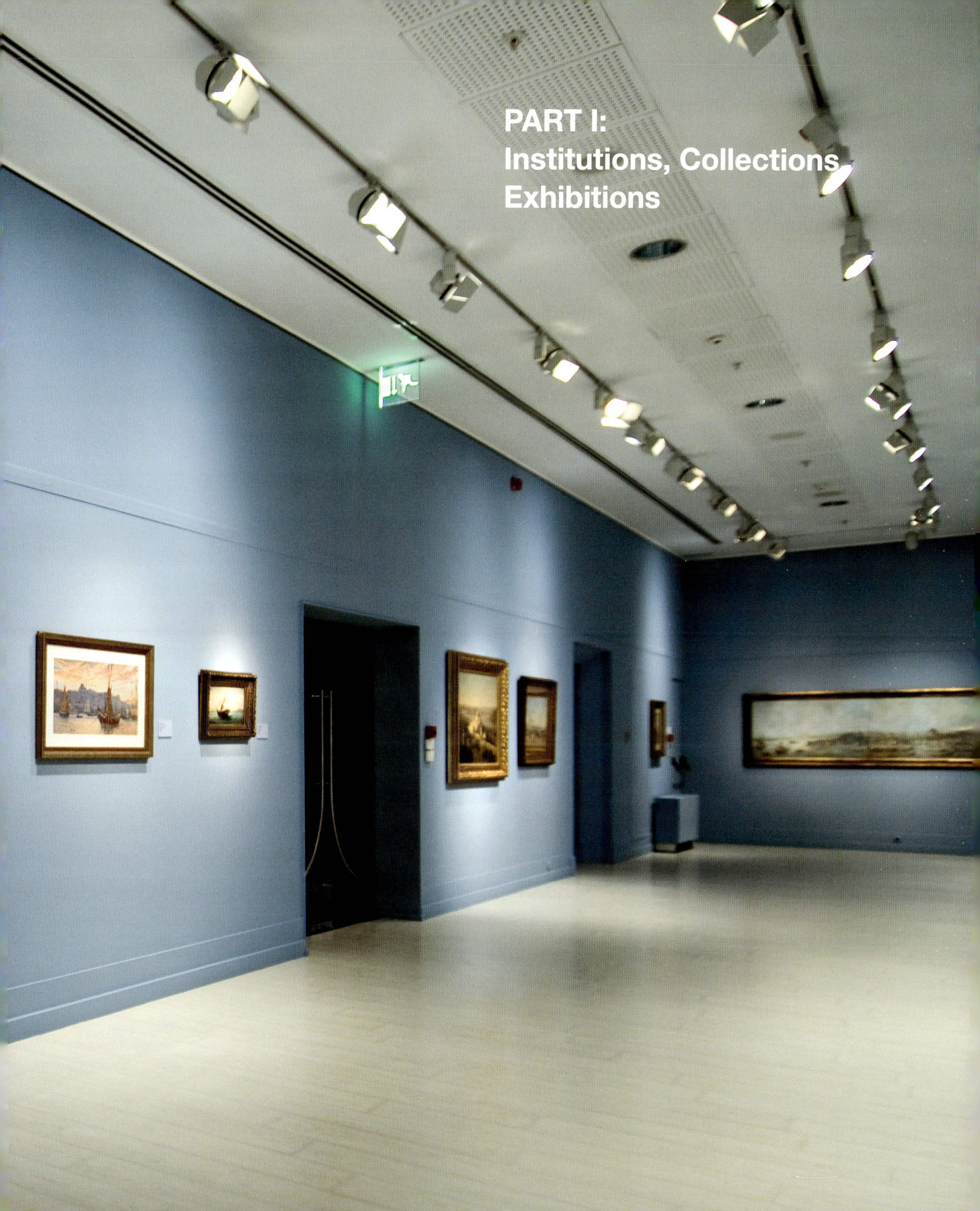

PART I: Institutions, Collections, Exhibitions

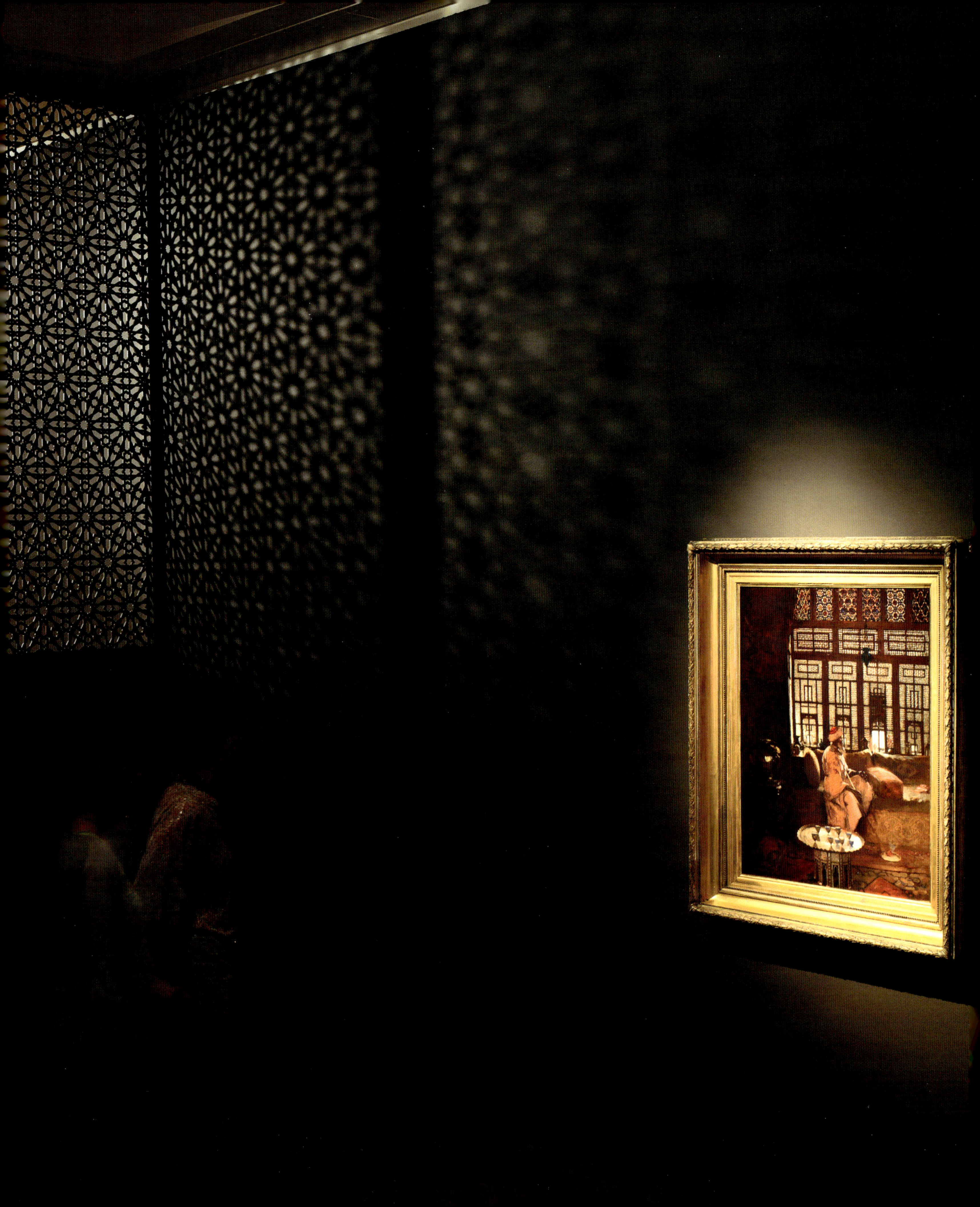

I

Staging *The Lure of the East* Exhibition Making and Orientalism

Christine Riding

The primary impetus and rationale behind Tate Britain's *The Lure of the East* exhibition was to stage the first, large-scale survey of British Orientalist painting. It was not the first to address Orientalism in the visual arts, of course. The largest exhibitions on this subject held in art galleries (as opposed to auction houses and dealer galleries) in the last thirty years were *Orientalism: The Near East in French Painting, 1800–1880* at the Memorial Art Gallery in Rochester NY (1982), *The Orientalists: Delacroix to Matisse* at the Royal Academy in London (1984), *Orientalism: Delacroix to Klee* at the Art Gallery of New South Wales (1997) and *Noble Dreams, Wicked Pleasures: Orientalism in America, 1870–1930* at the Clark Art Institute (2000). As the titles suggest, none of these exhibitions focused specifically on British art and those that did include British artists gave emphasis to other European artists and in particular nineteenth-century French artists, whose reputations are more widely known and in some instances specifically associated with Orientalist art. For Tate Britain, the National Collection of British Art, the exhibition was (in conventional exhibition terms) appropriate, unprecedented and timely, given that the Royal Academy exhibition, the last major exhibition of its kind in London, was held twenty-three years before.

Content was also of primary interest with an eye, as ever, on an exhibition as a quality-led, esthetic and spatial experience. It has often been observed that Orientalism is "not a movement or a style; it is more in the nature of a tradition with its base in a common fascination and, uniquely, that common factor is the place."[1] Hence the 1997 exhibition in New South Wales, mentioned above, could contain artists as dissimilar and unlikely to be shown together in any other context as Eugène Delacroix and Paul Klee. Similarly, the Tate exhibition included a wide range of artists, a number of whom are considered significant enough to be the focus of monographic exhibitions in Britain and North America, from David Wilkie and David Roberts, Richard Dadd, William Holman Hunt and Frederic Leighton, to John Singer Sargent, David Bomberg and Stanley Spencer. When discussions first began at the Tate in 1999, the idea was to stage an exhibition on John Frederick Lewis—perhaps the only British artist who can be described as a career Orientalist—a project that remains long overdue. Although Lewis continued to be a major component, the exhibition project developed and changed significantly to the extent that, across the whole tour in New Haven, London, Istanbul and Sharjah, over forty artists of varying style, experience and approach were represented.

Many of the curatorial decisions made during the project are common to all exhibitions. How many of these decisions were self-contained and autonomous and how many were in response to external factors is central to this essay. Above all, in what way did the subject of Orientalism itself influence these decisions? In developing an exhibition project, curators must work within certain parameters and restrictions, such as gallery space and budget, as well as developing an argument through themes and content that is concise, transparent and methodical. This involves strict decision making for me as the project leader and the others who made up the curatorial team, primarily Nicholas Tromans as the lead curator. It was decided, for example, to structure *The Lure of the East* exhibition not chronologically, not by artist/artists or by location, but by categories specifically associated with art production. The exhibition was structured according to the categories of portraiture (including self-portraiture), genre (scenes of everyday life), religious subjects, interior and harem subjects and finally landscape. This choice foregrounded the theoretical premise of the exhibition as primarily an exploration of how artists—that is painters and watercolorists not photographers—adapted long-established conventions and practice to new subjects and environments. A related decision was to focus on nineteenth- and early twentieth-century artists who had traveled to the eastern Mediterranean. Another decision was to exclude conventional historical or biblical subject paintings. Thus history painting, long understood in Western academies to be the most prestigious and demanding of artistic genres, as well as by convention the least anchored in reality, did not feature here (except for one or two examples). The exhibition concentrated on the period 1830 to 1920, from the rise of steamboat travel that facilitated and encouraged journeys to Turkey, Palestine and Egypt to the aftermath of the World War I. It was decided, however, that the first gallery, entitled "Travellers and Sitters: The Orientalist Portrait," would function as an introduction to the subject and the exhibition as a whole and thus range more widely, chronologically and artistically. This allowed us to use portraiture not only as a key artistic genre, exploring specific biographies and strategies behind the adoption of Eastern dress by British artists, travelers and expatriates, but also to establish a useful historical framework for the exhibition visitor, through the sitters themselves. This section commenced with pre-1830 portraits of diplomats, scholars, merchants and so on, through to Wilkie's portraits of Sultan Abdülmecid (1840) and Muhammad 'Ali, Pasha of Egypt (1841), and Jean-Léon Gérôme's *Napoleon in Egypt* (about 1863) and ended with Augustus John's portrait of Colonel T. E. Lawrence (1919).

Some factors were, however, beyond our control. For example, the "wish list" of works compiled by the curators included a substantial number of paintings and watercolors in private hands. Often the ownership and locations of these works were not known to us, as works of art changed hands via auctions and private sales. Through the assistance of dealers and auction-house specialists, we were able to secure Henriette Browne's *Harem Visit, Constantinople* (1860, Private Collection). This inclusion introduced a female artist with privileged access to a harem in contrast to the approximations and imaginings offered up by professional, male artists who otherwise dominated the display. We were also very fortunate to be made aware that the Qatar Museums Authority owned three "wish list" paintings, Lewis's *An Armenian Lady, Cairo* (1854), Edward Lear's *Damascus* (1861) and Gustav Bauernfeind's *Entrance to Temple Mount, Jerusalem* (1886). However we became aware of this so late in the project that the paintings were not included at the New Haven venue nor in the catalog. Conversely, despite our best efforts, we were not able to secure the loan of Lewis's *The Mid-Day Meal* (1875, Private Collection) and *The Hhareem* (1850, Private Collection). Both paintings would have been centerpieces, both visually and interpretatively, of their respective galleries, "Genre and Gender" and "Harem and Home." Such challenges, successes and disappointments are the norm. They are pertinent here, in that they underline the often unpredictable manner in which works of art are assembled. Thus we did not, for example, edit out "difficult" works from the selection in order to play down the worst excesses within British art, or to make any special pleas in favor of the British approach as opposed to that of the French. The aim was to be representative, not partial, within the parameters established by the curatorial team described above. However, the failure to secure such works as Lewis's *The Hhareem*, which seems to tick all the boxes in terms of "Eastern extravagance" and "sexual despotism," or John Faed's *Bedouin Exchanging a Slave for Armour* (1858, Private Collection), although included in the catalog, meant that the actual display of works in London could have been read as conveniently "backing up" the exhibition's curatorial premise. That is, the idea, suggested in the catalog and exhibition interpretation, that British representations tended to lean towards the domestic and the sentimental, when compared to the overt eroticism and violence exhibited by the likes of Delacroix, Ingres and Gérôme. Comparing and contrasting national schools is, perhaps, largely superfluous when engaging with a subject as sensitive as Orientalism. Instead it is the broader context and reception of Orientalist art, specifically in London in 2008, that is my primary focus here.

All public-facing organizations in Britain, especially those that receive funding from central or local government, have a duty and responsibility to understand, communicate with and interact effectively with people across cultures on a local and global level. This is especially pertinent for London-based institutions: Greater London Authority estimates in 2006, for example, suggested that thirty-two percent of Londoners were born outside the UK (2.3 million people). Unlike the majority of exhibitions staged at the Tate, the subject of *The Lure of the East* was extremely topical and resonated well beyond the art and academic worlds. These "external" conditions were of fundamental importance, not to the selection and themes, but the manner in which the exhibition was presented, the contents interpreted and the product marketed. This was, after all, an exhibition that focused on Near and Middle Eastern subjects and included a whole gallery devoted to religious subjects, with a focus on the three Abrahamic faiths, Jerusalem and British proto-Zionism, as well as a whole section on the harem, and its time-honored association in the West with segregation, oppression and inequality and images of women veiled. It is often stated that the world is a different place post 9/11. This was the first major Orientalist art exhibition in a public institution in the "new era," which is important here for a number of reasons. In the immediate aftermath of the 9/11 attacks, to quote Professor Alan Richardson, "it seemed that the old binaries—East and West, fanatic and secular, Islam and, what, the "free world," Christendom?—were destined to become reasserted as simplistically as ever before."[2] Such binaries are, of course, central to Edward Said's critique of European and American Orientalism and in turn are also central to negative criticisms of Said's methodology. But importantly his thesis, "written with 'saintly rage'" as one commentator has put it, was, in a sense, reenergized by current events.[3] This is exemplified by the organizers of the Courtauld Institute of Art's "Framing the Other: 30 Years after *Orientalism*" (April 26, 2008) advertising the conference call for papers, which focused on Said and his legacy, with two highly suggestive images, one historic, Ingres' *Odalisque with a Slave* (1839–40) and one contemporary, *Um Ahmed, July 5, 2006* by Emilio Morenatti, representing (to quote the website) "the indolent and submissive odalisque" and "the fierce and dehumanised suicide bomber."[4]

As an art-gallery professional working within this period of heightened political tension and cultural wariness, what was important to me was the perception of the West as ignorant of and insensitive to Islam and Muslims. This perception is as relevant to the cultural sector as to politics and the media. I can quote two examples at Tate Britain relating to this that had an impact on how *The Lure of the East* project developed. The first, which I was personally involved in, was the display of Val Prinsep's *Ayesha* (1889, Tate) in the permanent collection galleries in 2003. The accompanying label text caused offense to some in the Muslim community, because it was interpreted as stating that the painting was a portrait of one of the Prophet Mohammad's wives. The second was the decision to withdraw John Latham's *God is Great (no.2)* (1991, Tate) from an "in focus" exhibition in 2005. Both episodes were highly instructive. The case of *Ayesha*, underscored the need for clarity and intellectual rigor in composing interpretive material—after all, it was the text not the painting that suggested a specific identity. So too, a need for an awareness of one's own limitations when evaluating images. The episode involving Latham's *God is Great (no.2)*, which had been presented to the Tate by the artist in 2005, was different. The work, a freestanding sculpture comprising a large glass panel with three used editions of the Bible, the Qur'an and the Talmud, was judged too sensitive to be exhibited in the immediate aftermath of the London bombings of July 7. On both occasions, Tate Britain was judged (on the whole) to have "got it wrong." Thus Aaffreen Khan, speaking for the Muslim Public Affairs Committee, was quoted in *The Guardian* newspaper as saying that the *Ayesha* episode "just shows the level of ignorance there is about Islam and its practice."[5] But on the issue of the Latham work, representatives of the Muslim Council of Great Britain were reported on the BBC News website as saying that they had not "received any complaints about this piece of artwork." Furthermore having not been consulted by the Tate, they concluded that "Sometimes presumptions are incorrectly made about what is unacceptable to Muslims and this can be counter-productive."[6]

The development of *The Lure of the East* project must be understood within this rather tangled political, social and cultural landscape. After the Labour Party victory of 1997 government directives and initiatives were issued concerning multi-culturalism and diversity strategies—that is, diversifying both audiences to and staffing of government-funded arts organizations. Within British museums and art galleries these diversity strategies have been paralleled by unprecedented programming of exhibitions, displays and events that focused on, or addressed in some way, Islam, Britain's Muslim communities or, broadly speaking, Middle Eastern themes. When I say unprecedented, I do not mean simply how many there have been, but that the impetus and ambition of this programming goes beyond general "edutainment" towards that of self-consciously encouraging participation, dialog and debate and engendering greater understanding and awareness. This was certainly the intention of Tate Britain's *East West: Objects Between Cultures* (September 1, 2006 to February 18, 2007) which coincided with the Festival of Muslim Cultures. What is interesting here is not so much the installation of Islamic or "Islamic" objects within the permanent displays of historic British art, but that the introductory text should proclaim the organizers' "hope" that "this project will challenge static ideas of national history, art and identity."[7] A bolder exhibition initiative in this sense was the British Library's *Sacred: Discover What We Share* (April 27 to September 23, 2007) an exhibition that focused on the holy books of the Abrahamic faiths. As the title and the strap-line—"How Judaism, Christianity and Islam have so much in common"—make absolutely clear, this was not simply a display of "treasures" as might well have been the case, say, ten years ago. To quote the institution's website, this was considered to be an "inter-faith initiative" and "the first in a series of exhibitions celebrating religious diversity in Britain."[8] Such initiatives could not fail, in the current climate, to register outside the institution. In a review dated July 6, 2007, for example, Yasmin Khan noted that "by its sheer nature of subject matter, the exhibition *shoulders a grave responsibility* (whether intended or not) in facilitating community cohesiveness; a case in point in *demonstrating the critical role that cultural institutions have the potential to play* [my emphasis]."[9] What such exhibitions, displays and interventions demonstrate is thus a strong imperative in Britain today, in certain contexts, to explore and acknowledge the past as having direct relevance and influence on the present and future. The reverse, of the present impacting on the past, is also being acknowledged. The British Museum's *Babylon: Myth and Reality* exhibition (November 13, 2008 to March 15, 2009) for example, was, in many ways, a "straight-forward" presentation of an ancient and once powerful Middle Eastern civilization (represented by artifacts and archaeological finds) falling foul of Western/Orientalist myth making, represented by Western art and popular culture. The promotional material noted, however, that "Since 2003, our attention has been drawn to new threats to the archaeology of Mesopotamia, modern day Iraq." This comment gestured towards the destruction and alleged looting, reported world-wide, during and after the 2003 Iraq invasion. The issue was represented within the final gallery of the exhibition with film footage of British Museum staff and archaeologists "in the field" accompanied by Allied troops.[10]

If Alan Richardson, as a university professor, can claim "that the conditions for teaching Orientalism [post 9/11] changed significantly and perhaps permanently" and that "[presenting] Orientalism critically remains one of our important tasks," then it is surely true of exhibiting Orientalist art in a public gallery.[11] Indeed one can detect a change of emphasis in language and tone, just by reading through the various directors' forewords—the institutional "voice" rather than curatorial "voice"—within the Orientalist exhibition catalogs previously mentioned, which date from 1982 to 2008. The foreword to *The Lure of the East* catalog, co-signed by Stephen Deuchar and Amy Meyers (directors of Tate Britain and the Yale Center for British Art) and then by Stephen Deuchar and Andrea Rose (Head of Visual Arts, British Council) for the Istanbul and Sharjah catalog versions, are the only ones to make direct reference to contemporary events. They note pointedly, if diplomatically, that "the political dimension of our subject—and indeed of each object within it—is never very far from the surface" and that the exhibition tour coincided "with a moment when European and American political relations with the Middle East have been particularly difficult."[12] Furthermore these are the only forewords to mention Edward Said by name, let alone summarize his treatise in any conspicuous way. This too is interesting, as all these exhibitions were staged after the publication of *Orientalism* in 1978. I do not mean to imply that mentioning Edward Said in a foreword, i.e. "from the start," is a useful short-hand for being understood to be "on message" with the subject of Orientalism. But rather that one can detect a gathering momentum within these catalogs in engaging with Said. It is worth remembering in this context that Linda Nochlin's oft-quoted rallying cry to art historians, also mentioned in *The Lure of the East* catalog foreword, was first made at a conference during the tour of *Orientalism: The Near East in French Painting*. Nochlin criticized the exhibition's curator, Donald Rosenthal, for refusing to evaluate the "political uses" of French Orientalist painting.[13] That was 1982. The situation has since changed. In his "Introduction" to the *Consuming the Orient* exhibition catalog, for example, published in 2007, the curator Edhem Eldem noted that

> my efforts at "tempering" Said's accusations should not be perceived as a questioning or a criticism of his findings. Rather, in a somewhat opportunistic way, I would like to assume that, by now, Said's message has been to a large extent well received and understood across most of the intellectual spectrum, and that, from now on, one can look at Orientalist production in a more dispassionate way.[14]

Message received and understood. However, Eldem's "Introduction" is by far the longest and most complex explanation of the curatorial rationale and process behind an exhibition that I have personally read and I wonder, therefore, to whom these comments were addressed. Fascinating and informative as they are, was the author mindful of any adverse criticisms that might come his way, perhaps from those who do not appreciate the challenges and limitations of exhibition making when tackling a subject as complex, loaded and sensitive as this? In any case, for those engaged with Orientalism, the world post-1978 is similarly a different place.

What exactly can an exhibition be *expected* to achieve? Essentially it is a visual/esthetic experience and a physical forum for communicating ideas. But the *process* of making an exhibition is by nature and necessity one of summarizing and thus reducing information. The largest body of information, textual and visual, associated with an exhibition is the catalog. In the case of *The Lure of the East*, it contained about 100,000 words and 170 images (there were 108 works of art at the London venue). From here, information is extracted for the exhibition leaflet (about 1,500 words), which is given to all exhibition visitors, and the textual interpretation within the exhibition space. At Tate Britain, the standard is a 300 word introduction or mission statement for the whole exhibition, 250 words per introductory text per gallery and 100 words per individual work of art. And what is potentially lost in this dramatic compression of information? Complexity? Nuance? Variables? The challenge of presenting Orientalism adequately was compounded by the fact that we could not assume prior knowledge or awareness from exhibition visitors. We could not assume, for example, that the terms

Orientalist or Orientalism registered at all, or that anyone had heard of Edward Said. We could not assume that a UK-based audience had any concept of the *Ottoman Empire*, let alone any grounding in the history of British involvement and influence in these territories. Perhaps most importantly, despite the likelihood of visitors having absorbed countless Orientalist themes and representations, given their lingering presence in modern and contemporary popular culture and media, we could not assume that our public would "have any sense of the genealogy of such representations" and thus make connections with the works of art on display.[15] Given the limited word length, therefore, great care had to be taken over words, phrases and sentences. Even so, there was every potential for misunderstanding and controversy. Take, for example, the first part of a sentence from the introductory text of the third gallery entitled "The Holy City:" "As the balance of population of Jerusalem shifted towards a Jewish majority in the nineteenth century ..." Straightforward? Factual? Contentious? The comment represents a consensus of academic opinion, in the opinion of the curators. But does this consensus include Palestinian and Israeli academics? Given the sensitivities surrounding religion and territory in the present, the layout of "The Holy City" in particular was carefully thought through. Works of art relating to each faith were grouped and subdivided, for example for Islam, exteriors and interiors of mosques, prayer and study, pilgrimage. And each group was linked by an appropriate image. Thus Islam was linked to Christianity through Lewis's watercolor of Hagia Sophia (then a mosque converted from a church) and Christianity to Judaism by William Holman Hunt's watercolors of Nazareth and Bethlehem, settlements associated in the Christian narrative with the birth and childhood of Jesus. Because Jerusalem is sacred to all three faiths, however, works relating to it were grouped separately. In other words, there was nothing arbitrary about the layout. Even so, in planning the interpretation of the exhibition and its catalog it was decided that the works of art could not "stand alone," despite a careful installation plan, and that the standard interpretation format was inadequate. The result was, to my knowledge, the most diverse interpretation strategy that Tate Britain has yet employed within an exhibition. For example, in order to bring other "voices" (that is, alternative readings and opinions) into the galleries, the display incorporated thirty audio and textual comments that were directed at a variety of works of art, and in addition to the curatorial texts. The commentators were international, some of whom were based in Ankara, Baghdad, Beirut, Istanbul, Jerusalem, Tehran, Tel Aviv and so on, and came from broad professional and academic backgrounds, covering archaeology, history, art history, travel, politics, current events, religion, literature, music, law, sociology and feminist studies. The complex history of the Ottoman Empire, up to the formation of the Turkish Republic, was presented in an animated map projection, interjected with four journeys made by British travelers Lady Mary Wortley Montagu (1716–18), Lord Byron (1809–11), David Roberts (1838–39) and Arthur Melville (1880–82).

Everything I have described so far concerns the exhibition itself. The real challenge for the Tate, I would argue, was to convey these often carefully framed and complex curatorial messages into the wider public domain. This is especially true of marketing, which is an important activity for any institution, and guided by particular aims, methods and conventions. Thus much of what I am about to say is relevant to all exhibition marketing strategies. The primary marketing tool of any exhibition project is the poster image. The standard for the Tate, and many other institutions, is the exhibition title (in this case, eight words) and an image selected from the works of art within the exhibition. Importantly the poster image represents and characterizes the whole project beyond the physical location of the institution. In *No Logo: Taking Aim at the Brand Bullies*, Naomi Klein has observed that "[it is] important for any healthy culture to have public space—a place where people are treated as citizens instead of as consumers."[16] The question here, I would suggest, is who should take priority, "citizen" or "consumer"? The general belief in the marketing world is that advertising works, that is, it directs consumption behavior. For the purposes of this essay, let us assume that there are only two audiences for an exhibition poster. Audience one, the kind of people that attended the Symposium at the Pera Museum, the kind of people reading this essay, people who are curious about, knowledgeable of, and alive to the complexities of the subject matter of Orientalism and Orientalist art, its broader cultural impact, resonance, poignancy, and so on. Then there's audience two, namely, everybody else. And "everybody else" is a numerically immense, intellectually, economically and culturally diverse and complex group of people, anyone walking in the street, anyone traveling on pubic transport, anyone reading a newspaper, anyone surfing the internet, anyone, that is, who may encounter the poster image of the exhibition. The Tate's marketing campaign, I would suggest, was not devised for audience one, the assumption being that that group would be interested anyway, but directed at audience two. The aim would be to get as many of audience two into the exhibition itself. So the primary function of a poster is to promote the product and boost visitor figures, as well as promote and sustain brand awareness of the institution itself. It is fair to say that attendance figures remain the primary indication by which exhibitions are judged successful or not. This is predominantly because of associated income, sponsorship, profile and more broadly speaking a clear if somewhat simplistic indication that the institution is relevant and popular (i.e. not elitist) and thus in general terms justifies its public funding. The visitor target for *The Lure of the East* exhibition was 70,000 individual visits. The potential number of people seeing the poster campaign, however, ran into millions. The London Underground service alone accommodates about one billion individual journeys per year—there are approximately one million journeys made per day through Oxford Circus, one of the stations where the exhibition poster was displayed—and the Tate website has seventeen million unique users per year. Simply put, one could have predicted that the vast majority of those who had seen the poster would not attend the exhibition. Should that fact influence the choice of image and title? Lauren Rosewarne has noted, in her analysis of gender, advertising and public policy, that "outdoor advertising is the most public and unavoidable of all advertising yet is seldom approached as an issue of public importance."[17] She continues that "while it may be elitist to see a media audience as a homogeneous mass who unthinkingly absorb media messages, it is equally elitist to assume that audiences have the time, inclination or cultural studies education to enable them to 'negotiate' messages until they become palatable."[18]

This point is worth pursuing, as it mirrors the discussions between me and the Tate's marketing team concerning *The Lure of the East*. (For the sake of brevity and clarity, I am aware that I am here reducing our discussions down to very basic "positions".) The marketing team's position was that their job was to focus primarily on "the consumer," and get people through the door, and my job was to focus on "the citizen" and enlighten them once they had arrived. My position was that the crossover from consumer to citizen, at the point of entry to the exhibition, was too late, and (given the relatively low visitor predictions) arguably irrelevant. These respective positions were encapsulated, in my opinion, by the images selected for consideration. The two images, from a marketing perspective, were Lewis's *Hhareem Life, Constantinople* (Fig. 1.1) and Frank Dicksee's *Leila* (Fig. 1.2, 1892, Private Collection). The image chosen by the curatorial team was Arthur Melville's *The Arab Interior* (Fig. 1.3, 1881, National Gallery of Scotland). These choices need unpacking, in view of my comments above. In devising any advertising campaign, the standard marketing model utilized by the Tate, as quoted to me by the Tate marketing team, is "AIDA": A = Attract, I = Interest, D = Desire, A = Action. The poster first attracts attention, then awakens interest (in the product), which develops into a desire or craving (for the product), which results in action, in this case, paying and entering the exhibition. In choosing *Hhareem Life* and *Leila*, it must be stated, the Tate marketing team were simply operating within long established and accepted patterns of gender stereotyping in public advertising, which (to quote Lauren Rosewarne) "routinely employs sexualised and objectified images of women to sell products and sexualise public space." It has been estimated that about ninety percent of sexual content in UK advertising represents women.[19] I can give one example of the kind of advertising—admittedly on the extreme end of the spectrum—that profoundly influenced my thinking. Just after the run of *The Lure of the East* in London, photographs were published of the British model Kate Moss in a fashion shoot "as a sultan's concubine" for the US magazine *W* (September 2008, by Mert Alas and Marcus Piggott). The location was the Cağaloğlu Hamamı in Istanbul. The *Daily Mail* newspaper published an article on August 28, 2008, titled "Kate Moss Gets Steamy in Turkish Baths for ANOTHER Sexy Shoot" noting that the event had "raised a few eyebrows in the predominantly Muslim country."[20]

Although not a default position, it should certainly be borne in mind that images of attractive, young women often feature on posters and catalogs for art exhibitions. Occasionally these are overtly sexualized. To make the subject of British nineteenth-century academic nude paintings enticing, for example, *The Victorian Nude* exhibition (Tate Britain, 2001–2) was firstly given the suggestive pre-title, *Exposed*, and secondly the catalog cover sported a close detail of Leighton's *Bath of Psyche* (1891, Tate Collection). The exhibition's title was printed on a removable paper band wrapped around the cover, which, when ripped apart, "exposed" the female figure's nipple. Interestingly, all but one of the Orientalist exhibitions mentioned earlier in this essay had females on the front cover of the catalog: Auguste Renoir's *Girl with a Falcon*, Lucien Lévy-Dhurmer's *Evening Promenade, Morocco*, and Frederick Arthur Bridgman's *The Siesta* of 1878. But the question here, I would suggest, is whether the selection of female images, even (or especially) those that to our eyes (i.e. Tate staff) seem innocuous, was advisable or even appropriate in the pubic sphere, given the broader context described above and given that the position of women remains at the center of debate and criticism about, and justification for intervention in, Muslim cultures and states. If a reminder were needed of the contemporary resonance of this subject in Britain, in the years leading up to the exhibition opening, it was the then Home Secretary, Jack Straw's call for women to remove their face veils during his weekly constituency surgery, much reported upon and hotly debated in the British press in October 2006.[21] Hence William Holman Hunt's *The Lantern Maker's Courtship* (1854–57,

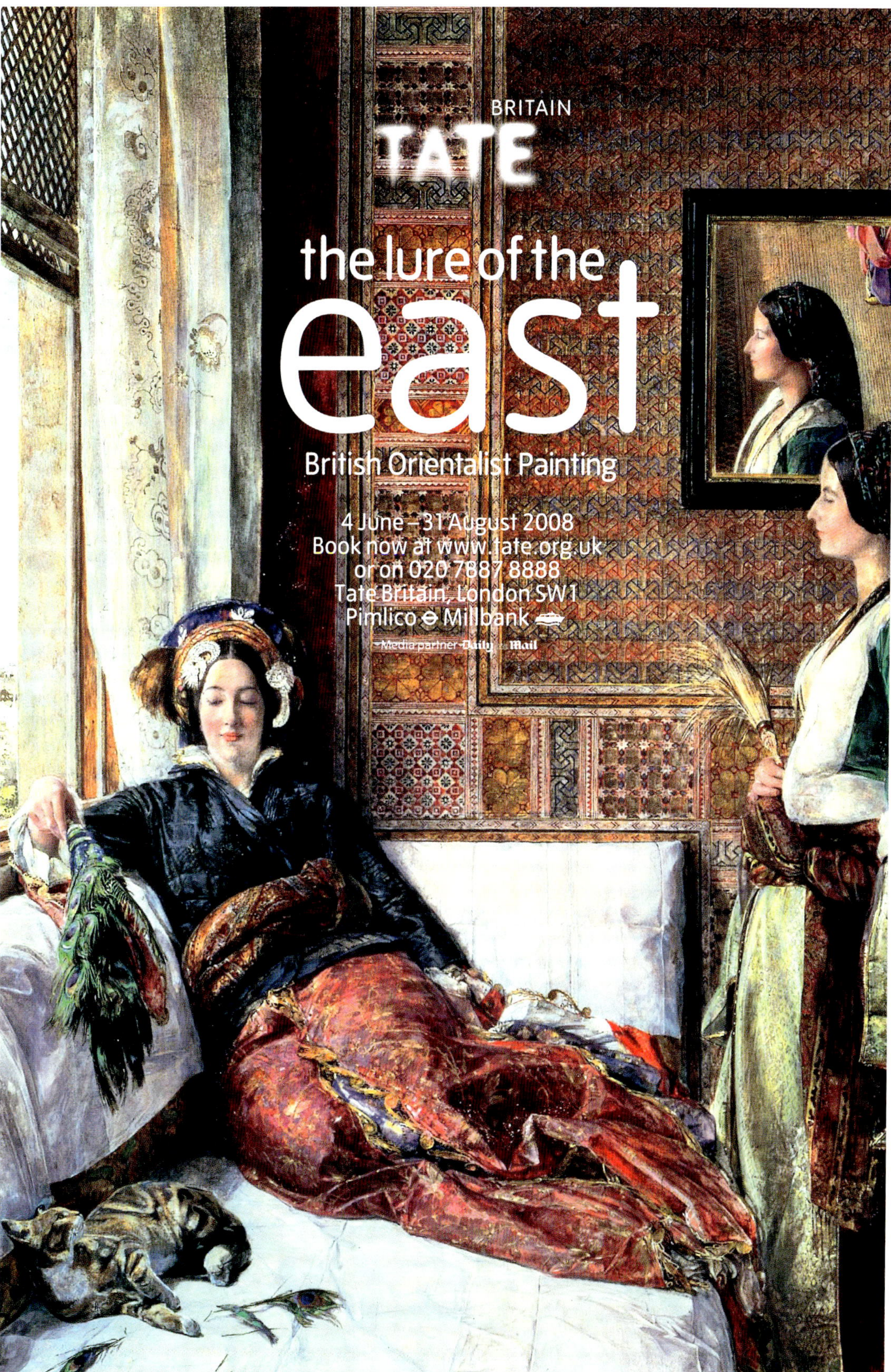

Figure 1.1 Draft poster design for *The Lure of the East: British Orientalist Painting* exhibition at Tate Britain showing a detail of *Hhareem Life, Constantinople*, John Frederick Lewis (1804–1876), 1857, watercolor, 61.2 x 48.1 cm, Laing Art Gallery, Newcastle-upon-Tyne (Tyne and Wear Museums). (Design by Rose, London UK.)

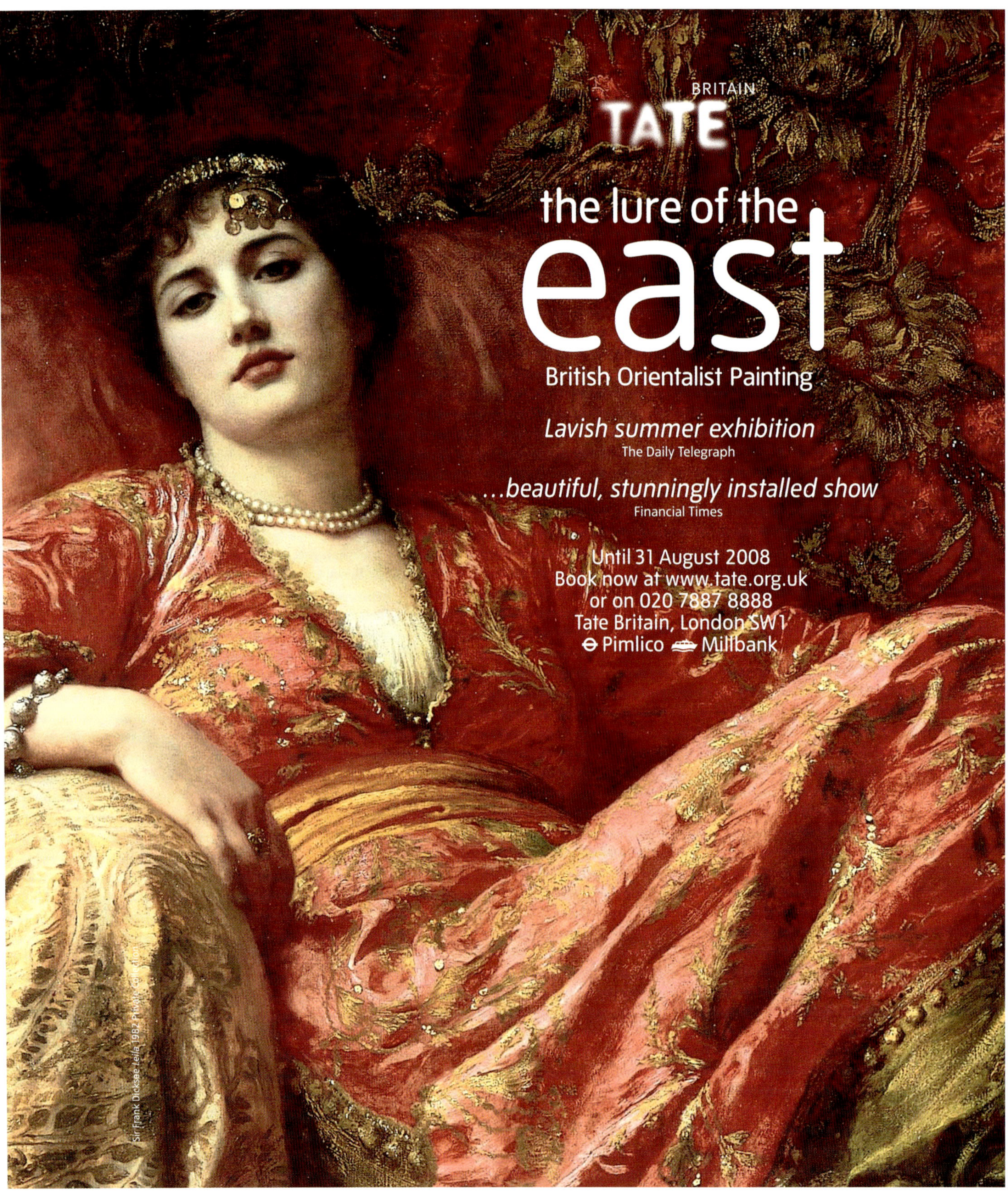

Figure 1.2 Advertisement design for *The Lure of the East: British Orientalist Painting* exhibition at Tate Britain showing a detail of *Leila*, Frank Dicksee (1853–1928), 1892, oil on canvas, 100 x 126 cm, Private Collection. (Design by Rose, London UK.)

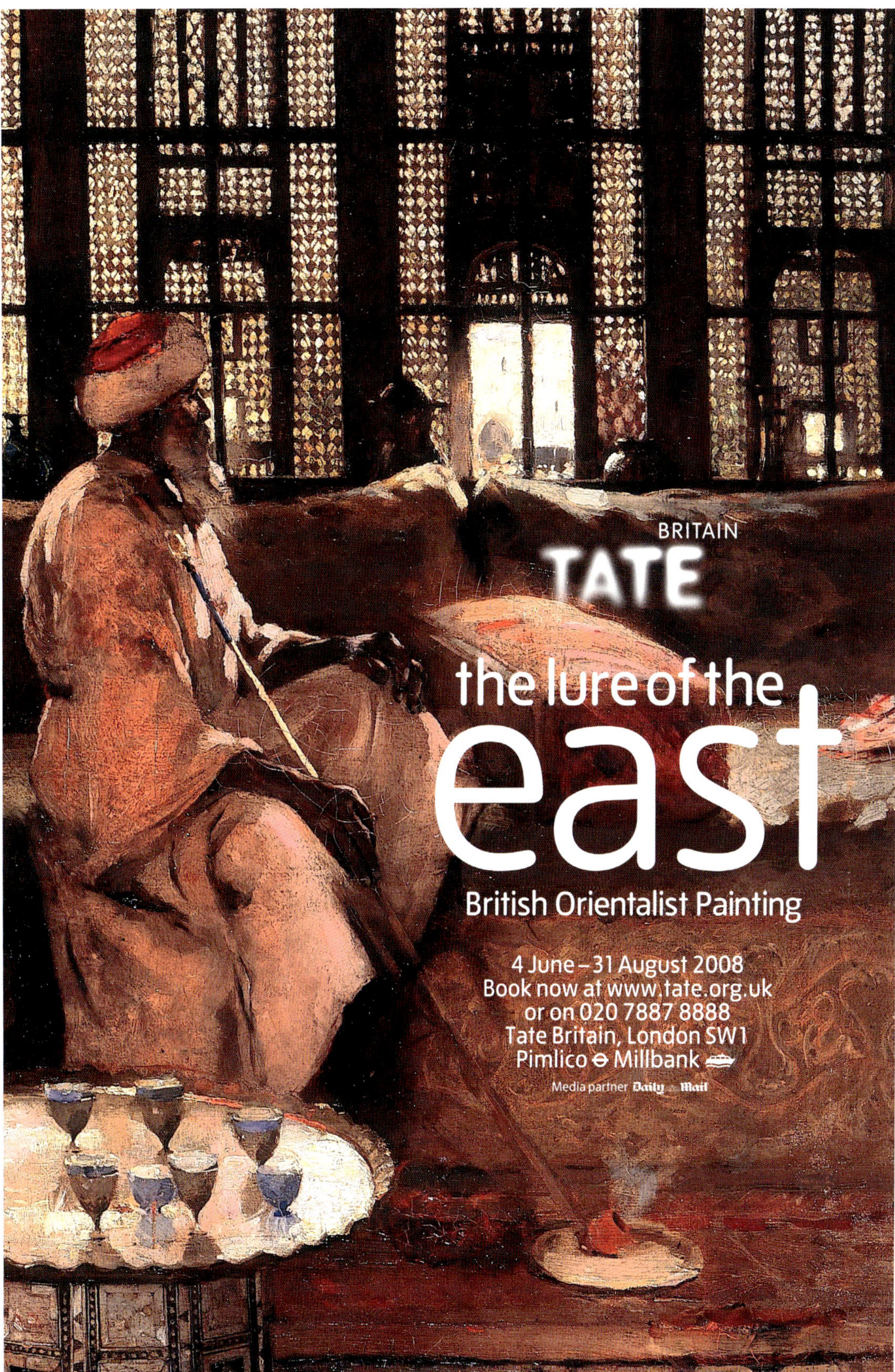

Figure 1.3 Poster design for *The Lure of the East: British Orientalist Painting* exhibition at Tate Britain showing a detail of *The Arab Interior*, Arthur Melville (1855–1904), 1881, oil on canvas, 95 x 72.8 cm, National Gallery of Scotland, Edinburgh. (Design by Rose, London UK.)

Birmingham Museum and Art Gallery) was never going to be the poster image for *The Lure of the East* exhibition, with its suggestion of the frustrated male gaze.

This issue was made additionally pertinent to my mind, once the pre-title, *The Lure of the East*, was agreed in December 2007. This was after two years' deliberating over such terms as *Traveling East*, *Looking East*, *Going East*, *Journeying East*, *Eastern Encounters*, *Arabesque*. The marketing clichés, as far as a British audience is concerned, of phrases such as *Turkish Delight* or *Eastern Promise* were deliberately avoided. The latter phrases refer to a well-known advertising campaign for Fry's "Turkish Delight" confectionary, which, as a sequence of three advertisements from the 1960s to the 1980s, marshaled as many Orientalist clichés as the creators could muster—the harem female, the sheikh, desert dunes, tents, snakes, swords, etc.—with the strap line, "full of Eastern promise." The Tate exhibition needed a pre-title, so it was argued by the press and marketing teams, because it was felt that the main title, "British Orientalist Painting," was dry and academic—thus unappealing in a popular, commercial sense—and that "Orientalist" would not register with many people. Thus "East," problematic as the term is, at least functioned as a geographical indicator. But what does "Lure of the East" suggest? Is it any better than "Eastern Promise"? The dictionary definition of "lure" reads "a) the power of attracting or enticing, b) anything having this power—to attract, entice." Imagine then, *Leila* or *Hareem Life*, unmediated, unexplained, over which is mapped a title suggesting enticement that is, by definition, non-Western, and in the process regurgitating an Orientalist cliché, namely a "depiction of non-productive excess secluded from view."[22] The East as female? The East as harem? The lure of that East?

The study of Orientalism has, of course, generated some stereotypes of its own. I am guessing that everyone reading this essay will have an opinion of what would be the visual clichés of Orientalist studies. What would they be? How many of us would choose a landscape painting? I suspect, not many. How many of us would choose a figurative work? Most of us? Delacroix's *Death of Sardanapalus* (1827), perhaps, or Ingres' *Turkish Bath* (1862)? How many of us already have in our minds Gérôme's *The Snake Charmer* (about 1880) as a contender for our shortlist? How much of the notoriety of this painting, in curatorial and academic circles at least, comes from it appearing as an early front cover to Said's *Orientalism*? In a review of *Orientalism*, first published in *The Journal of Middle East Studies* in 1980, Martin Kerr noted that much of the author's "outlook" was "neatly represented by the picture on the dust jacket, resourcefully unearthed by Said."[23] We should be particularly attentive to how Kerr then describes Gérôme's image, "in which a boy of fourteen or so, *stark naked*, displays a cobra wrapped around himself to a *bearded oriental potentate* and his *murderous-looking retinue slumped* at the base of a wall of richly painted oriental tile, while a *cadaverous musician* plays a reed instrument [my emphasis]." Thus the "picture itself *speaks volumes*, calling to mind all the *lurid distortions* of the Muslim East offered up by Hollywood and Herblock [my emphasis]."[24] Whether he did or not, Kerr assumes that Said chose the image, because it was material evidence to his argument and then "neatly," to use Kerr's word, encapsulates that argument. So can we conclude that the reader, whether fresh to the subject or not, can and will anticipate the content of the book? Interestingly Linda Nochlin, who was the first to analyze *The Snake Charmer* in a Saidian context made the same assumption: "No wonder Said used it as the dust jacket for his critical study of the phenomenon of Orientalism!"[25] Clearly a front cover, like a poster, is a powerful statement. Or tool? Thus in countering Said, should we expect equal attention paid by authors to cover images? In *Defending the West: A Critique of Edward Said's* Orientalism (2007), Ibn Warraq, amongst others, attempts to demonstrate how Said's supporters have used his arguments to remove thousands of works of art, particularly nineteenth-century Western paintings, from the displays of major art museums. The cover image is a detail from Lewis's *The Mid-Day Meal*, a visual counterpoint to Gérôme's image and its suggestions (one might summarize) of stagnation, exploitation and degeneracy, with a contrasting all-male scene, this time a respectful image (one might suggest) of good-natured *bonhomie* and egalitarian sociability, embracing servants, masters and guests—replacing a negative with a positive? While we might guess at the motivation behind using *The Mid-Day Meal*, we have Daniel Martin Varisco's own testimony. The author of *Reading Orientalism: Said and the Unsaid* (2007)—an "in-depth critical analysis of Said's unrevised text"—deliberately chose a cover image of a snake charmer by Etienne Dinet, which, he claims, would be "an uncomfortable fit for Said." For Varisco, the image underlines Dinet's "compassion with recognition of humanity of those he painted." He concludes, "What a difference a picture can make."[26] Indeed. But will Varisco's readership appreciate the image in the same way?

It was for all these reasons that the exhibition curators pushed for Arthur Melville's *Arab Interior*, an atmospheric scene with a seated male figure, to be used for the marketing campaign. Indeed the painting had already taken a central role in the design treatment of the catalog (Fig. 1.4) and the

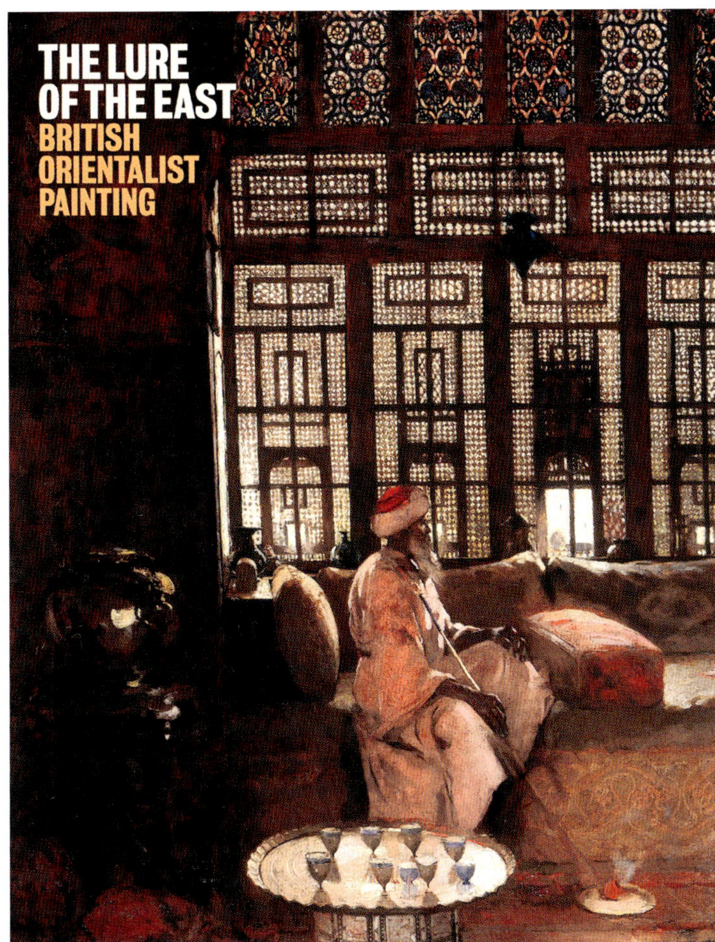

Figure 1.4 Front cover of *The Lure of the East: British Orientalist Painting* exhibition catalog showing a detail from *The Arab Interior*, Arthur Melville (1855–1904), 1881, oil on canvas, 95 x 72.8 cm, National Gallery of Scotland, Edinburgh. (Catalog cover designed by Atelier Works.)

exhibition itself, the curators and designers having developed together a design creative that was (we hoped) restrained, thoughtful and structured. Colors were used that were, to our eyes at least, fresh and natural (the colors were in fact copied from works of art) and, for the catalog title and text, fonts that were neat and simple to counteract the more decorative, "Arabian Nights" scripts associated with "the East." The Tate's own font was used for the exhibition graphics and the poster campaign. Although the catalog was designed before the title, *The Lure of the East*, had been devised and confirmed, the style adopted was meant to temper rather than encourage or reaffirm any clichéd associations. Combined with the detail from Melville's *Arab Interior*, the result was intended to offer an alternative, less loaded form of attraction to "the East," that was provoked by the traditional Cairene interiors that British artists visited, sketched and painted, and in particular the effect of strong sunlight through the latticed woodwork screens or *mashrabiyya* that were positioned across windows. This, as the catalog states, was a "favourite motif" of British painters, and could be seen by readers and visitors in numerous paintings within the catalog and exhibition itself, by Frank Dillon, Lewis and, of course, Melville.[27] After the title was confirmed, we decided to extend the motif into the exhibition design. We used a detail from a traditional Islamic pattern book, as a patterned light over the title at the exhibition entrance (Fig. 1.5), as background to the exhibition leaflet and within the exhibition itself, as a large-scale screen subdividing the "Harem and Home" gallery space into

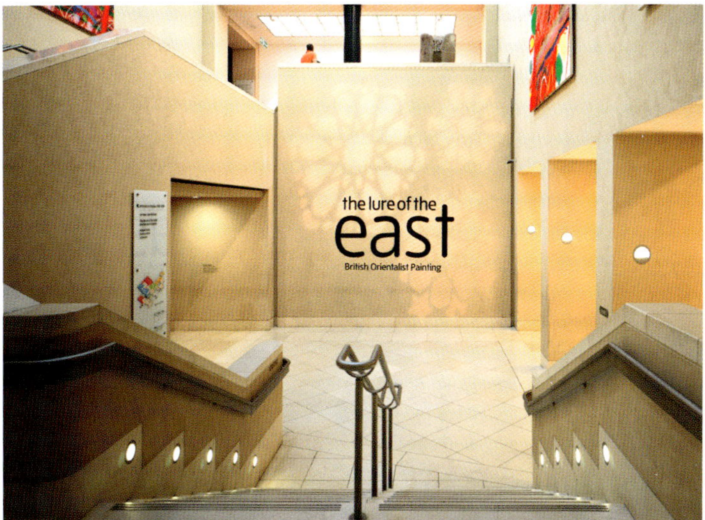

Figure. 1.5 Installation photograph taken at the entrance of *The Lure of the East: British Orientalist Painting* exhibition at Tate Britain. (Exhibition designed by Atelier Works. Photography © ChrisGascoigne.)

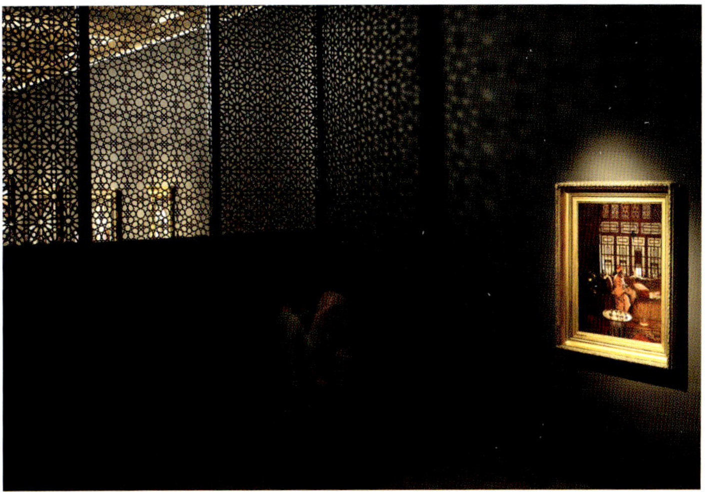

Figure. 1.6 Installation photograph taken within the "Harem and Home" gallery of *The Lure of the East: British Orientalist Painting* exhibition at Tate Britain. (Exhibition designed by Atelier Works. Photography © ChrisGascoigne.)

"interiors" and "harem" sections (Fig. 1.6). The screen was not intended to be a recreation but was an architectural conceit that, it was hoped, would give the effect of a traditional interior, casting patterned shadows across the walls of the gallery. Whether we succeeded or not in these ambitions is ultimately a decision for the exhibition visitor.

Once the various issues raised by this particular exhibition had been discussed, the curatorial and marketing teams were unanimous in agreeing to a detail from Melville's *Arab Interior* as the poster campaign at Tate Britain. There is, however, a coda to this story. In an attempt to bolster visitor figures, it was decided that a fresh, focused marketing campaign was necessary, utilizing a more consumer friendly image. As a result four advertisements were placed in *The Daily Telegraph* during August 2008, the readership of this conservative newspaper being an important audience for Tate Britain exhibitions. The image chosen was *Leila*.

Notes

1 Edmund Capon, "Director's Introduction" to *Orientalism: Delacroix to Klee*, ed. Roger Benjamin (Sydney: The Art Gallery of New South Wales, 1997), 5.

2 Alan Richardson, "Byron's *The Giaour*: Teaching Orientalism in the Wake of September 11," in *Interrogating Orientalism: Contextual Approaches and Pedagogical Practises*, ed. Diane Long Hoeveler and Jeffrey Cass (Columbus: Ohio State University Press, 2006), 214.

3 Quoted in Edhem Eldem, *Consuming the Orient* (Istanbul: Ottoman Bank Archives and Research Centre, 2007), 13.

4 "Call for Papers. Framing the Other. 30 Years after *Orientalism*," Courtauld Institute of Art, April 26, 2008, http://www.courtauld.ac.uk/researchforum/calls_paper/orientalism.shtml (accessed May 5, 2010).

5 Hugh Muir, "Fantasy Queen Mistaken for Prophet's Wife: Tate Apologises for Gaffe which Offended Muslims," *The Guardian*, November 10, 2003, http://www.guardian.co.uk/uk/2003/nov/10/arts.religion1 (accessed May 5, 2010).

6 "Tate 'Misunderstood' Banned Work," BBC News Channel, September 26, 2005, http://news.bbc.co.uk/1/hi/entertainment/4281958.stm (accessed May 5, 2010).

7 *East West: Objects Between Cultures*, Tate Britain, September 1, 2006 to February 18, 2007, http://www.tate.org.uk/britain/exhibitions/eastwest/default.shtm (accessed May 5, 2010).

8 *Sacred: Discover What We Share*, British Library, April 27 to September 23, 2007, http://www.bl.uk/onlinegallery/featuressacred/homepage.html (accessed May 5, 2010).

9 Yasmin Khan, "Sacred: Discover What We Share at the British Library," *Culture24*, July 6, 2007, http://www.culture24.org.uk/history+%2526+heritage/work+%2526+daily+life/faith+and+belief/art48762 (accessed May 5, 2010).

10 *Babylon: Myth and Reality*, British Museum, November 13, 2008 to March 15, 2009, http://www.britishmuseum.org/the_museum/museum_in_london/london_exhibition_archive/archive_babylon/babylon/exhibition_overview.aspx (accessed May 5, 2010).

11 Alan Richardson, "Byron's *The Giaour*," 214 and 222.

12 "Foreword" in *The Lure of the East: British Orientalist Painting*, ed. Nicholas Tromans (London: Tate Publishing, 2008), 6 and 7.

13 Linda Nochlin, "The Imaginary Orient" [1983] in *The Politics of Vision. Essays on Nineteenth-Century Art and Society* (New York and London: Harper and Row, 1989), 34.

14 Eldem, *Consuming the Orient*, 13.

15 I am here utilizing comments made in Edward Ziter, "Teaching Nineteenth-Century Orientalist Entertainments" in *Interrogating Orientalism*, 224.

16 Naomi Klein, *No Logo: Taking Aim at the Brand Bullies* (New York: Knopf Doubleday Publishing Group at Random House, 2000), 2.

17 Lauren Rosewarne, *Sex in Public: Women, Outdoor Advertising and Public Policy* (Cambridge: Cambridge Scholars Publishing, 2007), 4.

18 Ibid., 146.

19 Ibid., 31. The percentage is quoted in Tom Reichart, *The Erotic History of Advertising* (Amberst: Prometheus Group, 2003), 11.

20 "Kate Moss Gets Steamy in Turkish Baths for ANOTHER Sexy Shoot," *Daily Mail*, August 28, 2008, http://www.dailymail.co.uk/tvshowbiz/article-1050012/Kate-Moss-gets-steamy-Turkish-baths-ANOTHER-sexy-shoot.html (accessed May 5, 2010).

21 See, for example, "Straw's Veil Comments Spark Anger," BBC News Channel, October 5, 2006, http://news.bbc.co.uk/1/hi/5410472.stm (accessed May 5, 2010).

22 Ziter, "Teaching Nineteenth-Century Orientalist Entertainments," 228.

23 Malcolm Kerr, review of Edward W. Said, *Orientalism*, in *International Journal of Middle East Studies* 12, no. 4 (December 1980): 544.

24 Ibid.

25 Nochlin, "The Imaginary Orient," 35.

26 Daniel Martin Varisco, "The Other Half of Edward Said's Orientalism—and of Three Decades of Polemics," April 3, 2009, http://www.rorotoko.com/index.php/article/daniel_martin_varisco_book_interview_reading_orientalism_edward_said_unsaid/ (accessed May 5, 2010).

27 *The Lure of the East: British Orientalist Painting*, 129.

Bibliography

Babylon: Myth and Reality, British Museum, November 13, 2008 to March 15, 2009. http://www.britishmuseum.org/the_museum/museum_in_london/london_exhibition_archive/archive_babylon/babylon/exhibition_overview.aspx (accessed May 5, 2010).

"Call for Papers. Framing the Other. 30 Years after *Orientalism*," Courtauld Institute of Art, April 26, 2008. http://www.courtauld.ac.uk/researchforum/calls_paper/orientalism.shtml (accessed May 5, 2010).

Capon, Edmund. "Director's Introduction" to *Orientalism: Delacroix to Klee*, edited by Roger Benjamin. Sydney: The Art Gallery of New South Wales, 1997.

East West: Objects Between Cultures, Tate Britain, September 1, 2006 to February 18, 2007. http://www.tate.org.uk/britain/exhibitions/eastwest/default.shtm (accessed May 5, 2010).

Eldem, Edhem. *Consuming the Orient*. Istanbul: Ottoman Bank Archives and Research Centre, 2007. Published in conjunction with the exhibition *Consuming the Orient* shown at the Ottoman Bank Archive and Research Centre, Istanbul.

Exposed: The Victorian Nude. Edited by Alison Smith. London: Tate Publishing, 2001. Published in conjunction with the exhibition *Exposed: The Victorian Nude* shown at Tate Britain, Haus der Kunst, Munich, Brooklyn Museum of Art, Kobe City Museum and Geidai Museum (The University Art Museum).

Hoeveler, Diane Long and Jeffrey Cass, eds. *Interrogating Orientalism: Contextual Approaches and Pedagogical Practises*. Columbus: Ohio State University Press, 2006.

Ibn Warraq. *Defending the West: A Critique of Edward Said's Orientalism*. Amherst NY: Prometheus Books, 2007.

"Kate Moss Gets Steamy in Turkish Baths for ANOTHER Sexy Shoot," *Daily Mail*, August 28, 2008. http://www.dailymail.co.uk/tvshowbiz/article-1050012/Kate-Moss-gets-steamy-Turkish-baths-ANOTHER-sexy-shoot.html (accessed May 5, 2010).

Kerr, Malcolm. Review of Edward W. Said, *Orientalism*, in *International Journal of Middle East Studies* 12, no. 4 (December 1980): 544–47.

Khan, Yasmin. "Sacred: Discover What We Share at the British Library," *Culture24*, July 6, 2007. http://www.culture24.org.uk/history+%2526+heritage/work+%2526+daily+life/faith+and+belief/art48762 (accessed May 5, 2010).

Klein, Naomi. *No Logo: Taking Aim at the Brand Bullies*. New York: Knopf Doubleday Publishing Group at Random House, 2000.

Muir, Hugh. "Fantasy Queen Mistaken for Prophet's Wife: Tate Apologises for Gaffe which Offended Muslims." *The Guardian*, November 10, 2003. http://www.guardian.co.uk/uk/2003/nov/10/arts. religion1 (accessed May 5, 2010).

Nobel Dreams, Wicked Pleasures: Orientalism in America, 1870–1930. Edited by Holly Edwards. Princeton NJ: Princeton University Press, 2000. Published in conjunction with the exhibition *Nobel Dreams, Wicked Pleasures: Orientalism in America, 1870–1930* shown at the Sterling and Francine Clark Art Institute, the Walters Art Gallery and the Mint Museum of Art.

Nochlin, Linda. "The Imaginary Orient" [1983] in *The Politics of Vision. Essays on Nineteenth-Century Art and Society*, 33–59. New York and London: Harper and Row, 1989.

Orientalism: Delacroix to Klee. Edited by Roger Benjamin. Sydney: The Art Gallery of New South Wales, 1997. Published in conjunction with the exhibition *Orientalism: Delacroix to Klee* shown at the Art Gallery of New South Wales and Auckland City Art Gallery.

Reichart, Tom. *The Erotic History of Advertising*. Amherst: Prometheus Group, 2003.

Richardson, Alan. "Byron's *The Giaour*: Teaching Orientalism in the Wake of September 11." In *Interrogating Orientalism: Contextual Approaches and Pedagogical Practises*, edlted by Diane Long Hoeveler and Jeffrey Cass, 213–233. Columbus: Ohio State University Press, 2006.

Rosewarne, Lauren. *Sex in Public: Women, Outdoor Advertising and Public Policy*. Cambridge: Cambridge Scholars Publishing, 2007.

Sacred: Discover What We Share, British Library, April 27 to September 23, 2007. http://www.bl.uk/onlinegallery/features/sacred/homepage.html (accessed May 5, 2010).

Said, Edward W. *Orientalism.* London: Routledge and Kegan Paul, 1978.

"Straw's Veil Comments Spark Anger," BBC News Channel, October 5, 2006. http://news.bbc.co.uk/1/hi/5410472.stm (accessed May 5, 2010).

"Tate 'Misunderstood' Banned Work," BBC News Channel, September 26, 2005. http://news.bbc.co.uk/1/hi/entertainment/4281958.stm (accessed May 5, 2010).

The Lure of the East: British Orientalist Painting. Edited by Nicholas Tromans. London: Tate Publishing, 2008. Published in conjunction with the exhibition *The Lure of the East: British Orientalist Painting* shown at the Yale Center for British Art, Tate Britain, Suna and İnan Kıraç Pera Museum and the Sharjah Art Museum.

The Orientalists: Delacroix to Matisse, European Painters in North Africa and the Near East. Edited by MaryAnne Stevens. London: Royal Academy of Arts, 1984. Published in conjunction with the exhibition *The Orientalists: Delacroix to Matisse, European Painters in North Africa and the Near East* shown at the Royal Academy of Arts, London and the National Gallery of Art, Washington.

Varisco, Daniel Martin. *Reading Orientalism: Said and the Unsaid*. Seattle and London: University of Washington Press, 2007.

Varisco, Daniel Martin. "The Other Half of Edward Said's Orientalism—and of Three Decades of Polemics," April 3, 2009. http://www.rorotoko.com/index.php/article/daniel_martin_varisco_book_interview_reading_orientalism_edward_said_unsaid/ (accessed May 5, 2010).

Ziter, Edward. "Teaching Nineteenth-Century Orientalist Entertainments." In *Interrogating Orientalism: Contextual Approaches and Pedagogical Practises*, edited by Diane Long Hoeveler and Jeffrey Cass, 224–44. Columbus: Ohio State University Press, 2006.

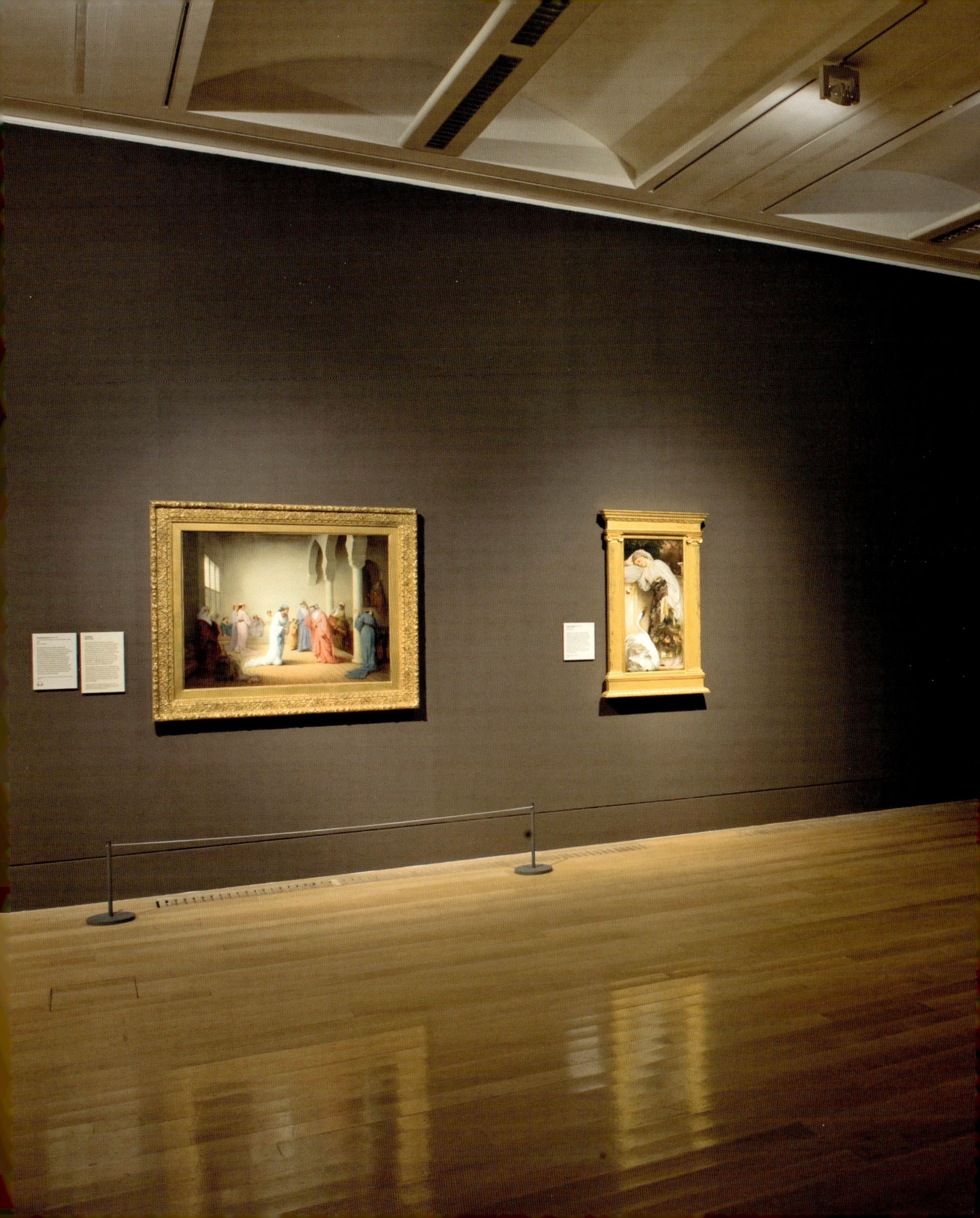

II

Cultural Exchange and the Politics of Pleasure

Reina Lewis

Thirty years after the publication of Edward Said's seminal polemic *Orientalism* a major exhibition of Orientalist paintings toured the East and West in 2008.[1] Starting at the Yale Center for British Art, a gallery located within a scholarly research center at an elite Western university, and moving to Tate Britain in London, a national public museum, this significant reprisal and reconsideration of mainly British Orientalism then crossed to Istanbul, the heart of the erstwhile Orient as was known to or imagined by the artists in the exhibition. Installed in the privately endowed Pera Museum, *The Lure of the East* was now seen alongside the museum's permanent collection of Western Orientalist art and Ottoman artifacts. In its final destination, *The Lure of the East* went to the United Arab Emirates, opening as one of the earliest exhibits at the Sharjah Art Museum.

Responding to this exhibition and contributing to associated academic and public events was of tremendous personal significance for me. My engagements with all but the final installation of *The Lure of the East* brought me back into the orbit of the very images whose mesmeric pull first prompted me to engage with the Orientalist paradigm as a young researcher. The combination of timing and display allowed me to look afresh at some cherished artifacts and to ask myself if, and how, I would approach them differently now. In indulging in my renewed reflections on these paintings I am not, of course, proposing that my response be seen as in any way unique: rather, it is precisely how that response is made possible and informed by new developments in the related fields of enquiry that surround these objects and their display that merits attention.

Orientalism Reviewed

The most exciting moment for me when *The Lure of the East* opened was the chance to actually see Henriette Browne's 1861 painting *A Visit: Harem Interior, Constantinople, 1860* (Fig. 2.1). This painting, exhibited to great acclaim in the Paris Salon of 1861 had formed the centerpiece of my PhD research and subsequently of my first book, *Gendering Orientalism*.[2] But I had never seen it in real life, or even had access to a color reproduction. Whilst many researchers in women's history (visual or otherwise) and those working on colonial and minority histories will be similarly familiar with the challenges of researching in the absence of preserved archives, it was unusual to spend so many years working on material that was unavailable to view. Operating before the advantages offered by the internet, I spent a long time tracing and evaluating the ways in which these (to me unseen) paintings were consumed, discussed, and circulated. And, suddenly, here it was, in full living color (Fig. 2.2).

Were I now to be starting on my project on Henriette Browne, I would also have the benefit of a vastly expanded "canon" in which to situate her. It is not just that so much more is known about the professional (and amateur) contribution of Western women artists, but that the expansion of the field challenges us to think more broadly about the impact of Orientalism on popular, material, and consumer cultures.[3] Art historians have put these new sources in a dynamic domain, attending to interactions between Ottoman and Western travelers, writers, artists, and patrons.[4] Reframing previous orthodoxies about Orientalism in the visual arts, literary, and material culture, we are more likely now to talk about multiple Orientalisms and their different, overlapping, and contradictory audiences, purposes, and pleasures. This significant change in what counts as Orientalism and how we approach it informs and is informed by what are for me two key developments in critical and cultural studies and art history since Said's first formulation. First, the ways in which postcolonial studies has turned to cultural production emanating from communities previously positioned as the objects of colonial or Orientalist enquiry. And, second, the ways in which the emphasis on pleasure that was such a

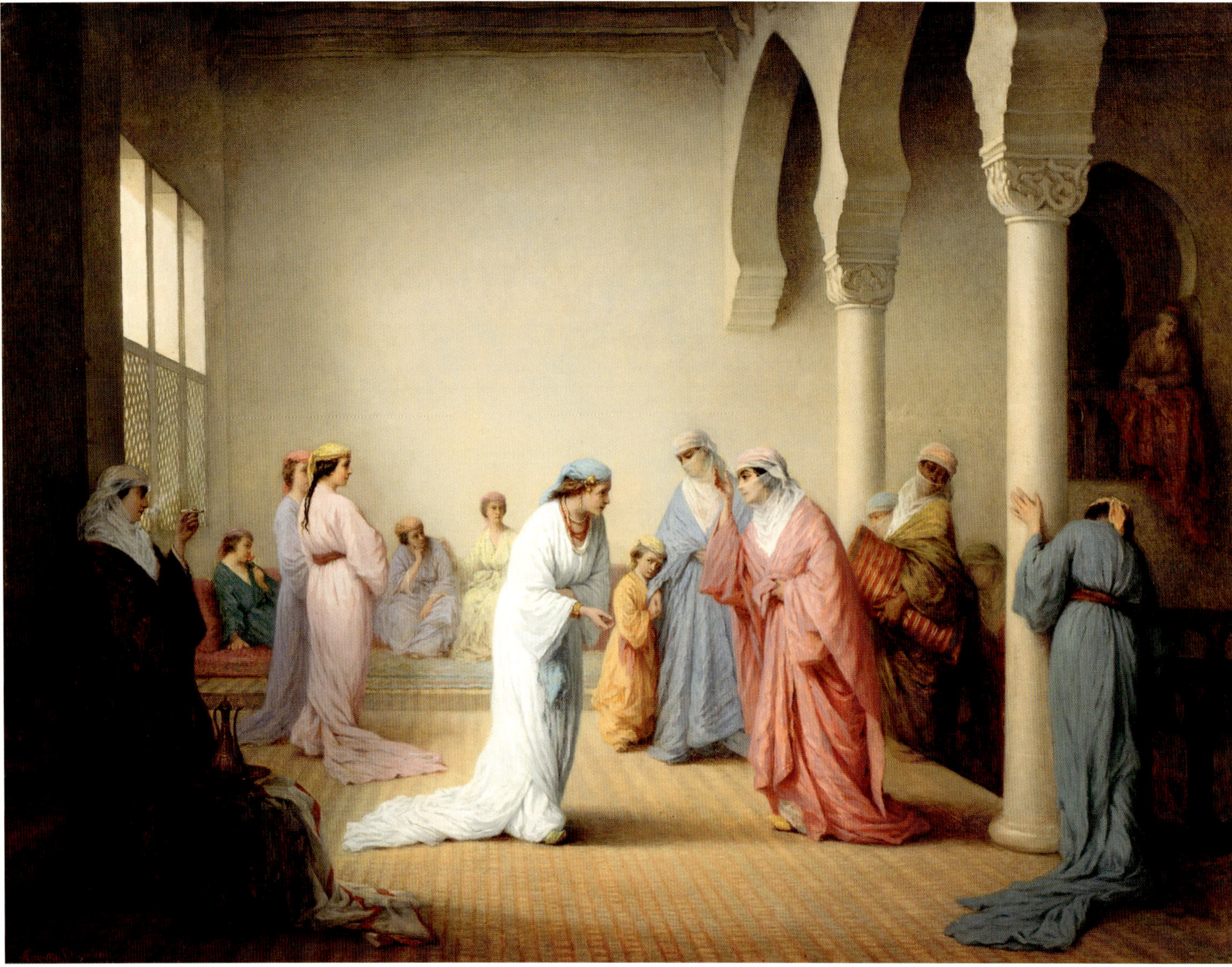

Figure 2.1 *A Visit: Harem Interior, Constantinople, 1860*, Henriette Browne (1829–1901), 1861, oil on canvas, 89 x 114 cm, Private Collection. Courtesy of Marco Frignati Art Advisory, London.

predominant feature of earlier postmodern theory has been critically taken up in the fields of gender and transnational studies, and feminist art history. Challenges to normative Western masculinist presumptions by feminist and postcolonial decenterings of the colonial subject have effectively repositioned pleasure as socially and historically contingent. At the same time, postcolonial feminist and queer interventions into earlier theories of the female gaze have dramatically widened the social and geographical scope of discussion, drawing attention to diverse, marginal, and contradictory modes of cultural production and consumption.

Focusing on colonial or postcolonial cultural production brings forward as subjects those populations previously classified as the objects of imperial, or in my case, Orientalist cultures. This motivated my shift in focus from Western women to Ottoman and Turkish women writers.[5] Foregrounding sources produced outside the Western imperial centers does indeed expand the domain of Orientalism and its—to some—troublesome pleasures. But changing the roster of images or texts is not of only empirical importance: redefining the objects of enquiry simultaneously alters their modes of explication, requiring and responding to new methodologies.

In my case, the desire to bring into view the cultural and political agency of women who would have been classified as "Oriental" (with all that that implied) took me to books rather than to pictures in a study of memoirs and travelogs by

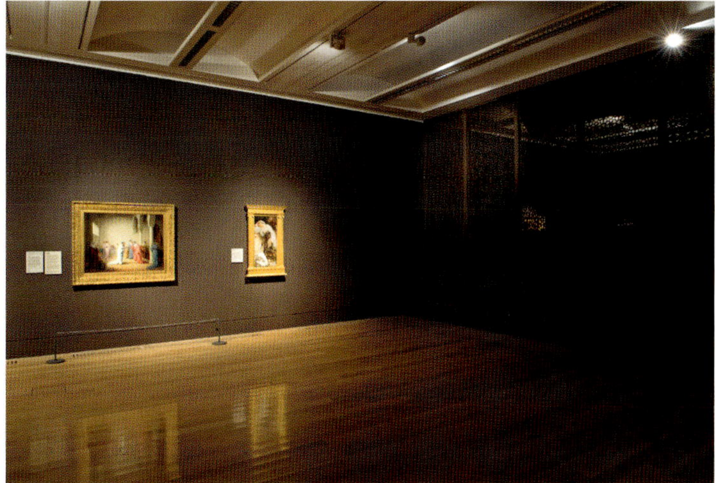

Figure 2.2 *The Lure of the East*, installation shot showing *A Visit: Harem Interior, Constantinople, 1860*, Henriette Browne, at Tate Britain, June 2008. © Tate, London, 2010.

Ottoman women from the late nineteenth and early twentieth centuries. Looking at publications written in English for a European and North American readership abroad, and for the educated Ottoman elite at home, I took as my sources volumes by authors such as Halide Edib, Zeyneb Hanım (or Hanoum as she styled herself), Demetra Vaka Brown, and Selma Ekrem.[6] Unlike Browne's paintings these books were available to me in their original form, though they had merited little critical attention, generally being disregarded as middle-brow literature. Popular enough in their day to garner reviews and selling into second and third editions, their peculiar literary and evidential status places them on the edge of literary respectability.

For their authors the books had serious intent; to counter Western stereotypes and simultaneously contribute to discussions about social change at home. But the Orientalizing challenges of participating in a Western genre like harem literature were unavoidable. In a cultural field reliant on gendered codes of authenticity,[7] women produced as Oriental faced the double bind of having to commodify themselves as Oriental in terms recognizable to their consumers, at the same time as they sought to undercut the prejudicial knowledges of that discourse. These written sources all use claims to authenticity as a selling point, just like Henriette Browne whose paintings were exhibited with validating details of time and place; *A Visit* was paired with the similarly titled *A Flute Player (Harem Interior, Constantinople, 1860)* (1861). Browne's claim to have seen the harem forbidden to Western men gave her works a premium. Théophile Gautier famously declared that "only women should go to Turkey"[8] —though another (woman) reviewer argued that she was "despite herself, influenced by the harem's enervating atmosphere" and so compromised her artistic judgment.[9]

For both Western and Middle Eastern women the claim to authenticity was essential to the value of their work and provided the framework within and against which they could function. Challenges to the validity of these sources continue today. On one hand I am driven mad by the perpetual need to defend my sources from charges of inauthenticity, but on the other hand I see it as part of the discourse. Attempts at invalidation on the grounds of disputed authenticity are characteristic of the field and come to bear especially in relation to women's lives, and most particularly in relation to the harem. So for example, as I have argued elsewhere,[10] it is not stupidity that prompts Zeyneb Hanım in 1913 to punctuate a book full of critical analyses of European stereotypes with potentially eroticizing photographs of herself in veils of various descriptions: rather, it is an indication of the discursive limitations that framed the emergence of a non-Western authorial voice.

The growing recognition of the nuance and importance of cultural exchange has motivated my recent work. When Teresa Heffernan and I started to republish these sources, we called the book series *Cultures in Dialogue* to highlight the reciprocal nature of colonial, imperial, and Orientalist cultures.[11] It was clear to us that these sources needed to be seen in dialog with each other, just as they were at the time. The nature of this dialog was personal, textual, and commercial. For example, Zeyneb Hanım's evaluation of European society is presented as a series of often acerbic letters exchanged with the British feminist and traveler Grace Ellison, who for some of the time was herself staying in an Ottoman harem while publishing her reports in the *Daily Telegraph* in 1912/13.[12]

But exchange is never simple or straightforward. Just as indigenized cultural forms are not a mirror image of the "original," each party in an exchange has different things to gain or lose and different ways of evaluating the experience. As several of the essays in this book demonstrate, there is increasing awareness of the delicate and sometimes hard to detect ways in which the global power inequalities of imperialism are recalibrated, even if briefly, by local hierarchies and value systems. In the context of British Orientalism and Ottoman Istanbul, there are several examples of how local power was exercised in and through the Ottoman patronage of Western artists; such as the ways in which Sultan Abdülmecid intervened to direct the portrait he had commissioned in 1840 from British artist David Wilkie.[13] This type of information is important for two related reasons. First, revealing the uneven and shifting social relations brought about by elite Ottoman patronage reinforces why attention to the particulars of the Ottoman empire are important for accounts of imperialism, providing a comparative corrective to the largely binarized models of Western imperialism. Second, demonstrating that Ottoman patrons were not simply passive consumers of Western culture contributes to debates about cultural authenticity by showing how both Western and Ottoman cultural forms were reciprocally altered through this interactive process of cultural production and display, illuminating the impact of localized cultural hybridity on the Western "original." This was often denigrated at the time by imperially nostalgic Westerners as a misplaced and failed attempt to be "modern," seen typically in the tendency of women travel writers like Annie Jane Harvey in 1871 to decry as vulgar and garish the mix of Ottoman and Western fashion found in elite harems, or in Julia Pardoe's critique in 1837 of the provincial "absurdity" of Ottoman Greek women's attempts at "European" fashion.[14] In contrast, current scholarship recognizes the potential pleasures and paybacks of such cultural bricolage for both local and Western actors.

Orientalism turns out to have incorporated far more viewpoints and varieties than might initially have been thought. The value in knowing about different manifestations is not simply one of train-spotting, of adding more examples to the archive. The benefit lies in how these diverse sources help us differently to understand the cultural relations that forged and still forge Orientalism. As someone with an abiding interest in discussions about the female gaze (necessarily understood in the plural), the expanded store of knowledge about women's Orientalism provides opportunities to deepen understandings of gendered visuality. It is increasingly possible to factor into a gender analysis the other social and imperial differentials that created and constrained conditions of cultural production and consumption. The evident diversity of female Orientalist viewpoints can be animated with reference to the collaborative and contestatory esthetic and social interactions that formed their moments of creation and reception.

Contestations like those between Fatma Sultan and Mary Walker over what the princess would wear in the portraits she commissioned in the 1850s. A decade after Abdülmecid intervened in Wilkie's portrait, his daughter was frustrating the Orientalist desires of another British artist by insisting on being painted in her European wardrobe. This deal-breaker was just one of the several conditions on the manufacture and display of Walker's portraits, as Mary Roberts and Zeynep İnankur reveal in their discussions of these still missing works.[15] As Roberts demonstrates, by the mid century the combination of generic Orientalist knowledges and the emerging protocols of women's ethnographic reportage were creating opportunities for the operation of a distinctively female scopic gaze. Utilizing especially details of dress and body management, Western women subjected the Ottoman female body to a coded eroticized surveillance. But the desire for this controlling gaze was just as likely to be frustrated by the interventions of Ottoman women for whom participation in the construction of Orientalist cultural forms may simultaneously create opportunities for the exercise of cultural agency.

This type of uneven cultural and personal exchange can also inform thinking in the domain of sexuality. Roberts's work on the relationship between Elisabeth Jerichau-Baumann and her patron the Ottoman-Egyptian princess Nazlı Hanım provides new material on the Polish-Danish artist, locating the two women within professional and friendship relationships characterized by complementary and conflicting artistic and personal motivations.[16] In my earlier work on Jerichau-Baumann I had initially positioned her as a corollary to Henriette Browne, featuring her as another prominent woman painter of Oriental scenes whose sometimes risqué images—often coded by critics as ethnographic—troubled the parameters of what we would have thought possible for respectable lady artists. I struggled to attend further to the homoerotics that seemed evident to me in her work.[17] Roberts's introduction of Jerichau-Baumann's literary renditions of her royal friend plus the photographs of Nazlı Hanım cross-dressed as an Ottoman bey[18] augment considerations of female homosociality and homoeroticism in the depiction of segregated life then and now. When connected to queer theory and the growing scholarship on Middle Eastern histories of sexuality,[19] the extension of the primary field can create new matrices within which to investigate sources whose relationship to gender, audience, power, and pleasure continue to defy straightforward or comprehensive readings.[20]

Postcolonial Audiences: Authenticity and Display

The UK version of *The Lure of the East* was quite different to its initial installation at the Yale Center for British Art. Not just because some pictures could not travel, but because Tate Britain was concerned about how a show that was mainly about the Muslim Middle East would play in postcolonial multicultural Britain, post 9/11, post 7/7.

The Tate gallery augmented its usual interpretive apparatus with a set of secondary captions and audio responses.[21]

Designed specifically to go beyond the usual suspects from the field of art history, this supplementary material included contributions from many not usually specializing in visual culture. As well as several art historians, the wall panels and audio accompaniment included creative writers and public figures with some connection to the territories represented, or with expertise in Middle Eastern history, Arabic arts and literature, and Islamic studies. Also featured was former BBC (and now al Jazeera) correspondent Rageh Omar. The captions and audio worked well, providing additional details about Muslim cultures of the Middle East and imperial history. But the choice of respondents was not casual—as well as subject experts and those notable for their interfaith work (like Rabbi Julia Neuberger who provided audio on Thomas Seddon's *Jerusalem and the Valley of Jehoshaphat from the Hill of Evil Counsel*) it was important for the gallery to field a visibly Muslim presence as an antidote to the roomfuls of Orientalist paintings that otherwise presented Muslims and Muslim cultures as objects rather than owners of the gaze. In the British context it was notable that this strategy went more broadly to issues presumed to be of widespread Muslim concern, especially British military engagements in the region. In this category would fall non-Muslim individuals such as the journalist Robert Fisk, Middle East correspondent for the *Independent*, whose name would be instantly recognizable as an outspoken opponent of the war in Iraq. Responding to Edward Lear's *Beirut* (c. 1861), Fisk's panel, "dictated from Beirut on 9 May 2008," brings an immediacy to the historical painting: "[the view in Lear] is geologically identical to the very same Mount Sannine which I am looking at from my balcony as I speak to you ... [Lebanon remains] a place of sectarian crisis on this day that I am speaking to you." Like Rageh Omar, a popular and prominent Muslim commentator with publicized regrets about his role as an embedded war reporter in Iraq, Robert Fisk is celebrated among the anti-war communities of Britain.

Looking at who was recruited, it was clear to me that authenticity was again center stage—this time driven by a desire for cultural sensitivity.

It is, however, a high risk strategy when individuals are asked, or offer, to represent a collective view, especially one that in this context is likely to be racialized, ethnicized, Orientalized—despite the obvious multi-ethnicity of Islam as a faith. I see the same dynamic across the historical period I study: the women who published accounts of segregated Muslim life at the start of the last century knew absolutely that their individual stories were also going to be read as emblematic of a whole society. In my own work I oscillate between using sources evidentially and reading them as creative artifacts. I cannot entirely avoid positioning Middle Eastern writers as "native informants," given that they almost inevitably adopt some version of this role—generic conventions and market conditions require it of them. One way out of this potential conundrum—of facing attacks on them as unreliable witnesses—is to emphasize that these books, or paintings, or photographs are historically contingent in their form as well as content. Technique is ideological, is historical, is located. The same can be said of curation.

The need to consider moments and mechanisms of cultural exchange in the context of Orientalism does not have significance for Orientalist cultural forms only at their point of production. Thinking about the historical materiality of, in this instance, paintings as mediated cultural objects also directs attention to the embodied and located nature of experiences of them at the point of consumption. Though the Yale show set out with considerable finesse the key debates about Orientalism, I can understand why Tate Britain was concerned about replicating in London the more straightforward interpretation provided by the hang at Yale. This was an exhibition commissioned before 9/11 that came to fruition in a different and difficult moment. In the UK, it might have been predicted that a Muslim and multi-cultural audience, as well as prevailing public sector cultural policy, would produce more overtly politicized modes of consumption. By the time the show was being installed in 2008 images of, or understood to be about, Muslims and the history of British relations with "the Muslim world" were highly fraught.

In the aftermath of the London bombs in July 2005 anxiety about the radicalization of "home-grown" jihadi youth had brought a pronounced scrutiny to bear on discernible Muslim communities. Working often from a securitizing discourse of containing potential threat, the perceived lack of integration of UK Muslim communities preoccupied national and local politicians, educationalists, security services, and welfare organizations, with an attendant shift in British multi-culturalism from a focus on race/ethnicity to one concerned increasingly with differences understood in terms of faith.[22] In a variety of ways, especially for a younger second and third generation Muslim population, a sense of religious identity began to augment and replace previous modes of anti-racist community activism whose cross-ethnic affiliations had been largely secular in character. The politicized reactivation of the concept of the *umma* (the world community of Muslim believers) offered a globalized affiliation that transcended the natal and regional attachments of their parents. Many in the UK came to recognize themselves within a religiously inflected internationalized world view that found connections with other Muslims as Muslims across geography and time (seen, for example, in both the increased interest in the Palestinian cause among the South Asian UK Muslim population and in the international response in 2005 to the Danish cartoons found to be offensive about the Prophet).[23] In a complex mix of community activism and state governance, resources and modes of political representation in the UK were organized more overtly than before along religious lines. Arts services were not immune, especially as images of Muslims played a key role in media and popular debates about citizenship, belonging, and nationality. Significantly for *The Lure of the East*, it was images of "visibly" Muslim women—i.e. women in hijab—that served as the key visual for any aspect of these discussions. With increasing numbers of young women in Britain taking hijab, often as a direct riposte to negative stereotypes of Islam, a pre-9/11 programming decision to mount a show full of minarets and odalisques had become a potential flashpoint.

In the end, however, most of these anxieties proved "unnecessary" in that the show, as Tate's Cross Cultural Curator Paul Goodwin noted, mainly attracted the usual (read non-Muslim) Tate audience of well-educated, visually literate habitual museum goers,[24] with good attendance at related public and educational events. While some broadsheet readers will have been drawn in by (*The Lure of the East* caption contributor) Yasmin Alibi Brown's favorable review in the *Independent* (the newspaper she shared with Fisk), the Muslim or Middle Eastern descent viewers that the Tate was concerned about were not especially present in the galleries. As both Goodwin thought and as Christine Riding (Chapter 1 in this volume) confirms, this may have had more to do with marketing than with curatorial decisions. Nominated not by the curatorial team but by the marketing department, the title *The Lure of the East* with its nostalgic associations was designed to appeal to the typical Tate Britain audience rather than, for example, to Muslim families in Tower Hamlets (a poor immigrant neighborhood of East London with a large Bengali Muslim population). Would another form of branding, perhaps based on appeals to cultural heritage or community "ownership," have drawn a different audience?

With fairly mainstream branding and a set of paintings that could be presented as a predominantly art historical intervention, it was the Tate's interpretation strategy and surrounding events that provided the postcolonial critical perspective to which the museum is committed. Now, one might argue that the Tate's desire to get recognizably Muslim names around the gallery had something in common with the desperate scramble in UK museums to install some sort of "Islamic trail" around their permanent collections. The renewed interest this prompted in previously unfashionable or disregarded Orientalist items paradoxically made it harder for the Tate to borrow pictures for *The Lure of the East* from other UK national collections.[25] It was not only for the Tate that the contents of *The Lure of the East* had become more overtly ideologically significant. Suddenly, paintings were being asked to do a lot of work—as noted by those critics of *The Lure of the East* who objected to the references to Said. Whilst all exhibitions have an interpretation strategy, some more clearly scholarly than others, the fact that this exhibition made the politics of interpretation overt from the start was bound to be contentious. For some, as Nicholas Tromans discusses here, the very inclusion of academic "cant" was anathema, for others, the attempt to politically mollify the presumed sensibilities of Muslim or Middle East descent viewers could only fall short.

As someone who is frequently invited to comment on all things queer because I am an out lesbian, regardless of whether I have any expertise in the given subject, I feared that the need for recognizably Muslim names might result in a similarly generic use of individuals as cultural intermediaries. But I need not have worried: the Tate's interpretation strategy was actually very successful in a possibly quite surprising and I think very important way. Formulated in a moment of postcolonial recognition that national collections need to reflect more adequately the diversity of the population, I welcome the attention to the historical and material circumstances in which the curators knew the show would be seen. As Goodwin pointed out, whilst the curatorial rationale behind the exhibition mounted an art historical case for the distinctiveness of British Orientalism in the last two centuries, when it came to installation the anxieties the show raised for in-house curatorial and interpretation teams illustrated the distinctiveness of contemporary UK postcolonial concerns. As a national British institution, the Tate needed to demonstrate sensitivity to local "Muslim" opinion at the same time as knowing full well that Muslim viewers do not have a single or shared interpretive approach. In the face of the constant demand for British Muslim "representatives" to provide the government with a vision of a manageably homogenous community (one that, in the prevailing terms, can distinguish between "extremist" and "moderate" Muslims), the clashing critical and creative registers featured in the secondary responses to the exhibition effectively disallowed any singular sense of a "British," or even an international, Muslim opinion.

The Pleasures of Looking/Commissioning/Owning

If we return, then, to the politics of pleasure, how do we figure pleasure in the complex reasons why these objects were commissioned, why they were then and are still now collected, and enjoyed by their various publics?

Thinking about why people like things enjoins us to recognize the diverse meanings available to the viewers of these works. One of the major contributions of *The Lure of the East* is that it foregrounds the historical role of Middle Eastern patrons—highlighting how commercial and personal interactions might reposition the power of the gaze in the representation of Oriental subjects and spaces.

Said initially factors in only a perverse, colonial pleasure—his putative Orientalist gaze is masculinist and monolithic. In this framework it would be almost impossible to explain, for example, that the strongest market for Orientalist paintings has for the last several decades consisted of buyers from the Middle East and North Africa and particularly, more recently, the Gulf.[26] To avoid resorting to a model of false consciousness we need to consider what different types of pleasures may be at play in the recuperation of this corpus by buyers from the region. Thirty years after the publication of *Orientalism* we do not need to replicate the dichotomous view laid out by the younger Said—instead, building on the work on Ottoman Orientalism by Ussama Makdisi and Edhem Eldem (see also Ahmet Ersoy, Chapter 9 in this volume),[27] we can incorporate into the frame the distinctive versions of Othering and Orientalizing that were projected onto different local populations by the Ottoman and subsequently Kemalist elites. In the same way as the colonial experience was instrumental in the formation of the Western self as (gendered, classed, sexualized) subject, the rendering of internal "Orientals" was instrumental to the fashioning of a preferred modern self for the urban elites of the Middle East.

Whilst Orientalism's paradigmatic eroticized harem scenes and nudes may be less assiduously collected by current Gulf and regional buyers, nostalgia—plus the relative rarity of indigenous pictorial images of the region—adds value to Western paintings. Sometimes, as colleagues in this book point out,[28] this gives enhanced value to the documentary potential of realist paintings as chronicles of a "lost" world. Anecdote also suggests that some images are found to be so spectacularly "wrong"' in their detail that they be bounced into the domain of desirable bad taste—allowing the sophisticated buyer the pleasure of discernment in reclaiming as kitsch material that might otherwise simply offend.[29]

The list of loans for *The Lure of the East* tells the story of the different ways in which and by whom Orientalist paintings have been valued. That more than usual came from private loans indicates that Orientalism was not always considered a valuable genre for acquisition in national collections in the West. That many more than usual came from first-time lenders indicates a pattern of private collection particular to this field. The developing collecting practices of the Middle Eastern and Arab buyers that have kept up the market for Orientalist painting can also be seen in a historical context in which location and generation inform changing consumption practices that have a significance beyond the initially small elite of actual buyers.

The characterizations above of the regional market for Orientalist art may apply to an older generation but not necessarily to their children. As Robin Start of the Park Gallery in London suggests, the next generation of buyers in the Gulf have much in common with elite buyers in Europe, or with the also more recently emergent Russian market.[30] Fewer, in his opinion, of the younger generation are buying Orientalist paintings, most purchase modern art including contemporary regional artists (a generational trend seen also in Turkey).[31] Women are also increasingly buyers in their own right, or an overt driving force behind their husband's/family collections. If the local interest in Western Orientalism has historically been driven in part by a desire for images of the region—given that there are few locally produced images for the pre-twentieth-century period—what happens when this appetite can now also be met by local modern art (figurative and abstract)? For younger buyers aiming also to distinguish themselves from their parents through the development of distinctive art buying habits, the increasing size and quality of the regional contemporary art scene may lead to a decline in interest in historic Orientalist paintings. Start, who also acts as an agent for/advisor to private collectors, has diversified his range accordingly, and sees contemporary Arab art "becoming internationalized, similar to what we have seen happen with Indian art and Chinese art." Whilst collectors at the moment are mainly local, he hopes that regional contemporary art will develop value on the global art market helped quite possibly by the establishment of super museums in the Gulf region[32] that might become newly significant for their potential to create a market for local art of international status.

The hesitation of some among the first generation of Arab collectors to reveal their holdings in public is not just about value (though there is an argument that works gain in resale value if they have not been seen for many years), but it is also connected to different notions of public and private and of display. For an older generation, of different habitus, the public display of wealth may be coded in relation to cultural conventions forged in the absence of a routinely experienced museum culture. For younger generations, educated and acculturated abroad, and demonstrating discernment locally through participation in global consumer culture, it remains to be seen whether the social and cultural capital of participating in the international circuit of loaning will form a valuable and desirable mode of distinction.

Conclusion: The Located Viewer, Time and Place

Aside from elite buyers, how do we think about the viewing experiences of the wider local and diaspora Middle Eastern and Muslim audiences who encounter these pictures on their travels around the world? Whilst for those living in non-Muslim majority territories there may be an intrinsic interest in finding material of some relevance to a cultural background rarely given center stage, Orientalist paintings can be difficult for those who feel themselves to be represented/misrepresented by them—even in a show that avoided, through its British focus it would argue, the worst cases of Orientalist sexualization. For this audience, Orientalist paintings are not necessarily devoid of pleasure—it just may be a different type of pleasure. I find helpful here bell hooks' emphasis on the "pleasures of interrogation"—her phrase to describe how black women in the USA can find a way to consume Hollywood movies without being obliterated by the endemic negative racial and gender stereotyping.[33] Making alternative, oppositional readings, politicized black women, she argues, can view the movie "on guard"—resisting the normatively white viewer position set up by the film and deriving a different pleasure through resistant reading. Explicit in her account is a historicized sense of a collective political identity forged through the histories of American racism and resistance.

For my discussion, this commitment to opposition may be less significant than the impact of generation—among both mainstream and minority ethnic consumers of Orientalism. The international internet generation raised on world music, world food, and world art, tends to be far less inhibited by the anxieties about cultural appropriation that restricted the habits of some of my peers. Whilst, in the West, the fleeting fashion for things ethnic temporarily deracinates the culturally specific for mainstream consumption,[34] young people of diasporic heritage move across a complex consumptionscape in which they constantly re-invent the "authentic."

On the international stage, new forms of local nostalgia that appear unproblematic to visiting tourists might have significant political nuance for local participants. In Damascus, as Christa Salamandra illustrates, the commodification of the Old City as a leisure destination is aimed at the traditional dynastic Damascene elite (now living in modern suburbs and facing the new power base of an incoming business elite) as much as at tourists.[35] With "traditional" food and clothing operating as stylish retro for the established elite, the depiction in literature and film of an idealized version of Old City life is rendered emblematic not just, she argues, for the city but for the city qua the nation. In a context of highly contested, coded, discussions about national identity an idealized Damascene past is packaged as a national Syrian past, in ways that resonate with the complex and contradictory recuperations of Ottoman Istanbul in contemporary Turkey.

In Turkey, the Ottoman past provides design inspiration in interiors, fashion, and leisure for both chic secular urbanites and for religious revivalists. Sometimes this is a generic admixture of seemingly random elements that goes to make up a vague cool "pastness" for secular local consumers and foreign tourists alike. This new form of heritage culture is often linked to the cycles of global fashion which in some cases especially lend themselves to the quasi-Oriental. A key contemporary example is the long-running boho trend, whose nouveau bohemian hippyness gave value-added fashionability to "Eastern" items. Dominating taste in interiors and fashion in the first decade of this century, boho's incorporation of Eastern textiles and Victoriana within an eclectic "more is more" approach to adornment and decor would have permeated the social and commercial worlds of many visitors to *The Lure of the East*, most especially in London and Istanbul. Gallery goers to the Tate and to the Pera museum would not have had to travel far to find cafés and restaurants that mixed on-trend squishy sofas and opulent velvet scatter cushions, lit quite possibly by inlaid metal work lantern light fittings, with inlaid tables on which they could eat modern interpretations of "traditional" Middle Eastern/Mediterranean or Ottoman dishes. In Istanbul especially, this international fashion story coincided with local nostalgias as part of the revitalization of Beyoğlu, where the Suna and İnan Kıraç Foundation perspicaciously chose to open the Pera Museum as part of the renovation of the district. The old European quarter has become again a residential and leisure destination. One block away, İstiklal Caddesi bustles with branches of global fashion brands and stylish Turkish multiples, alongside independent shops selling "traditional" foods and artifacts. On the main thoroughfare and in restored Ottoman passages tourists and locals alike can similarly re-value the

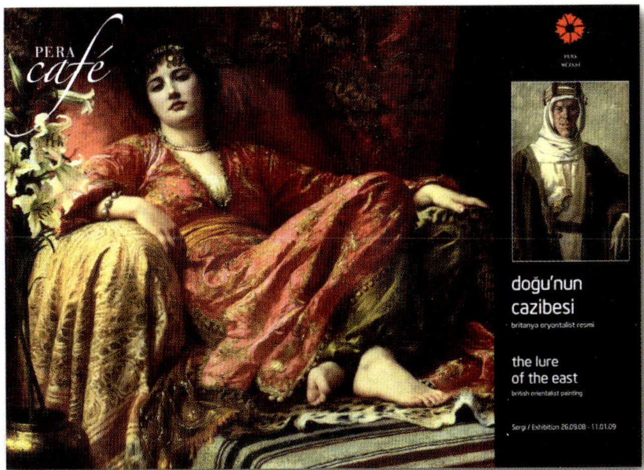

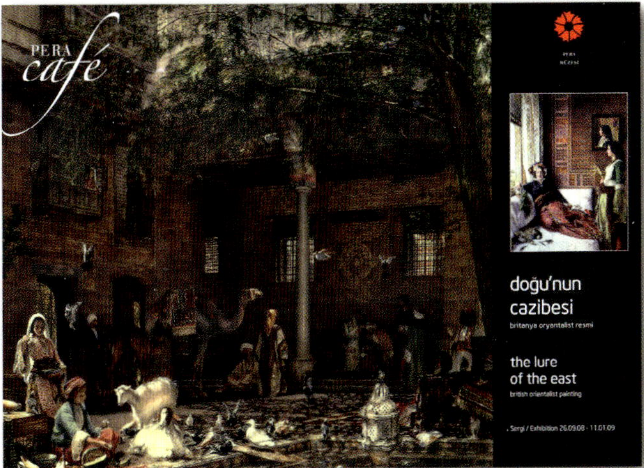

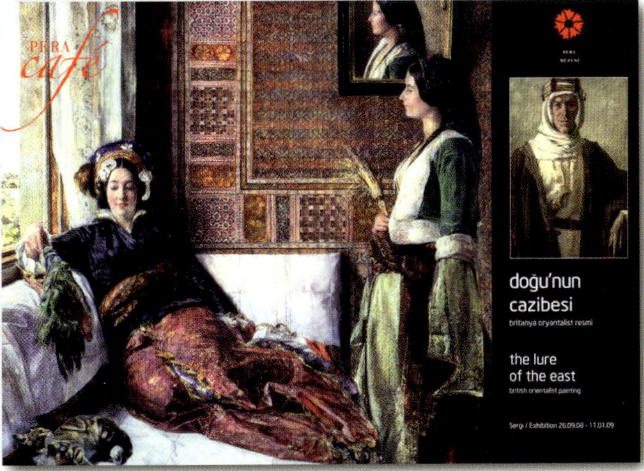

Figure 2.3 *The Lure of the East* placemats from Pera Museum café, 2008, showing (top to bottom): Frank Dicksee, *Leila* (with Augustus John, *Colonel T. E. Lawrence* detail); John Frederick Lewis *The Courtyard of the Coptic Partiarch's House in Cairo* (with John Frederick Lewis *Hhareem Life, Constantinople* detail); John Frederick Lewis *Hhareem Life, Constantinople* (with Augustus John, *Colonel T. E. Lawrence* detail). Courtesy of Suna and İnan Kıraç Foundation.

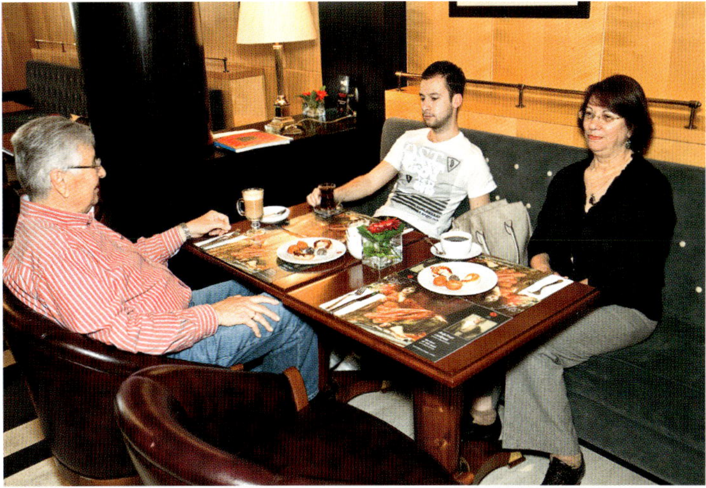

Figure 2.4 Location shot, Pera Museum café, Istanbul, showing *Leila* placemat in use. Courtesy of Suna and İnan Kıraç Foundation.

old through nostalgic recuperations coded variously as exotic or ironic, all available to be consumed and displayed as fashionable lifestyle bricolage.

In Istanbul *The Lure of the East* was an outstandingly successful show in terms of visitor numbers; the second most popular exhibition since the museum opened, with almost double the daily visitor numbers than the previous best seller.[36] The biggest draw at the exhibition, which repeated the structure of the Tate hang, was the harem display, followed by the portrait and landscape sections. The popularity of the harem images was echoed in the museum café where Frank Dicksee's *Leila* (1892) proved most popular of the three paper placemats printed with images from the exhibition (Figs. 2.3 and 2.4), with museum café staff besieged by customers begging for spare copies. Whilst Christine Riding in London had fought hard to stop Leila being used in the Tate advertising campaign to prevent the show being sold through stereotypically eroticized images of Oriental women, the *Leila* proved popular with punters, coming second in the top three best-selling postcards.[37] In Istanbul, the demand for *Leila* was possibly, as museum curators noted, fuelled by an existing local familiarity and affection; they had spotted the image reproduced in cafés and kebab shops and on sale as a jigsaw in the market. Western Orientalist paintings take on new significance when indigenized into local forms of nostalgia and exotica as part of the development of differentiated regional consumer cultures which in turn impact on the viewing conditions of an international touring exhibition.

But not all versions of nostalgia are the same. Much of the current popular Turkish cultural investment in the past has widened the frame beyond those more safely distant moments of Ottoman greatness (notably the sixteenth-century "magnificence" of Süleyman I) favored by the republican historiographical project. Whilst it was initially in the 1970s and 1980s the religious revivalists who fostered a popular interest in the last years of the caliphate before the secularization of the republic, popular secular discourse (informed by interventionist scholarship) has now re-incorporated the previously disfavored nineteenth century as one of the sources for the social, educational, and gender emancipations associated with the republic. These revaluations, however, rarely celebrate the role of religion in the Ottoman state. In the secular Turkish republic, it may be only the religious revivalists who are overtly ideological in their desire for stylistic links to the Ottoman caliphate in general, and to its pan-Islamic politicization under Abdülhamid in particular.

Istanbul has been central to the imagination of a recuperable Ottoman past with a material role in the liberalization of the Turkish economy. In this, the increasingly visible presentation of Istanbul, qua Turkey in the world, goes directly to the politics and poetics of place.[38] In the early twentieth century the Ottoman city of Istanbul and its diverse population was replaced by the nationalists with the newly built Ankara; a Turkish capital of the Anatolian heartland. By the end of the century a combination of market liberalization, mass rural migration, and resurgent Islamist politics had again brought Istanbul center stage. Reflecting on this in the late 1990s, Martin Stokes detected two distinct Istanbuls: the populist Islamism of the rural migrants and the secular commercialism of the liberalizing business elites, keen to promote Istanbul as a global city of "commerce and culture" in the post-Soviet economies of the region. Globalizing strategies served to legitimate both "liberal and new Islamist city managers; for the former, 'opening up' Turkey to the wider global traffic in commodities, ideas, and opportunities, and for the latter evoking the golden age in which Turks dominated Europe and the Middle East."[39]

By the time *The Lure of the East* reached Istanbul in 2008, the Islamist AKP, Justice and Development Party, were in power (with former Istanbul mayor Recep Tayyip Erdoğan as Prime Minister). Increasing, if still hotly contested, overlaps between the secular and the religious were marked by the emergence into the mainstream Turkish economy of Islamic or "green" businesses, previously geographically and economically marginalized into regional Anatolian bases.[40] The design and manufacture of conservative or modest fashion (often called *tesettür*) has been a prominent element, with the assertive presence of women in headscarves in the public spaces of the modern Turkish city often held to symbolize the shift to religiosity in the secular republic.[41] Just as in the mid-1990s, the appropriation today of selected Ottoman and Orientalist pasts is available to both secular urban elites and Islamists with implications for commerce and popular culture that extend beyond national boundaries. Leading Turkish modest fashion brands such as Tekbir and Armine distribute in international territories notable for their Turkish diaspora populations (such as Germany and the UK), but are, like the secular business elites, also exploring new regional markets. These commercial reconnections with territories of previous Ottoman interest or control are also prompted by an affective commitment to serving the needs of Muslims in minority or politically sensitive situations, underwriting commercially precarious markets.[42] In their local, regional, and international sales campaigns, these fashion companies utilize modern marketing and merchandising methods with visuals that can veer between modernist esthetics and appropriations of Ottoman nostalgia and Orientalist kitsch. Seen not only on billboards but in the streets and malls of Istanbul's consumer and leisure spaces, women in modish modest fashion join the parading throng in the streets around the Pera museum, helping Istanbul to feature as one of the key sites for the international performance of Muslim cool.

Whilst the politicized reactivation of the *umma* has been less pronounced in Turkey than elsewhere, the development in Turkey of national politics and new regional affiliations based on faith is extremely contentious. In relation to neighboring Arab states, popular sentiment is rarely neutral about secessionist Arab nationalism at the turn of the previous century.[43] When the Pera Museum used Augustus John's 1919 portrait of T. E. Lawrence as one of the promotional posters for *The Lure of the East*, a mix of strong and contradictory responses illustrated with immediacy the polysemic power of images to provoke. The billboard placed in the passage next to the museum was literally defaced with slashes to Lawrence's visage and graffiti labeling him an "English spy" (Fig. 2.5). Appearing very soon after commentary on the use of this picture by Ertuğrul Özkök in *Hürriyet* (October 18, 2008),[44] the street action appeared to be a (mis) reading of the former editor's positive report. Surprised to see the Lawrence image on a billboard at Istanbul's Ataturk airport, Özkök interpreted the visual as an encouraging sign of increasingly open, democratic, public debate: Lawrence's image, he noted, had for a long time been discouraged (if not formally banned) because of his role in the collapse of the Ottoman Empire for which he was generally known as a British spy. Whilst the physical poster was quickly replaced by the museum, and not reported in the press, in the virtual

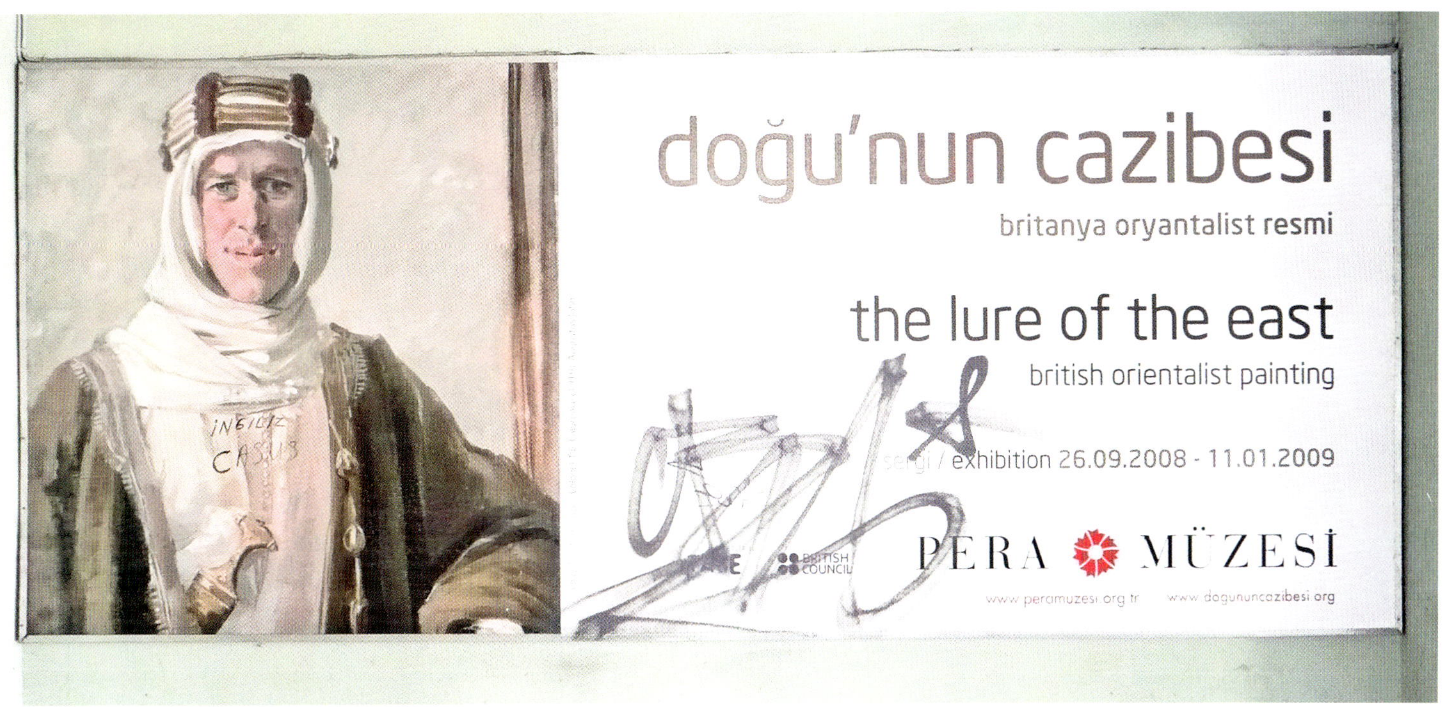

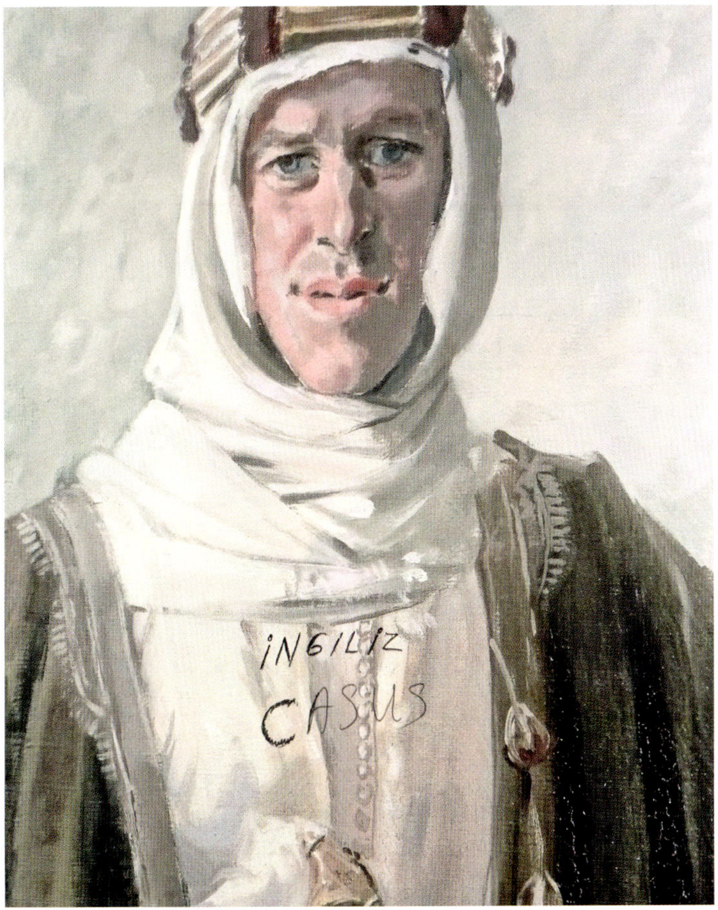

Figure 2.5 *The Lure of the East* poster featuring Augustus John, *Colonel T. E. Lawrence*, with graffiti reading "English spy," and detail, Istanbul 2008. Photograph by Nicholas Tromans.

world the debate continued with counter arguments on the internet criticizing Özkök's approach.

We can never, as Said would have told us, evacuate the political from the creation and consumption of Orientalist cultures. As *The Lure of the East* moved onto its final installation in Sharjah, we can wonder what other forms of collective identity will be sponsored, permitted, contested, and authenticated through the possible pleasures of consuming Orientalist art.

Notes

1 Edward W. Said, *Orientalism* (London: Routledge and Kegan Paul, 1978).

2 Reina Lewis, *Gendering Orientalism: Race, Femininity and Representation* (London: Routledge, 1996).

3 I make no attempt at an exhaustive list, but see, for example: John M. Mackenzie, *Orientalism: History, Theory and the Arts* (Manchester: Manchester University Press,1995); Anne McClintock, *Imperial Leather: Race, Gender and Sexuality in the Colonial Contest* (London: Routledge, 1995); Ella Shohat and Robert Stam, *Unthinking Eurocentrism: Multiculturalism and the Media* (London: Routledge, 1994).

4 Julie F. Codell and Dianne Sachko Macleod, eds., *Orientalism Transposed: The Impact of the Colonies on British Culture* (Ashgate: Aldershot, 1998); Mary Roberts, *Intimate Outsiders: The Harem in Ottoman and Orientalist Art and Travel Literature* (Durham: Duke University Press, 2007).

5 Reina Lewis, *Rethinking Orientalism: Women, Travel and the Ottoman Harem* (London: I.B. Tauris, New York: Rutgers, 2004).

6 Halidé Edib Adivar, *Memoirs of Halidé Edib* [1926] (Piscataway, NJ: Gorgias Press, 2005); Zeyneb Hanoum, *A Turkish Woman's European Impressions, edited and with an introduction by Grace Ellison* [1913] (Piscataway, NJ: Gorgias Press, 2004); Demetra Vaka, (Mrs. Kenneth Brown), *Haremlik* [1909] (Piscataway, NJ: Gorgias Press, 2004); Selma Ekrem, *Unveiled* [1931] (Piscataway, NJ: Gorgias Press, 2005).

7 See also Billie Melman, *Women's Orients: English Women and the Middle East, 1718–1918. Sexuality, Religion and Work* (Basingstoke: Macmillan, 1992).

8 Théophile Gautier, *Abécédaire du Salon de 1861* (Paris: Libraire de la Société des Gens de Lettres, 1861), 72–77.

9 Claude Vignon (pseud. Noémi Cadiot), "Une visite au Salon de 1861," *Le Correspondent* 18 (May 25, 1861): 137–60.

10 Reina Lewis, "'Oriental' Femininity as Cultural Commodity: Authors, Authority and Authenticity" in *Edges of Empire: Orientalism and Visual Culture*, ed. Jos Hackforth-Jones and Mary Roberts (Oxford: Blackwells, 2005), 95–120.

11 See http://culturesindialogue.com/main/home.

12 Ellison's reports subsequently appeared as *An Englishwoman in a Turkish Harem* [1915] (Piscataway, NJ: Gorgias Press, 2009).

13 See also Emily Weeks, "About Face: Sir David Wilkie's Portrait of Mehemet Ali, Pasha of Egypt," in *Orientalism Transposed: The Impact of the Colonies on British Culture*, ed. Julie F. Codell and Dianne Sachko Macleod (Ashgate: Aldershot, 1998), 46–58.

14 See Reina Lewis and Nancy Micklewright, *Gender, Modernity and Liberty: Middle Eastern and Western Women's Writings: A Critical Sourcebook* (London: I.B. Tauris, 2006); Rosaldo Renaldo, *Culture and Truth: The Remaking of Social Analysis* (London: B.T. Batsford Ltd, 1993).

15 See Roberts, *Intimate Outsiders*, and Zeynep İnankur, Chapter 13 in this volume.

16 Roberts, *Intimate Outsiders*.

17 Reina Lewis, "Women Orientalist Artists: Diversity, Ethnography, Interpretation, *Women, a Cultural Review* 6, no. 1 (1995): 91–106.

18 Roberts, *Intimate Outsiders*.

19 For an excellent account of new work in the field see, Leslie Peirce, "Writing Histories of Sexuality in the Middle East," *American Historical Review* (December 2009): 1325–39.

20 These ideas are developed in my conference paper "Sapphism and the Seraglio" delivered at College Arts Association (Chicago 2010) and will be published in a volume edited by Joan DelPlato and Julie Codell.

21 I am grateful to members of the curatorial and education teams at Tate Britain for discussing the evolution of this material and providing me with copies. Unless specifically stated, all opinions are mine alone.

22 Tariq Modood, "British Muslims and the Politics of Multiculturalism," in *Multiculturalism Muslims and Citizenship: A European Approach*, ed. Tariq Modood, Anna Triandafyllidou, Richard Zapata-Barrero (London: Routledge, 2006), 37–56; Bikhu Parekh, *Rethinking Multiculturalism: Cultural Diversity and Political Theory*, 2nd edn (London: Palgrave Macmillan, 2005).

23 The Rushdie Affair in 1988 is often cited as the flashpoint for Muslim mobilization over cultural politics in the UK. See, Lisa Appignanesi and Sara Maitland, eds. *The Rushdie File* (London: Fourth Estate, 1989).

24 This and all subsequent references, personal conversation with Paul Goodwin, December 18, 2008.

25 Tate Britain itself had mounted a similar trail in 2006–7 called *East/West: Objects Between Cultures*.

26 See also, Roger Benjamin, "Post-Colonial Taste. Non-Western Markets for Orientalist Art," in *Orientalism. Delacroix to Klee*, ed. Roger Benjamin (Sydney: Art Gallery of New South Wales, 1997).

27 Ussama Makdissi, "Ottoman Orientalism," *The American Historical Review* 107, no. 3 (June 2002): 768–96; Edhem Eldem, *Consuming the Orient* (Istanbul: Ottoman Bank Archive and Research Centre, 2007).

28 As well as Sarah Searight, Briony Llewelyn, Christine Riding, and Nick Tromans in this volume, I am also indebted to the generous responses of Brian MacDermot at the Mathaf Gallery London, Robin Start of the Park Gallery, London, Rose Issa of Rose Issa Projects, London, artist Hassan Hajjaj, and other collectors, curators and dealers, not all of whom are named here, with whom I have shared discussions over several years.

29 Similarly, the amateur and auction house trade in what is now

packaged as "Black Americana" (Aunt Jemima merchandise, material relating to historic black lives...) is supported by high profile black American celebrities such as Oprah Winfrey, Bill Cosby, and Whoopi Goldberg.

30 This and subsequent references, personal interview with Robin Start, London, October 21, 2008.

31 I thank Zeynep İnankur for pointing this out.

32 See Tromans, Chapter 3 in this volume

33 bell hooks, *Black Looks: Race and Representation* (London: Turnaround, 1992), 126.

34 Nirmal Puwar, "Multicultural Fashion ... Stirrings of Another Sense of Aesthetics and Memory," *Feminist Review* 71, no. 1 (Jan 2002): 63–87.

35 Christa Salamandra, *A New Old Damascus: Authenticity and Distinction in Urban Syria* (Bloomington: Indiana University Press, 2004).

36 Over a period of 92 active days (September 25, 2008 to January 11, 2009), *The Lure of the East* saw 44,000 visitors, with an average weekday number of 478 visitors per day, nearly double the usual number, and a weekend average of 800–1200, far exceeding the usual weekend head count of 350–450. The attendance for *The Lure of the East* was only superseded in the following year by the 48,150 visitors to the *Chagall: Life and Love* exhibition that ran at the museum for 80 active days (October 22, 2009 to January 24, 2010). Visitor numbers at Tate Britain for *The Lure of the East* were 60,530, on target for a themed show expected to have fewer visitors than exhibitions on a single artist or school (*Hogarth* had 200,000, *Turner, Whistler and Monet* over 300,000).

I am indebted to Özalp Birol, General Manager of the Suna and İnan Kıraç Foundation Culture and Art Enterprises and Christine Riding of Tate Britain for information in this section.

37 However Riding's battle to replace the *Leila* with Arthur Melville's more sober *An Arab Interior*, 1881, as poster image was vindicated when this proved to be the biggest selling postcard.

38 Martin Stokes, "'Beloved Istanbul': Realism and the Transnational Imaginary in Turkish Popular Culture," in *Mass Mediations: New Approaches to Popular Culture in the Middle East and Beyond*, ed. Walter Armbrust (Berkeley: University of California Press, 2000), 224–42.

39 Stokes, "'Beloved Istanbul'" 226.

40 Ömer Demir, Mustafa Acar and Metin Toprak, "Anatolian Tigers or Islamic Capital: Prospects and Challenges," *Middle Eastern Studies* 40, no. 6 (November 2004): 166–88.

41 Nilüfer Göle, *The Forbidden Modern: Civilization and Veiling* (Ann Arbor: University of Michigan Press, 1996).

42 Personal interviews with CEO and head office teams Tekbir and Armine, Istanbul, 2009.

Though, as we go to press, news that Louis Vuitton has opened a flagship store in Ulaanbaatar, emphasizes that territories previously seen as too impoverished or politically unstable are now targeted as potential markets by the global luxury brands. As well as Mongolia, Central Asia (notably Azerbaijan), Malaysia, and Vietnam join the roster of emergent markets in China, Russia, and India that marked the expansion of the international luxury consumer in the first decade of the twentieth-first century. (See Jo Craven, "Luxury Pioneers: Paris, Milan, Mongolia… What's a Brand like Louis Vuitton doing in a Place like Ulaanbaatar?" *The Times Luxx Magazine*, (March 13, 2010): 47–48.)

43 Eldem, *Consuming the Orient*, ch. 5.

44 See:
http://hurarsiv.hurriyet.com.tr/goster/haberaspx?id=10151028&yazarid=10.

Bibliography

Appignanesi, Lisa and Sara Maitland, eds. *The Rushdie File*. London: Fourth Estate, 1989.

Benjamin, Roger. "Post-Colonial Taste. Non-Western Markets for Orientalist Art." In *Orientalism. Delacroix to Klee*, edited by Roger Benjamin, 32–40. Sydney: Art Gallery of New South Wales, 1997.

Codell, Julie F. and Dianne Sachko Macleod, eds. *Orientalism Transposed: The Impact of the Colonies on British Culture*. Ashgate: Aldershot, 1998.

Craven, Jo. "Luxury Pioneers: Paris, Milan, Mongolia … What's a Brand like Louis Vuitton doing in a Place like Ulaanbaatar?" *The Times Luxx Magazine*, March 13, 2010, 47–48.

Demir, Ömer, Mustafa Acar and Metin Toprak. "Anatolian Tigers or Islamic Capital: Prospects and Challenges." *Middle Eastern Studies* 40, no. 6 (November 2004): 166–88.

Edib, Halidé Adivar. *Memoirs of Halidé Edib* [1926]. Piscataway, NJ: Gorgias Press, 2005.

Ekrem, Selma. *Unveiled* [1931]. Piscataway, NJ: Gorgias Press, 2005.

Eldem, Edhem. *Consuming the Orient.* Istanbul: Ottoman Bank Archive and Research Centre, 2007.

Ellison, Grace. *An Englishwoman in a Turkish Harem* [1915]. Piscataway, NJ: Gorgias Press, 2009.

Gautier, Théophile. *Abécédaire du Salon de 1861*. Paris: Libraire de la Société des Gens de Lettres, 1861.

Göle, Nilufer. *The Forbidden Modern: Civilization and Veiling.* Ann Arbor: University of Michigan Press, 1996.

Hanoum, Zeyneb. *A Turkish Woman's European Impressions, edited and with an introduction by Grace Ellison* [1913]. Piscataway, NJ: Gorgias Press, 2004.

hooks, bell. *Black Looks: Race and Representation*. London: Turnaround, 1992.

Lewis, Reina. "Women Orientalist Artists: Diversity, Ethnography, Interpretation." *Women, a Cultural Review* 6, no. 1 (1995): 91–106.

Lewis, Reina. *Gendering Orientalism: Race, Femininity and Representation*. London: Routledge, 1996.

Lewis, Reina. *Rethinking Orientalism: Women, Travel and the Ottoman Harem*. London: I.B. Tauris, New York: Rutgers, 2004.

Lewis, Reina. "'Oriental' Femininity as Cultural Commodity: Authorship, Authority and Authenticity." In *Edges of Empire: Orientalism and Visual Culture*, edited by Jos Hackforth-Jones and Mary Roberts, 95–120. Oxford: Blackwells, 2005.

Lewis, Reina and Nancy Micklewright. *Gender, Modernity and Liberty: Middle Eastern and Western Women's Writings: A Critical Sourcebook*. London: I.B. Tauris, 2006.

Makdissi, Ussama. "Ottoman Orientalism." *The American Historical Review* 107, no. 3 (June 2002):768–96.

Mackenzie, John M. *Orientalism: History, Theory and the Arts.* Manchester: Manchester University Press, 1995.

McClintock, Anne. *Imperial Leather: Race, Gender and Sexuality in the Colonial Contest*. London: Routledge, 1995.

Melman, Billie. *Women's Orients: English Women and the Middle East, 1718–1918. Sexuality, Religion and Work*. Basingstoke: Macmillan, 1992.

Modood, Tariq. "British Muslims and the Politics of Multi–culturalism." In *Multiculturalism Muslims and Citizenship: A European Approach*, edited by Tariq Modood, Anna Triandafyllidou and Richard Zapata-Barrero, 37–56. London: Routledge, 2006.

Parekh, Bikhu. *Rethinking Multiculturalism: Cultural Diversity and Political Theory.* 2nd edn. London: Palgrave Macmillan, 2005.

Peirce, Leslie. "Writing Histories of Sexuality in the Middle East." *American Historical Review* (December 2009): 1325–39.

Puwar, Nirmal. "Multicultural Fashion ... Stirrings of Another Sense of Aesthetics and Memory." *Feminist Review* 71, no. 1 (January 2002): 63–87.

Roberts, Mary. *Intimate Outsiders: The Harem in Ottoman and Orientalist Art and Travel Literature*. Durham: Duke University Press, 2007.

Rosaldo, Renaldo. *Culture and Truth: The Remaking of Social Analysis*. London: B. T. Batsford Ltd, 1993.

Said, Edward W. *Orientalism*. London: Routledge and Kegan Paul, 1978.

Salamandra, Christa. *A New Old Damascus: Authenticity and Distinction in Urban Syria*. Bloomington: Indiana University Press, 2004.

Shohat, Ella and Robert Stam. *Unthinking Eurocentrism: Multiculturalism and the Media*. London: Routledge, 1994.

Stokes, Martin. "'Beloved Istanbul': Realism and the Transnational Imaginary in Turkish Popular Culture." In *Mass Mediations: New Approaches to Popular Culture in the Middle East and Beyond*, edited by Walter Armbrust, 224–42. Berkeley: University of California Press, 2000.

Vaka, Demetra (Mrs. Kenneth Brown). *Haremlik* [1909]. Piscataway, NJ: Gorgias Press, 2004.

Vignon, Claude (pseud. Noémi Cadiot). "Une visite au Salon de 1861," *Le Correspondent* 18, (May, 25 1861): 137–60.

Weeks, Emily. "About Face: Sir David Wilkie's Portrait of

Mehemet Ali, Pasha of Egypt." In *Orientalism Transposed: The Impact of the Colonies on British Culture*, edited by Julie F. Codell and Dianne Sachko Macleod, 46–58. Ashgate: Aldershot, 1998.

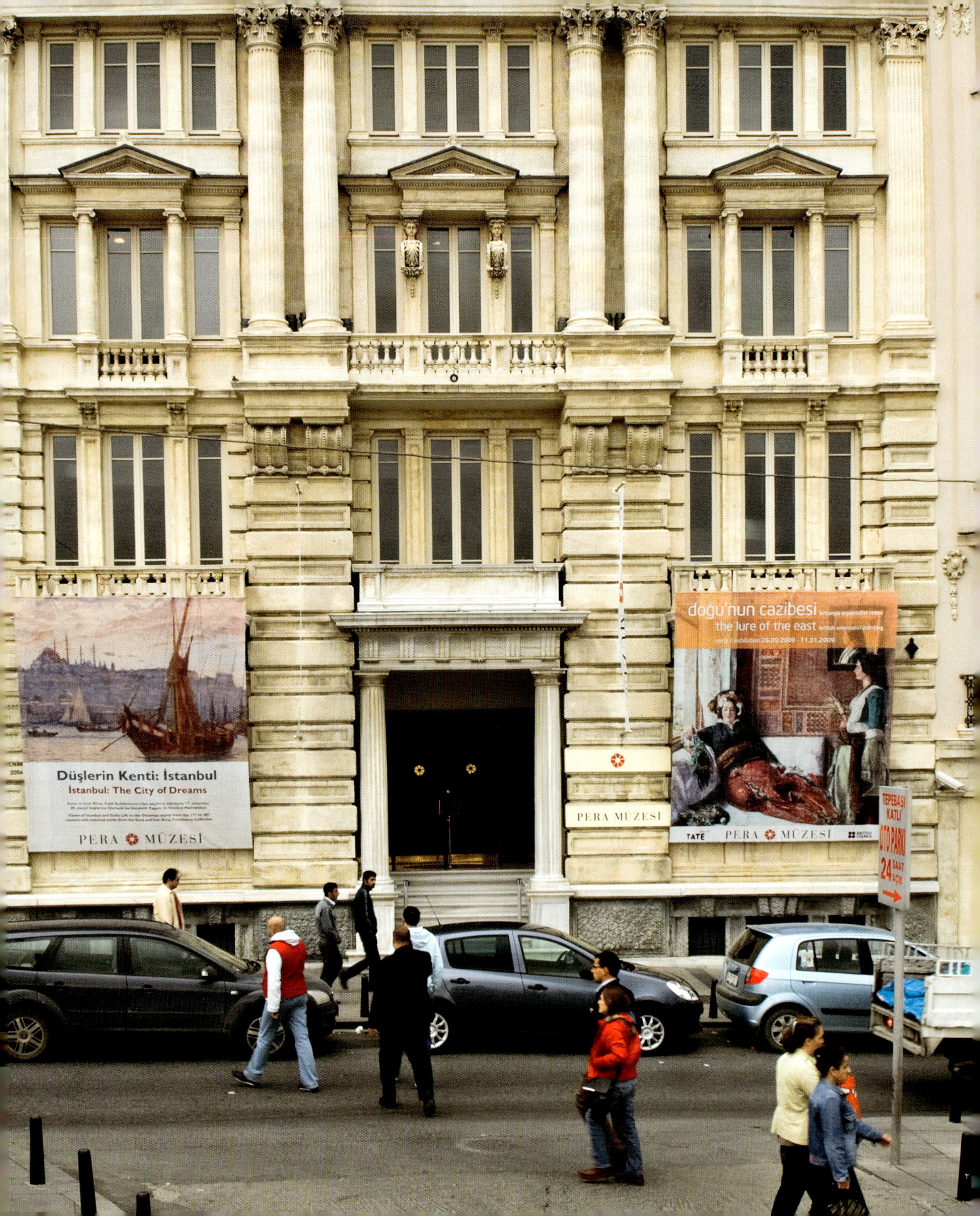
Düşlerin Kenti: İstanbul
İstanbul: The City of Dreams
PERA MÜZESİ
doğu'nun cazibesi
the lure of the east
26.09.2008 - 11.01.2009
TATE
PERA MÜZESİ
PERA MÜZESİ
TEPEBAŞI
KATLI
OTO PARKI
24 SAAT AÇIK

III

Bringing it Home? Orientalist Painting and the Art Market

Nicholas Tromans

The exhibition *The Lure of the East: British Orientalist Painting* came to Istanbul in September, 2008, after showing at the Yale Center for British Art in New Haven and at Tate Britain in London, and before moving on to its final venue, the Sharjah Art Museum in the United Arab Emirates (February to April, 2009). As the second part of the show's title made plain, the intention of the project was to survey British paintings of the Eastern Mediterranean world. It was also always the intention to seek to bring to the interpretation of this body of work some of the fruits of the torrential debates that have surrounded Western representations of the East since the 1970s. Finally, again from the beginning, it was the ambition of the exhibition's organizing institution, Tate Britain, to show British Orientalism in those parts of the world from which its inspiration had originally been drawn (Figs. 3.1 and 3.2).

The process of selecting exhibits for *The Lure of the East* was guided by the need to offer a representative survey of the main artists and most popular themes, but also by the desire to investigate particular aspects of iconography in depth—for example the city of Jerusalem, or tensions between the sexes in genre painting. The emphasis was consistently but not exclusively upon *paintings*—that is, finished and exhibitable pictures, rather than sketches or photographs—so that the exhibition would be able to explore how the characteristics of this specific European medium were challenged, developed or frustrated in the new environments of the Ottoman and Arab worlds, rather than dealing in more abstract generalizations about visual culture or the like. The concentration upon exhibited works also allowed a greater sense of what British Orientalist painting meant to its contemporary publics. A few exceptions to the British content of the selection were made in order to provide a little more international context. So, for example, works by Gustav Bauernfeind and Jean-Léon Gérôme were included, although in each case there were strong British connections with the specific pictures selected. For those to whom the entire genre of Orientalism in European art is deeply politically suspect, manifesting Said's model of culture-as-violence in its most garish modes, this effort of the exhibition to identify the particular qualities of the British contribution to that genre was an obvious point at which to open criticism.[1] Wasn't it complacent to risk implying that Orientalism was safe in the hands of the British because they tended to eschew the explicit sex and violence that are conventionally associated with the French version?[2]

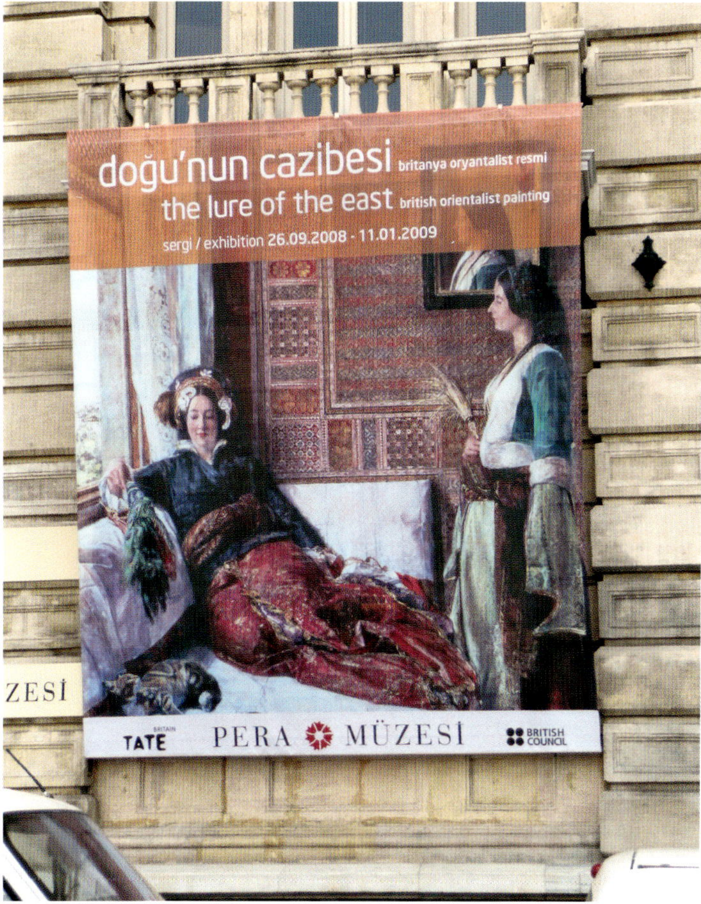

Figure 3.1 Poster for *The Lure of the East* outside the Pera Museum, September 2008. (Photo: author.)

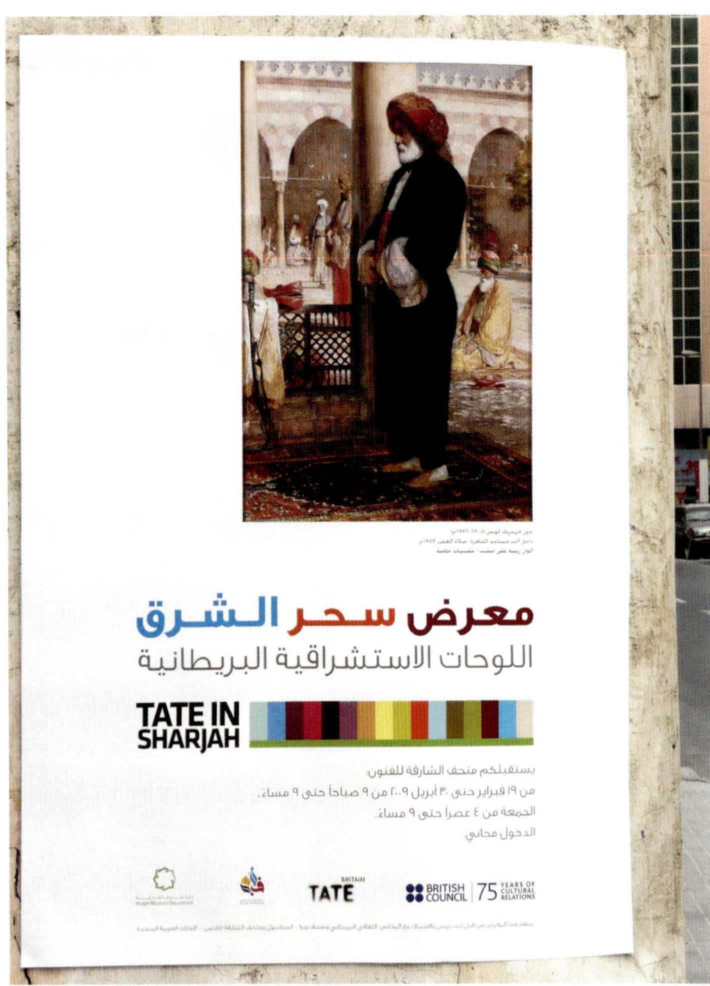

Figure 3.2 Poster for *The Lure of the East* near the Sharjah Art Museum, February 2009. (Photo: author.)

The opening of the exhibition coincided with the thirtieth anniversary of Edward Said's *Orientalism*, a milestone commemorated by conferences around the world.[3] Said's presence in the academic humanities had become virtually ubiquitous in the 1980s, and since then his arguments have of course been developed, countered and nuanced in such an extremely rich diversity of work across the world that it would now be impossible to even summarize here the scholarly literature relevant to "Orientalism" in general.[4] As the first attempt to survey British Orientalist painting in an exhibition, *The Lure of the East* thus was faced with the problem of seeking simultaneously to introduce Said's work as a relevant body of theory, as well as suggesting how the debates had since developed. Hence the ambitiously complex interpretation strategy in London which involved the presence of texts and audio commentaries contributed by a long list of individuals with different interests in the subject matter on show. If this rather diffused or devolved approach sought to echo the tenor of recent academic work in the field, which often emphasizes conversation and situation in its analyses of Orientalist structures, the wider media coverage of the exhibition was nevertheless often couched in cruder pro- or anti-Said terms.[5] In recent years, as conservative commentators in Europe and the USA have come to feel a more urgent need to "defend" the West (often against a supposed Islamic threat), the writings of Said (who died in 2003) have been attacked with renewed vigor. While the exhibition was being planned, several full-length assaults on his intellectual legacy appeared.[6] This background helps explain why it was that the mere mention of Said on the show's opening text panel was enough to reduce to apoplexy the art critic of the conservative *Daily Telegraph*, Richard Dorment, who accused those of us who had worked on the show of ruining a display of beautiful art with our "cant" (he later elected *The Lure of the East* the worst British exhibition of 2008).[7] Dorment recommended to his readers Ibn Warraq's recent vituperative critique of Said, *Defending the West*, and the author of that book returned the favor by writing to the *Telegraph* to praise Dorment's review.

Much of the media debate that took place around *The Lure of the East* in London turned on whether or not the representations of the "Orient" in the pictures on display were flattering or demeaning, it often being assumed that academics, under the thrall of the fashionable and politically correct Said, were programmed to see insults everywhere. A clinching argument was therefore regularly said to be that the well-attested phenomenon of Turkish and Middle Eastern art collectors choosing to buy European Orientalist pictures must prove that these images cannot be offensive.[8] It is this line, or circle, of thinking that I want to discuss here. But first I would like very briefly to scroll back through the history of the Orientalist debates to ask about the attitude of Said himself to images, given that his name is evoked so often in the media (and, in a curiously knowing way, in the art market also, as I will be suggesting below) as shorthand for a supposedly supercilious academic stance toward Orientalist art.

The conventional early history of the Orientalist debate would have it that, given Said's exclusive attention to literature and music, it was left to the art historian Linda Nochlin to begin the application of the basic arguments of his 1978 book to images in her now classic 1983 paper, "The Imaginary Orient." In fact Said made various references to images during his career, and while hardly adding up to a theory of visual culture, these certainly imply a position. Within the fine arts, Said expressed a preference for dynamic, expressive, perhaps masculine artists such as Goya, Rodin and Cézanne.[9] Beyond this, his scattered comments on pictures suggest an exasperation at the image's irresponsibility—at its capacity to be easily appropriated. For example, in *Covering Islam* of 1981, Said noted how a painting by Gérôme of a Cairene *muezzin*—which Said introduces as kitsch but harmless—so readily gave itself up to become a hopelessly crude cover for *Time* magazine. Captioned now with the headline "Islam: The Militant Revival," the image was put to work to equate the Iranian revolution with Islam in general.[10]

Said became, I think, deeply suspicious of the character of images: they were not to be trusted, shifting their meanings as they did from situation to situation. In retrospect, we can perhaps now see that this perspective was, in regard to Orientalist painting, nearer to some of the site-specific interpretations of recent years than the explicitly politicized "New" Art History of the 1980s, when critics such as Nochlin and Rana Kabbani attributed a greater degree of semantic stability to the Orientalist painting—albeit a character conceived very much in negative terms. Nochlin described the Orientalist picture as being bad both because it proclaimed a "real" transparency that more progressive artists such as Manet had abandoned, and because it quietly introduced, under its film of taut but gauzy realism, the messy old family of European prejudices against Islamic societies. A problem with this latter iconographic approach can be that it becomes hard to think of something a person in an Orientalist painting might be shown doing that could *not* be construed as demeaning. The nature of genre painting necessarily requires human types, which are inherently disdainful of the individual. *The Lure of the East* was concerned precisely with such questions of the limitations of the basic structures of the European painted image, and with the history of the act of traveling abroad to stare at other people in the name of truthful art, given that, in the memorable phrase of the nineteenth-century Egyptian educationalist Rifa'a al-Tahtawi, "one of the beliefs of the Europeans is that the gaze has no effect."[11]

Such intractable historical issues as the responsibility of the gaze, however, are not easily worked out in an exhibition that is able to show only the end-products of the artists' journeys, products almost invariably actually executed back home in the studio. Only a small minority of the works shown in *The Lure of the East* were actually painted in the East. Naturally the attention of visitors to the exhibition's several manifestations at its different venues focused primarily on the individual pictures—their style, subject matter and their ownership. By the standards of a London national museum exhibition, which would normally consist principally of "museum quality" works, *The Lure of the East* had a high proportion of loans from private collections, several of which belonged to individuals or institutions of Middle Eastern domicile or origin. Some of the most exciting—because least known—loans fell into this category, including pictures by Lewis, Lear and Roberts. An especially generous Middle Eastern lender, although not quite a private collection, was the Qatar Museums Authority, which made available, among other important paintings, Bauernfeind's picture of the Dome of the Rock in Jerusalem.

Qatar's ruling family were among the leading players on the London art market during its boom years around the turn of this century, acquiring extraordinary numbers of objects in many different categories, always of the highest quality. The intention was to create a series of museums in Qatar, although to date the only one to have opened (in 2008) is the wonderful Museum of Islamic Art in Doha. The larger project to launch a whole museum sequence was postponed after 2005 when it was claimed that Qatar's chief buyer had been agreeing artificially inflated prices with London art dealers in order, allegedly, to profit himself.[12] But Qatar still holds a magnificent collection of Orientalist paintings, and it is hopefully only a matter of time before this is given its own public museum.[13] Meanwhile, similar initiatives to create, virtually from scratch, entire museum complexes have been under way in two of the Emirates, Abu Dhabi and—on a much more modest scale—Sharjah (Dubai's neighbor), often generating in the Western media narratives of Oriental wealth, splendor and autocracy that have more to do with Beckford's gothic novel *Vathek* than with the realities of Gulf politics.[14] Among these state collections, only Qatar presently plans to create a museum of Orientalist painting, which would indeed, if and when it opens, be the first of its kind in the world. This would certainly be appropriate, as a summary review of the history of collecting Orientalist painting will soon confirm that the notion of a *collection* of painted European images of "Oriental" motifs is an "Oriental" invention. Perhaps the first such pioneer could be said to have been none other than the early-nineteenth-century Pasha of Egypt, Mehemet Ali, who loved to collect images of himself by visiting European artists (without ever aspiring to be a collector of Western painting in general). During the mid-nineteenth-century heyday of Orientalism as a species of academic art, it was scarcely heard of for British or French collectors to specialize in the genre. Rather, Orientalist paintings by the likes of Lewis or Gérôme were purchased, displayed and then dispersed again at auction in the company of all the other standard categories of contemporary canvas. Not even the establishment in France of a Société des Peintres Orientalistes in the 1890s seems to have changed this situation.

The history and context of the Société has been described by Roger Benjamin in his 2003 book *Orientalist Aesthetics*, and Benjamin is also the author of an important early effort to outline the history of non-Western markets for Orientalist pictures which concludes by seeing in that history "an act of repossession."[15] Certainly, the art market has provided new homes for these commodities in the collections of Turkish and Arab elites, a process that again can be traced all the way back to the nineteenth century, when the leading Parisian dealers Goupil had among their clients the Ottoman Court. Plenty has been said, in detail and in theory, about the West collecting the East, and about the styles of interpretation and possession that have come with this.[16] But much less has been said about the history of the reverse process.

In Europe, the ubiquity of museums has evolved into a fevered archivism whereby curating seems to have become one of our primary means of engaging with the world, museums supplying in the process further grist to the mills of contemporary artists and of the lumbering academic exercise of museum studies. Beyond the Western world, practices of collecting European art are by and large dominated, in the general absence of museums of such art, by the commercial market and by private collections, phenomena with which the academic world finds it extremely difficult to deal. Few scholars write theses on the commercial aspects of the history of the art, or on existing private collections. This is due to the difficulty of obtaining reliable data, but also to a more fundamental problem with the art market from an historical point of view, that is, its semantic flatness. The art market may be defined as the point of exchange of unique commodities, and therefore, at the same time, as the machine by which the uniqueness of those goods is erased through their being gathered in the category that the art market itself constitutes. The art market is ostensibly so endlessly rich in its produce, in the impossibly lush sequence of wares placed on offer in its metropolitan showrooms week after week throughout the year. But yet what is the history of the market itself, rather than that of its commodities? This is a question for historians of commerce and economics, but to date few have taken it up: the serious literature on the history of the art market still comprises only a modest bibliography.[17] The West's saturation in the modes of the museum, which define themselves *against* the commercial, has accustomed us to ignore the market as an unanalyzable "other," a strange place populated by young men and women who may resemble estate agents but who can tell a Watteau from a Lancret. And how much more opaque to analysis is the market when its clients are the very wealthy, and hence very discrete, people who can afford to buy the top-of-the-range Orientalist paintings in which we are interested.

Having lamented the lack of serious study of the art market, we can at least follow up Benjamin's outline of the development of the market for Orientalist pictures in the regions where the Orientalists originally traveled. No sooner had the British left the Gulf as Imperialists in 1971 than they returned as art dealers. Following the massive marking-up of oil prices after 1973, the Gulf States quickly developed into a significant market for Orientalist paintings, a market managed from London. There, the specialist Mathaf Gallery was established in 1975, and in 1978 (the year of Said's *Orientalism*), the Fine Art Society held what was probably the first selling exhibition of top-quality Orientalist paintings in London.[18] Christa Salamandra has recently analyzed this development in the larger context of the role of London as a primary site for the generation of new Arabian cultural identities. This relationship was predicated in part upon the projection of a shared Anglo-Arabian monarchical tradition, and underwritten historically by a longstanding body of British art and literature offering romanticized images of Arabian cultures. These more picturesque connections, suggests Salamandra, have helped develop positive images around a vigorous economic relationship based in reality upon the trade of oil and arms. As Salamandra puts it: "In contemporary London, a (post)imperial symbiosis of elites lives on in an industry of Arabian heritage."[19]

As a function of this process, the art market itself has developed a ready public-relations language with which to speak of the "Oriental" market for Orientalism. Arab collectors are said to cherish the European pictures on account of their recalling what has been lost in terms of culture, architecture and landscape. Here for example is Brian MacDermot of the Mathaf Gallery in his introduction to the catalog of the Najd Collection, a Saudi collection of European Orientalist pictures assembled during the 1980s:

> [H]istory will show that development came so fast that it was a challenge to try to keep intact the culture and traditions of a great Arab country. As part of this process the collector gathered together an astounding number of Orientalist paintings of top quality showing the traditions of the past.[20]

The same suggestion is made in comments by Dale Egee, another London dealer to Arab collectors from the late 1970s: "Our Gulf clients love Orientalist works; they remind them of what they've lost."[21] But, qualifies Egee, "they have to be genuine." Genuine? What might that mean? What the market wants it to mean is that their clients are fine connoisseurs of Orientalist painting, able to spot the difference between an image cobbled together from studio props on one hand, and something "genuine" on the other. One auction house expert in the field hints that the more exotic Orientalism was a Western taste, the more documentary type now an Eastern one.[22] Thus it is in effect suggested that the process of collecting Orientalism, and Arab collecting in particular, does the genre a favor by filtering out the kitsch from the authentic reportage. Collecting, then, refines representation and gives us a new, a better, reality, finally producing such a carefully curated auction preview as the *Orientalist Masterpieces* being shown in London as I write.[23] This process is in turn taken up as aspiring to a more significant level of cultural diplomacy by some collectors, such as the Egyptian businessman M. Shafik Gabr, a leading collector of European Orientalism, who sees the more documentary artists whom he admires as having been brave and sincere "early globalists."[24]

The intriguing thing here is the recognition that the product needed refining. Of which other category of art would the market itself admit such a thing? In fact, the system of institutions that we label "the art world" has ever been adept at digesting criticism of itself, indeed it has long been able to assimilate to its own purposes ostensibly alien or even antagonistic material. In the public sphere we think of those conceptual artists whose work critiques the museum mentality but which easily becomes part of the museum's discourse of itself. The private, commercial art world, meanwhile, has always been able to celebrate the authentic provenance of an object—to generate sentiment around its roots in a special place—while simultaneously transforming that object into a commodity floating free along the highways of global capital. In the case of Orientalist pictures, this trope is given a reverse twist in that the market likes to talk about the pictures being allowed, courtesy of the salesroom, to regain a lost homeland. But also we can identify an even more ingenious subtext according to which the market itself tacitly adopts a 1980s-style art-historical critique of Orientalism—that it is artificial, academic, and culturally divorced from its subject matter—as part of its own narrative of rediscovery and restitution. In a nutshell, Said and his followers are supposed to have accused Orientalism generally of falsity, thus requiring the market and its Middle Eastern clients to go to work to rescue the reputations of those carefully selected artists around whom a specialist sale might be built.

To be an art dealer you need plenty of money to establish your stock before you can open your gallery, a space itself likely to be located somewhere rents are not cheap. To be an auctioneer, on the other hand, all you really must invest in is a grand room hired for the day and some very sharp staff. This means that the leading brands of the international auction industry can move nimbly when exploring new venues for their offices and salerooms (the former charged with recruiting sellers and buyers, the latter being where the auctions themselves take place, either in permanent business premises or in hotels hired for the event).

The big story of the last few years in the development of the art market's relationship with Turkey and the Middle East has been the two leading auction houses' arrival there themselves. Joining the global rush to the Gulf, Christie's led the way, opening an office in Dubai in 2005 as part of a general push at that time to put clear distance between the company and its competitors in the pursuit of Gulf trade. Christie's Dubai auctions, which began in May 2006 with an offering of contemporary art from all over the world (plus jewelry), have however yet to include Orientalist painting, despite the company claiming to have first adapted the genre as a dedicated auction category back in the 1990s.[25] Sotheby's were of course not to be left behind, and held their own first Gulf auction in Qatar in March 2009, having shortly beforehand opened an office in Doha. This first sale did include Orientalist pictures, but the leading two auction houses both seem to remain wary of carrying their specialist sales in this category to the Gulf itself, leaving the resurgent third-placed Bonhams to boast that they are the only company presently planning to hold regular (annual) auctions of Orientalist paintings in the Gulf (Dubai), the first of which took place in May 2009.[26]

In Turkey, meanwhile, the international art market identifies a very healthy appetite among wealthy collectors, a demand which recently caused a picture by Osman Hamdi Bey to set, at a sale in London, a dramatic new record for a Turkish painting at auction.[27] But Turkey also offers a vital contemporary art scene from which the market hopes to benefit. At the time of writing, Christie's has no dedicated office in Istanbul, where however Sotheby's announced their formal arrival early in 2009, in time to promote their first London sale to be devoted to modern and contemporary Turkish art (held in March 2009, the same month as the company's first Gulf sale).[28] The catalog cover and prime promotional image for that sale was Taner Ceylan's photorealist painting of a bloodied boxer, *Spiritual* (2008), a visceral work by an artist who has been controversial in his home country on account of the explicit homoerotic content of his pictures.[29] Evidently the Sotheby's marketing people felt the need to launch the new auction category of contemporary Turkish art with a deliberately "edgy" spin that would (with consummate art market paradox) reassuringly align the novelty with established European and American modern art.

The Lure of the East, then, arrived in Istanbul and the Gulf from London's Tate Britain at the same time as those other grand old brands of the European art world, the giants of the auction market. We should recognize that the exhibition on one hand and the art market's commercial initiatives on the other were responding to, and making their respective ways through, similar cultural and political contexts. Pessimistic complaints over globalization emphasize the placelessness easily engendered by such brand-managed international cultural interaction. In a recent number of the journal *Third Text* devoted to Turkey, the art critic and curator Beral Madra complained that "The corporate art system is financially and officially dominating the art scene in Istanbul."[30] But while in Turkey and the Gulf some observers perceive the public and private artistic spheres interpenetrating in ways that appear raw or wrong, nevertheless these evolving power relations around the image will surely become naturalized and eventually appear as picturesquely settled as in Europe.

The extreme form of globalized placelessness is of course supposed to be Dubai, a venue where, according to conventional narratives, there is only money and preposterous architecture. The Gulf's explosion of wealth is often said to have caused its art-world to have been born backwards—it is acquiring museums, and now auction houses, before having raised artists and dealers.[31] At Abu Dhabi, so many signature architects and branded museum-chains are slated for compression into Saadiyat ("Happiness") Island, that the architect of the new Guggenheim there, Frank Gehry, has likened the project to "a cabinet of horrors," a phrase suggesting an early experiment in the history of collecting gone horribly wrong, but also implying a revulsion at the experience of himself *being collected*.[32] However, a new generation of architects are assuming that we all should—or even must—learn from the Gulf experience, accepting that, in the words of Brian Ackley:

> in fact the non-place has established a sort of authenticity especially evident in Dubai. It is a city that is unencumbered by vernacular architecture or traditional design practices ... The new authenticity is at once controlled and irrepressible, scripted and disorientating, unique and derivative, amusing and depressing.[33]

On the face of things, Sharjah (sometimes described as a suburb of Dubai) has gone to the opposite extreme, seeking in its "heritage quarter" not only to reconstruct the port's architecture as it might have been in the early nineteenth century, but also adding in recent years more than twenty-five museums to this ambitious initiative, plus the revamped Sharjah Biennial which since 2003 has become perhaps the leading such event in the Middle East. As a team of Emirates-based scholars recently suggested, "If Dubai symbolizes the 'virtual' then Sharjah symbolizes the concrete within a postmodern sense of complementary opposition among competing lineages," that is, Sharjah's gambit is to constitute itself an archive of heritage in order to achieve differentiation from—and at the same time the necessary supplement to—its neighbors' better-financed bids for global significance.[34] While the Sharjah Art Museum felt it inappropriate, for reasons of local culture and tradition, to emphasize the theme of the harem in its installation of *The Lure of the East* as strongly as it had been at the show's other venues, or to translate more than brief extracts of the catalog into Arabic for local audiences, it did very strongly emphasize the positive, intercultural interpretation of Orientalist painting, and its advertising celebrated the physical presence of "Tate in Sharjah."[35]

As for Istanbul and the exhibition's reception there, then this book of essays speaks to the range and depth of that conversation. In Istanbul there was a more tangible sense of "homecoming" in that the exhibition was shown in the Pera district where the Orientalist painters typically stayed in the nineteenth century. Here it was also possible to add to the display not only the Pera Museum's own works by Osman Hamdi Bey, but also an important British picture that had remained in Istanbul since having been painted there in 1840—David Wilkie's portrait of Sultan Abdülmecid, lent from the Topkapı Palace Museum. My own impression, which can only be subjective, was that the exhibition's presence in Istanbul felt like a politely explicit affirmation of an aspect of the city's European heritage made in the context of a wider cultural and political landscape in which that heritage is not the only one on offer.

Notes

1 For an outspokenly negative critique of Orientalist painting see Rana Kabbani, *Imperial Fictions: Europe's Myths of Orient* (London: Saqi, 2008), a new edition of a book first published in 1986. Kabbani was invited to return to the topic for the catalog of *The Lure of the East*: see Nicholas Tromans, ed., *The Lure of the East: British Orientalist Painting* (London: Tate Publishing, 2008), 40–45.

2 This is one of the challenges made by Ali Nobil Ahmad in his political critique of the exhibition, "What did you expect old boy? This is the Tate Britain!" *Dark Matter. In the Ruins of Imperial Culture* (July 7, 2008), http://www.darkmatter101.org/site/2008/07/07/ (accessed November 24, 2009).

3 An especially wide-ranging, cross-disciplinary event, *Orientalism 30 Years Later*, was held at the University of York, UK, on November 1, 2008.

4 I will note here just three books of the 1990s that indicated some of the paths taken by later participants in the Orientalist debates, by, respectively, articulating national and regional differences; by "gendering" Orientalism; and by insisting that specialist historians need not defer to cultural critics in historical debates: Lisa Lowe, *Critical Terrains: French and British Orientalisms* (Ithaca, NY: Cornell University Press, 1992); Reina Lewis, *Gendering Orientalism: Race, Femininity and Representation* (London: Routledge, 1996); John MacKenzie, *Orientalism: History, Theory and the Arts* (Manchester: Manchester University Press, 1995).

5 Some examples of academic literature emphasizing conversation, contradiction and situation in the analysis of Orientalism include: Todd Porterfield, *Allure of Empire: Art in the Service of French Imperialism, 1798–1836* (Princeton, NJ: Princeton University Press, 1998); Jill Beaulieu and Mary Roberts, eds., *Orientalism's Interlocutors: Painting, Architecture, Photography* (Durham, NC and London: Duke University Press, 2002); Semra Germaner and Zeynep İnankur, *Constantinople and the Orientalists* (Istanbul: Türkiye İş Bankası Kültür Yayınları, 2002); Frederick N. Bohrer, *Orientalism and Visual Culture: Imagining Mesopotamia in Nineteenth-Century Europe* (Cambridge: Cambridge University Press, 2003); Roger Benjamin, *Orientalist Aesthetics: Art, Colonialism, and French North Africa, 1880–1930* (Berkeley, CA and London: University of California Press, 2003); Ivan Davidson Kalmar and Derek J. Penslar, eds., *Orientalism and the Jews* (Waltham, MA: Brandeis University Press, 2004); Nicholas Tromans, "Palestine: Picture of Prophecy" in *William Holman Hunt*, ed. Carol Jacobi and Katherine Lochnan (Toronto: Art Gallery of Ontario, 2008), 135–60.

6 Robert Irwin, *For Lust of Knowing. The Orientalists and their Enemies* (London: Penguin, 2006); Ibn Warraq, *Defending the West. A Critique of Edward Said's* Orientalism (Amherst, NY: Prometheus, 2007); Daniel Martin Varisco, *Reading Orientalism. Said and the Unsaid* (Seattle, WA: University of Washington Press, 2007).

7 *Daily Telegraph*, June 10 and December 22, 2008. The exhibition fared better in the liberal press: see for example the review by Jonathan Jones in the *Guardian*, June 4, 2008.

8 For a typical expression of this argument—not specifically in relation to *The Lure of the East*—see Ibn Warraq, *Defending the West*, 301–4.

9 Edward W. Said and W. J. T. Mitchell, "'The Panic of the Visual': A Conversation with Edward W. Said," *Boundary 2* 25, no. 2 (1998): 11–33.

10 Edward W. Said, *Covering Islam. How the Media and the Experts Determine How we See the Rest of the World* [1981] (2nd edn, London: Vintage, 1997), 16–17.

11 Timothy Mitchell, *Colonising Egypt* [1988] (Berkeley, CA and London: University of California Press, 1991), 2.

12 Georgina Adam, "World's Biggest Art Collector Under Arrest in Qatar", *Art Newspaper* no. 157 (March 2005): 48.

13 See the Qatar Museums Authority website: http://www.qma.com.qa/eng/.

14 For a compendium of clichés of Gulf culture amounting to a gothic horror story, see Rod Liddle, "Sordid Reality behind Dubai's Gilded Façade", *The Sunday Times*, July 12, 2009.

15 Roger Benjamin, *Orientalist Aesthetics*, chapter 3; Benjamin, "Post-Colonial Taste. Non-Western Markets for Orientalist Art," in *Orientalism. Delacroix to Klee*, ed. Benjamin (Sydney: Art Gallery of New South Wales, 1997), 32–40.

16 For a lively recent overview of this theme, see Maya Jasanoff, *Edge of Empire. Conquest and Collecting in the East 1750–1850* (London: Fourth Estate, 2005).

17 There is no space here to sketch such a bibliography, but to be recommended is Olav Velthuis, *Talking Prices. Symbolic Meanings of Prices on the Market for Contemporary Art* (Princeton, NJ: Princeton University Press, 2005).

18 See Lynne Thornton, *Eastern Encounters. Orientalist Painters of the Nineteenth Century* (London: Fine Art Society, 1978).

19 Christa Salamandra, "Cultural Construction, the Gulf and Arab London," in *Monarchies and Nations: Globalisation and Identity in the Arab States of the Gulf*, ed. Paul Dresch and James Piscatori (London: I.B. Tauris, 2005), 74; cf. 78: "London serves as the construction site for the production of a local heritage from a globally circulating body of antiquities." Note also Salamandra's important argument regarding the role of the cultural intermediary, who seeks to stand outside the "dialogue" to effect "understanding": this new profession of cultural or commercial diplomacy in itself develops "vested interests in maintaining reified notions of difference—most obvious perhaps in art and publishing" (75).

20 Caroline Juler, *Najd Collection of Orientalist Paintings* (London: Manara, 1991), 1.

21 Quoted by Salamandra, "Cultural Construction, the Gulf and Arab London," 78–79.

22 Ali Can Ertug, "Orientalist Art, Worldwide. The Rise of the East," *Sotheby's Preview Online* (September–October 2008), http://www.sothebys.com/liveauctions/sneak/article/pdf/sept2008/rise.pdf. Cf. Benjamin, "Post-Colonial Taste", 37. Nina Siegal claims that "modern-day collectors can tell the difference between works rooted in the culture and those composed from a hodgepodge of exported exotica": see "Welcome to the Bazaar," *Art+Auction* (October 2008), http://www.artinfo.com/news/story/28702/welcome-to-the-bazaar/ (accessed November 24, 2009).

23 See *Orientalist Masterpieces*, auction catalog, Christie's, London, November 25, 2009.

24 Adrian Dannatt, "Orientalism and the Art Market," *artnet* (March 2009), http://www.artnet.com/magazineus/features/dannatt/dannatt3-17-09.asp (accessed November 24, 2009). Perhaps, Gabr hints, the artists' individualism may have allowed a greater transparency than today's media images processed through the news corporations—a line of thought also followed in Yasmin Alibhai-Brown's review of *The Lure of the East*: "Pride and Prejudice: In Praise of Britain's Colonial Artists", *Independent*, May 30, 2008. There now exists a luxurious catalog of *The Shafiq Gabr Collection*, ed. Ahmed-Chaouki Rafif (Paris: ACR, 2008).

25 Christie's launched their *Ottomans and Orientalists* sale category in 1998, although there were various one-off sales at both main houses before this, for example the *Important Orientalist Paintings* from the collection of Coral Petroleum, Inc., sold by Sotheby's in New York in 1985, several of which had only the year before formed a central attraction of the major exhibition *The Orientalists: Delacroix to Matisse. European Painters in North Africa and the Near East* at the Royal Academy in London and the National Gallery of Art in Washington.

26 Bonhams established an office in Dubai 2007 and held their first sale there—of contemporary art—in March 2008.

27 Hamdi Bey's *Tortoise Trainer*, now at the Pera Museum, fetched a huge price when sold at the Antik auction house in Istanbul in 2004, but his *Lady of Constantinople* almost doubled that result when it achieved £3.38m. at Sotheby's, London, May 30, 2008, lot 100. I do not intend to suggest that Hamdi forms part of the category of Orientalist painting in any straightforward way, for of course his relationship to that European tradition is a complex and vigorously debated question. Here I am merely noting his status as a Turkish phenomenon of the international art market.

28 In London, the main auction houses and various dealers have recently begun showcasing contemporary art from Turkey and the Middle East.

29 *Contemporary Turkish Art*, Sotheby's, London, March 4, 2009, lot 13.

30 Beral Madra, "The Hot Spot of Global Art. Istanbul's Contemporary Art Scene and its Sociopolitical and Cultural Conditions and Practices," *Third Text* 22, no. 1 (January 2008): 107.

31 Antonia Carver, "Are Auction Houses Moving onto Gallery Turf?" *Bidoun* 13 (Winter 2008), http://bidoun.com/bdn/magazine/13-glory/are-auction-houses-moving-onto-gallery-turf-by-antonia-carver/ (accessed May 5, 2010).

32 John Arlidge, "Art and Architecture in the Middle East," *The Sunday Times*, August 3, 2008.

33 In Shumon Basar, Antonia Carver and Markus Miessen, eds., *With/Without. Spatial Products, Practices and Politics in the Middle East* (Dubai: Bidoun and Moutamarat, 2007), 36.

34 John W. Fox, Nada Mourtada-Sabbah and Mohammed el-Mutawa, "Heritage Revivalism in Sharjah," in *Globalization and the Gulf* ed. John W. Fox, Nada Mourtada-Sabbah and Mohammed el-Mutawa (London and New York: Routledge, 2006), 277. The Ruler of Sharjah, Sheikh Sultan al-Qasimi, is himself a published diplomatic historian: see for example his *Omani–French Relations 1715–1900* (Exeter: Forest Row, 1996).

35 See Sylvia Smith, "Emirates Art Lovers Welcome Orientalism," *BBC News* (April 27, 2009), http://news.bbc.co.uk/1/hi/world/middle_east/8020421.stm (accessed November 24, 2009). To accompany The *Lure of the East*, the Sharjah Art Museum produced its own booklet in Arabic and English with an introduction by Dr. Elisabeth Stoney of the University of Sharjah.

Bibliography

Adam, Georgina. "World's Biggest Art Collector Under Arrest in Qatar." *Art Newspaper,* no. 157 (March 2005): 48.

Ahmad, Ali Nobil. "What did you expect old boy? This is the Tate Britain!" *Dark Matter. In the Ruins of Imperial Culture* (July 2008). http://www.darkmatter101.org/site/2008/07/07/(accessed November 24, 2009).

Alibhai-Brown, Yasmin. "Pride and Prejudice: In Praise of Britain's Colonial Artists." *Independent*, May 30, 2008, review section.

Arlidge, John. "Art and Architecture in the Middle East." *The Sunday Times*, August 3, 2008.

Basar, Shumon, Antonia Carver and Markus Miessen, eds. *With/Without. Spatial Products, Practices and Politics in the Middle East*. Dubai: Bidoun and Moutamarat, 2007.

Beaulieu, Jill and Mary Roberts, eds. *Orientalism's Interlocutors: Painting, Architecture, Photography*. Durham, NC and London: Duke University Press, 2002.

Benjamin, Roger. "Post-Colonial Taste. Non-Western Markets for Orientalist Art." In *Orientalism. Delacroix to Klee*, edited by Roger Benjamin, 32–40. Sydney: Art Gallery of New South Wales, 1997.

Benjamin, Roger. *Orientalist Aesthetics: Art, Colonialism, and French North Africa, 1880–1930*. Berkeley, CA and London: University of California Press, 2003.

Bohrer, Frederick N. *Orientalism and Visual Culture: Imagining Mesopotamia in Nineteenth-Century Europe*. Cambridge: Cambridge University Press, 2003.

Carver, Antonia. "Are Auction Houses Moving onto Gallery Turf?" *Bidoun* 13 (Winter 2008). http://bidoun.com/bdn/magazine/13-glory/are-auction-houses-moving-onto-gallery-turf-by-antonia-carver/ (accessed May 5, 2010).

Dannatt, Adrian. "Orientalism and the Art Market." *artnet* (March 2009). http://www.artnet.com/magazineus/features/dannatt/dannatt3-17-09.asp (accessed November 24, 2009).

Ertug, Ali Can. "Orientalist Art, Worldwide. The Rise of the East." *Sotheby's Preview Online* (September–October, 2008). http://www.sothebys.com/liveauctions/sneak/article/pdf/sept2008/rise.pdf (accessed November 24, 2009).

Fox, John W., Nada Mourtada-Sabbah and Mohammed el-Mutawa. "Heritage Revivalism in Sharjah." In *Globalization and the Gulf*, edited by John W. Fox, Nada Mourtada-Sabbah and Mohammed el-Mutawa, 266–87. London and New York: Routledge, 2006.

Germaner, Semra and Zeynep İnankur. *Constantinople and the Orientalists*. Istanbul: Türkiye İş Bankası Kültür Yayınları, 2002.

Ibn Warraq. *Defending the West. A Critique of Edward Said's* Orientalism. Amherst, NY: Prometheus, 2007.

Irwin, Robert. *For Lust of Knowing. The Orientalists and their Enemies*. London: Penguin, 2006.

Jasanoff, Maya. *Edge of Empire. Conquest and Collecting in the East 1750–1850*. London: Fourth Estate, 2005.

Juler, Caroline. *Najd Collection of Orientalist Paintings*. London: Manara, 1991.

Kabbani, Rana. *Imperial Fictions: Europe's Myths of Orient* [1986]. London: Saqi, 2008.

Kalmar, Ivan Davidson and Derek J. Penslar, eds. *Orientalism and the Jews*. Waltham, MA: Brandeis University Press, 2004.

Lewis, Reina. *Gendering Orientalism: Race, Femininity and Representation*. London: Routledge, 1996.

Liddle, Rod. "Sordid Reality behind Dubai's Gilded Façade". *The Sunday Times*, July 12, 2009.

Lowe, Lisa. *Critical Terrains: French and British Orientalisms*. Ithaca, NY: Cornell University Press, 1992.

MacKenzie, John. *Orientalism: History, Theory and the Arts*. Manchester: Manchester University Press, 1995.

Madra, Beral. "The Hot Spot of Global Art. Istanbul's Contemporary Art Scene and its Sociopolitical and Cultural Conditions and Practices." *Third Text* 22, no. 1 (January 2008): 105–112.

Mitchell, Timothy. *Colonising Egypt* [1988]. Berkeley, CA and London: University of California Press, 1991.

Nochlin, Linda. "The Imaginary Orient" [1983]. In *The Politics of Vision. Essays on Nineteenth-century Art and Society*, 33–59. New York and London: Harper and Row, 1989.

Porterfield, Todd. *Allure of Empire: Art in the Service of French Imperialism, 1798–1836*. Princeton, NJ: Princeton University Press, 1998.

al-Qasimi, Sultan Muhammad. *Omani–French Relations 1715–1900*, translated from the Arabic by B. R. Fridham. Exeter: Forest Row, 1996.

Rafif, Ahmed-Chaouki, ed. *The Shafiq Gabr Collection*. Paris: ACR, 2008.

Said, Edward W. *Orientalism*. London: Routledge and Kegan Paul, 1978.

Said, Edward W. *Covering Islam. How the Media and the Experts Determine How we See the Rest of the World* [1981]. 2nd edn, London: Vintage, 1997.

Said, Edward W. and W. J. T. Mitchell. "'The Panic of the Visual': A Conversation with Edward W. Said." *Boundary 2* 25, no. 2 (1998): 11–33.

Salamandra, Christa. "Cultural Construction, the Gulf and Arab London." In *Monarchies and Nations: Globalisation and Identity in the Arab States of the Gulf*, edited by Paul Dresch and James Piscatori, 73–95. London: I.B. Tauris, 2005.

Siegal, Nina. "Welcome to the Bazaar." *Art+Auction* (October 2008). http://www.artinfo.com/news/story/28702/welcome-to-the-bazaar/ (accessed November 24, 2009).

Smith, Sylvia. "Emirates Art Lovers Welcome Orientalism." *BBC News* (April 27, 2009). http://news.bbc.co.uk/1/hi/world/middle_east/8020421.stm (accessed November 24, 2009).

Thornton, Lynne. *Eastern Encounters. Orientalist Painters of the Nineteenth Century*. London: Fine Art Society, 1978.

Tromans, Nicholas. "Palestine: Picture of Prophecy." In *William Holman Hunt*, edited by Carol Jacobi and Katherine Lochnan, 135–60. Toronto: Art Gallery of Ontario, 2008.

Tromans, Nicholas, ed. *The Lure of the East: British Orientalist Painting*. London: Tate Publishing, 2008. Published in conjunction with the exhibition *The Lure of the East: British Orientalist Painting* shown at the Yale Center for British Art, Tate Britain, Suna and İnan Kıraç Pera Museum and the Sharjah Art Museum.

Varisco, Daniel Martin. *Reading Orientalism. Said and the Unsaid*. Seattle, WA: University of Washington Press, 2007.

Velthuis, Olav. *Talking Prices. Symbolic Meanings of Prices on the Market for Contemporary Art*. Princeton, NJ: Princeton University Press, 2005.

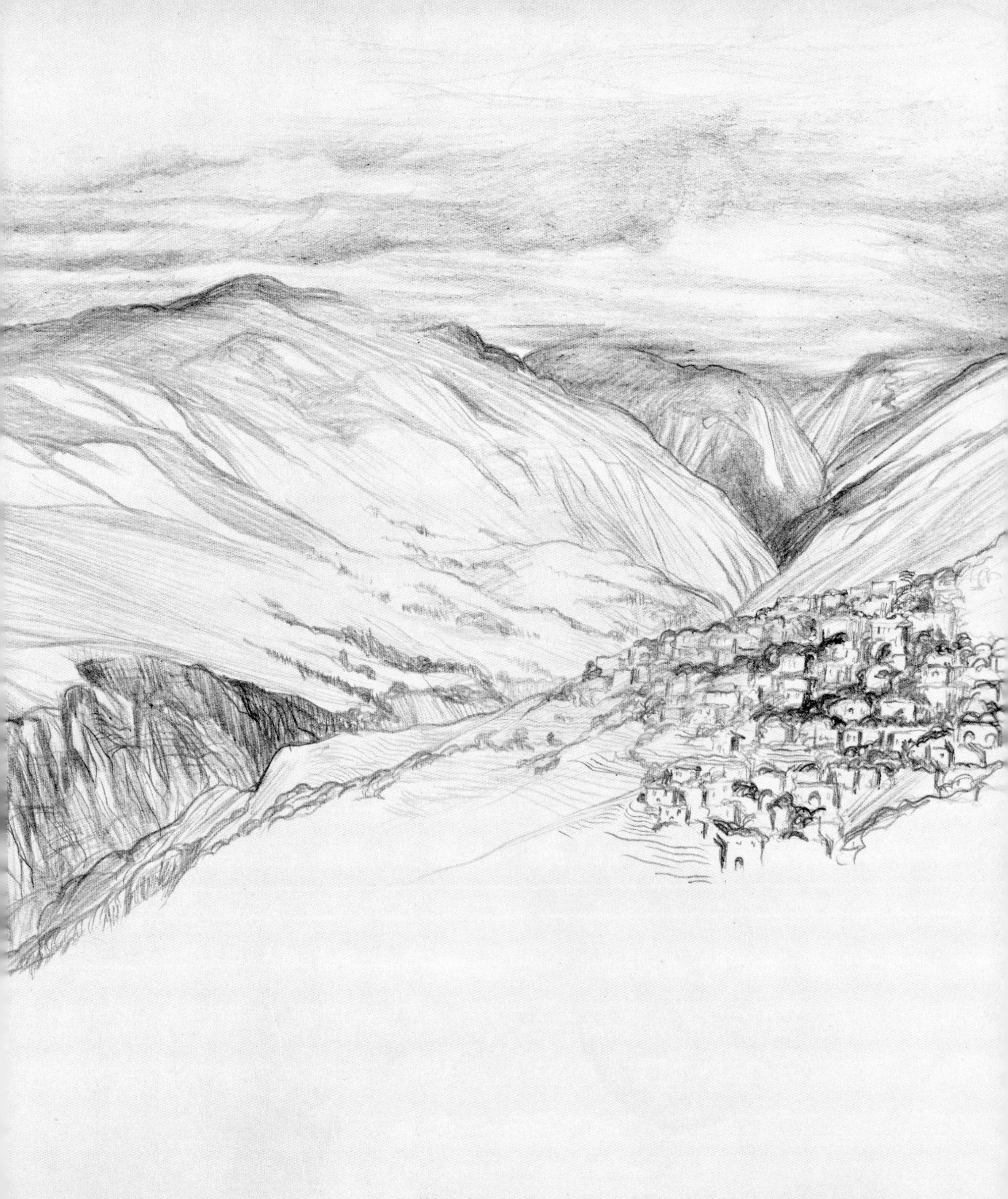

IV

The Searight Collection

Sarah Searight

The Searight Collection, by its size and range, is a unique record of Europe's vision, conception and understanding of the sixteenth- to the nineteenth-century Middle East, in particular the Ottoman Empire. In many ways the collection reflects the life and career of the collector, Rodney Searight, as much as it does that of the merchants, engineers, soldiers, antiquarians, travelers who shared his own wide-ranging interest in the region and whose depictions fill the collection. Admirers of the collection, such as Lynne Thornton in her book, *The Orientalists*, were inclined to place it in an "Orientalist" context. Its very catholicity counters the specificity of "Orientalism."[1]

The collection, now in the Victoria and Albert Museum (V&A), London consists of watercolors, drawings, prints, books of prints and printed travel accounts. It was mainly developed by Searight between the mid 1960s and mid 1980s and was acquired by the V&A in 1987. There are over 2,000 watercolors, over 5,000 prints and over 300 books. Many of the books are illustrated with engravings whose originals are also in the collection.

By background and career my father Rodney Searight was part of the European upper class. Well-educated, well-traveled, interested in the wider world, his approach was typical of many of those whose works he collected; paternalist perhaps in attitude to the Middle East but pragmatic—neither imperialist nor Orientalist. Born in 1909 Searight had a typical British private education in the aftermath of World War I, with its emphasis on classical history as well as on Britain's imperial role in the world. History was a principal interest throughout his life and, combined with his career, this explains his interest in the ramifications of European involvement in the Middle East whether through trade, religious zeal, antiquarian concerns, or the sheer pleasure of traveling through lesser known parts of the world. Much of his career was spent either in the Middle East or involved with it from London. Arriving in Cairo in the mid 1930s he found his mother already ensconced and deeply involved in founding the Brooke Hospital for Horses and Donkeys; today this remarkable charity functions at Luxor, Edfu, Aswan and also in India, Pakistan and Ethiopia. He then worked in Palestine but returned to Cairo for much of World War II, when he was involved in the armed forces, and again afterwards, only returning to London in 1952. He was later involved in oil negotiations in Iran and spent two years in Baghdad in 1958–60 negotiating with the new regime on behalf of the Iraq Petroleum Company.

On his return to London he began to spend his spare time in small out-of-the-way art galleries, initially buying watercolors of familiar scenes—Albert Goodwin and George Clausen among them—and life drawings by the great Victorian draughtsmen. At this point the Middle East hardly featured among his purchases although he did manage around 1960 to buy a David Roberts watercolor of Cairo for "the exorbitant price" of £52, which he came to regard as the foundation of his collection. In an essay in the catalogue of the V&A exhibition he pointed out that the Middle East was at that time an unpopular subject both in terms of theme but also in regard to the artists and "such drawings and watercolors as did appear were disgracefully cheap."[2] He began buying them wherever he went, then voraciously acquiring objects from well-known dealers as well as in the salerooms. Many more of these topographical drawings were available then.

My own book, *The British in the Middle East*, published in 1969, needed illustrations, these were now provided by what was becoming "a collection."[3] Moreover gathering the illustrations sparked a new interest in what he had accumulated, resulting in an exhibition at Leighton House in 1971. This was extremely well received and served to turn accumulation into The Collection.[4] It was quite a shock, he wrote, to realize he had already amassed a remarkable assemblage of British and foreign artists, both amateur and professional. The attractions that had drawn them to the Middle East (eased by the mid-nineteenth-century development of steam transport across the Mediterranean) also drew Searight's interest—architectural, archaeological, topographical and human subjects. After retirement, the collection grew from being a part-time hobby to become a full-time activity. Searight omnivorously scoured art galleries big and small as well as sale rooms, each purchase leading to the detailed research in libraries, print rooms, etc. Searight also sought out obscure archives and descendants, often discovering artists little known before.

It is crucial to recognize how much of a pioneer Searight was in developing his collection. He retired from Shell Oil in the mid 1960s, just as the art market was beginning to show interest in studies of the Middle East, especially the Ottoman Empire, by mostly unknown but nevertheless extremely fine artists. He lived in a large apartment in London's Kensington where the walls were covered with favorite watercolors and prints. Masses more were organized into large map chests. The magnificent book collection filled the bookshelves. He knew exactly where everything was and loved showing it to visitors. However, the oil price rises of the late 1970s led to changes in the art market—more money in different pockets. Europeans flocking to the region came home looking for appropriate pictorial images. Buyers from the region also became interested. And through his purchases my father had unfortunately drawn attention to certain artists, so prices of their paintings were now soaring. Having searched for several years for a safe home for the whole collection, in 1987 the whole lot was acquired by the Victoria and Albert Museum, thanks to a sympathetic reception for the collection by such individuals within the Museum as Michael Kauffman, head of the V&A's Prints & Drawings Department, and Michael Darby and Charles Newton, both also in the Department and familiar with the collection.

This paper is partly concerned with the drawings, watercolors and books in the collection and partly drawing attention to the collector's attitude to his collection, its development, its disposal and its use today. Back in the early 1930s, as a young man embarking on a career in oil, Searight had time to spare in the evenings to attend drawing classes at the Chelsea Polytechnic, later always maintaining that his own skill as an amateur draughtsman enabled him to recognize an unattributed or mis-attributed artist. Time and again this enabled him to spot the hand of a fellow draughtsman that others failed to notice, that eye of the draughtsman was essential to his assessments. It is interesting to compare the hands at work in Figure 4.1 by Searight on holiday in Lebanon in 1935 and the second Figure 4.2 by Edward Lear.

The collection portrays the wider Middle East from the Maghrib as far east as Afghanistan; its principal focus is on the nearer parts of the Ottoman Empire but there are some extremely interesting paintings of further east and west. The majority date from the nineteenth century and over half are by British artists. Most importantly in my opinion, the subjects reflect European involvement in the region from the sixteenth to the twentieth century, ending at World War I. This involvement was similar to Searight's own, in terms of trade and travel, aspects particularly significant when viewing the collection as a whole. One is continually reminded of the factors that brought artists—amateur as well as professional—to the region.

For the early period of links between the Ottoman Empire and Europe, the collection depends on some remarkable travel accounts. Trade links between Europe and the "orient," from the late sixteenth century, are illustrated, for example, with an engraving of Alexandria, c. 1575, from Georg Braun and Franz Hogenberg's *Civitas Orbis Terrarum*. This is a rather fanciful view of Alexandria but emphasizes nevertheless the longstanding trading connection between Mamluk and Ottoman Egypt on the one hand and Venice in particular on the other. However, Europe in general was becoming more involved in Ottoman trade, leading to the establishment of French and English trading companies with bases in such cities as Aleppo, a major terminus of the "Silk Road." In the collection is the account by the Reverend Henry Maundrell (chaplain to the Levant Company in Aleppo) of his 1697 journey from Aleppo to Jerusalem, including descriptions of contemporary Aleppo, thus providing an insight into the somewhat circumscribed life of Europeans in that city as well as the religious zeal of a Protestant pilgrim en route for Jerusalem.[5] Another remarkable account is by the Dutchman Cornelius le Bruyn, *A Voyage in the Levant or, Travels in the Principal Parts of Asia Minor* published in London in 1711.[6] Unlike the watercolors the books are not yet on the V&A website but can be consulted in the Prints & Drawings Department there. They provide a most significant background to the development of European interest in the region.

The headquarters for European traders was Istanbul. Foreigners living in Pera on the opposite shore of the Golden Horn from the Topkapı Sarayı were fascinated ever since the time of Süleyman, called by them the Magnificent, by the paraphernalia of the Ottoman court. Manners, customs and costumes were portrayed by several European artists and include, in the collection, an anonymous mid-eighteenth-century watercolor probably of a "feneriotes" or Phanariots family, wealthy Greeks who often acted as go-betweens for European merchants trading with Ottomans. By the late

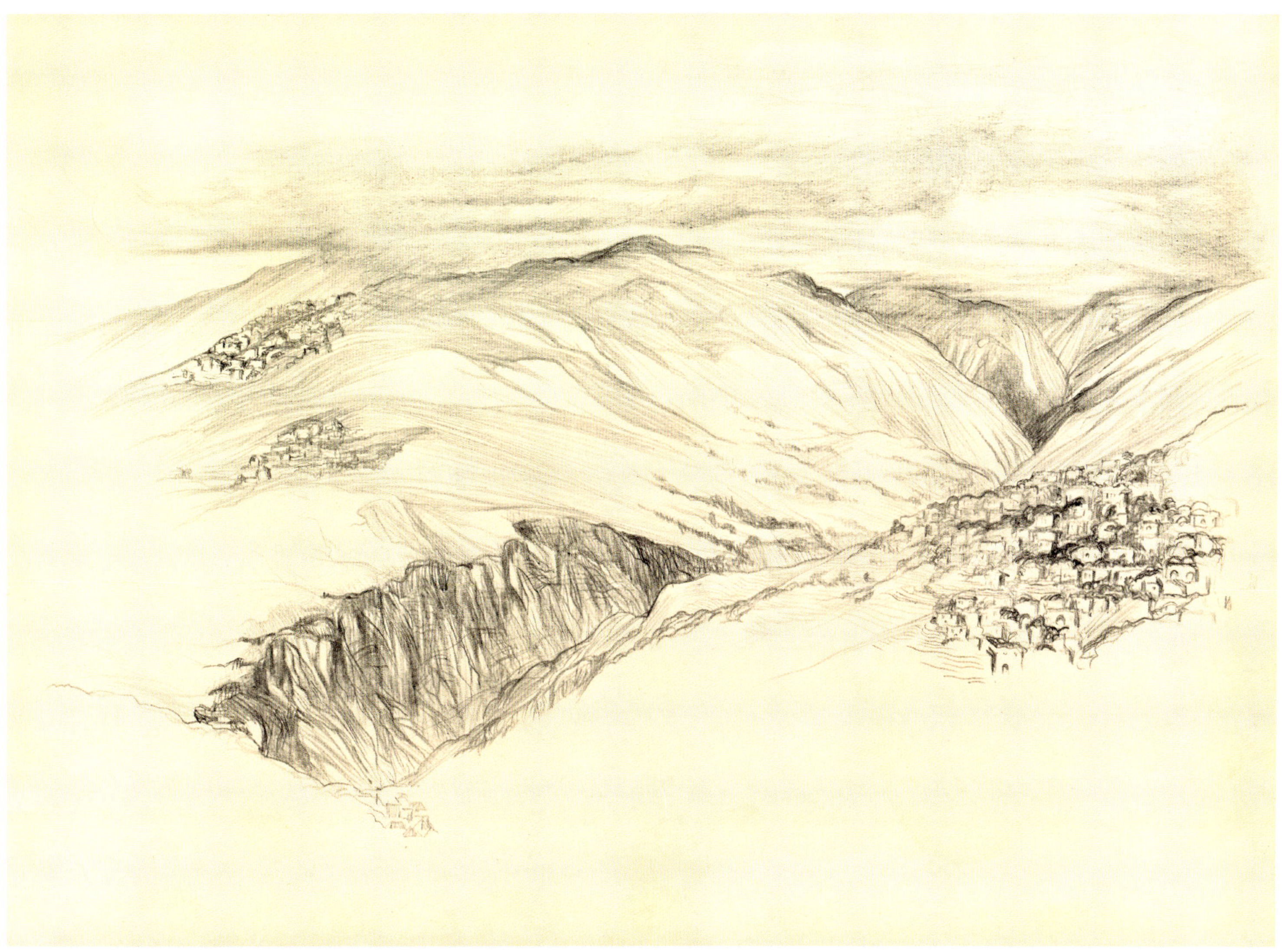

Figure 4.1 *Mountain Villages in Lebanon*, Rodney Searight (1909–1991), 1935, pencil, 26 x 35.5 cm. Trustees of the Victoria and Albert Museum.

eighteenth century increasing European political interest in the Ottoman Empire resulted in a number of images commissioned by an early generation of diplomats, such as an engraving of the French ambassador Comte Choiseul-Gouffier being received by an Ottoman official in the 1780s when he was ambassador in Istanbul. There is also a colored aquatint by Luigi Mayer of an Ottoman ambassador returning from a St Petersburg meeting in 1794. Sir Robert Ainslie, British Ambassador in Constantinople/Istanbul, had employed the artist, Luigi Mayer (for 50 pounds a year). Mayer was one of the first professional artists to travel all over the Ottoman Empire, including Egypt; several of his watercolors are in the collection as well as several volumes of his aquatints.[7]

There was also growing interest in the antiquities of the Ottoman Empire. Europeans were in the grip of the Enlightenment and now began exploring the ancient classical world. Greater curiosity and greater security led the more intrepid to the extension of the Grand Tour, producing on their return some of the most valuable books that are now in the Searight Collection. Two of these are Robert Wood's account of the journey he and James Dawkins made to Palmyra in 1751 and to Baalbek later the same year (*The Ruins of Palmyra, otherwise Tadmore, in the Desert* and *The Ruins of Balbec, otherwise Heliopolis in Coelosyria*). The faintly ridiculous engraved frontispiece to the mammoth Palmyra tome shows the two travelers clad most unsuitably in *togas*, with Palmyra very much in the background.[8] The original of the engraving was painted by Gavin Hamilton from sketches by the artist Giovanni Borra who accompanied the travelers and who is also in the picture. Other sketches by Borra are also in the collection. In 1764 the British Society of Dilettanti dispatched the antiquarian Richard Chandler, the artist William Pars and architect Nicholas Revett to Asia Minor to record antiquities.

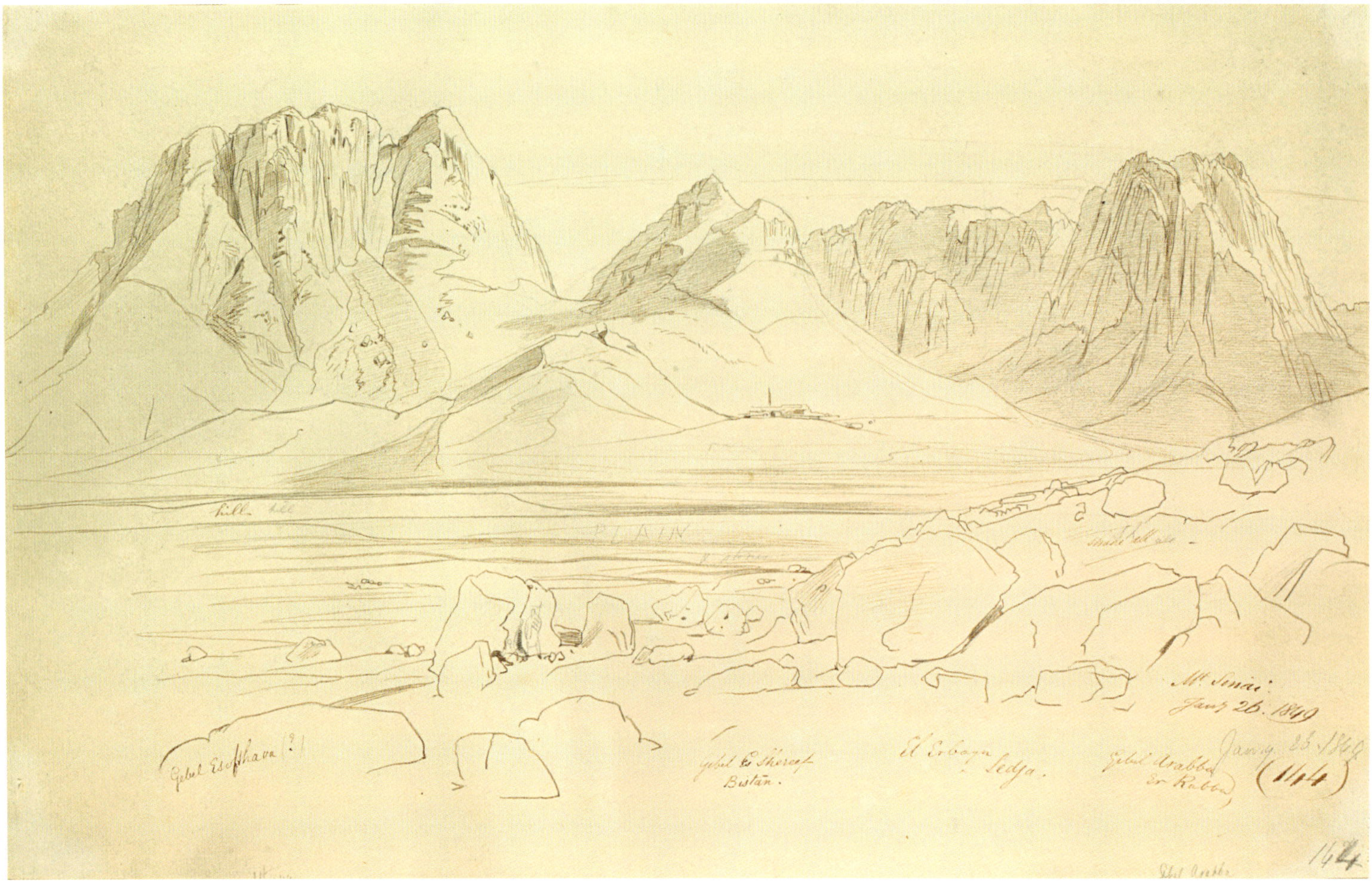

Figure 4.2 *Mount Sinai,* Edward Lear (1818–1888), 1849, pen and brown ink and pencil, 33.1 x 51.1 cm. Trustees of the Victoria and Albert Museum.

Pars's watercolors, including one of the theatre at Miletus in the collection, were subsequently etched and aquatinted by Paul Sandby, some of the earliest aquatints to appear in Britain.[9] Two other watercolors of Miletus are in the collection—a romanticized view by Louis Francois Cassas and a more prosaic view by Luigi Mayer.

Europe's involvement in the region changed dramatically in the aftermath of Napoleon's invasion of Egypt in 1798. Arguably this could be seen as the event that triggered the development of "Orientalism" as travel in the area for a wide variety of purposes became more widespread. Nelson caught up with the French fleet in Aboukir Bay just east of Alexandria. An observer of the battle, which resulted in the sinking of much of the French fleet, was the Reverend Cooper Willyams (chaplain and surgeon on board one of Nelson's fleet, as well as artist) who in a watercolor in the collection depicted the first day's attack on Aboukir fort by Turkish gunboats. In the painting Turkish officers are shown taking time off to have a smoke—much as one sees today on London's pavements now that smoking is forbidden inside offices.

Napoleon foolishly then advanced into Syria, but left his army to besiege Acre while he himself headed back to France. Turkish land forces defeated the French with the help of a British fleet commanded by Admiral Sir William Sidney Smith. The collection contains an album of hand-colored stipple engravings of original watercolors by Francis Spilsbury, the surgeon on the fleet; one of them shows Sir Sidney sitting down with the roguish governor of Acre, Jazzar Pasha.[10] It is worth noting that neither Cooper Willyams nor Spilsbury were professionally qualified as artists, but nevertheless show remarkable skill in their depictions of momentous events. The role of so-called "amateurs" in depicting the growing significance of the Ottoman Empire is particularly important, a reminder of how draughtsmanship was an important part of professional education for those such as surgeons, engineers, sailors, soldiers (there are also a number of skilled amateur women artists in the collection).

Back in Britain a much wider public was being aroused to interest particularly in ancient Egypt, initially by the discovery of that ancient world by Napoleon's cultural army of scholars, busy recording Egyptian monuments. Among them was Dominique Vivant Denon, first director of the Louvre as a museum; a watercolor by Denon in the collection depicts himself and Napoleon probably watching the hauling of a French flag to the top of the obelisk generally known as Pompey's Pillar (actually commemorating Diocletian). Despite the military failure of Napoleon's expedition Denon himself made a remarkable voyage up the Nile which he described in his *Voyage dans la Basse et la Haute Égypte* published in 1802.[11] The British tendency to mock the French venture and its influential aftermath is demonstrated by an etched cartoon (one of several cartoons in the collection that reflect Searight's interest in the politics of the period) by the British artist James Gillray. It is entitled *L'insurrection de l'Institut Amphibie or The Pursuit of Knowledge*, and is dated 1799. Gillray is satirizing the efforts of that army of scholars to impose French culture on the Egyptians. The manual *Sur l'education du crocodile* lies in tatters on the ground. Meanwhile Londoners were flocking to the British Museum to view the trophies dispatched by the British consul in Egypt, Henry Salt (with the help of a remarkable ex-muscle man, Giovanni Battista Belzoni). Belzoni's triumphalist account is in the collection.[12]

To focus briefly on a few other topics or events that drew amateur and professional artists to Egypt, chief among these was the development of communications across the Mediterranean, between Europe and India as well as up and down the Nile, using the new technology of the marine steam engine.[13] By the 1830s the Overland Route had developed through Egypt, matching steamers through the Mediterranean with others steaming through the Red Sea from Bombay. A number of aspects of the Route are depicted in the collection. The Overland Route was soon outmaneuvered by a new route—the Suez Canal. A watercolor of Ferdinand de Lesseps' yacht *Mathilde* anchored in Lake Timsa was painted by William Simpson, the first great war artist from his Crimea experience, and now in Egypt to cover the opening of the Canal in 1869.

The French scholars accompanying Napoleon had alerted Europe to the glories of ancient Egypt and soon everyone was hurrying up the Nile to grab spoils. Several of the engineers who accompanied Napoleon's expedition, stayed behind to work for the Viceroy. They were trained as expert draughtsmen and their fine watercolors in the collection depict the European penetration of the lands of the Nile: Figure 4.3 shows one of them, Linant de Bellefonds, at Abu Simbel. Another French engineer Prisse d'Avennes painted a watercolor of a *kanja*, showing the usual means of transport up or down the Nile. Tourists also began to be attracted. A notable individual in the collection is Mrs. Selina Bracebridge, a fine amateur draughtswoman who accompanied her friend Florence Nightingale up and down the Nile in 1849–50.

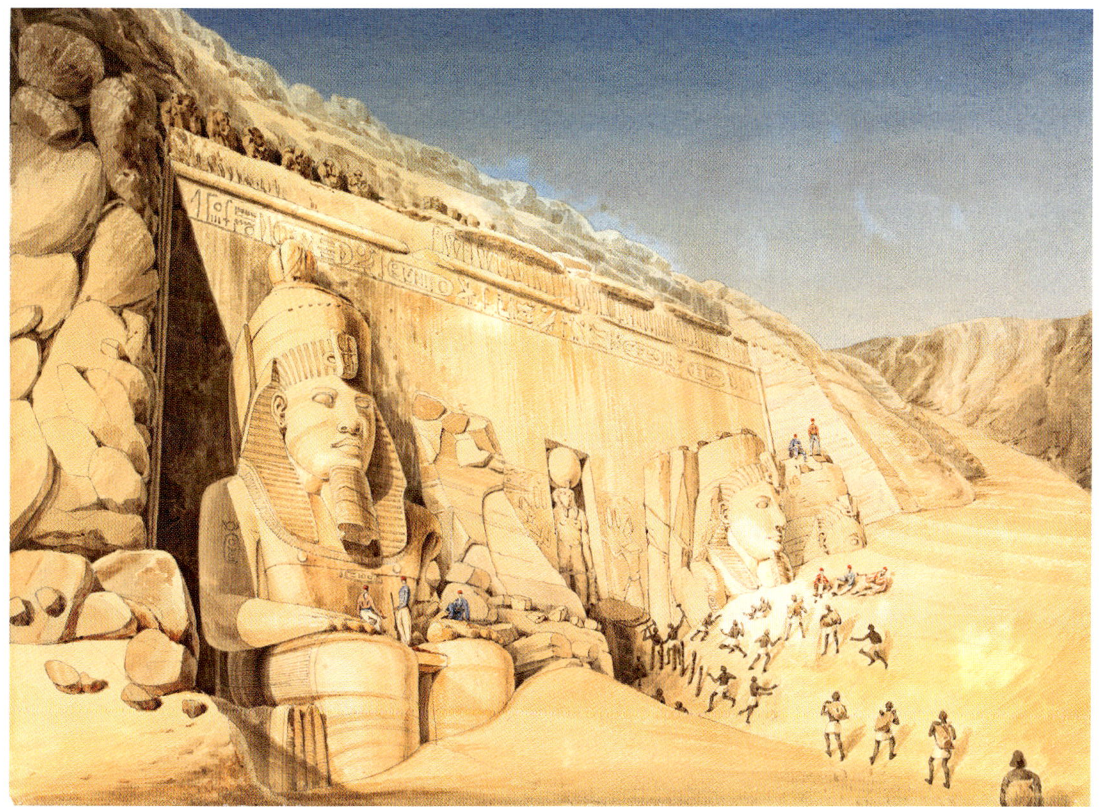

Figure 4.3 *Excavation of the Great Temple of Ramesses II at Abu Simbel*, Louis Maurice Adolphe Linant de Bellefonds (1799–1883), probably 1818–19, watercolor over pencil 17.1 x 23.9 cm. Photo © Victoria and Albert Museum, London.

Europeans were also showing a growing interest in Islamic decorative art and architecture. The great British missionary of Islamic decoration, Owen Jones, visited Egypt in the 1830s, spent some time sketching in Luxor and also, more importantly, in Cairo where he fell under the spell of Mamluk architecture. Several watercolors of Mamluk tombs are in the collection as is Jones's volume of lithographed views of the Nile.[14] Jones was particularly influential in stimulating mid-nineteenth-century British interest in Islamic architecture and its decoration, in particular through his *Grammar of Ornament*. Another enthusiast for Cairo's Islamic architecture was Pascal Xavier Coste whose magnificent album of drawings is in the collection.[15] Another British artist, focusing uniquely on Cairo's domestic architecture, was Frank Dillon; his watercolors include a number of paintings of the interiors of Cairo houses, particularly interesting in view of their subsequent disappearance.

Moving rapidly northwards we pass by that great pilgrimage site, St Catherine's Monastery in Sinai, including one image by that most prolific of topographical artists William Bartlett painted around 1848. Petra began to be on the itineraries of the more intrepid including Bartlett and also Edward Lear whose watercolor sketch of the site is very different from the colorful oil exhibited in *The Lure of the East*, more suited to the famous exclamation by Lear's servant Giorgio: "O master, we have come to a world where everything is made of chocolate, ham, curry powder and salmon!"[16]

Bartlett typifies the journeyman artist, meeting the demands of the armchair traveler back home, filling volumes with finely engraved biblical references based on his watercolors, several of which are in the collection.[17] These coffee-table books for a righteous Victorian readership give some idea of this indefatigable traveling artist. Numerous watercolors by Bartlett are in the collection, that were subsequently engraved as illustrations in the books. Sadly, perhaps worn out by meeting the insatiable demands of the non-traveling public back home, Bartlett died half way home from his *fifth* visit to the "Orient."

Jerusalem figures extensively in the collection with interiors of the Holy Sepulchre by Thomas Allom and others, also of the Haram al-Sharif including an interesting over-view painted around 1853 by Henry Warren (who was probably working from a sketch by architect-cum-archaeologist Joseph Bonomi as Warren himself never went east). There is also a superb watercolor of the interior of the Dome of the Rock painted in 1863 by the German artist Carl Werner. Moving on to the Mount Lebanon area and back to the gifted amateurs, we come to the traveler Godfrey Vigne and his portrait of Daoud Pasha, the remarkable Ottoman official who brought relative peace to the Mount Lebanon area in the 1830s. Vigne's travels took him through Anatolia, Iran and Afghanistan where he painted portraits of some of the more significant personalities of the region, again catching Searight's historical "eye".

So back to Istanbul and from the 1830s the so-called "Eastern Question," at the heart of which lay the rivalry of the major European powers—France, Britain and Russia—to safeguard their individual interests often at the expense of the Ottoman Empire. The greater involvement of Europe in the affairs of the Empire had led to the establishment of embassies, the arrival of tourists, a demand for images of the great city and a flourishing art market. In principle Searight excluded artists who had never visited the Middle East but an exception were some original drawings by Sir John Tenniel for his cartoons that appeared regularly in *Punch*.

Both the "Eastern Question" and easier transport increased the popularity of the "Near" East with artists. Those represented in the collection from this period are most likely to be professionals. Their nineteenth-century popularity was much revived in the mid-twentieth-century art market by Searight's interest. There is a sense, in no way belittling, that many of these artists were catering both for the visitors to Istanbul—some of those attracted in mid-century by the events of the Crimean War—as well as for the armchair traveler back home. The Italian artist Carlo Bossoli produced an album of colored lithographs of Crimean scenes published in 1856, while the French artist Camille Rogier produced an album of hand-colored lithographs of scenes in Istanbul itself in the 1840s, effectively conveying a sense of the bustle and liveliness of the great city, a kind of superior "post-card" art.[18]

European artists (and—just as important—their clients) were as fascinated as ever by the customs and costumes of the Ottoman world, as for instance shown in several studies by the artist William Page who was in Constantinople in the 1820s. His fine watercolor of the Tophane Fountain is in the collection. Thomas Allom was also a topographical artist who produced a whole volume on *Character and Costume in Turkey and Italy*. His watercolors of the tomb of Mehmed I in the Yeşil Cami complex in Bursa, a particularly good example of early Ottoman architecture, and his representations of houses along the Bosporus, now disappeared (Fig. 4.4), are significant contributions to the architectural history of the Ottoman world.[19] Two of the best-known artists to visit the city were John Frederick Lewis and Sir David Wilkie. Lewis sketched the interior of Aya Sofya in 1840–41 during a year which he spent in Istanbul prior to his decade in Cairo. A most prolific artist was Count Amadeo Preziosi who lived and worked in Constantinople for forty years from 1842 and painted innumerable watercolors of the city, that were popular with visitors of the period. Several of these were acquired by Rodney Searight who commented how Preziosi even had the dubious honor of being much copied. He was visited by both the Empress Eugènie of France and the Prince of Wales, both of whom bought paintings from him. It seems fair to say that Preziosi's twentieth-century reputation was much improved by the Searight interest as well as by an exhibition of his works held in the V&A.[20] (See Fig. 4.5.)

The aftermath of World War I brought so great a change in political relationships that Searight decided to draw back from collecting the work of post-war artists. His own subsequent involvement in those relationships, mainly in the field of oil negotiations in Egypt, in Iran and in Iraq, also reinforced his aim to remain with pre-war paintings.

Reverting now to the history of the Searight Collection, a number of other exhibitions followed the Leighton House exhibition in the 1970s and 1980s, some exclusively the Searight Collection, some a selection accompanied by input from other sources. In 1975 the Royal Academy hosted a major Orientalist exhibition[21] and in 1985 an exhibition of Edward Lear.[22] A significant exhibition that included a number of items from the collection was held in Brighton in 1983.[23] *The People and Places of Constantinople: watercolours by Amadeo Count Preziosi 1816–1882* was organized by Briony Llewellyn and Charles Newton at the V&A in 1985. Other exhibitions, more focused on stimulating interest among collectors from the region (with loans from the Searight Collection) also followed: *Romantic Lebanon: the European View 1700–1900* was held at Leighton House in 1986; *On the Banks of the Jordan* was held in Amman (where there were already several collectors) in 1987.[24] There was also a growing commercial interest, often stimulated by Searight's interests and sometimes employing him as consultant (nevertheless encouraging prices to rise beyond his purse). Commercial galleries were

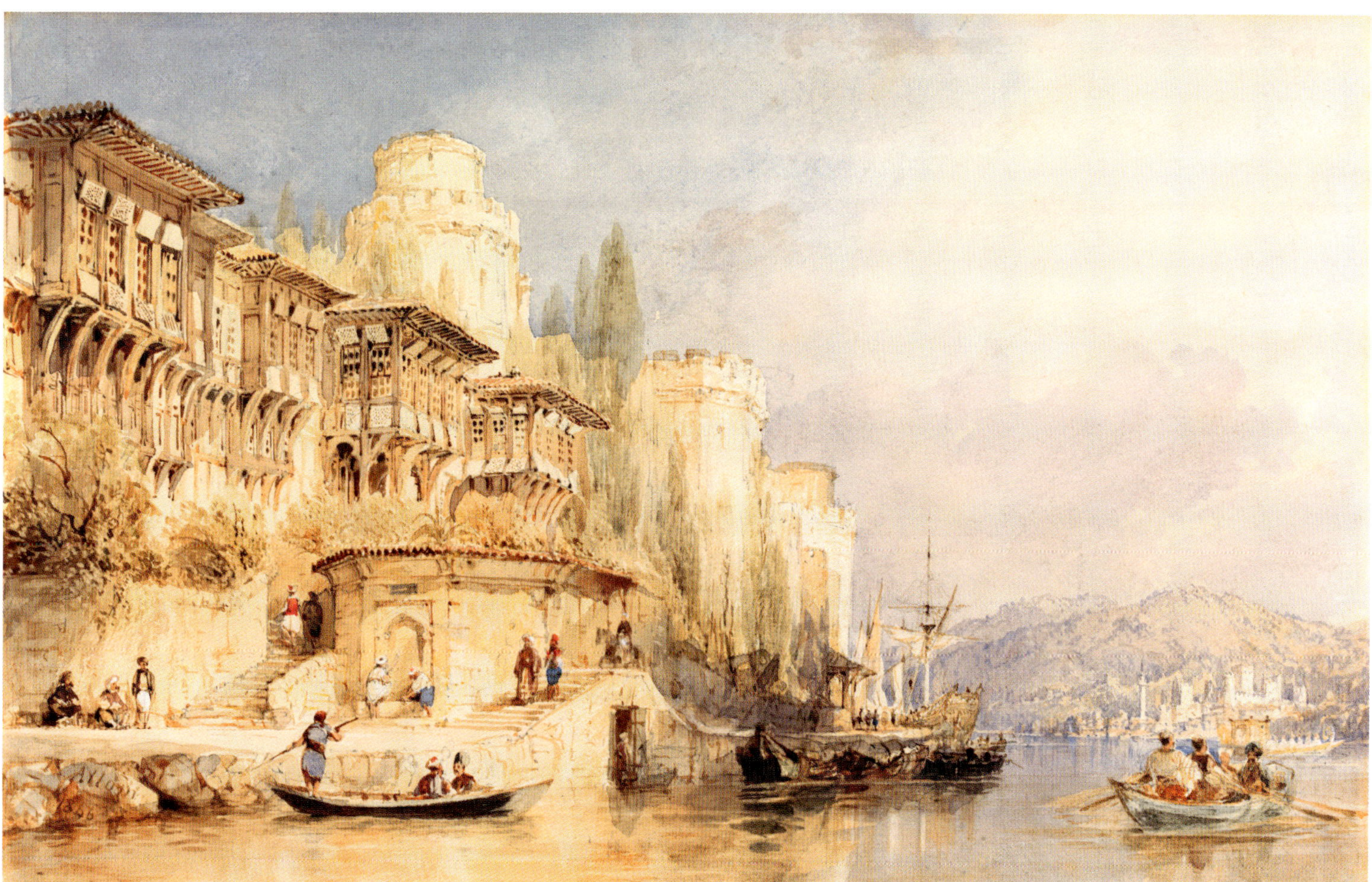

Figure 4.4 *Summer Houses and the Castle of Europe on the Bosphorus*, Thomas Allom (1804–1872), 1846, watercolor heightened with white, over pencil, 19.4 x 30.7 cm. Photo © Victoria and Albert Museum, London.

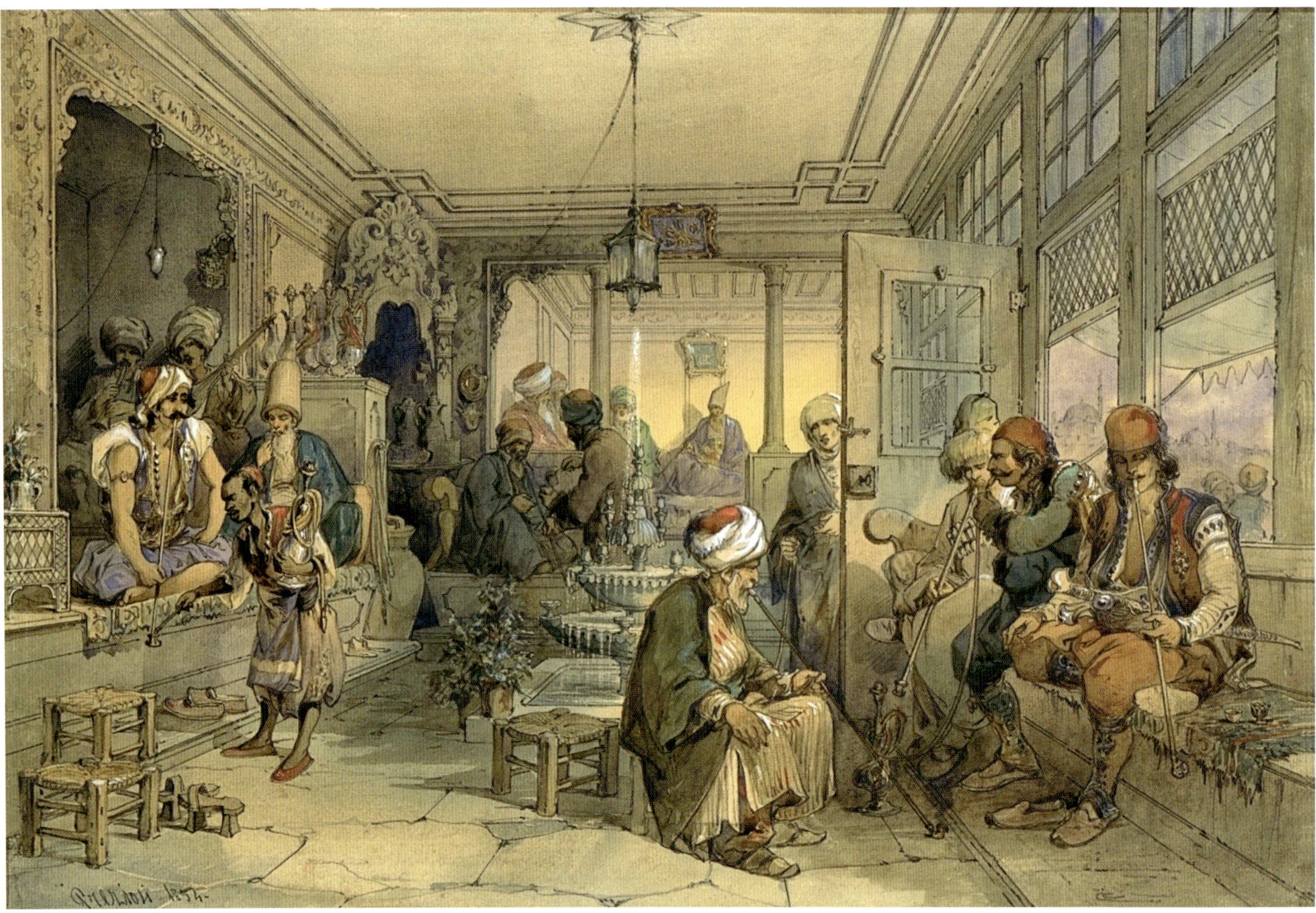

Figure 4.5 *A Turkish Coffee House*, by Amadeo Preziosi, 5th Count (1816–1882), 1854, pencil and watercolor heightened with white, 40.7 x 58.8 cm. Photo © Victoria and Albert Museum, London.

recognizing the purchasing power of the new oil money, resulting in such exhibitions as Agnew's *Sketches in the Holy Land 1839* by David Roberts in 1976. Others at the Fine Art Society included *Eastern Encounters: Orientalist Painters of the Nineteenth Century* in 1978, *Travellers beyond the Grand Tour* in 1980, *The Travels of Edward Lear* in 1983. American interest was aroused by such exhibitions as *A Grand Tour in the Ottoman Empire* of watercolors by Luigi Mayer (c. 1755–1803) held in New York in 1983.

Those involved in setting up these exhibitions invariably consulted Searight as well as borrowing from his collection. On one occasion he asked me to take a recently acquired drawing to the British Museum Prints & Drawings Department to see if anyone could identify the artist; I did so, without identifying the owner, and was strongly recommended, "Show it to Rodney Searight: he's sure to know the artist." He became an advisor to the Royal Geographical Society on its enormous store of watercolors and drawings, which had never seen the light of day since they were bequeathed to the Society by well-meaning descendants of the artists; some of these the Society was able to put on the market thereby raising funds for its library.

By the 1980s the art market had changed considerably from the early 1970s. It is instructive when consulting the collection on the V&A website to note how the curator, Charles Newton, has included the often astonishingly low figure meticulously recorded by Searight on the reverse of nearly all his purchases. These prices were partly due to the "hand" not being recognized by dealers, as well as to the subject matter being unfashionable. Now, partly due to interest stimulated by Searight himself, far more items were coming on the market. The oil price rise and the huge structural development of the Arabian world in particular resulted in much greater interest in the region as a whole. Not only were more foreigners employed in the regional development but also the new rich citizens of that world were interested in artistic depictions of the Middle East. All this interest led inevitably to price rises to levels Searight could no longer afford.

Meanwhile, already nearly 80 years old, Searight was deeply concerned to find a home for the collection. There were certain criteria for its disposal. His aim was to ensure the collection remained intact, in particular that the books stayed with the art, and the entire collection remained within the UK, despite a number of offers from overseas or for the watercolors and drawings minus the books. Searight was also determined that it must also remain accessible to the public. He was therefore greatly relieved when the V&A offered to acquire the collection which it did in 1985 thanks to individuals within the Museum who knew it well—notably Michael Kauffman, Michael Darby and Charles Newton. The acquisition came with a generous grant from Searight's old employer Shell International, the National Heritage Memorial Fund, the National Art Collections Fund, the Friends of the V&A and Gianni Versace. The watercolors and drawings were then cataloged by Briony Llewellyn (who had worked with Searight over many years), Jenny Elton and Tanya Szraiber. The entries were updated by Charles Newton in 2007–8 and these are now accessible on the V&A website. The prints were cataloged by the same team and together with the books can be accessed via microfiche in WID, formerly the Prints and Drawings Department at the Museum. A major exhibition—*The Orient Observed*—was organized by Briony Llewellyn and Charles Newton following the cataloguing.[25] There was a subsequent traveling exhibition of watercolors from the collection—*Voyages and Visions*—organized by the Smithsonian Institute throughout the USA, which went on show on its return to London in the Brunei Gallery at the School of Oriental and African Studies, under the title *Looking East*.[26]

In more recent decades there has been the remarkable growth of interest in "Orientalist" art in the Gulf countries. Rodney Searight would have been fascinated by this new generation of collectors—many of whose purchases have been on display in London's and Istanbul's *The Lure of the East: British Orientalist Painting* from Qatar, from Oman, from Jordan, Sharjah—acquiring some of the finest paintings. He would also have been intrigued by the fact that Sharjah hosted the final installment of the exhibition. The swings and roundabouts of the art market are one of the most intriguing aspects of art history and this latest movement of so-called Orientalist paintings actually to the region is part of that history. While reluctant to let his own collection head eastwards, he would certainly enjoy the regional interest in those he collected.

Artists in the collection were trying to document a world that *was*—a time when artists sought to capture their own responses to new and unfolding experiences. Thus to study collections such as the Searight Collection is to recognize the significant role which trade, diplomacy, antiquarianism, even tourism have played in our and our forebears' comprehension of the region. While on the one hand this pioneering collection represents the very personal and artistic eye of someone who spent much of his life involved with the region, it should also be seen as contributing to a wider historical comprehension of European involvements with that same part of the world.

Notes

1 See Lynne Thornton, *The Orientalists: Painter-Travellers 1828–1908* (Paris: ACR Internationale, 1983), 13–23.

2 Rodney Searight, "Recollections of a Collector" in *The Orient Observed: Images of the Middle East from the Searight Collection*, compiled by Briony Llewellyn (London: Victoria and Albert Museum, 1989), 11.

3 Sarah Searight, *The British in the Middle East* (London: Weidenfeld & Nicolson, 1969).

4 Leighton House, *The Middle East: Watercolours and Drawings by British and Foreign Artists and Travellers 1750–1908 from the Collection of Rodney Searight Esq.* (January 27 to February 20, 1971).

5 Henry Maundrell, *A Journey from Aleppo to Jerusalem at Easter AD 1697*, 6th edn (Oxford: The Theatre 1749).

6 Cornelius le Bruyn, *A Voyage in the Levant or, Travels in the Principal Parts of Asia Minor, the Isles of Scio, Rhodes, Cyprus etc.* (London: Jacob Tonson and Thomas Bennet, 1711); see also le Bruyn, *Travels in Muscovy, Persia and Part of the East Indies*, 2 vols (London: A. Bettesworth & C. Hitch etc., 1737).

7 Luigi Mayer, *Views in Europe and Asia* (London: William Watts, 1801); *Views in Egypt* (London: R. Bowyer, 1804); *Views in Palestine* and *Views in the Ottoman Empire, chiefly in Caramania* (London: R. Bowyer, 1804); *Views in The Ottoman Dominions, in Europe, in Asia, and some of the Mediterranean Lands* (London: R. Bowyer, 1810); *Interesting Views in Turkey* (London: Bensley and Son, 1819).

8 Robert Wood, *The Ruins of Palmyra, otherwise Tadmore, in the Desert* and *The Ruins of Balbec, otherwise Heliopolis in Coelosyria* (London, 1757).

9 Richard Chandler, Nicholas Revett and William Pars, *Ionian Antiquities*, 2 vols (London: Society of Dilettanti, 1769 and 1797).

10 F. B. Spilsbury, *Picturesque Scenery in the Holy Land and Syria* (London: Thos. McLean, 1819).

11 Dominique Vivant Denon, *Voyage dans la Basse et la Haute Égypte* (London: Samuel Bagster, 1809). The definitive *Description de l'Égypte* was published in 24 volumes between 1809 and 1829.

12 Giovanni Battista Belzoni, *Narrative of the Operations and Recent Discoveries within the Pyramids, Temples, Tombs and Excavations, in Egypt and Nubia* (London: John Murray, 1820).

13 See Sarah Searight, *Steaming East: the Forging of Steamship and Rail Links* (London: Bodley Head, 1991).

14 Owen Jones and Jules Goury, *Views on the Nile from Cairo to the Second Cataract* (London: Graves and Warmsley, 1843).

15 Pascal-Xavier Coste, *Architecture Arabe ou Monuments du Kaire, measurés et dessinés de 1818 à 1826* (Paris: publisher unknown, 1839).

16 See Vivienne Noakes, *Edward Lear: The Life of a Wanderer* (London: Collins, 1968), 160.

17 William Bartlett, *Forty Days in the Desert …* (London: Arthur Hall & Co., c.1849); *Walks about the City and Environs of Jerusalem* (London: Arthur Hall, Virtue & Co., c.1845); *The Nile Boat* (London: Arthur Hall. Virtue & Co., 1850); *Gleanings … on the Overland Route* (London: Arthur Hall, Virtue & Co., 1859); *Footsteps of Our Lord* (London: Arthur Hall, Virtue & Co., 1859); *Jerusalem Revisited* (London: Arthur Hall, Virtue & Co, 1859).

18 Carlo Bossoli, *The Beautiful Scenery and Chief Places of Interest throughout the Crimea* (London: Day & Son, 1856); Camille Rogier, *La Turquie* (Paris: Lemercier, 1846).

19 For example, Thomas Allom and Emily Reeve, *Character and Costume in Turkey and Italy* (London: Fisher, Son & Co., c. 1840).

20 Organized by Briony Llewellyn & Charles Newton, *The People and Places of Constantinople: Watercolours by Amadeo Count Preziosi 1816–1882* (London: V&A Museum, 1985).

21 The Royal Academy, *The Orientalists: Delacroix to Matisse: European Painters in North Africa and the Near East* (London: The Royal Academy, 1984).

22 The Royal Academy, *Edward Lear 1812–1882* (London: The Royal Academy, 1985).

23 See Patrick Conner, ed., *The Inspiration of Egypt its Influence on British Artists, Travellers and Designers* (Brighton: Brighton Borough Council, 1983).

24 *Romantic Lebanon: the European View 1700–1900* (London: The British Lebanese Association, 1986); *On the Banks of the Jordan: British Nineteenth Century Painters* (Amman: Jordan National Gallery, 1987).

25 *The Orient Observed: Images of the Middle East from the Searight Collection* (London: V&A Museum 1989).

26 Esin Atil, Charles Newton and Sarah Searight, *Voyages and Visions; Nineteenth Century European Images of the Middle East from the Victoria and Albert Museum* (Seattle and London: Smithsonian Institution, 1995).

Bibliography

Atil, Esin, Charles Newton and Sarah Searight. *Voyages and Visions; Nineteenth Century European Images of the Middle East from the Victoria and Albert Museum*. Seattle and London: Smithsonian Institution, 1995.

Allom, Thomas and Emily Reeve. *Character and Costume in Turkey and Italy*. London: Fisher, Son & Co., c. 1840.

Bartlett, William. *Walks about the City and Environs of Jerusalem*. London: Arthur Hall, Virtue & Co., c.1845.

Bartlett, William. *Forty Days in the Desert …* (London: Arthur Hall & Co., c.1849).

Bartlett, William. *The Nile Boat*. London: Arthur Hall, Virtue & Co., 1850.

Bartlett, William. *Footsteps of Our Lord*. London: Arthur Hall, Virtue & Co., 1859.

Bartlett, William. *Gleanings … on the Overland Route*. London: Arthur Hall, Virtue & Co., 1859.

Bartlett, William. *Jerusalem Revisited*. London: Arthur Hall, Virtue & Co, 1859.

Belzoni, Giovanni Battista. *Narrative of the Operations and Recent Discoveries within the Pyramids, Temples, Tombs and Excavations, in Egypt and Nubia*. London: John Murray, 1820.

Boppe, Auguste. *Les Peintres du Bosphore au dix-huitième siècle.* Paris: Hachette, 1911.

Bossoli, Carlo. *The Beautiful Scenery and Chief Places of Interest throughout the Crimea*. London: Day & Son, 1856.

Chandler, Richard, Nicholas Revett and William Pars. *Ionian Antiquities*, 2 vols. London: Society of Dilettanti, 1769 and 1797.

Conner, Patrick, ed. *The Inspiration of Egypt its Influence on British Artists, Travellers and Designers*. Brighton: Brighton Borough Council, 1983.

Coste, Pascal-Xavier. *Architecture Arabe ou Monuments du Kaire, measurés et dessinés de 1818 à 1826*. Paris, 1839.

Denon, Dominique Vivant *Voyage dans la Basse et la Haute Égypte*. London: Samuel Bagster, 1809.

Germaner, Semra and Zeynep İnankur. *Constantinople and the Orientalists.* Istanbul: Türkiye İş Bankası Kültür Yayınları, 2002.

Jones, Owen. *Grammar of Ornament*. London: Quaritch, 1910.

Jones, Owen and Jules Goury. *Views on the Nile from Cairo to the Second Cataract*. London: Graves and Warmsley, 1843.

Julian, Philippe. *The Orientalists: European Painters of Eastern Scenes*. Oxford: Phaidon, 1977.

le Bruyn, Cornelius *A Voyage in the Levant or, Travels in the Principal Parts of Asia Minor, the Isles of Scio, Rhodes, Cyprus etc.* London: Jacob Tonson and Thomas Bennet, 1711.

le Bruyn, *Travels in Muscovy, Persia and Part of the East Indies*, 2 vols. London: A. Bettesworth & C. Hitch etc., 1737.

Llewellyn, Briony and Charles Newton. *The People and Places of Constantinople: Watercolours by Amadeo Count Preziosi 1816–1882*. London: V&A Museum, 1985.

Maundrell, Henry. *A Journey from Aleppo to Jerusalem at Easter AD 1697*, 6th edn. Oxford: The Theatre, 1749.

Mayer, Luigi. *Views in Europe and Asia*. London: William Watts, 1801.

Mayer, Luigi. *Views in Egypt*. London: R. Bowyer, 1804.

Mayer, Luigi. *Views in Palestine*. London: R. Bowyer, 1804.

Mayer, Luigi. *Views in the Ottoman Empire, chiefly in Caramania*. London: R. Bowyer, 1804.

Mayer, Luigi. *Views in The Ottoman Dominions, in Europe, in Asia, and some of the Mediterranean Lands*. London: R. Bowyer, 1810.

Mayer, Luigi. *Interesting Views in Turkey*. London: Bensley and Son, 1819.

Noakes, Vivienne. *Edward Lear: the Life of a Wanderer.* London: Collins, 1968.

Rogier, Camille. *La Turquie*. Paris: Lemercier, 1846.

Royal Academy. *The Orientalists: Delacroix to Matisse: European Painters in North Africa and the Near East*. London,, The Royal Academy, 1984.

Royal Academy. *Edward Lear 1812–1882*. London: The Royal Academy, 1985.

Searight, Rodney. "Recollections of a Collector." In *The Orient Observed: Images of the Middle East from the Searight Collection*, compiled by Briony Llewellyn, 11–16. London: Victoria and Albert Museum, 1989.

Searight, Sarah. *The British in the Middle East.* London: Weidenfeld & Nicolson, 1969.

Searight, Sarah. *Steaming East: the Forging of Steamship and Rail Links*. London: Bodley Head, 1991.

Spilsbury, F. B. *Picturesque Scenery in the Holy Land and Syria*. London: Thos. McLean, 1819.

Thornton, Lynne. *The Orientalists: Painter-Travellers 1828–1908*. Paris: ACR Internationale, 1983.

Tromans, Nicholas, ed. *The Lure of the East: British Orientalist Painting.* London: Tate Trustees, 2008. Published in conjunction with the exhibition *The Lure of the East: British Orientalist Painting* shown at the Yale Center for British Art, Tate Britain, Suna and İnan Kıraç Pera Museum and the Sharjah Art Museum.

Woods, Robert. *The Ruins of Palmyra, otherwise Tadmore, in the Desert*. London, 1953.

Woods, Robert. *The Ruins of Balbec, otherwise Heliopolis in Coelosyria*. London, 1957.

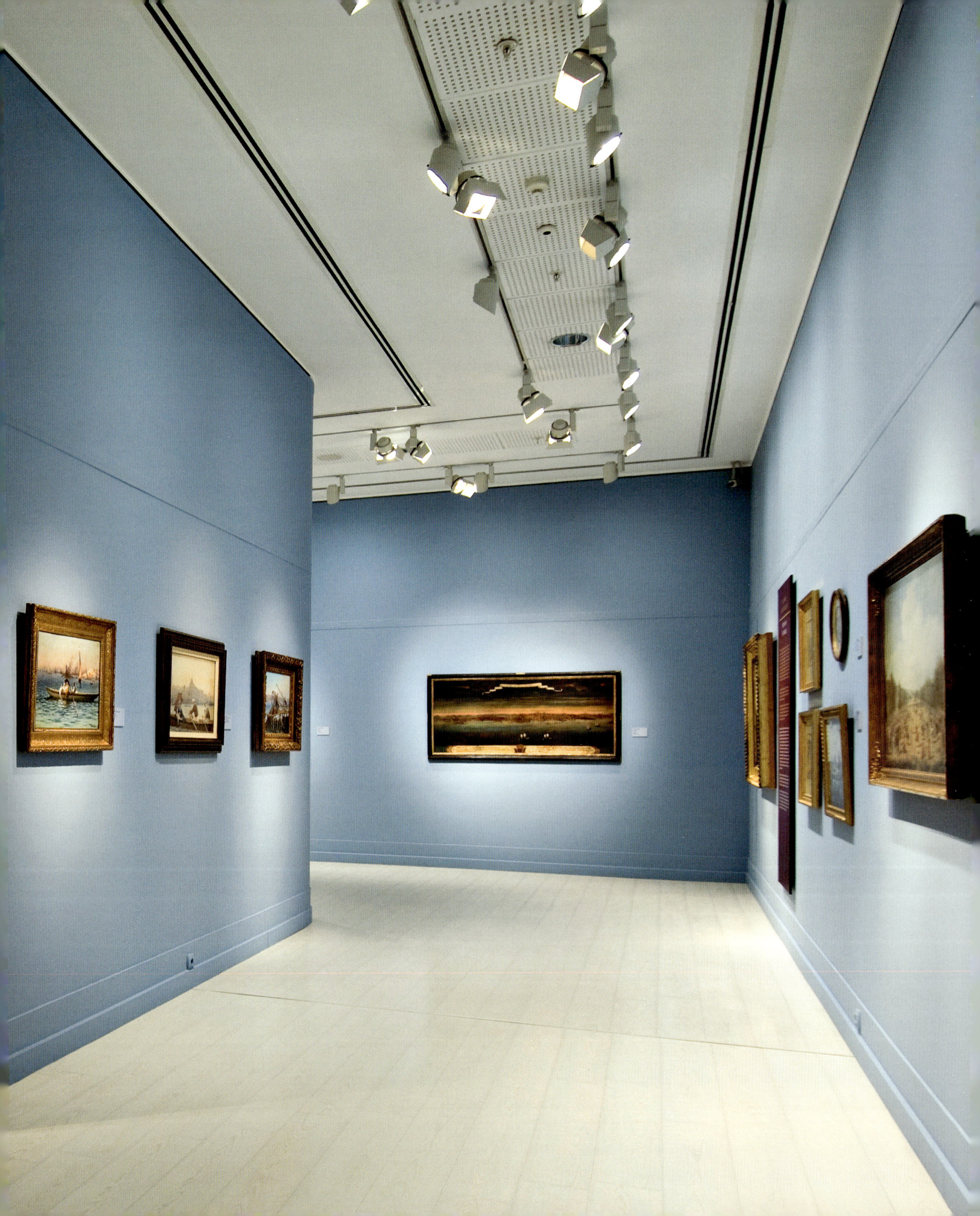

V

Cultural Consignment and Cultural (Ex)Change

Donald Preziosi

Synopsis

The most enduring controversy at the heart of many areas in the humanities and social sciences, and impacting especially on museum history and theory, concerns the nature of representation. This is a controversy played out over many centuries not only in diverse academic fields, but across the wider social and political spectrum in many societies. Concerns over representation were at the core of the ancient ambivalence voiced by Plato about the world of artifice in service to the ideal state and its social, political, and religious orders, given the ability of human craft to simultaneously create *and* problematize those orders. Such an ambivalence has underlain not a few religious controversies in ancient and modern societies. This chapter investigates some of the current fundamental beliefs about the nature and significance of objects that underlie and shape the dramaturgy and stagecraft of modern museums, and particularly institutions engaged in promoting narratives of national or regional or ethnic identity and history.

Introduction

Every claim that has been made about museums or could be made today rests upon beliefs about the nature and significance of objects.[1] The use of material objects to "exemplify" or embody ideas or lessons about virtually anything and everything is common to most societies: every object is always potentially an object-lesson, and the artifactual environment of every culture is semiotically organized and articulated, however materially minimal or extensive. The significance of any object can be made to appear a uniquely powerful "witness" to past or present events, or to the character, mentality, or spirit of a person, people, place, or time. Museums are uniquely powerful semiotic instruments for the creation, maintenance, and dissemination of meanings by fielding together and synthesizing objects, ideas, and beliefs.

Generally speaking, the stagecraft and dramaturgy of the modern museum rests upon two historical foundations. First, upon a two and a half millenniums' long history in Europe of instrumental technologies of what had once been called the "arts of memory," addressed to the production, formatting, storage, and retrieval of knowledge using material objects and their assemblages.[2] And secondly upon a co-extensive history of philosophical and religious problems and controversies, often distilled into legally enforced doctrines, regarding the proper or correct or "true" meanings and functions of objects in individual and social life. In short, the modern museum is an epistemological technology producing knowledge by fielding relationships amongst objects that ostensify individual and collective human relationships. But these two foundations, the technological and the philosophical, have always been co-constructed and co-extensive, and neither can be adequately understood in isolation.

One of the principal products of museum stagecraft is a belief in the independent existence and agency of what its objects are taken as signifying. Indeed, it might be claimed that museums exist in the first place to manufacture belief in what their collected and assembled contents are staged as implying or exhibiting. In fact, museums manufacture a *twofold* belief: in what their contents or collected objects signify, *and* in the independent existence or agency of what is signified. The latter can be as various as the soul, spirit, character, or mentality of a single individual, or that of an entire tribe, gender, class, race, nation, climate, or species. If artifacts collected and organized together in a narrative or historical fashion suggest a certain common style or mentality in the products of a person or people, or of a time and place, then it would seem reasonable to conclude that the objects are the product and effect of that spirit or mentality, which seems to suffuse the artifacts so assembled and staged.

This is one of the central articles of faith in modern disciplines such as art history, art criticism, esthetic philosophy, or museology, where it is not uncommonly believed that there is or should be a common style or spirit to the products of a person or people. It is essential to stress the word belief here, for all of this rests upon foundations that are essentially theological and ethical—discussed in more detail below. What is (or should be) common to the corpus of work by British Orientalist painters in Istanbul in the nineteenth century? To what extent are we exhorted to believe in the reality of such imputed commonalities? Is what is common a collective hallucination; a dreamworld that lures them eastward?

How reasonable is such a conclusion or belief, and what other conclusions can be made from reading museum stagings, and not least that staged at the Pera Museum in Istanbul through *The Lure of the East* and the exhibition that accompanied it *Istanbul: City of Dreams*?

There are in fact at least two different yet equally substantial problems here: that of the potential arbitrariness of given readings of a particular exhibitionary staging, and the potential arbitrariness (and the national, cultural and historical specificities) of notions of "reading" as such. Both problems co-exist, and they reflect problems that are both deeply philosophical and religious and also very ancient and intractably controversial in a number of societies. They cannot be adequately addressed separately from each other. While these controversies are quite ancient, in fact they continue to play a powerfully decisive role in the social and political struggles in the current era of transnational corporate neo-feudalism euphemistically called globalization.

A productive critical investigation of the phenomenon of museum narratives, as well as of museum narratives focused upon a particular time, place, or person(s), must engage with the historical, philosophical, and religious foundations of the problem if it is to yield a more than superficial and disingenuously innocent academic taxonomy.

Because of its complex nature as both a kind of thing and a way of using things; as an artifact operating on other artifacts so as to fabricate stories which are then made legible as causal agents of artifacts themselves, the problem before us in Istanbul facing an apparently collective dreamworld about "the east," is a difficult one. How can we engage in truly effective critical investigations of the problems—the mythologies, if you will—of museum narratives focused upon national identity and patrimony without simultaneously engaging in a critical interrogation of the epistemological and ideological presuppositions of which modern museum and collecting practices are themselves both product and producer? In other words, any critique of what is represented is inseparable from a more fundamental critique of what is understood by representation itself. But then what we understand by representation is itself a culturally specific matrix of mutually reinforcing theories and practices and professions with a long and complex and varied history in many societies. Things simply "mean" differently in different societies, and also in the same society at different times and places and for different meaning-makers.

The Object in and of the Museum

I'd like to begin by returning to the point where I began—the problem of the nature and significance of objects, which underlies everything to do with museums and museology. It was the architectural critic and historian Robert Harbison who some three decades ago observed rather laconically that "Art is troublesome not because it is not delightful, but because it is not *more* delightful: we accustom ourselves to the failure of gardens to make our lives as paradisical as their prospects."[3]

It is the very *troublesome* and challenging nature of things—as the ancient Roman philosopher Lucretius termed it, the inherent sadness of and in things [*lacrimae rerum*]—that in one sense might be claimed to be the deeper underlying problem that a consideration of museum stagecraft and dramaturgy should address. This concerns the indeterminacy, fragility, mutability, or mortality of the relationships between objects and their meanings—the fact that significance is evasive, that meanings evolve, or slightly or radically drift or shift with different perceptions or viewers and users. The fact, in other words, that the relationship between forms and meanings is neither one of autonomy nor determination, but one of semi-autonomy; of adequation rather than equation.

This phenomenon is at the same time at the heart of the socially sanctioned need (or even the legally enforced obsession in many societies) to discipline and "fix" the meanings of things; to give each entity an appropriate historical, political, chronological, geographic, and ethical locus or "address." And to do so ideally by embedding objects in a story or narrative; in an unfolding evolutionary history or teleology: a linked series of entities fabricating an overall shape to the time of a time and place. This has always been a facet of a social and political *decorum* with respect to the appropriateness of claimed links or connections between what are epistemologically and ideologically distinguished as form and content or meaning.

Which is another way of reaffirming that the subject is of very great importance, touching as it does upon some of our most fundamental beliefs, and not only about institutions such as museums. Cultural, social and political narratives, as spectacled in and by both modern museums and in their co-dependent professions such as art history, anthropology, and archeology, or the fashion, tourist, and heritage industries, have long been linked to ideological beliefs which amplify and perpetuate earlier religious narratologies, to be considered in a moment.

In the spatio-temporal dramaturgy of the modern historical museum, a rather extraordinary fusion takes place in institutional practice between historical time rendered in space as *sequence and succession* and a certain sense of time as *aspect*: time as a syntactical relation between "present" and the "past" connected in a causal relation of *incompletion and fulfillment*. In this regard, the "past" of the artifact/relic is not uncommonly staged as an incomplete manifestation of or a prologue to what has now come to pass in the present place of observation. Every artifact is thus the relic of an absence: of an absent past which at the same time *pre-figures* our present, which in turn fulfills, completes, or "proves" what the past imagines as its future. That is: us, here and now, in Istanbul and our current social, political, economic, and religious circumstances. The present is the artifact and effect of absent past causes that remain palpable to us *in and by their remaining as relics*. We are induced to imagine ourselves as what our historical relics (both individual and communal) can be read as implying we have long been in the process of becoming. The management and control of how this is to be made legible is centrally and crucially important to any society's sense of its own present and future. This social management of memory and desire is the central business of the modern public museum.[4] This is no less the case with the exhibition at the Pera Museum, an instrument in the ongoing fabrication and re-fabrication of Istanbul.

The production of that from which a society wishes to be descended is in fact precisely what museum narrative stagings seek to demonstrate and naturalize as truth: the facticity of its fictions. This is precisely the mythological core of all modern museum narratives, and of the uncanny space-time of museology across all cultures. It is very deeply grounded in a simulacrum of the structural logic and rhetoric of monotheistic religiosities, with their particular maps of time, history and causality-as-anticipation, fulfillment, and the vanquishing-whilst-retaining of what has been superseded. Where, in other words, the past (of a people or nation) is articulated, framed, or co-opted as a precursor of what it will have become in a new religious, national, social, or political order of things which constitutes our present time.[5]

There is a unique facet of this which is directly related to the birth and development of the museum as an epistemological technology and instrument designed to produce the modern nation-state, and which came to specify a particular attitude towards the past and its relics. It duplicates and uncannily repeats the founding gestures of the new post-tribal monotheism that came to be called Christianity, which is also echoed in the self-designated successor to both Judaism and Christianity, Islam.

Every political regime, both ancient or modern, has always been fundamentally devoted to managing and controlling collective memory. This normally entails a retrograde fabrication and projection of "cultural memories" focused upon lost or obscured entitlements claimed as having been granted by eponymous ancestors or even imaginary forces or beings such as one's own tribal gods. Such entitlements are still commonly used to justify the "ethnic cleansing" of an unwanted indigenous population from land wanted by present colonists, countless examples of which abound across the contemporary world on every continent.

But historically there is a specifically theological dimension to this which has had a decisive impact on the foundations, motivations, and functioning of museums as peculiarly modern inventions. It relates to the problem of the nature and significance of objects, and also concerns the phenomenon of *collecting* in both ancient and modern times. And of recollecting, and also of what might be called *de-collecting*. By which I mean the deliberate erasure (by "facts on the ground") of past meanings and functions through the liquidation or sequestering of what are taken as their relics or monuments. An obvious recent example being the deliberate vandalism in parts of South and Central Asia of Buddhist, Christian, Hindu, and other non-canonically Islamic imagery, directed against what are defined by those wielding or wishing to claim power as evil fetishes or "idols." Which is of course an obvious yet ironic instance precisely of an inverse idolatry; of investing power—taken to be somehow "evil"—as magically *actually existing in* images or monuments, requiring their destruction, and commonly also the murder of individuals or even whole populations who "believe in" or "worship" such evil idols (and thus who are imagined to "worship (the) evil" imagined as inhabiting those idols which the iconoclasts paradoxically both do and do not themselves "believe" in.[6] It would be well to reflect on the potential idolatry hidden in the envelope of the exhibitions under consideration here.

The point is that collection always co-exists, and is co-defined and co-determined by, recollecting and de-collecting or de-accessioning. The present exhibition in Istanbul is also related (by its differences) to the collections that have been exhibited in New Haven and London. But such differences are less related to the purported colonialism, orientalism, or "postcoloniality" of a given exhibition (dynamically shifting relationships, to be sure) than to other, more palpable dramaturgical circumstances. It is with a clear appreciation of this *matrix* of relational attitudes—collecting as but *one facet* of co-existing attitudes toward the nature and significance of objects and of subject–object relations—that it may be possible to critically investigate the phenomenon of the nationally linked or ethnically invested museum narrative. Significant differences amongst institutions which may be palpable on the level of stagecraft (the fielding of viewing subjects or audiences with respect to artifactual phenomena in museological contexts) may not necessarily align neatly or clearly with purported rhetorical, political, cultural, national, class, gender, or ethnic and national differences, despite occasional claims to the contrary. In short, purported homologies between these phenomena are themselves artifacts of the aims to which such claims are situationally put.

Our task, then, is basically twofold: *First*, to critically investigate the inherently mythological or phantasmatic structure of national (or ethnic or regional) museum narratives in both "public" and "private" (or secular and religious) institutions, archives, or collections (a problematic distinction in its own right today, given the increasingly hybrid nature of museum institutions globally). And our task, *secondly,* is to articulate possible ways to cure such pathologies by articulating potentially effective alternatives in given contexts. The use of the term pathology is neither accidental nor incidental, but is intended to signal that national or ethnic narratives are always, everywhere, simultaneously positive and negative in their effects and implications. As with the ancient Greek term *pharmakon*, which meant both poison and cure.[7] The fabrication of any identity or social reality is a function of its imagined relationships to "alternative" identities, and so may rightly be understood as a function or artifact of its imagined othernesses. Creating an identity simultaneously erases and problematizes others, and consequently each co-exists as a kind of artifact or effect of its other.

But this is not exactly what museums explicitly do, and this is what connects this set of issues to the question of the theological substrate of modern museology (or more exactly, the problematizing of distinctions between theological and "secular"). This is the retention, as part of the larger story of what is being historically superseded, of its antecedents or "past." In a crucially important sense, the *non-erasure* and the *re-framing* of the past by the *retention of what is rejected* or historically or theologically superseded as its memorial or monument is essential to making legible the legitimacy of what one wants the present to be understood as being. The museum's contents thus also serve to legitimize what is outside the museum: its contemporary social contexts.

The narratives crafted by modern museum institutions are universally indebted to a deeply disingenuous belief in the inherent power of objects to convincingly *bear witness* to the origins and evolution of state polities. All of which is made possible by an epistemological and semiotic hypothesis or belief inherited from pre-modern religious doctrines regarding the *proper* nature of relationships between subjects and objects—in which there was imagined to be a direct or determinate connection between the intentions of a maker and the perceived meanings of a made object or artifact. In the face, then, of the essential semiotic indeterminacy and mortality of objects staged as re-presentations of absent truths, investiture in the truth of a national narrative (or in its multiculturalist repetitions and alternatives) is tantamount to a pathology founded in what can perhaps best be termed a *coy idolatry*—one that lurks beneath the surface of the effect of maintaining such fictions as if they were re-presencing pre-existent (and independently existing) truths. It is with the acknowledgement of such idolatries that we may then finally begin to deal cogently, ethically, and effectively with what exactly museums are made of, and with why we should continue to care about them, both in Istanbul and everywhere else.

The Tomb at the Museum's Centre

So let me finally present an image which continues these observations by example.

At the center of any museum, any archive, is a *tomb*.[8]

All of the above has dredged up for me an event in another museum in another country: another traumatic rift, which insists itself here. This is an 1841 lithograph of a scene in the Jewish cemetery in the Kasımpaşa district of Istanbul, depicting the reading of prayers for the deceased, whose tomb we may believe is that represented here, next to which is seated a woman whom we may also believe to be the grieving widow. A grieving widow whose very powerful engagement with the viewer—and, we may also believe, the young painter, who was to marry in Istanbul, the city he had come to settle in and deeply love, the following year—elicits desire in the midst of death, framed by death, rejecting death whilst juxtaposed to it, superimposed on it, and the dead body in his tomb—which itself is juxtaposed as foreground to the great city visible in the background.

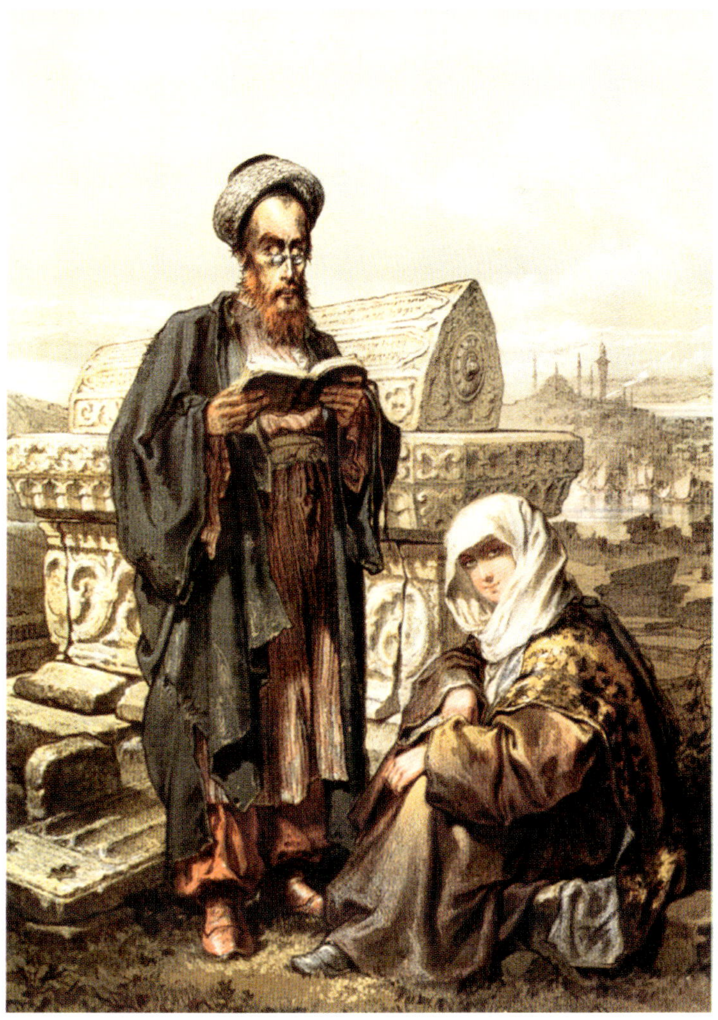

Figure 5.1 *Woman Dressed in Yasmak in Istanbul*, Amadeo Preziosi, 5th Count (1816–1882), 1841, engraving on paper, 51.5 x 61.7 cm. Collection of the Jewish Museum of Greece.

I first saw this lithograph by Amadeo Preziosi in the Jewish Museum of Greece in Athens,[9] and remain haunted by it for various reasons. Some of these reasons are impossible to speak of here and not only because of space but also for two reasons that relate directly to what I've already said and about which this essay is continually trying to talk, that is, to circum-locute; to circle around and wrestle with.

The *first* reason concerns the relationship between archival activity, and indeed museology at large, and the death drive: the impulse to flee a death which always pursues us like a night that never ceases rolling up behind our backs and which *consequently* propels us forward archivally, which is to say, perforce, erotically. The economy of *eros* is that of the archive; of the museum; *eros* properly denoting want or lack; a sign of what is missing. Both love (what the late Roland Barthes called the pure elixir of anxiety) and archives depend for their perpetuation on maintaining a state of tension that guarantees the non-achievement of final closure or completion, beyond the transitory satisfactions of answers; beyond the satisfactions of being sated. This is not unrelated to my own perambulatory wandering around this nexus of proliferating memories (or my own wanderings over the years through what are now Greece and Turkey), a spiralling, centripetal walk whose center point continually recedes into smaller dimensions, fractally connected. Like a picture of someone looking at a picture which contains someone looking at a picture of someone looking at a picture.

The *second* reason concerns the double tension between understanding subjects as homogeneous and heterogeneous, and between the desire for a synoptic point of resolution in which all things disparate are resolved into uniformity lest they dissolve into multiplicity. Like some kind of religious "Last Judgment," where all the dispersed body-part relics of a Christian saint are imagined to be rejoined together, not now, not here, but in an "after"-life, and the desire for its antithesis, in which all uniformities are construed as masking a more fundamental heterogeneity and disjunctiveness. There is a related art historical phenomenon called up by this tension, which I've alluded to above: the practice of explanation by "origins," not uncommonly taken to refer to a progression of states from a simpler unity or *punctum* to a complex, compounded, evolved (or degraded and chaotic) current condition.

In fact, this was an unusual scene in the oeuvre of this recently arrived, 25-year-old European painter, a British subject who lived the rest of his life in Istanbul, recording the costumes, customs, and scenes of daily life both in Istanbul and in Egypt, Palestine, and the Balkans. It is unusual not only in its somber narrative character—he made his living painting colorful scenes of the city and its characters for visiting European and especially British tourists—but also in its unabashedly direct engagement of a figure (and a female figure at that) with the viewer. The widow is a player in a highly charged emotional scene in which her behavior contradicts artistic conventions and social expectations. What might be expected as a depiction of grief and mourning is transformed by the woman's direct gaze toward the viewer into not only a defiance of death but a challenge to the viewer which is not simply proprietary but erotic. She is not merely a person challenging our presence as intruders into a private scene of family mourning; she is a woman erotically engaging the viewer directly and openly, whilst prayers of remembrance are being read right in front of her.

Of course I am projecting into this scene, perhaps, something that may be wholly fictitious? She—and I like to imagine that her name is Hannah—may be the daughter of a dead parent, or the sister of a deceased sibling or other relative, performing filial duty on a day of remembrance. She may not in fact be the widow of a husband just recently dead. Yet precisely because of the manner of her engagement of the viewer/artist, not long after to be married in this community, the speculation may not be off the mark.

What I want to call attention to is the presumed (auto)biographical and archival act of an artist depicting (semi-fictional?) characters; the dramaturgy and stagecraft presented here very closely engages what I've just been writing about. I've dredged up into the present certain "historical" matter. I've foregrounded the depiction of a singular act in its ceremonial setting; seizing a piece of something—an erotically engaging gaze—that for a variety of intensely personal reasons is *absolutely present and alive*; and staging it here as a beginning, an *arche*, of a life. In fact it is *I* who is seized up by this seizure, in recognizing a moment of drama and danger in an act that ruptures the ceremony taking place in what was, an instant earlier, in front of her. She's seated with her body facing the depicted reader, but her turned head changes the entire topology: her eyes are outside the frame. She no longer attends to the reader looming over her with his book; she is engaging us, or at least the young foreign painter. She functions like a character in a novel directly addressing the reader while remaining on the whole within the third or "historical" person: describing while problematizing and ironicizing the objectivity of description itself. In fact the scene is a picture of desire and its effects on the frame of life in what Lacan called the Symbolic Order of daily life; de-stabilizing, blasting open, flooding out beyond the boundaries of social propriety.

This raises several obvious questions regarding the nature of pictorial figuration; questions of integrity and homogeneity; and of the interdependence of artifacts or objects and subjects: which, again, is the key issue haunting this essay. Here, the picture surface is a screen that both separates and connects the past and present. This woman looks away from the man reading; away from the tomb of her relative (or late husband?), toward a future on our side of the screen; a future she engages with, but not in some general way. She's not merely looking out over the city in the background, meditating on her future, but she engages very specifically and concretely with the eyes of the viewer, the artist, us. Her future as our reading of her. Of my reading of her. Of my reckoning with her effect on my shifting subject position(s) here, in this essay you are reading.

An understanding of the depiction is dependent upon a concept of the image as essentially incomplete, as part of a process, perhaps indefinite or infinite, linked to the future. To "read" the image is to sew together the pieces of a *rebus* of disparate things into an archive which by its nature is dependent on the concept of the future; of futurity; in which parts of this artifact are composed into an *arche*, a beginning, a firstness, eliciting, calling forth and engendering, *what shall henceforth be subsequent*. So where is the archive's beginning; its *arche*? What this figure I'm naming "Hannah" ostensifies in short is the indeterminacy of beginnings and ends. To "read" an image, an archive, undoes it. To remember is to literally dis-member memory.

A common rebus is sewn into sense by pronouncing it in a way which takes literally certain elements, say letters, and the sounds of the names or parts of the names of objects or part-objects interspersed with them. What sews *this* rebus into sense is not voice as such, even though my art historical/museological voice is narrating this tale. Rather it is the tracing of a trajectory; a lineage, a history, of desire: of female desire and its eliciting engagement; the inscription of a line, an arc, linking the remains of a man being committed to memory by the reading of a text—being transformed into and becoming (a) text. This is a *phylactery* even—through the surviving partner whose turning away from him articulates him as past, rendering him dead—into a future elicited, seized up by a gaze engaging the eye of the viewer, and initiating a chain of events which will have led to this act being legible here, at this moment and in this place, as a beginning; not least that which I am voicing here, in this essay, and not at all anonymously, and for the first time, as *my own*, in a painting by a man who is painting the distracted mourning of his future wife for her previous husband. Let's be clear about this man.

Let's be clear about this woman: she embodies at the same time, but in different *directions*, mourning and desire; melancholia and performativity. She is at the same time a relay and a link in an endless chain of episodes, of men, stretching back to a compact with a God who demanded that henceforth there should be worn on the male body a sign of futurity, the phylactery, devised out of a sign-token of the severed piece of flesh which rendered the appearance of the remaining phallic organ a pointer to future potency and power in its impotent or quiescent state.

I have been attempting here to articulate some of the implications of understanding the roles of art, artifice, artistry, art history, and musicology in fabricating, factualizing, and maintaining realities that in our modernity they seem merely to patently reflect and recount. It remains to foreground the contemporary situation of this image, as one piece in the collection of the Jewish Museum of Greece in Athens, a "national" public institution dedicated to collecting and displaying memories of one ethnic community in Greece: ironically, by displaying an image of a scene in an Istanbul cemetery. Further problematizing the "national" (Hellenic) specificity of that ethnically focused public institution. Which may finally return us to the paradoxical unity of a collection of essays devoted to an Istanbul exhibition on "The Lure of the East." Is Istanbul a "City of Dreams" for this Athenian museum? Who here dreams?

Our promised (lured) selves always seem hidden in the holes in discourse, or just around the next corner, or outside the frame of the painting, or in the next gallery of the museum, or beyond, before, or posterior to, the margins of our lives. In an after-life. We are carried along a continuously twisting Moebius strip making up the modernist dramaturgy of "subjects" and their "objects," whose opposition is itself the artifact of a *refusal* to see them as the dynamically variable effects of the forces of power and desire; as the two anamorphic states of the artifice of the same modern self; each invisible to the other from the place of the other: each the ghost of the other's ghost.

Appreciating the inextricability; the differential intricacy; of artist and archive, of poet and poetry, of a self and its others is dangerous and terror-laden to be sure; and is always to be found lurking around the next corner of the museum. Of this museum.

Notes

1 See Donald Preziosi, *Brain of the Earth's Body: Art, Museums, and the Phantasms of Modernity*, The 2001 Slade Lectures in the Fine Arts at Oxford (Minneapolis and London: University of Minnesota Press, 2003); see also Preziosi and Claire Farago, eds., *Grasping the World: The Idea of the Museum* (London: Ashgate, 2004); as well as the essay "The Art of Art History," in *The Art of Art History: A Critical Anthology*, ed. D. Preziosi (Oxford: Oxford University Press, 1998; 2nd edn, 2008), 507–25.

2 See especially Mary Carruthers, *The Book of Memory: A Study of Memory in Medieval Culture* (Cambridge: Cambridge University Press, 1990), and Giorgio Agamben, *Stanzas: Word and Phantasm in Western Culture*, trans. Ronald L. Martinez (Minneapolis: University of Minnesota Press, 1993).

3 Robert Harbison, *Eccentric Spaces* (Cambridge, MA: MIT Press, 2nd edn, 2000), Foreword, vii.

4 This contrast between different senses of time and duration recalls the structural and epistemological distinction once made by Michel de Certeau between history-writing and psychoanalysis; see de Certeau, "Psychoanalysis and its History," *Heterologies*, trans. Brian Massumi (Minneapolis: University of Minnesota Press, 1986), 3–16. See also David Nirenberg, "The Politics of Love and its Enemies," *Critical Inquiry* 33 (Spring 2007): 600*ff.* for a discussion of syntactic differences between Greek and Semitic notions of past and present.

5 A useful recent critical introduction to some of these issues is Hent de Vries and Samuel Weber, eds., *Religion and Media* (Stanford: Stanford University Press, 2001), especially Jean-Luc Nancy, "The Deconstruction of Christianity," 112–30, and Gertrud Koch, "Mimesis and the Ban on Graven Images," 151–62.

6 See Koch, op. cit., n. 20, p. 584.

7 Perhaps the most famous critical discussion of this is Jacques Derrida's "Plato's Pharmacy," appearing as parts I and II of Derrida, *Dissemination*, trans. Barbara Johnson (Chicago: University of Chicago Press, 1981), 61–172.

8 An earlier attempt to articulate some of the issues and conundrums described below was in one of my Slade Lectures at Oxford in February, 2001, subsequently published as part of the fourth chapter in Preziosi, *Brain of the Earth's Body*.

9 As of this writing I have been unable to ascertain from the museum the provenance of the piece.

Bibliography

Agamben, Giorgio. *Stanzas: Word and Phantasm in Western Culture*, translated by Ronald L. Martinez. Minneapolis: University of Minnesota Press, 1993.

Carruthers, Mary. *The Book of Memory: A Study of Memory in Medieval Culture*. Cambridge: Cambridge University Press, 1990.

de Certeau, Michel. "Psychoanalysis and its History." In *Heterologies*, translated by Brian Massumi, 3–16. Minneapolis: University of Minnesota Press, 1986.

Derrida, Jacques. *Dissemination*, translated by Barbara Johnson. Chicago: University of Chicago Press, 1981.

deVries, Hent and Samuel Weber, eds. *Religion and Media*. Stanford: Stanford University Press, 2001.

Harbison, Robert. *Eccentric Spaces*. Cambridge, MA: MIT Press, 2nd. edn, 2000.

Koch, Gertrud. “Mimesis and the Ban on Graven Images.” In *Religion and Media*, edited by Hent de Vries and Samuel Weber, 151–62. Stanford: Stanford University Press, 2001.

Nancy, Jean-Luc. “The Deconstruction of Christianity.” In *Religion and Media*, edited by Hent de Vries and Samuel Weber, 112–30. Stanford: Stanford University Press, 2001.

Nirenberg, David. “The Politics of Love and its Enemies.” *Critical Inquiry* 33 (Spring, 2007): 573–605.

Preziosi, Donald. “The Art of Art History.” In *The Art of Art History: A Critical Anthology*, edited by D. Preziosi, 507–25. Oxford: Oxford University Press, 1998; 2nd edn, 2008.

Preziosi, Donald. *Brain of the Earth’s Body: Art, Museums, and the Phantasms of Modernity*. The 2001 Slade Lectures in the Fine Arts at Oxford. Minneapolis and London: University of Minnesota Press, 2003.

Preziosi, Donald, and Claire Farago, eds. *Grasping the World: The Idea of the Museum*. London: Ashgate, 2004.

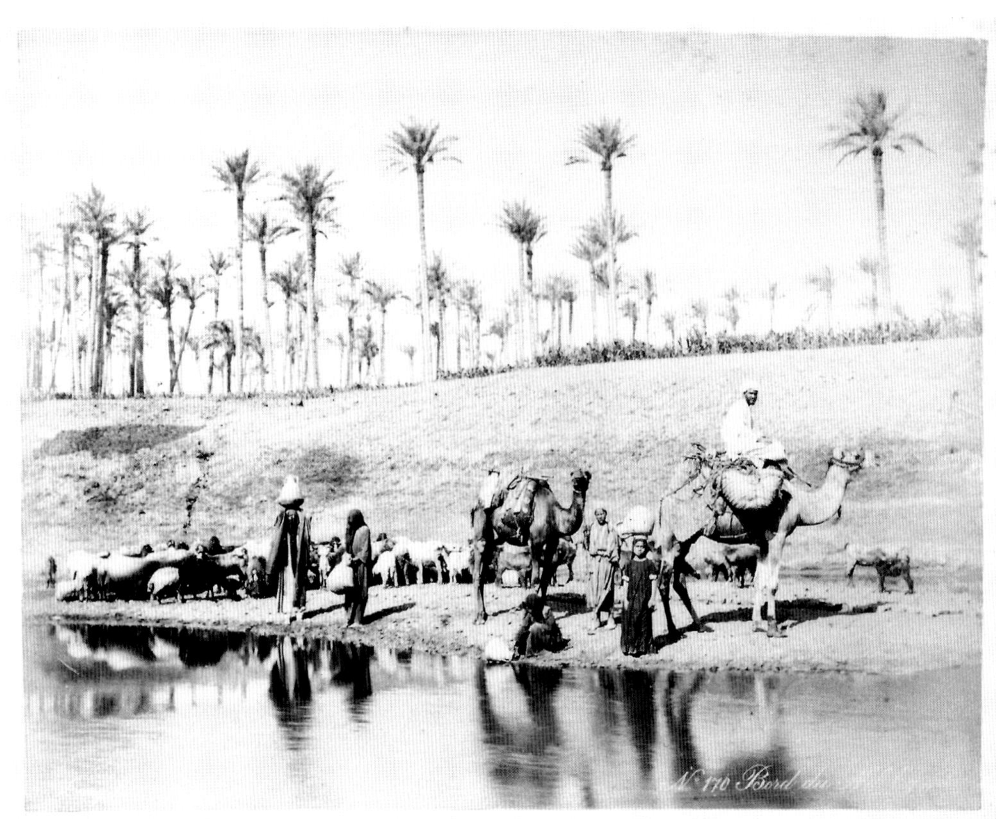

On the banks of the Nile.

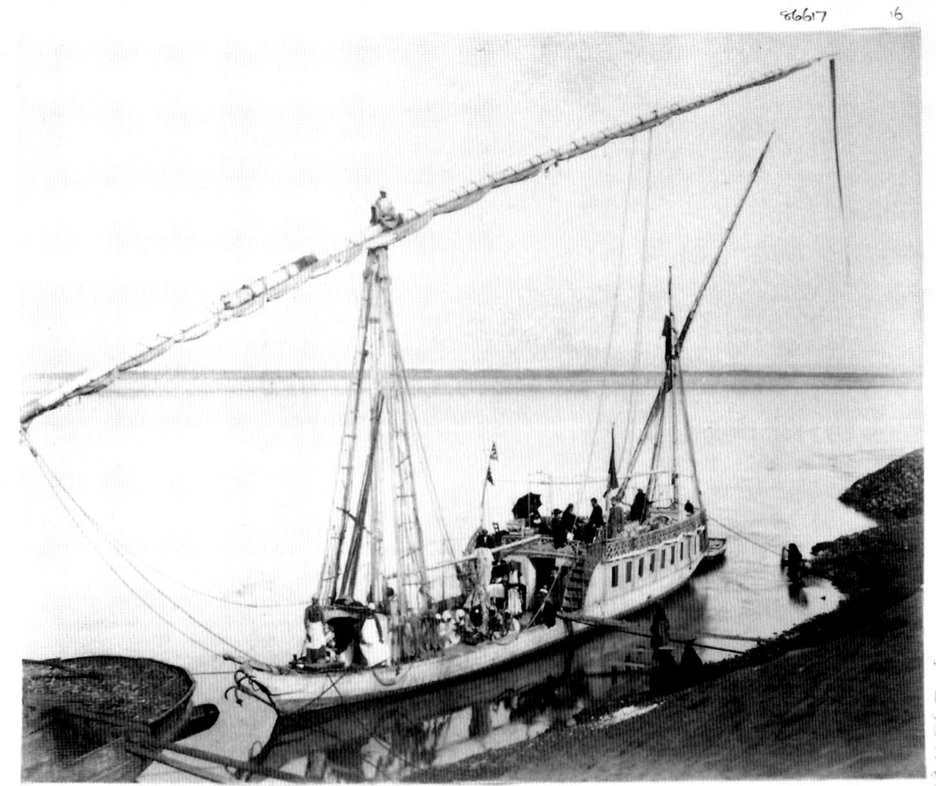

"Dahabiyeh" for Tourist's or private use.

VI

Orientalism and Photography

Nancy Micklewright

The study of photographs from the nineteenth-century Middle East[1] is a relatively recent phenomenon. This enormously compelling body of material has developed as a serious field of study only within the last few decades, with the publication of numerous articles and books where before there were very few, with major exhibitions, with conferences, with the formation of private collections and the other kinds of activity that characterize an active scholarly and economic enterprise. As this work has emerged, a "canon" of photographs has been identified, cited, recited and generally accepted as an accurate reflection of the historical record. The photographs in this canon (harem women, erotically posed or not; "types" or people engaged in traditional occupations; views of antiquities and views of historic urban sites, often in a state of near ruin) are familiar to anyone with even a passing interest in the subject.

Photographs of the nineteenth-century Middle East occupy a complex site where the overlapping and often competing claims of popular taste, scholarship, the market and even voyeurism are all at play in identifying and explaining iconic images. The photographs that capture public attention and that are repeatedly cited,[2] make up a part of the historical record, but they are a small part. This focus on a small subset of the complete archive marginalizes entire categories of images, such as the modern cityscapes of the region, personal photographs produced by or for local residents, and photographs produced in the service of the empire (Fig. 6.1). Scholarship engaged with these images has begun to demonstrate the complex and multivalent relationship that residents of the Middle East had with photography.[3] The study of photographs such as the portrait of the Ottoman bureaucrat in Figure 6.1, with its precise signaling of modernity and careful presentation of the subject, have a great deal to contribute towards our understanding of the period. By omitting these types of photographs and the scholarly analysis of them from this oft-cited "canon," there is a significant distortion of the historical record, both in terms of the history of photography in the region, and the history of the region more generally. The two books that will be analyzed at the end of this chapter are exemplary of this tendency and demonstrate the pitfalls such an approach to this material presents for researchers and general readers alike.

In part because of the competing claims on this body of material, a problematic (and often unquestioned) relationship between Orientalism and photography has developed. The word "Orientalist" is often used, without critical reflection, as an adjective to describe photographs from the Middle East. Is there an Orientalist subject matter? An Orientalist style? Does every photograph produced in the Middle East in this period exist within the framework of Orientalism?[4]

In the three decades that have elapsed since the publication of Edward Said's *Orientalism*, the fields of study touched by his book have changed almost beyond recognition, his work has been interpreted and re-interpreted, and Said's monolithic Orientalism has been reframed into multiple orientalisms. The 2008–9 exhibition *The Lure of the East: British Orientalist Painting*,[5] and its accompanying publications and symposia provided the opportunity to re-assess many aspects of the Orientalist paradigms in the light of contemporary scholarship. The relationship between Orientalism and photography, the subject of this essay, is long overdue for such a re-assessment.[6]

Photographs are a deceptively simple medium to study, not least because they are objects with which we all feel familiar—nearly everyone has taken photographs and owns them, which is not the case, for example, with painting which is the focus of many essays in this collection. However despite, or perhaps because of this shared sense of ownership and understanding of this medium, I want to begin by problematizing the study of historical photographs and lay

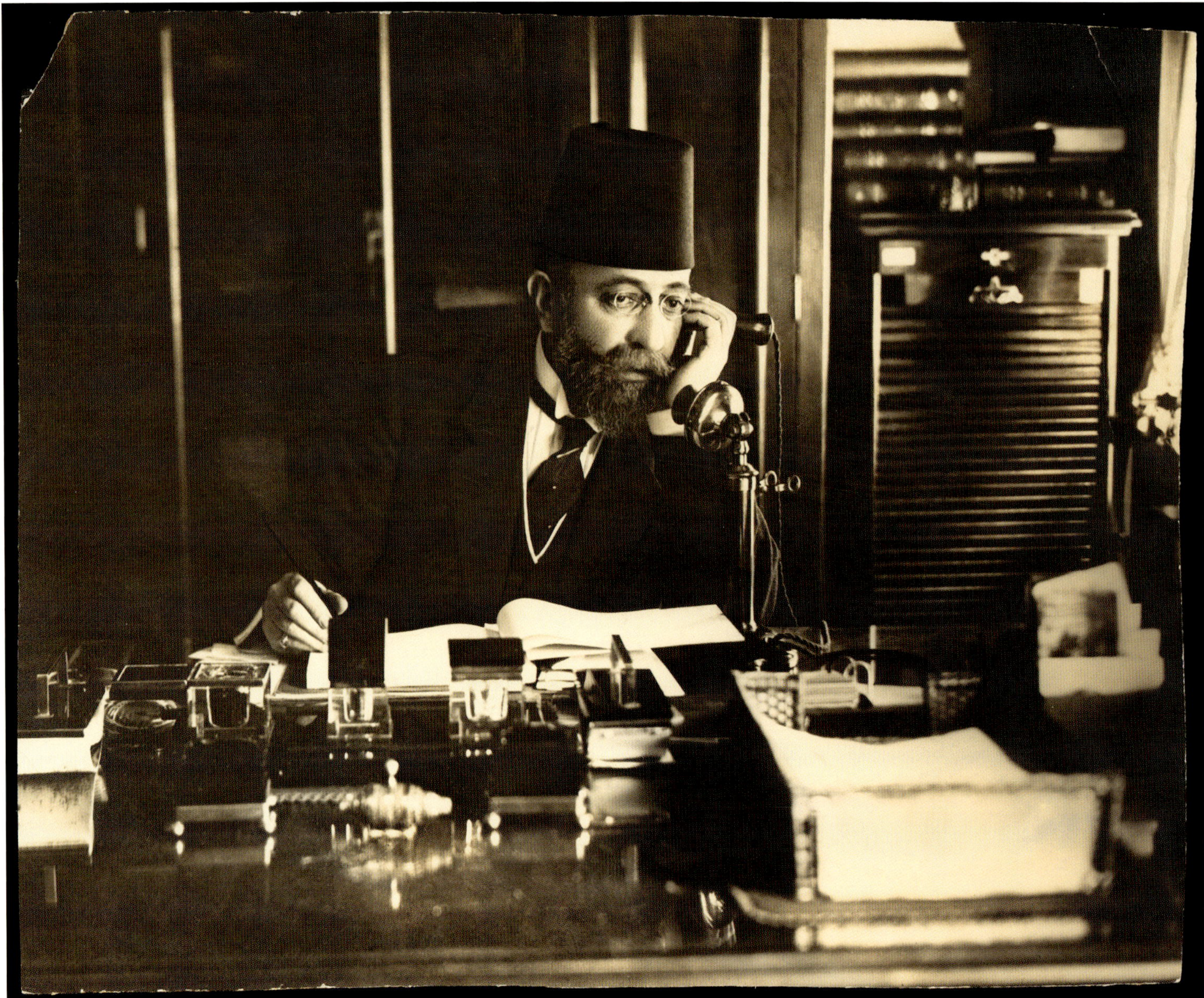

Figure 6.1 Photograph, photographer unknown, c. 1881–1910, gelatin silver print, 40 x 33 cm, Pierre de Gigord Collection. The Research Library, Getty Research Institute, Los Angeles, California (96.R.14).

out four parameters that I feel must frame any consideration of this material.

First is the apparent indexicality of the image. Even today, despite our intellectual understanding of the ways that photographs can be manipulated, we respond on an emotional level to the truth value of the photograph. This was even more so in the nineteenth century when photographs were still relatively novel and the technical possibilities for the manipulation of the image were less sophisticated. This issue, the "truth" value of historical photographs, and the various kinds of manipulation of the image, both behind and in front of the lens, is widely understood and discussed in the critical literature[7] and so I won't dwell on it here. In the context of nineteenth-century photographs from Istanbul, appearances were clearly sometimes meant to mislead, as for example in the case of a well-known image by the Swedish photographer G. Berggren.[8] Presumably a studio shot for the tourist market intended to invoke a harem interior, it is in fact a group of Swedish friends, Anders Zorn, the well-known painter and his wife, and a Swedish politician and his son who visited Berggren's studio to dress up in the costumes he kept in his studio and have their photograph taken. Because the occasion was mentioned in a letter we know the background of the photograph, but in many other cases, this happy combination of text and image does not occur and we are left to guess at, and perhaps misinterpret, the circumstances surrounding the production of an image.

Second is the unique position occupied by the photograph as an object of consumption.[9] Photographs are, and were right from the time of their invention, modestly priced goods, similar in value to ephemeral things like magazines, flowers or other low-priced commodities. But photographs are valued, not for their ephemerality, but because we expect them to last, to remind us of people, places and events long past. And in fact, photographs do often survive much longer than goods which require a significantly greater initial investment (housing, clothing, jewelry) but which are sold, worn out or somehow become separated from their owners.

Third, photographs are small, portable and treasured for their visible connection to people and places distant in time or space, or both. At the moment of their production, they document a particular relationship between subject and photographer, and perhaps patron. Photographs are meant to be shared, to serve as the illustrations of a personal or occasionally public story, and thus have an implicit performative aspect which is an essential characteristic of their materiality. As time passes, that original story may be lost or may acquire additional layers as the photograph moves from one context to another. In all but the most unusual of circumstances, at some point maybe three or four generations away from its creation, a photograph slips from being an object of personal history to a less specific historic document. Originally often a record of a particular occasion, the image eventually becomes one of a group of pictures given away or sold, with no information about the occasion that is being celebrated or the people who are pictured.[10] Recognizing the complex role that photographs play in multiple and ever-changing narratives is a crucial aspect of positioning them as objects of study.

Fourth, given their low cost and importance as holders of memory, it is not surprising that huge numbers of historical photographs have survived. Indeed the photographic record is disorganized and chaotic, a massive multiplication on a global scale of the crammed drawers, overflowing boxes, and now computers full of photographs that exist in our houses, waiting for that time when we will label our photographs and put them neatly, even chronologically, in albums, or at least folders in our computers. While the state of the photographic record presents a number of challenges for scholars, the essential point here is that because of the volume of what survives, the study of historical photographs is unlike nearly all other aspects of art history. The challenge for photo historians is not to find enough of a sample of the objects of their study to claim a representative examination, but to know when they've seen enough to be able to claim knowledge. If a certain collection has 5,000 images, can one stop after looking at 3,000?

The size of the photographic corpus also means that we are always looking at a set of images that has been mediated by some kind of selection process. This is generally true to some extent with any published research, but the fact of this mediation takes on a much greater significance for photography than for other media because of the numbers involved. Just to lay this out as clearly as possible, if an artist is known to have produced 250 paintings and sixty are reproduced in a publication, we are seeing more than twenty-five percent of the work. On the other hand, if there are 3,000 photographs in a collection and 100 are reproduced, we are not even seeing four percent of the whole. Considering the impact of the selection process involved in any publication, exhibition or collection on the viewer's understanding of the photographic record, ideally we would only study photographs in a situation where an unmediated examination was possible. Since such an ideal circumstance is rarely possible, deconstructing the selection process is essential in understanding how the photographic record has come to be known to us. Examining a collection from the point of view of its assembly and context is a crucial aspect of working with historic photographs.

For the nineteenth century, photograph albums are the best way to get a sense of the universe of images that existed and how album compilers chose among them for their albums. For the late-twentieth- and early-twenty-first century, collections could also include exhibitions curated in a museum, private collections, and the images chosen to illustrate photography books or exhibition catalogs.[11] Comparing the nineteenth-century albums to contemporary collections of photographs about the Middle East allows us to see at first hand the different kinds of choices made by compilers (album makers, collectors, curators, book editors) in representing the region through photographs over a distance of a century or more.

As a construction which orders a visual record, the album is a means by which the compiler organizes a particular subject for presentation to an audience. I assume that an album begins with an implied or explicit narrative, which may or may not have been carried through the entire album. In some cases, depending on the arrangement of the images and the presence of additional labels, the narrative, and the hand of the compiler are more obvious. Using the arrangement of photographs as a way of ordering time and experience, the compiler is also constructing history, and often also knowledge of a particular situation or place. The choice of image and their sequential relationships serves to reproduce a dominant ideology or to subvert it, or both. If a single photographic image embodies shifting meanings, then an album of multiple photographic images is even less likely to present a fixed and stable view of its subject.[12]

There are hundreds of commercially assembled photograph albums from the nineteenth century surviving in various collections, but my research has focused on unique products assembled by different kinds of British visitors to the region—missionaries, soldiers, political figures and travelers—in order to track the differences in the kinds of images they chose to include in their albums, how they arranged the photographs and the kind of text that was added to accompany the photographs. Looking at these mediated collections of images, assembled by people from different classes and who visited the region for different reasons allows us an understanding of the nineteenth-century photographic record quite unlike what we see in twentieth- and twenty-first-century collections. In this chapter I will explore the idea of the album as a photographic collection through the examination of a very closely related group of five albums, all assembled by British soldiers who either passed through or served in Egypt in the 1880s. These albums are now in the collection of the National Army Museum in London.[13] They are tangible evidence of the manner in which some subjects of the British Empire perceived and constructed the discursive categories of imperialism and Orientalism as shifting and unstable.

Of these five albums, three belonged to men who spent a relatively short period of time in Egypt, and views of Egypt comprise only a small part of their albums, between about six and nine images in albums containing between forty-nine and ninety photographs. In all three cases, the albums are filled with a combination of the commercial images the soldiers could have purchased in shops, as well as photographs taken by the men themselves. Their albums thus provide a good sense of how each man understood Egypt and what they found of interest there. The photographs illustrating Egypt are more or less evenly divided among the ancient monuments, the old city, and modern Egypt, for example a page from one of the albums that illustrates a

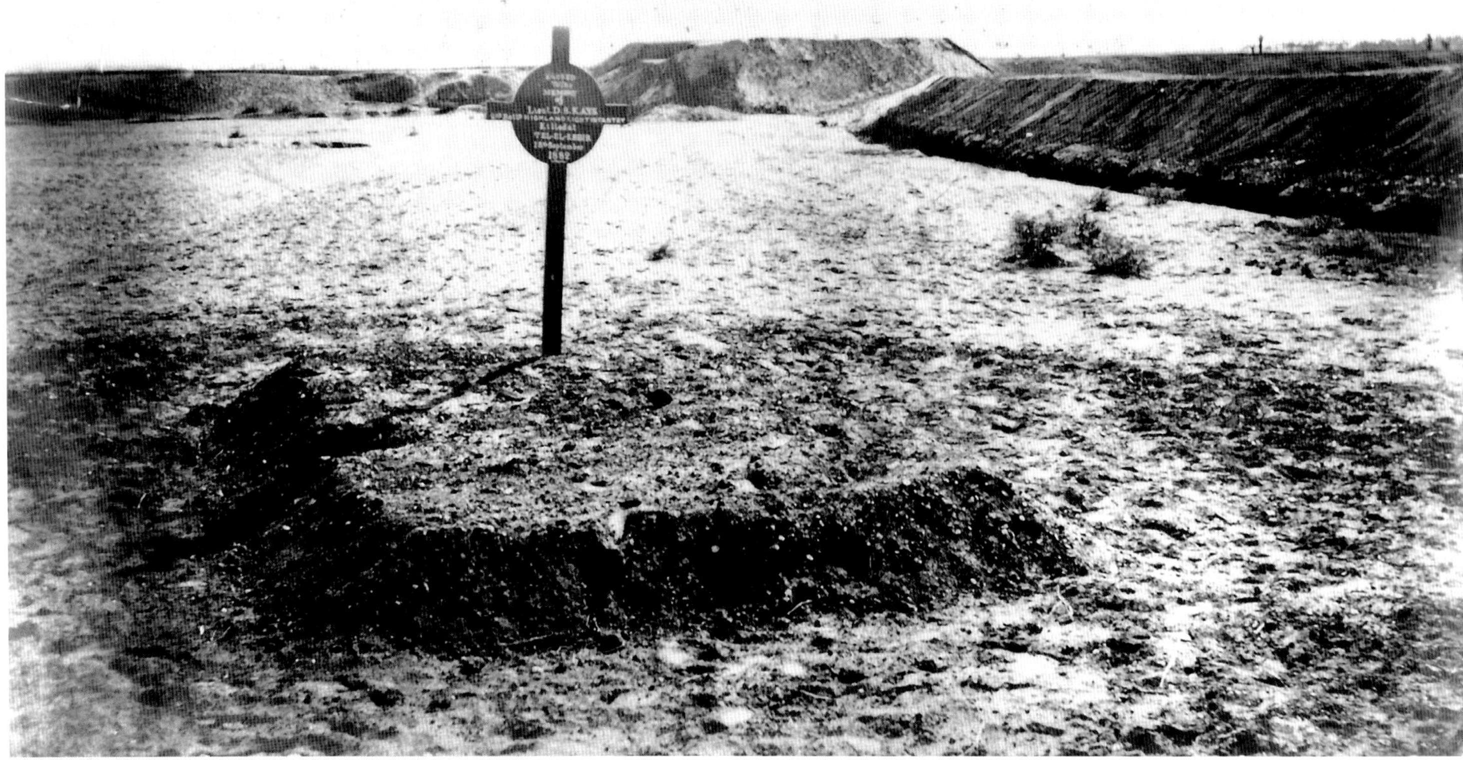

Figure 6.2 Album page from album belonging to an officer of 1st BN King's Shropshire Light Infantry, photographer unknown, c. 1882–85, albumen print, album page dimensions 31 x 37 cm, Album 7612-112, no. 3. Courtesy of the Council of the National Army Museum, London.

panoramic view of Cairo by the photographer P. Sebah. The page has notations in two different hands, below the picture identifying the subject "Cairo, Mokkatam Hills in Background," and along the side, with an arrow pointing to the specific location: "Whirling dervishes in cave!" This reference to seeing the whirling dervishes is the only indication in the entire album of any interaction between the album owner and the people of Cairo, and it seems to have taken place in the context of a staged performance for a tourist audience. In contrast to their prevalence in present-day compilations of nineteenth-century photographs, only three views in the three albums are commercial images of people. Native Egyptians, whether picturesque or modern, apparently did not interest these three British men to any great degree. Egypt for them seems to have been a place through which they passed, whose ancient ruins, desert landscapes and capital city served as a backdrop for their own lives.

Photographs of military life are much more numerous than images of Egypt, and there are occasional views that refer to the recent military action, as we see in Figure 6.2, a page from the same album. The photograph shows a grave in the desert, with a cross in the center of the picture which reads "sacred to the Memory of Lieut. D. S. Kaye, 2nd Battalion Highland Light Infantry, Killed at Tel el-Kabir. 13th September 1882." For this album owner, the death of British men in the course of the Egyptian campaign was clearly a defining feature of his representation of Egypt.

In contrast, the last two albums of this group include many more photographs of Egypt. Assembled by British officers who were posted there for longer periods of time and compiled within a few years of each other, both contain just over fifty photographs. Yet their choice of images was very different. The owner of the first album, Colonel S. D. Cleeve, took part in the 1882 bombardment of Alexandria, and assembled a compelling series of images to document that experience, including a gruesome photograph of the rotting bodies of soldiers and camels in the desert. Egypt as a whole seems to have made less of an impression on Cleeve, for he included only ten photographs of Egypt apart from the military base and scenes of the bombardment. The Holy Land, on the other hand, was of great importance to Colonel Cleeve; he managed to go to Jerusalem and bought a relatively large number of photographs, nearly all of religious sites, to remember his visit there.

The owner of the second album, a member of the 1st Dorset Regiment, having arrived after the bombardment, was not so interested in Alexandria, although the images which record the British military presence in Egypt act as a framing device for his further experience of Egypt. He was fascinated by the sites of ancient Egypt and that is what most of the photographs in his album illustrate, including several that document a trip that he and some of his fellow officers took on the Nile (Fig. 6.3). The album page contains two photographs, the upper one a view of the Nile by the photographer Zangaki, and

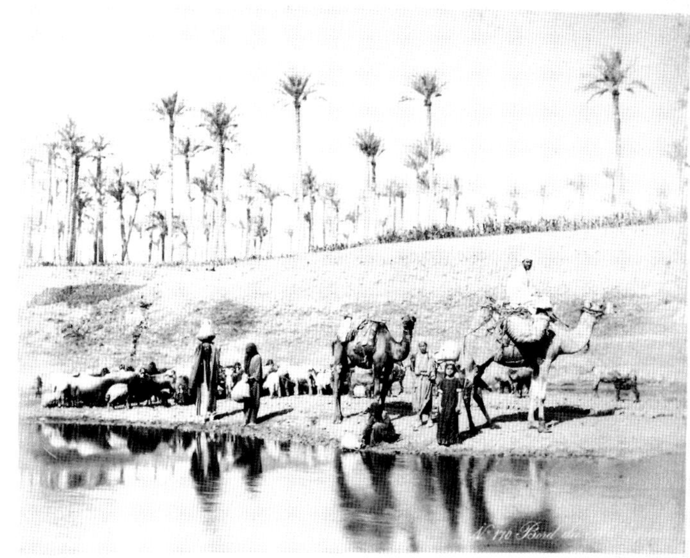

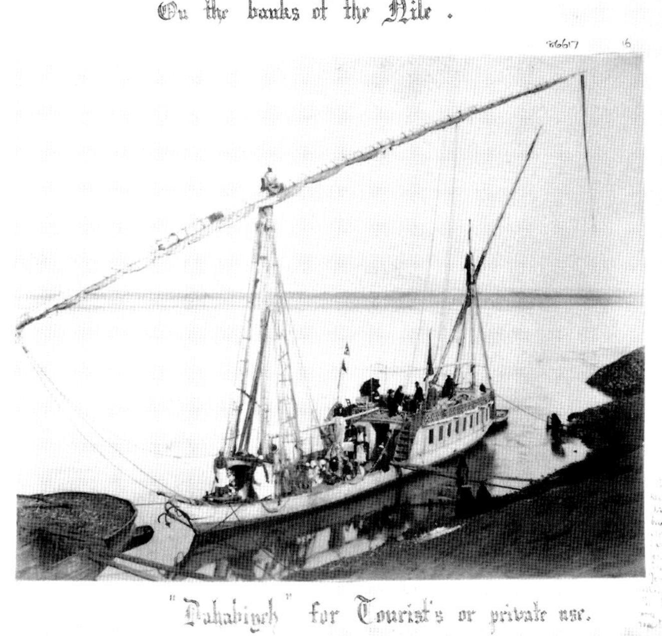

Figure 6.3 Album page from album belonging to an officer of 1st Dorset Regiment, Zangaki (upper image), lower image photographer unknown, c. 1885–86, albumen print, album page dimensions 55 x 37.5 cm, Album 8408-98, nos 15 and 16. Courtesy of the Council of the National Army Museum, London.

the lower one a boat on the Nile. Each photograph is neatly labeled in ink, and there is an additional extensive note written to the right of the lower image describing the voyage.[14] He apparently did not visit the Holy Land, and included only one image of Cairo.

Each of these albums documents to a greater or lesser extent the experiences of their owners as members of the British military, involved in implementing the foreign policy of an imperialist colonial power. While their common military identity, as well as of course their common British, late nineteenth-century masculine identities shaped much of their world view and thus their experiences of Egypt, it does not explain why their photograph albums differ from one another. The differences among the photographs they chose must be tied to differences of class, education, interest, and self-image. By looking carefully at each of their albums, five different views of Egypt and military life emerge, related but not identical, producing a nuanced and complex index of how these five men saw their surroundings and their experiences.

There is at best a minor overlap between the photographs which appear in these albums compiled by people who participated in the British imperial project and were informed by the colonial/Orientalist cultures of their times, and those typically included in twentieth- and twenty-first-century published collections of "Orientalist" photographs. We see very few images of people and none of the eroticized views of women so popular in contemporary presentations of historic photographs from the Middle East, as for example in Alloula's previously mentioned work, *The Colonial Harem*, or Alan Fleig's *Rêves de papier. La photographie orientaliste 1860–1914*.[15] Photographs of places provide a backdrop for the personal experiences of the album compiler, or as an *aide-mémoire* for specific events, without particular regard for the esthetic qualities of the photograph, or the need to include a comprehensive presentation of the site. The disparity that exists between the Orientalist canon of Middle East photography and the full archive of surviving images, as well as the privileging of the Orientalist canon in the contemporary context distorts the historical record. Even at a distance of well over a century, when the specific personal narratives embedded in these albums have mostly been lost, the photographs speak to a British engagement with Egypt and individual encounters with the region that convey impressions far removed from the more familiar Orientalist canon of images.

This brings us back to the second kind of collection I want to consider, the private collections that have been assembled in the past few decades and the exhibitions, catalogs and other publications from the same period which explicitly refer to "Orientalist" photographs.[16] These allow us a means of understanding how collectors, curators, and editors working in the last 25 years or so with historical photographs from the Middle East understand the word "Orientalist" and use it as a defining criterion for selecting images and constructing a vision of the region. While my ideas regarding these more contemporary collections have been shaped by a close examination of a range of material, our attention here will be focused primarily on two such collections, one of which is an actual collection accompanied by a publication (the collection is now housed in a scholarly research center). The second is a recent publication, a virtual collection, assembled by the author from a number of archives and other sources and brought to the public by means of a glossy coffee-table book.

The Getty Research Institute recently acquired a collection of "Orientalist" photography assembled by Ken Jacobson. Mr. Jacobson, a scientist by training, was led into historical photographs and the amassing of a substantial collection over the past thirty years by a "captivation with exotic photography" as he stated in the preface of the book he wrote about his collection, *Odalisques and Arabesques, Orientalist Photography 1839–1935*.[17] The collection now in the Getty Research Institute numbers about 4,500 images, and includes photographs primarily from North Africa and the Ottoman Empire, as well as photographs of Orientalist subject matter produced in Europe.[18] In describing the criteria which governed his collecting, Jacobson wrote that his "intention is to capture the daily life of the region, both real and that sometimes visualized by Western travellers,"[19] and thus he focused on images of people because "the evocation of the exoticism of the East compared to the West is readily provided through depiction of the people who inhabited these countries." He adds, though, that he does not ignore "evocative Islamic architecture, nor the archaeological remains of more ancient civilizations." Exoticism is a compelling aspect of this material for Jacobson: he used the word five times in a short three and a half page preface. He also privileges esthetics, acknowledging uneven coverage of the region because he chose striking imagery or beautiful and highly evocative images.

The choices that Jacobson made in shaping his collection and his approach to interpreting them are laid out in his book. In addition to looking for the evocative and the exotic to convey the essence of the Orient, and his esthetic criteria, he also wanted, via his collection and his book, to claim a place for this photography on its esthetic and emotional merits within the larger history of photography. Finally, through the last section of his book, "Biographies," he provides a valuable addition to our state of knowledge concerning the careers and work of many of the photographers active in the region.

The existence of a publication in which the collector describes the parameters which governed his collecting is extremely useful in terms of scholarship, as is the clear delineation of the period in which the collection was assembled. Given his desire, stated in the book's preface, to make a serious contribution to the history of what he calls Oriental photography, it is however disappointing that Jacobson deliberately places himself and his work outside current theoretical debates and some contemporary scholarship regarding photography from the regions, which complicates the reception of his work. While on the one hand he seems to have endless patience (and considerable skill) at tracking down details of the photographers' careers whose work he collects, he is unwilling or unable to acknowledge the complexity and the possibility of multiple readings of the images he presents.

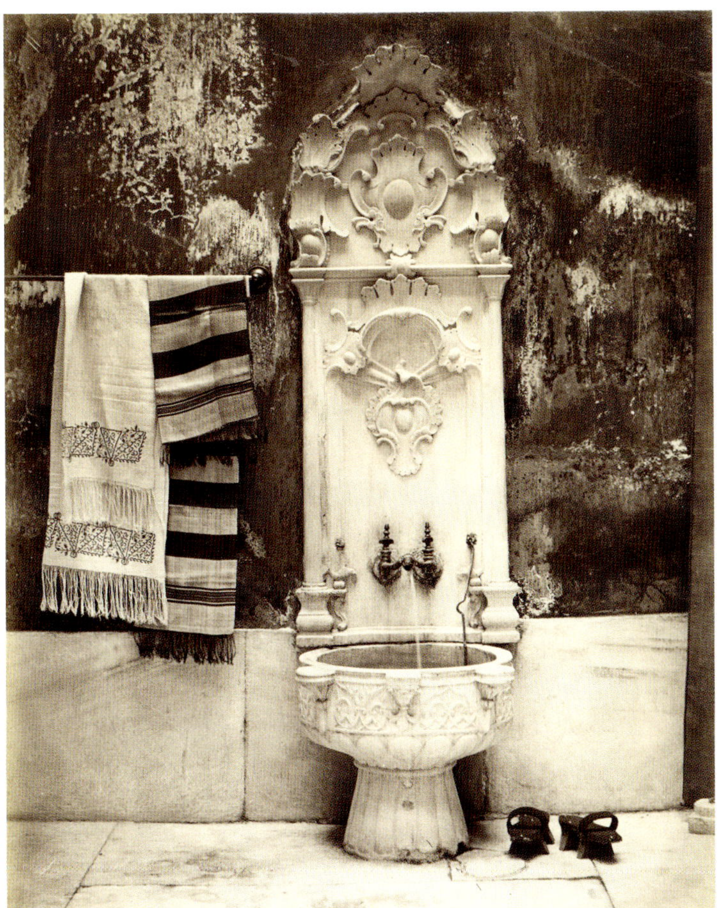

Figure 6.4 Photograph, Abdullah Frères, c. 1860s, albumen print. Courtesy of the Getty Research Institute, Los Angeles, California.

Thus for example, some of the most interesting photographs from the point of view of the historical record are relegated to the back section of the book, while the more familiar and often-reproduced Orientalist material is given prominence. Jacobson's insistence on seeing the region and the photographs as exotic means that in some cases, the content of the image or its context are misrepresented, as for example when he describes a photograph by Abdullah Frères depicting a fountain in the bath of the Topkapı Sarayı harem (Fig. 6.4) as part of the "sultan's forbidden harem," going on to say that "The extreme scarcity of 1860s prints of the harem suggests the possibility that they were only initially available to the Sultan and his friends and may not have been generally for sale to the public."[20] While it is true that such images from the Topkapı Sarayı in this period are rare and valuable documents of the history of the site, it is also true that by the time of this photograph, the court had moved from the Topkapı Sarayı to the new Dolmabahçe Palace and the Topkapı, empty of residents, had already begun its gradual transformation into a tourist destination. Limiting the reading of these photographs to the beautiful and the exotic allows the significance of the images as documents of the complex history of the nineteenth-century Ottoman sultanate to be overlooked or erased altogether.

Ultimately this refusal to engage with the complexity of the subject matter or acknowledge the range of approaches to this material limits the scholarly usefulness of Jacobson's otherwise painstaking written work. The presentation of his collection and by extension the historical record is unbalanced, privileging an "exotic" which is never clearly defined, and serving to mislead those readers of his book or viewers of his collection who are seeking a critical reading of these images. There are no doubt others who will be entirely content with his approach to the consumption of "Orientalist" photographs. Jacobson's book occupies an uneasy position at an overlap of the scholarly and the popular, a site occupied by numerous exhibitions and publications of nineteenth-century photographs from the Middle East. While the continuing popularity of "Orientalist" photographs has meant that this material continues to be accessible through exhibitions and new publications, the overlap of audience has complicated its presentation and interpretation.

Jacobson's approach to his collection stands in sharp contrast to a recently published volume on the subject, *Orientalist Photographs 1870–1950*, by the French photographer and travel writer Éric Milet.[21] An elegant but almost completely ahistorical presentation of approximately a hundred images, the book is organized into six sections, with titles such as "The Mirror of Al-Andaluz" and "Siba: Land of Resistance." Within these sections, each photograph is accompanied by a short essay on the facing page. In some cases, relevant passages from literature of the past or present are included. The subject of the photograph (as identified by the author) is given under the image, along with information about the photographer if known, the date and the location. It is not immediately clear whether it is the subjects of the brief essays, which cover topics from aspects of Islamic religious practice to traditional cuisine to the French colonial presence, or the photographs themselves which are the main point of this book. Moreover, there are few direct references in the texts to the images accompanying them, and in some cases the pairing of text and image seems almost random, as for example an early-twentieth-century photograph of an irrigation system in a wadi that is placed alongside an essay about the practice of giving gifts in the North African market. The photograph, with all of its potential value for understanding local economies, agriculture, and technology, to mention only the most obvious, appears with no comment or context.

The book is introduced by a one-page essay, "The Disoriented Orient," in which the author describes the Maghrib as a place about which nothing was known by the French before their 1830 invasion of Algeria, and the Orient as a concept, a foretaste of paradise which was revealed in photographs "to the public at large by men and women who were delighted to have crossed to the 'other side' in their lifetime, constantly evoking the delights of this earthly paradise."[22] No information is provided about the selection process which resulted in the specific contents of the book, or even of the book's objective. We learn of the sources of the photographs in the credits in the back pages (which also include a glossary and eight footnotes but no bibliography).

While Milet brings a great deal of knowledge about the region to this work and has assembled a stunning collection of photographs, including some rare autochromes, the presentation of the images is ahistorical and eroticizing. The publisher of the book claims it as a work of scholarship, a claim which may or may not be taken seriously, but like Jacobson's book serves as a reminder of the messy and potentially confusing overlap of audiences for works on nineteenth-century photographs from the Middle East.[23]

As a result of photography's widespread appeal, acknowledged at the beginning of this essay, and the obvious allure of the images generally included in exhibitions and publications of "Orientalist" photography, these continue to find a ready audience. At the intersection of the popular and the scholarly, there is significant slippage between these categories, which means that historical photographs can easily lose aspects of their history, becoming merely curious or beautiful or exotic. Given the inevitability of this slippage between categories of viewing and analysis, and the ensuing complexity of interpretation, collections, whether exhibitions, publications or actual collections, need to be positioned as clearly as possible. Photographs carry multiple identities, as historic documents, as elements of popular culture, as pieces of personal histories or *aide-mémoires*; the interpretive possibilities embodied in these shifting and multiple identities need to be embraced by those who collect, exhibit and publish them, not elided into a vague and poorly defined category such as Orientalist.

The corpus of photographs surviving from the nineteenth-century Middle East is unruly and chaotic, resisting a neat definition, even one as unwieldy as "Orientalist." In this period photographs were produced for a diverse audience of tourists and local residents, in some cases by the same photographers. Their subject matter is also extremely diverse, overlapping with Orientalist painting, but also encompassing the modern, the personal, and the political. As I have shown here, even within a category of image loosely defined as Orientalist, nineteenth-century and twentieth/twenty-first-century assemblages look very different, which is an important and complicating factor in attempting a classification of this material and something that deserves more attention. Photography and Orientalism have an uneasy and complex relationship, but one which merits our critical attention if we are to derive the full benefit of this extraordinary legacy from the past.

Notes

1 "Middle East" is a term of convenience used to define a region characterized by a variety of languages, ethnicities and religions. The history of photography has unfolded differently throughout the region, with North Africa, Egypt, the Holy Land, Istanbul and some aspects of Anatolia, and to a lesser extent, Iran, being much better studied than the rest of the Arabic-speaking world.

2 The photography from *The Colonial Harem* by Malek Alloula (Manchester: University Press, 1987) being the most obvious example of this trend, but certainly not the only one.

3 For examples of how the photographs taken and consumed by residents of the Middle East can be used in the exploration of specific aspects of history, see Edhem Eldem, *Pride and Privilige. A History of Ottoman Orders, Medals and Decorations* (Istanbul: Ottoman Bank Archives and Research Centre, 2004), and Zeynep Çelik, *Empire, Architecture and The City. French-Ottoman*

Encounters, 1830–1914 (Seattle: University of Washington Press, 2009). See Ahmet Ersoy, "A Sartorial Tribute to *Tanzimat* Ottomanism: the *Elbise-i "Osmaniye* Album," *Muqarnas* 20 (2003): 187–207; Nancy Micklewright, "Harem/House/Set: Domestic Interiors in Photography from the Late Ottoman World," in *Harem in History and Imagination*, ed. Marilyn Booth (Durham and London: Duke University Press, 2010), 336–57; and Frederick N. Bohrer ed., *Sevruguin and the Persian Image. Photographs of Iran, 1870–1930* (Washington, DC: Sackler Gallery, 1999), for three examples among many of studies focused on diverse aspects of the photographic record of the Middle East.

4 See Emily Weeks, "Cultures Crossed: John Frederick Lewis and the Art of Orientalist Painting," in *The Lure of the East. British Orientalist Painting*, ed. Nicholas Tromans (London: Tate Publishing, 2008), 22–32, for a discussion of the relationship of "Orientalism" and "Orientalist" in the context of painting. Similar confusions exist as far as historical photographs are concerned.

5 The exhibition opened in February 2008 at the Yale Center for British Art in New Haven, CT, then traveled to the Tate Britain in London, the Pera Museum in Istanbul and the Sharjah Art Museum, closing in April 2009.

6 I am very grateful to Zeynep İnankur, Reina Lewis and Mary Roberts, the organizers of the symposium, *The Ottoman Empire and British Orientalism*, held in Istanbul in November, 2009 for their kind invitation to participate in the symposium, as well as to our gracious host, Mr. Özalp Birol, the director of the Suna and İnan Kıraç Foundation and the Pera Museum.

7 The relationship between the photographic image and the real has been a concern of artists, scholars and theorists since the invention of photography and it is impossible to cite even a fraction of the important work published around this issue. Two classic texts are Roland Barthes, *Camera Lucida: Reflections on Photography* (New York: Hill and Wang, 1981) and Susan Sontag, *On Photography* (New York: Farrar, Strauss and Giroux, 1977). More recently, Gregory Batchen addressed the issue in his 2002 book, *Each Wild Idea: Writing Photography History* (Boston: MIT Press), and *differences: A Journal of Feminist Cultural Studies* devoted a volume to the subject of indexicality (vol. 18, no. 1, 2006). See also Mary Anne Doane, "Indexicality and the Concept of Medium Specificity" in *The Meaning of Photography*, ed. Robin Kelsey and Blake Stinson (New Haven and London: Yale University Press, 2008), among many others.

8 This photograph is published and its context explained in Leif Wigh, *Fotografiska vyer Från Bosporen Och Konstantinopel/ Photographic Views of the Bosphorus and Constantinople* (Stockholm: Fotografiska Museet, 1984), 72.

9 For a fuller discussion of photographs as objects of consumption, see Nancy Micklewright, "Personal, Public, and Political (Re) Constructions: Photographs and Consumption," in *Consumption Studies and the History of the Ottoman Empire*, ed. Donald Quataert (Binghamton: SUNY Press, 2000), 261–86.

10 There is an extensive literature concerning this aspect of photo history, of which only two examples will be cited here. For a good overview of the issues presented by snapshot photography, see Douglas Nickel, *Snapshots. The Photography of Everyday Life, 1888 to the Present* (San Francisco: San Francisco Museum of Modern Art, 1998). Anthony Lee's 2008 book, *A Shoemaker's Story: Being Chiefly about French Canadian Immigrants, Enterprising Photographers, Rascal Yankees, and Chinese Cobblers in a Nineteenth-Century Factory Town* (Princeton: Princeton University Press) is an excellent example of the challenges presented by historic photographs and the exciting scholarship that the search for their missing historical and social contexts may generate.

11 A full discussion of the culturally contingent and (often) politically charged practices of collecting and how these have changed over time is beyond what I can consider here. For the purposes of this chapter, I am considering the photograph collection as a sometimes permanent (as in the case of an album or an institutional collection) or temporary/virtual (as in the case of an exhibition or publication) assemblage of images, created within the framework of a personal, scholarly, commercial and/or institutional set of criteria (which may or may not be clearly or publicly articulated).

12 The photograph album as an object of study is discussed at greater length in Nancy Micklewright, *A Victorian Traveler in the Middle East. The Photography and Travel Writing of Annie Lady Brassey* (Burlington, VT: Ashgate, 2003), particularly 139–80.

13 For a more detailed discussion of a larger number of albums, see Micklewright, op. cit.

14 The note on the album page reads: "'Dahabiyeh' for Tourist's or private use. In July 1886 the officers of 1st Dorset Regt. travelled from Assouan to Assiout in a Dahabiyeh bringing up the rear of a procession of 2 iron barges and 5 native boats containing the regt.—all towed by steamer. Journey occupied 7 1/2 days—river being very low. The officers' Dahabiyeh broke loose on several occasions from the procession."

15 Alain Fleig, *Rêves de Papier. La photographie orientaliste 1860–1914* (Neuchâtel: Éditions Ides et Calendes, 1997).

16 Jacobson provides an excellent bibliography on this subject in his book: Ken Jacobson, *Odalisques and Arabesques: Orientalist Photography 1839–1925* (London: Quaritch, 2007), 283–301.

17 Ibid.

18 Jacobson's book provides a good sense of the scope of his collection. For more information, consult the Getty Research Institute Library Catalog: http://www.getty.edu/research/conducting_research/.

19 This and the following quotes are all from the Preface, Jacobson, *Odalisques and Arabesques*, 11–14.

20 Jacobson, *Odalisques and Arabesques*, 198.

21 According to his website, Milet has had an extensive career as a photographer, guide, and writer, with a particular focus on North Africa. He has a long-standing association with Éditions Arthaud, which is described as a leading publisher of travel, adventure, tourism, mountaineering, diving, trekking, sailing and photography books, and is a part of the Flammarion Publishing Group (Paris), which published *Orientalist Photographs* in 2008. Éric Milet website: http://monsite.wanadoo.fr/desertitude/.

22 Ibid., 8.

23 For example, an advertisement about the book on the internet reads in part: "This groundbreaking work is a privileged insight into the beliefs, culture, and traditions of Northern Africa … This collection of more than 100 autochrome, sepia, and black and white photographs captures delicate, lost details: the dusty, labyrinthine walls of the casbah; the dappled sunlight on the market stall of a souk; the intricate metal work of traditional jewelry. Each image is accompanied by an informative text that situates the photo in its historical reality …" Abbey's Bookshop. http://www.abbeys.com.au/items.asp?id=228975.

Bibliography

Allen, William. "Sixty-five Istanbul Photographers, 1887–1914." In *Shadow and Substance: Essays in the History of Photography*, edited by Kathleen Collins, 127–36. Bloomfield Hills, MI: The Amorphous Institute Press, 1990.

Alloula, Malek. *The Colonial Harem*. Manchester: University Press, 1987.

Appadurai, Arjun, ed. *The Social Life of Things. Commodities in Cultural Perspective*. Cambridge: Cambridge University Press, 1986.

Barthes, Roland. *Camera Lucida: Reflections on Photography*. New York: Hill and Wang, 1981.

Batchen, Gregory. *Each Wild Idea: Writing Photography History*. Boston: MIT Press, 2002.

Beauge, Gilbert and Engin Çizgen. *Images d'Empire. Aux origines de la photographie en Turquie*. Istanbul: Institut d'études françaises d'Istanbul, 1993.

Beaulieu, Jill and Mary Roberts, eds. *Orientalism's Interlocutors. Painting, Architecture and Photography*. Durham: Duke University Press, 2002.

Benjamin, Roger, ed. *Orientalism: Delacroix to Klee*. Sydney: The Art Gallery of New South Wales, 1997.

Bohrer, Frederick N., ed. *Sevruguin and the Persian Image. Photographs of Iran, 1870–1930*. Washington, DC: Sackler Gallery, 1999.

Bull, D. and D. Lorimer. *Up the Nile, a Photographic Excursion: Egypt 1839–1898*. New York: Clarkson Potter, 1979.

Çelik, Zeynep. *The Remaking of Istanbul. Portrait of an Ottoman City*. Seattle: University of Washington Press, 1986.

Çelik, Zeynep. *Empire, Architecture and The City. French-Ottoman Encounters, 1830–1914*. Seattle: University of Washington Press, 2009.

Chevedden, Paul. *The Photographic Heritage of the Near East*. Malibu: Undena Publications, 1981.

Chevedden, Paul. "Making Light of Everything: Early Photography of the Middle East and Current Photomania." *MESA Bulletin* 18, no. 2 (1984): 151–74.

Cizgen, Engin. *Photography in the Ottoman Empire*. Istanbul: Haşet Kitabevi A.Ş., 1987.

Cizgen, Engin. *Photographer/Fotoğrafçı Ali Sami, 1866–1936*. Istanbul: Haşet Kitabevi A.Ş., 1989.

Clammer, David. *The Victorian Army in Photographs*. London: David and Charles, 1975.

Clifford, James. *The Predicament of Culture*. Cambridge, MA: Harvard University Press, 1988.

Doane, Mary Anne. "Indexicality and the Concept of Medium Specificity." In *The Meaning of Photography*, edited by Robin Kelsey and Blake Stinson. New Haven and London: Yale University Press, 2008.

differences: A Journal of Feminist Cultural Studies. Special issue on Indexicality. Volume 18, no. 1, 2006.

Eldem, Edhem. *Pride and Privilige. A History of Ottoman Orders, Medals and Decorations*. Istanbul: Ottoman Bank Archives and Research Centre, 2004.

Edwards, Elizabeth, ed. *Anthropology and Photography 1860–1920*. New Haven: Yale University Press, 1992.

Edwards, Holly. *Noble Dreams, Wicked Pleasures. Orientalism in America, 1870–1930*. Princeton, NJ: Princeton University Press in association with the Sterling and Francine Clark Art Institute, 2000.

Ersoy, Ahmet. "A Sartorial Tribute to *Tanzimat* Ottomanism: The *Elbise-i 'Osmaniye* Album." *Muqarnas* 20 (2003): 187–207.

Faber, Paul, et al., eds. *Beelden van de Orient: Fotografie en Toerisme 1860–1900/Images of the Orient: Photography and Tourism 1860–1900*. Amsterdam: Fragment, 1986.

Fleig, Alain. *Rêves de papier: La photographie orientaliste, 1860–1914*. Neuchâtel: Éditions Ides et Calendes, 1997.

Gavin, Carney E. S. *The Image of the East: Photographs by Bonfils*. Chicago: University of Chicago Press, 1982.

Graham-Brown, Sarah. *Images of Women: The Portrayal of Women in the Photography of the Middle East 1860–1915*. New York: Columbia University Press, 1988.

Grant, Gillian. *Middle Eastern Photographic Collections in the United Kingdom*. Durham: Middle East Libraries Committee, 1989.

Hackforth-Jones, Jocelyn and Mary Roberts. *Edges of Empire. Orientalism and Visual Culture*. London: Blackwell, 2005.

Howe, Kathleen Stewart. *Excursions Along the Nile: The Photographic Discovery of Ancient Egypt*. Santa Barbara, CA: Santa Barbara Museum of Art, 1993.

Jacobson, Ken. *Odalisques and Arabesques: Orientalist Photography 1839–1925*. London: Quaritch, 2007.

Kabbani, Rana. *Europe's Myths of Orient*. Bloomington: Indiana University Press, 1986.

Khemir, Mounira. *L'Orientalisme. L'Orient des photographes au XIXe siècle*. Paris: Centre National de la Photographie and Institut du Monde Arabe, 1994.

Lee, Anthony. *A Shoemaker's Story: Being Chiefly about French Canadian Immigrants, Enterprising Photographers, Rascal Yankees, and Chinese Cobblers in a Nineteenth-Century Factory Town*. Princeton: Princeton University Press, 2008.

Lewis, Reina. *Gendering Orientalism. Race, Femininity and Representation*. London: Routledge, 1996.

Lewis, Reina. *Rethinking Orientalism. Women, Travel and the Ottoman Harem*. London: I.B. Tauris, 2004.

MacKenzie, John. *Orientalism. History, Theory and the Arts*. Manchester: Manchester University Press, 1995.

Makdisi, Ussama. "Ottoman Orientalism." *The American Historical Review* 107 (2002): 768–96.

Micklewright, Nancy. "Personal, Public, and Political (Re) Constructions: Photographs and Consumption." In *Consumption Studies and the History of the Ottoman Empire*, edited by Donald Quataert, 261–86. Binghamton: SUNY Press, 2000.

Micklewright, Nancy. *A Victorian Traveler in the Middle East: The Photographs and Travel Writing of Annie Lady Brassey*. Burlington, VT: Ashgate, 2003.

Micklewright, Nancy. "Harem/House/Set: Domestic Interiors in Photography from the Late Ottoman World." In *Harem in History and Imagination*, edited by Marilyn Booth, 336–57. Durham and London: Duke University Press, 2010.

Milet, Éric. *Orientalist Photographs 1870–1950*. Paris: Flammarion, 2008.

Mitchell, Timothy. *Colonising Egypt*. Cambridge: Harvard University Press, 1988.

Mollo, Boris. *The British Army from Old Photographs from the National Army Museum*. London: J. M. Dent & Sons, Ltd., 1975.

Nickel, Douglas. *Snapshots. The Photography of Everyday Life, 1888 to the Present*. San Francisco: San Francisco Museum of Modern Art, 1998.

Nir, Yeshayahu. *The Bible and the Image. The History of Photography in the Holy Land 1839–1899*. Philadelphia: University of Pennsylvania Press, 1986.

Nochlin, Linda. "The Imaginary Orient." *Art in America* 71 (1983): 120–29; 186–91.

Onne, Eyal. *The Photographic Heritage of the Holy Land, 1839–1914*. Manchester: Manchester Polytechnic, 1980.

Osman, Colin. *Egypt: Caught in Time*. Reading: Garnet Publishing Limited, 1997.

Özendes, Engin. *Abdullah Frères. Ottoman Court Photographers*. Istanbul: Yapı Kredi Culture, Art, Publications, 1998.

Özendes, Engin. *Sébah & Joaillier'den Foto Sabah'a: fotoğrafta Oryantalizm*. Istanbul: Yapı Kredi Yayınları, 1999.

Öztuncay, Bahattin. *James Robertson. Pioneer of Photography in The Ottoman Empire*. Istanbul: Eren, 1992.

Öztuncay, Bahattin. *The Photographers of Constantinople*, 2 vols. Istanbul: Aygaz, 2003.

Perez, Nissan.*Focus East. Early Photography in the Near East 1839–1885*. New York: Harry Abrams, Inc., 1988.

Phillips, Ruth and Christopher Steiner, eds. *Unpacking Culture. Art and Commodity in Colonial and Postcolonial Worlds*. Berkeley: University of California Press, 1999.

Pinney, Christopher. *Camera Indica. The Social Life of Indian Photographs*. London: Reaktion Books, 1997.

Pratt, Mary Louise. *Imperial Eyes. Travel Writing and Transculturation*. London: Routledge, 1992.

Quataert, Donald, ed. *Consumption Studies and the History of the Ottoman Empire*. Binghamton: SUNY Press, 2000.

Rosenthal, Donald. *Orientalism. The Near East in French Painting 1800–1880*. Rochester, NY: Memorial Art Gallery, 1982.

Roxburgh, David J. *Prefacing the Image. The Writing of Art History in Sixteenth-Century Iran*. Leiden: Brill, 2001.

Ryan, James R. *Picturing Empire. Photography and the Visualization of the British Empire*. London: Reaktion Books, 1997.

Said, Edward. *Orientalism*. New York: Vintage Books, 1979.

Said, Edward. *Culture and Imperialism*. New York: Alfred A. Knopf, 1993.

Scherer, Joanna. "Introduction. Historical Photographs as Anthropological Documents: A Retrospect." *Visual Anthropology* 3 (1990): 131–55.

Schwartz, Joan M. "*The Geography Lesson*: Photographs and the Construction of Imaginative Geographies." *Journal of Historical Geography* 22 (1996): 16–45.

Searight, Sarah. *The British in the Middle East*. London: East-West Publications, 1969.

Sontag, Susan. *On Photography*. New York: Farrar, Strauss and Giroux, 1977.

Stevens, MaryAnne, ed. *The Orientalists: Delacroix to Matisse: European Painters in North Africa and the Near East*. London: Royal Academy of Arts, 1984.

Thornton, Lynne. *The Orientalists: Painters-Travellers*. Paris: ACR Editions, 1994.

Tromans, Nicholas, ed. *The Lure of the East: British Orientalist Painting*. London: Tate Publishing, 2008. Published in conjunction with the exhibition *The Lure of the East: British Orientalist Painting* shown at the Yale Center for British Art, Tate Britain, Suna and İnan Kıraç Pera Museum and the Sharjah Art Museum.

Vaczek, Louis and G. Buckland. *Travelers in Ancient Lands*. Boston: New York Graphic Society, 1981.

Weeks, Emily. "Cultures Crossed: John Frederick Lewis and the Art of Orientalist Painting." In *The Lure of the East. British Orientalist Painting*, edited by Nicholas Tromans, 22–32. London: Tate Publishing, 2008.

Wigh, Leif. *Fotografiska Vyer Från Bosporen Och Konstantinopel/ Photographic Views of the Bosphorus and Constantinople*. Stockholm, Fotografiska Museet, 1984.

Yeğenoğlu, Meyda. *Colonial Fantasies. Towards a Feminist Reading of Orientalism*. Cambridge: Cambridge University Press, 1998.

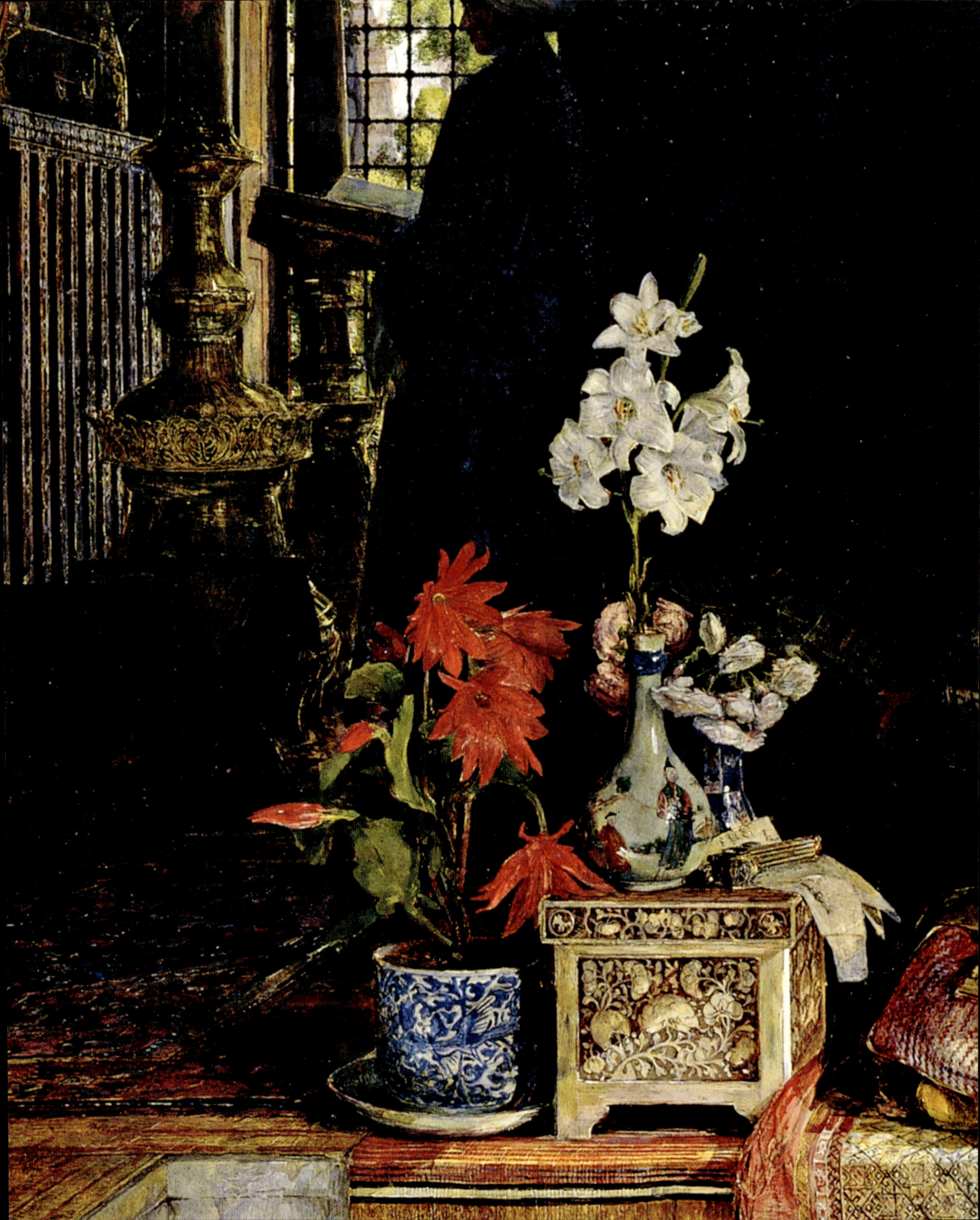

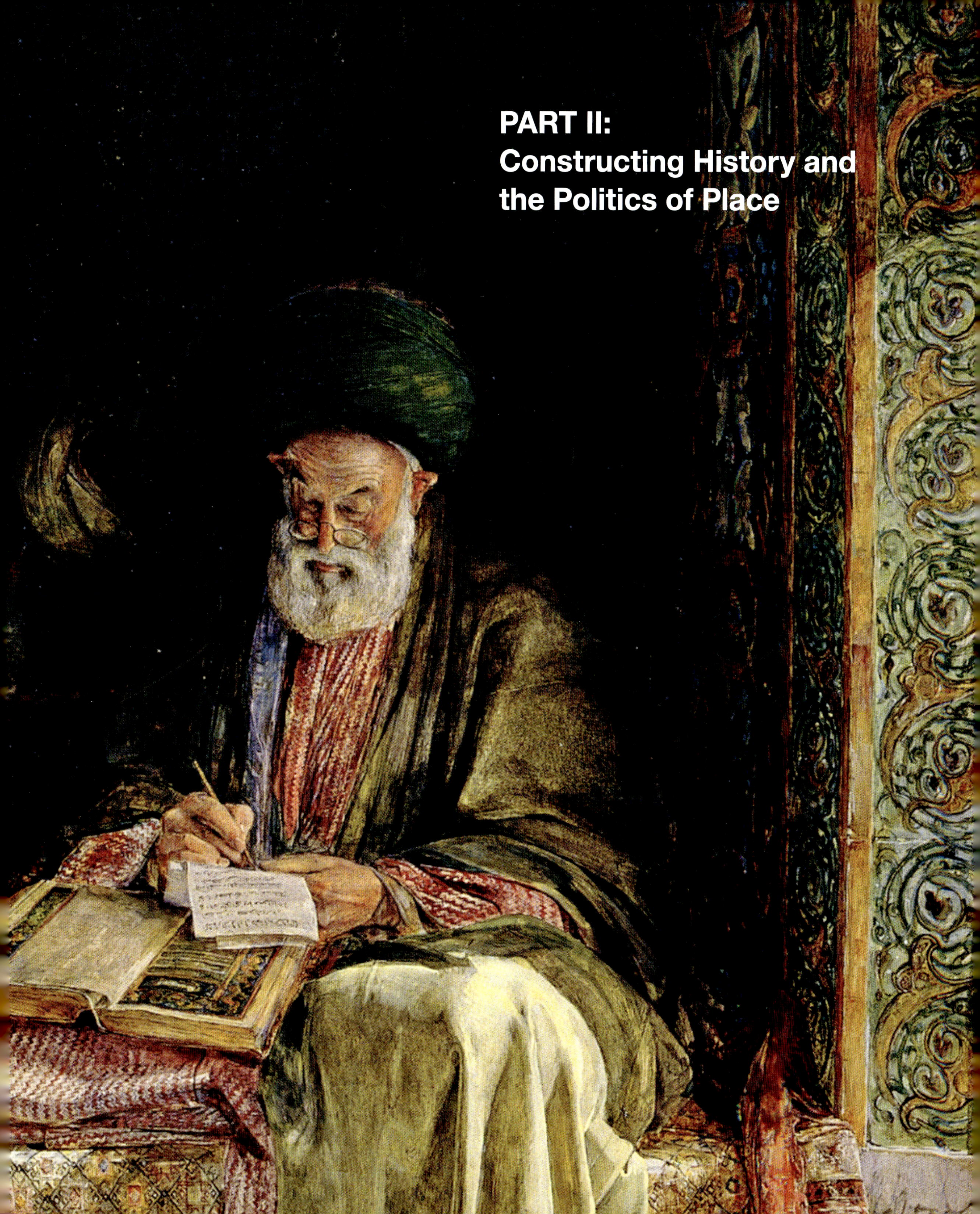

PART II:
Constructing History and the Politics of Place

FISHER'S ILLUSTRATIONS

OF

CONSTANTINOPLE

AND

ITS ENVIRONS.

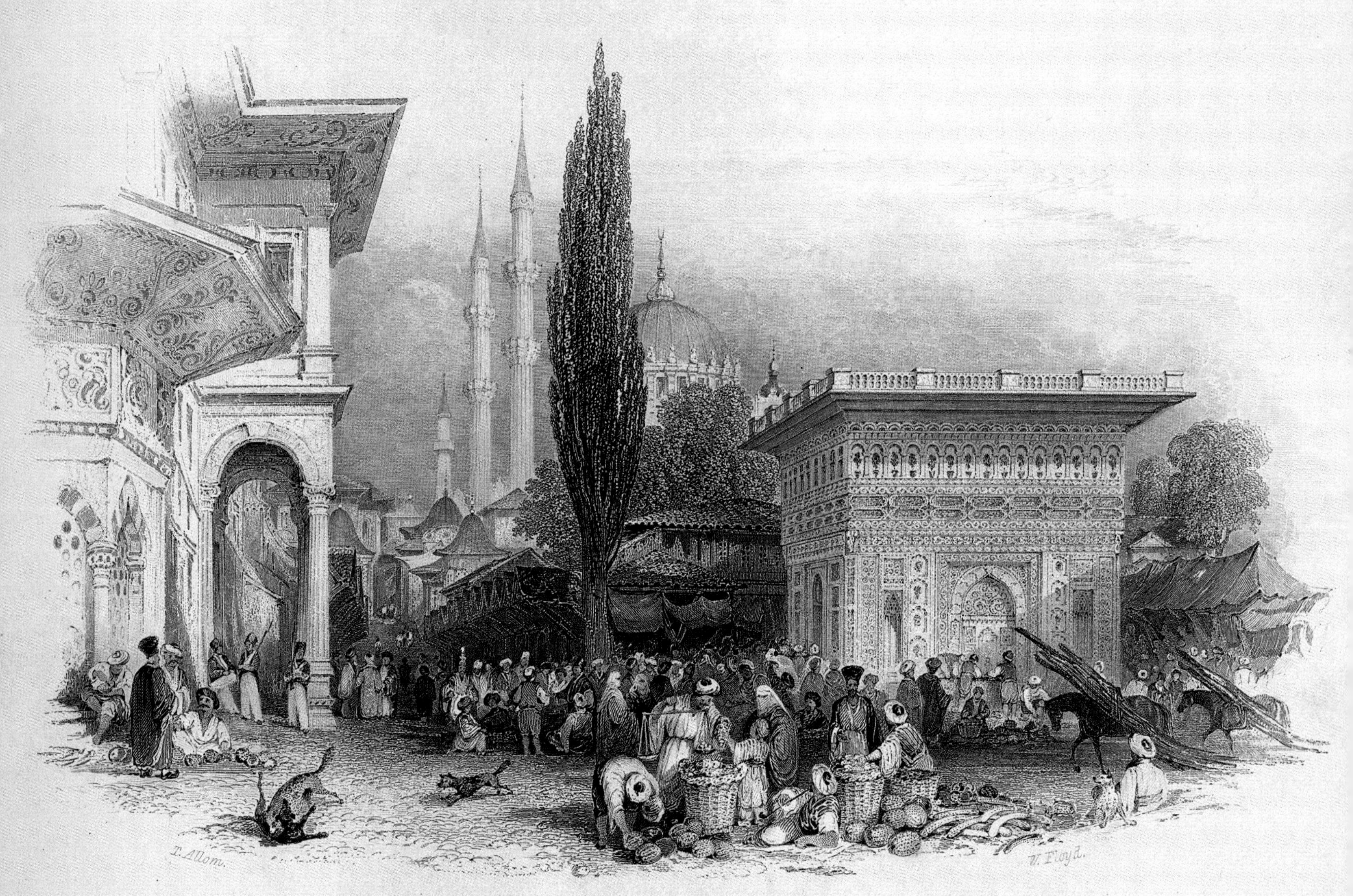

T. Allom. W. Floyd.

Fountain & Market-place of Tophana.

VII

Between the Sublime and the Picturesque

Mourning Modernization and the Production of Orientalist Landscape in Thomas Allom and Reverend Robert Walsh's *Constantinople and the Scenery of the Seven Churches of Asia Minor* (c. 1839)

Wendy M. K. Shaw

During the mid-nineteenth century, the confluence of increased ease of illustrated publication and of transportation enabled Western travelers to produce works that were avidly read by the curious back home. Such works served to normalize knowledge of the world and thereby enhance the perception of knowing about distant territories which could, in turn, serve to normalize possible imperial expansion.[1] Just as Orientalist painting could bolster broader assumptions about the East, published travel landscapes in the form of aquatint or engraving served to disseminate the image of the East through territorial tropes.[2] Orientalist painters created images of harems, Oriental despots, wild animals, Bedouin tribes, and slave markets that reified Western notions of Eastern delinquency while titillating the transparently sequestered desires of civilized male subjects to partake in the despotism and libidinous orgies they disparaged in others. In contrast, travel illustrations spoke the much more familiar and seemingly anodyne language of landscape, a genre that had become particularly popular in eighteenth-century England. Images corroborated textual representations of foreign lands by employing styles and conventions that were recognizable through paintings of local subjects. This mode of depicting the East that shifted the reader's attention from dramatic images of human subjects to landscape vignettes made their visual commentary no less political. If anything, the reduced scale of their work in comparison to Orientalist painting mimicked the casual sketch of that new being, the tourist, making it seem more accurate, a form of irrefutable reportage rather than interpretive representation. In its familiarity, landscape painting thus played a far more subtle game of constructing opinion of the East through established pictorial languages of beauty, the sublime, and the picturesque which could gain new meanings when transcribed onto distant lands. The relationship between text and images in *Constantinople and the Scenery of the Seven Churches of Asia Minor, illustrated in a series of drawings from nature by Thomas Allom, with an historical account of Constantinople and Descriptions of the plates by the Reverend Robert Walsh*, published in London and Paris around 1839 provides an example of how the visual tropes of the picturesque and the sublime served to frame the English image of the Ottoman Empire during an era of incipient European imperialism. Between romantic Orientalism and its critique, these small illustrations suggest a supplementary interpretation for imperialist ambitions couched in artistic forms, revealing instead an ambivalence both towards imperialism and the progress it proffered.

Constantinople and the Scenery of the Seven Churches of Asia Minor provides a ready example of the utility of pictorial tropes developed in the eighteenth century for the depiction of Britain to take on a new political role in the imagination, rendition, and domestication of foreign lands. Through judicious employment of the sublime and the picturesque, Allom and Walsh produce an overview of the Ottoman Empire ambivalent towards its modernization. Military and administrative reform represented the universalist success of the civilizing ideals of the white man's burden, so one might expect Europeans to celebrate it. Yet just as the Barbizon artists in Paris and the pre-Raphaelites in England looked respectively to the countryside and to the medieval past to find succor in a rapidly changing world, European travelers sought refuge in a timeless and unchanging East that could eternally satiate their nostalgia. Thus such travel literature supports the tropes of the timeless Orient built into the Orientalist genre, but instead of implicitly supporting the imperial power of Europe, questions its desire to modernize the East in the preservationist impulse to thwart the predations of progress. The Ottoman Empire provided a perfect field in which to explore this type of ambivalence. Unlike in British India, modernization did not represent European imperial power and superiority, but a practice that could theoretically be applied by any state and which thus threatened hierarchies of racial and/or cultural superiority on which imperialism often relied.

Widely reproduced today as part of contemporary Turkish and touristic nostalgia for the Ottoman past, these images were in their time already nostalgic for a present which their creators anticipated as soon to be lost. For 1839, the year in which many of the prints in the undated volume were printed, was not just any year in the Ottoman Empire: it was the year of the announcement of the *Tanzimat*, the decree of "Reordering" rooted in the French Declaration of the Rights of Man which established a modern bureaucratic government and the rights of a modern citizenry undifferentiated by ethnicity or religion in the Ottoman Empire. Preceded by the loss of Greek territories in 1829, as well as several decades of architectural, technological, sartorial, and military change, particularly under the rule of Sultan Mahmud II (r. 1808–39), during which Allom and Walsh traveled in the Ottoman Empire, 1839 would become the first of many cornerstones which would mark the empire's, and later the Republic of Turkey's, adoption of European political and social ideologies.

The work's mode of viewing Constantinople on the cusp of change is made immediately apparent from the first engravings illustrating the volume. Even before the frontispiece, the authors present a prospect view (Fig. 7.1) of the iconic, minaret-pierced city skyline and its bustling harbor. For centuries, the view of Constantinople as seen from the port of the Golden Horn had been the most frequently represented image of the city, used in numerous travelogs. Its iconicity was heightened in 1801–2, when the city became one of the first urban cityscapes made available through the new technology of the panorama (a term coined in 1787 by Robert Barker to designate a landscape painting providing a 360 degree point of view), which became a popular attraction at the Spring Gardens Arcades run by Joshua Crystal in 1801–2. Allom's illustration underscores the traditional aspect of the harbor, placing multi-oared rowboats and a raft in the foreground while placing the more modern steamships behind them, where they are less likely to interrupt the timeless view. Nonetheless, Walsh's text contravenes this

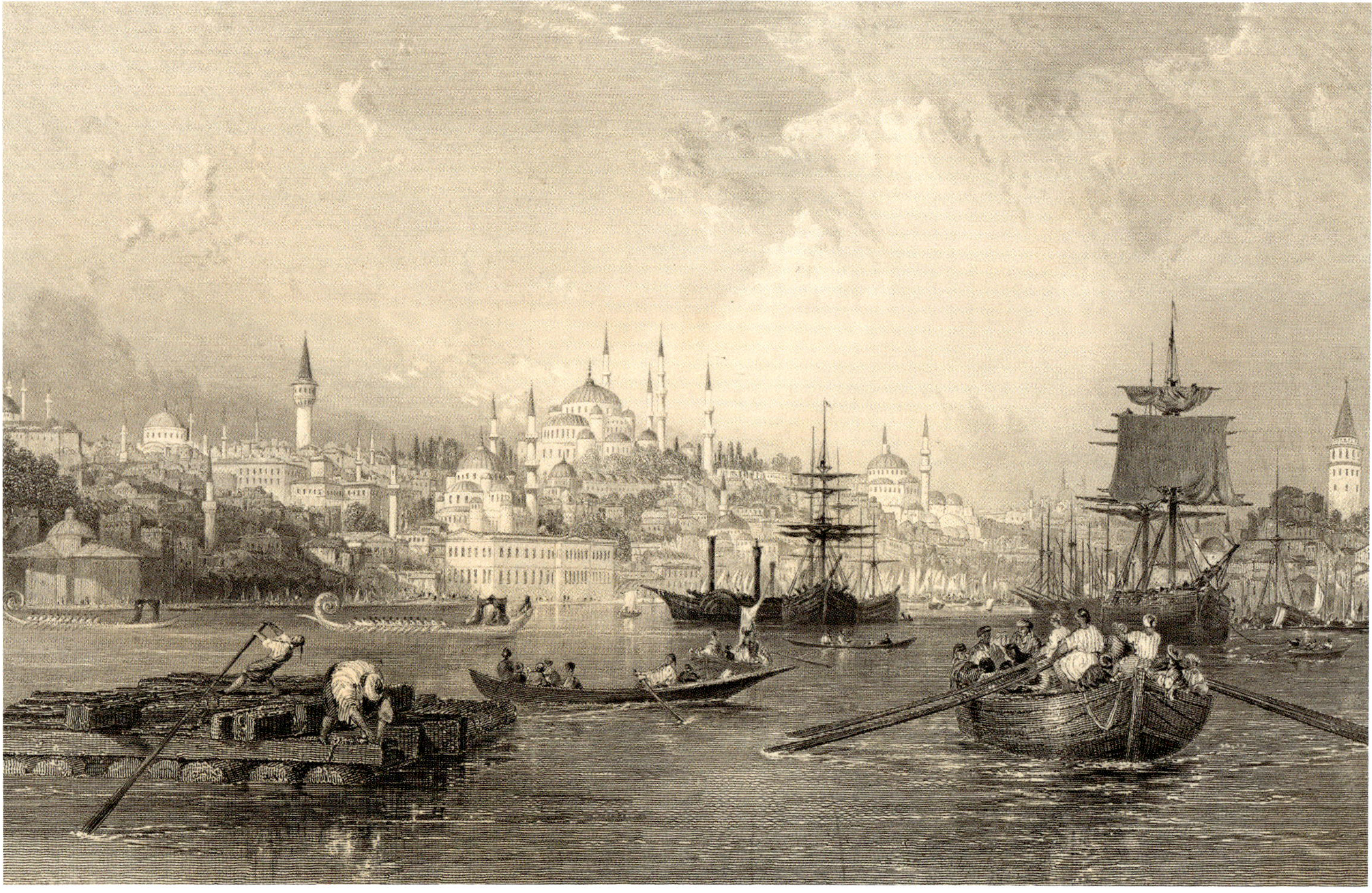

Figure 7.1 Constantinople viewed from the Golden Horn, Frontispiece of Allom and Walsh, *Constantinople and the Scenery of the Seven Churches of Asia Minor*, c. 1839. Universitätsbibliothek Basel.

subtlety in order to underscore the drama of recent events represented within the image while at the same time undermining the potential danger they might represent to enemies of the Ottoman Empire:

> The enormous vessels that compose the Turkish fleet are the most conspicuous objects … The first impression made by these great engines of naval warfare, is the vast superiority they possess, and the hopelessness of any opposition to them. Yet they are utterly powerless in the unskillful hands that guide them. The Turks, like their predecessors the Persians, are impotent by sea; and as the ancient Greeks with ease destroyed the fleets of the one, so did the modern Greeks those of the other with their tiny ships.[3]

Taking recourse to classical tropes of East and West, he casts the Ottoman Empire in the role of the despotic and the defeated already established in Aeschalus's *The Persians*. Nonetheless, modernity lurks around the bend, possibly threatening change for this hierarchy of civilizations.

> Within these few years a new feature has been added to the moving picture of the harbour. When steam-boats were adopted by all the nations of Europe, the tardy Turks alone rejected them … It was not uncommon to see lines of twenty or thirty men, with long cords passed over their shoulders, slowly dragging up ponderous merchantmen with a vast labour, which a single steamer would at once render unnecessary. It was among the first reforms of the sultan to introduce any European inventions which could assist human labour … this spacious and novel ship-yard is under the superintendance of the laborious and patient Armenians, who are the great mechanics of the Turkish empire. Here they not only build the boats, but cast the machinery, which the stupid Moslems could not comprehend, til they saw their own sultan embark in the wonderful self-moving machine, that issued from their own arsenal.

By emphasizing the role of Armenians over Turks as agents of modernization, Walsh creates a means of allowing for change without disturbing the longstanding characterization of the Muslim. The Ottoman Christian subject serves as a supplementary presence through which the timelessness of the East can be circumvented without altering the objectification of the Muslim Other of Europe.

The paradox of the idealized timelessness of the East and the modernizing reality of the empire reappears immediately in the vignette title page of the volume, featuring a scene of the Market Place of Tophane (Fig. 7.2). The scene

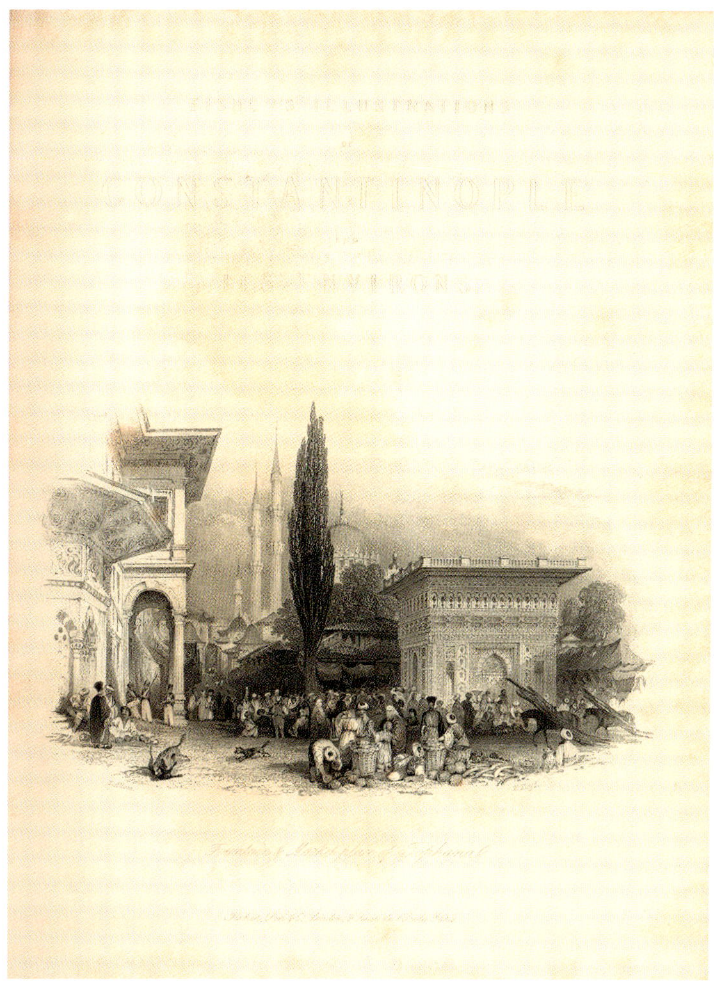

Figure 7.2 *Market Place of Tophane*, Title page illustration, Allom and Walsh, *Constantinople and the Scenery of the Seven Churches of Asia Minor*, c. 1839. Universitätsbibliothek Basel.

is dominated by the hustle and bustle of a market crowd, populated by minor characters such as sellers, women, street dogs, and donkeys carrying long plants in front of what Walsh identifies as one of the two fountains in the city where "the Turks seem to have exerted all their skill in sculpture" with a "beautiful specimen of the arabesque." This is the Tophane fountain erected in 1732 as part of Mahmud I's (r. 1730–54) modernization of the cannon foundry and barracks as part of an earlier phase of Ottoman military reform. Nonetheless, a century later, it could be understood by the casual observer as a sign not of modernization, but of traditional Ottoman urban form. Like the gypsies, beggars, and bandits whom William Gilpin (1724–1804), one of the early British theorists of the picturesque, suggested provided important foils for the ideal picturesque scene, the exotic figures populating the scene contribute to the seduction of the image. Walsh pointed out that this became all the more powerful "when the Other is so culturally—that is, when the picturesque being is not a marginalized portion of the observer's own culture but is, or represents, a wholly separate cultural formation." While Walsh presents this as an effect of isolation as a foreigner, the inclusion of figures who ignored the beholder and thus drew him into the work by establishing a fiction of his absence had already become a common strategy of drawing the viewer into an image.[4] If Oriental street scenes could be inherently picturesque because of the difference of their subjects, then the modernization of these subjects through the acquisition of "civilized," European behaviors, habits, and appearances could only make them more accessible and therefore reduce their attraction.

The image overdetermines the exoticism of the scene. The form of the monuments is framed by a layer of mist which separates foreground from background and indicates the picturesque focal point. In contrast to Orientalist paintings, which tend toward grand dramatic, domestic, or sublime scenes, this image promises the traveler light adventure. As Walsh explains, "a Frank, whose business leads him to the quarter, has reason to congratulate himself, if he shall escape the blow of a plank from the passing horse, or the laceration of his flesh by an irritated dog." What Walsh does not mention is the understated left side of the scene, where a group of three modern soldiers loiter under a suspiciously un-Arabesque neo-Classical arcade. Constructed between 1823 and 1826 as part of Sultan Mahmut II's larger project to rebuild the Tophane artillery barracks, which had been destroyed during the Firuzağa fire, the arcade and the soldiers serve as a clear indicator of the type of change creeping into the comfortably exotic picturesque realm which the intrepid traveler presumably sought and which Walsh exclusively describes.

Printed on the eve of the momentous declaration of the *Tanzimat*, the images accompanying the text render contemporary Constantinople as a ghost for the future, a place foreclosed to later travelers. While earlier travelers had suffered long journeys across land and sea, in future they would be able to take advantage of regular steamship schedules which began in 1840. This new breed of tourist would be able to arrive in Constantinople from Marseilles in only eight days.[5] This, along with the import of technology, would destroy the Constantinople captured in the book. As Robert Walsh explains in the preface:

> Constantinople, having for centuries exhibited the singular and extraordinary spectacle of a Mohomedan town in a Christian region, and stood still while all about it were advancing in the march of improvement, has at length, as suddenly as unexpectedly, been roused from its slumbering stupidity; the city and its inhabitants are daily undergoing a change as extraordinary as unhoped for; and the present generation will see with astonishment, that revolution of usages and opinions, during a single life, which has not happened in any other country in revolving centuries.

He goes on to explain the rapid transformation, in only ten years, of both the military, formerly a "mere rabble" and now one "as amenable to discipline as a corps of German infantry," and the Sultan, formerly "the model of an Oriental despot," and now "in a noble palace, on which the arts have been exhausted to render it as beautiful and commodious as that of a European sovereign." One might interpret all this change as positive, and indeed the text notes it with a charge of excitement. However, images provide a subtext of nostalgia.

A comparison of scenes representing the "Reception Room of the Seraglio" and the "Entrance to the Divan" reveals Allom and Walsh's ambivalent attitude towards these recent changes (see Figs. 7.3 and 7.4). On the one hand, the reception room of the Topkapı Palace, increasingly falling into disuse in the early nineteenth century, appears grand and orderly, marked by a clear hierarchy underscored by the perspectival emphasis of the image on the central figure. On the other, the recently constructed *Bab-ı Ali*, the "high gate" guarding the new administrative buildings that housed Sultan Mahmud II's modern bureaucracy, features lavish disarray. Although the increased public visibility of the monarch might seem a mark of increasing modern identity, the crowd of fighting dogs in the foreground, coupled with an idle soldier hiding behind the *Alay Köşkü* (Parade Pavilion) to the right uses picturesque tropes of disorder to underscore the perception of modernization as a loss rather than as a gain.

This nostalgic perception of progress as loss, complimenting the sublime glorification of the ruin, suffuses the entire book. Oscar Ortiz has noted that this reaction was common in the mid-nineteenth century, dubbing it "cultural hypochondria," an excessive anxiety over the possibility of the disintegration and death of a culture.[6] In the preface, and with an apparent note of admiration, Walsh describes how the people had been transformed from one that listened to mere stories to one that read newspapers. Nonetheless, the relatively infrequent images which focus on people rather than on landscapes emphasize such increasingly outdated aspects of Ottoman society as *The Sultana in her State Arrhuba, Circassian Slaves of the Harem,* or *The Medak or*

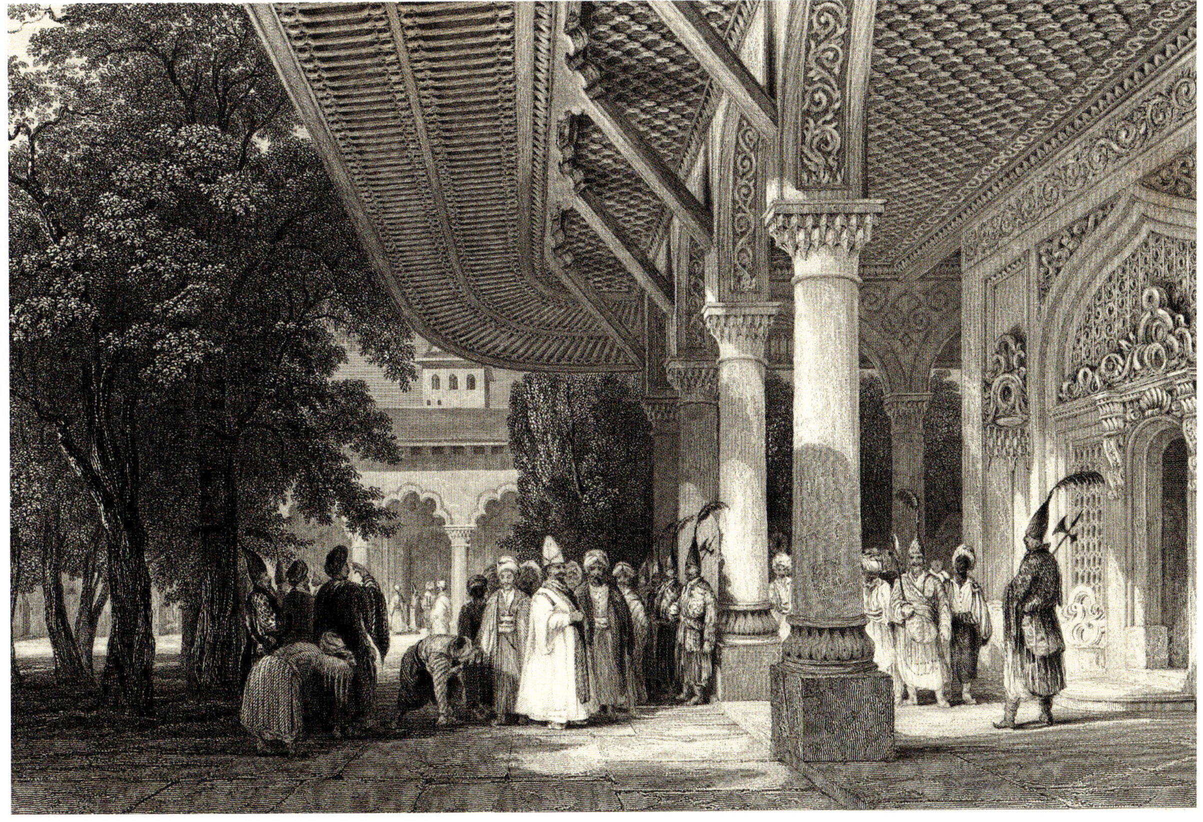

Figure 7.3 *Reception Room of the Seraglio*, Allom and Walsh, *Constantinople and the Scenery of the Seven Churches of Asia Minor*, c. 1839. Universitätsbibliothek Basel.

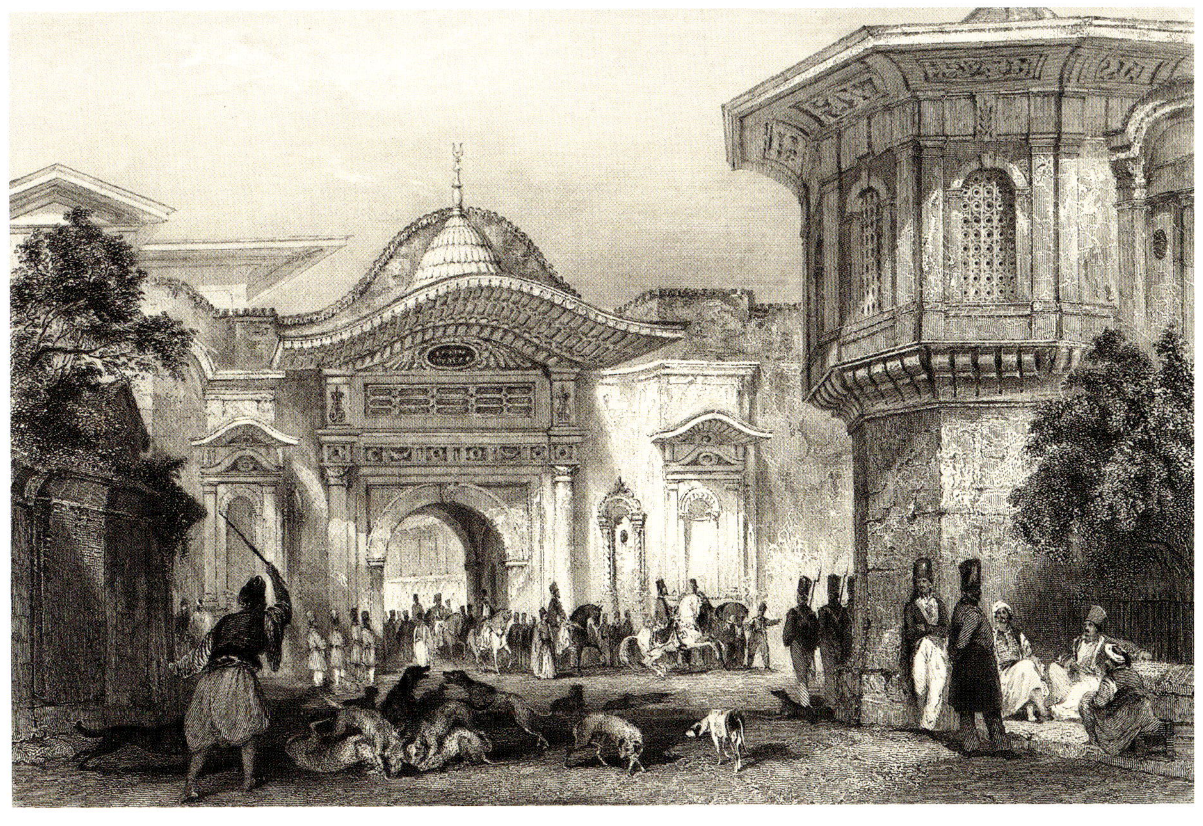

Figure 7.4 *Entrance to the Divan, Constantinople*, Allom and Walsh, *Constantinople and the Scenery of the Seven Churches of Asia Minor*, c. 1839. Universitätsbibliothek Basel.

Eastern Story-Teller. Indeed, having listed the remarkable progress of the empire, Walsh laments:

> It is thus that the former state of things is hurrying away, and he who visits the capital to witness the singularities that marked it, will be disappointed. It is true, it possesses beauties which no revolution of opinions, or change of events, can alter … but all the distinctive peculiarities of a Turkish town will soon merge into the uniformity of European things, and if the innovation proceed as rapidly as it has hitherto done, scarce a trace behind them.

The modernization of exotic lands was antithetical to the desire which propelled a traveler of the mid-nineteenth century seeking a respite from the modernization of his own society. As developed by Allom, the Orientalist landscape was designed precisely to sooth such concerns: to preserve difference in the face of modernization through the use of the visual, erasing the modern as necessary.

> To preserve the evanescent features of this magnificent city, and present it to posterity as it was, must be an object of no small interest: but the most elaborate descriptions will fail to affect it.
>
> It is, therefore, to catch the fleeting pictures while they yet exist, and transmit them in *visible* forms to posterity, that the present work has been undertaken, and, that nothing might be wanting, Asiatic subjects are introduced; and thus presenting, not only the Turk of one region as he was, but of another as he is, and will continue to be.

British travelers were particularly well-suited to such a task. Although comparable travelogs were produced by numerous European travelers to the Ottoman Empire from the seventeenth century to the twentieth, the British interest in the esthetics of landscape as developed in the eighteenth century enable Allom's illustrations to employ a language of landscape which would have been readily legible to his intended audience. Unlike earlier works, which often emphasized the employment of the picturesque in their titles, by the mid-nineteenth century, the tropes of the picturesque were so well established as the ready currency of depicting landscape in Britain that there would have been no need to point to them. Rather, they served as a marker of effective rhetorical exposition through which the artist could convey his construction of the land in its presentation to the viewer. Equipped with this clearly defined visual language, Allom could convey the sense of mourning expressed by Walsh's text, while producing an Orientalist landscape which held the promise of immortality.

Although seemingly anodyne, the development of the picturesque esthetic in eighteenth-century Britain was already deeply informed by contemporary political, social, and economic change, and remained so when applied to the depiction of foreign rather than local lands. As Ann Bermingham points out, "the picturesque vision represents an ideological as well as aesthetic commitment," focusing on the estheticization not of some abstract natural space but of a working agrarian land and those who worked it before and after it became scenery. She explains, "the fashion for the picturesque coexists with the ongoing depopulation of rural areas brought on by enclosure and progressive agricultural techniques."[7] It is within this context that the term *picturesque* was first used by William Gilpin in 1768 in *An Essay on Prints* in order to designate "that peculiar kind of beauty which is agreeable in a picture," a circular definition which defines the picturesque object through its ability to conform "to prior objects lodged in memory … mediated by representative works of art."[8] Gilpin's subsequent works published through the end of the eighteenth century provided formulaic instructions for producing picturesque landscape sketches for tourists to out-of-the-way places in Britain, particularly the lower gentry whose means provided them with the opportunity to travel but did not provide them with massive amounts of land to physically transform. The theory was further developed through several works by Richard Payne Knight and Uvedale Price, both squires in their own right, who developed Gilpin's ideas from a mode of depicting the land to one of forming it through large-scale landscaping projects on the vast enclosures of the remaining landed gentry. Gilpin's earlier understanding of the picturesque focused on the needs of the traveler, unable to mark the land except by re-imagining it through the image. In contrast, later promoters of the picturesque such as Knight, Price, and the landscape designer Humphrey Repton saw themselves as improvers of the land, engineers of a real landscape which could conform to the requirements of the picturesque.[9]

The traveler who took on the tropes of the picturesque to depict foreign lands during the nineteenth century was caught between these two modes, that of depiction and that of improvement. Of course, in order to "improve" land through landscaping, one had to own or control it. Thus when, Thomas and William Daniell depicted Oriental buildings through the picturesque mode in their *Select Views of India* of 1788 and *Picturesque Voyage to India* of 1810, they depicted a place which, while exotic, was enough under British control that it could be subject to British Aesthetic improvement.[10] In contrast, Allom and Walsh had no hope of "improving" or modifying the Ottoman landscape according to the strictures of picturesque taste. Unlike the actual imperialist, their enterprise within Constantinople, the capital of the Ottoman Empire, was purely that of the traveler, who could compose images of desire by pruning less pleasing aspects of reality and by focusing instead on those they found attractive. Just as the readers of travel literature back in England might be called "armchair tourists," figures like Allom and Walsh might be considered itinerant imperialists. Their imperialism was virtual, enacted through the controlled representation of landscape painting rather than the construction of physical landscape. As such, instead of improvement towards an ideal of progress, it sought the opposite. For them and like-minded travelers seeking in the exotic refuge from the predations of industrialization, the Orient was to be a refuge from change, a repository of the picturesque. Yet the picturesque held within it an implicit irony: the scenes which it searched for—of decay, abandonment, idleness, and even minor criminality—were directly opposed to the values modern civilization, the premise of imperial civilizing missions, was supposed to promote.[11] In favoring the picturesque view of his Ottoman Other, the British traveler favored the maintenance of the very disorder, inefficiency, and despotism which he claimed to despise.

In the work of Allom and Walsh, the sublime steps in to remedy this seeming contradiction. From spectacular mountain passes and waterfalls in the Balkans to the ruins scattered throughout Asia Minor, the sublime supplies the timeless quality which the traveler still seeks despite the "unhoped for" change of the urban Orient, where "men and things still display the permanency of Oriental usages; and they are now as they have been, and will probably continue to be, for an indefinite period." Yet it is not people whom the traveler seeks outside the city, but ever broader views of sublime landscape, in which nature and grand ruins conspire to strike the viewer with a sense of awe not possible in the picturesque, ever-changing urban melee. There, Ottoman modernization, which might be understood as a metonymic trope for all non-Western attempts at self-generated progress, is rendered as ineffectual an agent of change as the traveler himself.

This is perhaps nowhere more apparent than in one of the few scenes of Constantinople which employs the sublime, entitled "Baluk Hane and Method of Fishing for the Red Mullet," with the sub-caption "At this spot state criminals are thrown into the Bosphorus from the Seraglio" (Fig. 7.5). On a lightly clouded moonlit night, between the shadows of moored ships on the horizon and the city walls, Allom depicts the romantic forms of a fishery on stilts, a common element of fishing on the Bosporus until the mid-twentieth century. This, despite the title, is clearly not the main objective of the scene. The moonlight illuminates a small group standing in a rowboat, sending a dead body to a watery grave. Reminiscent of a biblical deposition, the scene uses European painting conventions to sympathize with the criminal, cast in place of a potential Jesus executed by an Oriental potentate. In contrast to nearly every other scene in the book which actually might conceivably have been witnessed by the authors, this scene of secrecy, veiled by moonlight and excluded from the realms of both tourist and citizen, recapitulates myths of Oriental despotism which, despite any promise of change, ironically comfort the traveler in the belief that the fundament of the Orient, underscored in painting, remains constant: dramatic, arbitrary, and attractively frightening.

If the traveler is unable to control the Oriental environment except through representation, then the sublime environment provides a place where the local subject is equally unable to affect change. As Michasiw explains, in the realm of theories of the picturesque, the sublime functions through the privileged prospect where

> the one seeking it must abandon spectatorship and enter the plane of representation ... This new beholder exists to be annihilated by the representation, either through exile from the scene or by absorption into it.
>
> Sublime scenes, especially in nature where human mediation is absent, constitute a clear and present case of this danger. In the face of the sublime, individual identity dwindles and can only be reasserted through representation.[12]

At the point where the possibility of change is erased, the traveler can relax, transforming the moment of sublime awe, a sense of powerlessness and loss of control, into one of equality with the Oriental owner of the land.[13] Like the criminal thrown into the water, or the Ottoman who might fear such a fate, the foreign traveler who observes the scene at the Baluk Hane can do no more than shudder in awe. Yet unlike the Orientals, his shudder contains not only fear but pleasure, both in his own liberty and civilizational superiority. While the tropes of extra-urban images recall the sublime, the texts that accompany them play down such grandeur, emphasizing the modern traveler's willingness to pass by mountains or decaying ruins. The moral power affected by the transcendence of impotence normally brought about by the sublime is thus altered as the Orientalist traveler transforms the sublime into yet another version of the picturesque.

The power to control the image itself can be seen within this framework. As Susan Sontag points out, "As photographs

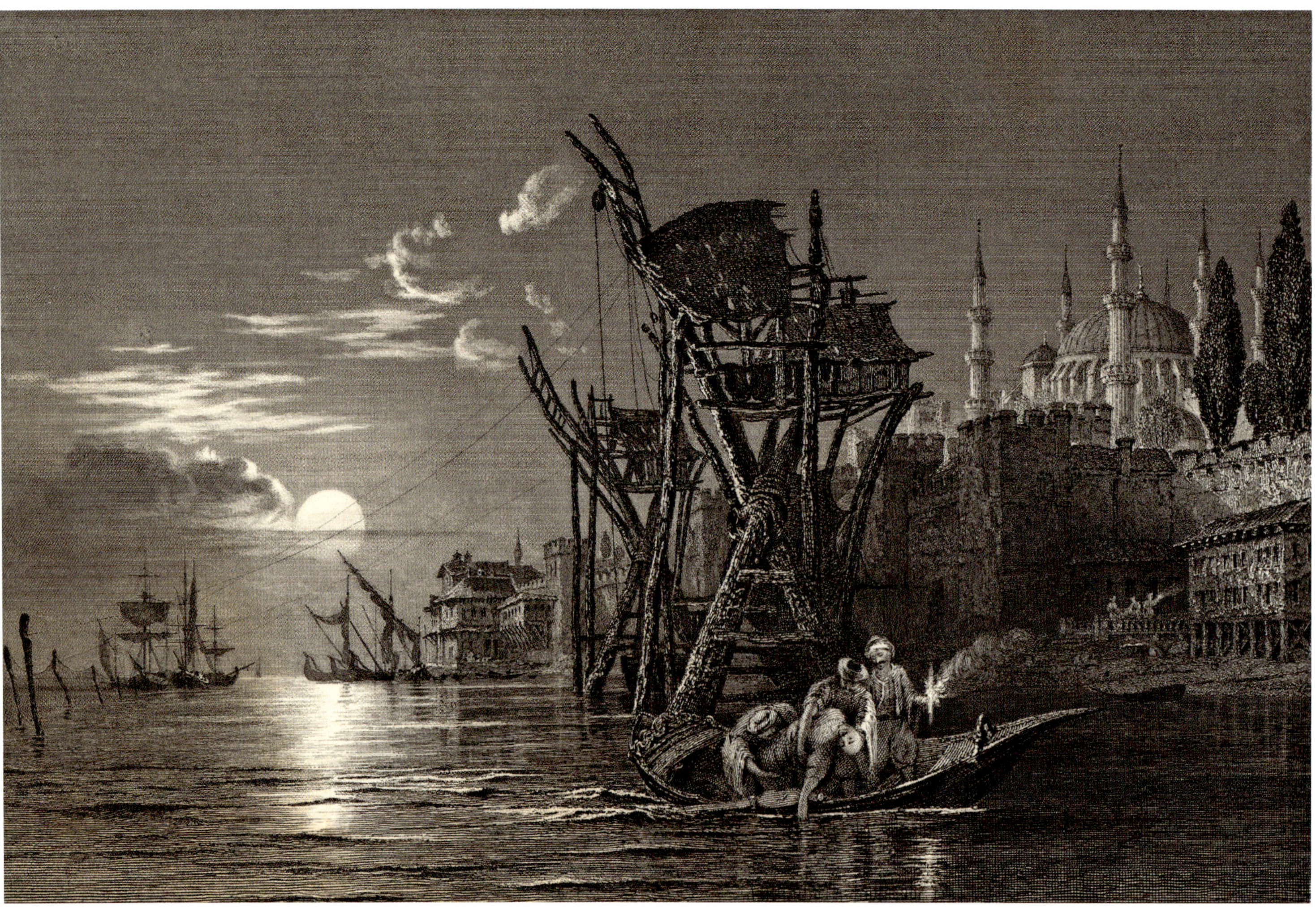

Figure 7.5 *Baluk Hana and Method of Fishing for the Red Mullet*, Allom and Walsh, *Constantinople and the Scenery of the Seven Churches of Asia Minor*, c. 1839. Universitätsbibliothek Basel.

give people an imaginary possession of a past that is unreal, they also help people to take possession of a space in which they are insecure. Thus photography develops in tandem with one of the most characteristic of modern activities: tourism."[14] However, this observation relies less on the technology of the photograph than on the process of image-making which creates an interface between the temporary interloper and the place where he or she is situated. The lag between the advent of the steam engine, which enabled relatively rapid travel, and the development of photography into a relatively portable technology in the 1860s, marked a period in which images, such as those of Allom, could serve as a mechanism of distancing and control which photography would later take on.

Thus Orientalist landscape creates a psychology of imperial control not through actual physical modification of the landscape, but through the modification of its perception. In contrast with Antoine Ignace Melling's *Voyage pittoresque de Constantinople et des rives du Bosphore* published in Paris between 1809 and 1819 which celebrated an earlier epoch of modernization, Allom frames scenes to the general exclusion or denigration of the modern. Thus the book produces the Oriental Other as a picturesque site of nostalgia inappropriate for modernization. This sense of timelessness is enhanced through an appeal to the sublime, where both the native and the traveler are equally impotent in the face of nature and antiquity. In this process, a new morality—rooted not in modernization, not in civilization, but in conservation—emerges. As Townsend explains:

> The picturesque, particularly as Ruskin re-forms it in the mid-nineteenth century, requires the actual presence of the past in the present. It is directly opposed not only to the new but also to the artificially restored and the imitations of the past … Conservation is only possible under the special conditions imposed by picturesque theory …

> the picturesque introduces both a temporal and a physical distance that influences the formulation of "distance" as an aesthetic term.[15]

Once created as the site of nostalgia, the Orient is caught in a double bind: although politically and socially bound towards notions of progress, it also must maintain the past as a site of nostalgia, like a zombie, in a kind of suspended death animated by artifice, rather than with a living and subsequently mortal relationship with the past. The practice of Oriental landscape, then, is not simply one of vision, but one of circumscription, a framing device which foreclosed a relationship between the future and its past.

The continued popularity of reprints of these images suggests a similar disjunction in modern Turkey between modernization and the history from which it diverged rather than emerged. For the most part, sites throughout Turkey are preserved and visited by foreign tourists, seeking within them the same type of sublime experiences as travelers of yore. In the meantime, every month of Ramazan (Ramadan), local municipalities throughout Turkey ignore entire neighborhoods of decaying historical residential architecture as they construct models of old streets to be used as commercial fair booths staffed by servers in cheap Ottoman costumes. In both cases, the past does not live within the present, but is set aside from it. Ruins become sites of sublime exoticism, while old neighborhoods rot away in favor of picturesque plywood sales stalls. Already produced as exotic nostalgia nearly two centuries ago, Thomas Allom's landscape paintings enable foreigner and local alike to imagine themselves within an alternate world in which the modern never happened. Such an economy of nostalgia can serve multiple functions. For the republican modernist, it bolsters the impression of Ottoman stagnation from which the republic emerged in 1923 as a phoenix from the ashes; for an Islamist or nationalist audience, it celebrates a pure past towards which a politics of return can be imagined. Particularly when disassociated from their original sequence and divested from the text which originally framed their imagery, what were once book illustrations become independent works which function only through the play of visual tropes, such as the picturesque, within them.

Such a potential for ambivalence within these images destabilizes their interpretation through tropes of British imperialist power and the Orientalist quest for knowledge. Technology, as much as the growing imperial might of Europe, would soon shift the possibility of such ambivalence within the representation of the East. Of course 1839 was not only the year of Ottoman reordering; it also marked the official announcement of the invention of photography with the patenting of the Daguerrotype in France. As suggested by one of its first promoters, François Arago, who compared the possibilities of photography with the encyclopedic project of Napoleon's *Description de l'Egypte*, one of the earliest uses of photography was the extensive documentation of the East, where travelers such as Frederic Goupil Fesquet (1843), Joseph Philibert Girault de Prangey (1842–45), and Maxime du Camp (1844, 1849) sought to document sites in the Holy Land, and the ancient monuments of the Near East and Egypt—all of which were part of the Ottoman Empire.[16] As James Ackerman points out, landscape photography was largely influenced by the tropes of the picturesque which preceded it. However, photography also led to shifts in artistic choices. With a reduced ability to place figures and objects within a scene at will, artists had to choose sites without human subjects or use posed subjects who could often not elicit the same range of picturesque response as imaginary figures placed within a scene.[17] Moreover, the long exposure times of early photographic technologies reduced the possibility of capturing lively urban scenes, and made the representation of remote sites more attractive. As photographers generally chose the ancient over the modern, the unpopulated or the remote over the crowded or the urban, and the still over the active, they ultimately translated many of the practices of landscape depiction in travel literature, as embodied in the work of Allom, to a new photographic age. Yet, as is often the case in translations, something was lost: whereas in the picturesque drawing, permanence was represented through images of timeless human activity, in photography, permanence became the province of architecture. Where they were included, human subjects, often in regional costumes or professional contexts, were artificially posed for photographs that could serve ethnographic rather than picturesque ends. By its nature, photography promised a less poetically framed and more positive vision of the world, leading to a more fully objectifying, less ambivalent portrayal of the East that fits more closely with the kind of institutional objectification categorized within Saidian Orientalism.[18]

Notes

1 Rhoads Murphy, "Bigots or Informed Observers? A Periodization of Pre-Colonial English and European Writing on the Middle East," *Journal of the American Oriental Society* 110, no. 2 (April–June 1990): 291–303.

2 Roger Benjamin, *Orientalist Aesthetics: Art, Colonialism, and French North Africa, 1880–1930* (Berkeley, CA: University of California Press, 2003).

Linda Nochlin, "The Imaginary Orient," *Art in America* (May 1983): 119–131, 187, 189, 191.

3 Due to the lack of page numbers in the original publication, this article does not indicate page numbers for quotations from Thomas Allom and Reverend Robert Walsh, *Constantinople and the Scenery of the Seven Churches of Asia Minor* (London: Fisher, Son and Co., c. 1839).

4 Kim Ian Michasiw, "Nine Revisionist Theses on the Picturesque," *Representations* 38 (Spring 1992): 85.

5 Reinhold Schiffer, *Oriental Panorama: British Travellers in Nineteenth Century Turkey* (Amsterdam: Rodopi Bv Editions, 1999), 5.

6 Oscar Rodriguez Ortiz, ed. *Imagenes de Humboldt* (Caracas: Monte Avila, 1983). See also Julia Ballerini, "Rewriting the Nubian Figure in the Photograph: Maxime du Camp's "cultural hypochondria," in *Colonialist Photography: Imagining Race and Place*, ed. Eleanor M. Hight and Gary D. Sampson (London: Routledge, 2002), 30.

7 Ann Bermingham, *Landscape and Ideology: The English Rustic Tradition, 1740–1860* (Berkeley: University of California Press, 1986), 66.

8 Quoted in Stephanie Ross, "The Picturesque: An Eighteenth-Century Debate," *The Journal of Aesthetics and Art Criticism* 46, no. 3 (Winter 1987): 271 and Michasiw, "Nine Revisionist Theses on the Picturesque," 87.

9 Mavis Batey, "The Picturesque: An Overview," *Garden History* 22, no. 2 (Winter 1994): 126.

10 Ibid., 127.

11 Francesca Orestano, "The Revd William Gilpin and the Picturesque: Or, Who's Afraid of Doctor Syntax?" *Garden History* 31, no. 2 (Winter 2003): 167; Dabney Townsend, "The Picturesque," *The Journal of Aesthetics and Art Criticism* 55, no. 4 (Autumn 1997): 370–72.

12 Michasiw, "Nine Revisionist Theses on the Picturesque," 85.

13 Kari Elise Lokke, "The Role of Sublimity in the Development of Modernist Aesthetics," *The Journal of Aesthetics and Art Criticism* 40, no. 4 (Summer 1982): 421–29.

14 Susan Sontag, *On Photography* (London: Penguin, 1977), 9.

15 Townsend, "The Picturesque," 368.

16 Alan Trachtenberg, *Classic Essays on Photography* (New Haven, CT: Leetes Island Books, 1980), 17.

17 James S. Ackerman, "The Photographic Picturesque," *Artibus et Historiae*, 24, no. 48 (2003): 73–94.

18 Edward W. Said, *Orientalism* (London: Routledge and Kegan Paul, 1978).

Bibliography

Ackerman, James S. "The Photographic Picturesque." *Artibus et Historiae* 24, no. 48 (2003): 73–94.

Allom, Thomas and Reverend Robert Walsh. *Constantinople and the Scenery of the Seven Churches of Asia Minor*, London: Fisher, Son and Co., c. 1839.

Ballerini, Julia. "Rewriting the Nubian Figure in the Photograph: Maxime du Camp's 'Cultural Hypochondria." In *Colonialist Photography: Imagining Race and Place*, edited by Eleanor M. Hight and Gary D. Sampson. London: Routledge, 2002.

Batey, Mavis. "The Picturesque: An Overview." *Garden History* 22, no. 2 (Winter 1994): 121–32.

Benjamin, Roger. *Orientalist Aesthetics: Art, Colonialism, and French North Africa, 1880–1930*. Berkeley: University of California Press, 2003.

Bermingham, Ann. *Landscape and Ideology: The English Rustic Tradition, 1740–1860*. Berkeley: University of California Press, 1986.

Daniell, Thomas and William Daniell. *Picturesque Voyage to India.* London: Longman, Hurst, Rees and Orme, 1810.

Lokke, Kari Elise. "The Role of Sublimity in the Development of Modernist Aesthetics." *The Journal of Aesthetics and Art Criticism* 40, no. 4 (Summer 1982): 421–29.

Melling, Antoine Ignace. *Voyage pittores*

Michasiw, Kim Ian. "Nine Revisionist Theses on the Picturesque." *Representations* 38 (Spring 1992): 76–100.

Murphy, Rhoads. "Bigots or Informed Observers? A Periodization of Pre-Colonial English and European Writing on the Middle East." *Journal of the American Oriental Society* 110, no. 2 (April–June 1990): 291–303.

Nochlin, Linda. "The Imaginary Orient." *Art in America* (May 1983): 119–91.

Orestano, Francesca. “The Revd William Gilpin and the Picturesque: Or, Who’s Afraid of Doctor Syntax?” *Garden History* 31, no. 2 (Winter 2003): 163–79.

Ortiz, Oscar Rodriguez, ed. *Imagenes de Humboldt*. Caracas: Monte Avila, 1983.

Ross, Stephanie. “The Picturesque: An Eighteenth-Century Debate.” *The Journal of Aesthetics and Art Criticism* 46, no. 3 (Winter 1987): 271–79.

Said, Edward W. *Orientalism*. London: Routledge and Kegan Paul, 1978.

Schiffer, Reinhold. *Oriental Panorama: British Travellers in Nineteenth Century Turkey*. Amsterdam: Rodopi Bv Editions, 1999.

Sontag, Susan. *On Photography*. London: Penguin, 1977.

Townsend, Dabney. “The Picturesque.” *The Journal of Aesthetics and Art Criticism* 55, no. 4 (Autumn 1997): 365–76.

Trachtenberg, Alan. *Classic Essays on Photography*. New Haven: Leetes Island Books, 1980.

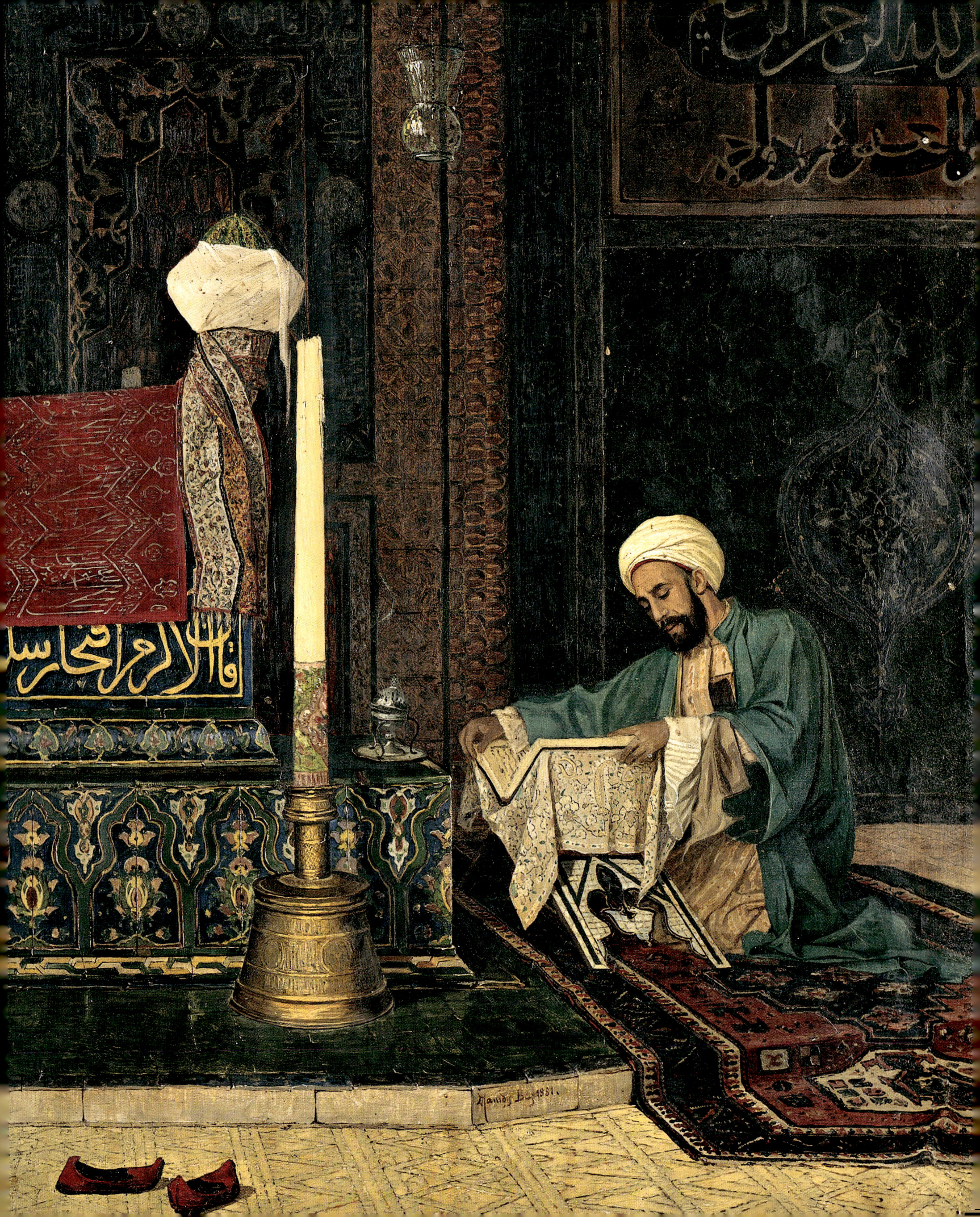
Hamdy Bey 1881.

VIII

Genealogies of Display

Cross-Cultural Networks at the 1880s Istanbul Exhibitions

Mary Roberts

In the summer of 1880 a dispute broke out in the Istanbul press around a collaborative art exhibition held in Tarabya on the shores of the Bosporus. This controversy between the Ottoman critic Abdullah Kâmil writing for *Osmanlı* and the anonymous reviewer for the local English-language paper *The Constantinople Messenger*, centered on how to characterize the artistic network that was formed through this event. Both claimants asserted the importance of this initiative for the development of an artistic community in Istanbul, but the precise terms of that alliance were fiercely disputed. The issue at stake in this contested politics of display was how to construe the geo-political allegiances of the varied participants and thus the overall significance of the event. On the one hand the critic for the English-language newspaper construed it as a collaboration forged from distinct national entities because the exhibition included "English, French, Italian, German, Belgian, Greek, Armenian and Turkish artists."[1] Strenuously rejecting this characterization, the Ottoman critic Abdullah Kâmil counterclaimed the event as an "Ottoman exhibition," because "nothing else but Ottoman themes could be seen there."[2] He reclassified the participants into the broader categories of Ottoman and non-Ottoman insistently incorporating the Muslim Ottoman and non-Muslim Ottoman–Armenian artists within the first category.

The heated nature of this debate about which terms to use to characterize the geo-political allegiances of the exhibition's participants can be interpreted in the broader context of contemporary international relations, specifically disputes about the territorial integrity of the Ottoman Empire. In emphasizing separate national identities, the English-language critic assumed a position that was antagonistic to the Ottoman critic who responded by asserting the more expansive category of "Ottoman." Invoked in this context by a member of the Empire's elite, the term expresses an ideal of an overarching Ottoman identity encompassing the Empire's heterogeneous religious, ethnic and regional groups.[3] Such questions of classification were particularly charged for the Ottoman State in this period in the face of the ongoing and urgent territorial threats to the Empire. As a result of the recent Russo-Turkish war and the Congress of Berlin of 1878, as Şükrü Hanioğlu argues: [in this decade] "European and Ottoman interpretations of the empire's territorial integrity had never been further apart." The most dramatic impact of these events for the Ottomans resulted from a shift in British foreign policy that signaled "the end of active British support for the Ottoman Empire."[4] The consequences of these events that occurred two years prior to the Istanbul exhibition makes sense of the Ottoman writer's strenuous rejection of *The Constantinople Messenger's* interpretation of the exhibition and why he reconfigures it according to the prevailing supranational ideology of Ottomanism, that asserts unity within a multi-religious and multi-ethnic Ottoman Empire; an ideological buttress for maintaining the Empire's territorial diversity.

Following the contours of this argument, the lines of this dispute could be drawn around two seemingly incompatible characterizations of the artistic network; Ottoman versus Orientalist. A closer study of this and other nineteenth-century Istanbul exhibitions, however, reveals a more complex set of engagements that cut across any dualistic interpretation of cultural alliances. I will argue that these Istanbul collaborations require a more complex understanding of network relations, that takes into account not just broader national allegiances but also cross-cultural connections premised on the pedagogic, gender-based and local alliances that intersected and at times cut across these broader political categories. An approach that emphasizes these alliances shifts us away from the tendency to conceptualize national cultures as circumscribed or self-contained entities and instead focuses our critical attention on nodes of cross-cultural contact. In other words it allows us to scrutinize critically what the organizing term British Orientalism might mean in the context of Ottoman Istanbul. This does not evacuate considerations of power from the analysis of these Istanbul art exhibitions. It does, however, construe the cultural field in terms of a more decentered and contested model of power relations and focuses us on the historical moments and particular sites where cross-cultural alliances were formed and renegotiated. Such an approach, I would argue, gets closer to an understanding of the complexity of the interactions that took place in the sphere of visual culture in the "contact zone" between Ottoman painters, visiting Europeans, European resident artists and non-Muslim Ottomans in the capital of the Ottoman Empire in the late nineteenth century.

* * *

The initiative for this exhibition in 1880 in Tarabya and the one the following year in Pera, came from the Reverend George Washington, the Anglican priest attached to Istanbul's British Embassy. The first exhibition prompted the formation of the "ABC Club," a suitably germinal acronym that encompassed the local nature of this collaborative venture in its full title: that is, the "Artists of the Bosphorus and Constantinople." A rudimentary catalog accompanied both exhibitions.[5] For Washington, his idea of an art society for Istanbul was modeled on the amateur clubs that flourished in England and its primary aim was rather loosely constituted as a "means for mutual improvement" for those involved.[6] The initiative was enthusiastically received by the critic for *The Constantinople Messenger*, who saw it as a springboard for fostering "culture, artistic taste and ability" among "Constantinople society" which, the critic claimed, "knows very little about itself or what it is really worth, owing to the fact of its being split up into colonies, and again into subdivisions of those colonies."[7]

The event was as much part of the world of diplomatic relations as of visual culture, with the presence of the French and British embassies prominently manifested. The current British deputation was well represented in the organizing committee while Albion's diplomatic lineage in the city was celebrated in the exhibition through a portrait of former ambassador, Sir Henry Layard. The British contributors were primarily long-term Istanbul residents. They included affiliates of the British embassy (Reverend George Washington and his wife) and other members of the Anglican church community such as Charles Curtis, Chaplain of Galata's Crimean Memorial Church and his sister Mary Adelaide Walker. The legal fraternity was also involved through the inclusion of paintings by Edwin Pears who was appointed to the European bar in Istanbul in 1873.[8] So too the exhibitions included wives of those who had established careers as Ottoman State employees, for example Edith Katherine Hobart-Hampden. She was the wife of Hobart Paşa who had served in the Ottoman navy from 1867. The exhibitor referred to only by his surname "Robertson" was James Robertson the painter and renowned photographer who had been the chief engraver to the Ottoman Imperial Mint from the early 1840s.[9] Despite their importance in Istanbul's art community, with the exception of Robertson, none of these amateur artists have been included in recent exhibitions of nineteenth-century British Orientalism. The French legation was also represented at the highest local levels in these Istanbul exhibitions with the ambassador himself, Tissot, exhibiting sixteen sketches of Morocco. The opening ceremony underscored these foreign diplomatic networks through the presence of these and other European national representatives.[10]

While the rituals of these 1880s exhibitions signaled their connection to the domain of foreign affairs and their integration within Istanbul's expatriate communities, they were preceded, and perhaps inspired, by two exhibitions in the 1870s that were embedded in Ottoman cultural politics. Although these two earlier exhibitions were not directly under the auspices of the palace or the Ottoman State, their organizer, Şeker Ahmed Paşa, the Ottoman painter, former student of Gérôme and Boulanger, and later aide-de-camp to Sultan Abdülaziz had made strategic overtures that ensured the exhibition openings were well attended by senior Ottoman bureaucrats.[11] Portraits of Sultan Abdülaziz and his son Şehzade Yusuf Izzedin Efendi were prominent in these exhibitions and in 1875, the Ottoman State provided the venue, the Dârülfünûn, University building.[12] Kargopoulo's photograph of the *Tombeau du Sul. Mahmoud* (Fig. 8.1) shows that the presence of the Resim Sergisi/Exposition des Beaux Arts in the Dârülfünûn building was promoted by a sign in Ottoman and French that was prominently displayed on the corner of the building visible from the busy thoroughfare the Divanyolu. As Mustafa Cezar argues, these exhibitions were part of a lineage of Palace support for the arts that was crucial for the emergence of art in the public sphere in the Ottoman capital and thus were important in the development of modern Turkish painting.[13] Such high level Ottoman support for the exhibitions of 1873 and 1875 contrasts with the 1880s exhibitions which, judging from press reportage, did not inspire, nor did the organizers solicit, the same level of official Ottoman engagement.

One could argue that these divisions between foreign diplomatic and Ottoman elite support are also mirrored in the spatial logic of the exhibition venues, with the first two organized by the Ottoman painter in the precincts of the old city

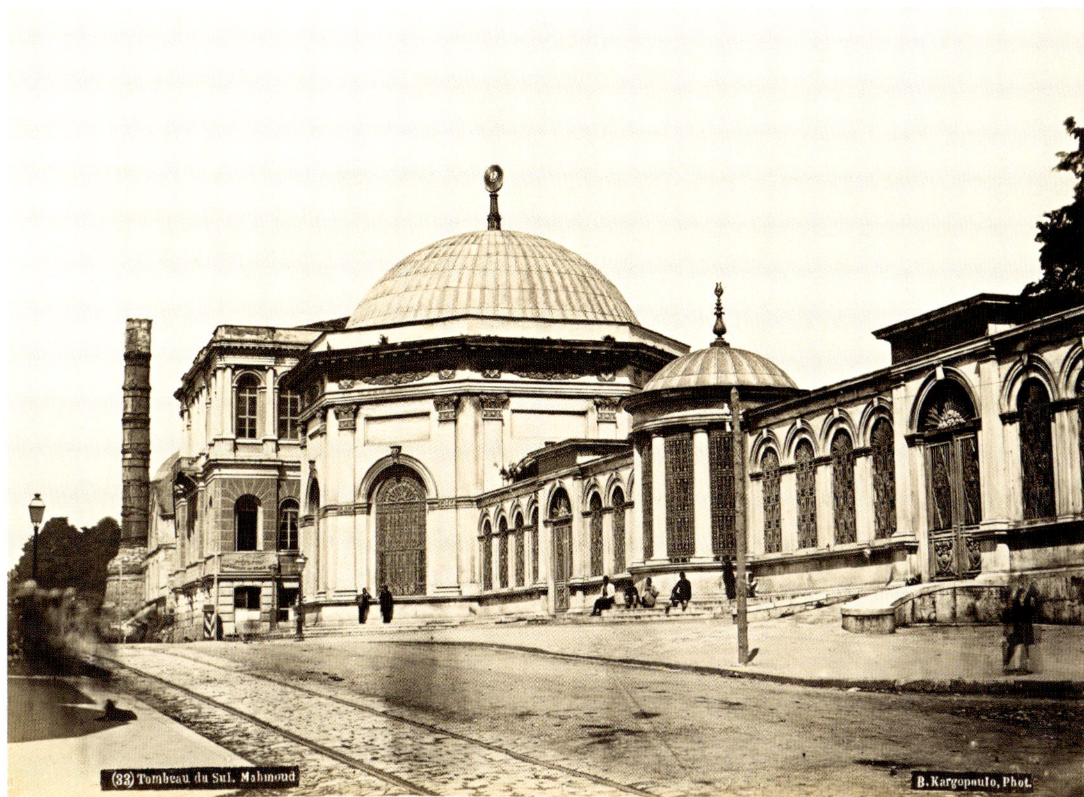

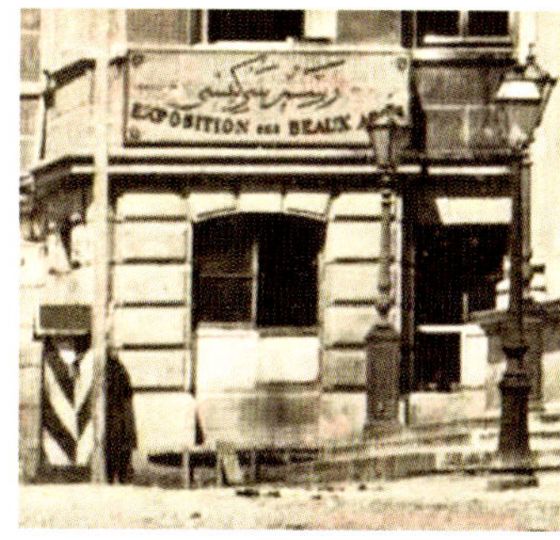

Figure 8.1 *Tombeau du Sul. Mahmoud*, and detail, Vassilaki Kargopoulo (1826–1886). Research Library, Getty Research Institute, Los Angeles, (96.R.14).

and the second two, in the hands of Istanbul's foreign residents, located in the spaces of the city associated with these foreign communities. So too each exhibition was held in institutional contexts that aligned them with the broader interests of these respective groups. The first two, held at the Imperial School of Arts and Trades and the University were locations that allied these art initiatives with contemporaneous Ottoman education reform.[14] In 1880, by contrast, the venue was the Greek School for Girls, a private educational institution in Tarabya the Bosporus village where the summer residences of the British and French legations were located. The Pera exhibition of 1881 was held in an entertainment venue in the Tepebaşı Municipal Gardens (across from where the Pera Museum is now located).[15]

Yet pursuing a rigidly dualistic reading of these four exhibitions is too simplistic in terms of the spatial divisions of the Ottoman capital, which as Zeynep Çelik has argued, does not conform to the divisions of other colonial cities.[16] Although the differing institutional contexts and nationalities of the organizers are significant, there was a complex mixture of exhibitors and a significant continuity of both Ottoman painters and foreign resident artists at each event. So too, it is clear that the organizers of all these exhibitions conceived of their audience as encompassing both Ottomans and foreigners with the dual signage advertising the venue in Ottoman and French. Also for the duration of the exhibition in 1881, a specific time was designated on a Saturday for attendance by women only in order to encourage Muslim women visitors.[17] This highlights the limitations of dichotomous thinking in relation to these Istanbul exhibitions. I would argue that it was the very openness of the structure of the event in 1880 that led to the claims and counterclaims in the local press about the geo-political alliances of its participants that I cited at the beginning of this chapter. Further exploration of the precise terms of the Ottoman critic's response to this exhibition enables insights into these intersecting networks.

Responding to the *Constantinople Messenger*'s division of the exhibition participants into separated national entities, the *Osmanlı* reviewer reclassified the artists as Ottoman and non-Ottoman. Where the foreign language newspaper claimed only two Turkish participants, Princess Nazlı Hanım and Osman Hamdi Bey, the *Osmanlı* critic contested this narrow categorization, objecting to the assumption that "a non-Muslim cannot be Ottoman," citing in evidence that "even though some of these people are not Muslim they have nevertheless become Ottoman state employees." At issue here were the Ottoman-Armenian painters and the three encompassed within this rubric were Verjin Serviçen, Krikor Köçeoğlu and Boğos Şaşiyan. Verjin Serviçen exhibited a portrait painting of her father, whom the Ottoman critic noted was a member of the Senate,[18] and in doing so this critic made a claim for the inclusiveness of the Ottoman Empire on the basis of non-Muslim political representation. (Figure 8.2 is a photograph of Dr. Serviçen.) The second artist, Krikor Köçeoğlu, was associated with the revival of Kufic script and he exhibited calligraphy in this style.[19] Both he and the third artist, Boğos Şaşiyan, had collaborated on the *Usûl-i Mimari-i Osmanî (l'architecture Ottomane)* project for the Ottoman Pavilion at the 1873 Vienna exhibition. Ahmet Ersoy characterizes this project as expressing "in distinctly architectural terms, the Tanzimat's official discourse on Ottoman identity."[20] It is hardly surprising then that the *Osmanlı* critic should encompass them as exemplars of Ottomanism in his 1880 review.

The foreign expatriate artists are also brought within this encompassing Ottoman interpretation of the event, praised as "friends of our country." The British resident artist, Mary Adelaide Walker was singled out in particular for rendering "a great service" to the Ottoman Empire as an art teacher to the Ottoman-Armenian Verjin Serviçen.[21] In signaling the pedagogic value of these women's networks, this critic underscores collaborations traversing national boundaries that had been in operation in Istanbul for several decades prior to the exhibition he was reviewing. By the 1880s Walker was well established as one of the city's key art teachers offering public lectures on drawing as well as ladies' drawing classes and publicly exhibiting her work in her studio in Pera on "Rue Terjiman."[22] She had been employed between 1870 and 1872 as the drawing and watercolor teacher at the *Dârülmuallimât*, Women's Teacher Training College.[23] This school established in 1870 was another important Ottoman State education reform initiative. These informal Istanbul women's art networks were also evident in the international arena when the work of both Walker and her pupil Serviçen was exhibited together, among a select group of Ottoman painters and photographers, at the Ottoman pavilion of the 1867 International exposition in Paris.[24] Serviçen exhibited a painting entitled *Circassian Girl Serving Coffee* while Mary Walker exhibited a portrait of Sultan Abdülaziz, an extremely prestigious commission because the Sultan himself attended this exhibition in Paris.[25] The fact that Walker was entrusted with such a distinguished commission is indicative of the respect with which she was held in the Ottoman capital among members of the imperial family, despite being an artist with no professional prestige in Europe. This advantageous connection for Walker was initiated by the women of the Ottoman royal family whose harem portraits she had painted soon after her arrival in Istanbul in the 1850s. Sultan Abdülmecid's

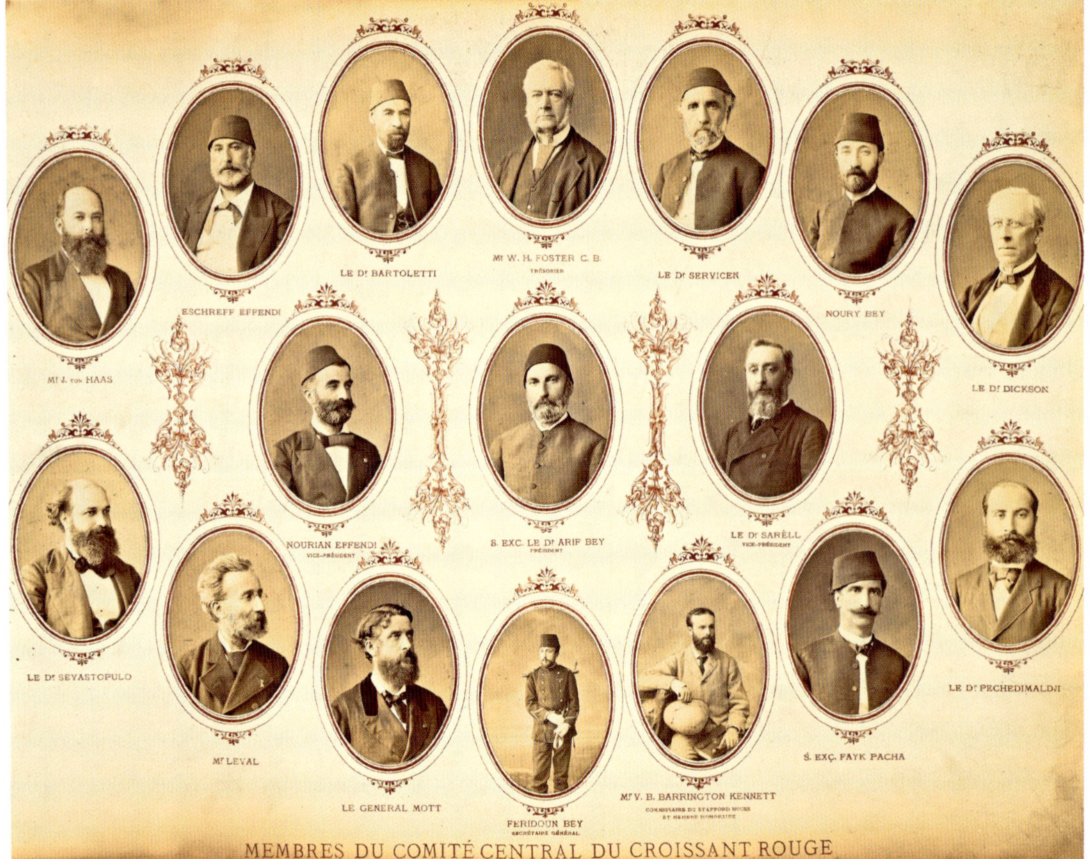

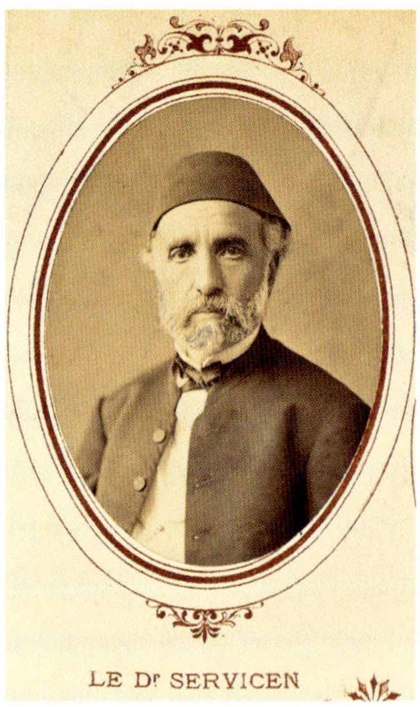

Figure 8.2 *Le Dr Serviçen, Membres du Comité central du Croissant Rouge*, in *Album de la Société ottomane de secours aux blessés militaires: Guerre 1877–1878*, folio 01, Research Library, Getty Research Institute, Los Angeles (96.R.14).

daughter, Fatma Sultan, was one of Walker's most powerful women patrons.[26]

Walker and Serviçen are by no means an isolated case of women's pedagogic networks at the Istanbul exhibitions. The inclusion of four still-life paintings by Mustafa Fazıl Paşa's daughter Princess Nazlı Hanım, points to further informal cross-cultural social ties. While Osman Hamdi Bey's painting in this same exhibition, *İki Müzisyen Kız* (Two Musician Girls), 1880 (Fig. 8.3) celebrates young women's accomplishment in

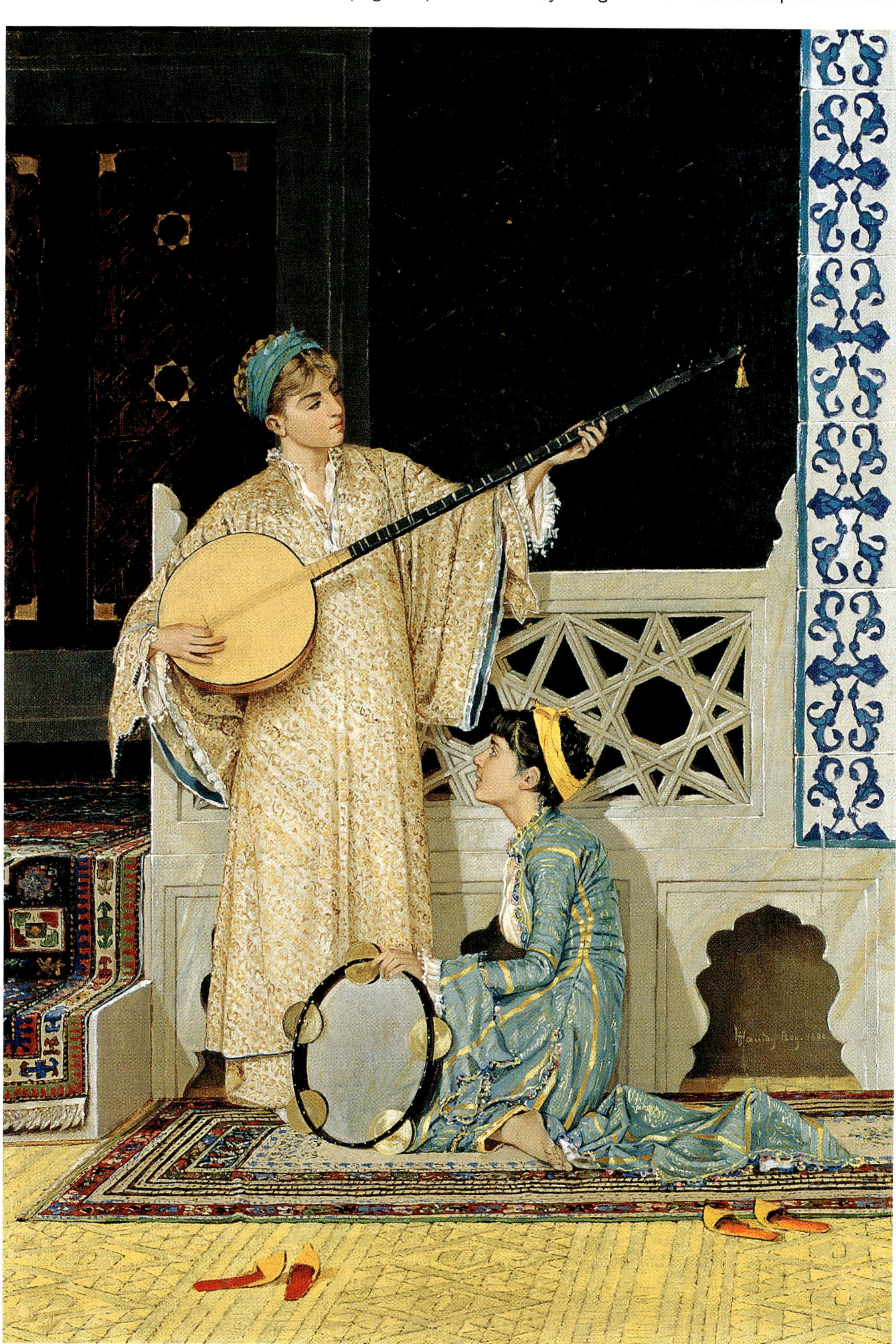

Figure 8.3 *İki Müzisyen Kız,* (Two Musician Girls), Osman Hamdi Bey (1842–1910), 1880, oil on canvas, 58 x 39 cm, Suna and İnan Kıraç Foundation Orientalist Paintings Collection, Istanbul.

the traditional arts of music, Nazlı's own contribution is evidence of a nascent interest in the practice of painting among elite Ottoman women. One of the early inspirations for her interest in art was the Danish/Polish painter Elisabeth Jerichau-Baumann who had been commissioned to paint the young Princess's portrait in 1870. Jerichau-Baumann had also been an art tutor for Nazlı's uncle, the Ottoman-Egyptian Prince Halim Paşa and his wife, and had exhibited two portraits in Şeker Ahmed Paşa's Istanbul exhibition in 1875.[27] These cross-cultural connections in Istanbul were reduced to Orientalist cliché in a report of the 1880 exhibition published in Denmark that year. Instead of reviewing the art, the report in *Dagbladet* focused on the personal lives of the two Muslim painters, Osman Hamdi Bey and Princess Nazlı. The reviewer was particularly fixated on rumors about Princess Nazlı Hanım and her famous husband Halil Şerif Paşa, the renowned art collector and Ottoman statesman, whose notoriety in Europe was summed up in a reference to his "[squandering] an enormous fortune during the wildest of escapades." Revealing a distinct preference for biography over art, the entire 1880 Istanbul exhibition is reduced to an Orientalist stereotype of Turkish despotism. Any serious consideration of Ottoman art practice or patronage was sidelined in this Danish review in favor of a rumor of Nazlı's virtual imprisonment by her so-called, "unworthy husband."[28]

Back in Istanbul in 1880, in his review of the ABC club exhibition, the *Osmanlı* reviewer by contrast cited a more elevated European response to his own art criticism. Specifically Abdullah Kâmil noted that his review published some months earlier of Osman Hamdi Bey's painting, *Türbe of Çelebi Sultan Mehmet*, which had been exhibited at the French embassy in Tarabya and again in the Abdullah Frères studio in Pera, had inspired the Austrian art Museum to contact the artist to purchase the work.[29] This painting was one of a number of Bursa's Yeşil Türbe that Osman Hamdi Bey produced in the 1880s including a work by the same title shown at the ABC club exhibition of 1881.[30] This work is likely to be the painting, *Yeşil Türbe'de Dua*, 1881 (Fig. 8.4). It was a theme that he revisited and reconfigured in the decades ahead representing both men and women within the Yeşil Türbe.[31]

Abdullah Kâmil's extended response to the painting exhibited in the Abdullah Frères photographic studio in 1880 offers a valuable insight into the reception of Osman Hamdi Bey's art in Istanbul. It reveals the contemporary political resonances of his Bursa religious paintings in this decade and clearly allies the ideology of Ottomanism with a particular esthetic response to the work. Abdullah Kâmil praised Sultan Mehmed I (r. 1413–1421) as a man who was:

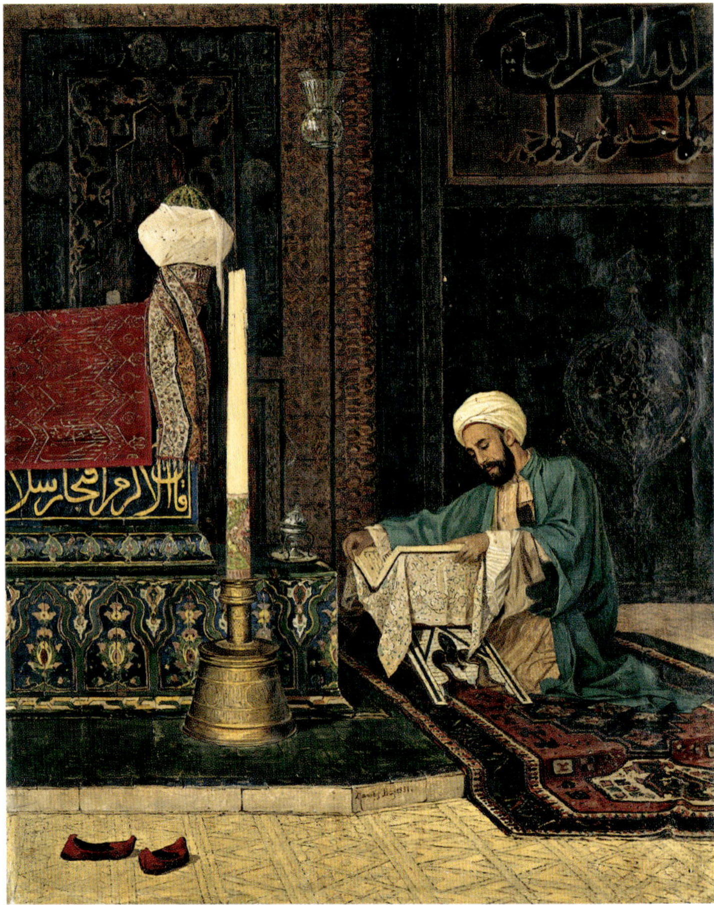

Figure 8.4 *Yeşil Türbe'de Dua* (Prayer in the Green Tomb), Osman Hamdi Bey (1842–1910), 1881. © Christie's Images Limited 2011.

> more illustrious than all our other illustrious sovereigns [and who] succeeded in rebuilding the State from its ruins, despite the complicated plots and intrigues which surrounded him on all sides … he reunited the Ottoman Empire in its entirety under his powerful rule and thus provided the precedent for the glorious victories of his successors by giving them back the way to Constantinople.[32]

Stressing the contemporary political import of this painting and the patriotism of the artist himself, the reviewer asserts that "In taking as a theme for his works of art the celebration of such men, a painter like Hamdy Bey, emulating the glorious Sovereign he thus recalls to our filial memory, adds to his merit as an artist another and even more praiseworthy merit: that of the true patriot." This critic articulates with great clarity what a number of scholars have identified as Osman Hamdi Bey's historical genre painting, where the "reality effect" of Orientalist painting is redeployed to represent Ottoman cultural history.[33] Osman Hamdi Bey's choice of the Yeşil Türbe in Bursa was particularly resonant in the context of a revivalist

Ottoman discourse where the restoration of the Ottoman-Islamic heritage of the former capital, was linked to emergent notions of Ottoman cultural patrimony.[34]

This critic's extensive visual analysis, however, also reveals a distinctive engagement with the language of academic art that inspired an affective spectatorial experience that we might call a "devotional effect." The critic responds to the pared down space of the türbe, the "noble simplicity" of the composition, "the generally pure and gentle tone that reigns within," the "complete truth of all its detail" as well as their "simple and conscientious execution." "Taken together" he asserts, "all these impressive qualities produce upon the soul of the viewer exactly the same profound and grave emotion it would experience, and the artist himself truly experienced, in contemplating the actual objects, the sacred place, and the moving scene that are the subject of his work."[35] The critic responds to the austere simplicity of Osman Hamdi's religious painting. This is not the sensuous pleasure in details that we associate with the Aestheticism of John Frederick Lewis's art and which we see in his 1869 painting of the Bursa Yeşil Türbe (Fig. 8.5) where the eye is diverted by the

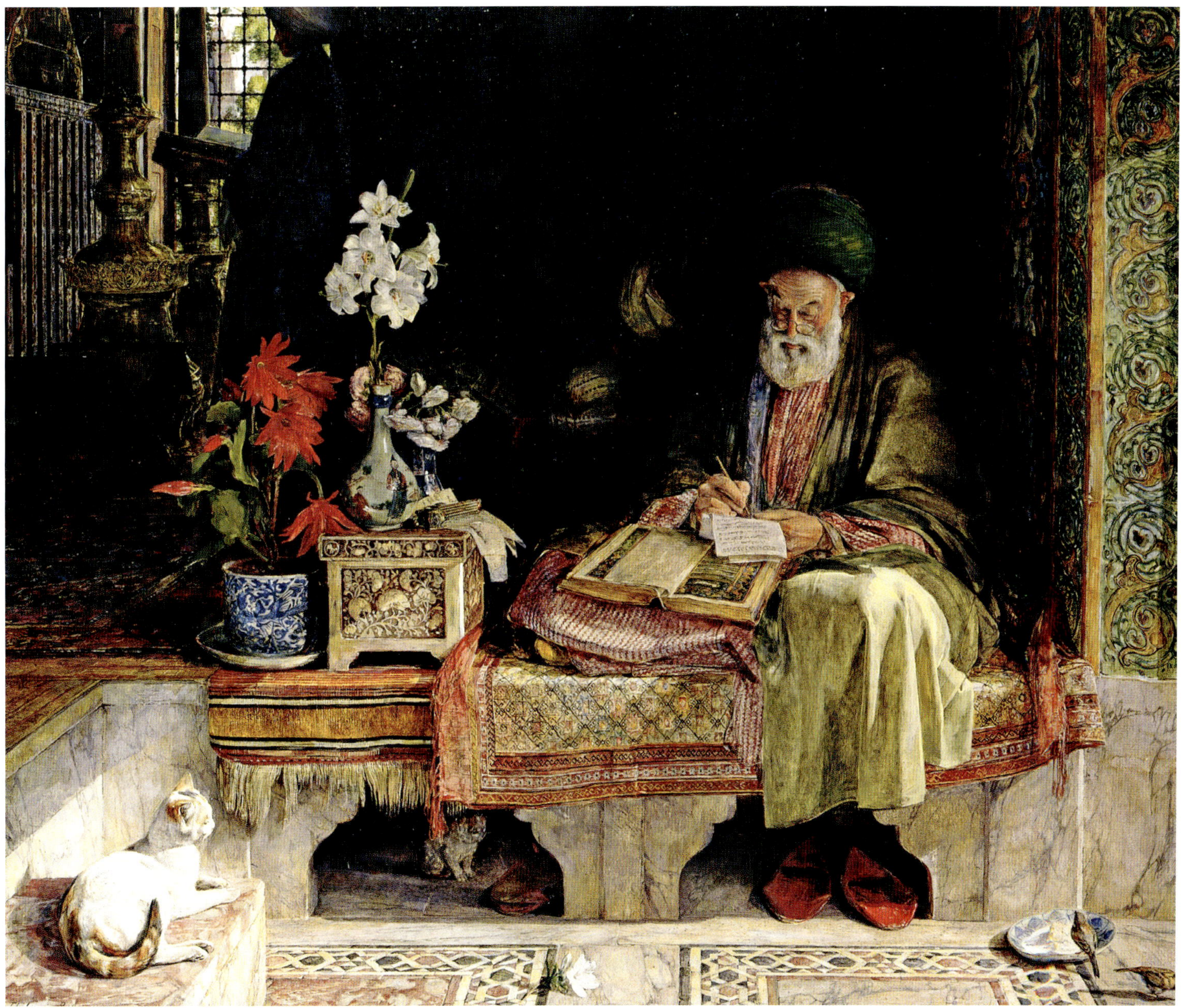

Figure 8.5 *The Commentator on the Koran: Interior of a Royal Tomb, Bursa, Asia Minor*, John Frederick Lewis (1804–1876), 1869, oil on wood, 62.5 x 75.5 cm, Elton Hall Collection.

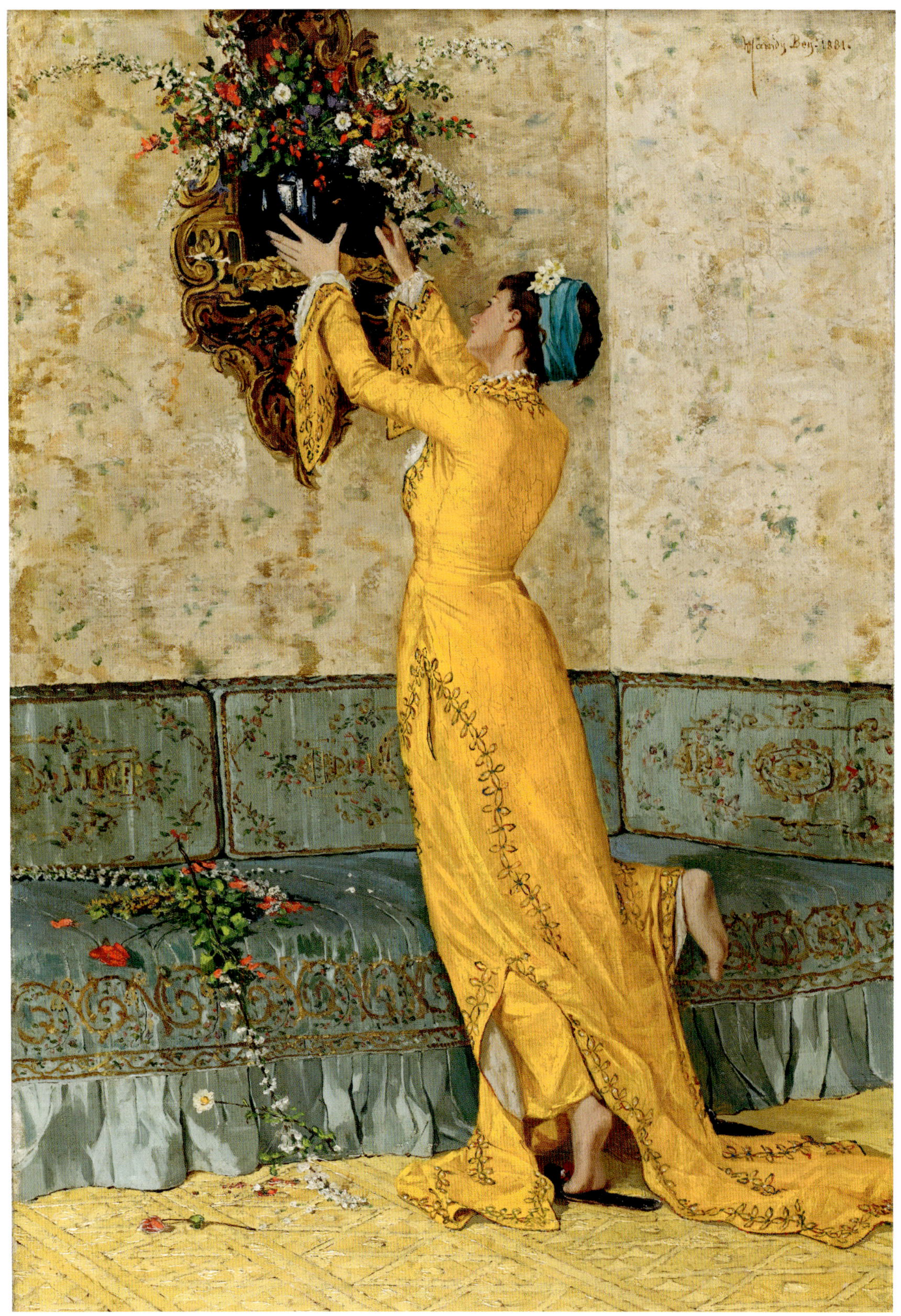

Figure 8.6 *Vazo Yerleştiren Kız*, (Young Girl Placing a Vase) Osman Hamdi Bey (1842–1910), 1881, oil on canvas, 55 x 37 cm, Feryal and Kemal Gülman Collection.

anecdotal details of exquisite flowers and the superbly rendered carpet on which the religious man is seated. The way the details operate in Osman Hamdi Bey's religious paintings also differs from the sensuous pleasures evident in his own images of women from these years, such as the one modeled on his wife Naile that he exhibited at the Istanbul exhibition of 1881 (Fig. 8.6). All the details in the türbe painting focus on the act of devotion, a devotion that the Ottoman critic articulates as encompassing both a political and religious dimension.[36] He writes:

> How could this emotion not communicate itself to every truly Ottoman heart with the same force as felt by the patriotic artist himself, for whom this ancient splendour, with its shawls, carpets, enamels, bronzes, book bindings, embroideries, and its stained glass—all these wonders of art and industry brought together by Sultan Mohammed Chelebi in his own turbé, his greatest and final work, are not magical objects of art and curiosities to make all the amateurs crazy; but rather they are august witnesses of our beginnings, of the glory of our ancestors, which invite us to remember their great history so that we might be like them.[37]

Through the invocation to venerate one of the Ottoman Empire's great forebears, Abdullah Kâmil's interpretation of Osman Hamdi Bey's painting articulates a clear sense of belonging via a shared devotion to cultural and political heritage. This is an invocation of the Ottoman past as a model for the future.

How then did foreign resident painters who participated in the Istanbul exhibitions articulate their relationship to the culture in which some of them had lived for over thirty years? In contrast to Osman Hamdi Bey's historical genre paintings, many of the works by the British artists were picturesque Istanbul landscapes, views of Büyükada, the Galata Kulesi and many of the familiar sites along the Bosporus. Although most of these paintings are untraced, several of these artists published Istanbul landscapes in their memoirs and accounts of the city. Edwin Pears, for example, published his watercolor *Constantinople from the Bosporus* in his memoir *Forty Years in Constantinople* of 1916 and a number of the same Istanbul sites that James Robertson represented in his hand-painted photographs exhibited in 1881, had earlier been published as prints in the English translation of Théophile Gautier's travelog, *Constantinople of Today* and, as Bahattin Öztuncay notes, in the *Illustrated London News*.[38] So too, Mary Adelaide Walker published her sketches of Istanbul in her 1897 travelog *Old Tracks and New Landmarks*. Through the unique conjunction of text and image in Walker's volume, rather than an invocation of belonging via cultural patrimony, Walker instead articulated an esthetics of attachment to the cosmopolitan capital that I would term the resident picturesque. This provides one way of thinking about the particular significance for the British expatriates of this cluster of Istanbul landscapes at the 1880s exhibitions.

Walker's choice of pronoun in her title for her chapter on Istanbul, "Our Beautiful Waterway: Bosphorus Vignettes," is both plural and possessive, signaling the writer's identification with, and claim upon, the city. In nineteenth-century Istanbul this is an expatriate's provisional identification based on long-term residence within a foreign sovereign state, not underpinned by the territorial claims of imperialism. At the outset Walker distinguishes between her own subject-position and that of the casual tourist. She contrasts her intimate knowledge of the city with their fleeting, often erroneous impressions, but above all she is repelled by their failure to anticipate the cosmopolitan sophistication of the city in which they have arrived. For Walker this is signaled through their sartorial miscalculation, "they climb the steep ascent to Pera, displaying with delightful unconcern the most impossible costumes, well suited, perhaps, to tent life and the ruins of Baalbec, but of startling eccentricity in the very modern and up-to-date High Street of our suburb."[39] This was the district where Walker lived, where her studio was located as well as the church in which her brother was the appointed Chaplain. The distinction that Walker invokes between tourist and travel writer is a familiar rhetorical device of the genre through which the author establishes her authority, and yet what is particularly interesting in Walker's text is that she aligns her critique with different ways of viewing Istanbul. What she disparages most in these frivolous visitors is that they look but do not see, and she counterpoints their blindness with her own insights. According to Walker, their desire for a singular vantage point from which to overview the city produces a superficial stereotypical European view that generalizes, exoticizes and bifurcates Istanbul. Instead she proposes an alternative mode of viewing, one that was familiar to any resident who traveled in the boats that regularly traversed the Bosporus. She characterizes this mode as a "moving panorama." Walker writes:

> To appreciate the beauties of this celebrated waterway, they should be taken in detail, and are best seen, if possible, from a caïque, or steam-launch, or from the cabin of a steamer, almost on a level with the water, where, through the little windows on the shore side, you obtain a moving panorama of exquisite vignettes.[40]

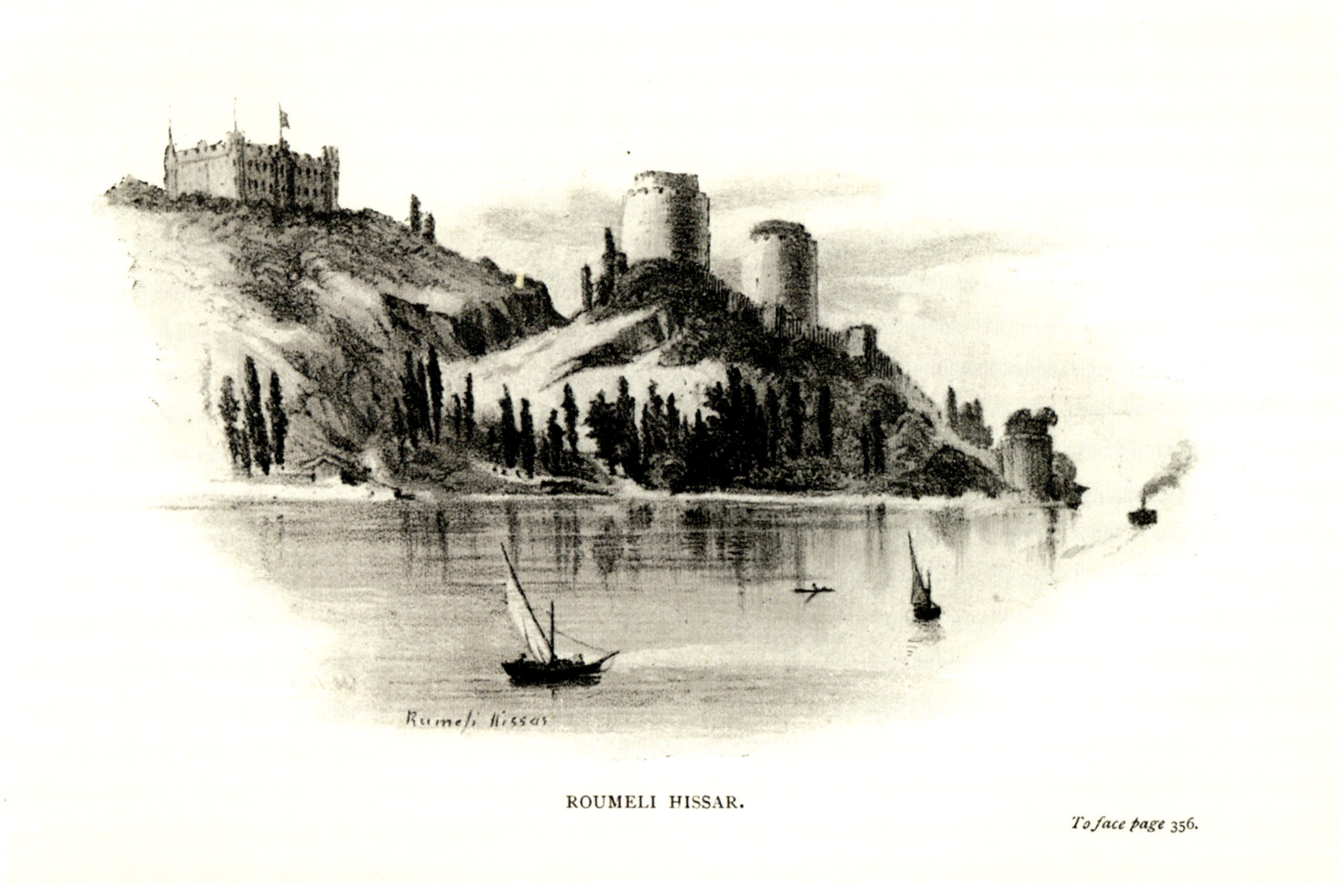

Figure 8.7 *Roumeli Hissar*, Mary Adelaide Walker, From Mary Adelaide Walker, *Old Tracks and New Landmarks. Wayside Sketches in Crete, Macedonia, Mitylene, etc*, (London: Richard Bentley, 1897), illustration facing page 356.

Through the descriptive flow of her chapter's narrative, Walker provides us this "moving panorama" of detailed and precise readings of the city. The accompanying sketch titled, *Roumeli Hissar* (Fig. 8.7) provides that water vantage point, framed as if from a larger ship looking down onto smaller water craft in the foreground, across to the edge of the shore and up to the landmark fortress towers. Her text illuminates the range of architectural details that are seen here, emphasizing that "to the old inhabitant, [this view] offers more startling contrasts, more clear evidence of change, than any spot on these historic shores."[41] Here Walker's text provides a great deal more specificity about place than is readily discernable in her accompanying illustration. Where the sketch contrasts the "modernity" of the American-funded Robert College with the historic fortress that was crucial to the Ottoman conquest of the city, her text presents a more complex view, including among her observations about the modernity of this site the yalı (waterside mansion) of the revered former Ottoman statesman and reformer Ahmed Vefik Paşa. Walker conveys her fond personal reminiscences of his "incorruptible integrity, his great learning, and his splendid library."[42] And yet Walker's textual and visual "tour" concludes in an elegaic tone that blends millennialism with what was by this point a familiar British vision of the inevitability of the Ottoman Empire's demise, through failures in leadership. Forecasting a bleak future, she characterizes it as "this fair land of 'lost opportunities.'"[43]

In Walker's vignettes, Istanbul is not represented as the timeless Orient, but rather as a city marked by contrasts between historic sites, traditional practices and modernization. The historic beauties of the city and its surrounds are suffused with the here and now of the modernity of a cosmopolitan city.[44] The picturesque and the fragmentary esthetics of the vignette becomes a way of sustaining these disjunctions without contradiction. Walker privileges the British and American contribution to this modernization but the avatars of progress in her text are not only European. She plays to

Orientalist notions of the city's exoticism, through tales of palace life and "the insensate luxury of the East"[45] but these moments of objectification are counterpointed with a more sympathetic view premised upon the bonds of friendship with individual men and women of the Ottoman elite. These contradictions between intimacy and distance disclose the conflicted sense of belonging of the foreign expatriate, who describes herself as an "old inhabitant" of the city but is nonetheless a foreigner. Between Walker's notion of the resident picturesque and Abdullah Kâmil's interpretation of Osman Hamdi Bey's historical genre painting, we see two very different definitions of belonging. Both are premised on personalizing a connection to place but with very different implications for the future. Walker's dwells on the failures of leadership and reform, whereas for Abdullah Kâmil the glorious Ottoman past with its exemplar of great leadership provides a model for the future.

* * *

In this chapter I have focused on the competing claims of two groups in these exhibitions. On the one hand the British resident painters and critics who claimed a commonality between the artists of different nationalities on the basis of a shared affinity with the city and who distinguished their notion of the resident picturesque from the superficial insights of the British tourist. This concept of artistic community based on an affinity among separate national entities in Istanbul was clearly incompatible with prevailing concepts of Empire for the Ottoman critic for whom this categorization too closely reflected the divisive foreign policy of the European powers that threatened the integrity of the Ottoman Empire in the political domain. Instead this critic reconfigured the 1880 exhibition as an exemplar of the prevailing supranational ideology of Ottomanism and embraced those Ottoman, Ottoman-Armenian and resident foreigners whose work was compatible with this ideal. Extending this approach into the realm of esthetic interpretation, the same critic had earlier argued that Osman Hamdi Bey's painting of the Bursa Türbe invoked an absorptive spectatorial experience that fused religious devotion with patriotism. My emphasis within this chapter on interpreting these exhibitions through the lens of the Ottoman critic's response in 1880 is not to read it as an "Ottoman" rather than an "Orientalist" event. Doing so would erroneously transform the relatively inchoate form of these amateur exhibitions into an ideological program. Rather my purpose has been to map the *multiplexity* of intersecting network structures that preceded, intersected and emerged out of these events, networks that informed the critical standoff that emerged in 1880 but cut across any neat separations along national boundaries.[46]

The distinctiveness of these Istanbul exhibitions is highlighted by situating them within the broader context of nineteenth-century exhibition culture. On the one hand, the contribution of a range of Ottoman artists and the contemporary critical response distinguishes them from European societies of Orientalist painting such as the one in France that Roger Benjamin has characterized as "a collectivity authoring Orientalism."[47] On the other hand, because these Istanbul exhibitions were loosely structured events that encompassed such a diverse range of agendas, including those of the resident expatriates, they are also to be distinguished from the official Ottoman exhibition projects at the European Worlds Fairs and the development of Istanbul's State-sponsored museums that emerged in the same period. Zeynep Çelik and Wendy Shaw among others have analyzed Ottoman museology and Ottoman pavilions at the Worlds' Fairs as the Empire's negotiated response to modernization and European imperialism.[48] The Istanbul exhibitions did not have such a programmatic agenda as did the State-sponsored Ottoman pavilions, although they intersected with contemporary Ottoman debates about the Empire's past as a resource from which to negotiate the contemporary context and to imagine its future.

While these Istanbul exhibitions have an important place in the histories of modern Turkish art, they have been absent from accounts of nineteenth-century British Orientalism. What might it mean to insert these exhibitions and their contested critical reception into a history of British Orientalist painting as part of the genealogy of the recent exhibition, *The Lure of the East: British Orientalist Painting*? That exhibition reassessed the legacy of British Orientalism which had previously been subsumed within a predominantly Franco-centric narrative. Addressing the Istanbul exhibitions challenges us to further expand the canon of British Orientalism by bringing into focus not just the professional British artists whose Orientalist paintings were produced for an audience in Britain, but the amateur British painters of Istanbul. These amateur resident artists were exhibiting their work to a more diverse audience, encompassing European expatriates and Istanbul's Ottoman elites. Drawing them into the analysis reveals a more sustained connection between British Orientalism and the initiatives of the Ottoman elites to develop art in the public sphere. So too, a study of these exhibitions highlights the limitations of the very project of studying Orientalism as bounded by national traditions because they bring into sharp focus cross-cultural networks and collaborations. A study of their fraught critical reception reveals some of the varied ways such collaborations were imagined, interpreted and contested in the Empire's capital in the late nineteenth century.

Notes

My sincere thanks to Evra Günhan, Nurullah Şenol, Hannah Williams, Gay McAuley, Samuel Williams and Rob Linrothe. The research for this essay was supported by the Australian Research Council and fellowships at the Getty Research Institute and the Sterling and Francine Clark Art Institute.

1 *The Constantinople Messenger*, Saturday, September 11, 1880.

2 Abdullah Kâmil, "Tarabya'da Sanayi-i Nefise Sergisi," *Osmanlı* 11 Şevval 1297, no. 14.

3 For a more extended analysis of debates about Ottoman identity and the ideology of Ottomanism across this period see Şükrü M. Hanioğlu, *A Brief History of the Late Ottoman Empire* (Princeton and Oxford: Princeton University Press, 2008), 104–8.

4 Ibid., 118 and 131.

5 The 1880 catalog remains untraced. My thanks to Garo Kürkman for making a copy of the 1881 catalog available to me.

6 *The Constantinople Messenger*, Saturday, September 11, 1880. The new club's proposed rules were published in *The Constantinople Messenger*, Thursday, September 16, 1880.

7 *The Constantinople Messenger*, Monday, September 13, 1880.

8 See Chandrika Kaul, *Dictionary of National Biography* online, Oxford University Press, 2004–8.

9 Robertson retired from the Imperial Mint in 1881 and departed Istanbul for Japan on November 9 that year. *James Robertson. Photographer of Istanbul* (Edinburgh: Scottish National Portrait Gallery, 1991), 9. On Robertson's Istanbul years see also: B. A. and H. K. Henisch, "Robertson of Constantinople," *Image. Journal of Photography and Motion Pictures of the International Museum of Photography at George Eastman House*, 17, no. 3 (1974): 1–11; B. A. and H. K. Henisch, "James Robertson of Constantinople," *History of Photography*, 8, no. 4 (1984): 299–313; B. A. and H. K. Henisch, "James Robertson of Constantinople: A Chronology," *History of Photography*, 14, no. 1 (1990): 23–32; Bahattin Öztuncay, *James Robertson Pioneer of Photography in the Ottoman Empire* (Istanbul: Eren, 1992); Luke Gartlan, "James Robertson and Felice Beato in the Crimea: Recent Findings," *History of Photography*, 29, no. 1 (2005): 72–80.

10 *The Constantinople Messenger*, Saturday, September 11, 1880.

11 The writer for *La Turquie* noted that the exhibition received the patronage of Mehmed Ruchdi Pacha (sic) (ex-Grand Vizier) and his Excellency Kemal Paşa (*La Turquie*, April 26, 1873: 2). The same paper later reported that the Sultan's son, Prince Youssouf (sic) Izzeddin Efendi planned to visit the exhibition (*La Turquie*, May 1, 1873: 1).

12 Ahmed Ali Bey announced in *La Turquie* that "The government ... put at our disposal the superb location of Darul-Fanoum (University) situated near the tomb of Sultan Mahmoud" (Ahmed, "Beaux-Arts. Deuxième exposition annuelle," *La Turquie*, May 11, 1875: 2). *La Turquie* later reported that the Sultan, himself a painter, requested that the exhibited works be brought to the palace for his examination (August 5, 1875: 2).

13 Mustafa Cezar, *Sanatta Batı'ya açılış ve Osman Hamdi*, 2 vols. (1971; Istanbul: Erol Kerim Aksoy Kültür, Eğitim, Spor ve Sağlık vakfı yayınları, 1995), 2, 422–45.

14 Şeker Ahmed Paşa was an art teacher at the *Sultanahmet Sanayi Mektebi* (Sultanahmet School of Arts and Trades) when the exhibition was held there in 1873. See Ömer Faruk Şerifoğlu and İlona Baytar, eds., *Şeker Ahmed Paşa, 1841–1907* (Istanbul: TBMM Milli Saraylar Daire Başkanlığı, 2008).

15 For an analysis of the education system in nineteenth-century Istanbul, see Carter Vaughn Findley, "Education," in *Ottoman Civil Officialdom. A Social History* (Princeton: Princeton University Press, 1989), 131–73.

16 Zeynep Çelik, *The Remaking of Istanbul: Portrait of an Ottoman City in the Nineteenth Century* (Washington: University of Washington Press, 1986).

17 The *Osmanlı* reviewer noted that the dual Ottoman and French signage was also used in the 1881 exhibition in Tepebası and that Saturdays from 3–5pm were designated as exclusively for women in order to encourage Muslim women's attendance. *Osmanlı* 5, Cumadelevvel 1298, no. 70.

18 *Osmanlı*, 11, Şevval 1297, no. 14. Dr. Serviçen, one of the officials of the medical school, was appointed by the Sultan to the Senate, Meclis-i Ayan in March 1877. When the elected parliament was disbanded in 1878 the members of the Senate were still in favor with the Sultan and continued to draw their salaries from the State (Yılmaz Kızıltan, "Meşrutiyetin İlânı ve İlk Osmanlı Meclis-i Mebusan'ı, *GÜ, Gazi Eğitim Fakültesi Dergisi*, 26, no. 1 (2006): 251–72). For a précis of the first Ottoman parliament see Hanioğlu, *A Brief History of the Late Ottoman Empire*, 118–21. For an analysis of the political ideals of Istanbul's Armenian elite in this period and Serviçen's prominent role in arguing for a culturally defined Armenian national awakening while maintaining the political status quo of the

Ottoman Millet structure, see Gerard J. Libaridian, "Nation and Fatherland in Nineteenth Century Armenian Political Thought," *Armenian Review*, Autumn (1983): 71–90.

19 For examples of his work in Kufic script see Garo Kürkman, *Armenian Painters in the Ottoman Empire, 1600–1923* (Istanbul: Matüsalem Uzmanlık ve Yayıncılık, 2004) 2, 532.

20 Ahmet Ersoy, "On the Sources of the 'Ottoman Renaissance': Architectural Revival and its Discourse during the Abdülaziz Era (1861–76)" (PhD diss., Harvard University, 2000), 198.

21 *Osmanlı*, 11, Şevval 1297, no. 14.

22 An article promoting Walker's art on display in her studio in "Rue Terdjiman" was published in *The Levant Herald*, Friday, April 23, 1875: 311; and her lectures on drawing and drawing classes are mentioned in *The Constantinople Messenger*, Wednesday, January 19, 1881: 2.

23 Walker recounts her experience as a teacher in this school in Mary Adelaide Walker, "The Turkish Girls School," *Eastern Life and Scenery. With Excursions in Asia Minor, Mytilene, Crete and Roumania* (London: Chapman and Hall, 1886), 1, 221–48.

24 Salahéddin Bey, *La Turquie à l'Exposition Universelle de 1867* (Paris: Libraire Hachette & Co., 1867), 139–46.

25 Walker's portrait was one of several portraits of Sultan Abdülaziz exhibited in the Ottoman pavilion—there were two others, one by Ahmed Ali Bey (at that time a young student in Paris) the other a photographic portrait by the Abdullah Frères while Amadeo Preziosi exhibited a watercolor entitled *La Garde noble de S. M. I. le Sultan.*

26 On Fatma Sultan's portrait commissions see Mary Roberts, "Contested Terrains: Women Orientalists and the Colonial Harem," in *Orientalism's Interlocutors. Painting, Architecture, Photography*, ed. Jill Beaulieu and Mary Roberts (Durham: Duke University Press, 2002), 179–203; and Mary Roberts, "The Politics of Portraiture behind the Veil," in *Art and the British Empire*, ed. Tim Barringer, Geoff Quilley and Douglas Fordham (Manchester: Manchester University Press, 2007), 223–36 and 399–402. See also Zeynep İnankur, Chapter 13 in the present volume.

27 Elisabeth Jerichau-Baumann writes about her experiences as painting tutor to Prince Halim Paşa in her memoir, Elisabeth Jerichau-Baumann, *Brogede Rejsebilleder* (Motley Images of Travel). (Copenhagen: Forlagsbureauet, 1881).

28 *Dagbladet*, November 11, 1880.

29 *Osmanlı*, 11, Şevval 1297, no. 14

30 In the catalog it is listed as number 170, *Tombeau à Brousse*. Both the reviews in *La Turquie* and *Osmanlı* identify it as the tomb of Çelebi Sultan Mehmed. *La Turquie* April 27, 1881: 1 and *Osmanlı* 5, Cumadelevvel 1298, no. 70.

31 Samuel Williams provides a very important analysis that interprets Osman Hamdi's 1882 painting of the Bursa Türbe in the context of contemporary Ottoman debates about historical consciousness, identity and perceptions of imperial belonging in his paper: Samuel Williams, "The Untimely Meditations of Osman Hamdi Bey: Competing Visions of History and Belonging in the Late Ottoman Empire," Turkish Studies Association Graduate Student Session, Middle East Studies Association Annual Meeting, November 17, 2006, Boston University, MA.

32 Abdullah Kâmil, "Le Turbé de Sultan Mohammed Tchélébi. Tableau par Hamdy Bey," *La Turquie*, August 20, 1880: 3.

33 For an historiographical account of the extensive debate about Osman Hamdi's engagement with academic realism see Edhem Eldem, "Osman Hamdi Bey ve Oryantalizm," *Dipnot* 2 (Winter/Spring 2004): 39–67.

34 On the transformation of Bursa in this period and its significance for notions of Ottoman patrimony see Beatrice St. Laurent, "Ottomanization and Modernization: the Architectural and Urban Development of Bursa and the Genesis of Tradition, 1839–1914" (PhD diss., Harvard University, 1989); and Ersoy, "On the Sources of the 'Ottoman Renaissance.'"

35 *La Turquie*, August 20, 1880: 3.

36 The absorptive effect of Osman Hamdi Bey's painting is further evident when we compare it with Lewis's watercolor sketch of a solitary worshipper in the same space, where the worshipper looks out of the picture, as if momentarily interrupted by the spectator/visitor. Illustrated in Nicholas Tromans, ed., *The Lure of the East. British Orientalist Painting* (London: Tate Publishing, 2008), 171.

37 *La Turquie*, August 20, 1880: 3.

38 Edwin Pears, *Forty Years in Constantinople. The Recollections of Sir Edwin Pears, 1873–1915* (London: Herbert Jenkins Ltd, 1916) illustration facing page 6. Théophile Gautier, *Constantinople of Today* (London: David Bogue, 1854). Bahattin Öztuncay, *The Photographers of Constantinople. Pioneers, Studios and Artists from Nineteenth-Century Istanbul* (Istanbul: Aygaz, 2003) 1, 150.

39 Mary Adelaide Walker, *Old Tracks and New Landmarks. Wayside Sketches in Crete, Macedonia, Mitylene, etc.* (London: Richard Bentley and Son, 1897), 331.

40 Ibid., 333.

41 Ibid., 356.

42 Ibid., 357. Walker's praise for Ahmed Vefik Paşa's civic reforms (in particular his restoration projects in the former Ottoman capital Bursa after the earthquake that caused so much destruction in 1855) is even more effusive in her chapter on Bursa. See Walker, *Eastern Life and Scenery*, 2, 107–9.

43 Walker, *Old Tracks and New Landmarks*, 360.

44 Walker notes, for example, evidence of the telegraph system, one of the indices of modern telecommunications, at the "Sweet Waters of Asia" (Ibid., 352). Such disjunctions are unfamiliar in the more well-known picturesque Orientalist representations of this leisure site. Walker's emphasis on an ideal of progress and the failures of this modernizing reform contrasts with the notion of "progress as loss" that Wendy Shaw identifies in Thomas Allom's picturesque Istanbul landscapes in her essay for this volume.

45 Walker, *Old Tracks and New Landmarks*, 343.

46 My approach here is influenced by the extensive debates over the last two decades about network theory. On the concept of multiplexity in particular see Roger V. Gould, "Multiple Networks and Mobilization in the Paris Commune, 1871," *American Sociological Review* 56 (1991): 716–29; and Mustafa Emirbayer and Jeff Goodwin, "Network Analysis, Culture, and the Problem of Agency," *American Journal of Sociology* 99, no. 6 (1994), 1411–54.

47 Roger Benjamin, *Orientalist Aesthetics. Art, Colonialism and French North Africa, 1880–1930* (Berkeley: University of California Press, 2003), 57.

48 Zeynep Çelik, *Displaying the Orient: Architecture of Islam at Nineteenth-Century World's Fairs* (Berkeley: University of California Press, 1992). Wendy Shaw, *Possessors and Possessed. Museums, Archaeology and the Visualization of History in the Late Ottoman Empire* (Berkeley: University of California Press, 2003).

Bibliography

Ahmed (Şeker Ahmed Paşa). "Beaux-Arts. Deuxième exposition annuelle." *La Turquie*, May 11, 1875.

Benjamin, Roger. *Orientalist Aesthetics. Art, Colonialism and French North Africa, 1880–1930*. Berkeley: University of California Press, 2003.

Çelik, Zeynep. *The Remaking of Istanbul: Portrait of an Ottoman City in the Nineteenth Century*. Washington: University of Washington Press, 1986.

Çelik, Zeynep. *Displaying the Orient: Architecture of Islam at Nineteenth-Century World's Fairs*. Berkeley: University of California Press, 1992.

Cezar, Mustafa. *Sanatta Batı'ya açılış ve Osman Hamdi* [1971]. Istanbul: Erol Kerim Aksoy Kültür, Eğitim, Spor ve Sağlık vakfı yayınları, 1995, 2 vols.

The Constantinople Messenger, September 11, 1880.

The Constantinople Messenger, September 13, 1880.

The Constantinople Messenger, September 16, 1880.

Dagbladet, November 11, 1880.

Eldem, Edhem. "Osman Hamdi Bey ve Oryantalizm." *Dipnot* 2 (Winter/Spring 2004): 39–67.

Emirbayer, Mustafa and Jeff Goodwin. "Network Analysis, Culture, and the Problem of Agency." *American Journal of Sociology* 99, no. 6 (1994): 1411–54.

Ersoy, Ahmet. "On the Sources of the 'Ottoman Renaissance': Architectural Revival and its Discourse during the Abdülaziz Era (1861–76)." PhD diss., Harvard University, 2000.

Findley, Carter Vaughn. *Ottoman Civil Officialdom. A Social History*. Princeton: Princeton University Press, 1989.

Gartlan, Luke. "James Robertson and Felice Beato in the Crimea: Recent Findings." *History of Photography* 29, no. 1 (2005): 72–80.

Gautier, Théophile. *Constantinople of Today*. London: David Bogue, 1854.

Gould, Roger V. "Multiple Networks and Mobilization in the Paris Commune, 1871." *American Sociological Review* 56 (1991): 716–29.

Hanioğlu, M. Şükrü. *A Brief History of the Late Ottoman Empire*. Princeton and Oxford: Princeton University Press, 2008.

Henisch, B. A. and H. K. "Robertson of Constantinople." *Image. Journal of Photography and Motion Pictures of the International Museum of Photography at George Eastman House* 17, no. 3 (1974): 1–11.

Henisch, B. A. and H. K. "James Robertson of Constantinople." *History of Photography* 8, no. 4 (1984): 299–313.

Henisch, B. A. and H. K. "James Robertson of Constantinople: A Chronology." *History of Photography* 14, no. 1 (1990): 23–32

James Robertson. Photographer of Istanbul. Edinburgh: Scottish National Portrait Gallery, 1991.

Jerichau-Baumann, Elisabeth. *Brogede Rejsebilleder* (Motley Images of Travel). Copenhagen: Forlagsbureauet, 1881.

Kâmil, Abdullah. "Tarabya'da Sanayi-i Nefise Sergisi." *Osmanlı* 11 Şevval 1297, no. 14.

Kâmil, Abdullah. "Le Turbé de Sultan Mohammed Tchélébi. Tableau par Hamdy Bey." *La Turquie* August 20, 1880: 3.

Kaul, Chandrika. *Dictionary of National Biography* online. Oxford: Oxford University Press, 2004–8.

Kızıltan, Yılmaz. "Meşrutiyetin İlânı ve İlk Osmanlı Meclis-i Mebusan'ı." *GÜ, Gazi Eğitim Fakültesi Dergisi*, 26, no. 1 (2006): 251–72.

Kürkman, Garo. *Armenian Painters in the Ottoman Empire, 1600–1923*, 2 vols. Istanbul: Matüsalem Uzmanlık ve Yayıncılık, 2004.

The Levant Herald, April 23, 1875.

Libaridian, Gerard J. "Nation and Fatherland in Nineteenth Century Armenian Political Thought." *Armenian Review* Autumn (1983): 71–90.

Osmanlı 5, Cumadelevvel 1298, no. 70.

Öztuncay, Bahattin. *James Robertson Pioneer of Photography in the Ottoman Empire*. Istanbul: Eren, 1992.

Öztuncay, Bahattin. *The Photographers of Constantinople. Pioneers, Studios and Artists from Nineteenth-century Istanbul*, 2 vols. Istanbul: Aygaz, 2003.

Pears, Edwin. *Forty Years in Constantinople. The Recollections of Sir Edwin Pears, 1873–1915*. London: Herbert Jenkins Ltd, 1916.

Roberts, Mary. "Contested Terrains: Women Orientalists and the Colonial Harem." In *Orientalism's Interlocutors. Painting, Architecture, Photography*, edited by Jill Beaulieu and Mary Roberts, 179–203. Durham and London: Duke University Press, 2002.

Roberts, Mary. "The Politics of Portraiture behind the Veil." In *Art and the British Empire*, edited by Tim Barringer, Geoff Quilley and Douglas Fordham, 223–36 and 399–402. Manchester: Manchester University Press, 2007.

Salahéddin Bey. *La Turquie à l'Exposition Universelle de 1867*. Paris: Libraire Hachette & Co., 1867.

Şerifoğlu, Ömer Faruk and İlona Baytar, eds. *Şeker Ahmed Paşa, 1841–1907*. Istanbul: TBMM Milli Saraylar Daire Başkanlığı, 2008.

Shaw, Wendy. *Possessors and Possessed. Museums, Archaeology and the Visualization of History in the Late Ottoman Empire*. Berkeley: University of California Press, 2003.

St. Laurent, Beatrice. "Ottomanization and Modernization: The Architectural and Urban Development of Bursa and the Genesis of Tradition, 1839–1914." PhD diss., Harvard University, 1989.

Tromans, Nicholas, ed. *The Lure of the East. British Orientalist Painting*. London: Tate Publishing, 2008. Published in conjunction with the exhibition *The Lure of the East: British Orientalist Painting* shown at the Yale Center for British Art, Tate Britain, Suna and İnan Kıraç Pera Museum and the Sharjah Art Museum.

La Turquie, April 26, 1873.

La Turquie, May 1, 1873.

La Turquie, May 11, 1875

La Turquie, August 5, 1875.

La Turquie, August 20, 1880.

La Turquie, April 27, 1881.

Walker, Mary Adelaide. *Eastern Life and Scenery. With Excursions in Asia Minor, Mytilene, Crete and Roumania*. London: Chapman and Hall, 1886, 2 vols.

Walker, Mary Adelaide. *Old Tracks and New Landmarks. Wayside Sketches in Crete, Macedonia, Mitylene, etc.* London: Richard Bentley and Son, 1897.

Williams, Samuel. "The Untimely Meditations of Osman Hamdi Bey: Competing Visions of History and Belonging in the Late Ottoman Empire." Turkish Studies Association Graduate Student Session, Middle East Studies Association Annual Meeting, November 17, 2006, Boston University, MA.

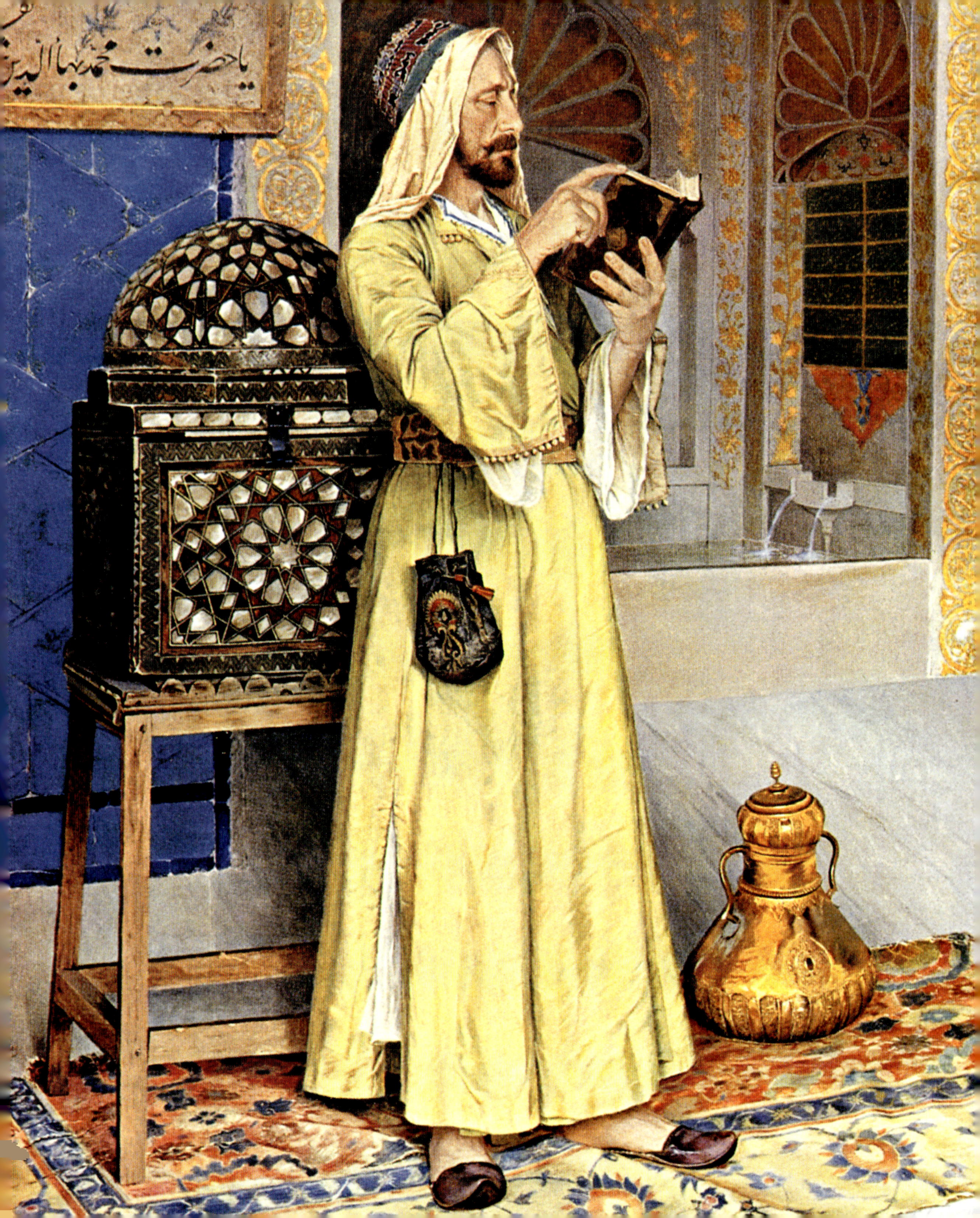
یا حضرت محمد بها

IX

Osman Hamdi Bey and the Historiophile Mood

Orientalist Vision and the Romantic Sense of the Past in Late Ottoman Culture

Ahmet Ersoy

For modernizing Ottomans, the complex dramaturgy of becoming Europeans also involved the prospect of becoming genuine "Orientals." In their historic stride towards political and cultural Westernization, nineteenth-century Ottomans were compelled to straddle conflicting poles of identification. Becoming habituated to myriad cultural and scholarly practices that were fraught with Eurocentric biases and alteritist binarisms, they were faced with the conflicting task of developing a novel awareness of their own "Oriental" identity and of their own place in the "Eastern" landscape. Thus, while striving to be incorporated into the Concert of Europe, the Ottoman elite were forced to redefine their own conceptions of the "East," to re-inscribe the word with new meanings in view of a complex set of European references, and to reconsider their own identity along the parameters of this novel definition. Even a cursory glance at nineteenth-century Ottoman historical writing reveals the profound impact of European Orientalist scholarship (such as the works of the Viennese historian Joseph von Hammer-Purgstall, or that of Louis Viardot on Islamic Spain) on the shaping of late Ottoman conceptions of the historical self.[1] The Orientalist scholarly establishment, with its overwhelming import and authority, was something with which the Ottoman intellectuals had to reckon and negotiate.

While European Orientalist scholarship made a strong imprint on the late Ottoman historical imaginary, in the realm of literary and visual representation, the growing awareness of European norms and conventions for imagining the Orient engendered within the Ottoman artistic milieu a diverse array of creative strategies, through which novel visions of the self and other were articulated. Especially after the 1860s, as the new *Tanzimat* generation began experimenting with new genres of literary and visual representation, such as the novel (more distinctively the thriving genre of the historical novel), the play, or academic painting, elaborate techniques of Orientalist displacement, illusion and fantasy allowed the Ottoman artists to concoct their own collective daydreams about a distant and resplendent Ottoman/Islamic past. While it is true that numerous late Ottoman intellectuals were adamant in maintaining a critical distance from the reductive tropes and inaccuracies embedded in Orientalist representation (particularly as regards the standard European rendition of the Oriental female as an object of erotic delectation[2]), it would nevertheless be far-fetched, and, I would argue, downright anachronistic, to assume that these confrontations, vociferous and astute as they might have been at times, amounted to a categorical and overtly "subversive" denunciation of the Orientalist establishment at large. Here, my position regarding the Ottoman engagement with Orientalist representation is largely informed by the insights of recent scholarship, abundantly represented in the collection of essays in the present volume, which accentuates the pressing need to historicize the field of Orientalism, to fracture it into its multiple voices, and to recognize its cross-cultural potential as a polyvalent discourse.[3] It is my contention, therefore, that the European Orientalist tradition, as a panoply of representative habits, artistic and literary tropes and stereotypes, was perceived by the Ottomans as an open and malleable field, a "hybrid" and contested space for fleshing out local agendas and for enunciating projected differences as well as internal alterities.[4] Orientalist dualistic imagination, positing the East and the West as mutually exclusive opposites, provided new and potent categories to the Ottomans through which they articulated their own cultural differences vis-à-vis the looming presence of the West in their everyday lives. As revealed by the studies of Selim Deringil and Ussama Makdisi, by the second half of the nineteenth century Orientalism had become part and parcel of the habitus of Ottoman modernity.[5] Inflected by the priorities and predilections of the dominant Muslim elite, Orientalism's techniques of exoticizing displacement, as well as its inherent archaisms and essentialisms, were recruited within the Ottoman domain in order to propagate the mission of imperial domination and to project archetypal visions of the Ottoman self. Orientalist representation, as a "universally" recognizable marker of cultural difference, was appropriated by the Ottoman center, as in the case of the "Orientalizing" idiom established in late Ottoman architecture, and embellished as an identifiable "dialect" in accord with the panoply of local European identities.[6] (See Fig. 9.1.)

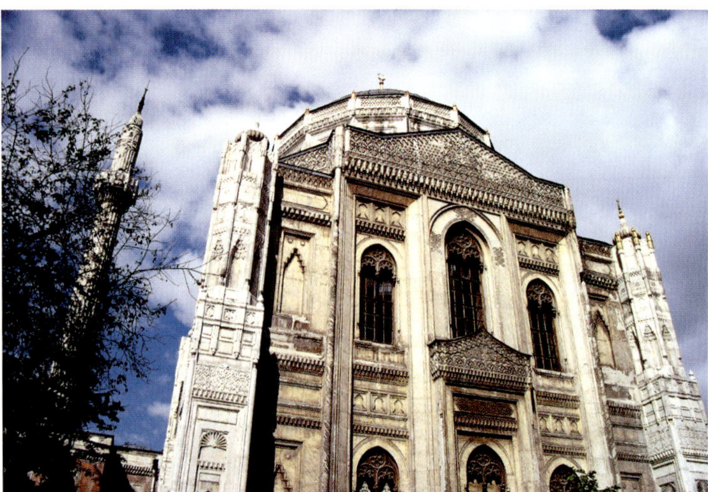

Figure 9.1 *Aksaray Pertevniyal Valide Mosque* (1871), Sarkis and Agob Balyan (architects). Photograph by the author.

Lying at the heart of the late Ottoman urge to appropriate Orientalist modes of perception and representation was the rise of a distinctively modern historical consciousness in the Ottoman realm. Although in many ways the *Tanzimat* was embedded in a complex internal dynamics of change linked to the "early modern" transformation of Ottoman state and society,[7] the era of Westernizing reforms did constitute a critical rupture, and a dramatic rift that separated the Ottoman present from the past. Ushering in a diverse array of novel institutions, reading practices, print cultures, and radically new modes of self-fashioning and expression, the *Tanzimat* instilled in the minds of many Ottomans a fundamental awareness of change, an irreversible sense of break and, especially in the scholarly and artistic field, a Romantic sensitivity towards irremediable loss. The increasing demand among the Ottoman reading public for a growing number of popular and scholarly works dealing with the past indicates that a passionate desire and need for history, that uniquely modern proclivity nurtured by rupture and intense yearning, started manifesting itself in the Ottoman lands in the wake of the tumultuous *Tanzimat* experience. With rising intensity, the Ottomans began to experiment with unprecedented forms and techniques of historical representation in order to overcome the irrevocable distance separating them from their past. Thus, a new and more versatile form of historical knowledge, what Stephen Bann calls the new "historical mindedness" of the nineteenth century,[8] made its way into the Ottoman world, replete with myriad practices of representation and popular diffusion it entailed for imagining the Ottoman present and the historical past. The new historical culture pertained not only to the field of academic historiography, but was manifested in the form of the museum, the exhibition, as well as the historical novel, play and painting. It is not only that every aspect of the past became a potential target of historical investigation after this transformation, but for a growing number of audiences, history, in all the disparate ways that it was envisaged and reanimated, became an indispensable object of emotional consumption. For the Ottoman public, a closer and more empathic relationship with the glorious days of yore offered relief from the grim realities of the present, helping overcome the sour deficiencies of living in an old-fashioned empire struggling to come to terms with the age of modern change. It is only with reference to the rising modern sensibility about the radical otherness of the past that one can explain the rising antiquarian urge among certain men of the *Tanzimat* to salvage, collect, and display objects, costumes and paraphernalia dating back to the pre-*Tanzimat* periods. The nascent Romantic anxiety concerning the perils and uncertainties of modern cultural change kindled a growing passion among the late Ottoman elites to reassess, document and cherish the "endangered" lifestyles and traditions of the pre-*Tanzimat* ages through the employment of various technologies and formats of representation, such as the museums (as in the case of the Janissary Museum, or the weapons and eventually the Islamic arts collections of the Imperial Museum), ethnographic/popular costume albums (such as Arif Paşa's *Mecmu'a-i Tesavir* or Osman Hamdi Bey and Marie de Launay's *Elbise-i 'Osmaniyye*), or novels, plays and paintings.[9] One should note, however, that all these attempts, scholarly or popular, to salvage a world threatened by the *Tanzimat*'s new life patterns were heavily laden with sensibilities of the exotic and the picturesque. The Ottomans tapped into the rich imaginary potential of Orientalism and invoked its esthetic or academic protocols in order to recapture and reanimate past experience in veristic form and authentic detail.

Driven by an acute awareness of being "expelled" from the past, the Ottomans employed Orientalist representation as a potent instrument in the post-Tanzimat period in order to penetrate, control, and re-enact history in view of their own image of empire and their changing visions of collective identity.[10] Orientalism, in accordance with the demands of modern historicizing vision, was subservient to the broader agenda of re-experiencing the past, and overcoming its ineluctable otherness. The standard Orientalist paradigm of former glory and a bygone "golden age," which felicitously overlapped with collective yearnings that were deeply rooted in the Ottoman historical imaginary (such as long-standing visions of the faultless ancient order of early Islam, or the resplendent age of Süleyman the Magnificent), engendered a new urge among Ottoman artists, scholars and intellectuals to reconnect to marked moments of power and glory in the Ottoman and Islamic past, and to make these available for emotional consumption. The past, in other words, was recast as an object of Romantic and exotic desire, and Orientalism was an appropriate means through which this desire was articulated, and made a ground of shared experience in the Ottoman domain.

Osman Hamdi Bey (1842–1910), the late-nineteenth-century Ottoman painter, must be among the earliest artistic figures in the non-Western world to define his creative standpoint through a complex engagement with the European Orientalist tradition. The Ottoman artist appropriated European techniques of looking in order to construct what he held to be "objective" scenes of a putatively native and pristine Ottoman/Islamic past. Drawing upon Orientalist conventions and techniques of representation, Osman Hamdi conjured up in his paintings a domesticated vision of the Orient; an Eastern fantasy space that appealed to the exoticizing sensibilities of European audiences, and was also heavily informed by late Ottoman agendas on self-identification and projection. As observed in the case of the painting *In the Tomb of the Princes*, a standard example representing the Orientalist oeuvre of Osman Hamdi (1908), the Ottoman artist was highly competent in employing the lingua franca of his trade as a painter of the East (Fig. 9.2). The setting, the dramaturgy and the meticulous technique of the painting, with its familiar Orientalizing contrivances, such as the dim and rundown atmosphere of the ornate tomb, the pseudo-Medieval outfit and the dramatic gesture of the dervish, as well as the inevitable leopard skin on the ground, make this a standard Orientalist work, with an enhanced feeling of remoteness and exotic charm that pervades the entire make-believe setting. Yet, Osman Hamdi also employs visual devices that help render the fantastic strikingly familiar in the eyes of the Ottoman observers. The unmistakably Ottoman cenotaphs from the "classical" period, and the glimpse of an eighteenth-century Istanbul fountain through the doorway, not to mention the tangible presence of the artist himself in stylish and exoticized outfit, compromise the radical otherness of the fantasy space, and transform this concocted setting into a "local" milieu through which the Ottoman viewers could recover and "authenticate" an ideal patrimonial past.[11] I believe that interrogating the status of Osman Hamdi as an Ottoman Orientalist and reflecting upon his creative engagement with European constructs of the East will contribute to our broader task of dismantling the assumed monolithic/univocal structure of the Orientalist tradition in art. It will also help us reconsider Orientalism as an uneven field of knowledge and practices that was expanded and inflected by alternative participants, allowing for the expression of multiple dreams, aspirations, and anxieties.

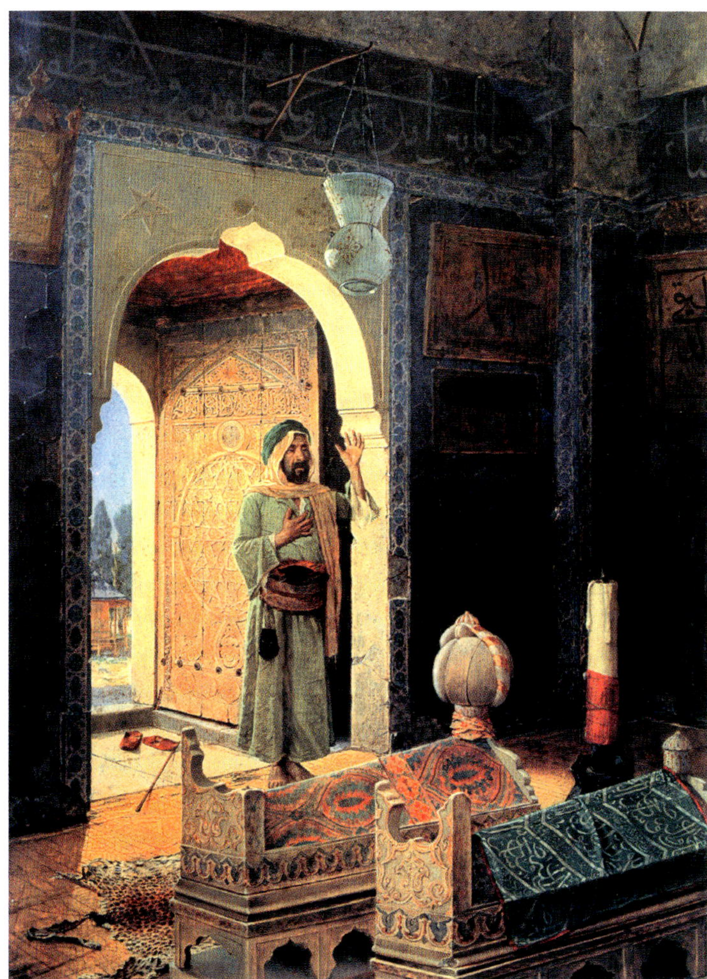

Figure 9.2 *In the Tomb of the Princes*, Osman Hamdi Bey (1842–1910), 1908, oil on canvas, 122 x 92 cm. Reproduced by permission of the MSGSÜ İstanbul Resim ve Heykel Müzesi.

Osman Hamdi's mode of negotiation with the Orientalist genre has been the subject of an ongoing debate in Turkish scholarship.[12] Above and beyond the unfulfilling discussion of whether Osman Hamdi Bey was a dyed-in-the-wool Orientalist (hence, a collaborator) or an embedded critic of the genre (hence, an anti-imperialist hero *avant la lettre*), I believe the debate has been constructive in terms of revealing the necessity (and the sheer difficulty) of historicizing the painter's works and his elusive artistic persona. Although Osman Hamdi's artistic career is primarily marked by the Orientalist paintings he displayed in exhibitions, Salons and expositions,[13] the painter's works need to be discussed beyond the reductive and generalizing attributes of a specific (and much maligned) genre, taking into consideration his individual sensibilities and particular esthetic choices as an artist and a highly Europeanized member of the Ottoman bureaucratic elite. The difficulty in endeavoring to contextualize these paintings, and thinking with them in order to make out what they must have meant to their audiences, is, as Edhem Eldem reminds us, the sobering fact that they were hardly acknowledged by contemporary European critics in their Salon appearances, and that the public presence they enjoyed in the Ottoman capital was extremely limited.[14] Although Osman Hamdi was among the most eminent figures of the late Ottoman cultural scene, his works were displayed in a limited number of exhibits that only catered to the small and cosmopolitan art public of Istanbul at that period.[15] Of course, one should not underestimate here the painter's much cherished public role as a director and studio teacher at the Imperial School of Fine Arts, for which he has been rightly venerated as a larger than life "founding figure" by generations of artists and art historians. But in considering the status and impact of Osman Hamdi Bey's works especially prior to the rise of a perceptible public debate on Westernized art, which materialized through a flurry of publications in the wake of the Young Turk Revolution (1908), one should pay heed to Eldem's cautionary note and refrain from overburdening these paintings with possible "messages" they might have contained about the painter's vision of late Ottoman society.[16] Of course, even if adequate documentary evidence were to exist on the production, reception and circulation of these paintings, it would still be downright naïve to expect to recover any originary meaning or intent lying behind their production, and to seal every work with a fixed and privileged interpretation. One, obviously, would have to explore how these works might have been intelligible within specific social and cultural contexts of viewing, and how certain meanings were determined in these different sites.

Although many of Osman Hamdi Bey's paintings are shrouded in silence, one can safely assert, judging from their most obvious thematic and esthetic attributes, that for the late Ottoman audiences these Orientalist compositions resonated with several other fields of artistic or scholarly representation, such as historical novels, plays, or museum displays, whereby the Ottoman/Islamic past was idealized and staged as a locus of desire. Among other products of the new historical culture of the post-Tanzimat period, one immediately recalls the popularly acclaimed historical plays of "the ultimate Romantic" ("romantik-i 'ulâ") Abdülhak Hamid (1852–1937), for instance, on the Islamic dynasties of Spain, such as *Tarık*, *İbn Musa*, or *Tezer*,[17] where the author entertains the image of an "impeccable" Muslim society embedded in a glorious Medieval past. In the exotic sensibilities they display, the costumes donned by contemporary Ottoman actors in these plays are akin to figures portrayed in solemn dignity in Osman Hamdi Bey's paintings (see Fig. 9.3). In the vein of his European counterparts, Hamdi Bey collated a diverse and anachronistic melange of historical fragments in his paintings—settings, costumes and paraphernalia culled from the broad geography of the Ottoman and Islamic world (from Medieval Syria and Mamluk Egypt to Early Ottoman Anatolia), most of which were housed in the Islamic collections of the Imperial Museum.[18] Despite remaining elusive in their deployment of temporal markers, these paintings nevertheless sustained a fundamental sense of historicity for viewers attuned to the Romantic sensibilities of late Ottoman culture. Conforming to the standard art historical template of painterly genres, one could argue that these Orientalist compositions (as well as those by many other foreign Orientalists, for that matter) were conceived as historical genre paintings, and cherished by their Ottoman viewers as visual reconstructions of everyday life in the Ottoman or Islamic historical past. These concocted scenes were meant to provide visual testimony to a quintessential historical milieu, an unblemished eastern Arcadia reinvented by late Ottoman culture as the legendary seedbed of its modern identity.

It was not only the deftly fabricated historical settings (mostly segments from late Medieval/early Ottoman architecture) that were deployed by Osman Hamdi in order to fabricate a persuasive atmosphere of local color and detail. The local costumes were essential in enhancing the reality of a remote and imaginary past, most of which seem to be stylized and exoticized versions of the traditional garments of the Arab provinces. Examples of these same costumes were documented by Osman Hamdi and Marie de Launay (in similarly Orientalizing manner) in their ethnographic study of Ottoman dress, the *Elbise-i 'Osmaniyye* (Fig. 9.4). Osman Hamdi was an admirer of the "endangered" sartorial traditions of the provinces that, he claimed, were redolent of the Medieval, or even Ancient past.[19] From the perspective of the privileged Ottoman center, the costumes of the eastern territories, these provincial markers of "authenticity" and difference, readily evoked the image of a distant and exotic past—since these regions were assumed to have remained "untarnished" by the ills of modernization, in a perpetual state of Medievalness. Conflating the idea of "suspended time," prescribed so

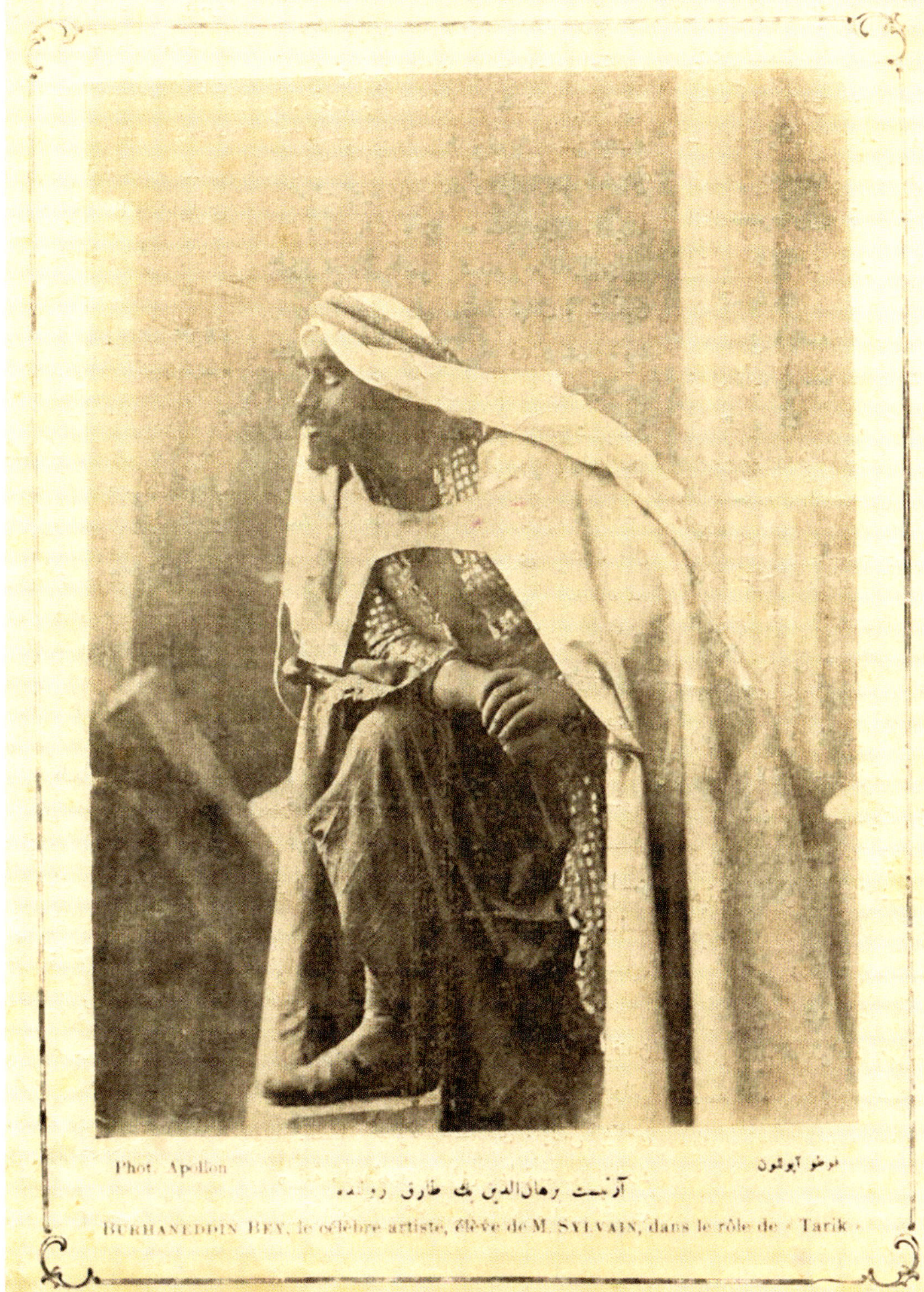

Figure 9.3 *Burhaneddin Bey in the Role of Tarık*, after the cover page of *Musavver Muhit* 1, no. 3 (6 Teşrin-i Sani 1324 [November 19, 1908]).

forcefully by Orientalist vision, with rooted imperial notions of geographic hierarchy, Osman Hamdi used Arab dress to dream up an idyllic Ottoman *Vorzeit*; a time of exemplary virtue and immaculate "Eastern" morality that was evoked recurrently in the period plays and novels.

Yet Osman Hamdi Bey's passionate interest in recapturing "local color" through a meticulous documentation of traditional costumes, fine artifacts and rarities cannot merely be attributed to an antiquarian urge to re-animate past experience. The Ottoman painter used what a contemporary critic

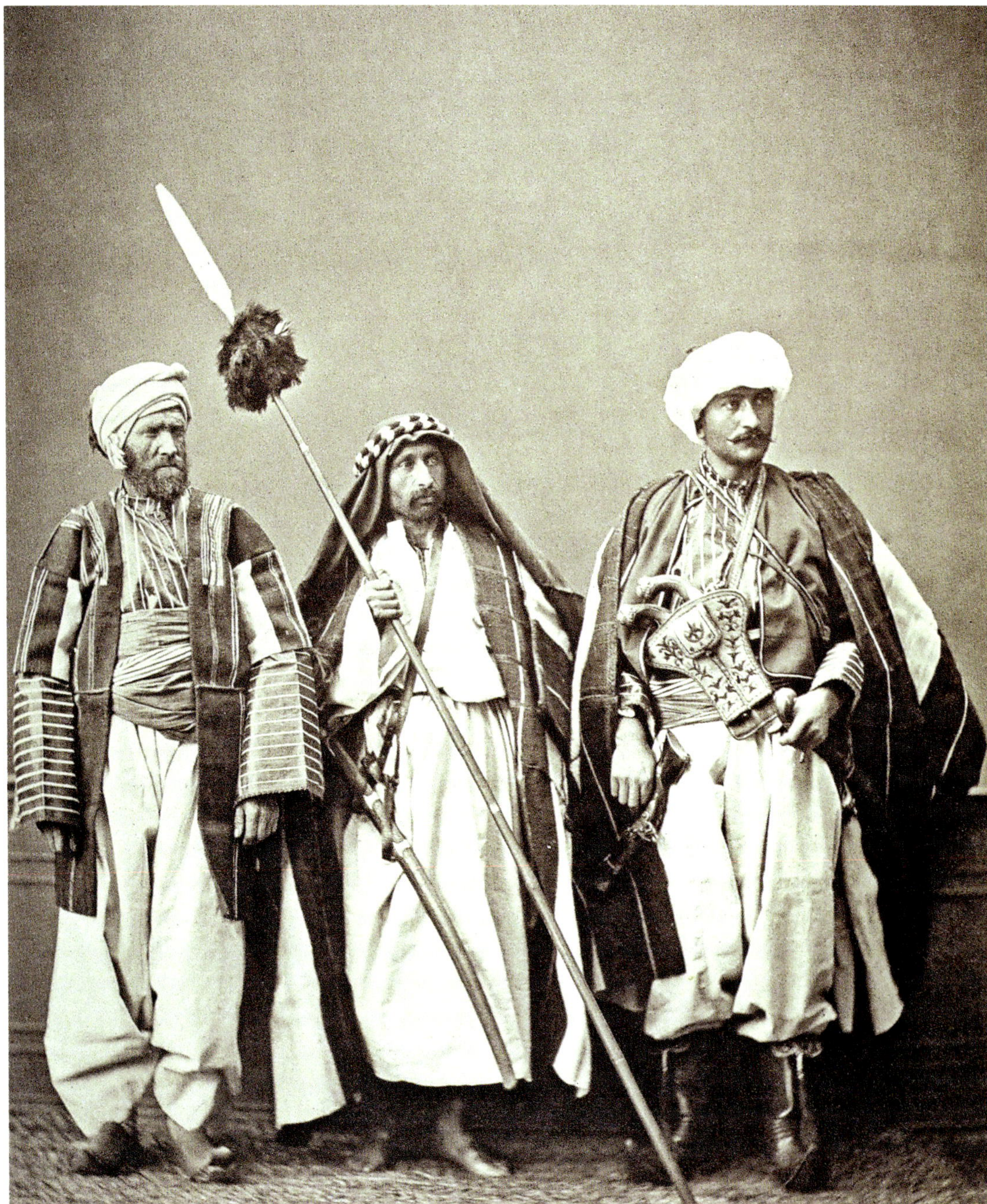

Figure 9.4 *Inhabitants of the Province of Syria*, in Osman Hamdi Bey and Marie de Launay, *Elbise-i 'Osmaniyye/Les Costumes populaires de la Turquie en 1873* (Istanbul: Levant Times and Shipping Gazette, 1873) Part 12, Plate 32.

called "la science du décor,"[20] the technical precision and photographic realism of the Orientalist genre, as a modern agent to display the splendor of traditional arts and commodities in their reconstructed context of use. This is observed markedly in the painting *The Miraculous Fountain* (1904), for instance, which seems almost to have been conceived as a showcase for displaying the authentic richness of rarities from the Ottoman and larger Islamic world, such as the uniquely colored fifteenth-century Ottoman tiles, a "classical" fountain from the sixteenth century with lavish decorative details, a gilded ewer and an elaborately designed Qur'an chest from the same period, a Persian rug, as well as exquisite textiles from the "oriental" provinces of the Ottoman Empire (Fig. 9.5).[21] In many of Osman Hamdi's Orientalist compositions, a carefully selected architectural décor (usually without a tangible depth of field) is animated by a few figures clad in glistening local outfits, who pose emotionlessly in solemn gestures, with an air of remoteness that recalls mannequins displaying rare ethnographic specimens in a museum. The space represented offers such a profuse display of crafts, fabrics, traditional artifacts that it smacks of the pedantic displays of the "national industries" galleries in the world

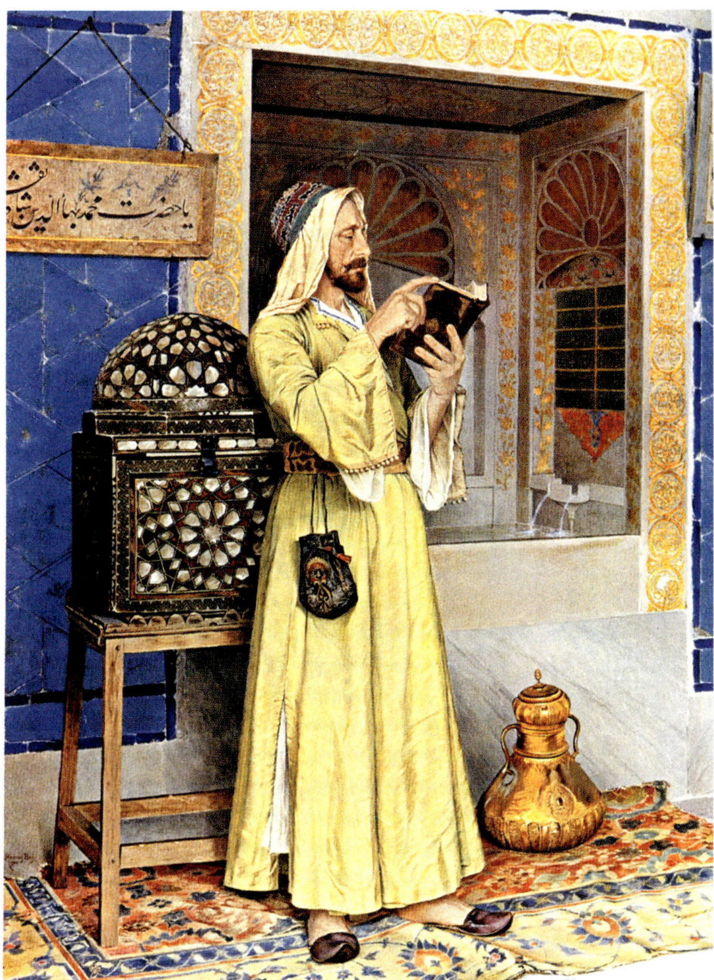

Figure 9.5 *The Miraculous Fountain*, Osman Hamdi Bey (1842–1910), 1904, oil on canvas. After Adolphe Thalasso, *L'Art Ottoman: Les peintres de Turquie* (Paris: Librairie artistique internationale, 1911).

expositions, or, for that matter, department store windows—all catering to the nineteenth century's bourgeois culture of comfort, with its intense visual appetite for material goods and commodities. Indeed, with the experience of serving as a museum director, an exposition commissary for the Ottoman displays at the 1873 Vienna Exposition, and as the author of an ethnographic costume album, Osman Hamdi must have been well versed in his period's advanced technologies of material display. He knew very well, for instance, that the myriad objects of daily use he depicted scrupulously in his paintings (or exhibited in organized displays) were observed by his Ottoman and European audiences with a keen eye on their decorative and utilitarian value, and as Romantic alternatives to the panoply of mass-produced goods that crowded their worlds. The preparatory reports of the Ottoman commission to the 1873 Exposition drafted under the direction of Osman Hamdi Bey clearly reveal such an awareness about the significance of traditional artifacts for Ottoman and international viewers as sources of inspiration and esthetic pleasure. In assembling the Ottoman exhibits, Hamdi Bey's committee expresses a strong determination to observe a methodical display strategy, and organize a show that would provoke "a serious interest on the part of the industrialists, traders, artists and scholars of other nations … [and hence make a positive impact on diagnosing] the real causes of the decline of craft guilds as well as on discovering the remedies that would bring back the prosperity of past ages, the splendor of ancient crafts and industries."[22]

It is important here to note that the question of applied arts reform in Europe, prompted by an artistic and social concern to revive the values of craftsmanship and to improve the esthetic standards of everyday commodities, was complemented in the Ottoman domain by a rising demand for the promotion of traditional crafts and local industries in the public domain.[23] Starting with the 1860s, in line with the launching of new protectionist measures for the Ottoman economy, many members of the Ottoman ruling elite and the burgeoning intelligentsia were engaged in a public debate about the negative effects of Western commercial penetration on Ottoman taste and consumption patterns. From the earlier years of his career as a bureaucrat Osman Hamdi was linked, through a web of personal and professional alignments, to a close network of Ottoman officials who played a prominent role in the efforts to revive and modernize local production and to raise the competitive value of Ottoman products in the local and international market. This privileged network included pioneering reformers like Midhat Paşa (Osman Hamdi's model statesman, whose modernizing agenda was centered on the consolidation and mobilization of the Ottoman middle class through the agency of vocational schools and trade organizations), as well as İbrahim Edhem (his father) and Ahmed Vefik Paşa, who ardently supported projects for the improvement of domestic crafts and industries in the empire, such as the revival of the Kütahya tile workshops, or the founding of the School of Industry, the Ottoman equivalent to the *Conservatoire des Arts et Métiers*.[24] The cohort also included lesser bureaucrats and friends, like the French expatriate Marie de Launay, whose entire career in the Ministry of Trade and Public Works was devoted to the cultivation and dissemination of a new sense of artistic appreciation in the empire concerning traditional objects of daily use, local costumes and vanishing decorative crafts.

The "descriptive mode" Hamdi Bey adopted in his paintings, and his genuine attentiveness to material detail testify to the rise of a connoisseurial interest in traditional arts and crafts in the late Ottoman Empire.[25] Osman Hamdi's flair for elaborate material display is not only traceable to his typical bourgeois susceptibilities, but was also informed by his distinctive predilections and political sensibilities as an Ottoman bureaucrat embedded in a particular social/professional milieu. I am not, of course, arguing that Osman Hamdi's Orientalist works were intended to propagate certain official cultural/political agendas that prescribed a particular vision of the past. My quite modest point is that Osman Hamdi's specific (and quite personal) mode of sensual engagement with the past was, nevertheless, highly inflected by a particular imperial vision that, in patriarchal and Orientalistic terms, sought to reassess Ottoman material culture and make it a locus for social and cultural regeneration. For the Ottoman audiences of Osman Hamdi's Orientalist works, the scopic pleasures of viewing these alluring scenes of everyday life also entailed new modes of esthetic engagement with the Ottoman past and material culture. The elite and historicist vision of the material environment propounded by Osman Hamdi Bey was later to be demystified and "democratized" by the likes of Hoca Ali Rıza, who, with similar antiquarian zeal, succeeded in registering the "quiet undercurrent" of Ottoman everyday life through their exacting portrayals of familiar settings and ordinary artifacts.[26] Many compositions of Ali Rıza, especially his interior sketches, depict the humble and mundane realities of middle-class Istanbul at the turn of the twentieth century. The unassuming spaces represented in these works, with their indiscriminate clutter of pots, pans, cups, threadbare shoes, smoldering braziers and water pipes, cannot be more different than the exquisitely contrived settings of Osman Hamdi Bey's paintings. Yet, in the genuine fondness for local color and material detail they reveal, these images speak of a common and dominant sense of Romantic engagement with a fading past, which seems to be the very longing that determined the lifelong artistic career of Osman Hamdi Bey.[27]

Notes

1 Of major impact among the works of Hammer-Purgstall was his colossal *Geschichte des Osmanischen Reiches*, 10 vols (Pest, 1827–32). The French translation, by J. J. Hellert, was published with the title *Histoire de l'empire ottoman depuis son origine jusqu'à nos jours*, 18 vols (Paris, 1835–43). A belated and incomplete Turkish translation by the historian Mehmed 'Ata appeared in nine volumes at the beginning of the twentieth century: *Hammer Tarihi Tercümesi* (Istanbul: Keteon Bedrosyan Matbaası, 1914–19). Ziya Paşa's translation of Louis Viardot's *Histoire des Arabes et des Mores d'Espagne* (Paris: Pagnerre, 1851) was momentous in terms of kindling romantic imagery on Arab Andalusia among the late Ottoman elites. Ziya Paşa, *Endülüs Tarihi*, vols 1–2 (Istanbul: Takvimhane-i Amire, 1859–63). On this publication see M. Halil Yinanç, "Tanzimattan Meşrutiyete Kadar Bizde Tarihçilik," in *Tanzimat* (Istanbul: Maarif Matbaası, 1940), 573–95.

2 One striking example quoted by Selim Deringil is the case of the Ottoman intellectual Ebuzziya Tevfik, who, in a memorandum to the palace on the occasion of the 1900 Paris Exposition, expresses the urgent need to counter demeaning European stereotypes in the depiction of historic Ottoman costumes. He is especially critical of the way Ottoman or Islamic women were portrayed in art or in various popular spectacles in the European context. See Deringil, *The Well Protected Domains: Ideology and the Legitimation of Power in the Ottoman Empire, 1876–1909* (London and New York: I.B. Tauris, 1998), 161–62.

3 Very illustrative of the state of the art in studies of visual Orientalism is an excellent collection of essays compiled by Jill Beaulieu and Mary Roberts with the title *Orientalism's Interlocutors: Painting, Architecture, Photography* (Durham and London: Duke University Press, 2002).

4 Here, of course, I use the term "hybrid" in the sense it is employed by Bhabha in his assessment of colonial representation. See Homi Bhabha, *The Location of Culture* (London and New York: Routledge, 1994).

5 Ussama Makdisi, "Rethinking Ottoman Imperialism: Modernity, Violence and the Cultural Logic of Ottoman Reform," in *The Empire in the City: Arab Provincial Capitals in the Late Ottoman Empire*, ed. J. Hanssen, T. Philipp and S. Weber (Beirut: Orient Institut der Deutschen Morgenländischen Gesellschaft, 2002), 29–48; Makdisi, "Ottoman Orientalism," *American Historical Review* 107, no. 3 (June 2002): 768–96; Selim Deringil, "'They Live in a State of Nomadism and Savagery:' The Late Ottoman Empire and the Post-Colonial Debate," *Comparative Studies in Society and History* 45, no. 2 (April 2003): 311–42.

6 Regarding experiments in Orientalizing and "neo-Ottoman" styles in late Ottoman architecture, see my dissertation, Ahmet Ersoy, "On the Sources of the 'Ottoman Renaissance': Architectural Revival and its Discourse During the Abdülaziz Era (1861–76)," (PhD diss., Harvard University, 2000). Also see: Ersoy, "Architecture and the Search for Ottoman Origins in the Tanzimat Period," *Muqarnas* 24 (2007): 79–102.

7 Rifa'at Abou-El-Haj re-examines the period of reforms as the culminating point of a lengthy "early modern" phase of transformation in the empire extending back to the seventeenth century. See Rifa'at 'Ali Abou-El-Haj, *The Formation of the Modern State: The Ottoman Empire, Sixteenth to Eighteenth Centuries* (Albany: State University of New York Press, 1991).

8 Stephen Bann uses the term "historical mindedness" to denote the nineteenth-century's new level of cultural awareness about history, and the ensuing popular demand for establishing closer empathic ties with the past. For changing modes and practices of historical reconstruction in nineteenth-century France and England, see his *Romanticism and the Rise of History* (New York: Twayne Publishers, 1995); and *The Clothing of Clio: A Study of the Representation of History in Nineteenth-Century Britain and France* (Cambridge: Cambridge University Press, 1984).

9 The Imperial Museum in Hagia Irene, which combined the functions of an archeological and a military museum, also housed a permanent collection of historic costumes ("Yeniçeri Kıyafethanesi") belonging to the members of the royal household and various divisions of the Janissary corps. During the Abdülaziz era (1861–76) the collection, displayed on one hundred and forty mannequins, was moved to one of the buildings of the School of Industry on the Atmeydanı (ancient Hippodrome). See Sermed Muhtar, *Müze-i 'Askeri-i 'Osmani* (Istanbul: Necm-i İstikbal Matbaası, 1920); and Edmondo de Amicis, *Constantinople*, trans. M. H. Lansdale, vol. 2 (Philadelphia: H.T. Coates, 1896), 232–35. On the history of museums and modern practices of display in the late Ottoman Empire, see Wendy M. K. Shaw, *Possessors and Possessed: Museums, Archaeology, and the Visualization of History in the Late Ottoman Empire* (Berkeley and Los Angeles: University of California Press, 2003). Costume albums and displays depicting the Ottoman bureaucratic and military elite of the *ancien régime* seem to have gained popularity in Europe and the Ottoman Empire especially after the Crimean War (1853–56). One noteworthy example in the Ottoman context is an album published by the Ottoman official Mehmed Arif Paşa (1808–65) with the title *Mecmu'a-i Tesavir-i 'Osmaniyye/Les anciens costumes de l'Empire Ottoman* (Istanbul: Tasvir-i Efkar, 1863). A more comprehensive study on Ottoman dress was published on the occasion of the 1873 World Exposition in Vienna. Osman Hamdi Bey and Marie de Launay's *Elbise-i 'Osmaniyye/Les Costumes populaires de la Turquie en 1873* (Istanbul: Levant Times and Shipping Gazette, 1873) was an ethnographic costume album that contained photographs of Ottoman subjects from all provinces of the empire dressed in their local garb. For a broader discussion of this publication, see: Ahmet Ersoy, "A Sartorial Tribute to Tanzimat Ottomanism: the Elbise-i Osmaniyye Album," in *Muqarnas* 20 (2003): 187–207.

10 I borrow the term "expelled" from Frank Ankersmit who argues that the modern consciousness of history involves the sense of being "ejected, expelled or exiled from the past." See his *Sublime Historical Experience* (Stanford: Stanford University Press, 2005), 327–28.

11 On the original location of the early seventeenth-century cenotaphs, as well as that of other objects in the painting, see Belgin Demirsar, *Osman Hamdi Tablolarında Gerçekle İlişkiler* (Ankara: Kültür Bakanlığı, 1989), 169.

12 See, for instance, İpek Aksüğür Duben, "Osman Hamdi ve Orientalism," *Tarih ve Toplum* 7, no. 41 (May, 1987): 283–90; Vasıf Kortun, "Osman Hamdi Üzerine Yeni Notlar," *Tarih ve Toplum* 7, no. 41 (May, 1987): 281–82; Semra Germaner and Zeynep İnankur, *Oryantalistlerin İstanbul'u* (Istanbul: İş Bankası Kültür Yayınları, 2002), 300–311; Wendy Shaw, "The Paintings of Osman Hamdi and the Subversion of the Orientalist Vision," in *Aptullah Kuran İçin Yazılar/Essays in Honour of Aptullah Kuran ed.* Çiğdem Kafesçioğlu and Lucienne Thys-Şenocak (Istanbul: Yapı Kredi Yayınları, 1999), 423–34; Zeynep Çelik, "Speaking Back to Orientalist Discourse," in *Orientalism's Interlocutors*, ed. Beaulieu and Roberts, 19–41; Edhem Eldem, "An Ottoman Archaeologist Caught Between Two Worlds: Osman Hamdi Bey," in *Archaeology, Anthropology and Heritage in the Balkans and Anatolia*, ed. David Shankland, vol. 1 (Istanbul: Isis, 2004): 121–49. Edhem Eldem, "Osman Hamdi Bey ve Oryantalizm," *Dipnot* 2 (Winter/Spring 2004): 39–67; Edhem Eldem, "Ressamlar, Kaplumbağalar, Tarihçiler…" in *Toplumsal Tarih* 185 (May 2009): 20–30.

13 Most contemporary accounts of Osman Hamdi Bey's art pertain to his Orientalist paintings. See the articles published in the *Journal of the Society of Ottoman Artists: Osmanlı Ressamlar Cemiyeti Gazetesi, 1911–1914*, abridged by Yaprak Zihnioğlu (Istanbul: Kitap Yayınevi, 2007); and Adolphe Thalasso, *L'Art Ottoman: Les peintres de Turquie* (Paris: Librairie artistique internationale, 1911).

14 Eldem, "Osman Hamdi Bey ve Oryantalizm," 56, 66.

15 On art exhibitions and their reception in the late Ottoman capital see Mustafa Cezar's comprehensive biography of Osman Hamdi Bey: *Sanatta Batıya Açılış ve Osman Hamdi*, vol. 2 (Istanbul: Erol Kerim Aksoy Vakfı, 1995): 422–45. One might be tempted to categorize Osman Hamdi's make-believe Oriental scenes, many of which featured the self-image of the artist in glaring pseudo-oriental outfit, as personal conceits and leisurely diversions. And to a certain extent, of course, many of these paintings were indeed personal and idiosyncratic, for Osman Hamdi was a "Sunday painter" who worked of his own accord and never received any commission for a work.

16 One is reminded here of Ernest Hemingway who is reported to have said: "If you're looking for messages, try Western Union." For the quotation, see http://www.litterascripta.com/bibliomania/quotes.shtml.

17 The plays were first printed with these titles: *Tarık yahud Endülüs'ün Fethi* (1879); *Tezer yahud Melik 'Abdurrahmanü's-Salis* (1880); *İbn Musa yahud Zatü'l-Cemal* (1919).

18 On the use of props in Hamdi Bey's paintings and their origins, see Demirsar, *Osman Hamdi Tablolarında Gerçekle İlişkiler.*

19 The archaizing outlook is prevalent throughout the text, but is more visible in the sections on the eastern provinces. In Plate 23 (Part III, Diyarbakır Province), for instance, the outfits and the elaborate headgear of a Kurd from Mardin are alleged to be identical to those represented in the Hellenistic reliefs and sculptures found in the Nimrud tumulus in Southeast Anatolia.

20 Thalasso, *L'Art Ottoman*, 21.

21 The space represented in the painting is "the fountain room" at the fifteenth-century Çinili Köşk (Tiled Pavilion), located in the Topkapı Palace grounds. The fountain is a sixteenth-century addition to the building. The mother of pearl inlayed Qur'an chest is located in the Islamic collections of the Ottoman Imperial Museum. See Demirsar, *Osman Hamdi Tablolarında Gerçekle İlişkiler* 131–34.

22 From the report presented to the official director of the Ottoman commission İbrahim Edhem Paşa on March 5, 1872. *Haus- Hof- und Staatsarchiv, Wien*, AR, F34 S.R. (Handelspolitische Akten, 1873–74) Karton 145, R. 25, 61/1.

23 On efforts for the revival of traditional crafts and industries and their broader cultural and economical context in the late Otoman Empire, see the first chapter in Ersoy "On the Sources of the 'Ottoman Renaissance.'"

24 On the School of Industry (Mekteb-i Sanayi) see Osman Nuri Ergin, *Türkiye Maarif Tarihi*, vols 1–2 (Istanbul: Eser Neşriyat, 1977), 627–37; Adnan Giz, "İstanbul'da İlk Sanayi Mektebinin Kuruluşu," *İstanbul Sanayi Odası Dergisi* 35 (January 15, 1969): 20–22; and Yaşar Semiz and Recai Kuş, "Osmanlıda Mesleki ve Teknik Eğitim," *Selçuk Üniversitesi Türkiyat Araştırmaları Dergisi* 15 (2004): 276–95.

25 The term "descriptive mode" is borrowed, of course, from Svetlana Alpers. See her article "Describe or Narrate? A Problem in Realistic Representation," in *New Literary History* 8 (1976): 15–41.

26 On the rising antiquarian interest in the material realities of everyday life in late Ottoman and early Republican culture see Yavuz Sezer, "The Perception of Traditional Ottoman Domestic Architecture as a Category of Historic Heritage and a Source of Inspiration for Architectural Practice (1909–1931)," (MA Thesis, Boğaziçi University, 2005).

27 On Hoca Ali Rıza (1858–1930), see Ömer Faruk Şerifoğlu (ed.), *Hoca Ali Rıza, 1858–1930* (Istanbul: Yapı Kredi Yayınları, 2005).

Bibliography

Abou-El-Haj, Rifa'at 'Ali. *The Formation of the Modern State: The Ottoman Empire, Sixteenth to Eighteenth Centuries.* Albany: State University of New York Press, 1991.

Alpers, Svetlana. "Describe or Narrate? A Problem in Realistic Representation" *New Literary History* 8 (1976): 15–41.

Amicis, Edmondo de. *Constantinople*. Translated by M. H. Lansdale. vol. 2. Philadelphia: H. T. Coates, 1896.

Ankersmit, Frank. *Sublime Historical Experience*. Stanford: Stanford University Press, 2005.

Bann, Stephen. *Romanticism and the Rise of History.* New York: Twayne Publishers, 1995.

Bann, Stephen. *The Clothing of Clio: A Study of the Representation of History in Nineteenth-Century Britain and France.* Cambridge: Cambridge University Press, 1984.

Bhabha, Homi. *The Location of Culture*. London: Routledge, 1994.

Beaulieu, Jill and Mary Roberts, eds. *Orientalism's Interlocutors: Painting, Architecture, Photography.* Durham and London: Duke University Press, 2002.

Çelik, Zeynep. "Speaking Back to Orientalist Discourse," in *Orientalism's Interlocutors: Painting, Architecture, Photography*, ed. Beaulieu and Roberts, 19–41. Durham and London: Duke University Press, 2002.

Cezar, Mustafa. *Sanatta Batıya Açılış ve Osman Hamdi*, 2 vols. Istanbul: Erol Kerim Aksoy Vakfı, 1995.

Demirsar, Belgin. *Osman Hamdi Tablolarında Gerçekle İlişkiler.* Ankara: Kültür Bakanlığı, 1989.

Deringil, Selim. *The Well Protected Domains: Ideology and the Legitimation of Power in the Ottoman Empire, 1876–1909.* London and New York: I.B. Tauris, 1998.

Deringil, Selim. "'They Live in a State of Nomadism and Savagery:' The Late Ottoman Empire and the Post-Colonial Debate." *Comparative Studies in Society and History* 45, no. 2 (April 2003): 311–42.

Duben, İpek Aksüğür. "Osman Hamdi ve Orientalism." *Tarih ve Toplum* 7, no. 41 (May 1987): 283–90.

Eldem, Edhem. "An Ottoman Archaeologist Caught Between Two Worlds: Osman Hamdi Bey." In *Archaeology, Anthropology and Heritage in the Balkans and Anatolia*, edited by David Shankland, vol. 1, 121–49. Istanbul: İsis Press, 2004.

Eldem, Edhem. "Osman Hamdi Bey ve Oryantalizm." *Dipnot* 2 (Winter/Spring 2004): 39–67.

Eldem, Edhem. "Ressamlar, Kaplumbağalar, Tarihçiler…" *Toplumsal Tarih* 185 (May 2009): 20–30.

Ergin, Osman Nuri. *Türkiye Maarif Tarihi*, vols 1–2. Istanbul: Eser Neşriyat, 1977.

Ersoy, Ahmet. "Architecture and the Search for Ottoman Origins in the Tanzimat Period." *Muqarnas* 24 (2007): 79–102.

Ersoy, Ahmet. "A Sartorial Tribute to Tanzimat Ottomanism: the Elbise-i Osmaniyye Album." *Muqarnas* 20 (2003): 187–207.

Ersoy, Ahmet. "Şarklı Kimliğin Peşinde: Osman Hamdi Bey ve Osmanlı Kültüründe Oryantalizm." *Toplumsal Tarih* 119 (November 2003): 84–89.

Ersoy, Ahmet. "On the Sources of the 'Ottoman Renaissance': Architectural Revival and Its Discourse During the Abdülaziz Era (1861–76)." PhD diss., Harvard University, 2000.

Germaner, Semra and Zeynep İnankur. *Oryantalistlerin İstanbul'u*. Istanbul: İş Bankası Kültür Yayınları, 2002.

Giz, Adnan. "İstanbul'da İlk Sanayi Mektebinin Kuruluşu." *İstanbul Sanayi Odası Dergisi* 35 (January 15, 1969): 17–19.

Hammer-Purgstall, Joseph von. *Geschichte des Osmanischen Reiches*, 10 vols. Pest, 1827–32.

Kortun, Vasıf. "Osman Hamdi Üzerine Yeni Notlar." *Tarih ve Toplum* 7, no. 41 (May 1987): 281–82.

Makdisi, Ussama. "Rethinking Ottoman Imperialism: Modernity, Violence and the Cultural Logic of Ottoman Reform." In *The Empire in the City: Arab Provincial Capitals in the Late Ottoman Empire*, edited by J. Hanssen, T. Philipp and S. Weber, 29–48. Beirut: Orient Institut der Deutschen Morgenländischen Gesellschaft, 2002.

Makdisi, Ussama. "Ottoman Orientalism." *American Historical Review* 107, no. 3 (June 2002): 768–96.

Mehmed Arif Paşa. *Mecmu'a-i Tesavir-i 'Osmaniyye/Les anciens costumes de l'Empire Ottoman*. Istanbul: Tasvir-i Efkar, 1863.

Osman Hamdi Bey and Marie de Launay. *Elbise-i 'Osmaniyye/Les costumes populaires de la Turquie en 1873*. Istanbul: Levant Times and Shipping Gazette, 1873.

Semiz, Yaşar and Recai Kuş. "Osmanlıda Mesleki ve Teknik Eğitim." *Selçuk Üniversitesi Türkiyat Araştırmaları Dergisi* 15 (2004).

Şerifoğlu, Ömer Faruk, ed. *Hoca Ali Rıza, 1858–1930*. Istanbul: Yapı Kredi Yayınları, 2005.

Sermed Muhtar. *Müze-i 'Askeri-i 'Osmani*. Istanbul: Necm-i İstikbal Matbaası, 1920.

Sezer, Yavuz. "The Perception of Traditional Ottoman Domestic Architecture as a Category of Historic Heritage and a Source of Inspiration for Architectural Practice (1909–1931)." MA Thesis, Boğaziçi University, 2005.

Shaw, Wendy M. K. *Possessors and Possessed: Museums, Archaeology, and the Visualization of History in the Late Ottoman Empire*. Berkeley and Los Angeles: University of California Press, 2003.

Shaw, Wendy M. K. "The Paintings of Osman Hamdi and the Subversion of the Orientalist Vision." In *Aptullah Kuran İçin Yazılar/Essays in Honour of Aptullah Kuran*, edited by Çiğdem Kafescioğlu and Lucienne Thys-Şenocak, 423–34. Istanbul: Yapı Kredi Yayınları, 1999.

Thalasso, Adolphe. *L'Art Ottoman: Les peintres de Turquie*. Paris: Librairie artistique internationale, 1911.

Viardot, Louis. *Histoire des Arabes et des Mores d'Espagne*. Paris: Pagnerre, 1851.

Yinanç, M. Halil. "Tanzimattan Meşrutiyete Kadar Bizde Tarihçilik." In *Tanzimat*, 573–95. Istanbul: Maarif Matbaası, 1940.

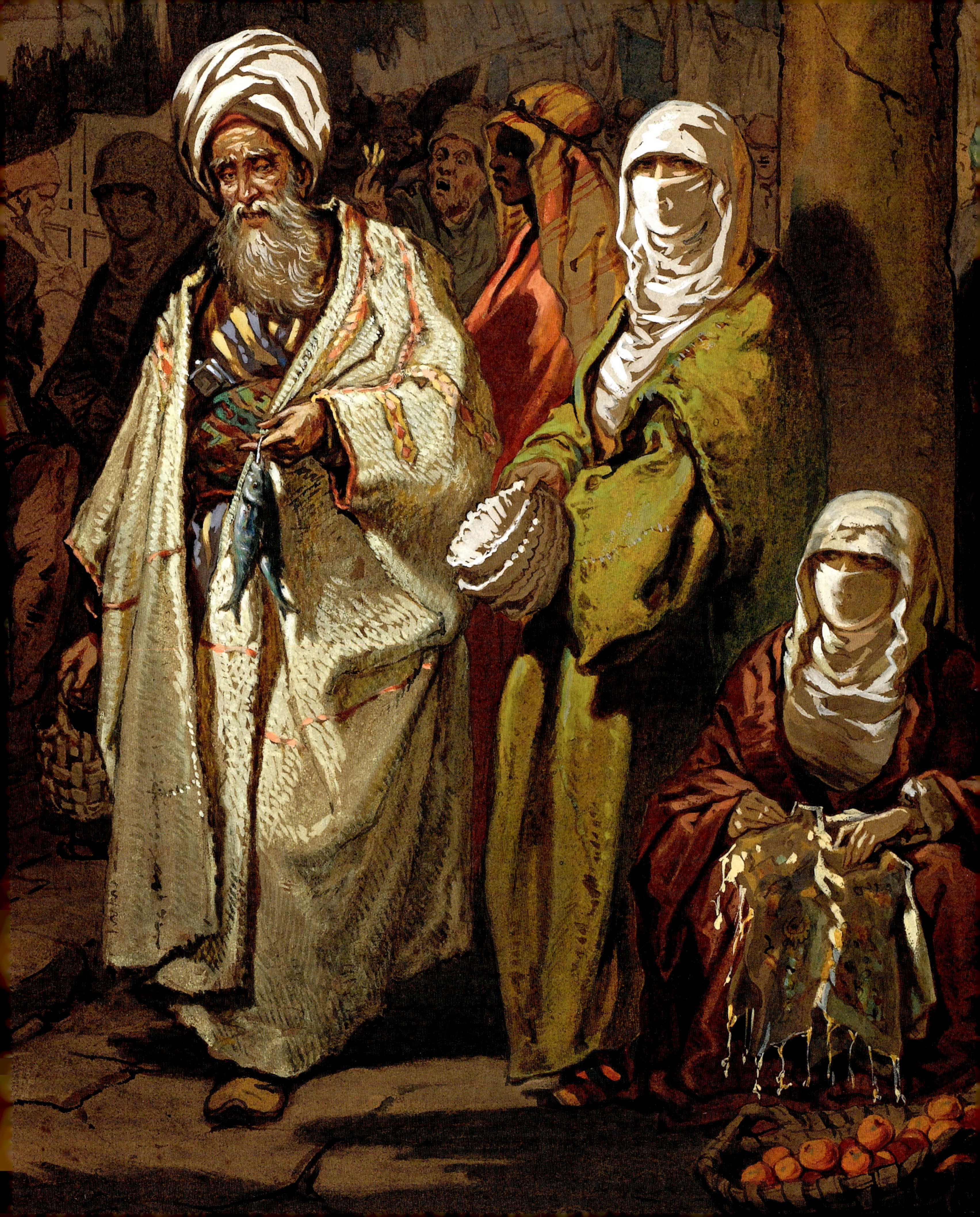

X

Traveling East
Veiling, Race, and Nations

Teresa Heffernan

While discussions of veils and harems are largely absent from medieval and Renaissance works about Muslim women, from the eighteenth century onwards (with the new gendering of public and private space in the West) they became standard tropes in Western travel narratives, often connoting Turkish women's oppression and in turn Ottoman barbarity.[1] Thevenot's 1687 account where the author announces: "the Turks do not believe that Women go to Heaven, and hardly account them Rational Creatures; the truth is, they take them only for their service as they would a Horse";[2] differs little in sentiment from William Hunter, who traveled to Turkey in 1792 and wrote: "the prejudices which the Turks entertain against their women, are, indeed, one of the great causes of their own inflexible barbarism."[3] So too, Stanley Lane-Poole noted in 1878: "It is quite certain that there is no hope for the Turks as long as Turkish women remain what they are ... they are choked by a pernicious system which destroys the moral force of the women and thereafter the men of the empire."[4] And the pervasiveness of the trope continues today in the debates over the veil; for example, Harriet Harman, the British Labour MP, joining and trumping Jack Straw's anti-niqab stance, insisted that the veil in Britain should be abolished, "because I want women to be fully included. If you want equality, you have to be in society, not hidden away from it."[5] What these sampling of statements from different historical periods share is a view of Muslim women as oppressed, obscure, hidden, and lacking in all agency.

This consistency in citation about Muslim women points not so much to the truth of their presumed collective, transhistorical, oppression but rather, as Edward Said has argued about repetition, works to consolidate a world view and speaks to the interests at play in the construction of the East/West divide. This representation of Turkish/Muslim women as enslaved in turn leads to the call to "liberate" them from their harems and veils, but this "rescue" mission invites some reflection as to what purposes are served by unveiling women at any given historical moment. What I will argue in this paper is that from the mid nineteenth to the early twentieth century, this call for unveiling is caught up with the desire to police race, class, and national boundaries as part of a larger imperialist strategy.

The Rise of European Nationalism

European travelers in the early modern period often used the term Turk to refer to Muslims, hence the term "to turn Turk." In *Travels in the Levant*, which was translated from French and circulating in London in 1686, Thevenot writes:

> Where I speak here of Turks, I understand Natural Turks, as no such as turn to their religion from another who are very numerous in *Turkie*, and are certainly capable of all sorts of Wickedness and Vice, as is known by Experience, and commonly as unfaithful to Men, as they have been to God; but the native Turks are honest people. And love honest people, be they Turks, Christians, or Jews.[6]

As problematic as the idea of a "natural/native Turk" is given that the Turks, a nomadic people, only began to convert to Islam in large numbers in the tenth century, Thevenot, reflecting his time, understands the world as "naturally" divided by religion. Yet, more than just suggesting the unsettling attractions of religious conversion and fears about the expansion of Islam, his statement also anticipates the new emphasis on territorial boundaries and place that will become a key marker of identity with the rise of racialized nationalism in the West. Accompanying this rise, the term "Turk" changes meaning: less and less used as a religious designation, travelers to the Ottoman Empire increasingly use it to refer to ethnicity and race rather than religion. Yet, this new focus on race, ethnicity, and nations needs to be considered in the larger context of their invention and solidification in the nineteenth century.

While nations are born in Europe at the dusk of the religious age, nationalism is more than a rational construct. The mythic dimension of the nation provides a sense of continuity, destiny, and meaning that fills the void left by the belief in a divinely ordered universe. Hence, while, as Benedict Anderson has argued, "nation-states are widely conceded to be 'new' and 'historical,' the nations to which they give political expression always loom out of an immemorial past."[7] Race or the idea of a people as a "natural" grouping participates in this invention of a past without record and comes to serve as the basis for the governance of the nation, displacing the classical notion of the citizen as the product of a complex political nexus. Michael Hardt and Antonio Negri write in *Empire*: "Many contemporary analyses of nations and nationalism from a wide variety of perspectives go wrong precisely because they rely unquestioningly on the naturalness of the concept and identity of the people," arguing that the idea of a "people" as a homogenous group is close to the "concept of race."[8] So too Vasant Kaiwar and Sucheta Mazumdar write in "Race, Orient, Nation" that "racism, as a system of social classification, is not passive, that is, simply recording difference already 'objectively' in existence in the world, but one that actively creates subjects ... turning mutable identities into fixed ones" and that, further, this creation of racialized subjects and the emergence of the nation are closely affiliated.[9] In *The Racial State*, David Theo Goldberg similarly argues that the social contract was also a racial contract and that: "Race qua otherness is as necessary and 'natural' to the logic and historical development of modern state formation as modern technologies of state governmentality are to racial formation."[10]

* * *

Turkey in its rapid transformation, from a multi-religious, multi-lingual, inter-racial and inter-ethnic cosmopolitan Empire into a racialized nation proves an exemplary case of this invention of a "people," and in the process exposes the workings of the modern nation. The remaking of Ottoman society involved radically transforming the very conception of community, from the Islamic understanding of the nation, the *umma*, to a modern Western model: the former based on a transhistorical, transgeographical membership and the latter based on birth and teleology. The Turkish reforms, which involved the adoption of a Western-style of governance, meant having to deal with the difficulties of a mutable diverse population that did not operate along the same lines as the "imagined communities" of Europe, which were able to foster the illusion of homogeneity through a strict policing of borders, both internally and externally, and through exclusive cultural and legal practices. Fighting on the side of Greece during the War of Independence and later fuelling other ethnic divisions in the Ottoman Empire, Britain and then America fostered the understanding of the nation as organic, homogenous and racially and linguistically coherent, turning the accident of birth into destiny and exposing in these conflicts the dark side of national independence movements—in other words, the purging, reviling, and expulsion of those who fall outside what is understood as the official members of the community, a legacy the Republic continues to grapple with. The early twentieth-century Turkish historian Yusuf Akçora rightly argued that both the Ottoman and Islamic imaginings of alternative versions of the nation were quickly displaced by the triumph in Germany and the rest of Europe of race based nationalisms.[11]

Heterogeneity and Fears of Miscegenation

If British travelers in the nineteenth century were no longer focused on the threat of religious conversion, many did express uneasiness about the Ottoman Empire's cosmopolitan mix. Murray's guidebook advised travelers to the Empire not to expect any national coherence or dominant "people," quoting the historian Lord Bryce: "Constantinople is 'a city not of one nation but of many, and hardly more than one than of another. You cannot talk of Constantinopolitans as you talk of Londoners or Parishioners, for there are none.'"[12] And Charles Eliot referred dismissively to the city's inhabitants as "one of the most mixed breeds in the world."[13]

Nineteenth-century newspapers, travel literature, and memoirs from Turkish sources are full of accounts of the porous borders that had long constituted the Empire. Halide Edib, a leading feminist and nationalist, adopts a complicated internalized racism as a child growing up in Istanbul in the 1880s. Her Anglophile father remarried a blue-eyed, blonde-haired wife, after the death of his first wife, and Edib writes in her memoir that in her first encounter with her stepmother and her new "fair" relatives, who mock her, she is made aware that her own "skin is not pink and her eyes are not blue."[14] "Having acquired an impression from [her] stepmother's relations that it is only fair people with blue eyes who are beautiful," she feels, at a very early age, inadequate.[15] Yet despite being brought up with this sense of a racial hierarchy and the "English-made" frocks, English diet, English novels, and "English ways" that her father so strongly admired,[16] Edib's memoir also serves as a record of the inter-racial and inter-ethnic society, where ever shifting boundaries and cultural fluidity countered and challenged strict racial hierarchies. Her black Nubian "milk-mother," Nevres Bacı is married to a "blond giant" from Trebizond, Ahmet Ağa. Her sister's father was Kurdish and had both a Syrian and an Abyssinian wife and "three white and three colored children."[17] Two Abyssinian girls are bought for Halide and her sister, and while at first both sets of girls are terrified that the other comes from a culture of cannibalism, they all grow up together and the slaves are treated as part of the family, as was typical of Ottoman households. On the boat to Egypt she meets an African-American from Pera who has a "white" daughter with a Frenchman (now dead) and is on the verge of marrying another Frenchman.[18] While Ottoman social structures were hierarchical, rigid, and formal, Islamic respect for equality and difference combined with the relative lack of concern with blood, family name, and birth allowed for a great deal of individual mobility within these structures and facilitated these mixed households. Western travelers were as disturbed by this social mobility as they were by the fluidity of race and ethnicity, and comments like Thomas Thornton's are common: "What would become of the other nations in Europe , if, in imitation of the Turkish government, the highest offices in the state were filled by men from the lowest ranks in society."[19]

Melek Hanım's memoir, *Thirty Years in the Harem* (1872), which covers the first half of the nineteenth century, also documents this unrestricted and unregulated mixing of cultural and ethnic identities in Ottoman society. Granddaughter of a woman from the island of Chios who married an Armenian, the daughter of a French father and Greek mother, wife of first a London-born Protestant and then a Cypriot-born Muslim, Maire converts to Islam in 1860 and changes her name to Melek. If Edib's Anglophile upbringing and nationalist leanings encourage a hyper-sensitivity to skin color and a privileging of fair hair and blue eyes, Melek's earlier narrative rarely comments on coloring, except in passing. At one point, she refers to a choosey Pasha for whom she is trying to find a bride who wants his future mate to have "black hair and eyes," refuting Edib's Anglo-influenced belief that there is a universal preference for blue-eyed women;[20] and, at another, Melek comments on an Abyssinian of "great beauty."[21] The newspapers of the period also suggest the equitable treatment of mixed race marriages. The *Levant Herald*, an English language newspaper circulating in Istanbul, for instance, posted a story in 1871 about an eccentric but wealthy Mahmud Bey who died leaving apparently no heirs, so his estate was passed onto the State and a grand nephew. A "negress" and her young son came forward, however, and after an investigation that proved she was his lawful wife, the estate was re-distributed and Molla Bey, like "an upright judge, awarded the whole succession, in pursuance of the Ottoman law of the *Sheri*, to the delighted negress and her child."[22]

Yet if the Ottomans seemed relatively unperturbed by inter-racial and inter-ethnic mixing, England was obsessed with questions of hybridity and in particular mixed race unions, which the scientific world was trying to measure, quantify, diagnose and place on a hierarchical scale. This obsession with race and nation was further intensified by the American civil war and the debates about abolition, that, in turn, produced a plethora of articles and books that spoke to fears of both racial contamination and trans-racial desire. I will briefly mention three of the more influential of these works. In the first part of the century, Josiah Nott's: "The Mulatto a Hybrid—Probable Extermination of the Two Races if the Whites and Blacks are Allowed to Intermarry" (1843) argued that the intermingling of these two different "species" could only result in sterility.[23] In *The Races of Man: A Philosophical Enquiry into the Influence of Race over the Destinies of Nations* (1862), Robert Knox also made a case for races as distinct species, with the Anglo-Saxons at the top of the hierarchy.[24] In *The Inequality of Races*, Joseph Arthur Gobineau argued in the 1850s that the mixing of superior races with inferior races could not but result in the decline of civilizations and that race and ethnicity were the most pressing issues of the day.[25] The mixed and mobile populations within Ottoman culture could not be anything but deeply disturbing to the Western traveler, whose entire perspective was shaped by the distorting lens of racial science, and by the nineteenth-century, all Western travel narratives, to varying degrees, reflect this obsession. Both the frequent complaints about hybrid populations and the attempts to organize, categorize, encourage, and invent racial and ethnic differences distinguish nineteenth-century travel narratives from earlier ones that focused primarily on religious differences.

Travel literature played an important role in the cataloguing of racial and national types, and England's increasing investment in policing national and race borders is evident. For instance, Julia Pardoe, in her *The City of the Sultan, and the Domestic Manners of Turks* (1837), is quick to distinguish between "faux" Europeans who inhabit Pera and "real" Europeans who are born within the national borders of England or France. She writes: "In my definition of European society, I must not omit to mention that Perotes, or natives of Pera, consider themselves as much Franks as though they had been born and nurtured on the banks of the Thames or the Seine; and your expression of amusement at this very original notion would inevitably give great offense."[26] Pardoe later goes on to suggest that you can always tell a Perote from a "genuine European," as despite similarity in dress, the Perote displays "an insurmountable taste for bright colours" and an "indescribable peculiarity of their toilette." The reference is clearly to a lesser, corrupted racial populous, but the fact that all that tells the "faux" from the "genuine" European is make-up and dress also points to the tenuousness of this boundary, undercutting the mythic dimension of nationalism by inadvertently exposing this "original notion" as no more than an accident of birth. This tenuousness, that is part of the liminal place Turkey holds between East and West, is made explicit in Charles Macfarlane's 1829 account of the Franks in İzmir, whom he describes as "of a strange hybridous nature, something neither Christian nor Turk, Asiatic nor European. ... A turban and a caftan would make the Frank a Turk; a hat and coat, the Turk a Frank."[27] While the modern nation invokes race as organic, Macfarlane seems, unintentionally, to beg the question is race nothing more than a sartorial performance, unsettled as he is by this "hybrid" population.

In her *Turkey of the Ottomans* (1911), Lucy Garnett, thoroughly educated in the racial sciences that dominated nineteenth-century England, literally "white washes" the Ottoman Empire. She writes that the Turks were "civilized" by their mixture with white blood and that this mixture could only happen as Turks were, in fact, not "coloured" but Aryan:

> The Osmanli race cannot, however, according to modern ethnologists, correctly be said to be "Turks" in the sense in which that term, in common with "Turanian," is ordinarily used, namely, to designate not only a non-Aryan, but a coloured race, and appear rather to have belonged originally to a branch of that white race of Western Asia variously termed Circassian, Alarodian, or Archaian. But whatever may have been the original stock from which they sprang, the Osmanlis have developed into the great nation they now constitute by admixture during more than six centuries with the best white blood both of Western Asia and Eastern Europe.[28]

She had already erased the "coloured" element from Turkey in her 1890 ethnographic study, which carefully categorized Ottoman women according to national/ethnic "types." Arguing that while the "best white blood" had resulted in a successful mix and a great nation, Garnett insisted the "bad" hybrid—the "higher races" mixed with the "lower races"—had failed to reproduce:

> The thousand upon thousands of negroes and negresses that have been imported into the country since the Turkish conquest might lead us to expect to find a considerable mixture of black blood in the lower classes especially of the population. This, however, is not the case. Though negresses and Abyssinians are often married, either to men of their own race or to the whites, the climate does not seem favourable to the propagation of the coloured races, and the few negro or mulatto children who come into the world generally die in infancy.[29]

Garnett's ethnography is thoroughly saturated by the many debates about nations, hybridity, mulattos, and race that filled the pages of Europe and America's nineteenth-century scientific journals and informed most cultural production.[30] These passages in her work cannot be properly unpacked without this context. Although she suggests rather vaguely that "climate" is the reason for the supposed decline of the black or mixed race population in the Ottoman Empire, Garnett's thesis favors the view that humans are polygenesis (multiple species), so that intermixture between "Aryan" and "coloured races" cannot but end in sterility just as the biological hybrid, the crossing of horse and donkey, produced the infertile mule. In other words, the true hybrid could not produce viable offspring, whereas Turks and Europeans, as they were of the same "white" species, successfully interbred. This thesis was, in turn, used to explain the sophistication of Ottoman civilization: Osmanlis as "white," were of the highest race, and thus capable of a great civilization. Garnett's argument about Osmanlis parallels the similar view of the period that the ancient Egyptians were a "white" race: "Ancient Egyptians were Caucasians" argued Nott.[31] The greatness of this ancient world in Africa, like that of the Ottoman, then could be explained in a way that did not disturb European theories about the hierarchy of races.

The monogenesis view (human as one species), which explained the success of sexual unions between races, with all its "negative" consequences, was also circulating and was equally informing readings of the Ottoman. These mixed populations were hence dismissed as corrupt and dissolute. The inter-mixing of races and ethnicities, as Gobineau had argued, inevitably led to degeneration and heralded the decline of a civilization. A correspondent for the *Near East* (an English newspaper that reported on events in the Middle East and India in the first decades of the twentieth century), voicing this theory, described Constantinople as a "medley":

> Turks, Greeks, Armenians, Circassians, Kurds, figure in it, all equally bad, mean, dishonest, and treacherous. ... The failure of Turkey is the failure of Rome. Rome fell because there remained no Romans, and Turkey will fall because in Constantinople there remain no Turks. They have become "Levantine-y." A Turk will trace in his family, perhaps, a Circassian mother, an Egyptian grandfather, here a rich Greek, always an Albanian or a Jew. ... Throughout the

> centuries many people have come to the city. The city of the Great Whore has sucked most of them in and spit most of them out Levantines—a people who are not a people, without patriotism, without honour, talking myriad tongues in jargon, the sole people in the world without one virtue.[32]

The writer concludes his piece with the suggestion Turkey is not about divided religions but is about the tensions between "pure" races and mixed breeds: "Turkey is represented in England as divided cleanly into the Turk and the Christian, eternally antagonistic. It is not. It is divided into Anatolian and Levantine, native inhabitant and bastard ruling race."[33] This mythic creation of "pure natives" is then offered as a credible basis for the nation and comes to displace earlier religious divisions.

Imperialism, Unveiling, and the Policing of Race and Class

The Western investment in homogenous nations is explicitly linked to imperialism, which needed to be able to order the world according to a hierarchical ranking of nations and races; as Paul Gilroy has written: "The commitment to an organic ordering of humankind was important also because it endorsed the claims of racial science to observe, organize and regulate the social body."[34] In the later part of the nineteenth century, Lady Annie Brassey traveled around the globe in a steam-powered yacht with her husband, Thomas Brassey, who was a Member of Parliament and responsible for ensuring that colonial rule was facilitating English commerce and trade abroad. With five travel books, Lady Annie also displayed the archeological, botanical, and ethnographical curiosities she collected on her voyages at various exhibitions at Hastings and South Kensington and was at work on establishing a private museum. Further, she produced, from both her own attempts and from prominent photographers of the day, seventy large gold-embossed photo albums, organized by nation and typically opening with representative photos of national types. Commenting on the heterogeneous population of Edirne in her 1880 travel narrative about Turkey, Lady Annie attempted to carefully categorize the various inhabitants by nationality, as was typical of the genre in the nineteenth century, invoking a hierarchal scale: "There are representatives of every nation under the sun here. ... Some are fine, handsome, intelligent–looking men, while others appear fitted to hold a position in the social scale but a little higher than the inhabitants of Tierra del Fuego."[35] Her endorsement of Disraeli's 1847 novel, *Tancred; or the New Crusade*, is telling since Disraeli, like Lady Annie, was committed to re-imagining the East in terms of racialized nations. He wrote: "nationality, without race as a plea, is like the smoke of this nagrilly, a fragrant puff"[36] and in another passage insists: "All is race; there is no other truth, and every race must fall which carelessly suffers its blood to become mixed."[37] Yet the hybrid populations, "the great medley of races" as Eliot referred to them, that comprised Ottoman culture, were resistant to this regulating and ordering of nations that Lady Annie was committed to.

In this 1880 travel narrative about the Ottoman Empire, Lady Annie also strongly encouraged Turkish women to "liberate" themselves from their yashmaks and harems and suspected that "the revolution" amongst these women was fast approaching.[38] However, she herself was opposed to women's suffrage in Britain and strongly in favor, along with her husband, of the British colonial mission, so why is she interested in Turkish women rebelling against Islamic paternalism? Moreover, if the overturning of feudalism was in part about the revolutionary possibilities of individuals disrupting a paternal order that situated them in a particular place in the social hierarchy and allowing them social mobility, a narrative that inspires Lady Annie's call for the emancipation of Turkish women, then Lady Annie should readily understand why the Sultan is, as she writes, very proud of his title "Son of a Slave." Instead she insists she can't fathom any reason for it.[39] She describes his mother as "a slave of the very lowest description" and as such "*naturally* bigoted and ignorant."[40] In part her call for the unveiling of Turkish women is about using feminism abroad as a colonial strategy. This investment in unveiling Turkish women, however, is also about re-structuring the heterogeneous population of the Ottoman into a racially unified version of the nation that could be slotted on a hierarchy and thus could accommodate the Brasseys' belief that the world should be "moulded" into and guided by the "Anglo-Saxon" character, even if its various populations can never, as a result of their place of birth, be that. The practice of veils and harems, however, actively frustrated this attempt as these hidden worlds and bodies could not be policed and seemed rather to facilitate the mixed populations of the Ottoman that Western travel writers found so disturbing. As Leslie Peirce has noted about the imperial harem "all royal consorts after the first two Ottoman generations (with one exception) were neither Muslim nor Turkish by birth."[41]

The Western anxiety about miscegenation that veiling and harems seemed to encourage is also evident in Anna Bowman Dodd's *In the Palaces of the Sultan*. Traveling to Istanbul as a guest of the United States Ambassador to France in 1901, Dodd writes an eclectic, contentious, and lyrical work that sketches the enormous changes that were occurring as the Ottoman world was collapsing and serves as a record of the last and controversial attempts of Sultan Abdülhamid II, with his Christian confidants and his revival of Islam, to preserve this racially, linguistically, and religiously diverse world that both fascinated and disturbed Dodd. She comments on how there is no dominant race on the streets: "Turk, Greek, Armenian, Khurd, Syrian, Jew, each and all these races, like the rags that draped them, seemed to have been inextricably mixed."[42] It is veiling itself, which conceals skin color, that contributes to this mixing. Commenting on the daughters and wives of the Sultan as they pass in a procession, she writes:

> The faces behind the veils might have been black, white, or yellow; none among those hundred onlookers would ever know their color. ... Within these silken mantles the secret shape or outline, even to the very color of the skin of the favorite wife, daughter, or Khadine, were secrets as closely guarded as though these ladies had never emerged from harem walls.[43]

Writing for a largely American audience for whom interracial marriages were explicitly outlawed in some States, Dodd's emphasis on the varied skin colors, hidden behind the veils of the daughters and wives, would have been read as the very source of Eastern decay. Yet, even if her earlier reference to the "inextricable mix" of the multitude would seem to undercut any attempt to organize it on a hierarchical scale of race, like Brassey, she is quick to support the idea of a dominant race, la raison d'être of imperialism. In her description of the crowd awaiting boats around the Galata Bridge, she writes of:

> The close, dense, packed crowd of Turks in loose, ill-fitting coats and scarlet fezes; of negresses with filthy white veils above whose tattered edges the glowing African eyes roamed wide and far, every turn showing the ivory-whites of their setting; of groups of showy Albanians in their blues and gold; of tattered vendors, carrying their wares to inland markets; and the group, above all others, that riveted the eye, the group centering about the correctly attired figure of the American ambassador, whose simple morning coat and black tie, whose collected repose and air of command, were the dress and the bearing of one of the ruling race.[44]

The appeal to a naturalized "ruling race" in this passage, again, seems to be undone, unwittingly, by the suggestion that it has more to do with performance and dress.

One way of understanding veils and harems is that they, amongst other things and at this historical moment, allowed for hybrid populations and facilitated modes of belonging that challenged modern nationalism and its invention of "natural" territories that housed homogeneous, fixed populations. Invested in establishing racial hierarchies and in policing national boundaries, which in turn fed imperialism, Western travelers in the nineteenth and early twentieth centuries found the cosmopolitan nature of Ottoman society deeply disturbing. The representation of the hidden worlds of veils and harems as tyrannical was, thus, not so much about an interest in the conditions of Turkish women, as it was about eradicating the very fluidity of Ottoman society.

As the model of the racial/ethnic/homogenous nation has increasingly proved itself untenable in the twentieth century, "new cosmopolitanism" has been offered up as a hotly debated post-nationalist version of community.[45] Yet, what I have been suggesting in this essay is that this move might also be understood as a return to an alternative model of modernity that was interrupted by Western imperialism. Roxanne Euben has convincingly argued that an Islamic cosmopolitanism, which has structured various Muslim societies at different historical moments, offers "resources for the reworking of contemporary culture," countering the "presentism," provincialism, and eurocentrism of some of the recent discussions of cosmopolitanism—both pro and anti—that make nationalism the focal point.[46] "The city of the Great Whore" with its "Levantine" populous pre-dates the naturalized and racialized models of nationalism, and offers a useful check to the ahistorical religious and national fundamentalisms that have erupted as anxious responses to the pressures of globalization.

Notes

Many thanks to Zeynep İnankur, Reina Lewis, and Mary Roberts for their deft readings and their valuable feedback, which has made this chapter a much stronger piece.

1 See for instance, Nancy Armstrong in *Desire and Domestic Fiction: A Political History of the Novel* (New York: Oxford University Press, 1987), 3. She discusses "the rise of the domestic woman" and the new gendering of public and private space in the eighteenth century as "a major political event."

2 Jean de Thevenot, *The Travels of Monsieur de Thevenot into the Levant: In Three Parts, viz. into I. Turkey, II. Persia, III. The East-Indies/newly done out of French* (London: Printed by H. Clark for H. Faithorne, 1687), 56–57.

3 William Hunter, *Travels through France, Turkey, and Hungary, to Vienna, in 1792* (London, 1803), 37.

4 Stanley Lane-Poole, *The People of Turkey* (London: John Murray, 1878), xxiii.

5 Mary Riddell, "Why I want to see the veil gone from Britain" [interview with Harriet Harman], *New Statesman*, October 16, 2006, 12.

6 Jean de Thevenot, *Travels in the Levant*, 63.

7 Benedict Anderson, *Imagined Communities: Reflections of the Origin and Spread of Nationalism* (London: Verso, 1983), 19.

8 Michael Hardt and Antonio Negri, *Empire* (Cambridge, MA: Harvard University Press, 2000), 102.

9 Vasant Kaiwar and Sucheta Mazumdar, "Race, Orient, Nation in the Time-Space of Modernity" in *Antinomies of Modernity: Essays on Race, Orient, Nation*, ed. Vasant Kaiwar and Sucheta Mazumdar (Durham and London: Duke University Press, 2003), 265.

10 David Theo Goldberg, *The Racial State* (Oxford: Blackwell 2002), 49.

11 See Ayse Gül Altinay, *The Myth of the Military-Nation: Militarism, Gender, and Education in Turkey* (New York: Palgrave Macmillan, 2004), 17.

12 *Murray's Handbook for Travellers in Constantinople, Brusa, and the Troad* (London: John Murray, 1900), 6.

13 Charles Eliot, *Turkey in Europe* (London: Edward Arnold, 1900), 97.

14 Halidé Adivar Edib, *Memoirs of Halidé Edib* [1926] (Piscataway, NJ: Gorgias Press, 2005), 22.

15 Ibid., 37.

16 Ibid., 23.

17 Ibid., 187.

18 Ibid., 287.

19 Thomas Thornton, *The Present State of Turkey* (London: 1807), 4.

20 Melek Hanım, *Thirty Years in the Harem* [1872] (Piscataway, NJ: Gorgias Press, 2005), 37.

21 Ibid., 51.

22 "A Romance of Stamboul," *Levant Herald*, January 22, 1871, 954.

23 J. C. Nott, "The Mulatto a Hybrid—Probable Extermination of the Two Races if the Whites and Blacks are Allowed to Intermarry," *American Journal of the Medical Sciences* 6 (July 1843): 252–56. Reprinted in the *Boston Medical and Surgical Journal* 29 (August 16, 1843): 29–32.

24 Robert Knox, *The Races of Man: A Philosophical Enquiry into the Influence of Race over the Destinies of Nations*, 2nd edn (London: Henry Renshaw, 1862).

25 Joseph Arthur de Gobineau, *The Inequality of Races*, trans. Adrian Collins (New York: G. P. Putnam's Sons, 1915).

26 Julia Pardoe, *The City of the Sultan, and the Domestic Manners of Turks* (London: Henry Colburn, 1837), 57.

27 Charles Macfarlane, *Constantinople in 1828. A Residence of Sixteen Months in the Turkish Capital and Provinces, with an Account of the Present State of the Naval and Military Power, and of the Resources of the Ottoman Empire* (London: Saunders & Otley, 1829), 14–15.

28 Lucy Garnett, *Turkey of the Ottomans* (London: Isaac Pitman, 1911), 3.

29 Lucy Garnett, *The Women of Turkey and their Folklore* (London: David Nutt, 1891), 414.

30 Robert Young skillfully lays out this history in his book, *Colonial Desire: Hybridity in Theory, Race and Culture* (London: Routledge, 1995).

31 J. C. Nott, *Two Lectures, on the Natural History of the Caucasian and Negro Races* (Mobile, AL: Dade and Thompson, 1844), 14.

32 *The Near East*, January 22, 1920, 115.

33 Ibid., 117.

34 Paul Gilroy, *Against Race: Imagining Political Culture Beyond the Color Line* (Cambridge, MA: Belknap Press of Harvard University Press, 2000), 63.

35 Lady Annie Brassey, *Sunshine and Storm in the East, or Cruises to Cyprus and Constantinople* (London: Longmans, Green, and Co., 1880), 361.

36 Benjamin Disraeli, *Tancred, or the New Crusade*, vol. 2 (London: Henry Colburn, 1847), 181.

37 Ibid., 157.

38 Brassey, *Sunshine and Storm in the East*, 190.

39 Ibid., 109.

40 Ibid., 68 (emphasis mine).

41 Leslie Peirce, *The Imperial Harem: Women and Sovereignty in the Ottoman Empire* (Oxford: Oxford University Press, 1993), 37.

42 Anna Bowman Dodd, *In the Palaces of the Sultan* [1903] (Piscataway, NJ: Gorgias Press, 2005), 169.

43 Ibid., 41.

44 Ibid., 237.

45 See for instance: Kwame Anthony Appiah *Cosmopolitanism: Ethics in a World of Strangers* (New York: Norton, 2006); Gita Rajan and Shailja Sharma, eds., *New Cosmopolitanisms: South Asians in the US* (Stanford, CA: Stanford University Press, 2006); Timothy Brennan, *At Home in the World: Cosmopolitanism Now* (Cambridge, MA: Harvard University Press, 1997); Peng Cheah and Bruce Robbins, eds., *Cosmopolitics: Thinking and Feeling Beyond the Nation* (Minneapolis: University of Minnesota, 1998). This list represents only a handful of the many recent works on cosmopolitanism.

46 Roxanne Euben, *Journey to the Other Shore: Muslim and Western Travelers in Search of Knowledge* (Princeton and Oxford: Princeton University Press, 2006).

Bibliography

"A Romance of Stamboul." *Levant Herald*, January 22, 1871.

Altinay, Ayse Gül. *The Myth of the Military-Nation: Militarism, Gender, and Education in Turkey*. New York: Palgrave Macmillan, 2004.

Anderson, Benedict. *Imagined Communities: Reflections of the Origin and Spread of Nationalism*. London: Verso, 1983.

Appiah, Kwame Anthony. *Cosmopolitanism: Ethics in a World of Strangers*. New York: Norton, 2006.

Armstrong, Nancy. *Desire and Domestic Fiction: A Political History of the Novel*. New York: Oxford University Press, 1987.

Brassey, Lady Annie. *Sunshine and Storm in the East, or Cruises to Cyprus and Constantinople*. London: Longmans, Green, and Co., 1880.

Brennan, Timothy. *At Home in the World: Cosmopolitanism Now*. Cambridge, MA: Harvard University Press, 1997.

Burton, Richard. *Five Footsteps in East Africa; or, an An Exploration of Harar*. London: Longman, 1856.

Cheah, Peng, and Robbins, Bruce, eds. *Cosmopolitics: Thinking and Feeling Beyond the Nation*. Minneapolis: University of Minnesota, 1998.

Disraeli, Benjamin. *Tancred, or the New Crusade*, vol. 2. London: Henry Colburn, 1847.

Dodd, Anna Bowman. *In the Palaces of the Sultan* [1903]. Piscataway, NJ: Gorgias Press, 2005.

Edib, Halidé Adivar. *Memoirs of Halidé Edib* [1926]. Piscataway, NJ: Gorgias Press, 2005.

Eliot, Charles. *Turkey in Europe*. London: Edward Arnold, 1900.

Euben, Roxanne. *Journey to the Other Shore: Muslim and Western Travelers in Search of Knowledge*. Princeton and Oxford: Princeton University Press, 2006.

Garnett, Lucy. *The Women of Turkey and their Folklore*. London: David Nutt, 1891.

Garnett, Lucy. *Turkey of the Ottomans*. London: Isaac Pitman, 1911.

Gilroy, Paul. *Against Race: Imagining Political Culture Beyond the Color Line*. Cambridge, MA: Belknap Press of Harvard University Press, 2000.

Gobineau, Joseph Arthur de. *The Inequality of Races*. Translated by Adrian Collins. New York: G. P. Putnam's Sons, 1915.

Goldberg, David Theo. *The Racial State*. Oxford: Blackwell, 2002.

Hardt, Michael, and Negri, Antonio. *Empire*. Cambridge, MA: Harvard University Press, 2000.

Hunter, William. *Travels through France, Turkey, and Hungary, to Vienna, in 1792*. London, 1803.

Kaiwar, Vasant, and Mazumdar, Sucheta. "Race, Orient, Nation in the Time-Space of Modernity." In *Antinomies of Modernity:*

Essays on Race, Orient, Nation, edited by Vasant Kaiwar and Sucheta Mazumdar, 261–98. Durham and London: Duke University Press, 2003.

Knox, Robert. *The Races of Man: A Philosophical Enquiry into the Influence of Race over the Destinies of Nations*, 2nd edn. London: Henry Renshaw, 1862.

Lane-Poole, Stanley. *The People of Turkey*. London: John Murray, 1878.

Macfarlane, Charles. *Constantinople in 1828. A Residence of Sixteen Months in the Turkish Capital and Provinces, with an Account of the Present State of the Naval and Military Power, and of the Resources of the Ottoman Empire*. London: Saunders & Otley, 1829.

Melek Hanım. *Thirty Years in the Harem*. [1872] Piscataway, NJ: Gorgias Press, 2005.

Murray's Handbook for Travellers in Constantinople, Brusa, and the Troad. London: John Murray, 1900.

Nott, J. C. "The Mulatto a Hybrid–Probable Extermination of the Two Races if the Whites and Blacks Are Allowed to Intermarry." *American Journal of the Medical Sciences* 6 (July 1843): 252–56. Reprinted in the *Boston Medical and Surgical Journal* 29 (August 16, 1843): 29–32.

Nott, J. C. *Two Lectures, on the Natural History of the Caucasian and Negro Races*. Mobile, AL: Dade and Thompson, 1844.

Pardoe, Julia. *The City of the Sultan, and the Domestic Manners of the Turks*. London: Henry Colburn, 1837.

Peirce, Leslie. *The Imperial Harem: Women and Sovereignty in the Ottoman Empire*. Oxford: Oxford University Press, 1993.

Rajan, Gita, and Sharma, Shailja, eds. *New Cosmopolitanisms: South Asians in the US.* Stanford, CA: Stanford University Press, 2006.

Riddell, Mary. "Why I want to see the veil gone from Britain" [interview with Harriet Harman]. *New Statesman*, October 16, 2006.

The Near East, January 22, 1920.

Thevenot, Jean de. *The Travels of Monsieur de Thevenot into the Levant: In Three Parts, viz. into I. Turkey, II. Persia, III. The East-Indies/newly done out of French*. London: Printed by H. Clark for H. Faithorne, 1687.

Thornton, Thomas. *The Present State of Turkey*. London, 1807.

Young, Robert. *Colonial Desire: Hybridity in Theory, Race and Culture*. London: Routledge, 1995.

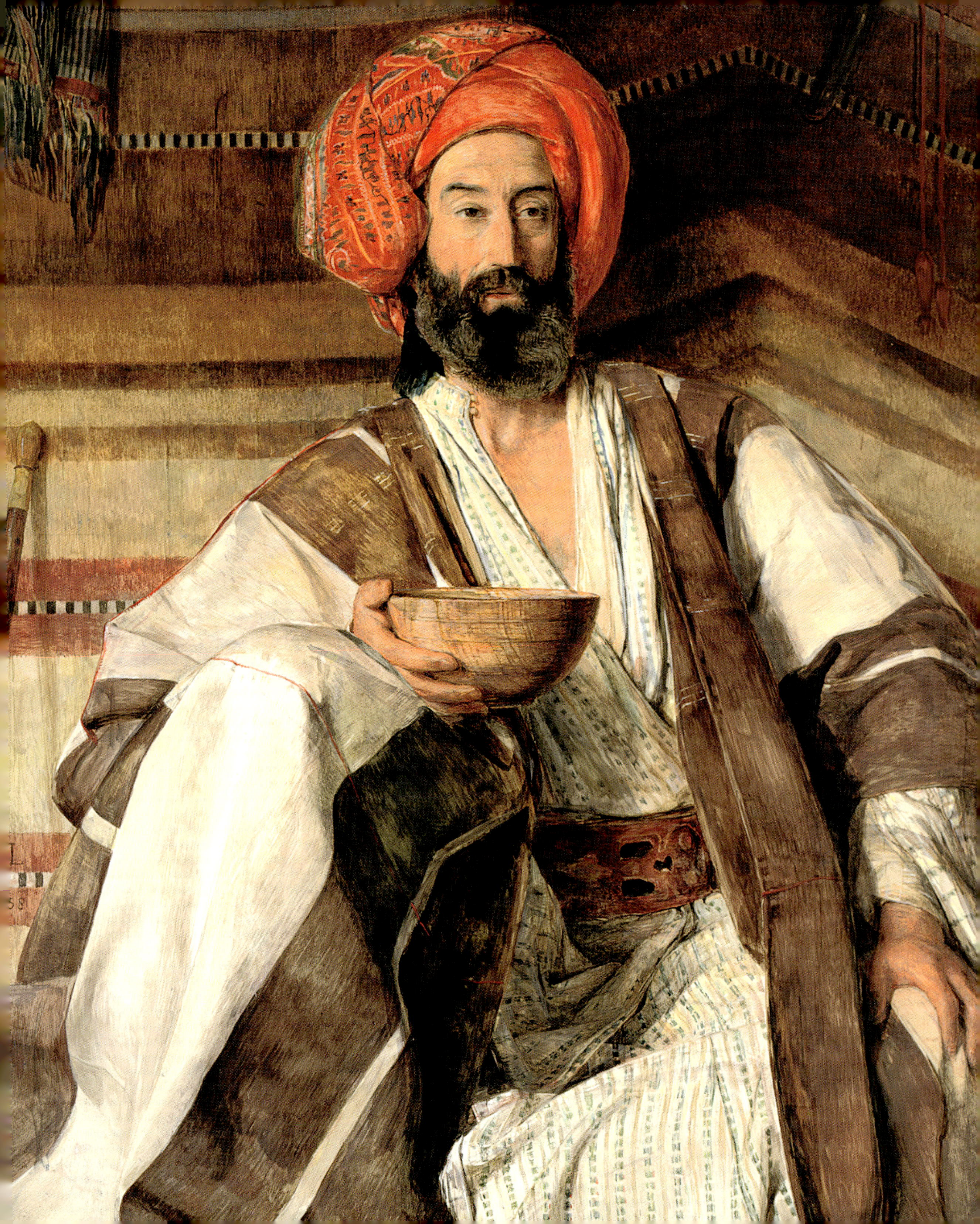

XI

"Solitary Eagle"?[1]

The Public and Private Personas of John Frederick Lewis (1804–1876)

Briony Llewellyn

In 1876, the year that John Frederick Lewis died, his fellow Royal Academician, Charles West Cope, exhibited a painting at that institution, entitled *The Council of the Royal Academy Selecting Pictures for the Exhibition, 1875*.[2] Lewis, seated on the left, is one of a number of eminent Royal Academicians, including Sir Francis Grant, Sir Frederic Leighton and John Everett Millais, selected by Cope to represent the Academy at this time. It was, in the opinion of a later Secretary of the Academy, Frederick Eaton, "a very representative group of some of the principal members of the Academy at the time it was painted, in 1875, and most of the likenesses are excellent," although this was not "a Council that ever actually existed—that is to say the members depicted never all served on the council together."[3] The painting shows Lewis in his public role as a distinguished member of the British art establishment of the mid nineteenth century, commensurate with the high standing he had achieved during a career of over a quarter of a century as the pre-eminent painter of meticulously observed and exquisitely rendered scenes of Oriental life. But in these paintings we can discern another, less orthodox, aspect of his life, a reference to the Oriental role that he had fashioned for himself. The tension between Lewis's two personas—his conventional "Western" face and a more outré "Eastern" obverse—will be explored in this chapter.

A widely disseminated portrait represents him in profile, with white hair and beard, wearing the jacket, stiff white collar and neck-tie that conformed to the expected attire of a respectable Victorian gentleman.[4] This image originated in a carte-de-visite print taken by the well-known photographer of famous artists, John Watkins, and presented to Lewis in 1864 (Fig. 11.1).[5] A further portrait indicative of Lewis's status as an artistic luminary is an unidentified caricaturist's watercolor of the white-haired, white-bearded Lewis, holding palette, paint-brushes and mahl stick (Fig. 11.2).[6] His steely profile is again derived from the Watkins photograph. From what little is known of this apparently amateur British caricaturist, signing with the monogram "SEM," the drawing of Lewis was part of a series of artistic and literary figures that included Edwin Landseer and Charles Dickens.[7]

In a celebratory article to mark Lewis's election as Royal Academician, the *Illustrated London News* styled him "the

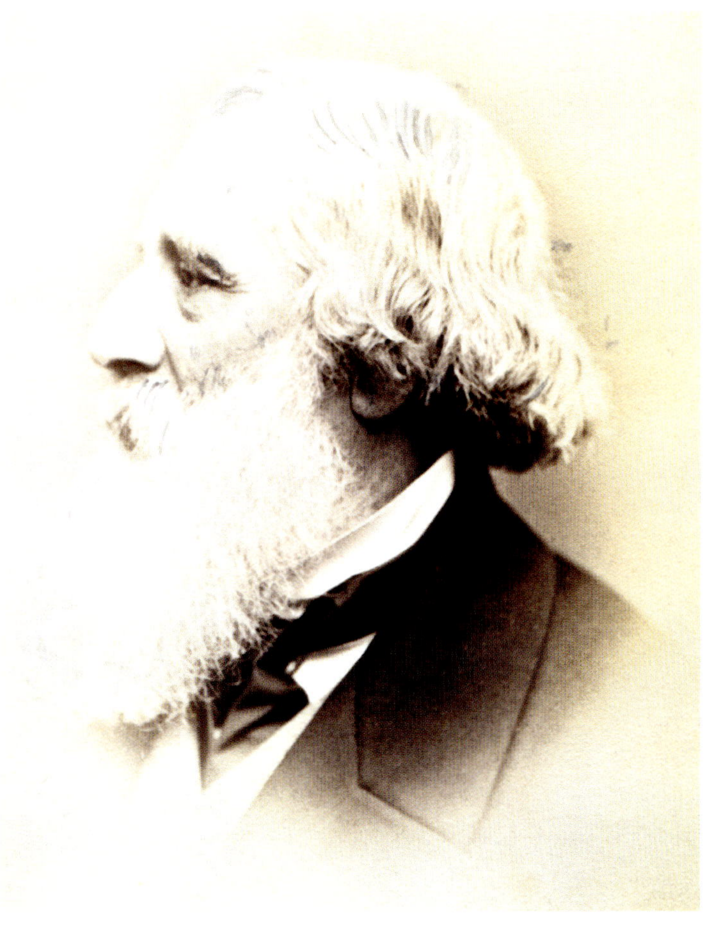

Figure 11.1 *John Frederick Lewis*, John Watkins (1823–1874), 1864, albumen print mounted on card as a carte-de-visite, 8.8 x 5.9 cm, Royal Academy of Arts, London.

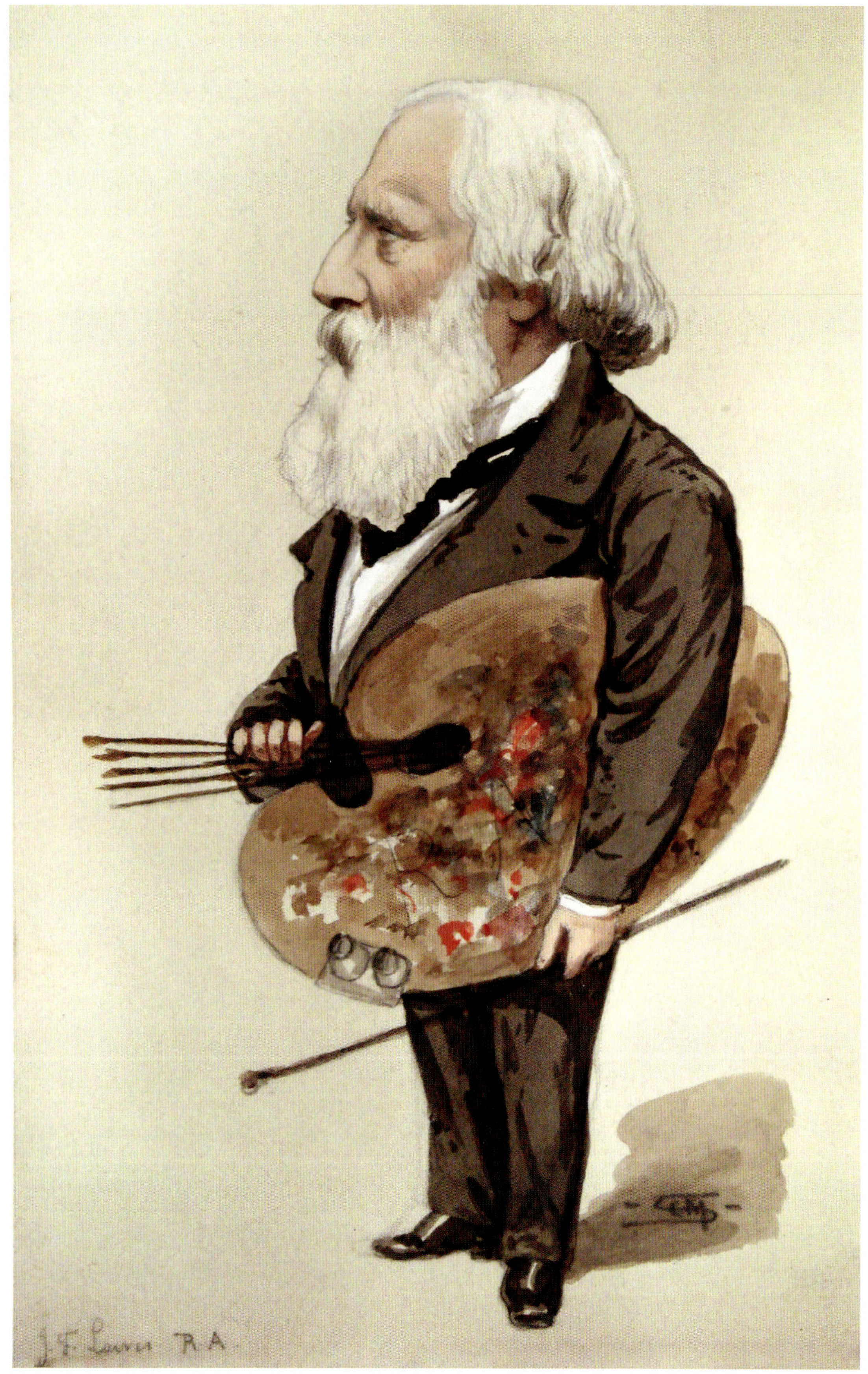

Figure 11.2 *John Frederick Lewis*, "SEM", 1868–74, pencil and watercolor on grey-green paper, 22.2 x 14.2 cm, signed with monogram SEM (or CSM, or CMS), inscribed J. F. Lewis R.A. © Ashmolean Museum, Oxford.

eminent Oriental painter" and underlined his success within the artistic establishment by noting that "his wonderful picture of the court of the Coptic Patriarch's Cairene house" had been hung in "the place of honour in the great East Room" at the previous year's exhibition.[8] For the last decade, the paintings that Lewis had shown at the Royal Academy had received plaudits from the critics. In 1861, for example, a notice in the *Art Journal*, though regretting Lewis's switch in medium from watercolors to oils, wound up on a high note: "there is no better artist in England than J. F. Lewis, while there is none to compare with him in the class of subjects which has made his reputation."[9] Earlier, Lewis's elaborate watercolors, exhibited at the Society of Painters in Water Colours in the 1850s, had drawn lavish praise from the fiery and influential critic, John Ruskin, who had pronounced his *A Frank Encampment in the Desert of Mt. Sinai, 1842* as "among the most *wonderful* pictures in the world."[10] Critical acclaim was matched by commercial success and his paintings sold well to middle-class collectors, newly rich from the manufacture of commodities, who were now enthusiastically acquiring contemporary British art. Few of the prices paid to Lewis himself by collectors are recorded, but his paintings were changing hands in sales later in the century for large sums.[11]

And yet, as his fellow artists well knew, the public role that came with the success of Lewis's Oriental paintings did not sit easy on his shoulders. He was elected President of the Society of Painters in Water Colours in November 1855, but resigned little more than two years later. When required to make an official speech at a members' dinner, he was tongue-tied: "I was *all* abroad—*depressed & spiritless* ... you have a President who whatever other qualities he may possess is evidently a very bad chairman," he wrote next day to the Secretary. In February the following year, he resigned both presidency and membership of the Society, on the grounds of over-work: his watercolor methods were "so laborious & unremunerative, that I now find it *imperative* to pursue it in another & more lucrative material."[12] The strain of juggling his efforts between watercolor and oil, producing work for both exhibiting institutions, had become too much for him. Ambition dictated that oil should be preferred, prompting his decision to resign from the Water-Colour Society in order to maneuver himself into a better position for election to the Royal Academy, since the institution's rules at this time precluded membership of another exhibiting society.[13] The artistic "club" that Lewis joined when he was elected, in 1859 as Associate and in 1865 as full member, of the Royal Academy, does not seem to have been a milieu in which he felt at ease. Ruskin later noted this dislocation from convivial life: "There was something un-English about him, which separated him from the good-humoured groups of established fame whose members abetted or jested with each other. ... He never dined with us, as our other painter friends did."[14] Nor did Lewis relish the obligatory teaching duties as a "Visitor" in the Painting School, where he was remembered by a student, William Silas Spanton, as "not a good teacher, being too fidgety, and particular as to materials."[15] His methods were too meticulous to encourage followers and he preferred to work alone away from the smoke and dirt of London, aided by his wife who is said to have "cleaned his brushes and set his palette."[16]

With this image of an aloof, unsociable Lewis in mind, apparently at a far remove from the dandified bon viveur of his younger days, the features of the Watkins photograph—craggy brow, large beaky nose and wary expression—which the "SEM" caricature brings more sharply into focus, construct an identity that seems aptly described, fifty years after his death, as "this solitary eagle."[17] The appellation may have arisen from comments made by John Frederick's elderly nephew, John Hardwicke Lewis, who had described his uncle as "a reticent man, easily irritated."[18] Despite his reclusive existence away from London, Lewis was sufficiently interested in the response to his Royal Academy exhibits for the Pre-Raphaelite sculptor, Thomas Woolner, a fervent admirer of Lewis's, to write him a long account of the 1874 private view: "You now live so much out of the world that such things must be to you like the faint sounds of a triumphal procession heard in the remote distance." According to Woolner, his lavish praise of Lewis's "Cairo picture," *The Bezestein Bazaar of El Khan Khalil, Cairo*, resulted in the elderly collector, John Graham, offering the owner, David Price, £10,000 for the painting, but to no avail, for "no money should tempt him to part with it."[19] Lewis's response to Woolner was immediate: "I am in dreamland."[20]

Public recognition and success in the market were undoubtedly of paramount importance to Lewis, and were goals that he actively pursued. His deliberate removal of himself and his wife away from the hub of artistic activity in London to the suburban seclusion of Walton-on-Thames, however, seems to indicate that contradictory impulses, propelling him towards a constructed public persona on the one hand and recoiling from it on the other, were at work within his personality. I would suggest that this dichotomy in Lewis's life between the seeking and the shunning of the limelight is reflected in the disguised auto-mimetic representations that recur so frequently in his work.[21]

The best known of these is Lewis's *In the Bezestein, El Khan Khalil, Cairo*, one of the paintings exhibited at the Royal

Academy in 1861 that prompted the *Art Journal* eulogy already cited.[22] Two photographs of Lewis himself in Ottoman dress and a pencil and watercolor self-portrait, wearing a turban, have been the basis for the identification of the figure as Lewis himself; as a result, this complex image has been the subject of substantive discussion by several scholars.[23] Various hypotheses have been proposed around the idea that this painting embodies a self-promotional construct on the part of the artist: that it is a visual expression for a Western audience of the experience and authority of an oriental traveler; that it is a Western artist's conscious or sub-conscious "desire for power" over the Orient; that it is a metaphor for the commercial dialog between the artist and his customers. To these theoretical arguments I wish to add some empirically based observations through an investigation of Lewis's other similarly "disguised" representations of himself and an examination of them in the context of Lewis's own biography.

A most puzzling aspect of this painting's launch on to the market, is, that if any of its viewers were aware that the figure represented Lewis, they made no comment, at least none that is extant. Leaving aside the most obvious indication of his identity—the resemblance to the physical presence of Lewis himself—there were other pointers by which he could have been recognized. The two photographs of Lewis in this same Ottoman dress probably date from the 1860s, and the costume is probably the very one in which, "dressed as a Turk," he is reported to have attended a fancy dress ball.[24] However, the audience for both events is likely to have been private rather than public.[25] In more general circulation, was the now much-discussed passage in William Makepeace Thackeray's *Notes of a Journey from Cornhill to Grand Cairo*, describing the novelist's visit to Lewis's house in the "Arab quarter" of Cairo and his outdoor costume "of dark blue, consisting of an embroidered jacket and gaiters, and a pair of trousers, which would make a set of dresses for one English family."[26] Published in 1846, this elaborate, apparent "advertisement," may have been "a calculated business deal between an author and an all-but-forgotten artist, about to re-enter the Victorian art world," but the document that supports this contention is second-hand rather than direct evidence, from a not wholly reliable source.[27] Moreover, the fact remains that even if Lewis had been intending to re-launch himself on to the art market in the form of a painting, shortly after Thackeray published his account, he did not in fact do so for another four years. It seems that Lewis's own motives, both in relation to Thackeray's beguiling description of his life in Cairo, and to the later photographs were ambiguous.

The same white-bearded man who appears in the *Bezestein* painting had been seen in a small panel exhibited at the Royal Academy three years earlier, *Interior of a Mosque at Cairo—Afternoon Prayer (the 'Asr)* (Fig. 11.3).[28] He seems to be wearing the same blue outfit (the pigment has darkened), with the slippers and sword put to one side, and a red patterned cloth wound round his head as a turban, instead of the cream-colored one. None of these garments can securely be identified as among the numerous items of Oriental clothing in the sale of Lewis's effects after his death, but the red Kashmir sash remained with Lewis's wife, Marian and has survived.[29] If, despite such pointers, neither Lewis nor anyone else, as far as we can ascertain, saw fit to publicize the identity of the principal figure in these images, then their purpose

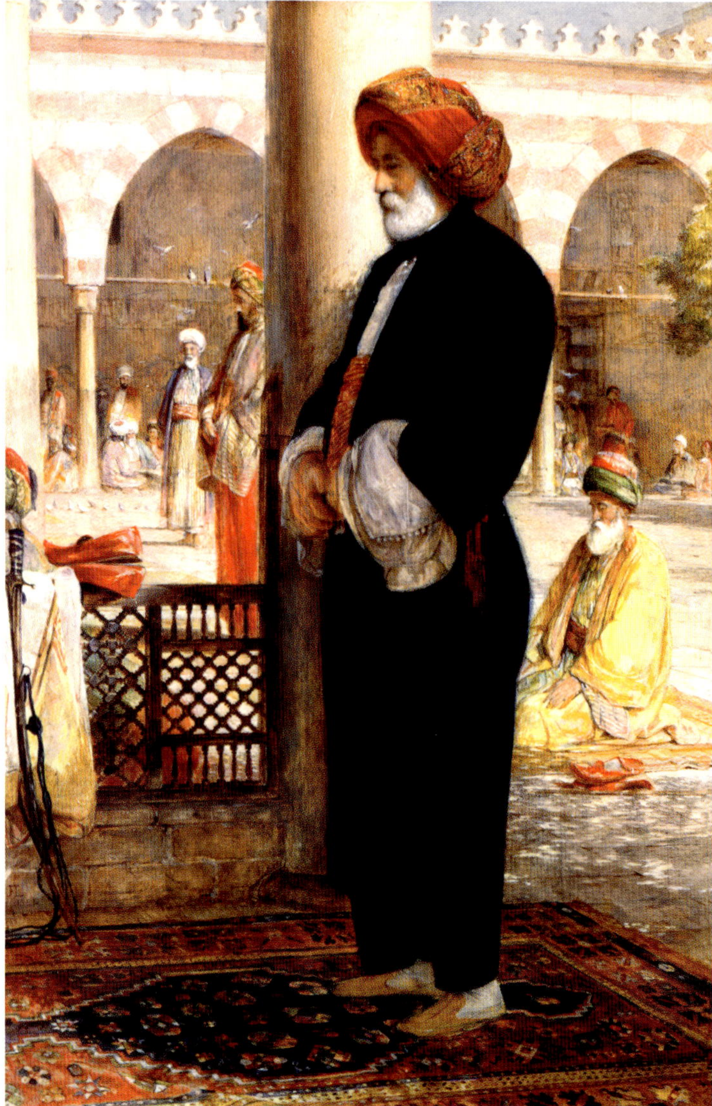

Figure 11.3 *Interior of a Mosque at Cairo—Afternoon Prayer (The 'Asr)*, John Frederick Lewis (1804–1876), 1857, oil on panel, 31 x 21 cm, signed and dated JFL/1857, Private Collection. © Mathaf Gallery, London.

in creating an elaborate "spinning" of his public image and an assertion of his authority as a painter of the Orient, was subtle indeed. It seems that there was a collective blindness to his identity, or perhaps a collective wish not to break the "Oriental spell" that Lewis had conjured.

It could be argued that artistic charades of this type were so well understood that no one thought it worth a mention. Artists and other prominent travelers in Oriental dress frequently appeared on the walls of the Royal Academy as a means of advertising their sitters' adventures overseas, often with titles suggesting "disguise," despite the widespread knowledge of their identity. The most obvious precedent was Thomas Phillips's portrait of Lord Byron, exhibited in 1814, with the title *Portrait of a Nobleman in the Dress of an Albanian*, which, "sought to confuse the division between his poetry and his own biography and identity."[30] Twenty-six years later, Robert Scott Lauder, taking his cue from what had become an iconic image, invested his portrait of *David Roberts Esq. in the Dress he wore in Palestine*, with a romanticism that the pragmatic Scot hardly possessed. Artistic license also applied to the costume, authentic in detail but not as an ensemble.[31] In fact, Roberts usually wore Western dress during his Eastern travels, only donning local garments on occasions for expediency or comfort,[32] and despite the propagandist potential of this portrait, it is notable that for the frontispiece of his *Holy Land* volumes Roberts chose to have himself portrayed in conventional Western clothes by a leading lithographic portraitist.[33] Although Roberts had initially been pleased with Scott Lauder's portrait, he later deplored "the representation of the Edinburgh callant in that outlandish dress."[34] Roberts's ambivalent attitude to the public association of himself with Oriental attire, may provide a clue to Lewis's diffidence in declaring his own identity.

While the role-playing and self-promotional aspects of Lewis's bazaar portrait, subtle as they were, may be part of the story, it is not the whole one. I suggest that he was practicing a sleight-of-hand with his identity, entirely in keeping with the coexistence in his personality of reticence and display, opposing traits that seem also to characterize his manipulation of his reputation. On the one hand, there is the absence of a substantial memoir either during or after his lifetime and of a commemorative exhibition at the Royal Academy that was accorded to several artists of similar stature, as well as the lack of a large corpus of correspondence, inferring an apparent disinterest in the opinion of posterity. On the other, surviving letters and the celebratory notices that were published during and after his lifetime, evince a concern with public opinion.[35]

Born into a prodigiously talented artistic family, Lewis was aware from a young age of the intensely competitive art market of early nineteenth-century London and the need to create an artistic niche for himself. An early pencil drawing, which shows him posing nonchalantly, with his two younger brothers behind, neatly encapsulates the dandyish persona that Lewis adopted as a young man.[36] The consciousness of self that was invaluable for a young, ambitious artist is evident in the numerous self-portrait drawings that are also contained within this album of Lewis's early drawings (Figs. 11.4 and 11.5). Like many artists before and since, Lewis used his own features to experiment with different poses as well as to communicate aspects of his self-image, adopting the practice later recommended by a younger contemporary, William Powell Frith.[37] Although, like Frith, Lewis was probably aware

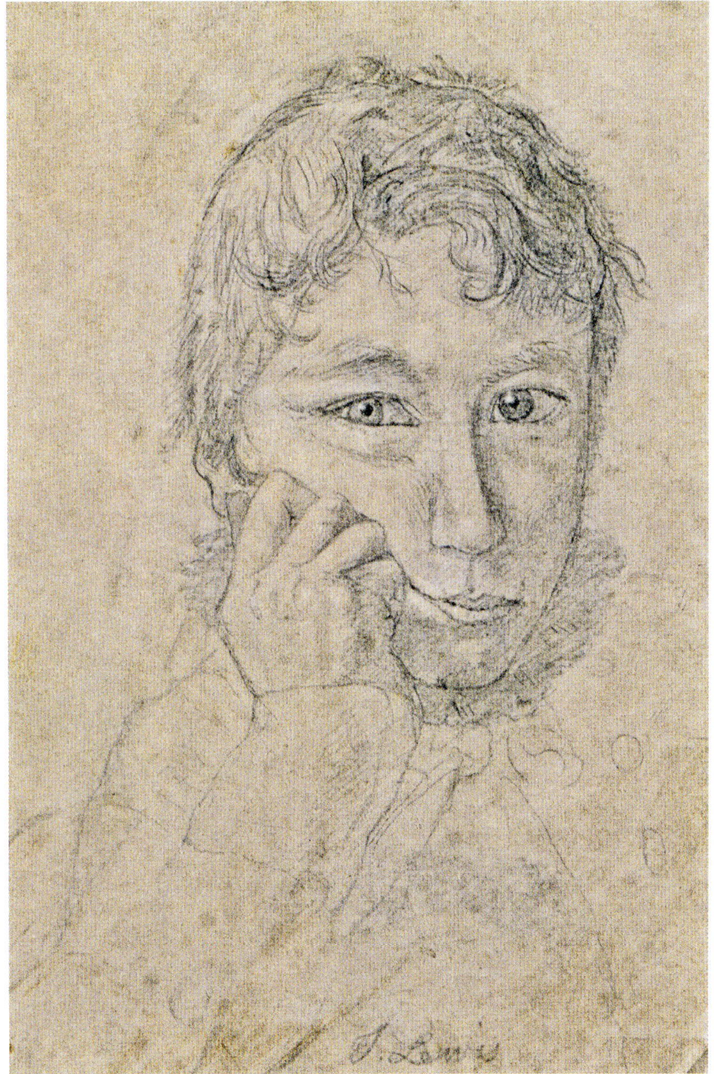

Figure 11.4 *Self-Portrait of the Artist as a Boy*, John Frederick Lewis (1804–1876), 1816–18, pencil on brown wove paper, 16.5 x 11.2 cm, inscribed J. Lewis, Royal Academy of Arts, London.

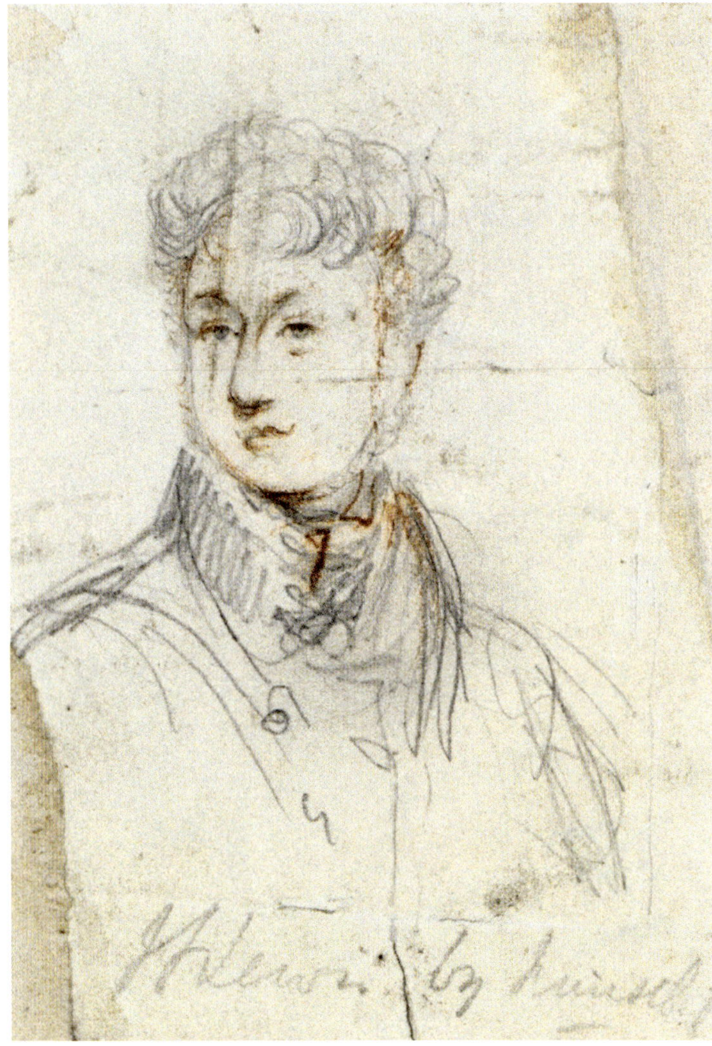

Figure 11.5 *Self-Portrait as a Young Man*, John Frederick Lewis (1804–1876), early 1820s, pencil and chalk on wove paper, 8.8 x 6.3 cm, inscribed JF Lewis by himself, Royal Academy of Arts, London.

that he was following established artistic tradition, his early self-portraits, unlike those of many other artists, did not enter the public arena, being made, it seems, solely for himself and his family.[38]

A wider audience was certainly intended for the flamboyant portrayal of Lewis in his early twenties, by the fashionable miniaturist Simon Jacques Rochard.[39] The stylish clothes, aquiline features and abundant whiskers convey an image of a self-assured man of the world, whose charm with women prompted Roberts's description of him as "quite a Blood"[40] and whose passion for fine clothes and good living elicited Thackeray's witty, if exaggerated, portrayal of him as "the exquisite of the Europa and the Trois Frères."[41] The confidence that Lewis displays here was well founded since his paintings of animals and sporting subjects were bringing him both critical and commercial success. The following year, in one of the changes of direction that marked his career, Lewis undertook the first of his sojourns abroad, donning the mantle of European artist-traveler. Glimpses of this character that he assumed are seen in a pencil sketch from the Royal Academy's album, titled *By Himself on the Rhine*,[42] and in a fellow-artist's description of his "huge pair of mustachios which had come to maturity during his tour in Germany, where he learnt to smoke much and shave little."[43] The portrait of Lewis by William Boxall, dating, according to Marian Lewis, from 1832, just before his visit to Spain, represents another subtle shift in identity.[44] Fashionable sideburns have replaced the "mustachios" in an image probably intended for a public display, but it remained unfinished and with the artist until given by him to Lewis's widow after 1876.[45]

Lewis's physical absence for over a decade from the London art scene was matched by a singular lack of information about what later seemed to his stay-at-home compatriots a life that was "strange and adventurous."[46] In Cairo from 1841 to 1851, he wrote few letters and sent no works back for exhibition; nor are there any securely identified portraits of him known. "How was he spending his time?," they asked, "And why were the talents of so great an artist as he had proved himself to be thus hidden under a bushel?"[47] Lewis's art-loving audience were dependent on Thackeray's colorful account of him as "an oriental nobleman" who "lives like a languid Lotus-eater—a dreamy, hazy, lazy, tobaccofied life,"[48] but his well-known hyperbole has now been both corroborated and undermined by more recently uncovered references from other European visitors and residents, rounding out the persona of indigenous Cairene that Lewis adopted in Egypt.[49] He was not alone in this, a partial adoption of Ottoman dress and life-style being the norm for Europeans living in, rather than just visiting, Cairo,[50] among whom the best known is Edward William Lane, author of the popular and authoritative compendium of Egyptian social life, *Manners and Customs of the Modern Egyptians*, published in 1836.[51] At the same time, these expatriates retained European habits, collected antiquities and formed societies.[52] Lewis appeared out at dinner "dressed in a handsome oriental costume," and, in his own house, served the Egyptian cuisine that Thackeray spoofs, but he also drank tea and, if Thackeray is to be believed, beer, supplied by English firms.[53]

If Thackeray fabricates an Arabian-Nights style glamour for Lewis's existence in Cairo, the French adventurer and long-time Eastern resident, Achille Constant Théodore Émile Prisse d'Avennes, paints a distinctly less flattering picture of him, centered around a transaction involving sex and money.[54] Against a background of Abolition in Britain, the continuation of the slave trade in Egypt was the source of both repugnance and fascination for Western visitors. David Roberts and William Muller had depicted the slave market in the Wikalat al-Gallaba in Cairo, but Lewis, with his customary ability to present topical subjects in a novel situation, made the purchase of a slave within a private home the subject of the picture with which he re-launched himself on to the London art market, with sensational results.[55] According to Prisse, the story behind the representation of this scene, reflects rather less well on Lewis. Seeing a beautiful slave in the market he asks Prisse to purchase her on his behalf, so that he can use her as a model, but the deal goes sour when the slave, whose name is given as Husné, objects to "that hateful Christian, that repellent old greybeard, whose touch and filthy caresses disgust me." Returning her to Prisse, Lewis demands his money back, and the situation descends to the level of a sordid farce. If Thackeray's image of Lewis as an "oriental nobleman" must be treated with skepticism, Prisse's tale of the lascivious, slave-owning Lewis may also be exaggerated. Although Prisse is described as a "friend" of Lewis's,[56] he was a Frenchman who made his living as a draughtsman, possibly with his own axe to grind against a successful British artist. The account was transcribed many years after the event and may have gained color with the passing of years. Whether embellished or not, the account highlights the equivocacy of Lewis's encounter with Islamic society, for, as we have seen, he, like Lane, Prisse d'Avennes, Henry Abbott and other European residents of long standing, adopted a hybrid lifestyle that placed him on the overlapping borders between East and West, occupying what Ahdaf Soueif has termed "the common ground."[57] This ground was itself unstable, since the reforms introduced by the Ottoman Sultan in Istanbul and his Viceroy, Muhammad Ali in Egypt were eroding cultural distinctions, and the Egyptian traditions that both Lewis and Lane were attempting to "fix" for posterity were giving way to European modernization.[58]

When he returned to England, I submit that Lewis attempted to perpetuate the cultural traverse that he had experienced in Egypt by painting a series of images that presented Oriental figures with features that were reminiscent of his own, at least an ideal version of them, as they were when he was living in Cairo—long face with large nose and dark, bushy beard. It can also be argued that there is a self-representational element in a great many of the male figures in Lewis's Orientalist paintings, some of them central to the narrative, some painted towards the edges of the picture space.[59] Not one of these disguised "portraits," whether single or part of a group, was declared as such. One of the earliest of the single figure sequence is *A Syrian Scheik, Egypt*, apparently a Bedouin Arab from one region displaced in another.[60] The same "Arab" wearing almost identical garments—striped *qumbaz*, woollen *abayeh*, and on his head a red and yellow silk *kuffieh*—but this time removed from the desert to the city, is also the subject of a small oil panel, dated 1857 (Fig. 11.6).[61] The most compelling image of all is *An Arab of the Desert of Sinai*, depicting the same "desert Arab," again wearing almost identical robes, but with a red turban head-dress (Fig. 11.7).[62] This time the figure is comfortably ensconced in a tent in the Sinai, relaxed and confident within his own sphere, and so placed, right at the front of the picture plane, as to connect with the viewer's space. His assurance perhaps reflects Lewis's own feelings of affinity for the perceived simplicity of desert life.[63]

This sequence of "Arab" figures thus represents disguised, retrospective portrayals of an idealized Lewis. They are images intended for public display and for sale to wealthy middle-class clients, exhibited at the Royal Academy in the late 1850s and 1860s, just at the time when he had again switched his principal exhibiting medium from watercolor back to oil, and was making his bid to join the ranks of that august institution. In seeking to combine the roles of British and Egyptian grandee, he appears to be revealing his own continuing sympathies with the culture he had partially adopted for ten years, and to be expressing a desire to dissolve the distinctions between East and West. The complexities of Lewis's intentions must remain speculative, since neither Lewis nor anyone else declared a connection between representee and representer, but it is possible that, as well as demonstrating publicly his familiarity with and understanding of Egyptian culture and his unique ability to portray this for a British audience, they were also a private conceit to enable him to relive his oriental experience. If his art seems to hover in a hinterland between artifice and actuality, cumulative hints from correspondents suggest that in his life too there was a blurring of the edges between fantasy and reality. While physically inhabiting a private world in a genteel suburb by the Thames, he and his wife, Marian, may have attempted to recreate the "terrestrial paradise" beside the Nile that they had left behind.[64] Its delights were experienced by Thomas Woolner, who, visiting Lewis the year before he died, wrote that he had "for a while lived the life of the Arabian Nights; with all its joys and without any of the evil."[65] In the same year, Lewis's old friend, Edward Coleridge, wrote fondly of "my little visit to your Oriental Tent at Walton."[66] By privately inhabiting the role of the character he was creating for public display in paint, he was attempting to mesh these opposing aspects of his life together. On one side of the coin is the "British Lewis": the official role that

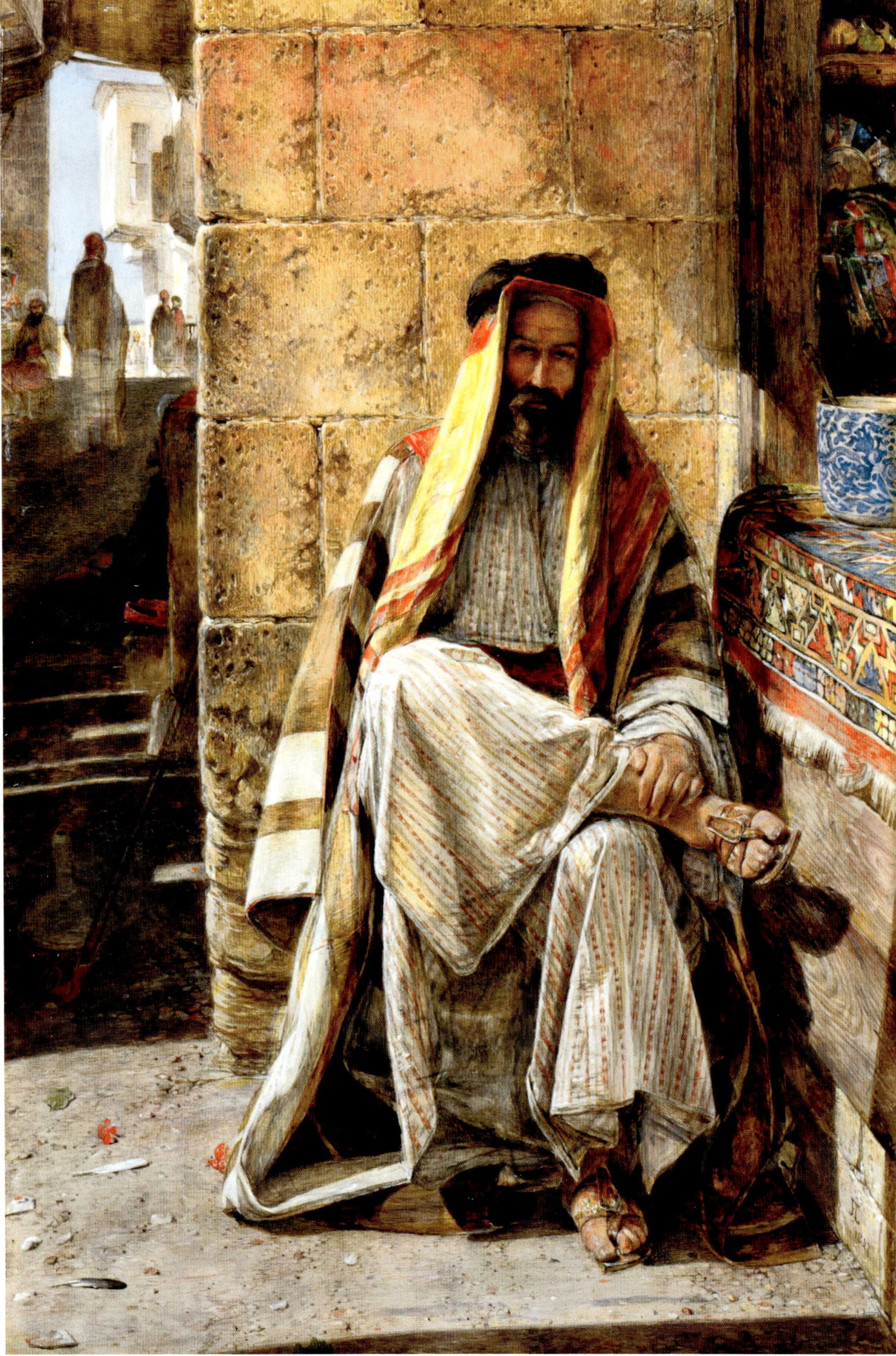

Figure 11.6 *An Arab, Seated in a Cairo Bazaar*, John Frederick Lewis (1804–1876), 1857, oil on board, 31.2 x 20.2 cm, signed and dated JFL/1857, Private Collection. © Christie's Images Limited 2010.

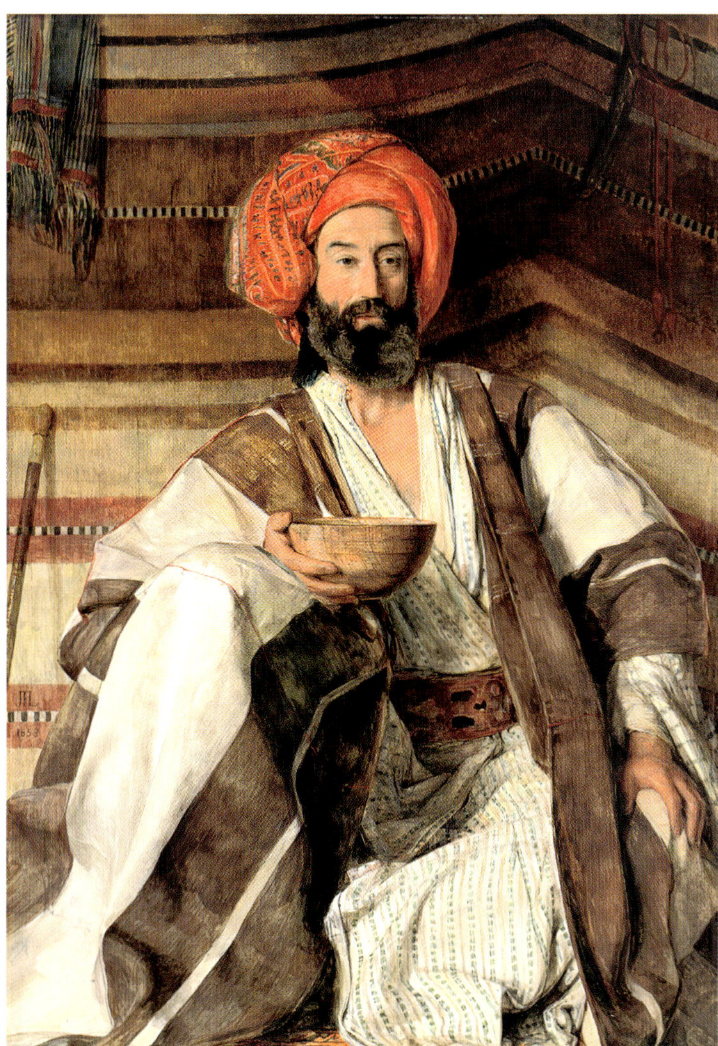

Figure 11.7 *An Arab of the Desert of Sinai*, John Frederick Lewis (1804–1876), 1858, oil on panel, 43.5 x 30.5 cm, signed and dated JFL/1858, Shafik Gabr Collection, Cairo. Reproduced by kind permission of Mr. Shafik Gabr, Chairman and Managing Director of ARTOC Group for Investment and Development, Egypt.

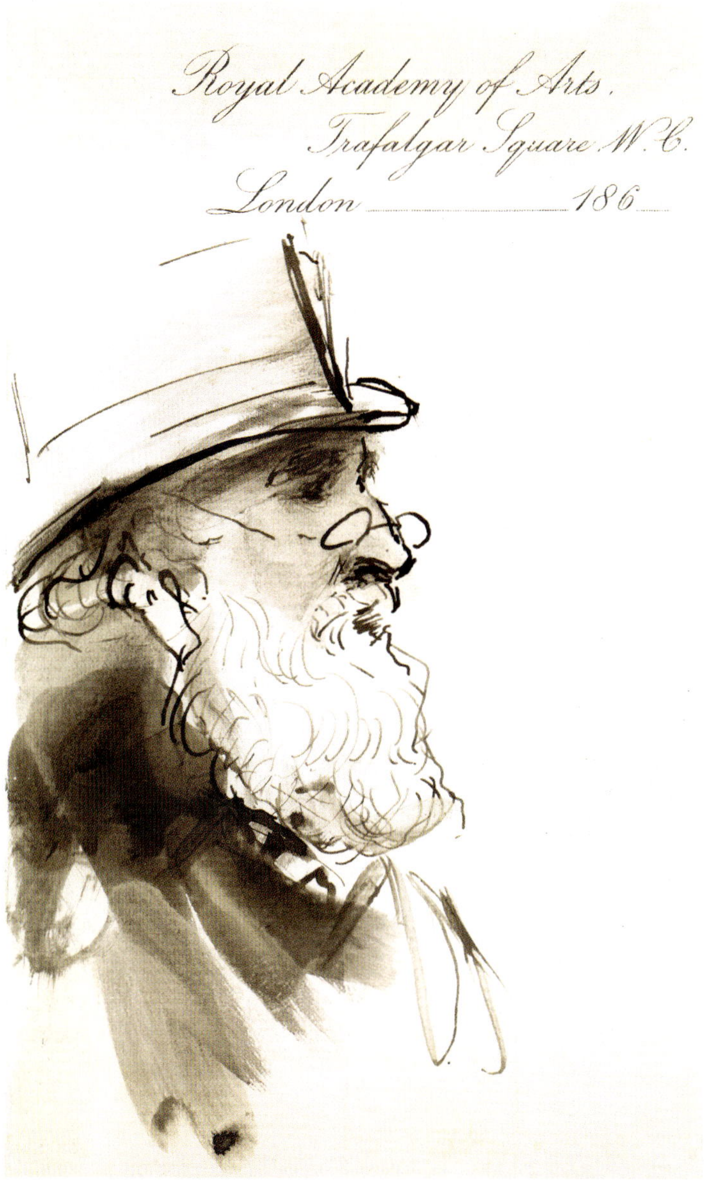

Figure 11.8 *Portrait Sketch of John Frederick Lewis*, Sir Francis Grant PRA (1803–1878), 1865–68, pen and ink wash on a sheet of Royal Academy stationery of the 1860s, 17.6 x 11 cm (sheet size), inscribed on the backing sheet JF. Lewis R.A, Private Collection. Courtesy of Lowell Libson Ltd, London.

he had fashioned for himself as respected member of the British art establishment and respectable Victorian gentleman. This aspect of Lewis's persona is represented in a more informal way than in the stiff Watkins photograph in a rapid sketch by Francis Grant, of Lewis attending Royal Academy business, c. 1866–67. With disheveled hair and beard, spectacles on the end of his nose and hat rammed on to his head, this seems to represent Lewis free from any of the guises that he assumed (Fig. 11.8). On the other side of the coin is his Oriental construct, as exhibited in the single "portraits" discussed above, and as figures inserted into compositions such as *The Doubtful Coin*, exhibited in 1869, where one might see the features of the "old" Lewis in those of the venerable *seraff*, and of his younger self in those of the merchant.[67]

Just as his career changed direction several times, so Lewis affected different personas at different times of his life, some of them conflicting, some complementary, reflecting the contrarities within his personality. Apparent non-productivity contrasts with painstaking attention to detail; the respected but aloof "great Oriental" was at the same time an uxorious husband;[68] the extrovert dandy who loved extravagant clothes and frequented clubs was also an introverted seeker of solitude, with a nervous disposition. He was, as his younger contemporary, Baudelaire, wrote in 1863, "an 'I' with an insatiable appetite for the 'non-I,'"[69] Nevertheless, in a career that was punctuated by intermittent translocations, one of the unifying themes might be the representations of himself that extend from his boyhood to his venerable old age.

Notes

I am indebted to many people for their assistance with the preparation of this chapter. For general comments: Nebahat Avcioğlu, Alexander Gimson, Charles Newton; for access to particular sources in museums and archives: Patricia Allderidge, Mark Bills, Paul Cox, Rosemary Crill, Sally Doust, Pat Eaton, Donato Esposito, Simon Fenwick, Colin Harrison, Penny Hatfield, Hannah Hawkesworth, Clive Lewis, Jan Marsh, Krystyna Matyjaszkiewicz, Jan Piggott, Mark Pomeroy, Jason Thompson, Mercedes Volait, Jennifer Wearden, Emily Weeks and Annette Wickham.

1 Randall Davies, "John Frederick Lewis, R. A. (1805–1876)," in *The Old Water-Colour Society's Club, 1925–1926*, 3 (1926): 40.

2 Royal Academy of Arts, London (03/1288).

3 Sir Frederick Eaton, "The Royal Academy," *Scribner's Magazine* 36 (October 1904): 564–65, 568–69. Lewis had served the required two years on the Council after his election as RA in 1865, and again in 1874, but resigned before the exhibition. He retired in 1876. See RA Archives.

4 Engraved in the *Illustrated London News*, Supplement, March 25, 1865, 285; in the *Graphic* obituary, August 26, 1876, 204. Engravings were presented by his brother Charles to friends and institutions (British Museum, London, 1878, 0914.35 and National Portrait Gallery, London, D36909 and D36910).

5 Lewis to Watkins, October 9, 1864, Watkins Album, National Portrait Gallery, London (NPGMS 113, p. 96). Royal Academy of Arts, London (04/262 and 05/2685) and another copy in the Rob Dickins Collection, Watts Gallery, Compton (COMWG2008.163.4364). Another set of carte-de-visite photographs were taken by Elliott & Fry in the later 1860s: National Portrait Gallery, London (Ax14823, Ax28933, Ax17262, Ax131897).

6 Bound into an extra-illustrated RA catalogue, 1874, compiled by Caleb Scholefield Mann, Ashmolean Museum, Oxford (with reg. no. WA1967.6.3).

7 Its style relates to the *Vanity Fair* artists, active from 1868 onwards. The caricature of Landseer, Victoria and Albert Museum, London (E.1355–1948) and of Charles Dickens, Charles Dickens Museum, London.

8 The *Illustrated London News*, op. cit. The painting referred to is *The Hòsh (courtyard) of the House of the Coptic Patriarch Cairo*, exhibited RA 1864 (110); Private Collection, see Sotheby's November 20, 1996 (253).

9 The *Art Journal*, June 1, 1861, 167–68.

10 John Ruskin, "Academy Notes," 1856, in *The Works of John Ruskin*, ed. E. T. Cook and Alexander Wedderburn (London: George Allen; New York: Longmans, Green, and Co., 1903–12) 14: 73–74. The watercolor, exhibited in 1856 at the SPWC (134), is at the Yale Center for British Art, New Haven (B1977.14.143).

11 For Lewis's patrons, see Dianne Sachko Macleod, *Art and the Victorian Middle Class: Money and the Making of Cultural Identity* (Cambridge: Cambridge University Press, 1996).

12 See Simon Fenwick, *The Enchanted River: Two Hundred Years of the Royal Watercolour Society* (Bristol: Sansom and Company, 2004), 57–64, and Simon Fenwick and Greg Smith, *The Business of Watercolour: A Guide to the Archives of the Royal Watercolour Society* (Aldershot: Ashgate, 1997), 193–95.

13 The ban was lifted in 1866: see Sidney C. Hutchison, *The History of the Royal Academy 1768–1986*, 2nd edn (London: Robert Royce, 1986).

14 John Ruskin, *Praeterita*, 1885–89, in *The Works of John Ruskin*, ed. E. T. Cook and Alexander Wedderburn (London: George Allen; New York: Longmans, Green, and Co., 1903–12), 35: 405–6. Lewis was a member of The Athenaeum Club in 1856, but, probably through necessity rather than inclination.

15 Cited in Hugh Stokes, "John Frederick Lewis R. A. (1805–1876)," *Walker's Quarterly* 28 (1929): 45. Lewis was a "Visitor" in 1866 and 1867.

16 W. S. Spanton, *An Art Student and his Teachers in the Sixties with other Rigmaroles* (London: R. Scott, 1927), 44.

17 Davies, "John Frederick Lewis, R. A.".

18 Ibid., 40. In preparing his short biographical article on Lewis, Davies, grappling with the dearth of biographical data that continues to perplex Lewis scholars, had written to John Hardwicke Lewis (1840–1927).

19 Woolner to Lewis, May 3, 1874, Lewis Family Collection (A27). See also Woolner to Lewis, May 17, 1874, Yale Center for British Art, New Haven, Paul Mellon Fund (MS. Woolner). The Bezestein Bazaar

(RA 1874, 332; Private Collection) is illustrated in Nicholas Tromans ed., *The Lure of the East: British Orientalist Painting* (London: Tate Publishing, 2008), 93.

20 Lewis to Woolner, May 4, 1874, in Amy Woolner, *Thomas Woolner, R. A., Sculptor and Poet: His Life in Letters* (London: Chapman and Hall, 1917), 293–94.

21 On auto-mimetic portraits, see Francis Ames-Lewis, *The Intellectual Life of the Early Renaissance Artist* (London and New Haven: Yale University Press, 2000), 209–43 and on the function of self-portraiture see Shearer West, *Portraiture* (Oxford: Oxford University Press, 2004), 163–85.

22 RA 1861 (266); Private Collection, see Sotheby's, November 20, 1996 (251). Reduced watercolor version in Blackburn Museum and Art Gallery (551), illustrated in Tromans, *The Lure of the East*, 68.

23 Briony Llewellyn, "A 'Masquerade' Unmasked: An Aspect of John Frederick Lewis's Encounter with Egypt," in *Egyptian Encounters*, ed. Jason Thompson, vol. 23, no. 3 of *Cairo Papers in Social Science* (Fall 2000): 133–51 and, more extensively, Emily M. Weeks, "The 'Reality Effect': The Orientalist Paintings of John Frederick Lewis (1805–1876)" (PhD diss., Yale University, 2004), 1–138. See also Tromans,*The Lure of the East*, 22–23, 56. The photographs are undated albumen prints by an unknown photographer or photographers; one 140 x 108 mm, Cyril Fry Collection, the other 111.5 x 114.5 mm, Royal Watercolour Society Archive, London (J57/80); both illustrated in Tromans, *The Lure of the East*, 23. Lewis's choice of dress is discussed in Mary Roberts, *Intimate Outsiders: The Harem in Ottoman and Orientalist Art and Travel Literature* (Durham and London: Duke University Press, 2007), 38–39.

24 W. S. Spanton, recalling events of c. 1866–67, cited in Stokes, "John Frederick Lewis R. A.," 45.

25 Only one copy of each photograph is known to survive, suggesting that few were produced, and although one is now in the collection of the Royal Watercolour Society, the date and circumstances of its acquisition are unknown; there is nothing in the RWS Archives to suggest that it was part of the series of members' photographs proposed by J. D. Harding in 1860, by which time Lewis was no longer a member. The photograph is more likely to have been a private gesture of friendship to his former colleague, Joseph Jenkins, Secretary of the Water-Colour Society, on the part of Lewis or his widow.

26 William Makepeace Thackeray [Michael Angelo Titmarsh, pseud.], *Notes of a Journey from Cornhill to Grand Cairo*, reprint (Heathfield, Sussex: Cockbird Press, 1991), 142–46.

27 Weeks, "The 'Reality Effect,'" 55; she also acknowledges its ambiguity. According to Jenkins, Lewis, in Cairo, had received a note from Thackeray: "I don't want much money—but any trifle you can bestow will be thankfully received by yours truly Thackeray" (RWS J107/196). Since separate documentary evidence has shown that the previous item (RWS J107/195), concerning the relationship between the young Lewis and Sir Thomas Lawrence, contains inconsistencies, this recall of a conversation should be treated with caution. See Fenwick and Smith, *The Business of Watercolour*, 273.

28 RA 1858 (245); Private Collection, illustrated in Tromans, *The Lure of the East*, 192.

29 Christie's, Manson & Woods, London, Catalog of the remaining works of that distinguished artist, John F. Lewis, RA., deceased, May 7, 1877, Costumes (478–524). Lot 484 included a "dark-blue Saltah jacket," but this sleeved, short coat was "embroidered with gold" not the blue silk thread that seems to embellish the Bezestein salteh; and there is no mention of the şalvar. The sash or shawl appears in many of Lewis's paintings; it is wool, embroidered with woollen thread, 260 x 71 cm, Kashmir, c. 1830, Victoria and Albert Museum (501–1907), bequeathed by Marian Lewis. It was acquired by her husband in Istanbul, 1840–41: VAM Registered Papers.

30 Christine Riding, "Travellers and Sitters: The Orientalist Portrait," in Tromans, *The Lure of the East*, 55.

31 Exhibited RA 1840 (169); Scottish National Portrait Gallery, Edinburgh (PG2466).

32 On Roberts's clothing while traveling, see his Eastern Journal and letters to David Ramsay Hay, National Library of Scotland, Edinburgh (Acc. 7223/1–2 and MS 2255, ff. 88–89 and 90–91).

33 Drawn on Stone from Life by C. Baugniet. London 1844, frontispiece to David Roberts, *The Holy Land, Syria, Idumea, Arabia, Egypt and Nubia* (London: F. G. Moon, 1842–49).

34 Cited in Lindsay Errington, *Master Class, Robert Scott Lauder and his Pupils* (Edinburgh: National Galleries of Scotland, 1983), 58. A "callant" is Scottish dialect meaning "chap" or "lad."

35 For example letters in Lewis Family Collection, including Woolner to Lewis, May 3, 1874, cited in note 19.

36 "John F. Lewis his Brothers Charles and Frederick," c. 1818, from album titled "Sketches by John Frederick Lewis," Royal Academy of Arts, London (07/2698 in album 05/880). See Briony Llewellyn and Sally Doust, *The Young Lion: Early Drawings by John*

Frederick Lewis RA (1804–1876) A Guide to the Display (London: Royal Academy of Arts, 2008), no. 2.

37 William Powell Frith, *My Autobiography and Reminiscences* (London: R. Bentley and Son, 1887–88), 2: 312.

38 Numerous examples in the album of Lewis's sketches (RA 05/880), for example 07/3100, 3102, 3136, 3339; see also Llewellyn and Doust, *The Young Lion*, nos. 4–6.

39 Dated July 1826; Private Collection. Rochard (1788–1872) was based in England for thirty years from 1816.

40 Roberts to D. R. Hay, January 6, 1831, National Library of Scotland (MS 3521, f. 27v).

41 Thackeray, *Notes of a Journey*, 144. The Europa was a hotel in Venice; Les Trois Frères Provençaux was a fashionable restaurant in the Palais Royal, Paris.

42 07/2769 in RA album 05/880. The artist is seated on a stool smoking a pipe, a sketchbook on his lap and a paint-box at his feet.

43 Tom Taylor, ed., *Autobiographical Recollections of Charles Robert Leslie, RA* (Wakefield, England: EP Publishing Ltd, reprint, 1978), 2: 186.

44 National Portrait Gallery, London (NPG 1470).

45 See Richard Ormond, *Early Victorian Portraits* (London: National Portrait Gallery, 1973), 270; illustrated plate 531.

46 *Illustrated London News*, 285.

47 John Lewis Roget, *History of the "Old Water-Colour" Society: now the Royal Society of Painters in Water Colours* (London: Longmans, Green, and Co., 1891), 2: 140.

48 Thackeray, *Notes of a Journey*, 146.

49 See Llewellyn, "A 'Masquerade' Unmasked," and Weeks, "The 'Reality Effect,'" 59–63, 93–138.

50 Several commentators refer to the European practice of wearing Ottoman dress, for example: "Monsieur Prieste [Emile Prisse d'Avennes] received us quite in the Oriental style, and was himself, in common with all Europeans who reside in the East, dressed à la Turque ...": Lucinda Darby Griffith, *A Journey Across the Desert, from Ceylon to Marseilles* (London: Henry Colburn, 1845), 1: 251.

51 Published in London by the Society for the Diffusion of Useful Knowledge. For portraits of Lane in Ottoman dress and a comprehensive biography, see Jason Thompson, *Edward William Lane 1801–1876 The Life of the Pioneering Egyptologist and Orientalist* (Cairo: The American University in Cairo Press, 2010).

52 For European residents in Cairo see Warren R. Dawson and Eric P. Uphill, *Who Was Who in Egyptology*, 3rd rev. edn by M. L. Bierbrier (London: Egypt Exploration Society, 1995).

53 Sir Thomas Phillips to his brother Benjamin, December 9, 1842, Private Collection. Phillips was the patron of the artist, Richard Dadd, traveling in the Near East, 1842. The reference to tea is in A. C. Harris to Joseph Bonomi, April 16, 1844, Yvonne Neville-Rolfe Collection of Bonomi Papers, and to the "sherberts" of "Hadji Hodson" and "Bass Bey" in Thackeray, *Notes of a Journey*, 145.

54 Bibliothèque nationale de France, Département des manuscripts occidentaux: nouvelles acquisitions françaises 20420, ff. 67–69; 13 janvier 1883.

55 *The Hhareem*, 1850, Corporate Collection, Japan. See Mary Roberts, *Intimate Outsiders*, 31–37. I have further discussed Prisse's narrative in "'These Inhuman Trafficers in Flesh & Blood': British Artists and the Slave Trade in Egypt" (paper presented at the Paul Mellon Centre for Studies in British Art, London, January 21, 2010).

56 Other known contacts between them include their membership of the Literary Association of Egypt, founded in 1842 by Henry Abbott and Prisse d'Avennes: see pamphlet in Wilkinson Library, Calke Abbey, Derbyshire and their attendance at a séance held by the notorious Egyptian Magician: see *Murray's Handbook for Travellers in Egypt* (London: John Murray, 1847), 151, text by Sir John Gardner Wilkinson.

57 Ahdaf Soueif, *Mezzaterra: Fragments from the Common Ground* (London: Bloomsbury, 2004), 1–23.

58 The process was incremental rather than comprehensive, affecting different levels of society at different times and in a variety of ways. Lane reported that the "'march' of European innovations here … has now become a gallop" but that although the "officers of the Government … have begun to put themselves into the complete Frank dress," "the sheykhs are very angry at all this" (Bodleian Library, Oxford, MS Eng. Lett d 165, f. 151).

59 For example the "Bey" in *The Hhareem*, 1850: see Caroline Williams, "John Frederick Lewis: 'Reflections of Reality,'" *Muqarnas* 18 (2001): 227–43. In this he was following well-established artistic tradition, from the Renaissance onwards. Contemporaries who also

inserted themselves into their compositions as bystanders included William Powell Frith (1819–1909) and Lawrence Alma-Tadema (1836–1912), but they advertised this presence whereas Lewis did not. See National Portrait Gallery, London, *Later Victorian Portraits*, forthcoming on-line. For parallels in the work of the Ottoman artist, Osman Hamdi Bey (1842–1910), see Ahmet Ersoy, Chapter 9 in this volume.

60 RA, 1857 (39): oil on panel, 1856, Fitzwilliam Museum, Cambridge (468); watercolor, Private Collection, UK; a related watercolor sketch is in a Private Collection (Christie's, November 12, 1991, 136). The image was chosen to illustrate a short biographical article on Lewis in the *Art Journal* (February, 1858, 42) but no connection was made between the two.

61 See Christie's December 12, 2007, lot 200.

62 RA 1858 (114); see Shafik Gabr, *The Shafik Gabr Collection* (Paris: ACR Edition, publication forthcoming). The turban seems to be the red, patterned sash, later owned by Marian Lewis (see note 29), that appears in other paintings by Lewis, including another disguised "self-portrait," *A Memlook Bey, Egypt*, RA 1869 (876), Private Collection, see MaryAnne Stevens, ed., *The Orientalists: Delacroix to Matisse: European Painters in North Africa and the Near East* (London: Royal Academy of Arts, 1984), 207. Another notable self-representation is the older man in *The Pipe Bearer*, 1856, Birmingham Museums & Art Gallery (1954P11).

63 As reported by Thackeray, *Notes of a Journey,* 146. Lewis exhibited several desert scenes in the 1850s.

64 Edward Stanley Poole to Joseph Bonomi, [1851], Cambridge University Library (Add. 9389/2/P/90).

65 Woolner to Lewis, July 18, 1875, Yale Center for British Art, Paul Mellon Fund (MS Woolner).

66 Coleridge to Lewis, August 28, [1875], Lewis Family Collection (A32). The Revd Edward Coleridge (1800–1883), nephew of the poet, was a master at Eton College, 1824–67 and Vicar of Mapledurham near Reading from 1862.

67 RA 1869 (97) as *The Seraff (Money-changer), A Doubtful Coin; A Scene in a Cairo Bazaar*, Birmingham Museums & Art Gallery (1891P28); illustrated in Tromans, *The Lure of the East*, 90–91.

68 Woolner to Marian Lewis, January 16, 1876, Yale Center for British Art, Paul Mellon Fund (MS Woolner).

69 Charles Baudelaire, 'The Painter of Modern Life', 1863, in *The Painter of Modern Life and Other Essays*, trans. Jonathan Mayne (London: Phaidon, 1964), 5–15.

Bibliography

Ames-Lewis, Francis. *The Intellectual Life of the Early Renaissance Artist.* London and New Haven: Yale University Press, 2000.

Baudelaire, Charles. "The Painter of Modern Life." In *The Painter of Modern Life and Other Essays,* translated by Jonathan Mayne, 5–15. London: Phaidon, 1964.

Cook, E. T., and Alexander Wedderburn, eds., *The Works of John Ruskin.* London: George Allen; New York: Longmans, Green, and Co., 1903–12, vols 14, 35.

Darby Griffith, Lucinda. *A Journey Across the Desert, from Ceylon to Marseilles*. London: Henry Colburn, 1845.

Davies, Randall. "John Frederick Lewis, R. A. (1805–1876)," in *The Old Water-Colour Society's Club, 1925–1926*, 3 (1926): 31–40.

Dawson, Warren R., and Eric P. Uphill. *Who Was Who in Egyptology*, 3rd rev. edn by M. L. Bierbrier. London: Egypt Exploration Society, 1995.

Eaton, Sir Frederick. "The Royal Academy." *Scribner's Magazine* 36 (October 1904): 564–65, 568–69.

Errington, Lindsay *Master Class, Robert Scott Lauder and his Pupils*. Edinburgh: National Galleries of Scotland, 1983.

Fenwick, Simon. *The Enchanted River: Two Hundred Years of the Royal WatercolourSociety.* Bristol: Sansom and Company, 2004.

Fenwick, Simon, and Greg Smith. *The Business of Watercolour: A Guide to the Archives of the Royal Watercolour Society.* Aldershot and Vermont: Ashgate, 1997.

Frith, William Powell. *My Autobiography and Reminiscences.* London: R. Bentley and Son, 1887–88.

Gabr, Shafik. *The Shafik Gabr Collection*. Paris: ACR Edition, publication forthcoming.

Hutchison, Sidney C. *The History of the Royal Academy 1768–1986,* 2nd edn. London: Robert Royce, 1986.

Lane, Edward William. *Manners and Customs of the Modern Egyptians*. London: Society for the Diffusion of Useful Knowledge, 1936.

Lewis, Michael. *John Frederick Lewis R. A. 1805–1876.* Leigh-on-Sea: F. Lewis, 1978.

Llewellyn, Briony. "A 'Masquerade' Unmasked: An Aspect of John Frederick Lewis's Encounter with Egypt." In *Egyptian Encounters*, edited by Jason Thompson, vol. 23, no. 3 of *Cairo Papers in Social Science,* Fall 2000: 133–51.

Llewellyn, Briony. "'These Inhuman Trafficers in Flesh & Blood': British Artists and the Slave Trade in Egypt." Paper presented at the Paul Mellon Centre for Studies in British Art, London, January 21, 2010.

Llewellyn, Briony and Sally Doust. *The Young Lion: Early Drawings by John Frederick Lewis RA (1804–1876) A Guide to the Display.* London: Royal Academy of Arts, 2008.

Macleod, Dianne Sachko. *Art and the Victorian Middle Class: Money and the Making of Cultural Identity.* Cambridge: Cambridge University Press, 1996.

Murray's Handbook for Travellers in Egypt. London: John Murray, 1847.

Ormond, Richard. *Early Victorian Portraits.* London: National Portrait Gallery, 1973.

Riding, Christine. "Travellers and Sitters: The Orientalist Portrait." In *The Lure of the East: British Orientalist Painting*, edited by Nicholas Tromans, 48–61. London: Tate Publishing, 2008.

Roberts, David. *The Holy Land, Syria, Idumea, Arabia, Egypt and Nubia*. London: F. G. Moon, 1842–49.

Roberts, Mary. "Cultural Crossings: Sartorial Adventures, Satiric Narratives and the Question of Indigenous Agency in Nineteenth-Century Europe and the Near East." In *Edges of Empire: Orientalism and Visual Culture*, edited by Jocelyn Hackforth-Jones, and Mary Roberts, 70–94. Oxford: Blackwell, 2005.

Roberts, Mary. *Intimate Outsiders: The Harem in Ottoman and Orientalist Art and Travel Literature.* Durham and London: Duke University Press, 2007.

Rodenbeck, John. "Dressing Native." In *Unfolding the Orient: Travellers in Egypt and the Near East,* edited by Paul and Janet Starkey, 65–100. Reading: Ithaca Press, 2001.

Roget, John Lewis. *A History of the "Old Water-Colour" Society: now the Royal Society of Painters in Water Colours*. London: Longmans, Green, and Co., 1891, 2.

Ruskin, John. "Academy Notes" [1856]. In *The Works of John Ruskin*, edited by E. T. Cook and Alexander Wedderburn, 14: 73–74. London: George Allen; New York: Longmans, Green, and Co., 1903–12.

Ruskin, John. *Praeterita* [1885–89]. In *The Works of John Ruskin*, edited by E. T. Cook and Alexander Wedderburn, 35: 405–6. London: George Allen; New York: Longmans, Green, and Co., 1903–12.

Soueif, Ahdaf. *Mezzaterra: Fragments from the Common Ground.* London: Bloomsbury, 2004.

Spanton, W. S. *An Art Student and his Teachers in the Sixties with other Rigmaroles*. London: R. Scott, 1927.

Stevens, MaryAnne, ed. *The Orientalists: Delacroix to Matisse: European Painters in North Africa and the Near East.* London: Royal Academy of Arts, 1984.

Stokes, Hugh. "John Frederick Lewis R. A. (1805–1876)." *Walker's Quarterly* 28 (1929): 3–53.

Sturgis, Alexander. *Rebels and Martyrs: the Image of the Artist in the Nineteenth Century.* London: National Gallery, 2006.

Taylor, Tom, ed. *Autobiographical Recollections of Charles Robert Leslie, RA*. Wakefield, England: EP Publishing Ltd, reprint, 1978.

Thackeray, William Makepeace [Michael Angelo Titmarsh, pseud.]. *Notes of a Journey from Cornhill to Grand Cairo*. Heathfield, Sussex: Cockbird Press, reprint 1991.

Thompson, Jason. *Edward William Lane 1801–1876: The Life of the Pioneering Egyptologist and Orientalist.* Cairo: The American University in Cairo Press, 2010.

Tromans, Nicholas, ed. *The Lure of the East: British Orientalist Painting.* London: Tate Publishing, 2008. Published in conjunction with the exhibition *The Lure of the East: British Orientalist Painting* shown at the Yale Center for British Art, Tate Britain, Suna and İnan Kıraç Pera Museum and the Sharjah Art Museum.

Weeks, Emily M. "The 'Reality Effect': The Orientalist Paintings of John Frederick Lewis (1805–1876)." PhD diss., Yale University, 2004.

Weeks, Emily M. "'For Love or for Money' Collecting the Orientalist Pictures of John Frederick Lewis." *Fine Art Connoisseur* 4, no. 1 (January/February 2007): 40–47.

Weeks, Emily M. *Cultures Crossed: John Frederick Lewis (1804–1876) and the Art of Orientalist Painting.* London and New Haven: Yale University Press, publication forthcoming.

West, Shearer. *Portraiture.* Oxford: Oxford University Press, 2004.

Williams, Caroline. "John Frederick Lewis: 'Reflections of Reality.'" *Muqarnas* 18 (2001): 227–43.

Woolner, Amy. *Thomas Woolner, R. A., Sculptor and Poet: His Life in Letters.* London: Chapman and Hall, 1917.

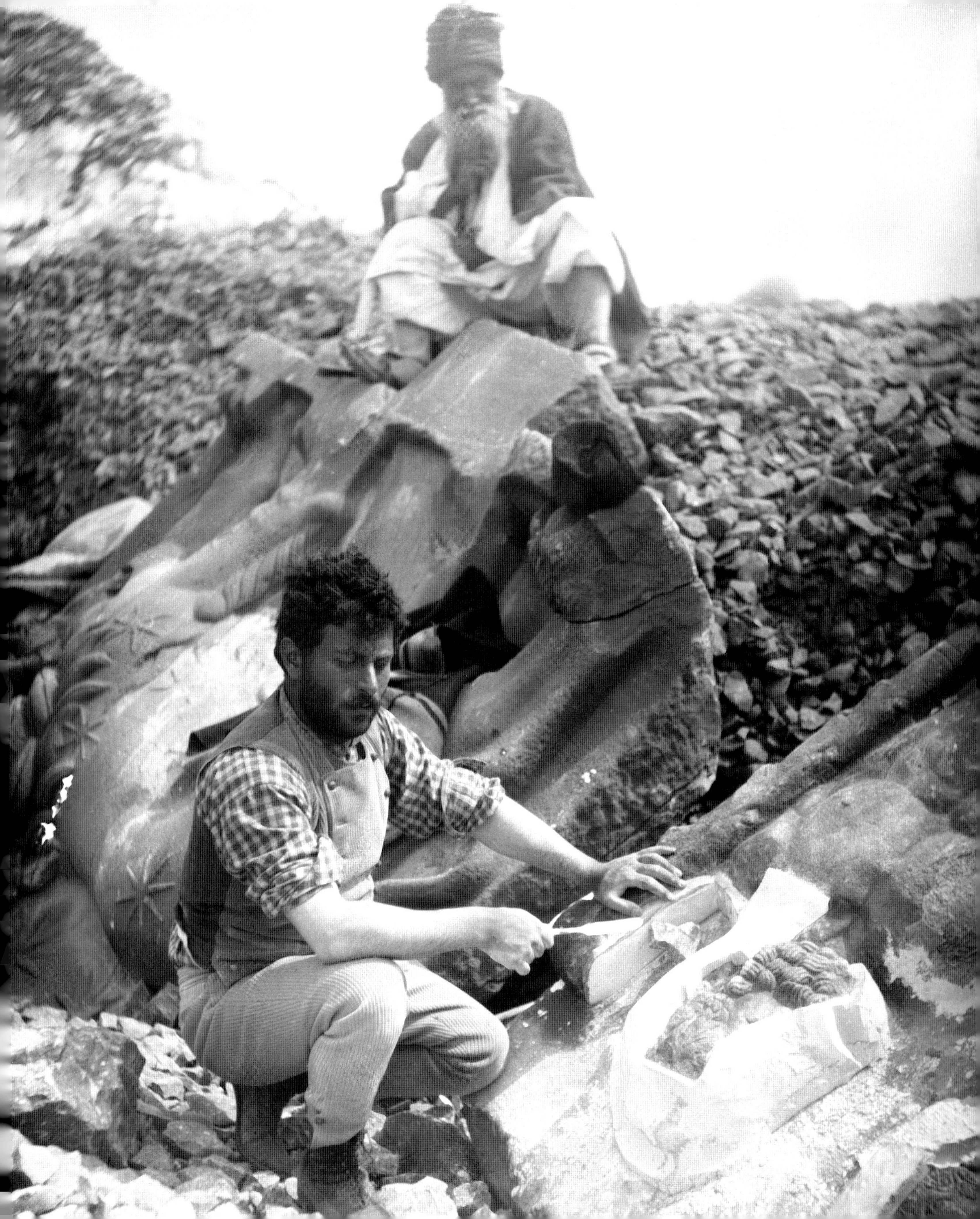

XII

An Ottoman Traveler to the Orient
Osman Hamdi Bey

Edhem Eldem

Introduction

About ten years ago, Christoph Herzog and Raoul Motika published a long and detailed article dealing with Ottoman travelers to the East in the nineteenth century. To define the larger phenomenon that they saw looming over the whole issue, the authors came up with the rather creative term of "Orientalism *alla turca*."[1] Whether this was really their intention or not is open to discussion, but this particular formulation had the advantage of suggesting that this Ottoman version of Orientalism was somewhat shallow and circumstantial, almost accidentally born from the context of travel, and that it lacked the kind of sophistication one would have expected from a more intellectual and ideological investment. I would even add that it was not without irony that the term *alla turca* was one of the catch words of Ottoman, and later Turkish, self-deprecation, in the sense that it was heavily loaded with a devaluing connotation, almost parallel with the contemporary French expression of "*bon pour l'Orient*."

A few years later, Ussama Makdisi coined the term that caught on with unequaled success, to the point of becoming the standard label used to describe a recognized cultural and ideological phenomenon: Ottoman Orientalism.[2] Makdisi's concept was much broader and much less "accidental" in nature: he saw it as "an Ottoman challenge to a European discourse," and considered it to be of a "specifically *Turkish* sensibility."[3] This is a powerful argument, and one that has contributed to the study of a new dimension of Orientalism, but even more, to the discovery of a new way to fathom the intricate cultural and ideological context of Ottoman modernization in the nineteenth century, much in line with the works of Selim Deringil.[4] Makdisi's—and to a certain extent Deringil's—vision of Ottoman Orientalism is almost exclusively geared towards explaining the quasi-colonial relationship that settled in the second half of the nineteenth century between the imperial center—Istanbul, as the seat of Ottoman political power, but also of culture—and the Arab periphery of the Empire, hence the emphasis on the "*Turkish* sensibility" of Ottoman Orientalism. While it is true that this binomial construct of "Turks vs. Arabs" feeds into the most evident, most powerful, and most convincing argument of an Ottoman version of Orientalism, it may be problematic to exclude, albeit implicitly, from the larger picture non-Turks—be they Muslims or non-Muslims—as producers, and non-Arabs—including Turks—as objects, of this new discourse.

My objective is not to start a discussion on the origins and possible limitations of the concept of Ottoman Orientalism as it developed in the past decade. Rather, I am concerned with setting a general framework within which I may analyze Osman Hamdi Bey's travels to the East, more specifically to Iraq in 1869–71, and to South-Eastern Anatolia in 1883. The possible links with Herzog and Motika's study of Ottoman travelers is, I think, quite obvious. As to Makdisi's Ottoman Orientalism, it is rather clear that Osman Hamdi Bey (1842–1910) is one of the most tempting case studies one can think of to illustrate the logic and functioning of this ideological curiosity. Indeed, Osman Hamdi Bey is one of the main characters referred to by Makdisi in his demonstration.[5] Nor is he the first to do so: before and after him, quite a number of scholars have studied Osman Hamdi Bey in relation to Orientalism, mostly from the perspective of his painting. I have myself participated in this discussion, countering some of the efforts made to "save" Osman Hamdi Bey from the stigma of accusations of Orientalism, claiming that his being an Orientalist was pretty much inevitable and not necessarily morally reprehensible in the Westernizing context of the time.[6]

Nevertheless, the match between Osman Hamdi Bey's personality and cultural inclinations, on the one hand, and the Herzog-Motika and Makdisi models of Orientalism, on the other, may not be as smooth as one might initially think. First of all, Osman Hamdi Bey was not included in Herzog and Motika's survey of Ottoman travelers, and understandably so, considering that he had not really left any real travel account. Moreover, as a French-educated, French-speaking, "super-westernized"[7] artist cum archeologist, he clearly had very little in common with the much more "local" profile of the travelers studied by Herzog and Motika. Makdisi's take on the issue is much closer to our concerns, if only because of the rather obvious overlap between his definition of Ottoman Orientalism and some of the dominant aspects of Osman Hamdi Bey's career and personality. Nevertheless, Makdisi uses only the 1892 Sidon report[8] and the 1873 publication on popular costume,[9] both of which were designed as official Ottoman publications targeting a French-speaking Western audience, which made them likely, especially for the *Costumes*, to bear some resemblance to propaganda material. Moreover, both these publications were co-authored by non-Ottomans, which brings up the question of the actual authorship of the lines used to illustrate Osman Hamdi Bey's political and ideological stand. This is particularly true of the *Costumes*, which Makdisi uses extensively without considering the possibility that some (or much) of the text may have been written by de Launay, who had already written a much shorter but similar text on the "popular costumes of Constantinople" to accompany an exhibit at the 1867 Paris world fair.[10] I have also recently discovered that much of the information on Baghdad was borrowed from Ferdinand Hoefer.[11] The attribution of this text to Osman Hamdi Bey may have to be reconsidered, even if the fact that he appeared as a co-author may be reason enough to argue that he embraced most, if not all, of the ideas they contained.

I can safely say, then, that my attempt at analyzing Osman Hamdi Bey as a traveler to the Orient stands somewhere halfway between Herzog-Motika and Makdisi. "My" Osman Hamdi is certainly much less "*alla turca*" than the formers' travelers—he would probably come closer to "*alla franca*"—and he is less of the textbook Orientalist than the latter seems to suggest. In actual fact, my intention is not to suggest that there may have been a single and consistent Osman Hamdi Bey, but rather to prove that, on the contrary, the same individual could show different attitudes towards the Orient, depending on the circumstances in which the actual events took place and/or were narrated. In no way do I suggest that there may have been three Osman Hamdi Beys, each distinct from the other in his perception of the East; there is only one dominant personality, best described in terms of the combined effects of a staunch belief in the West, an Orientalist perception of the East, and a patriotic, if somewhat condescending, stand with respect to the Empire. Yet this personality was exposed to a similar vision of the East at three different *moments* in time and in space, which led to the emergence of a slightly different discourse at each point. Moreover, these three moments correspond also to three different narrative styles: it is not only the discourse that changes, but the voice itself, which makes it necessary to add one more layer to the analysis.

Political Awakening: Baghdad, 1869–1871

The first of these three moments, and chronologically the earliest, corresponds to the two years Osman Hamdi Bey spent in Baghdad, from 1869 to 1871. Following almost ten years of residence in Paris as a young student and dilettante, Osman Hamdi Bey had been sent out to Baghdad by his somewhat disappointed and concerned father, Edhem Pasha, in the hope that a "hands-on" training as a junior bureaucrat in a remote province would bring back to his senses a young man who had started to show a dangerous inclination towards starting a career as a painter in Paris.[12] Under the watchful eye of Midhat Pasha, engaged in his civilizing mission, the young man discovered a remote province of the Empire from which he would write his father a number of letters—all in French—strongly imbued with a rather characteristic mix of Orientalism and patriotic ideals. Compared to the other two "moments," this is probably the rawest, for a number of reasons. First of all, quite understandably, the shock of discovering, after a decade spent on or near the boulevards, the realities of one of the most remote provinces of the Empire was clearly at work behind the overall tone of the letters. So was the enthusiasm, maybe faked to a certain extent in order to impress a (very) demanding father, but certainly genuine enough if one considers the frequent patriotic outcries and the rather convincing way in which he constantly refers to Midhat Pasha's—and by extension, his own—civilizing mission in this land of backwardness. From this perspective, one could argue that this is one of the instances where Osman Hamdi Bey's discourse—in *his* own words—comes closest to Makdisi's understanding of Ottoman Orientalism as an ideology targeting the Arab populations in the name of the reaffirmation of an implicitly Turkish and modern hold over the Empire. His use of the French language makes it even more tempting to view it in this way: "to have them see that Turkey still lives, to show to all peoples the Turkish flag, that is the flag of Muslims."[13]

"Arabs" is the blanket term he uses to describe the locals, and his first attempt at providing his father with a synoptic vision of the 'natives' starts with a rather demeaning tone: "[I will try] to describe to you this Arab people, initiate you to their character, and to their degree of civilization, if they have one!"[14] It soon becomes clear, however, that this generic term embodies two main categories, namely the town dweller and the nomad. The Bedouin had to be preferred to the urban Arab, "for if the latter leads a primitive and patriarchal life, the former leads a corrupt and vile one."[15] This was a rather typical distinction in Orientalism, between the "noble savage" and the degenerate urban masses. The former was dangerous and primitive, but worthy of an almost esthetic appreciation; the latter, on the contrary, had freed themselves from primitiveness, but in doing so had lost the raw purity of their essence. All in all, then, Osman Hamdi Bey seemed to have developed a four-tiered classification of the Orientals he was exposed to in Baghdad. At the moral top, but civilizational bottom, of the ladder, stood the idealized Bedouin: noble, but savage, honest, but primitive. Interestingly, when the Bedouin tribes became "real" and took up arms against the Ottoman Government, they could suddenly revert to the status of "Arabs."[16] Somewhat below the idealized Bedouin and the warring nomad/Arab came the urban scum, the half-civilized, conniving and treacherous inhabitants of the cities, who needed to be reminded of the imperial authority of the Sultan. Yet, surprisingly, there was still worse, the most despicable and dangerous of all: the Persians. "The Persians are perfidious and liars" was the way he introduced the matter to his father,[17] expanding later into a detailed account of the powerful influence exerted by Iran and its agents on the local population through Shi'ite networks and propaganda. This was a political and patriotic reaction to a serious threat to Ottoman authority in the region, but with a familiar moral and civilizational undertone:

> You have no idea what a Persian really is like. Do you believe that Persia has entered the path of civilization? Yes, it has, about a month ago. Until then, they did not even have printed laws. I enclose here a copy of the first laws they have promulgated, those very laws which all the representatives of foreign powers in Tehran have immediately rejected in perfect unanimity.[18]

The sarcastic and demeaning tone used to mock Iranian claims to modernity, and the enthusiastic siding with Western sentiments pointed at a very conscious instrumentalization of Orientalist arguments to counter a political threat by questioning its legitimacy from the perspective of Western standards of civilization, much like a number of European politicians and observers did with respect to the Ottoman *Tanzimat* movement.

Noble Bedouins, unruly nomads, corrupt Arabs, and perfidious Iranians, Osman Hamdi Bey clearly felt himself to be up against a rather hostile environment, to which he reacted by using differing degrees of Orientalist stereotyping. Much of this attitude was certainly inspired by nearly ten years of residence in Paris; it also looked very much like Makdisi's model of Ottoman Orientalism in its anti-Arab and pro-Turkish dimension. Yet, to what extent should one take this attitude to represent a consistent and conscious ideological construct? I have tried to show above that much of these stereotypes were circumstantial, in more than one way. The image of the "noble savage," a strong leitmotiv in Osman Hamdi Bey's correspondence is very likely to have been inspired by his French upbringing; on the contrary the negative perception of troublemaking tribes crisscrossing the border falls into one of the most typical and oldest Ottoman stereotypes applied to nomadic populations. The strong "Turkish" bias throughout the correspondence cannot be dissociated from the fact that it was written in French, while the anti-Iranian prejudices are obviously amplified by the very particular political context of Sunnite and Shi'ite tensions in Iraq. Most of all, however, I think one has to underline the fact that Osman Hamdi Bey's Orientalist critique ended up transcending the narrow context of the local population: his last letter to Edhem Pasha, dated April 27, 1870, brought the whole issue to a higher level of criticism, covering all of the Orient and of Islam in rather general terms. Incensed by what seems to have been a suggestion that he should marry, Osman Hamdi Bey suddenly felt an urge to rebel against tradition and conventions:

> With the exception of my dear family and a few others, please, Dear Father, just look around you! What do you see in families? Nothing but corruption, depravation, fights, divorces. They are infested by slavery and lose their morality to odalisques. The wife does not submit to her husband's will, and the husband fails to respect his wife. He goes his way, as she goes hers. They have never held hands. They have never formed a family. The children are abandoned. The mother has never thought of them. Entrusted to a slave who thinks s/he is movable property, these poor children are left to vegetate, while the mother goes to the Sweet Waters to dirty and roll in the mud a name she carries but hates. And all of this happens just because a ridiculous convention in our degenerate customs requires that a man should close his eyes before taking a wife. A convention which requires that marriage should not result from the free will of a man and a woman, but rather from an agreement between their parents.[19]

The target was no longer the Arab, the Bedouin, or the Persian, but rather the average Muslim or, for that matter, the average Ottoman subject. Through a modernist discourse of corruption and degeneration, he was attacking the very foundations of what he considered to be the essence of Oriental society. His reference was so obviously Europe and his discourse so strongly imbued with Western clichés that Osman Hamdi Bey felt the need to take a defensive stand against any possible accusation of blind submission to the West:

> Please note, my Dear Father, that by demolishing in such a way our customs, which are no longer those of the Muslim, I am not praising European customs either. I have many objections to them, too, but nevertheless, I must say that I prefer them if only because they are generally depraved, corrupt and immoral only outside the marriage. The rich do not keep alongside their wives a stream of young slave girls and if they do have illegitimate and illegal affairs, it is in the street with free women labelled as prostitutes, and therefore outside of the realm of law.
>
> Please note that I am speaking only of the powerful, of the rich, and not of the people, of the artisans. Bourgeois families are all more or less irreproachable, especially in Germany.[20]

Interestingly, Osman Hamdi Bey was resorting to the typically modernist—and rather crypto-secularist—argument of Islam having lost its original purity through centuries of degeneration. More importantly, however, it seems that his reference to the perfection of the bourgeois class in Europe had brought to his mind a possible, and rather damning, comparison with Ottoman society:

> Just go to the mosque on a Friday, and look at the artisan, at the bourgeois, the only source of wealth of a country. He is nothing but a wretch dressed in rags, a shadow that only inspires pity. No industry, no trade, nothing! Just a patient form of fatalism! Everything is God's making. He goes to a half-ruined hut he calls a shop and finds it robbed: it is God's making. He returns to a shanty he calls home and finds it in flames: it is again God's making. And never the administration's fault! There you have the artisan; there you have the taxpayer; there you have the people.[21]

It was clear, then, that Osman Hamdi Bey's Orientalist stand, at this early stage of his career, was an amalgamation of several tendencies, and as such could not be reduced to a single and consistent ideological inclination. Be it in the case of nomads rebelling against the pasha's authority, of Baghdadis showing signs of corruption, of Iranians exerting their influence over the Shi'ite population, the abusive treatment of the local population by Ottoman officials, or even his own family putting pressure on him, Osman Hamdi Bey's discourse was generally triggered by an idealist desire to redress a political wrong. In doing so, even though he would seem to target mostly the "local" population by stigmatizing it as backwards and corrupt, in actual fact the common denominator has to be sought in the very consistent way in which a much more varied Orient is set against an idealized model of the West and of modernity. Osman Hamdi Bey's prime concern was still predominantly about European standards and about the "civilizing mission" that should reform every sector of the population, including the Ottoman "Turkish" administrative elite. Therefore, if an obvious patriotic inclination seems to have tipped the balance against the Arabs, Bedouins, and Iranians, in actual fact, his statements targeted a much wider spectrum, accused of an incapacity, or an unwillingness to comply with the norms of—Western—civilization. Ottoman officials were corrupt, except for Midhat Pasha and, implicitly, himself; Ottoman society lacked integrity, except for Edhem Pasha and, of course, his own family. Clearly, the West and its civilization constituted the only chance for the Orient to redeem itself and break the vicious circle of backwardness and moral corruption.

Anthropological Maturity: Nemrud Dağı, 1883

A little more than a decade later, in 1883, Osman Hamdi Bey embarked upon his second major trip to the East, this time to South Eastern Anatolia and Kurdistan, more specifically to the recently discovered monumental tumulus of Antiochus of Commagene, on the summit of Mount Nemrud. In 1883, Osman Hamdi Bey was no longer the inexperienced young man struggling to find a vocation that might satisfy his desire to set up a life and a meaningful career that would answer both his and his father's expectations. Following a number of positions in the administration, he had finally been appointed director of the Imperial Museum in 1881, a position he would maintain until his death in 1910, and that would eventually turn him into the most powerful man of the Empire in matters related to archeology, art, and culture in general.

Nemrud Dağı had been spotted in 1881 by a German engineer, Sester, and was surveyed the following year by Otto Puchstein. Osman Hamdi Bey's mission was therefore not one of discovery, but rather an interesting attempt to claim this German discovery in the name of the Imperial Museum, which explains the very rapid publication of the report co-authored by Osman Hamdi Bey and his travel companion, the Armenian sculptor Osgan/Oskan Efendi (1855–1914).[22] The *Tumulus* was an archeological survey, rather than a travelog. However, I have had the chance to come across the actual diary of the journey and some eighty photographs accompanying it.[23] An important part of the diary covered the journey to and from the site, which made it a sort of travelog. Similarly, half of the photographs, most of them absent from the publication, documented the trip and local characters instead of the archeological site.

From the perspective of this particular study, the most important aspect of this document is that it differs greatly from Osman Hamdi Bey's earlier correspondence from Baghdad: correspondence versus diary, personal writing versus a text written by a collaborator, Osgan Efendi. However, the systematic use of a common "we" to express most of the opinions, observations, and feelings throughout the text allows us to assume that Osgan Efendi was truly writing in the name of the two, and that this "secretarial" duty was most likely the result of the hierarchy between the two. Nevertheless, the most significant difference between these two "moments" of Osman Hamdi Bey's discovery of the Orient had to do with the general context in which they were inscribed. His Baghdad experience was strongly political and idealist, reflecting the feelings and ambitions of a young man fresh out of Paris, who believed in the need for—and probably the possibility of—"civilizing" the system, from the administrators down to the nomadic tribes, and from the inhabitants of Baghdad to the middling classes of the Empire. This political stand is completely absent from the 1883 travelog, and replaced by a dominant ethnographic and anthropological mood. The two friends were clearly "discovering" a human environment that was extremely foreign to them. This had been true of Baghdad, too, but this time however, Osman Hamdi had no mission to fulfill, no war to fight, no rebellion to quell, no pasha to follow, no father to impress. The result was a much calmer narrative, dominated by curiosity, a desire to observe, and a certain quest for exoticism.

This "softer" context does not exclude a strong Orientalist, and even colonial, context. The cultural divide that separated the authors from their "fellow" Ottomans of the area put them in a position very similar to that of European travelers, down to some of the most typical clichés and expectations of Western travel literature. Contrary to Baghdad, where Osman Hamdi Bey's position of power and superiority overshadowed most romantic constructs with a pragmatic political discourse, Osgan Efendi and Osman Hamdi Bey were alone in the wilderness, two oddly misfit representatives of universal art and culture on their way to discover the remains of a late Hellenistic funerary tumulus. While they symbolized in every way the colonial division of labor between centre and periphery in terms of science and knowledge, the fact that they were alone may account for their more humane, less haughty attitude towards the locals. Moreover, this time, the "native" elements were no longer the Arabs and the Bedouins, but almost exclusively the Kurds. The tone was generally jovial, sympathetic to every sign of respect and affection shown to them by the local population. Hospitality and friendliness were the key words, with frequent references to "the patriarchal friendship that is so characteristic of these peoples,"[24] to the "eager hospitality one finds in all the peoples of the Orient,"[25] and to quaint scenes of interaction worthy of an anthology of nineteenth-century anthropology. A high point in the narrative was the crossing of the river Göksu:

> A group of these peasants headed by two dervishes playing the tambourine and singing at the top of their voice came to greet us, saluting and kissing Hamdi Bey's feet, hands and stirrups. I cannot think of anything more amusing and picturesque than the sight of all these chaps, some stark naked, others with only a shirt loading travellers and their baggage on their backs, or guiding horses under the sun through the quick waters of the river and the numerous pebble beds that crisscross it. We were the first to entrust ourselves into the hands of these deft and strong men who carried us across the river while at the same time shouting and sending fervent prayers to God and all the saints to obtain a safe crossing.[26]

This Orientalist/colonialist streak becomes even more evident, when they describe their arrival in Adıyaman, where they were hosted by the major in command of the local garrison. The contrast between the locality itself—"a large village, [where] apart from very few houses with more than one floor, all the rest consist of four walls and no windows, with roofs made of mud"—and the barracks—"outside the town is a rather large and very neatly kept barracks"—is already telling enough of the kind of colonial setting that characterized the coexistence of governmental forces and the local population.[27] Yet nothing could be more striking with respect to the colonial rift between Ottoman officials and the "natives" than the little fête set up by the major in honor of his guests, involving a dance show of local Kurds, reminiscent of French or British colonial amusements:

> The *binbashi* who invited us for supper offered us a very interesting show by having some twenty Kurds dance for us. This national dance of the Kurds consists in forming two lines following each other at some twenty paces distance, dancing and singing, and then facing each other, with each man clapping hands with the man facing him. The same operation is then done in reverse order, and so on.[28]

This colonial and Orientalist context was nevertheless less aggressive than in Baghdad. True, some of the remarks were clearly demeaning to the local population, or even openly insulting, as in the case of the decision to entrust the shoveling of the snow that covered the monuments "to a Kurd from Horik whose intelligence and goodwill seemed sufficient to carry it out with success."[29] Yet, the overall tone remained softer: the word "civilization" and its derivatives do not appear a single time in the diary; nor is there a single reference to unruliness, rebellion, or any form of incompatibility with a larger scheme of Ottoman rule or state control over the area. Orientalism is thus reduced to its purely anthropological and ethnographic dimension, with little, if any, direct political concern and civilizational judgment.

True, this smoother context could be partly explained by the fact that there was much less political tension in the region than in Baghdad, or by the fact that the actual author, Osgan Efendi, as an Armenian with no real governmental duties, may have been more inclined towards a less political and more "benevolent" form of Orientalism. Nevertheless, I believe that the latter argument also holds true for Osman Hamdi Bey in the context of his new occupation and of the identity of a man of science that came with it. Already an artist at heart, and now discovering the novel appeal of archeology and scientific missions, Osman Hamdi Bey seems to have been moving towards a more detached, more scientific, and more esthetic interest for things Oriental.

Perhaps the most telling aspect of this more laid-back position of a curious and esthetically minded observer is to be found in the photographs taken during the expedition. If one excludes the purely archeological images, most of the photographs depicted views involving a number of locals. Some combined archeology with ethnography, by having locals pose next to the monumental heads of the tumulus. While this may have been a practical way of giving a sense of scale, it seems that the concern was also to suggest similarities between the appearance of the locals and of their "ancestors" (Fig. 12.1), possibly with a certain degree of artistic license (Fig. 12.2). Such anachronistic shortcuts were fully consistent with one of the major tenets of Orientalism, namely the notion of a "frozen" Orient, incapable of changing over time, already suggested in the *Costumes*, by noting that the Kurds wore breeches similar to those of the Medes and Persians, and that their costume "seemed as if it had been removed from one of the low reliefs found in the so-called ruins of Nimrod."[30] The authors themselves would also pose next to the same monuments, but with a calculated nonchalance (Fig. 12.3) or a pensive mood (Fig. 12.4) giving a very "white" message to the viewer.

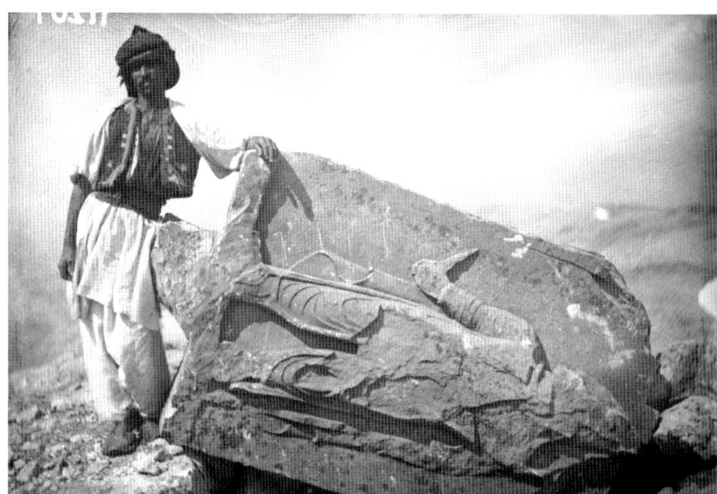

Figure 12.1 Kurdish worker standing by a plaque decorated with a low relief of [...] danes, son of Aroandes II, paternal ancestor of Antiochus I of Commagene, on the western terrace of the tumulus of Antiochus on Nemrut Dağı, Osman Hamdi Bey (1842–1910) or Osgan Efendi (1855–1914), May 1883, glass plate negative, 13 x 18 cm, Istanbul Archaeological Museums, photograph collection, negative 11201.

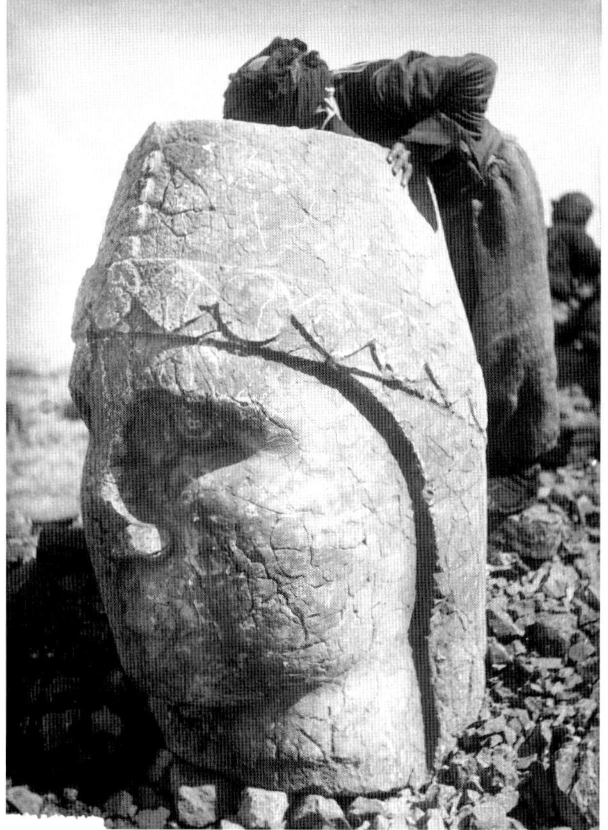

Figure 12.2 Kurdish worker and the monumental head of Apollo-Mithras on the eastern terrace of the tumulus of Antiochus on Nemrut Dağı, Osman Hamdi Bey (1842–1910) or Osgan Efendi (1855–1914), May 1883, glass plate negative, 18 x 13 cm, Istanbul Archaeological Museums, photograph collection, negative 11183.

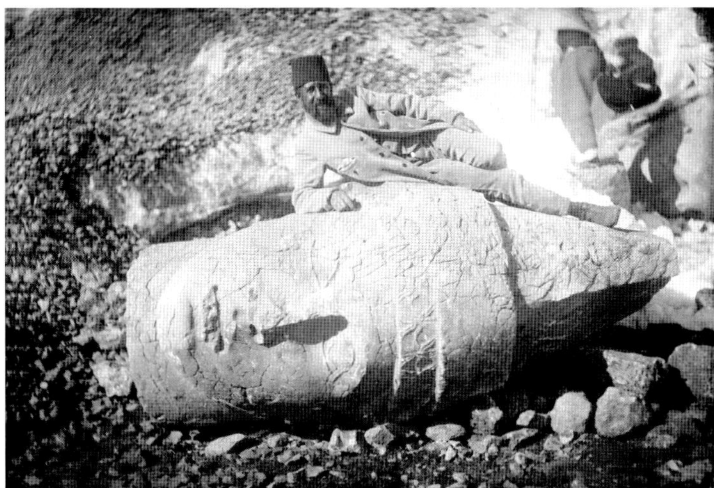

Figure 12.3 Osman Hamdi Bey reclining on Antiochus' monumental head on the western terrace of the tumulus of Antiochus on Nemrut Dağı, Osgan Efendi (1855–1914), May 1883, glass plate negative, 13 x 18 cm, Istanbul Archaeological Museums, photograph collection, negative 11190.

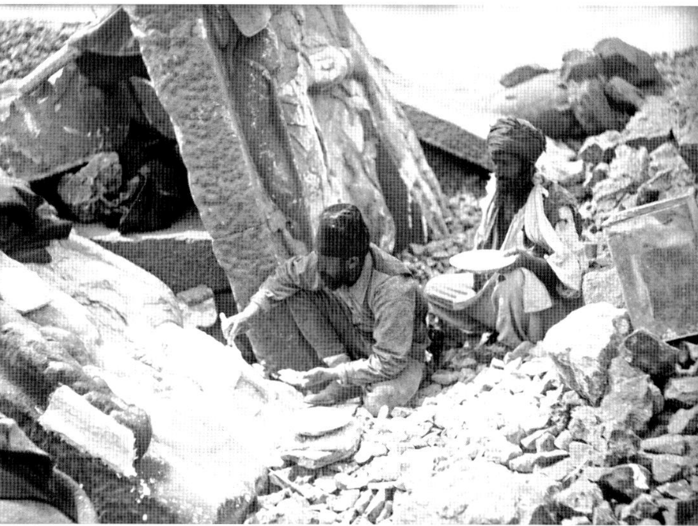

Figure 12.5 Osman Hamdi Bey preparing a cast of a plaque representing the dexioxis (handshake) between Antiochus and Hercules, on the western terrace of the tumulus of Antiochus on Nemrut Dağı, Osgan Efendi (1855–1914), May 25, 1883, glass plate negative, 13 x 18 cm, Istanbul Archaeological Museums, photograph collection, negative 11216.

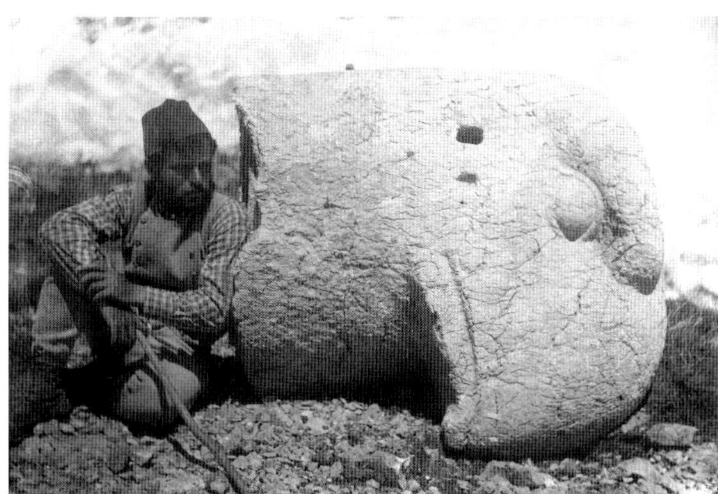

Figure 12.4 Osgan Efendi next to a monumental eagle head on the western terrace of the tumulus of Antiochus on Nemrut Dağı, Osman Hamdi Bey (1842–1910), May 1883, glass plate negative, 13 x 18 cm, Istanbul Archaeological Museums, photograph collection, negative 11203.

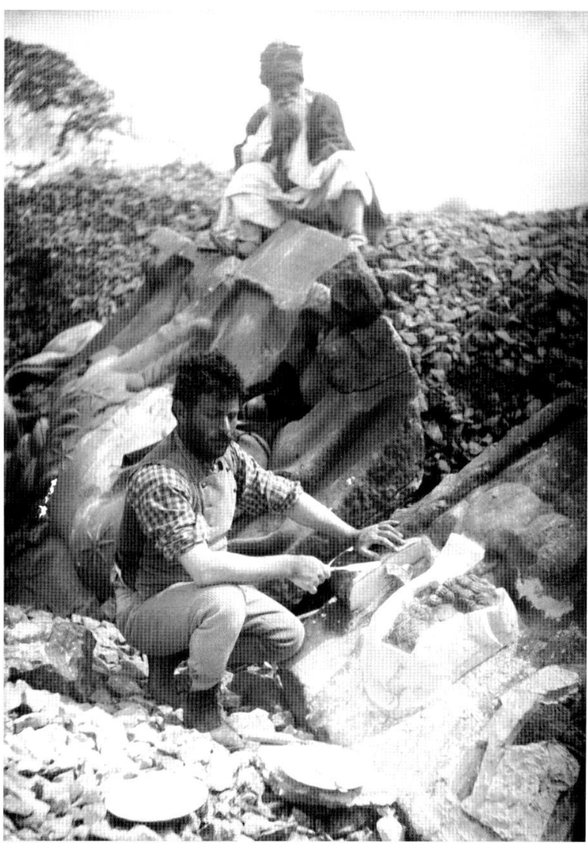

Figure 12.6 Osgan Efendi preparing a cast of a plaque representing the dexioxis (handshake) between Antiochus and Hercules, on the western terrace of the tumulus of Antiochus on Nemrut Dağı, Osman Hamdi Bey (1842–1910), May 25, 1883, glass plate negative, 18 x 13 cm, Istanbul Archaeological Museums, photograph collection, negative 11173.

Most of the photographs involving the locals were more openly ethnographic in nature. A few placed them in the specific context of the expedition, as in the documentary realism of a pan-holding local assisting Osman Hamdi Bey (Fig. 12.5), or the somewhat artistic effect created by the painting-like composition of an elderly Oriental pensively looking down on Osgan (Fig. 12.6). The rest was purely ethnographic, with no other subject than the locals themselves, photographed in a rather self-conscious pose (Fig. 12.7), or against the backdrop one of the columns of Karakuş (Fig. 12.8).[31] The locals thus became part of the photographic inventory of the region: "This

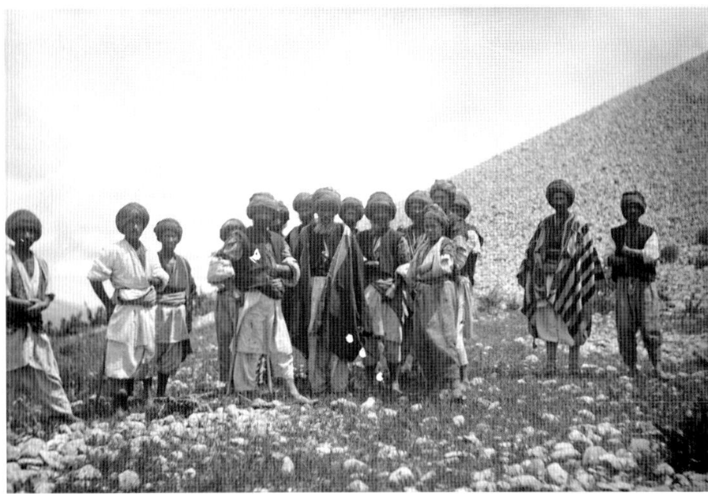

Figure 12.7 Group of Kurds at the tumulus of Karakuş. Osman Hamdi Bey (1842–1910) or Osgan Efendi (1855–1914), 18 May 1883, glass plate negative, 13 x 18 cm, Istanbul Archaeological Museums, photograph collection, negative 11175.

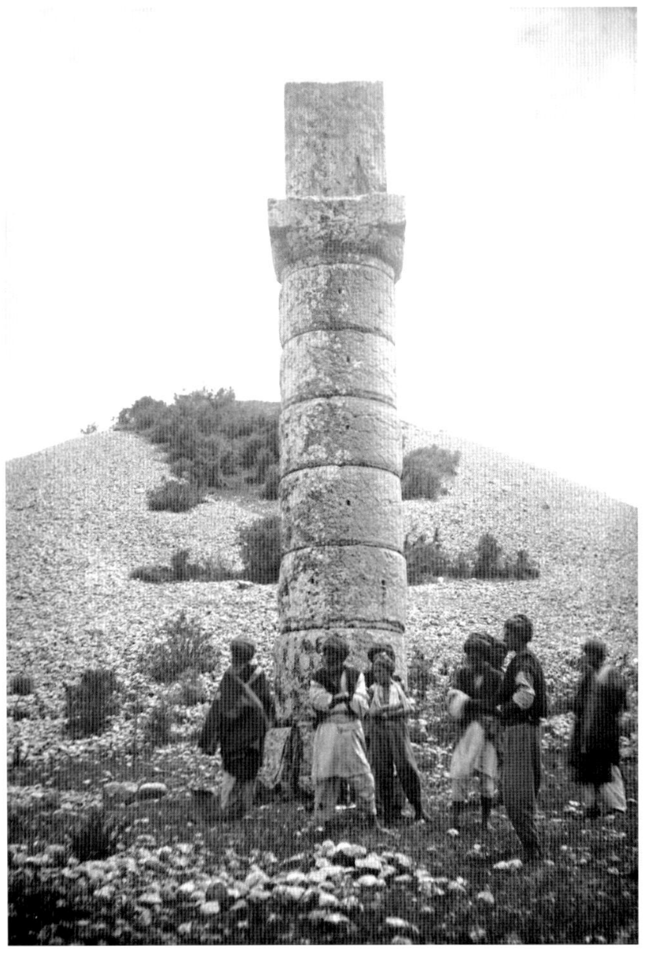

Figure 12.8 Group of Kurds in front of the north-western column of the tumulus of Karakuş, Osman Hamdi Bey (1842–1910) or Osgan Efendi (1855–1914), May 18, 1883, glass plate negative, 18 x 13 cm, Istanbul Archaeological Museums, photograph collection, negative 11193.

morning, we have photographed some Kurdish types, the castle, and the waterfalls."[32] Very few references in the diary allow for a reconstitution of the context in which these photographs were taken: "We photographed the Kurd İsmail Agha on horseback in the courtyard in two different poses" (Fig. 12.9).[33] Other poses, even more sophisticated in their effort of composition, stand as fascinating *tableaux vivants*, in a sense the ultimate Orientalist painting (Figs. 12.10 and 12.11).

Traveling Down Memory Lane: Remembering and Reinventing Baghdad, 1892–1896

The last "moment" in Osman Hamdi Bey's Oriental travels is probably the most fascinating and yet the most problematic of all. This journey was extremely different from the preceding two, in the sense that it was not a real one, but rather a nostalgic revisiting of his first contact with the Orient in 1869–71. However, these reminiscences did not take the predictable form of published memoirs based on recollections; instead, they took the form of five stories written by Rudolf Lindau (1829–1910), based on his conversations with Osman Hamdi Bey. Published in 1896, his *Erzählungen eines Effendi* (the Stories of an Efendi), included five stories: "Jinn and Mansur," the story of an Arab horse and its groom; "Hassan," the story of a young Chechen boy who wanted to enlist; "Saliha," the story of a love affair with a Bedouin woman; "Reyhan," the story of a young black child he saves from misery; and "Hattidja," the story of a woman devoted to inciting men to combat.[34]

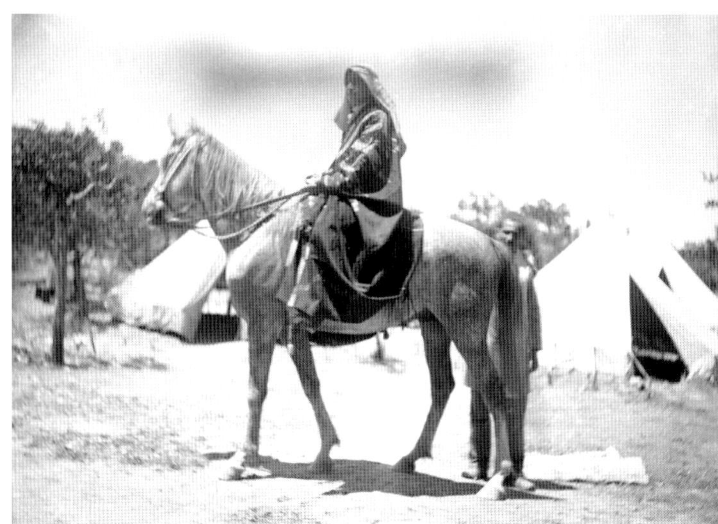

Figure 12.9 Local figure on horseback, Osman Hamdi Bey (1842–1910) or Osgan Efendi (1855–1914), May or June 1883, glass plate negative, 13 x 18 cm, Istanbul Archaeological Museums, photograph collection, negative 11247. One is tempted to imagine that the man on horseback is no other than Osman Hamdi Bey in local garb. However, the quality of the photograph does not allow for proper verification.

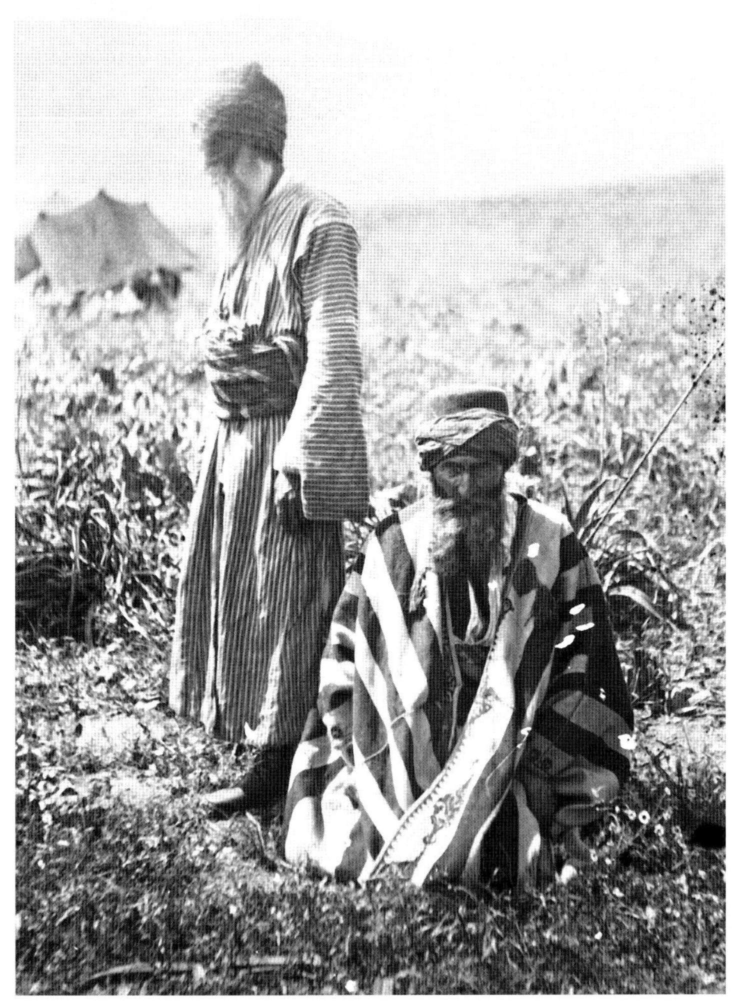

Figure 12.10 Two local figures, Osman Hamdi Bey (1842–1910) or Osgan Efendi (1855–1914), May or June 1883, glass plate negative, 18 x 13 cm, Istanbul Archaeological Museums, photograph collection, negative 11248.

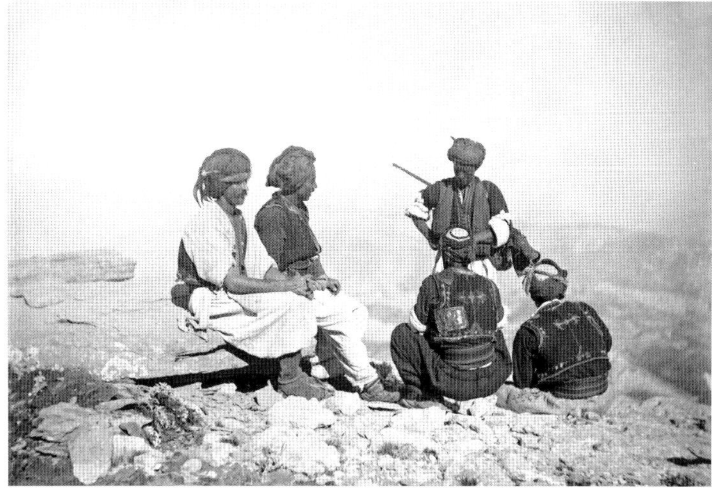

Figure 12.11 Group of armed Kurds, Osman Hamdi Bey (1842–1910) or Osgan Efendi (1855–1914), May or June 1883, glass plate negative, 13 x 18 cm, Istanbul Archaeological Museums, photograph collection, negative 11254.

While the text was evidently written by Rudolf Lindau, it remained to a sufficient degree faithful to what must have been Osman Hamdi Bey's narration in about 1892 to allow us to use it as a reflection of an interesting combination of actual recollections, creative reconstitution, and romantic reinvention to fit the purposes of an Orientalist construct. In a nutshell, the text includes enough verifiable details to ascertain that Osman Hamdi Bey had been closely involved in the building of this narrative, while, on the other hand, he was enough of an Orientalist at heart to actively participate in the process of reinvention that turned these memories into stories with an evident appeal to a Western audience. The point, then, is not to try to figure out whether these stories were true or not, or, more accurately, to understand to what extent a number of evidently authentic recollections had been adapted to the needs of Orientalist fiction. Rather, the point is to see where this new and remodeled vision of the Orient stood, compared to the two concrete examples studied above, and what this has to say about the mind of a fifty-year-old man looking back with apparent fondness at the adventures of his youth. If the Baghdad letters were dominantly political, and if the Nemrud travelog had moved toward ethnographic curiosity, where did Osman Hamdi stand in the 1890s, now that he was a well-established and respected figure of the intellectual and cultural milieu of the Ottoman capital, and a successful painter of (mostly) Oriental scenes?

Some of the "spirit of 1869" had definitely survived: the admiring references to Midhat Pasha's achievements, the frequent descriptions of the wars waged against unruly tribes, the scorn expressed for city dwellers by the noble nomads ... Yet, once these are set aside, the core of the narrative differs greatly from all the previous material in two novel ways: first, the way in which the local actors are brought to the forefront and romanticized through a real concern for their thoughts and feelings; and second, the emergence of an extremely heavy sense of doom hanging over the protagonists, ensuring that despite all affinities, attractions, and even love, East and West shall never meet.

The desire to grant a greater presence and dignity to the Oriental characters may have been a rather logical consequence of an evolution already felt during the Nemrud journey, from a harsh and political stand in Baghdad to a mellower form of curiosity and esthetic fascination for the quaintness and exoticism of Eastern Anatolia. Another decade later, now a recognized (and secure) artist, man of science, and bureaucrat, Osman Hamdi seemed eager to move one step further into exploring the fascinating world of the characters he had started romanticizing through photographic poses and compositions. This was an occasion to bring to life some of the characters he had until then only superficially observed and categorized. This recreation involved a lot of idealization, and a predictable tendency to borrow some European clichés: the beautiful Bedouin woman he falls in love with, the perfect couple formed by an Arab thoroughbred and its (almost animal) groom, the Bedouin woman who promises herself to the most valiant warrior, the little black child abused by an evil uncle … Each of these characters thus engage in a strong, even passionate, relationship with the Westerner who has come to their land and tries to transform their existence. In this way, not only is Osman Hamdi Bey able to give life to these characters, but he manages to promote himself from the status of a passive observer—as in Baghdad, or on the way to Nemrud—to that of an active participant in an Oriental adventure, clearly the dream of any Orientalist of the time.

Yet the most striking aspect of these stories was the constantly repeated notion, like a depressing leitmotiv, that despite all efforts to unite, separation was the ultimate and inevitable fate that awaited East and West, much in line with Kipling's "Ballad of East and West": "Oh, East is East and West is West, and never the twain shall meet/Till Earth and Sky stand presently at God's great Judgment Seat".[35] The difference, however, was that despite this pessimistic statement at the start of his poem, Kipling had tried to counter this belief by giving the example of two men of courage who ended up recognizing each other's worth, whereas in Osman Hamdi Bey's stories, recounted by Lindau, mutual esteem or even love, fail to avert the painful separation that befalls the two protagonists. In most cases the West is represented by Osman Hamdi Bey himself, who, feeling a strong attraction for a "native" character, ends up pulling both of them into the abyss. In the case of Jinn, the Arab thoroughbred, and Mansur, its Bedouin groom, he had been responsible for uprooting them both from their natural environment, just because he wanted to have them with him in Istanbul; but his lifestyle there had made him gradually neglect and eventually betray these two objects of his Oriental fantasies. One recognizes a typical transposition of a well-known Western Orientalist discourse of disgust with the materialism of Western culture and civilization.

The story of Saliha, the beautiful Bedouin maiden, goes in the same direction of a passion ending in doom. This time, Osman Hamdi Bey falls in love with a young local woman; he convinces her to elope and live with him in Baghdad. Following several months of bliss, fate strikes again: when her father claims her back to replace her late sister as her brother-in-law's wife, Saliha yields to her destiny and abandons her lover to fulfill her duty. This time, the evil lies in the East, which imposes the force of its tradition on the fragile union that had formed for just a fleeting moment between the two worlds.

This is the reason for Osman Hamdi's cynical—but in fact cautious—attitude in another amorous adventure, again with a Bedouin woman, but this time of a very different character: Hattidja, the war-lady, the woman who leads entire tribes to war by promising herself to the bravest of all. Knowing from experience that they will never be able to come together, he will consciously limit himself to flirting with Hattidja, and will manage to bid her farewell, while still declaring his love. This time, the separation is a pre-emptive one, for both know well that they will not be able to live their love freely and prefer, therefore, to avoid the inevitable rupture by simply putting an end to their relationship.

Last in this tragic series of gloomy destinies, the sad story of Reyhan, the little black child saved by Osman Hamdi Bey from the claws of an abusive uncle, whom he brings back to Istanbul with him, adopts, and educates as his own child. This time, fate does not immediately destroy the child's life; instead, it seems at first that Osman Hamdi may have been able to stall fate by saving the child from the violence of the Orient and entrusting him to the care of civilization, again embodied in the context of modern Istanbul. Reyhan is thus given the chance to embark on the privileged path once followed by his adoptive father, and ends up finding true and mutual love in the person of a young Turkish woman. That was the moment that Fate had been waiting for to catch up with Reyhan and remind him that he was different. What followed is a long descent into hell, as the young man sees all his dreams of happiness crumbling one after the other, and ends up finding the only possible solace in death. Once again the West—in its Ottoman version, of course—has managed to defeat the Orient, destroying any hope that may have remained of seeing the accomplishment of the miracle of a true union between the two worlds.

In Way of Conclusion

Three different moments, three different contexts, three different attitudes of the same man towards the Orient: from his first discovery of Iraq in 1869 to his reminiscences of those days some twenty-five years later, Osman Hamdi Bey's vision of the East had greatly changed over time. As an idealist and politically motivated young man sent out to Baghdad, he had started by believing that the government should—and that Midhat Pasha would—bring progress and civilization to this Oriental backwater of the Empire. About a decade later, when, as the recently appointed director of the Imperial Museum, he set out, as it were, to plant the Ottoman flag on top of Mount Nemrud, his vision had softened greatly, moving from an overenthusiastic desire to control and civilize to a much more relaxed attitude made of a blend of curiosity, condescension, and estheticism. This was also his last major journey to the Orient—Sidon was a much shorter and *ad hoc* matter—that signaled a passage to a much more sedentary life divided between his office at the museum and his studio at home. Not surprisingly, then, the very late pilgrimage he made, through Rudolf Lindau's pen, into the memories of his early years in Baghdad took a completely different turn, abandoning realism for the sake of fantasy, replacing observation with feelings, finally telling the intimate stories he had never been able to tell his father and inventing those he wished had been true.

Nevertheless, what these three distinct phases still had in common was the strong Orientalist context that permeated at practically every level. This, however, should not be understood as an indication of Osman Hamdi Bey's subscribing to a single and monolithic form of Orientalism. His early years in Baghdad probably come closest to Makdisi's definition of Ottoman Orientalism, largely due to the political dimension that dominated his concerns at that point in his life and career. It is doubtful, however, that the same label can be used with some accuracy to describe the direction in which Osman Hamdi Bey's Orientalism evolved from the 1880s on. It seems that the more he was able to withdraw from the political and governmental scene into the protective cocoon of art and science, his Orientalism moved gradually away from a local version to a more Western one. One of the main differences between Osman Hamdi Bey and his fellow countrymen of the Orientalist creed may well have been that while the latter still believed in the necessity of actively participating in the civilizing mission that would bring progress and modernity to the Empire, he had gradually distanced himself from this "activist" stand in order to enjoy the full freedom of a well-protected microcosm he had transformed into an extension of that Western civilization he admired so much. Under these circumstances, one may claim that, starting as an Ottoman Orientalist, Osman Hamdi Bey had gradually become a "real" Orientalist.

Notes

1 Christoph Herzog and Raoul Motika, "Orientalism 'alla turca': Late 19th/Early 20th Century Ottoman Voyages into the Muslim 'Outback,'" *Die Welt des Islams*, 40, no. 2 (July 2000): 139–95.

2 Ussama Makdisi, "Ottoman Orientalism," *The American Historical Review* 107, no. 3 (June 2002) 768–96.

3 Makdisi, "Ottoman Orientalism," 787.

4 Selim Deringil, *The Well-Protected Domains. Ideology and Legitimation of Power in the Ottoman Empire 1876–1909* (London: I. B. Tauris, 1998); Deringil, "'They Live in a State of Nomadism and Savagery': The Late Ottoman Empire and the Post-Colonial Debate," *Comparative Studies in Society and History* 45, no. 2 (April 2003): 311–42.

5 Makdisi, "Ottoman Orientalism," 783–87.

6 Edhem Eldem, "Osman Hamdi Bey ve Oryantalizm," *Dipnot*, 2 (Winter/Spring, 2004): 39–67. The article gives a detailed list of previous contributions to the subject.

7 Şerif Mardin, "Super Westernization in Urban Life in the Ottoman Empire in the Last Quarter of the Nineteenth Century," in *Turkey: Geographic and Social Perspectives*, ed. Peter Benedict, Erol Tümertekin and Fatma Mansur (Leiden: Brill, 1974), 404–46.

8 Osman Hamdy Bey and Théodore Reinach, *Une Nécropole royale à Sidon, fouilles de Hamdy Bey* (Paris: E. Leroux, 1892–96).

9 Osman Hamdi and Marie de Launay, *Les Costumes populaires de la Turquie en 1873. Ouvrage publié sous le patronage de la commission impériale ottomane pour l'Exposition Universelle de Vienne* (Constantinople: Imprimerie du Levant Times and Shipping Gazette, 1873).

10 Marie de Launay, "Costumes populaires de Constantinople," *L'Exposition Universelle de 1867 illustrée* (Paris: E. Dentu, 1867), 133–35.

11 Ferdinand Hoefer, *Chaldée, Assyrie, Médie, Babylonie, Mésopotamie, Phénicie, Palmyrène* (Paris: Firmin–Didot Frères, 1852).

12 For a discussion of his years in Paris, see Eldem, ed., *Un Ottoman en Orient. Osman Hamdi Bey en Irak, 1869–1871* (Paris: Actes Sud, 2010), 26–34.

13 Osman Hamdi to Edhem Pasha, Baghdad, August 18, 1869 (Eldem, *Un Ottoman en Orient*, 80).

14 Osman Hamdi to Edhem Pasha, Baghdad, August 25, 1869 (Eldem, *Un Ottoman en Orient*, 83).

15 Ibid.

16 Ibid.

17 Osman Hamdi to Edhem Pasha, Baghdad, July 13, 1869 (Eldem, *Un Ottoman en Orient*, 72).

18 Osman Hamdi to Edhem Pasha, Baghdad, August 18, 1869 (Eldem, *Un Ottoman en Orient*, 79).

19 Osman Hamdi to Edhem Pasha, Baghdad, April 27, 1870 (Eldem, *Un Ottoman en Orient*, 99).

20 Ibid., 100.

21 Ibid.

22 Osman Hamdy Bey and Osgan Efendi, *Musée impérial ottoman. Le Tumulus de Nemroud-Dagh. Voyage, description, inscriptions* (Constantinople: F. Loeffler, 1883).

23 My thanks go to Mrs. Cenan Sarç, Osman Hamdi Bey's granddaughter, for the original notebook.

24 Wednesday, April 20/May 2, 1883.

25 Sunday, April 24/May 6, 1883.

26 Saturday, April 30/May 12, 1883.

27 Sunday, May 1/13, 1883.

28 Sunday, May 1/13, 1883.

29 Wednesday, May 4/16, 1883.

30 Osman Hamdi and de Launay, *Costumes populaires*, 235 and part III, pl. XXIII. This point was made earlier by Ahmet Ersoy, "A Sartorial Tribute to Tanzimat Ottomanism: The *Elbise-i Osmaniyye* Album," *Muqarnas*, 20 (2003): 194. However, he wrongly assumed that this was a reference to the tumulus of Nemrud Dağı—which would be discovered almost a decade after the publication of the *Costumes*—whereas what was meant by the "so-called ruins of Nimrod" was the site of Birs Nimroud, near Hilla, in northern Iraq.

31 These two particular shots are commented in the diary in the following terms: "We also give a photograph of a group of nomadic Kurds whose tents were set next to the tumulus and who had come there out of curiosity. These are people of very soft character, very friendly and most of all helpful" (Friday, May 6/18, 1883).

32 Sunday, May 8/20, 1883.

33 Samsat, Saturday, May 21/June 2, 1883.

34 Rudolf Lindau, *Erzählungen eines Effendi* (Berlin: F. Fontane & Co., 1896). For a commentary and a French translation, see Eldem, *Un Ottoman en Orient*, 51–63, 103–96.

35 Rudyard Kipling, "The Ballad of East and West," *The Writings in Prose and Verse of Rudyard Kipling. Verses 1889–1896*, New York: 1899, 61.

Bibliography

Deringil, Selim. *The Well-Protected Domains. Ideology and Legitimation of Power in the Ottoman Empire 1876–1909*. London: I.B. Tauris, 1998.

Deringil, Selim. "'They Live in a State of Nomadism and Savagery': The Late Ottoman Empire and the Post-Colonial Debate." *Comparative Studies in Society and History* 45, no. 2 (April 2003): 311–42.

Eldem, Edhem. "Osman Hamdi Bey ve Oryantalizm," *Dipnot*, 2 (Winter/Spring, 2004): 39–67.

Eldem, Edhem, ed. *Un Ottoman en Orient. Osman Hamdi Bey en Irak, 1869–1871.* Paris: Actes Sud, 2010.

Ersoy, Ahmet. "A Sartorial Tribute to Tanzimat Ottomanism: The *Elbise-i Osmaniyye* Album." *Muqarnas* 20 (2003): 187–207.

Herzog, Christoph, and Raoul Motika. "Orientalism 'alla turca': Late 19th/Early 20th Century Ottoman Voyages into the Muslim 'Outback.'" *Die Welt des Islams* 40, no. 2 (July 2000): 139–95.

Hoefer, Ferdinand. *Chaldée, Assyrie, Médie, Babylonie, Mésopotamie, Phénicie, Palmyrène*. Paris: Firmin–Didot Frères, 1852.

Kipling, Rudyard. "The Ballad of East and West." *The Writings in Prose and Verse of Rudyard Kipling. Verses 1889–1896*, vol. 11, New York: C. Scribner's Sons, 1899.

Lindau, Rudolf. *Erzählungen eines Effendi*. Berlin: F. Fontane & Co., 1896.

Makdisi, Ussama. "Ottoman Orientalism." *The American Historical Review* 107, no. 3 (June 2002): 768–96.

Mardin, Şerif. "Super Westernization in Urban Life in the Ottoman Empire in the Last Quarter of the Nineteenth Century." In *Turkey: Geographic and Social Perspectives*, edited by Peter Benedict,

Erol Tümertekin, and Fatma Mansur, 404–46. Leiden: Brill, 1974.

Osman Hamdi and Marie de Launay. *Les Costumes populaires de la Turquie en 1873. Ouvrage publié sous le patronage de la commission impériale ottomane pour l'Exposition Universelle de Vienne.* Constantinople: Imprimerie du Levant Times and Shipping Gazette, 1873.

Osman Hamdy Bey and Osgan Effendi. *Musée impérial ottoman. Le Tumulus de Nemroud-Dagh. Voyage, description, inscriptions*. Constantinople: F. Loeffler, 1883.

Osman Hamdy Bey and Théodore Reinach, *Une Nécropole royale à Sidon, fouilles de Hamdy Bey*. Paris: E. Leroux, 1892–96.

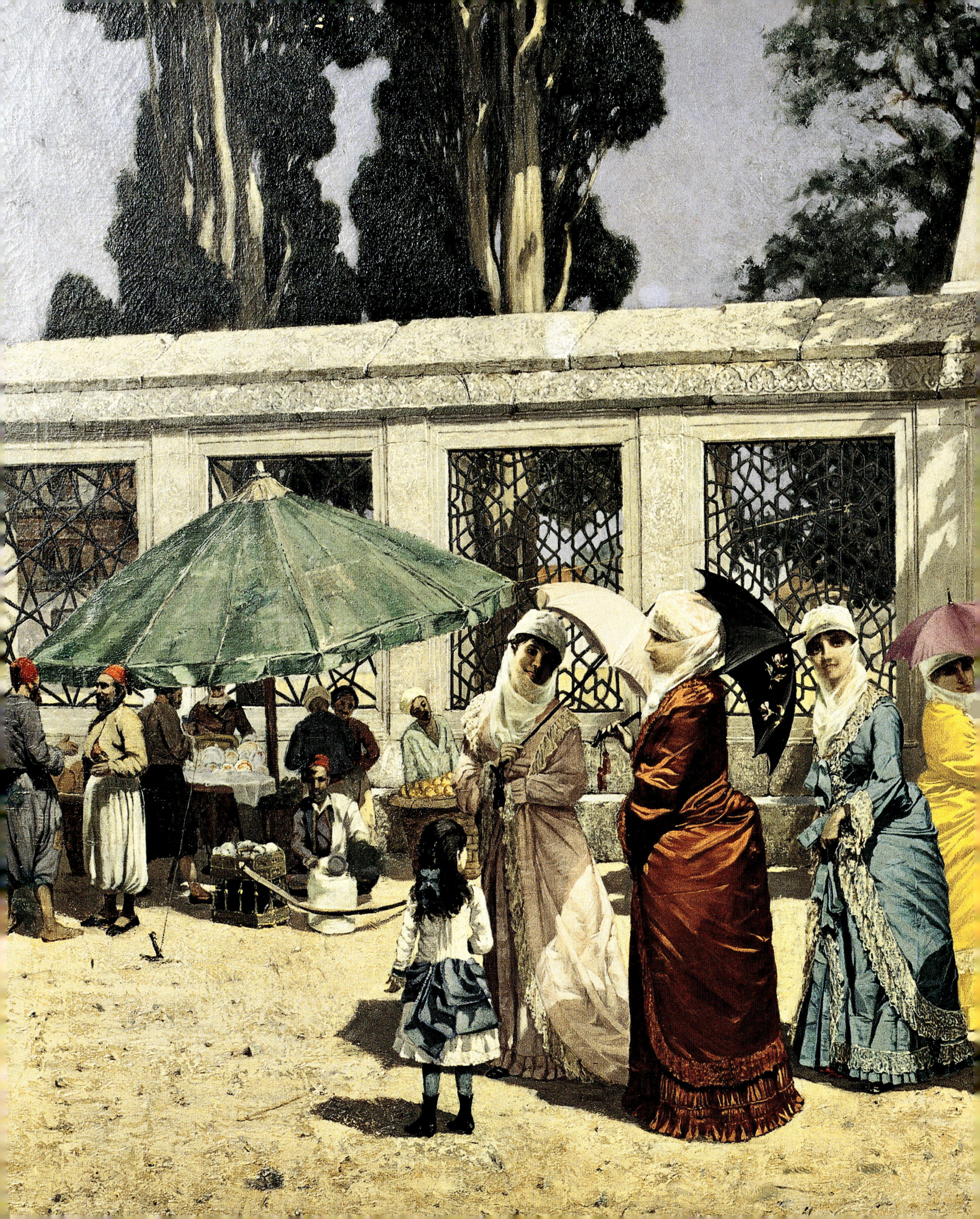

PART III:
Cultural Mediators, Boundaries, Exchanges

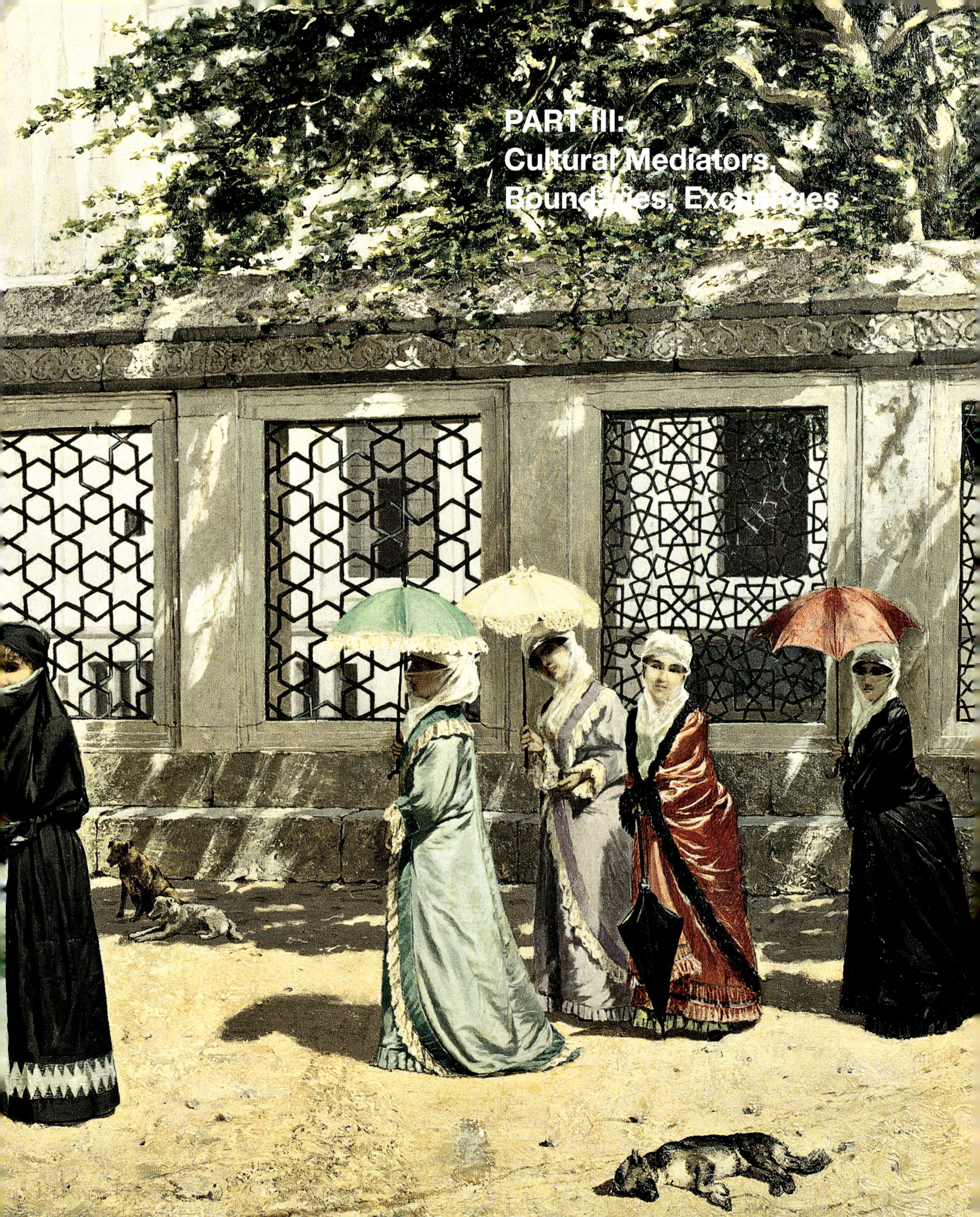

Conventual Church of St John Studius (Emir Akhor Djamissi
Founded by Studius, a Consul in the reign of the Emperor Leo = 5th cent.y
known as the Studium, contained 1000 monks called "acæmeti" (the unsle
perpetual Psalmody maintained there, night and day. The great school of Gr
confessors during the Iconoclastic controversy.

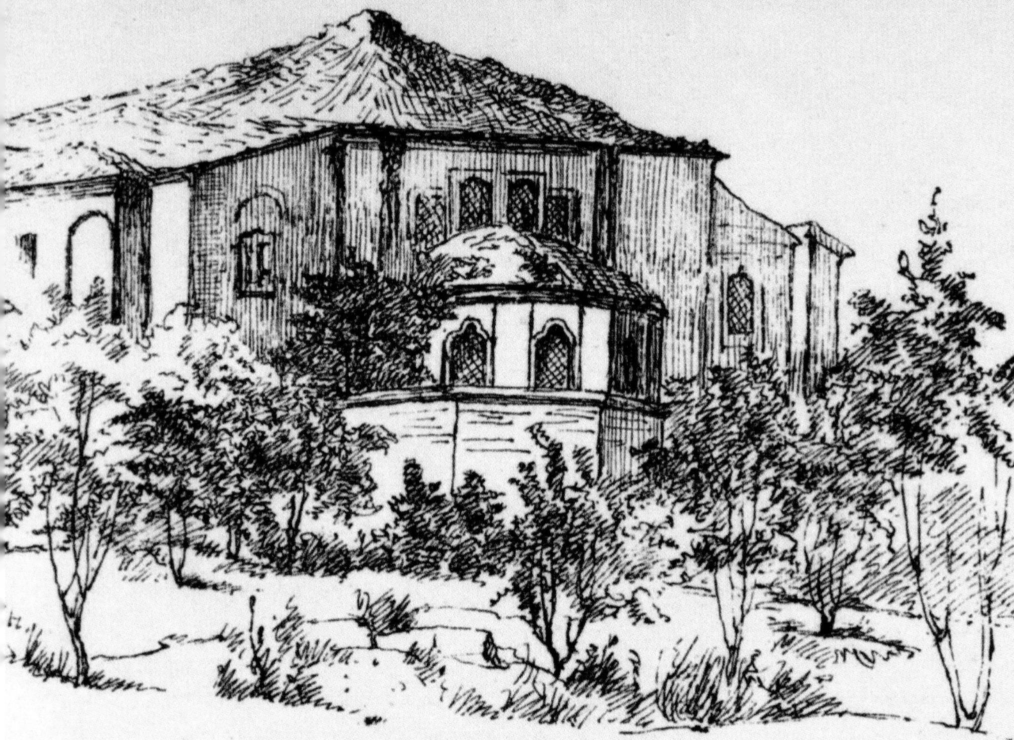

43

On west front

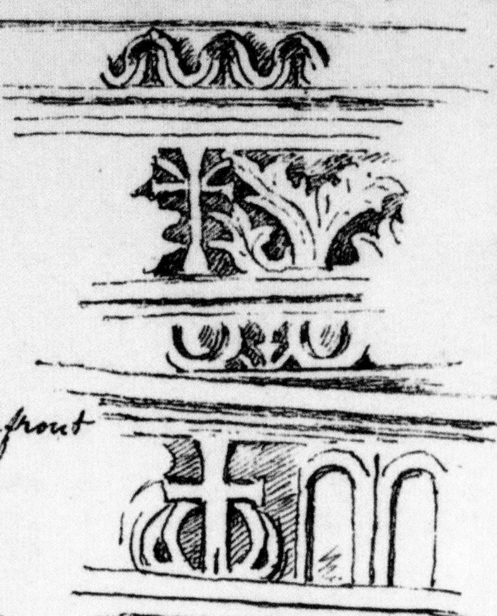

Fragment of
two entablatures: compare
cross and foliation in the
upper entablature, with
similar remains of the
Palace of Theodosius the Younger
(No 28). C G C 1887

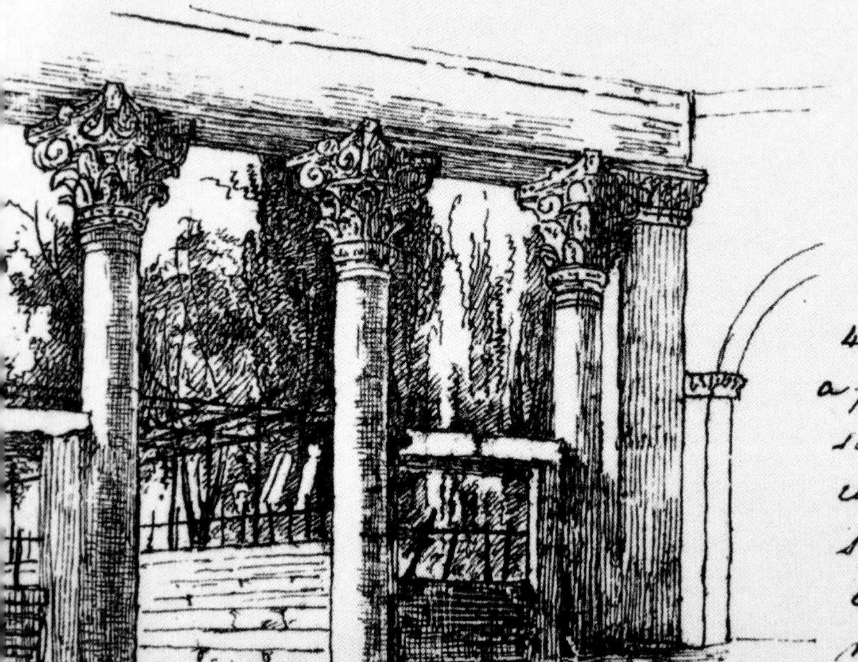

42) Remark
a portion of the
same earlier
construction as is
seen outside, in
contrast with the
more ornate work
of the later
entablature

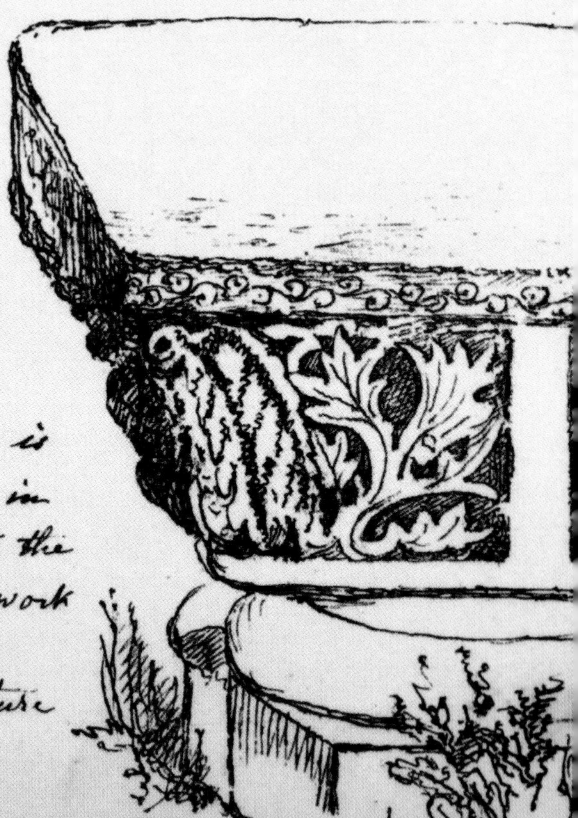

John Studius, from Within. M W. 1857
tween the columns were filled up several years ago.

Capital in front of west

XIII

Mary Adelaide Walker

Zeynep İnankur

Mary Adelaide Walker (née Curtis, 1820–1905) was a British painter who lived in Istanbul for nearly half a century and held a significant place in the art milieu of the Ottoman capital. She was from an ancient Cornish family whose origins go back to the period of Edward the First. Her father was a lawyer, John Curtis, her mother was Fanny Wilson. Both Londoners, the couple married in 1814 and had nine children. Their eldest child Mary Adelaide was born in 1820.

Mary Adelaide's brother Charles George Curtis who was one year her junior, was educated at Merton College, Oxford. After obtaining his degree he became a Master of Charterhouse and held that office for about eleven years. In 1855 the *Society for the Propagation of the Gospel in Foreign Parts* (SPG) offered him a Missionary Chaplaincy in Constantinople. He came to Constantinople in 1856, just at the end of the Crimean War and began to work at Ortaköy Church.[1] In 1868, the Bishop of Gibraltar licensed him as the chaplain of the Crimean Memorial Church[2] which was erected as a memorial to the Crimean War (Fig. 13.1). Mary Curtis came to Istanbul with her brother.

During her stay in Istanbul Mary described her life in the city, her travels in Anatolia and in the Balkans in a series of

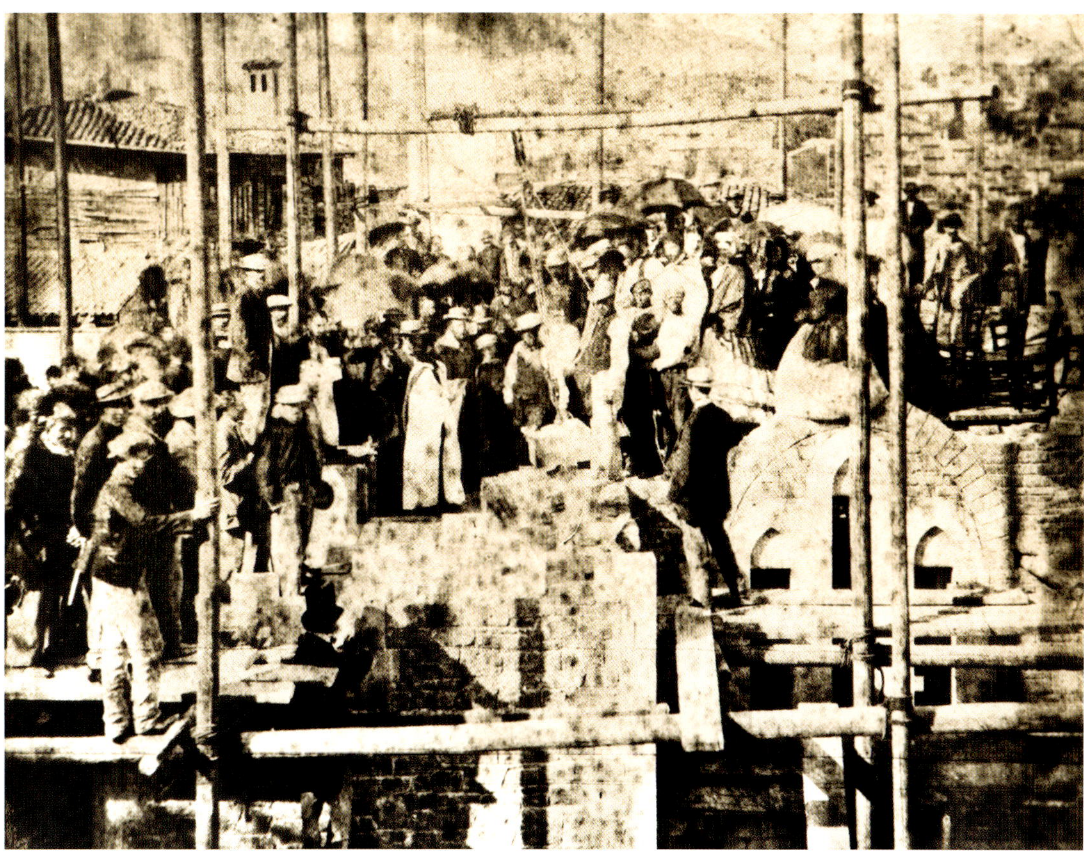

Figure 13.1 Photograph taken midway through the construction of the Crimean Memorial Church, 1864–65, Crimean Memorial Church's Inventory.

books that she illustrated herself. These were *Through Macedonia to the Albanian Lakes* (1864), *Eastern Life and Scenery, with Excursions into Asia Minor, Mytilene, Crete, and Roumania* (1886), *Untrodden Paths in Roumania* (1888) and *Old Tracks and New Landmarks* (1897). We learn from an advertisement in the *Examiner* that Walker, "went with her brother to Salonica, where he was invited to act as a clergyman to the English community, and thence, in company with some friends she made two summer tours among the Albania Lakes at the confines of Macedonia."[3] The result was her first book, *Through Macedonia to the Albanian Lakes*. It was published in 1864 by Chapman and Hall in London and she received the sum of one hundred guineas on June 15, 1863, for the copyright and sketches.[4] *Untrodden Paths in Roumania* and *Eastern Life and Scenery, with Excursions into Asia Minor, Mytilene, Crete, and Roumania* were also published by Chapman and Hall. *Eastern Life and Scenery* is of special importance since it is about her sojourn in Istanbul and her impressions about the home life of the Turks. In her last book, *Old Tracks and New Landmarks* published by Richard Bentley and Son, "Walker returns to some of the regions explored in her earlier works, 'Through Macedonia' and 'Eastern Life and Scenery,' showing them now in the changed aspects which intervening years have brought about."[5] Apart from her reminiscences about Istanbul, her excursions in İzmit, Ankara and Bursa are described in detail. As the critic in *The Levant Herald and Eastern Express* points out Mrs. Walker is an artist and a scholar. "She sees everything with an artist's eye ... she also brings ample historic knowledge to bear upon all that strikes her observation."[6] Apart from these four books, she wrote in British journals such as *Good Words*, *Temple Bar*, *London Society* and *The Morning Post* and also for a French periodical. The factual and historical information in these books and articles are very detailed and accurate. Walker was an intrepid traveler. The fact that she had settled in Istanbul and resided there for almost half a century, and her travels in the neighboring countries where she visited places which no other foreign woman traveler had set foot in, makes her a pioneer. In her obituary she was defined as "the doyenne of the British colony in Constantinople"[7] but interestingly her name is rarely mentioned in the society news of the British colony. In *Old Tracks and New Landmarks* Walker herself offers some indication of why this might be. Talking about a brief summer holiday spent with friends at Chalcedon during the absence of her husband in England, she says:[8]

> We are a very happy little party of four ladies in this morning room: in fact we are so well satisfied with each other's society and with our various useful or ornamental occupations of painting, music, needlework and reading, that I am afraid we do not stand very high in the estimation of the rest of the colony for preferring these to the prevailing habit of strolling listlessly into each other's houses and to tell Mrs. M. or N. "that those Miss X. Y's have actually got new dresses again, though, to be sure they are only imitation, and very flimsy; they won't wash, for certain, but how her father affords so much finery is more than one can imagine;" or to state an opinion of "that idle Greek maid Calliope, who instead of sweeping her rooms, has taken her parasol and gone for a stroll down Moda, in the very heat of the day, too."[9]

The reason why she stayed away from these circles might lie in her lifestyle because as soon as she arrived in Istanbul she started working as a professional painter and earned her living which was quite unusual for the British female expatriates of her time.

Her brother Canon Curtis took a leading part in the foundation of the Sailors' Home, and subsequently opened the first school in Constantinople for the benefit of English-speaking boys. He was one of the founders of the Mechanics' Institution[10] and used to give lectures about the history of Constantinople[11] either in the rooms of the British Literary and Mechanics' Association of the Sailors' Home in Galata or at their recreation hall in Hasköy. Curtis had a great interest in archeology and he soon became a prominent authority on the antique remains of Istanbul. He published the results of his thirty years of research into the Byzantine monuments of Constantinople in a book entitled *Broken Bits of Byzantium*. The sketches in the book were executed partly by him and partly by Mary (Figs. 13.2 and 13.3). In a letter he sent to the editor of *The Levant Herald and Eastern Express* in July 6, 1887, Curtis says:

> Sir, in thanking you for your notice in yesterday's paper of the little book lately put forth by my sister, Mrs. Walker, and myself, I beg to state that several pieces are from her pen and pencil, and are specially distinguished by the initials MW.[12] We supposed that the preface explained the object of it. It illustrates not text by drawings but drawings by text. We should of course, be glad if it could serve the purpose of a handbook to tourists, in showing them the way to what they must not expect to see; but we mean it for any who are interested in the history of the place. We propose, if permitted, to continue this treatment of the subject in other parts, so as to reproduce the image of several memorials that either have been lost to sight, or are on the way to oblivion and to present our fragments not only of the land-walls of the city, but of monuments

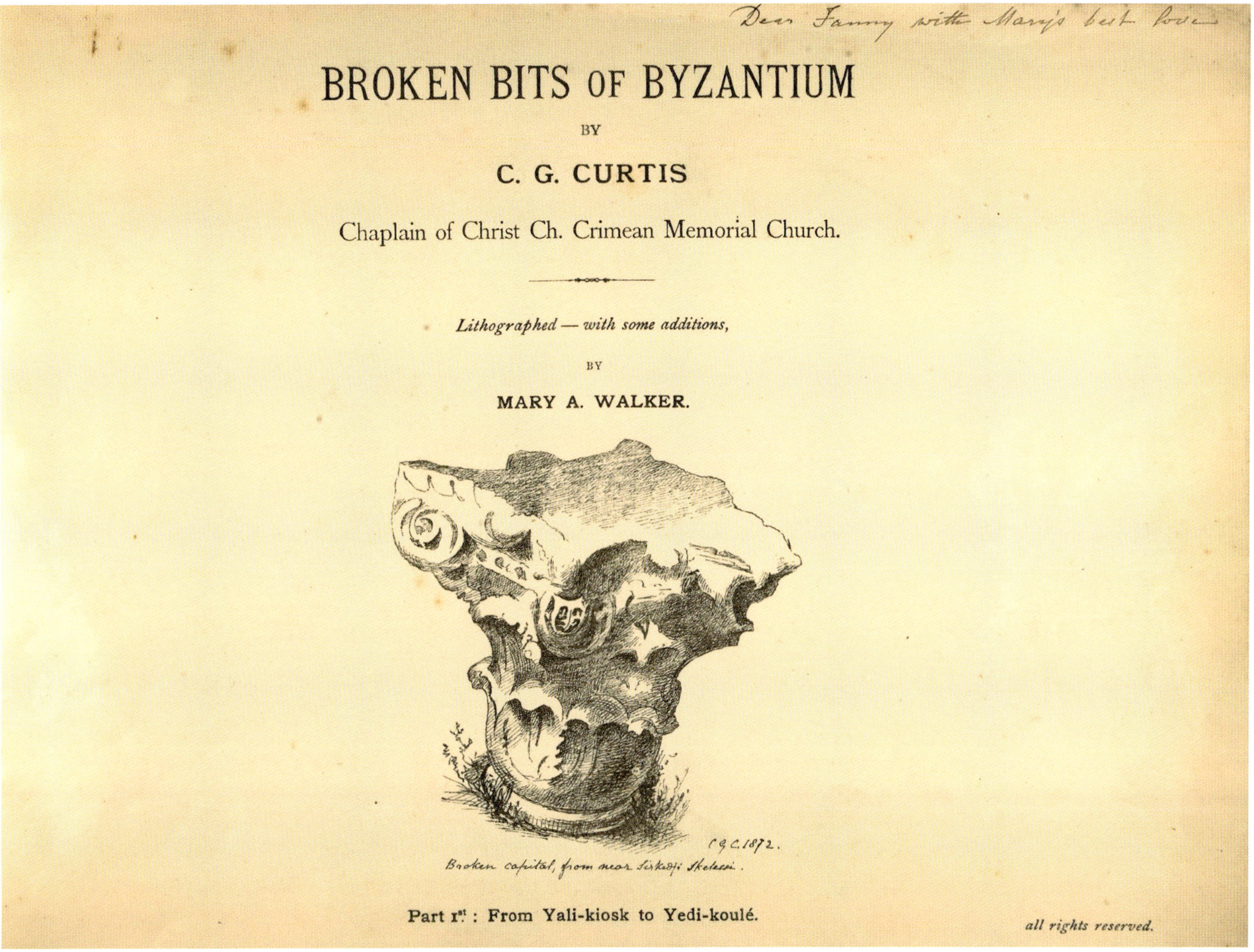

Dear Fanny with Mary's best love

BROKEN BITS OF BYZANTIUM

BY

C. G. CURTIS

Chaplain of Christ Ch. Crimean Memorial Church.

Lithographed — with some additions,

BY

MARY A. WALKER.

C.G.C. 1872.

Broken capital, from near Sirkedji Skelessi.

Part 1st: From Yali-kiosk to Yedi-koulé.

all rights reserved.

Figure 13.2 Title page of *Broken Bits of Byzantium* by C. G. Curtis and M. Walker (London, 1861), dedicated to Fanny Montrose Curtis by Mary Walker.

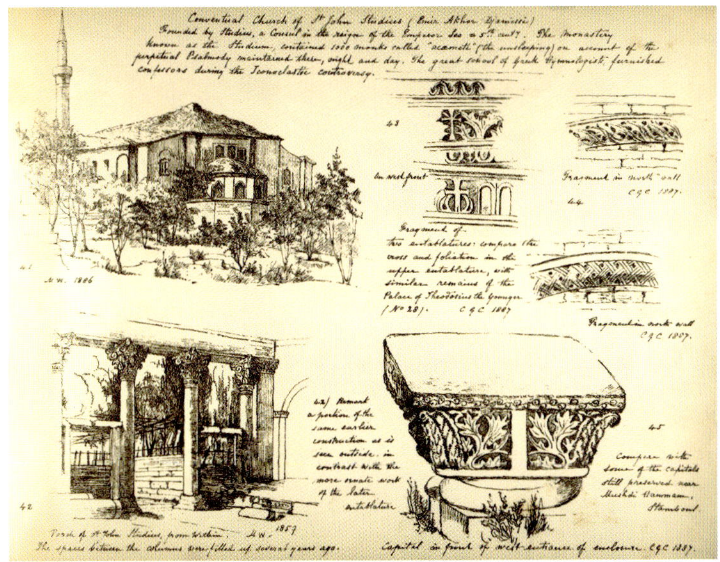

Figure 13.3 Illustration by Mary Walker, signed MW. In *Broken Bits of Byzantium* by C. G. Curtis and M. Walker (London, 1861).

> within it and then pass to this side of the Golden Horn, and gather up precious debris from Galata and Pera and aimed to reproduce the monuments of Istanbul which were rapidly falling into ruin.[13]

Canon Curtis served as the Chaplain of the Crimean Church for forty years and died on August 13, 1896 and was buried at Haidar Pasha cemetery.[14]

Mary continued to live in Constantinople after her brother's death, accompanied by her sister Clara Fanny Montrose Curtis, who must have joined them in the 1860s. She continued to travel, went to Macedonia, Crete and Mytilene and described these excursions in her last book *Old Tracks and New Landmarks* published in 1897. Throughout her stay in Constantinople, Mary frequently went back to her home country. In 1904 she went again intending to return soon but family bereavements prolonged her stay. She died in Dover, on September 28, 1905, after a serious illness.

Unusually for her time, when middle-class women were not expected to have a career, Mary supported herself through art. As Susan Casteras points out, in the Victorian period, "creating art was deemed a source of edification, entertainment and beauty, a suitable undertaking or genteel hobby for young women; it was not, however, intended as pre-professional, serious training for an aspiring artist. Making art was part of the initiation process of becoming a lady."[15] Mary, in contrast, took art beyond accomplishment, working professionally and earning her living by teaching painting. For instance, in relation to one of the paintings she executed, she says, "I may mention here the fact that in all my transactions with the Turks, this is the only instance I failed to receive—with more or less of delay, but always, in the end, honestly and faithfully—the sum of money agreed upon between us.[16] She received an artistic education in Paris in her early youth, specialized in portrait and landscape painting and quickly made a reputation in Istanbul. She lived at Pera near the *Mekteb-i Sultani*, present day Galatasaray High School, in a stone house on the sharp slope of a hill descending to Tophane. This was the Yeni Çarşı Street[17] where artists like Amadeo Preziosi and Jean Brindesi had their studios. Interestingly, although they were neighbors and also members of the same jury at the ABC Club exhibition, she doesn't mention Preziosi's name in her accounts, there is also not a single reference to the artistic milieu of Istanbul. Mary married Robert Walker who was also from the Pera parish, on December 7, 1862. They were married by Reverend Charles Besly Gribble, Canon of Gibraltar and Chaplain to the British Embassy at Constantinople, at the Crimean Church.[18] She was a widow when she died.

In the preface of her book *Eastern Life and Scenery* which was published in 1886, Walker says that every rule and custom of harem life mentioned in the book would be found exemplified in the varied scenes that had been drawn from notes of personal experience during a residence of nearly thirty years in the East. Mary, most probably through the mediation of her brother's acquaintances at the beginning, had the unique opportunity to visit and consequently portray the Ottoman harem into which no male Orientalist painters were allowed to enter. Conveying her impressions of this particular theme in her memoirs and depicting Turkish home life with unprecedented accuracy Walker presented to the West a world that was vastly different from the harem image that the male Orientalists chose to portray.

In the spring of her arrival in Constantinople and shortly after the end of the Crimean War, Mary was invited to the *konak* (mansion) of one of the chief functionaries of the Palace to paint the portrait of his wife. This statesman whom Mary calls R… Pasha is probably Mustafa Reshid Pasha[19] who was six times appointed Grand Vizier, Minister of Foreign Affairs and twice appointed Ottoman ambassador to Paris and London. The British ambassador in Constantinople, Sir Henry Layard praised him by saying that he was amongst the first Turkish statesmen who adopted, to a certain extent, European manners and habits.[20] The lady featuring in the portrait must have been Reshid Pasha's second wife, Adile Hanım. This indicates the presence of a certain group of people in the Ottoman capital who easily opened up their harems to foreigners and moreover commissioned the portraits of their family members. Mary who complained about the difficulty of setting up an easel for the first time in a Turkish harem, says,

> as it would be quite contrary to the rules of orthodox Mussulman society that a lady should visit a painter's studio or expose her portrait in any way to be seen by men, it becomes necessary to execute the whole work within the harem, even to the last finishing touch of varnishing and framing—a labour of difficulty and fatigue—rarely undertaken by a lady artist in the case of very large canvases.[21]

After completing the three-quarters life-size portrait of the Pasha's beautiful Circassian wife in oils, Mary received her second harem commission from the daughter of the Sultan married to the son of a celebrated statesman. Although Walker doesn't give the real name of this princess, both her description and the information supplied about her palace suggest that the princess in question was Sultan Abdülmecid's daughter Fatma Sultan (Fig. 13.4) who was then married to Ali Galip Pasha, son of Mustafa Reshid Pasha. During her first

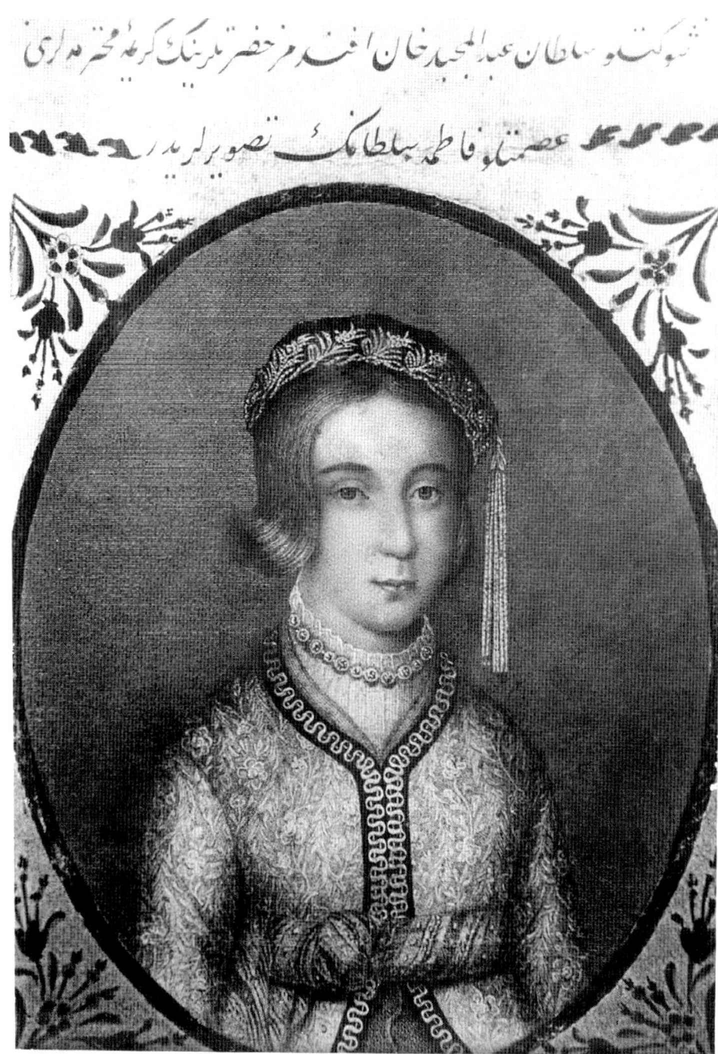

Figure 13.4 *Princess Fatma, Daughter of Sultan Abdülmecid, Ruben 1266*, Engraving, Topkapı Palace Museum Library.

visit to Mustafa Reshid Pasha's residence Walker found him, "most anxious for the success of the work, as it was to be followed by a likeness of one of the sultanas."[22] So this new commission was most probably realized through the agency of Mustafa Reshid Pasha. Walker's first meeting with the princess took place at her palace on the Bosporus. This stone mansion which was quite modern for its time is the Baltalimanı Coastal Palace built by the architect Sarkis Balyan for Mustafa Reshid Pasha. When his son married Fatma Sultan, the palace was bought by the treasury and given to the married couple. The description of the interior decoration of the building as told in the memoirs of Leyla Saz, the daughter of Sultan Abdülmecid's doctor is quite similar to Walker's. Walker when describing the palace says: "A vast hall, the ceiling supported on columns of many-coloured marble, the walls gorgeous with slabs of malachite, agate, and alabaster, rose-coloured porphyry, and lines of lapiz-lazuli; the floor, a beautiful parqueterie of inlaid woods; mirrors, gilding, dazzling lights from high branched stands of richly wrought silver."[23] Leyla Saz's version is very close to Walker's:

> The Palace of Baltalimanı is the most beautiful of all the sultan palaces. The central hall of this strong stone building is illuminated by the thick, ornamented clearstory, while the interior hall which is divided by columns is illuminated by windows overlooking the sea. Fireplaces of colored marble, parquetry decorated with small pieces and the ornaments of the ceiling are of the best craftmanship.[24]

Walker stayed at Fatma Sultan's summer palace for five or six months and one of the rooms of the palace was converted into a studio for her. Fatma Sultan's portrait in oil was quite large and since her "varying taste wandered … amongst the different articles of dress, jewellery, or furniture which she took a sudden fancy to see represented," it was painted three times over before it was finally finished. According to Walker:

> The costume chosen for the important occasion was deplorable; no line of Oriental grace, or even of splendour in the dress. She had robes stiff with gems, draperies of fairy tissue, yet she stood for her portrait in a dress of the poorest French silk, because it was "moda" "a la franca." It was dead unlovely white, the upper part made like a European lady's ball dress, while from the waist downwards it was fashioned into the orthodox antary and schalwars.[25]

[The] "ease, the grace, the dazzling magnificence of the East was lost and dimmed by a painful striving after Western fashions."[26] When the portrait was finished and hung on the wall a large curtain of white silk was fastened on to the frame so that the men working at the palace wouldn't see it. None of the paintings Mary Walker did at this palace have survived but the French artist, Henriette Browne who was presented to Fatma Sultan by Walker executed a painting entitled *A Visit: Harem Interior, Constantinople, 1860* which was inspired by her visit to the Baltalimanı Palace. With its authentic depiction of an Ottoman harem, this painting became a great success when it was exhibited in Paris and London and shook the foundations of stereotyped harem fantasies.[27]

After several years Walker was summoned to the winter palace of Fatma Sultan who requested the artist repaint the dress she wore in her portrait in the style of a fashion book she has just received from Paris.[28] This new taste for Western fashion increased in the second half of the nineteenth century and the women of the court began to dress according to the Parisian dress patterns they acquired in Istanbul.[29] These dresses were so in vogue that Fatma Sultan hearing that Walker was depicting the harem ladies in their traditional outfits in her pocket sketch-book, ordered the book to be brought to her and it was returned to Walker with "one of the most cherished sketches of the classical draperies scored all over with pencil marks and nearly torn away, and a polite message from the Sultana, who begs that I will not do any more pictures of her women in their morning dresses, 'with their robes all twisted about them; it is ugly, and the Franks will think her harem very ill-dressed.'"[30]

Following the portrait of Fatma Sultan, the artist painted a miniature oil portrait of Serfiraz Hanım, a favorite of Sultan Abdülmecid's, and then the portraits of the wife and children of a high-ranking army officer. This commission came from the wife who wanted her husband stationed at the camp at Schumla to have some visual reminders of the family ties left behind in Istanbul.[31] Most of these portraits were kept at the harem, and as Mary Roberts points out, it is the harem woman who exercised control in their production, in contrast to the pervasive stereotype of the passive odalisque.[32] In fact Fatma Sultan who was short and plump asked Walker to depict her as tall and slim and, when the artist objected, she "stamped her foot, said I [Walker] did not care to please her, and that the portrait must be done according to her wishes, or—not at all."[33]

In 1870, Walker who had a good command of Turkish was appointed as a professor of drawing at the first girls' vocational school, *Dersaadet Darülmuallimat* (Women's Teacher Training College of Istanbul). The school was established in a wooden house situated in the Yerebatan quarter on April 26. It was founded by the Minister of Public Instruction, Saffet Pasha with the aim of training teachers for girls' schools. After the 1839 Tanzimat Firman (Noble Reform Script), primary schools for girls (*Sıbyan*) were restructured, secondary schools for girls (*Rüşdiye*) and vocational schools came onto the scene. As the number of girls' schools increased, there was more need for female teachers, since even in Istanbul many families were reluctant to send their daughters to schools with a male staff. The consequence was the founding of the *Darülmuallimat*, teacher training colleges for women. The education commenced with thirty-two girls.[34] Pupils of this school were not from the upper classes, but the children of modest social origin who were to graduate into the first female professions of teaching. The advertisement which announced the opening of *Darülmuallimat* in *Takvim-i Vekayi* said that the students would be given a monthly salary of thirty *kuruş* in the first class and sixty *kuruş* in the second class.[35] The duration of education was two years for *Sıbyan* and three years for *Rüşdiye* school teachers. The curriculum of three years consisted of religion and ethics, grammar, arithmetic, domestic science, embroidery, drawing, calligraphy, Ottoman history and geography. Twenty-one students entered the graduation exams in 1873, and seventeen passed; the eldest was thirty, the youngest was fourteen years old.

Walker taught there for two years and her students did not have the faintest idea about drawing at the beginning. Talking about her classes, Walker says that simple landscape studies were in vogue, that the students made still lives or sketches from nature first by pencil and then by watercolor. Vere Foster's series of models which was a present from Lady Hobart who was a painter herself were also in great demand among the students. After two years Walker resigned partly for personal reasons and partly because of the lack of discipline at school.[36] We also learn from the *Constantinople Messenger* dated November 24, 1880 that Mrs. Walker would be giving drawing lessons at the "Ladies Classes"[37] at the British Mechanics and Literary Institute in Istanbul. The committee members of the Ladies' Classes were Reverend C. G. Curtis, M. A. Chairman, J. H. Fawcett, Rev. Albert Long, E. Pears, Rev. George Washington, and Rev. G. Washburn. Its curriculum consisted of "History of Constantinople" by Rev. Canon Curtis, "Elementary Physiology" by John Patterson, "Early History" by Edwin Pears, "Natural Science" by Rev. Albert Long, "Astronomy and Physical Geography" by Capt. Woods and drawing by Mrs. Walker. The lectures were given at the Francis Memorial Institute and tickets were to be obtained either at Mr. Jew's, the British Post Office or at Mr. Baker's, Grand Rue de Pera.[38]

Walker participated in the Fine Arts exhibitions organized by the ABC Club, first at the Greek Girls' School in Tarabya in 1880 and then at the chalet of Petit Champs in Pera, in 1881. In an article about the first exhibition published in the *Constantinople Messenger*, the author says that Mrs. Walker was the only artist who exhibited in so many different styles.[39] From this article we learn that Walker contributed a picture of a negro boy carrying fruit, portraits in oils, a head of a boy in pastels and also sketches of the Bosporus in watercolor and black and white.[40] Abdullah Kâmil who wrote a review of the exhibition in the newspaper, *Osmanlı*, praised Miss Serviçen who participated in the exhibition with a portrait of her father, Serviçen Efendi. He also emphasized Mrs. Walker's contribution to Ottoman cultural life by remarking, "at the same time we give our thanks to Mrs. Walker because by training Miss Serviçen through her drawing lessons, she performed a service to our country."[41] Walker was one of the jury members of the 1881 exhibition of the ABC Club together with Rev.

Washington, Mr. Wrench, Mr. Köçeoğlu, Mr. Preziosi, Jr., Mr. Pears and Mr. Mavrogordoto.[42] She also exhibited six of her works, two of which were landscapes.[43] An anonymous writer in the *Constantinople Messenger* who introduced himself as a recent visitor in Constantinople and a well-known figure in the art circles of London, praised her but also criticized the position of the head in the pastel study belonging to Mme Onou and the lack of proportion in the *Montenegrin Woman* and in *The Sweet Waters of Asia*.[44] The same year, Walker donated a painting to an exhibition organized by an Armenian Union called *Tibrotzaser Dignantz Ingerutyun* (Association of Women in Favour of Education).[45] The artist participated in the 1867 Paris Universal Exhibition with a portrait of Sultan Abdülaziz. We don't know whether this portrait was made from life but if it is, this is the first and the last instance of an Ottoman Sultan's portrait painted by a woman. In the booklet published for the occasion, *La Turquie dans l'Exposition Universelle*, the curator of the Ottoman section, Selâhaddin Bey, mentions Walker in connection with Miss Serviçen. He says that with her pretty painting, *A Circassian Slave Serving Coffee*, Miss Serviçen had proved her talent to Mrs. Walker who executed a portrait of Sultan Abdülaziz which was noticed in spite of its closeness to Osman Hamdi Bey's painting, *Halt*.[46]

Apart from Miss Serviçen, one of Walker's private students was Enid Layard, wife of the British ambassador, Henry Layard. We learn from Lady Layard's journals that Mary gave her lessons in portrait painting, and even brought her a little girl as a model for her picture of a Circassian slave.[47] These lessons which started in December 1879 continued until May 1880 when Sir Layard retired and the couple left for Venice. They remained in contact and Walker sent Lady Layard some drawings which she paid for with a cheque.[48] Lady Layard also mentions Princess Vijdane Halim, wife of Mohamed Abdel-Halim Pasha, who was going to Paris and London and asked her to ask Mrs. Walker to go with her as *dame de compagnie*.[49] From this information we may deduce that Mrs. Walker sometimes worked as an artistic guide as well.

In spite of all the information about Mrs. Walker's paintings, only one has been located so far. This is a watercolor picture of Thomas Sandwith's house and its surroundings in Khalépa, looking down towards Chania in Crete and it is signed "Mary Walker." Sandwith was the British Consul there in 1870–85 and Walker in *Eastern Life and Scenery*[50] mentions that she was entertained at his house at Khalépa.[51] We know from Mary Walker's testament that she gave all her books, manuscripts and pictures to her sister Clara Fanny Montrose Curtis[52] but unfortunately a full list is not available. Thus the illustrations in her brother's book *Broken Bits of Byzantium* or in Lady Emelia Hornby's[53] memoirs *Constantinople during the Crimean War* (Figs. 13.5 and 13.6) or in her own books are the only sources

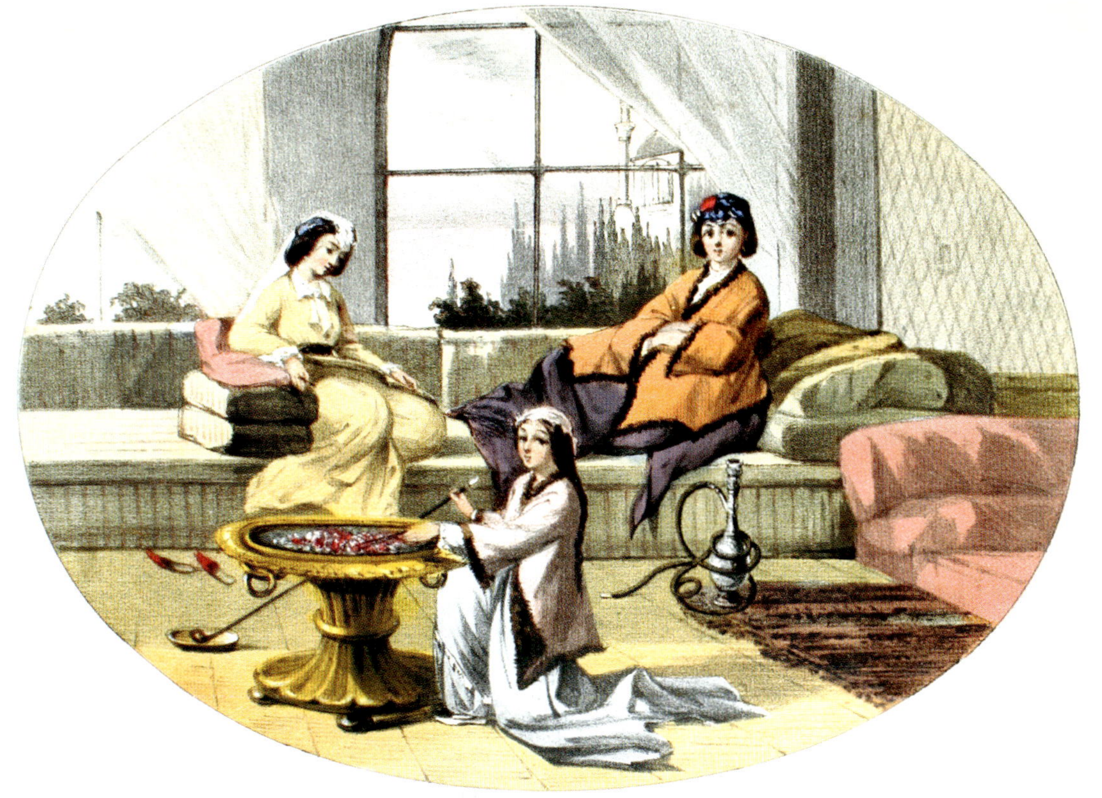

Figure 13.5 Illustration facing page 321 by Mary Adelaide Walker from Lady Hornby, *Constantinople during the Crimean War* (London: Richard Bentley, 1863).

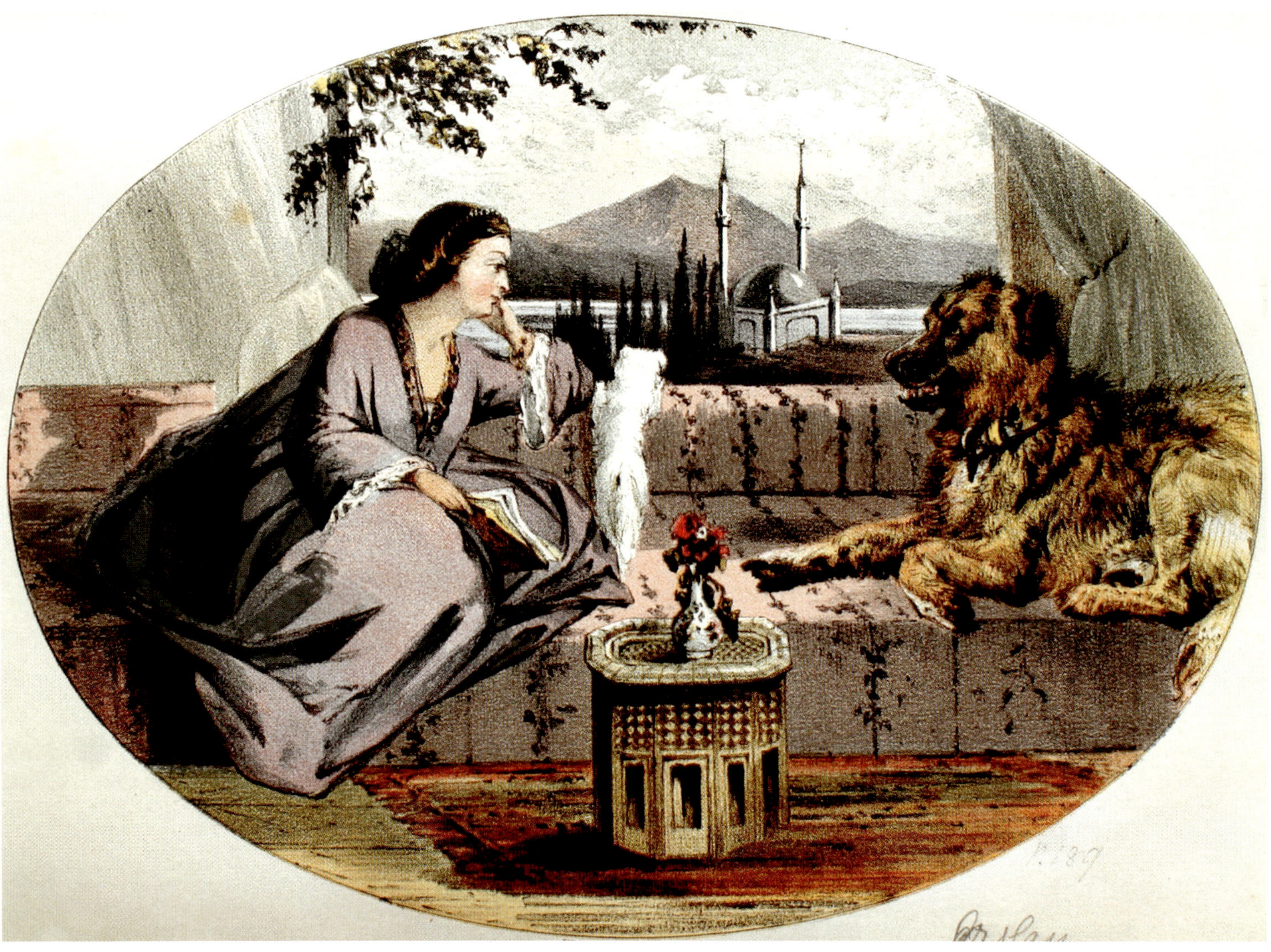

Figure 13.6 Illustration facing page 38 by Mary Adelaide Walker from Lady Hornby, *Constantinople during the Crimean War* (London: Richard Bentley, 1863).

that can give us an idea about her art.[54] Hornby's memoirs were first published as *In and Around Stamboul* in 1858. After she returned to England in 1862 she made some additions to the book, had it illustrated by Mary Walker and republished it in 1863 under the name *Constantinople during the Crimean War*. We learn from the advertisement by the publisher that Walker was Hornby's friend, although they don't mention each other's names in their books.[55] As can be seen from all these pictures, Walker is an illustrator rather than a first class painter (Fig. 13.6). But in spite of this it is difficult not to agree with Sir Donald Mackenzie Wallace's[56] comments regarding the illustrations in Walker's book, *Old Tracks and New Landmarks*. Wallace says that these sketches were

> very carefully drawn little pictures by one who has a keen, practised eye for picturesque little details, and an intimate knowledge not only of the past history of the country, but also of the character and customs of the various sections of the population, the keenness of observation and accuracy of knowledge being always tempered by that kindly sympathy which helps an outsider to see things from the inside.[57]

Mary Walker's affection and sympathy for the Turks can indeed be felt in her writings. The fact that she entitled the chapter where she talks about the Bosporus in *Old Tracks and New Landmarks* as "Our Beautiful Waterway"[58] shows that she felt like a native citizen. When she went to Britain in 1904, it was with the intention of returning to Constantinople. If she hadn't fallen ill she would have ended her days in this city that she loved so much.

Notes

1 He was the Missionary Chaplain at Constantinople from 1856 to 1868, at Pera from 1868 to 1896 and Canon of Gibraltar from 1879 to 1896.

2 *The Levant Times*, November 23, 1868.

3 *The Examiner*, January 14, 1865.

4 http://www.ilabdatabase.com/db/detail.php?booknr=332646438&source=ilaborg

5 *The Levant Herald and Eastern Express*, January 24, 1898.

6 *The Levant Herald and Eastern Express*, July 28, 1886.

7 *The Levant Herald and Eastern Express*, October 9, 1905.

8 This chapter was originally written for *Good Words* in 1866.

9 Mary Adelaide Walker, *Old Tracks and New Landmarks* (London: Bentley and Son, 1897), 88.

10 *The Levant Herald and Eastern Express*, August 17, 1896. The inaugural meeting of the British Literary and Mechanics Association was held on January 4, 1872.

11 Some of his lectures were, "Traces of English who were in Constantinople and the Greek provinces before the arrival of the Turks," "Traces of English Guards in the Service of the Greek Emperors of Constantinople," "The Hippodrome at Constantinople," "Broken Bits of Byzantium, or Curiosities," "Rambles among the Ruins of Constantinople." This last talk was accompanied by drawings and sketches.

12 The editor of the *Levant Herald and Eastern Express* had stated the sketches and the accompanying text were by Canon Curtis, see *The Levant Herald and Eastern Express*, July 6, 1887.

13 *The Levant Herald and Eastern Express*, July 6, 1887.

14 *The Chapel of Her Majesty's Ambassador at the Sublime Porte: Register of Burials*, no. 1528, 191.

15 Susan P. Casteras, "With Palettes, Pencils and Parasols: Victorian Women Artists Traverse the Empire," in *Intrepid Women: Victorian Artists Travel*, ed. Jordana Pomeroy (Aldershot: Ashgate Publishing, 2006), 12.

16 Mary Adelaide Walker, *Eastern Life and Scenery* (London: Chapman and Hall, 1886) 1: 40–41.

17 Henry James Hanson Collection (GB165-0135), Archive library, Middle East Centre, St. Anthony's College, Oxford, http://www.levantineheritage.com/note27.htm and *Levant Times*, February 3, 1870. See also the description in Walker, *Eastern Life and Scenery,* 1: 77.

18 The *Chapel of Her Majesty's Ambassador at the Sublime Porte: Register of Marriages*, no. 186, 62. I am grateful to Reverend Canon Ian Sherwood for letting me into the archives of the Crimean Memorial Church in Istanbul.

19 He was the Grand Vizier from September 1846 to April 1848; August 1848 to January 1852; March 1852 to August 1852; November 1854 to May 1855; November 1856 to August 1857; October 1857 to January 1858.

20 Sir A. Henry Layard, G.C.B., D.C.L, *Autobiography and Letters from His Childhood Until His Appointment as H. M. Ambassador at Madrid* (London: John Murray, 1903), 2: 87.

21 Walker, *Eastern Life and Scenery*, 1: 2.

22 Ibid., 1: 2.

23 Ibid., 1: 35.

24 Leyla Saz, *Harem'in İçyüzü* (Istanbul: Milliyet Yayınları, 1974), 148.

25 Walker, *Eastern Life and Scenery*, 1: 15.

26 Ibid., 1:16.

27 On the critical reception of Henriette Browne's harem painting see Reina Lewis, "'Only Women Should go to Turkey': Henriette Browne and Women's Orientalism," *Third Text* 7, no. 22 (Spring 1993): 53–64.

28 Walker, *Eastern Life and Scenery*, 1: 311.

29 Hülya Tezcan, "Batılılaşma Döneminde Saray Kadının Modası," *P. Dergisi* (Winter 1998–99): 84.

30 Walker *Eastern Life and Scenery*, 1: 312.

31 Ibid., 1: 99.

32 Mary Roberts, *Intimate Outsiders* (Durham: Duke University Press, 2007), 116. See also, Mary Roberts, "The Politics of Portraiture Behind the Veil," in *Art and the British Empire*, ed. Tim Barringer, Geoff Quilley and Douglas Fordham (Manchester: Manchester University Press, 2007), 223–36 and 399–402; Mary Roberts, "Contested Terrains: Women Orientalists and the Colonial Harem,"

in *Orientalism's Interlocutors: Painting, Architecture, Photography*, ed. Jill Beaulieu and Mary Roberts (Durham: Duke University Press, 2002), 179–203.

33 Walker, *Eastern Life and Scenery*, 1: 17.

34 Osman Ergin, *Türkiye Maarif Tarihi*, vols 1–2 (Istanbul: Eser Matbaası, 1977), 669. This number is forty in Walker, *Eastern Life and Scenery*, 1: 226.

35 *Takvim-i Vekayi,* 24 Eylül 1285, Defa 1148.

36 Walker, *Eastern Life and Scenery,* 1: 221–22, 225, 227, 231–33, 246.

37 These classes were most probably for the families of the members.

38 *The Constantinople Messenger*, November 24, 1880.

39 *The Constantinople Messenger*, September 11, 1880.

40 Ibid.

41 Abdullah Kâmil, *Osmanlı*, 11 Şevval, 1297, no. 14.

42 *The Constantinople Messenger*, March 9, 1881.

43 *Young Bulgarian*, *Jerry*, *Study in Pastel Portrait of Mme C.*, *Portrait in Pastel Belonging to Mme Onou*, *Vlanga Bostan in Pastel*, *Zeibek Dancers of the Balkans*, *Montenegrin Woman*, *Galata Tower and Istanbul*, *Sweet Waters of Asia*, *Molovo*, *Island of Métélin*. See *ABC Club Exposition des Beaux Arts au Chalet des Petits Champs* (Constantinople: Imprimerie B. J. Q., 1881).

44 *The Constantinople Messenger*, April 27, 1881.

45 *Stamboul*, February 2, 1882.

46 Salâhaddin Bey, *La Turquie dans L'Exposition Universelle de 1867* (Paris: Hachette, 1867), 143.

47 "Lady Layard's Journals," December 9, 1879, March 20, 1880; available at http://www.browningguide.org.

48 Ibid., August 25, 1882.

49 Ibid., September 4, 1879.

50 Walker, *Eastern Life and Scenery*, 2: 295.

51 Stephen Boys Smith who kindly provided me with this valuable information and who is the present owner of the painting, also possesses a number of Walker's drawings, put together in an album with "Crete" emblazoned on the front in gold. These drawings are signed "MW." Some of them are the illustrations in *Old Tracks and New Landmarks* by Mary Adelaide Walker.

52 Clara Fanny Montrose Curtis who died on October 18, 1906, left all the pictures in her possession to her nephew's widow, Mary Annie Louisa Wigan.

53 Lady Hornby was the wife of Edmund Hornby, Judge of the Supreme Consular Court at Constantinople.

54 On Walker's illustrations of Emilia Hornby's book, see Mary Roberts, *Intimate Outsiders*, 125, 126.

55 Lady Hornby, *Constantinople during the Crimean War* (London: Richard Bentley, 1863).

56 Donald Mackenzie Wallace, *The Times* Istanbul correspondent.

57 Mary Adelaide Walker, *Old Tracks and New Landmarks* (London: Richard Bentley and Son, 1897), vii–viii.

58 Ibid., 331.

Bibliography

ABC Club Exposition des Beaux Arts au Chalet des Petits Champs. Constantinople: Imprimerie B. J. Q., 1881.

Abdullah Kâmil. *Osmanlı* 11 Şevval, 1297, no. 14.

Casteras, Susan P. "With Palettes, Pencils and Parasols: Victorian Women Artists Traverse the Empire." In *Intrepid Women: Victorian Artists Travel*, edited by Jordana Pomeroy, 11–26. Aldershot: Ashgate Publishing, 2006.

Curtis, Charles George. *Broken Bits of Byzantium*. Constantinople: Lorentz and Keil, 1887.

The Constantinople Messenger, September 11, 1880; November 24, 1880; March 9, 1881; April 27, 1881.

Ergin, Osman. *Türkiye Maarif Tarih*. Istanbul: Eser Matbaası, 1977.

The Examiner, January 14, 1865.

The Levant Herald and Eastern Express, July 28, 1886; July 6, 1887; August 17, 1896; January 24, 1898; October 9, 1905.

The Levant Times, November 23, 1868; February 3, 1870.

Henry James Hanson Collection (GB165-0135), Archive library, Middle East Centre, St Anthony's College, Oxford, http://www.levantine.plus.com/link.htm.

Hornby, Lady. *Constantinople during the Crimean War*. London: Richard Bentley, 1863.

Kuneralp, Sinan, ed. *Twixt Pera and Therapia: The Constantinople Diaries of Lady Layard*. Istanbul: The Isis Press, 2010.

Layard, Sir A. Henry, G.C.B., D.C.L. *Autobiography and Letters from His Childhood Until His Appointment as H. M. Ambassador at Madrid*. London: John Murray, 1903.

"Lady Layard's Journals." December 9, 1879; March 20, 1880, http://www.browningguide.org.

Lewis, Reina. "'Only Women Should Go to Turkey': Henriette Browne and Women's Orientalism," *Third Text* 7, no. 22 (Spring 1993): 53–64.

Roberts, Mary. "Contested Terrains: Women Orientalists and the Colonial Harem." In *Orientalism's Interlocutors: Painting, Architecture, Photography*, edited by Jill Beaulieu and Mary Roberts, 179–203. Durham: Duke University Press, 2002.

Roberts, Mary. *Intimate Outsiders. The Harem in Ottoman and Orientalist Art and Travel Literature*. Durham: Duke University Press, 2007.

Roberts, Mary. "The Politics of Portraiture Behind the Veil." In *Art and the British Empire*, edited by Tim Barringer, Geoff Quilley and Douglas Fordham, 223–36 and 399–402. Manchester: Manchester University Press, 2007.

Salâhaddin Bey, *La Turquie dans L'Expositon Universelle de 1867*. Paris: Hachette, 1867.

Saz, Leyla. *Harem'in İçyüzü*. Istanbul: Milliyet Yayınları, 1974.

Stamboul. February 2, 1882.

Takvim-i Vekayi. 24 Eylül 1285, Defa 1148.

Tezcan, Hülya. "Batılılaşma Döneminde Saray Kadının Modası." *P. Dergisi* (Winter 1998–99): 84.

Twixt Pera and Therapia The Constantinople Diaries of Lady Layard. Edited by Sinan Kuneralp. Istanbul: Isis Press, 2010.

Walker, Mary Adelaide. *Through Macedonia to the Albanian Lakes*. London: Chapman and Hall, 1864.

Walker, Mary Adelaide. *Eastern Life and Scenery, with Excursions into Asia Minor, Mytilene, Crete, and Roumania*. London: Chapman and Hall, 1886.

Walker, Mary Adelaide. *Untrodden Paths in Roumania*. London: Chapman and Hall, 1888.

Walker, Mary Adelaide. *Old Tracks and New Landmarks*. London: Richard Bentley and Son, 1897.

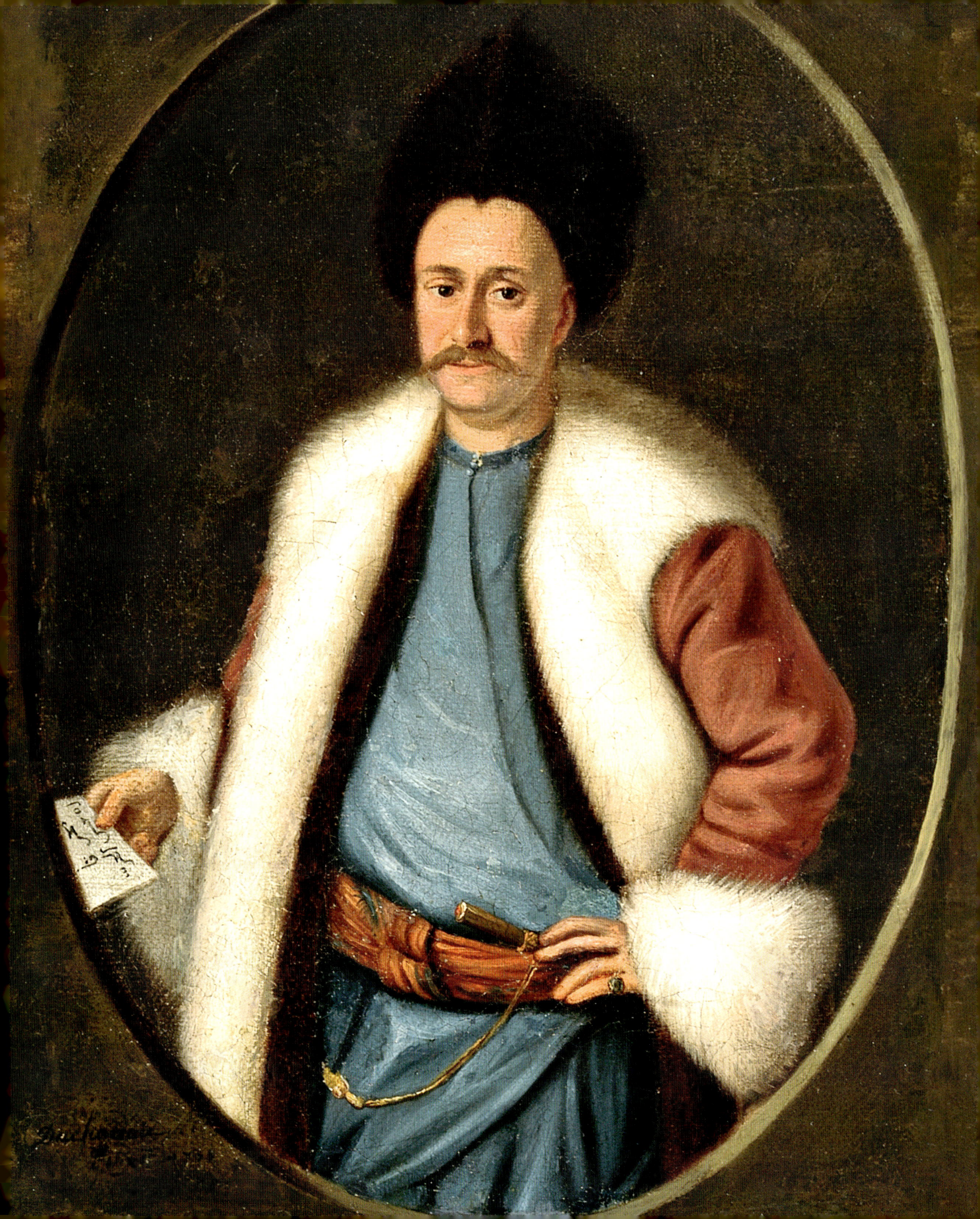

XIV

The Dragoman who Commissioned His Own Portrait

Aykut Gürçağlar

This chapter explores a specific aspect of the interpreter's agency. It looks at the dragomans in the Ottoman Empire as active agents in the act of communication and as patrons of artists—commissioning their own portraits. The study also examines the representation of the dragomans in costume albums by Ottoman painters. These albums feature generic pictures of dragomans and use stereotyped images. I will discuss the implications of both of these kinds of representations for a study of the image and self-image of dragomans. This chapter starts out by offering a general overview of the profession of the dragoman in the Ottoman Empire and contextualizes dragomans at the intersection of translation studies and art history. It also includes a look at the origins of portraiture in the West and the Ottoman Empire. The second part of the chapter presents a detailed study of several dragoman representations by Western and Ottoman painters.

The profession of interpreting in the Ottoman Empire was mainly performed in diplomatic services, trade missions and the Sublime Porte. One of the earliest known interpreters at the service of the Porte was Yunus Bey, who was a Greek convert. He is reported to have died in 1551, which shows that the position of the court interpreter already existed in the Ottoman Empire in the sixteenth century.[1] The term used to denote interpreters in the Ottoman Empire was etymologically Syriac and developed from the word *tercuman* which entered first Arabic and then Turkish. The Italian was *dragomanno*, while the French called the profession *drogman* or *truchemen*.[2]

The dragomans were one of the elements who carried out cultural mediation in the early modern Mediterranean. They played a double role by both marking and maintaining cultural boundaries and acting as bridge builders among different cultures. Dragomans also assumed important roles in the establishment and shaping of political relations among the leading empires in the sixteenth and eighteenth centuries; therefore they have often been referred to as "trans-imperial subjects"[3] and cultural intermediaries.[4] Dragomans were the forerunners of the early Enlightenment Orientalists through the observations and reports they wrote and the Eastern works they translated.[5] Dragomans always integrated into the social structures in which they lived or adopted in later stages of their lives, therefore it can be argued that they had the unique skill of straddling at least two cultures at the same time; their original culture and the one in which they worked as an interpreter. Their status as cultural intermediaries made dragomans into a type of news source and the reports they drafted circulated in major European capitals which coincided with a curiosity in current affairs and international relations triggering the rise of the newspaper in Italy, particularly in Venice in the seventeenth century.[6]

Interpreters at the Porte translated treaties and interpreted at the meetings between statesmen. They also held occasional diplomatic responsibilities. As the ties between the Ottoman Empire and the Western world became closer, there arose more need for interpreters at the Porte and their status became more important especially after the seventeenth century.[7] The interpreters were essential to the Ottoman Empire's ability to establish and maintain its contacts with the Western world. The social status of the court interpreters started rising in the second half of the seventeenth century, especially after the Grand Vizier Köprülü Fazıl Ahmet Paşa and his adviser and friend Panayoti Nikosios Efendi set up the post of the chief interpreter at *divan-ı hümayun*. Panayoti Nikosios became the first chief interpreter, enabling him to start enjoying many privileges not conventionally granted to non-Muslims. These privileges include growing a beard, exemption from the *cizye* (poll) tax, riding a horse and wearing a fur cap. They were also granted the right to employ servants.[8] Panayoti Nikosios was not only given the post of the chief interpreter but was also given an office which would report to him. Grand Vizier Köprülü Fazıl Ahmet Paşa also created another post for Panayoti Nikosios which did not exist in the Porte: the Chief Interpreter of the Navy.[9]

Panayoti Nikosios was a Phanariot—in other words he was of Greek origins and came from the Phanar region in Istanbul. His office was run by Phanariots until 1821. The office was a key post in the Ottoman administration as it was the point of contact with Europe. Chief interpreter Phanariots were also appointed as *voivodes* (governor generals) of Wallachia and Moldavia starting from 1709 which is evidence of the high socio-political status of the post of the chief interpreter.[10]

The Phanar (Fener) neighborhood in Istanbul was inhabited by merchant families from Albania, Epirus, Trabzon, Wallachia and the Aegean Islands. The Ottoman State held a monopoly over goods that yielded a high income and held important trade routes. Both of these factors enabled trade to develop in the Ottoman Empire so much so that in the eighteenth century, ships owned by Ottoman-Greek merchants could sail to the American continent for trade purposes.[11] The Phanariots held great wealth generated by their commercial activities and started exercising their influence over the Patriarchate which was relocated to the Phanar area in the seventeenth century. It was common for Phanariot children to receive university education in France and Italy. They also attended the Patriarchate Academy which continued its activities after Istanbul was taken over by Turks. Phanariots studied medicine, philosophy, political sciences and theology but also fostered a special interest in languages, many learned Ottoman, Arabic, Persian, Greek, French and Italian.[12] Their linguistic competence helped them maintain their presence in the office of the Chief Interpreter at the Porte and hold the post for a century.

Not all interpreters, however, worked at the Porte. Western embassies or merchants also needed interpreters to establish contacts with the Ottoman State. The first state which started training its own interpreters was the Venetian republic in 1551.[13] Venice was later followed by France, Austria and Poland.

Portraits of Dragomans

Dragomans have traditionally appeared in three main types of paintings. The first one is the audience scenes showing the Ottoman Sultan or the Grand Vizier receiving a Western ambassador accompanied by a dragoman. We know that Western ambassadors who were received by the Sultan or the Grand Vizier commissioned audience scenes. In these scenes dragomans are among the indispensable figures along with ambassadors, the Sultan or the Grand Vizier. These audience scenes were multi-purpose documents, serving as a witness to the ambassador's reception by the Sultan, a major achievement in his career. These paintings often accompanied the reports sent home as a visual depiction of the lived experience as exemplified by the two audience scenes commissioned by Gustaf and Ulric Celsing during their posts as Swedish ambassadors to Istanbul.[14] There was a need to make a realistic portrait of the ambassador, so either the artist was taken to the court along with the delegation or, more often, the ambassador posed for the artist who would then insert his portrait in the audience scene which had its own conventions. In the meantime, although the dragomans were not the commissioners of these paintings, they still had an indispensable place, position and role in these audience scenes—a fact which underlines their high social status in the court. I have studied these scenes and published my findings.[15] For the purposes of the present chapter, I will look at the remaining two types of paintings, namely dragoman depictions in costume albums and portraits commissioned by dragomans themselves.

Costume albums have been commissioned by Western ambassadors since the early sixteenth century as sources of information regarding the attire of the Ottoman subjects. The artists were either Western artists brought over to the empire by the embassies or local artists based in Istanbul.[16] The interest in costume albums spread to European courts in the eighteenth century and albums featuring folkloric garbs as well as royal attire started to be produced for the West. Costume albums prepared for Europeans carried explanations in English, French and German. In some costume albums, figures are placed in front of a plain background, while in others, there is scenery serving as a background. Most costume books are reproduced copies of a master book. It is generally believed that the artists are Ottoman painters who more or less knew about the Western techniques but were inexperienced in drawing human figures, especially women. There are two different styles in these albums—one entails the use of pastel colors, soft curves and a better anatomical depiction. The second one involves the use of brighter colors and darker outlines, and a more naïve anatomical approach. One of the albums in this style is attributed to an Ottoman-Greek subject who wrote explanations in Turkish using the Greek alphabet.[17] Most of these costume albums feature a dragoman figure.

Let us now move on to the specific examples. The first example is the figure called *The Interpreter of the French Ambassador* by Fenerci Mehmet Efendi (Fig. 14.1). This album offers valuable information in the sense that it has a known painter and because the painter indicates in the album that he has a workshop in Bayezid, Istanbul. The album dates back to 1811.[18] The background of the painting is light blue and empty. The figure is drawn from the front. This is the second type of style with bright colors, thicker brush strokes, prominent under-eye bags, a fixed gaze and a poorer knowledge of human anatomy. Nevertheless, the artist has a certain knowledge of the Western art of painting, implied by the creation of volume through the use of chiaroscuro and the inclusion of the folds of fabrics in the painting. We know that dragomans in the service of the Ottoman State wore crimson coats with fur collars as represented here. The dragoman wears a flower-patterned shirt and yellow boots or shoes. He has a long mustache.

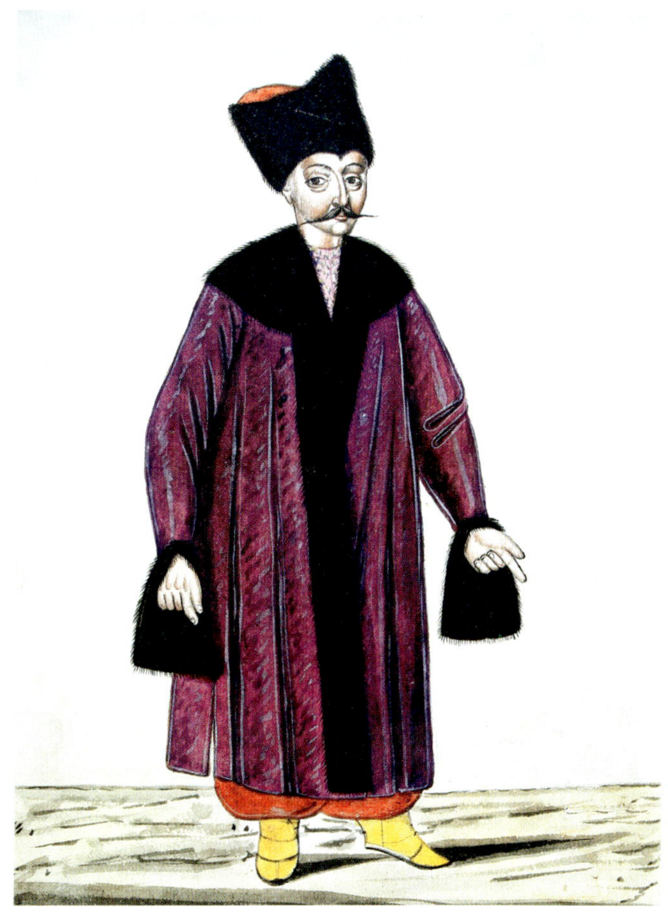

فرانسز ايلچيسنك ترجمانى
Fransız Elçisinin Tercümanı

Figure 14.1 *The Interpreter of the French Ambassador*, Fenerci Mehmet Efendi, 1811, gouache on paper, 23 x 17 cm, from the Fenerci Mehmed Album, Private Collection of Rahmi M. Koç.

Let us now move on to the next example. It is entitled *Interprète de la Porte/Dragoman* (Fig. 14.2). This comes from an album taken from the print collection of the King of Poland Stanisław August Poniatowski in 1818. The album describes the rituals, festivals, daily lives, buildings of Ottoman subjects as well as the life in the palace. The paintings are done in gouache and placed in threes or fours in boxes. Over half of the collection was lost in World War II and what remains is held by the Library of Warsaw University today. Although we don't know who the artist is, the style of the paintings suggests that the album was made by Ottoman artists working in Istanbul who were in touch with Western art conventions. On the other hand, the pictures have Turkish explanations in Latin characters, carry Ottoman titles and even notes in French which shows that the album was a co-production by various artists including Muslim, Greek or Armenian subjects.[19] The pose of the dragoman fits the same scheme as the previous painting. This time the face is bearded and the artist has worked with a finer brush stroke. The cape is blue and the dragoman wears a fur cap worn on top of another cap that is red like the previous example. The interpreter holds a paper which is most likely a *berat*, a royal edict authorizing him to work as an interpreter. We see the word Stanislaus written in Ottoman script. According to one source, Stanisław Kotska Pichelstein (1742–1820) was the only interpreter of the Republic of Poland in Istanbul starting from 1779.[20] The commissioner of this painting wanted to have an image of an interpreter symbolizing Stanisław Kotska Pichelstein. However, without the inscription of his name, it would be impossible for us to guess who the figure was because this depiction was also created based on the conventions of the miniature painting tradition. We know why the cape is blue, because the dragomans wore crimson while on official duty and wore blue in daily life.[21]

Whereas the costume book representations of dragomans are mostly unidentified figures and are generically represented, those portraits commissioned by the dragomans themselves have a more specific attribution. The first example is *Portrait of Jacobus Tarsia* at the Koper Regional Museum in Slovenia (Fig. 14.3). Jacobus Tarsia belonged to the prominent Tarsia family and continued the family profession of interpreting. His brother Thomas Tarsia was the chief dragoman at the Venetian Embassy in Istanbul.[22] The picture belongs to the second half of the seventeenth century and is among the oldest known dragoman portraits. Jacobus Tarsia served at the delegation of the Venetian Ambassador Alvise Molino. He translated a number of works on Ottoman history in 1675. The Tarsia brothers fell victim to a diplomatic dispute and were left behind by their employer who fled Istanbul in

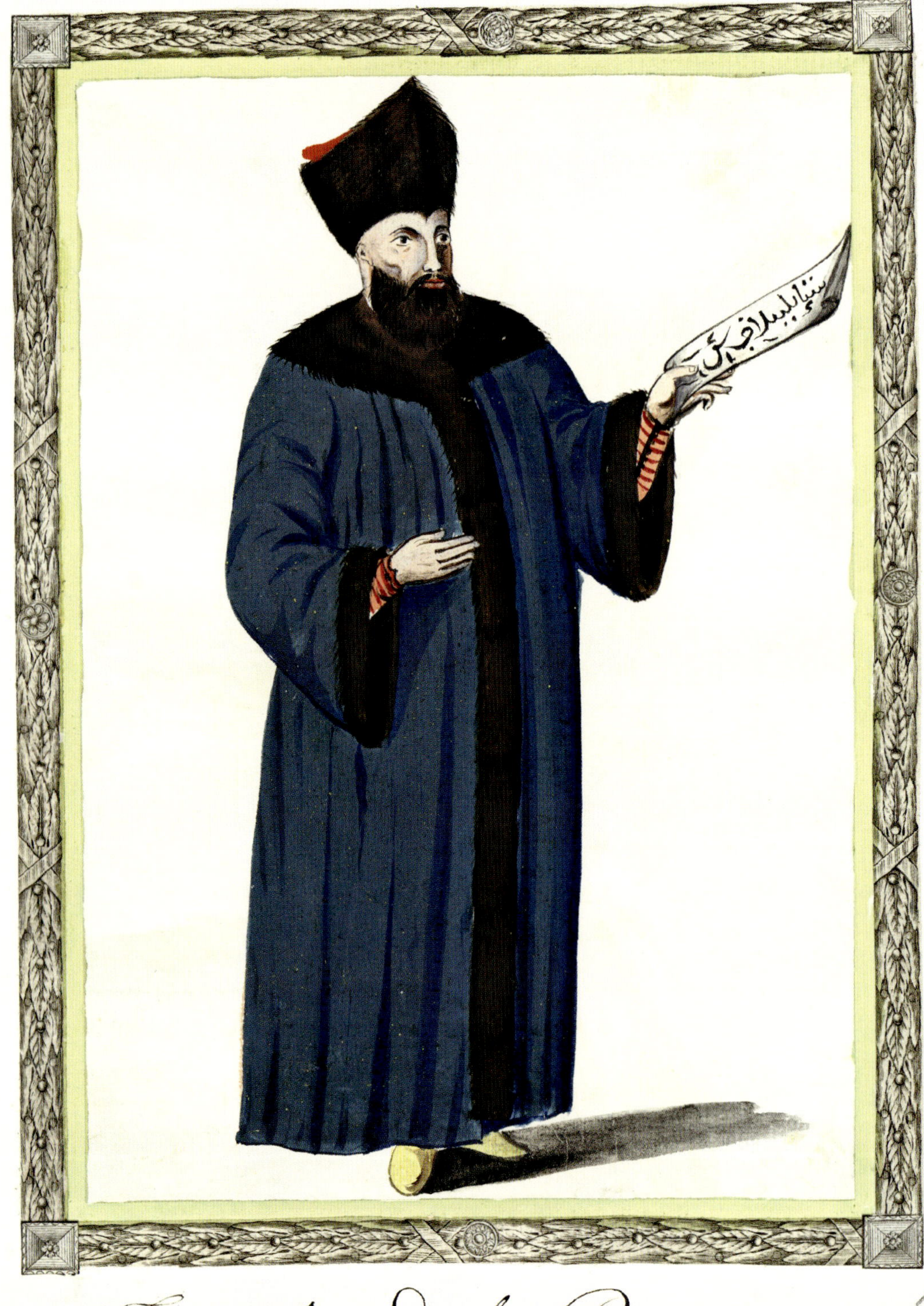

Figure 14.2 *Interprète de la Porte/ Dragoman*, unknown Ottoman artist, c. 1779–80, gouache on paper, 20.8 x 14.8 cm, from an album taken from the print collection of the King of Poland Stanisław August Poniatowski to the Library of Warsaw University in 1818. Courtesy of the University of Warsaw Library.

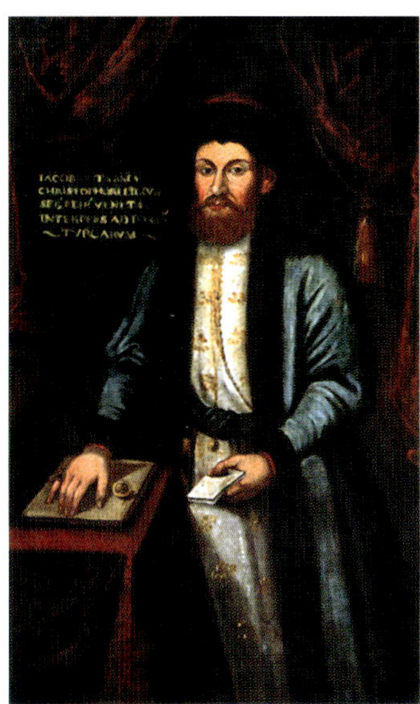

Figure 14.3 *Portrait of Jacobus Tarsia*, unknown painter, second half of the seventeenth century, oil on canvas, 148 x 94.5 cm, Koper Regional Museum.

1684.[23] The portrait is nearly full-length and is by an unknown painter. It is likely that Tarsia posed for the artist. The model turns slightly to the left in this frontal portrait. He is placed in an interior space that is divided by a curtain which represents wealth with its rich fabric and tassels. His use of dramatic light, thick brush strokes and the rich velvet curtain in the background indicates that the painter knows the Baroque conventions in art. This may be taken as an indication that the anonymous but brilliant painter was educated in the West. Jacobus Tarsia has posed with his blue cape, everyday attire for dragomans. The professional symbol, the fur cap with the red cap underneath, is present here too. The golden stamp is clearly visible. He holds a bundle of papers while one of his hands rests on a leather covered and stamped folder. In the background we see the inscription "Iacobvs De Tarsia/Christophori Filivs/Ser.e Reip.ae/Interpres Ad Porta./ Tvrcarvm," confirming the identity of the dragoman.[24] The painting which could only be commissioned by a well-to-do individual, not only includes the established professional and social symbols pertaining to the dragomans but also depicts Tarsia realistically, with his physical and character traits.

The final dragoman portrait I will be taking up is *The Portrait of Antoni Łukasz Crutta* presently at the Warsaw Royal Castle (Fig. 14.4). Crutta (1727–1812) was a Venetian of Albanian origin who served as the dragoman of the King August Poniatowski. He accompanied Numan Bey, who was sent to Poland as a diplomatic envoy in 1777 and published the diary of his travels. He was decorated as a nobleman by the Polish state in 1775.[25] The portrait painter is Jean-François Duchateau (1750–1796), a French artist who also painted other dragomans.[26] The portrait is included in an oval frame and only shows the upper body of the model. This painting made about 110 years after the portrait of Jacobus Tarsia, in 1775, features the dragoman and all of the signs surrounding him once more. This time the style is Rococo, rather than Baroque; the Rococo elements can be seen in the playful folds in texture of the fabrics and the casual posture of the dragoman. Crutta wears the crimson cape, with a fur collar, showing a rich blue fabric underneath. He is also wearing a red belt on his waist and his writing gear is attached to it. The chain around his neck must be carrying his stamp. Crutta has one hand on his waist, and the other hand holding a paper inscribed with the word interpreter in Arabic letters. His fur cap completes his costume. The posture of Crutta is much more informal. In the century that had passed since the last painting there had been a change not only in the artistic style but also in conventions pertaining to the pose of the sitter. Despite this difference, the two portraits share a similarity in that they both depict real individuals. The artist of this painting not only offered a realistic representation of his subjects but also depicts the self-confidence of the dragoman.

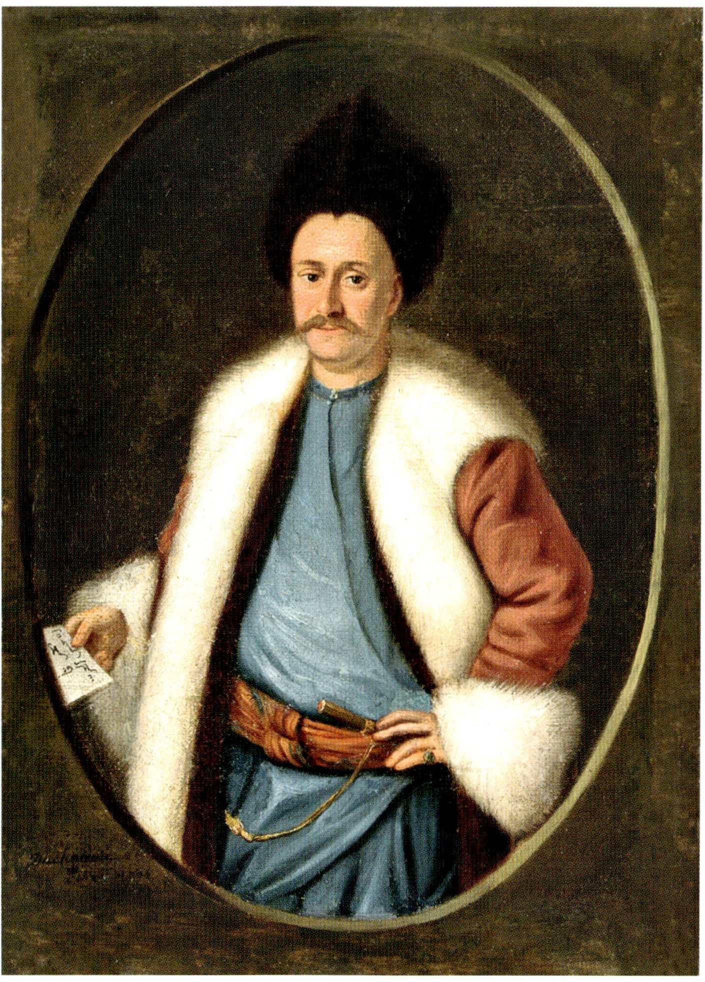

Figure 14.4 *Portrait of Antoni Łukasz Crutta*, Jean-François Duchateau, (1750–1796), 1775, oil on canvas, 28.7 x 20.9 cm, Warsaw Royal Castle. Photographed by Andrzej Ring.

However, one should not be misled into thinking that dragomans in the Ottoman Empire kept their status. In time their official costumes became obsolete, so did the high political influence they enjoyed vis-à-vis their respective government. The change in the dress code may seem like a trivial shift. I would argue, however, that it is highly symbolic and coincides with the demotion of dragomans from the political ranks in the nineteenth century. The shift in the dress code also became visible in visual representations of Ottomans as exemplified by an engraving by David Wilkie in *Sir David Wilkie's Sketches in Turkey, Syria & Egypt 1840 & 1841* printed in 1843.[27] The engraving shows Sotiri, the principal Albanian dragoman to the British Consul General at Bucharest, Mr. Colquon. The figure is accompanied by two others, a boy and a woman. Nevertheless, for the purposes of the present chapter, it is the dragoman figure which is of interest. The dragoman in the picture is dressed in daily Ottoman attire, wearing a fez, which was very much the fashion of the day as a result of the Ottoman dress reforms. He also wears a long jacket, again a popular garment among Ottoman men. The professional symbols present in the dragoman portraits described previously are missing from this picture. There is nothing in the engraving proving the man's status as a consulate dragoman unlike the previous representations whose semiotic structure relied on such professional status created by the use of not only the professional symbols, such as the dictionaries, the decree, and the ink holder but also the costumes and the confident postures of the sitters. This indicates the gradual disappearance of a professional dragoman culture which was created and maintained in the "contact zones"[28] between the Ottoman Empire and other states in the West. This culture which was marked by hybridity and indigeneity was phased out in the nineteenth century as the Ottoman *Tanzimat* took hold of ways of interacting with the West and led to the establishment of a professional foreign service where diplomats and chancellery, instead of dragomans, took on the role of interpreters.

There is little doubt that the dragomans commissioning their own portraits intended to immortalize themselves. On the other hand, the dragomans in costume albums do not feature a specific individual but serve to signify the concept of a generic dragoman with the standard costumes. These paintings are stereotypes, changing little from one to the next. The painter of costume albums usually had workshops around the Bayezid district like Fenerci Mehmet Efendi who wrote down his address on the album. The format of these costume albums suggest that these painters were in contact with their European counterparts such as Jean-Baptiste van Mour. The clients for these costume albums prepared by local artists were Westerners in Istanbul. The seventeenth-century costume albums do not present any dragoman depictions. However, they seem to have made their way into the albums by the eighteenth century as relations between the West and the Ottoman Empire became more intense and the importance of dragomans in political contacts was understood. By contrast dragomans had already started commissioning their own portraits in the second half of the seventeenth century. In addition to their close contacts with ambassadors, grand viziers and the Ottoman elite, dragomans also kept touch with artists as mentioned previously. Their dealings with artists can be associated with their social status and prestige.

Western embassies in the Ottoman capital served as initial points of contact for Western artists traveling to the Orient whose numbers started rising in the seventeenth century and onwards. Some Western envoys even brought along artists with them who were expected to serve as documenters of the ambassadors' diplomatic deeds in Istanbul. This provided the artists with an occasion to meet the dragomans who were an indispensable part of the embassy staff. Neither the artists nor the dragomans remained indifferent to these encounters which meant that artists fostered a fresh interest and curiosity in this professional group which was distinguished from other professions by their privileges and fascinating costumes. This resulted in the ample space provided to dragomans in audience scenes. On the other hand, dragomans also started to commission their own portraits as explored in the present chapter creating a vogue among their colleagues. This should not come as a surprise: Dragomans were an intellectual group by virtue of their provenance and education, therefore they were sensitive to new currents in arts and culture. As argued previously, they mastered the codes of at least two cultures at the same time and were more open to cultural influences from outside the Ottoman Empire which explains their immediate adoption of the art of portraiture as a way of asserting their professional positions. They created a common professional culture which was reflected in their costumes. Their costumes appeared rather Oriental in the eyes of the Western visitors, while their flamboyant garments were not really a part of the Ottoman dress codes either. The inbetweenness of their attire embodied the inbetweenness in their cultural standing as intermediaries occupying a contact zone[29] between the West and the Ottoman Empire.

Dragomans and artists became the carriers of a new tradition in portraiture which reflected the cultural intermediary roles they both played. Artists were sources of visual proof (although often marked by fictive rather than factual data) with the various depictions of the Oriental world they offered the West. Therefore they served as visual and artistic intermediaries between the Orient and the West. Interestingly enough, they found the role of dragomans very pertinent to their own role as a professional group. Nowhere is this better demonstrated than in the two self-portraits made by the leading Western artists carrying images of the Ottoman Empire to the Western world: Jean-Baptiste Van Mour and Antoine de Favray. Both artists painted themselves in dragoman costumes.[30]

The dragoman portraits are larger paintings executed in oil on canvas, and they were probably intended to be hung by the dragoman in his house. The costume books present a stereotyped watercolor designed as a small painting to fit the pages of an album. The commissioned portrait presents a figure whose identity is known and uses text to support and confirm this identity, whereas the costume album paintings feature anonymous figures whose professional signs are expressed in simplified stereotypes. The explanation under the painting is generic and does not identify the figures. The dragoman portraits are early indicators of the professional and social status held by interpreters in the Ottoman Empire. Dragomans have been depicted as a wealthy class of professionals who have a high level of professional identity. Examples are the members of the Tarsia and Brutti dragoman families who received noble titles and reached the highest echelons of the European aristocracy in the seventeenth century.[31] The portraits not only display the privileged position of the dragomans for the countries they worked for, as the audience for these paintings would have been the family and colleagues of the dragomans. The combination of professional symbols with individual traits was observed in the portraits of the sultans only in the late eighteenth century. These paintings prove the strong agency and status enjoyed by the dragomans in the Ottoman Empire as members of a wealthy professional class.

In the meantime, costume albums have been instrumental in the adoption of a Western perspective on art in the Ottoman Empire. The artists of these albums, however, were within the sign system of the miniature tradition and therefore do not show individuality or character traits in the paintings. The dragomans they represent are but standard images and reflect no identity or individuality unlike the portraits commissioned by the dragomans themselves.

Notes

1 Frédérick Hitzel, ed., *Enfants de langue et Dragomans/Dil Oğlanları ve Tercümanlar* (Istanbul: Yapı Kredi Yayınları, 1995), 17.

2 Ibid., 17.

3 E-N. Rothman, “Between Venice and Istanbul: Trans-Imperial Subjects and Cultural Mediation in the Early Modern Mediterranean” (PhD diss., The University of Michigan, 2006), 2, 219.

4 Ibid., 1, 7.

5 Ibid., 213.

6 Ibid., 214; Brendan M. Dooley, *The Social History of Skepticism: Experience and Doubt in Early Modern Culture* (Baltimore: Johns Hopkins University Press, 1999), 10.

7 Hitzel, *Enfants de langue et Dragomans*, 17.

8 Zeynep Sözen, *Fenerli Beyler 110 Yılın Öyküsü (1711–1821)* (Istanbul: Aybay Yayınları, 2000), 46.

9 Ibid., 46–47.

10 Ibid., 44–45.

11 Suraiya Faroqhi, *Osmanlı Kültürü ve Gündelik Yaşam Ortaçağdan Yirminci Yüzyıla*, trans. Elif Kılıç (Istanbul: Tarih Vakfı Yurt Yayınları, 1997), 51, 54.

12 Sözen, *Fenerli Beyler*, 40–41.

13 Hitzel, *Enfants de langue et Dragomans*, 19.

14 Merit Laine, “Audienstavlarna paa Biby”, in *Minnet av Konstantinopel Den Osmansk-turkiska 1700-talssamlingen paa Biby*, ed. Karin Aadahl (Stockholm: Atlantis, 2003), 124–25.

15 Aykut Gürçağlar, “Representations of Ottoman Interpreters by Western Painters,” *Acta Orientalia Scientiarum Hungaricae* 57 (2004): 231–42.

16 Günsel Renda, *Batılılaşma Döneminde Türk Resim Sanatı 1700–1850* (Ankara: Hacettepe Üniversitesi Yayınları, 1977), 45.

17 Ibid., 52–55.

18 İlhami Turan, ed., *Osmanlı Kıyafetleri Fenerci Mehmed Albümü/Ottoman Costume Book Fenerci Mehmed* (Istanbul:Vehbi Koç Vakfı, 1986), 31.

19 Jolanta Talbierska, “Kral Stanisław August Poniatowski Koleksiyonu’ndan Osmanlı Giysileri ve Sahneleri İstanbul ve

Varşova, 1779–1780 civarı," in *Savaş ve Barış 15–19.Yüzyıl Osmanlı-Polonya İlişkileri*, ed. Selmin Kangal (Istanbul: T.C. Kültür Bakanlığı ve Polonya Kültür ve Sanat Bakanlığı, 1999), 273.

20 Ibid., 288.

21 Hitzel, *Enfants de langue et Dragomans*, 59.

22 Edvilijo Gardina, "Thomas Tarsia'nın Portresi," in *17. Yüzyıl Avrupasında Türk İmajı*, ed. Ksenija Vidic et al. (Istanbul: Sabancı Üniversitesi Sakıp Sabancı Müzesi, 2005), 282.

23 Edvilijo Gardina, "Jacobus Tarsia'nın Portresi," in *17. Yüzyıl Avrupasında Türk İmajı*, ed. Ksenija Vidic et al. (Istanbul: Sabancı Üniversitesi Sakıp Sabancı Müzesi, 2005), 284.

24 Ibid., 284.

25 Hanna Małachowicz, "Antoni Łukasz Crutta'nın Portresi," in *Savaş ve Barış 15–19. Yüzyıl Osmanlı-Polonya İlişkileri*, ed. Selmin Kangal (Istanbul: T. C. Kültür Bakanlığı ve Polonya Kültür ve Sanat Bakanlığı, 1999), 246.

26 Hitzel, *Enfants de langue et Dragomans*, 74–75.

27 David Wilkie, *Sir David Wilkie's Sketches in Turkey, Syria & Egypt 1840 & 1841* (Pall Mall: Graves and Warmsley, 1843), 12.

28 Mary L. Pratt, *Imperial Eyes: Travel Writing and Transculturation* (New York: Routledge, 1992), 4.

29 Ibid., 4.

30 Hitzel, *Enfants de langue et Dragomans*, 55; Semra Germaner, "Sultan III. Mustafa Dönemi'nde İstanbul'da Bir Malta Şövalyesi Antoine de Favray," *Antikdekor* 117 (2010): 53.

31 Rothman, "Between Venice and Istanbul," 231–32.

Bibliography

Dooley, Brendan M. *The Social History of Skepticism: Experience and Doubt in Early Modern Culture*. Baltimore: Johns Hopkins University Press, 1999.

Faroqhi, Suraiya. *Osmanlı Kültürü ve Gündelik Yaşam Ortaçağdan Yirminci Yüzyıla*. Translated by Elif Kılıç. Istanbul: Tarih Vakfı Yurt Yayınları, 1997.

Gardina, Edvilijo. "Jacobus Tarsia'nın Portresi." In *17. Yüzyıl Avrupasında Türk İmajı*, edited by Ksenija Vidic et al. Istanbul: Sabancı Üniversitesi Sakıp Sabancı Müzesi, 2005. Published in conjunction with the exhibition 17. Yüzyıl Avrupasında Türk İmajı shown at the Sabancı Üniversitesi Sakıp Sabancı Müzesi, Istanbul.

Gardina, Edvilijo. "Thomas Tarsia'nın Portresi." In *17. Yüzyıl Avrupasında Türk İmajı*, edited by Ksenija Vidic et al. Istanbul: Sabancı Üniversitesi Sakıp Sabancı Müzesi, 2005. Published in conjunction with the exhibition 17. Yüzyıl Avrupasında Türk İmajı shown at the Sabancı Üniversitesi Sakıp Sabancı Müzesi, Istanbul.

Germaner, Semra. "Sultan III. Mustafa Dönemi'nde İstanbul'da Bir Malta Şövalyesi Antoine de Favray." *Antikdekor* 117 (2010): 52–61.

Gürçağlar, Aykut. "Representations of Ottoman Interpreters by Western Painters." *Acta Orientalia Scientiarum Hungaricae* 57 (2004): 231–42.

Hitzel, Frédérick, ed. *Enfants de langue et Dragomans/Dil Oğlanları ve Tercümanlar*. Istanbul: Yapı Kredi Yayınları, 1995.

Laine, Merit. "Audienstavlorna paa Biby." In *Minnet av Konstantinopel Den Osmansk-turkiska 1700-talssamlingen paa Biby*, edited by Karin Aadahl, 113–45. Stockholm: Atlantis, 2003.

Małachowicz, Hanna. "Antoni Łukasz Crutta'nın Portresi." In *Savaş ve Barış 15–19. Yüzyıl Osmanlı-Polonya İlişkileri*, edited by Selmin Kangal. Istanbul: T. C. Kültür Bakanlığı ve Polonya Kültür ve Sanat Bakanlığı, 1999. Published in conjunction with the exhibition Savaş ve Barış 15–19. Yüzyıl Osmanlı-Polonya İlişkileri shown at the Türk ve İslam Eserleri Müzesi, Istanbul.

Pratt, Mary L. *Imperial Eyes: Travel Writing and Transculturation*. NewYork: Routledge, 1992.

Renda, Günsel. *Batılılaşma Döneminde Türk Resim Sanatı 1700–1850*. Ankara: Hacettepe Üniversitesi Yayınları, 1977.

Rothman, E-N. "Between Venice and Istanbul: Trans-Imperial Subjects and Cultural Mediation in the Early Modern Mediterranean." PhD diss., The University of Michigan, 2006.

Sözen, Zeynep. *Fenerli Beyler 110 Yılın Öyküsü (1711–1821)*. Istanbul: Aybay Yayınları, 2000.

Talbierska, Jolanta. "Kral Stanisław August Poniatowski Koleksiyonu'ndan Osmanlı Giysileri ve Sahneleri İstanbul ve Varşova, 1779–180 civarı." In *Savaş ve Barış 15–19. Yüzyıl*

Osmanlı-Polonya İlişkileri, edited by Selmin Kangal. Istanbul: T. C. Kültür Bakanlığı ve Polonya Kültür ve Sanat Bakanlığı, 1999. Published in conjunction with the exhibition Savaş ve Barış 15–19. Yüzyıl Osmanlı-Polonya İlişkileri shown at the Türk ve İslam Eserleri Müzesi, Istanbul.

Turan, İlhami, ed. *Osmanlı Kıyafetleri Fenerci Mehmed Albümü/Ottoman Costume Book Fenerci Mehmed*. Istanbul: Vehbi Koç Vakfı, 1986.

Wilkie, David. *Sir David Wilkie's Sketches in Turkey, Syria & Egypt 1840 & 1841*. Pall Mall: Graves and Warmsley, 1843.

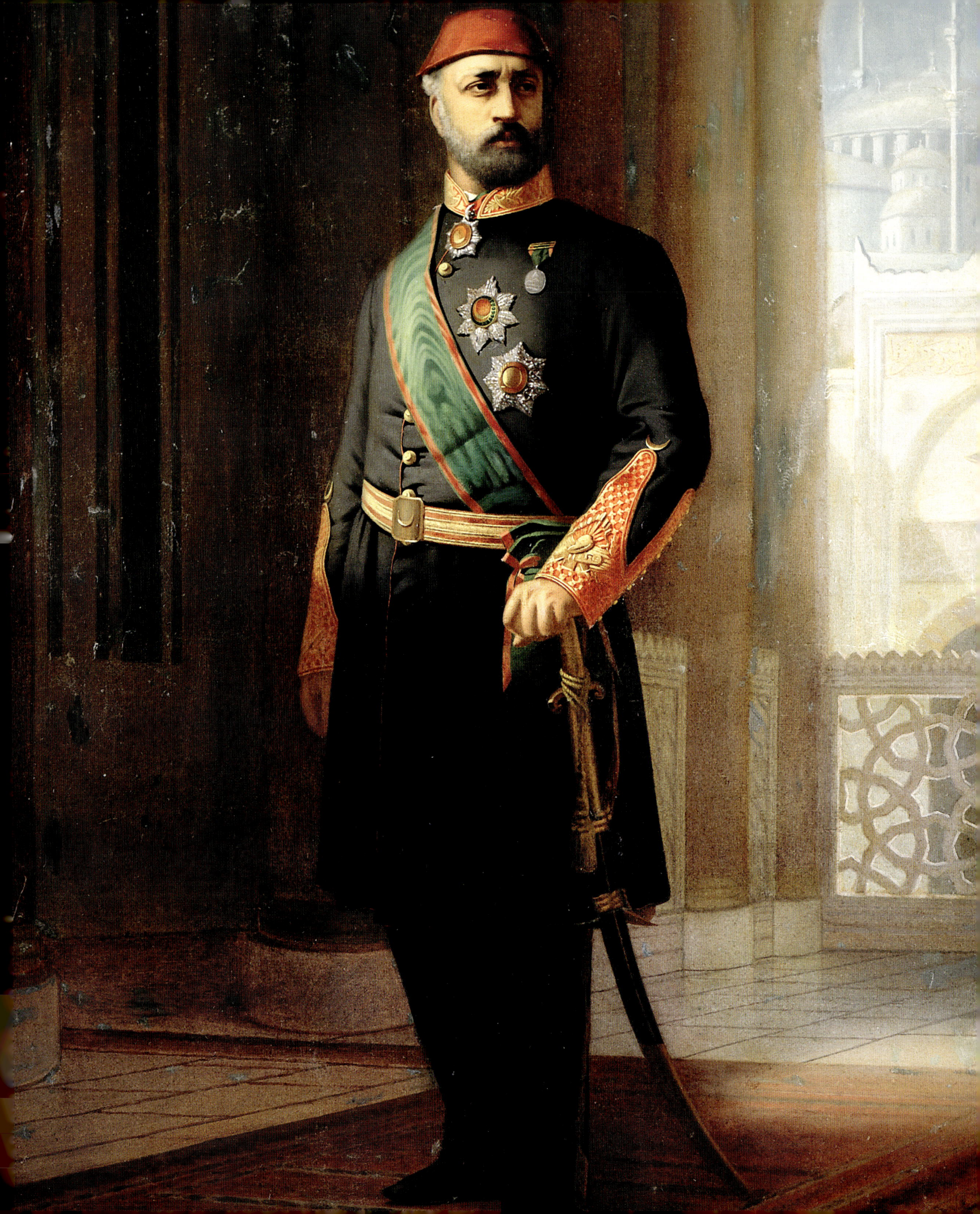

XV

European Artists at the Ottoman Court

Propagating a New Dynastic Image in the Nineteenth Century

Günsel Renda

The nineteenth century was a period of Westernization and modernization in the Ottoman Empire. The political balances in Europe necessitated an intense Westernization, institutionalized with reforms in governmental organization, education and the military. Especially after the 1839 *Tanzimat Firman* (Noble Reform Script) the diplomatic and commercial relations with the Europeans also followed a different course. Europeans became influential in commercial and cultural life in the Empire and Westernization became a lifestyle in the Ottoman palace circles and the elite class. European styles were now adopted both in architecture and painting. The nineteenth-century sultans had palaces built one after another such as the Dolmabahçe, Beylerbeyi, Çırağan and Yıldız, with monumental gates and decorative facades displaying an eclectic style, a blend of the neo-baroque and the neo-classical of the nineteenth-century European palaces. Their interiors displayed gilded reliefs, carton-pierre decoration panoramic wall paintings and European-made furniture and porcelain. The nineteenth-century sultans not only commissioned buildings and paintings but they also formed a collection of European paintings for the palace. A large number of European architects and artists worked for the Ottoman sultans, some officially appointed as court painters. This paper will discuss the nature of the commissions made to the European artists working at the Ottoman court and their impact on imperial portraiture shifting away from Eastern concepts to a new sultanic image in the contemporary European manner, thus propagating a new dynastic image.

The Ottoman sultans' interest in their past history and their preoccupation with the image of their ancestors had led to a tradition of sultanic portraiture continuing through the centuries. What is so distinctive about Ottoman royal portraiture is that it is based on both Asian-Turkic and European traditions blending purposefully and successfully these opposing modes of representation to propagate the dynastic image through various media and techniques. Initiated during the reign of Mehmed II (1451–1481) the genre of imperial portraiture continued in the following centuries with a distinctive iconography showing the sultan seated on his legs in the Eastern fashion or on a throne, often in the case of the reigning sultan, but in the more Western three-quarter pose with an attempt at individualization in spite of the preset Eastern idiom in portraiture. This iconography stayed with the Ottoman artists and common physical features of the sultans and their attributes remained invariable until the nineteenth century in the historical manuscripts, genealogies and portrait albums usually as series of sultans.[1]

Imperial portraiture took a new form in the eighteenth century. New types and media made their appearance in the second half of the eighteenth century and single portraits of the sultans were now painted in oil on canvas to be hung on walls in the palace or in the residences of the palace members. The sultans started to commission both local and European artists to paint their portraits in new techniques and media. The first single portraits started to be produced by European artists working in Istanbul for embassy circles. For example the Italian artist Ferdinando Tonioli who came to Istanbul with the Venetian bailo in 1785 painted a portrait of Sultan Abdülhamid (1774–1789) in bust form.[2] The French artist Jean-Baptiste Hilair also painted portraits of the sultan. Hilair (d. after 1822) worked in 1776–77 for Comte de Choiseul-Gouffier on his expedition to Greece, the Aegean and is known for his illustrations of Turkey and Greece as well as costume pictures.[3] Hilair painted the portrait of the reigning Sultan Abdülhamid I standing in the palace on a porch and also depicted him in the harem gardens.[4] Recent research has shown that he also painted a genealogical tree with the portraits of the sultans in medallions hung from the branches of a tree with the names inscribed above or below.[5] This is highly probable because while in Istanbul Hilair also worked for Mouradgea d'Ohsson, a native of Istanbul from a family of French-Armenian origin who was the dragoman (interpreter) to the Swedish embassy in Istanbul and who wrote the book *Tableau Général de l'Empire Othoman* that was published in Paris in 1787–88. It is one of the best sources on the history of the Ottoman Empire.[6] Recently discovered documents in Sweden indicate that three large-sized family trees were painted in Paris while d'Ohsson was there publishing his book. The Swedish King Gustav III who happened to be in Paris in 1784, impressed by the sultans' portraits d'Ohsson had with him to use as illustrations in his book, requested them to be painted as a family tree. It is highly possible that d'Ohsson commissioned Hilair for these trees as he knew the artist well while he was in Istanbul. Upon his return to Istanbul, d'Ohsson presented one of them to the reigning Sultan Selim III (1789–1807), who was deeply impressed by this new form of portraiture and ordered local artists to paint smaller sized family trees to be distributed.[7] With these trees painted in oil, a new medium was introduced as well, a medium that had been popular in the European pictorial tradition for centuries. Genealogical trees continued to be produced by the succeeding sultans indicating that the sultans now wished to propagate the Ottoman dynastic image through portraits painted in the European manner.[8] (See Fig. 15.1.)

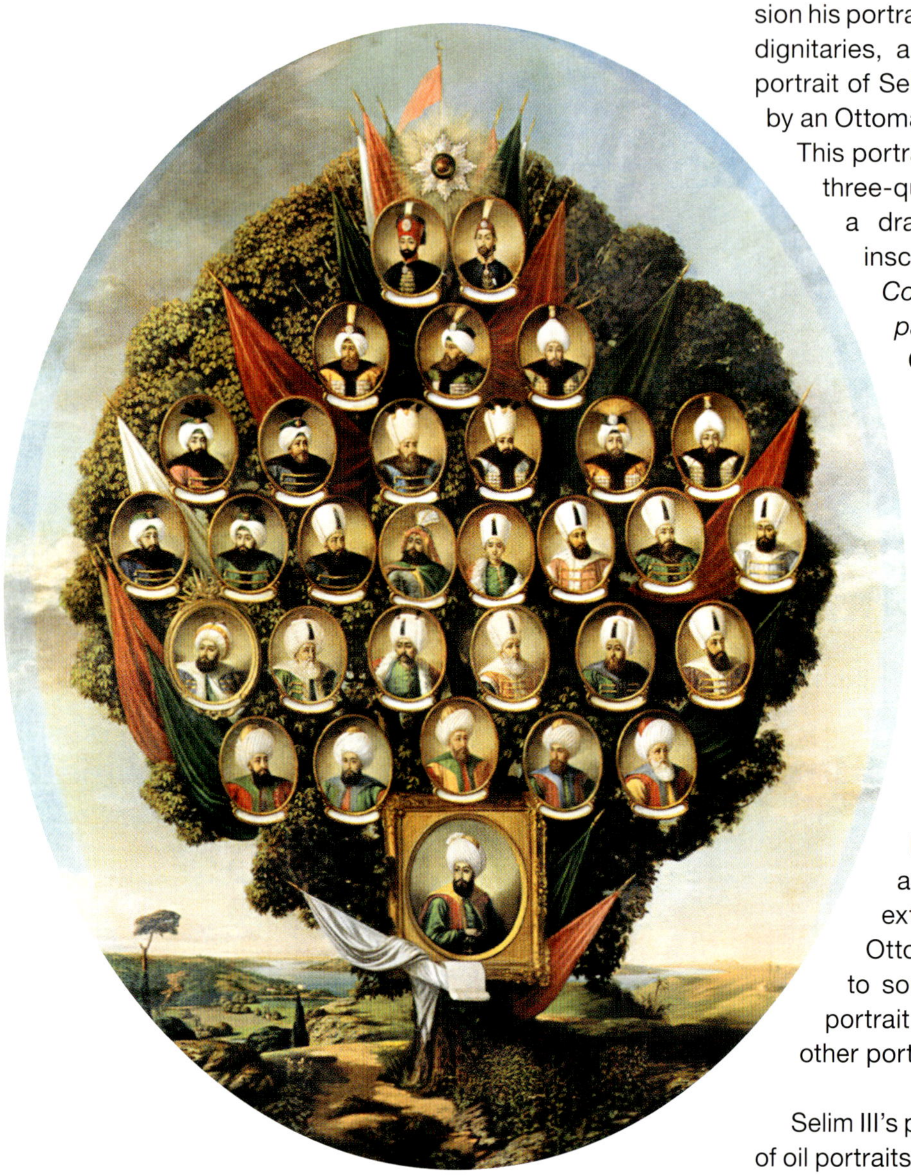

The reign of Selim III was certainly a turning point in Ottoman royal portraiture. He is the first sultan to commission his portrait to be painted and distributed among Ottoman dignitaries, ambassadors and foreign rulers. An engraved portrait of Selim III dated 1793 is the first commission made by an Ottoman sultan for his portrait to be printed in Europe. This portrait shows the sultan standing half-length and in three-quarter view framed in a medallion crowned by a draped curtain in the European manner. The inscription below the portrait reads "*dessiné par Constantin Capoudaghlé sujet ottoman, gravée par Schiavonetti à Londres.*"[9] Constantin Capoudaghlé (Kostantin Kapıdağlı in Turkish and Konstantinos Kyzikenos in Greek), a well-known Greek artist from Kapıdağı on the southern shore of the Marmara Sea, was active in Istanbul from about 1780–1810 working for the Ottoman court. His mastery in the use of Western techniques of painting suggests that he must have had some training in Europe.[10] This portrait printed in England in 1793 in black and white and in color was distributed among dignitaries and foreign rulers. Selim III was fully aware of the European custom of exchanging portraits among emperors as a token of diplomacy as he had already received a portrait of Napoleon as a gift. Therefore, this printed portrait was extended to Napoleon in Paris through the Ottoman ambassador Muhib Efendi and according to sources Napoleon was highly impressed by the portrait and placed it in a cabinet where there were no other portraits.[11]

Figure 15.1 *Genealogical Tree of the Ottoman Sultans*, anonymous, 1866–67, oil on canvas, Topkapı Palace Museum 17/135.

Selim III's patronage resulted in the production of a number of oil portraits not only individual portraits but also ceremonial scenes revealing his interest in new functions for painting. His single portraits painted both by European and local artists introduced a new iconography in imperial portraiture. The majority of his portraits are in the bust-form, the most common type for portraiture in Europe. One of the earliest portraits of the sultan was painted in 1792 by Jean-François Duchateau inscribed "*sultan regnant*" (reigning sultan), it was engraved in London in 1798.[12] Duchateau was a French artist working in Istanbul between the years 1775 and 1797 for embassy circles and he may well have been commissioned to paint a portrait of the sultan (Fig. 15.2).[13] Selim III must have commissioned other artists in order for his portraits to be presented to ambassadors and even to European rulers. Such a present was made to Napoleon as it is indicated on a printed portrait in the Bibliothèque Nationale in Paris "*gravé après un tableau original envoyé à l'Empereur*" (engraved after an original painting sent to the Emperor).[14] The years 1806–7 were significant for diplomatic relations between Europe and the Ottoman Empire as the French and the Ottomans were forging a new alliance after battles in Egypt and Acre. A printed portrait in the Topkapı Palace has an inscription indicating that it was engraved in London in 1807 after an original portrait brought from Istanbul by Spencer Smith. John Spencer Smith was the younger brother of Sidney Smith who had fought for Turkey in Egypt and Acre against the French. This portrait must have been based on an original painted by a European artist residing in Istanbul in the 1790s as Spencer Smith was chargé d'affaires in the British Embassy in Istanbul until Ambassador Lord Elgin's appointment in 1799.[15]

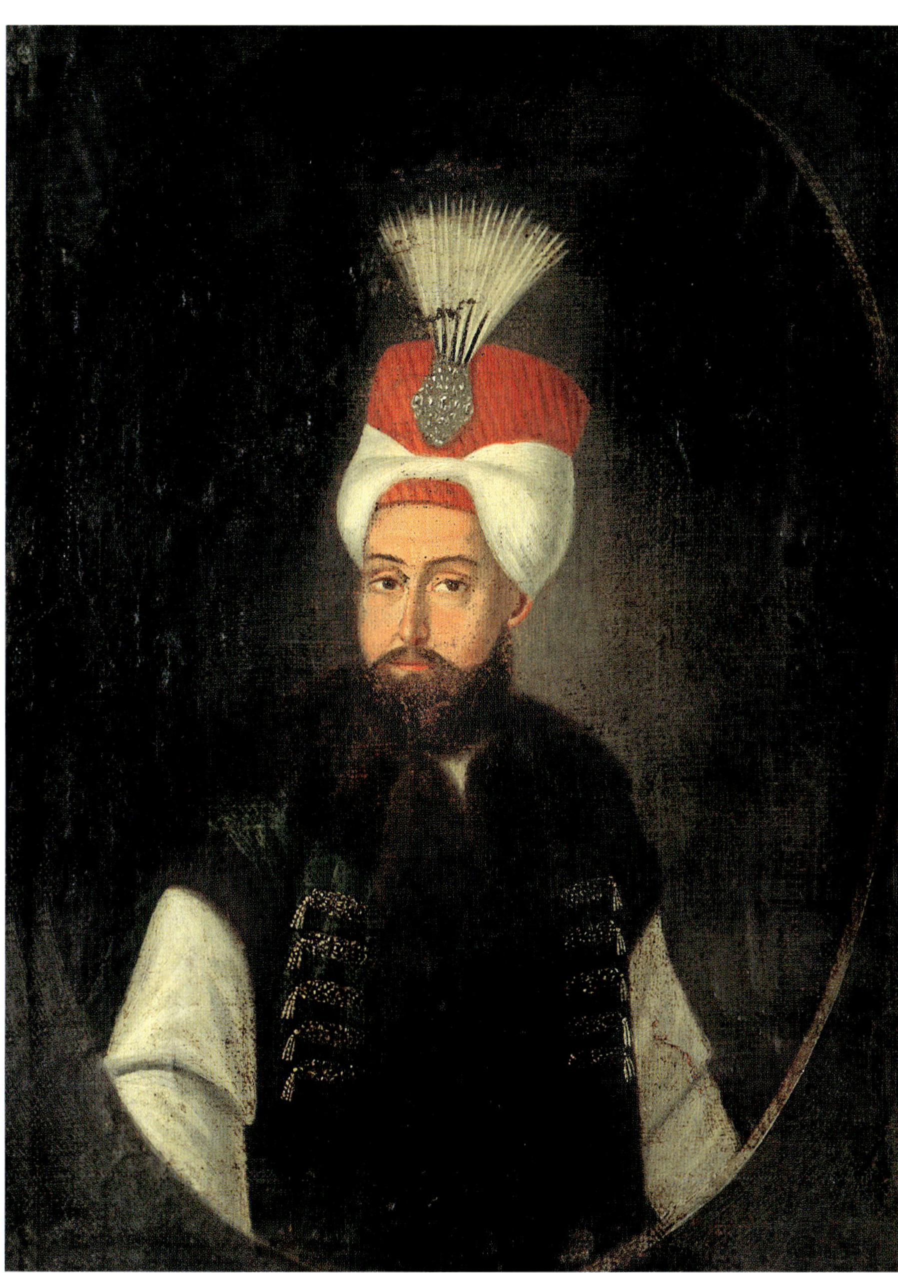

Figure 15.2 *Sultan Selim III*, Jean-François Duchateau, 1792, oil, 33 x 24 cm, Topkapı Palace Museum 17/32.

With Mahmud II (1808–1839) another era started in Ottoman royal portraiture with the introduction of more Western iconography. Mahmud II was a great reformist following the path of Selim III and during his reign Westernization in the empire was institutionalized. He established a new army the *Asakir-i Mansure-i Muhammediye*, the 'Victorious Mohammedan soldiers', and one of the new regulations was the European type of uniform—tunic, trousers, boots—and fez with a tassel replacing the turban and the kaftan. The clothing reform was extended to the public in 1829 and he commissioned his portraits in the new uniform which came to be called *tasvir-i humayun* (imperial portrait), to be hung on the walls of government offices. Travelers like Julia Pardoe and Robert Walsh describe the ceremonies organized on the occasion of hanging the sultan's portraits in official buildings.[16] Mahmud II even went further, minting coins with his engraved portraits. In spite of some political opposition to his official use of portraits going as far as labeling him as the "infidel sultan," the reign of Mahmud II witnessed great artistic production.[17] The most important portraits of this sultan were executed during the last decade of his reign after these reforms.

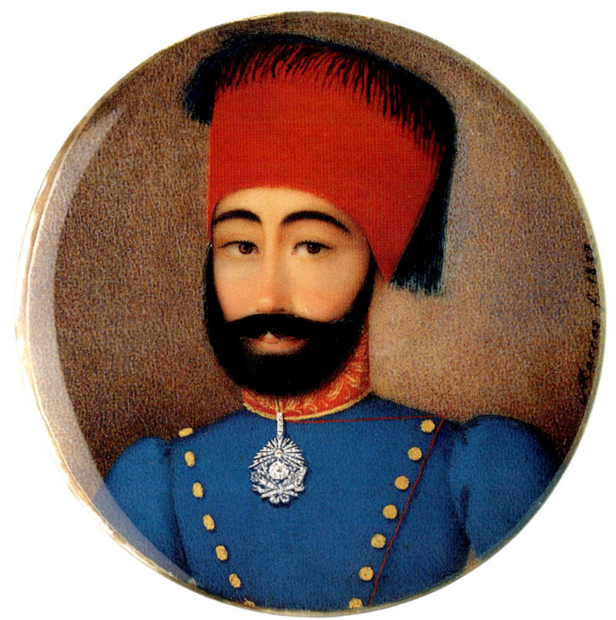

Figure 15.3 *Sultan Mahmud II*, Marras, 1832, oil on ivory, 6 cm in diameter, Topkapı Palace Museum 17/208.

One new genre of sultanic portraiture initiated during his reign was the small size portrait medal. These portrait medals, about six centimeters in diameter and mostly painted on ivory, were designed to be presented as gifts or as decoration to the high officials as *tasvir-i humayun*. One of these portraits signed "*Marras f. 1832*" indicates that he must have been the initiator of these portrait medals in the tradition of European miniature portraits of the time (Fig. 15.3).[18] Marras was a French artist of Spanish origin and sources indicate that he had been in New York and in Istanbul for some time.[19] The portraits on these small medals some of which have jeweled frames, or are placed in boxes, show the sultan wearing a similar medal around his neck. They were worn as decoration on a chain or pinned on uniforms. Julia Pardoe mentions seeing such a portrait pinned on a pillow in the house of an official.[20] Archive documents indicate that they were presented to several officers of high rank and foreigners including the Austrian Prince Metternich who received it through the Ottoman Ambassador Rıfat Bey in Vienna.[21]

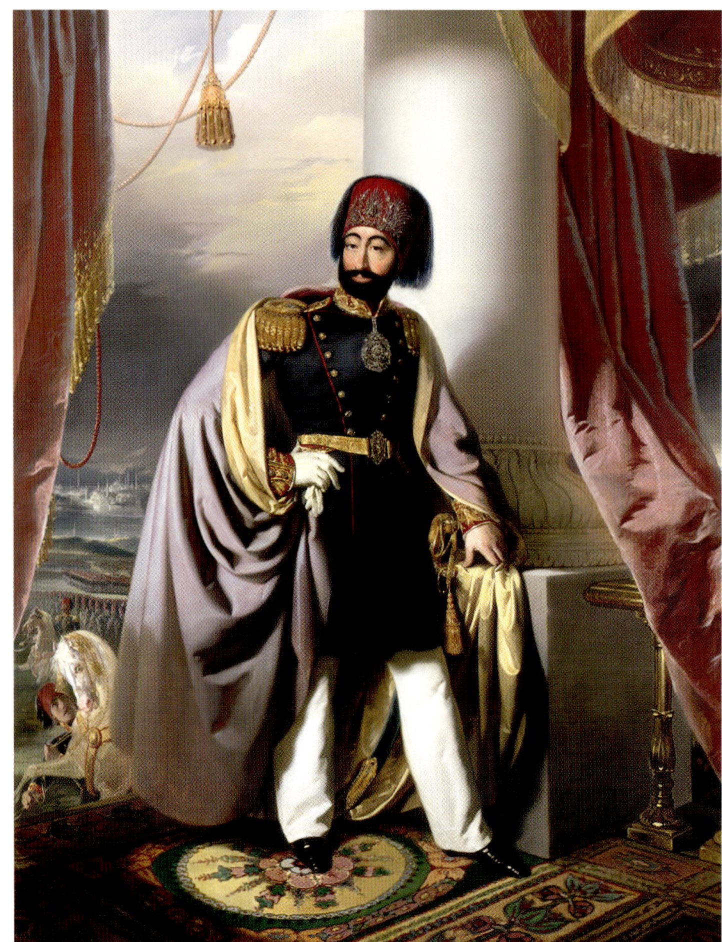

Figure 15.4 *Sultan Mahmud II*, Henri-Guillaume Schlesinger, 1839, oil, 2.56 x 1.93 cm, Musée de Versailles, 4842.

More significant are the sultan's oil portraits executed after his reforms. These reflect a completely new iconography. One type is the equestrian portrait showing the sultan on a galloping horse leading his newly formed troops, his hand pointing ahead.Such a portrait in the Topkapı Palace painted by Henri-Guillaume Schlesinger (d. 1893) indicates that he must have introduced this type.[22] A French artist of German origin, Schlesinger is reported to have made this portrait in

1837, two years after which he painted the sultan in his new uniform standing on a porch behind which are officers of his army on galloping horses and in the distance a silhouette of the Seraglio point (Fig. 15.4).[23] This portrait held in Versailles Palace has an inscription stating it was painted in Paris, and sources indicate that it was presented to King Louis-Philippe by the Turkish ambassador, Ahmed Fethi Paşa in Paris. Ahmet Fethi Paşa is reported to have been in Paris between 1835 and 1837 and also in Vienna in 1836.[24] He might have recommended Schlesinger as a renowned portrait artist. Two different engravings have survived after Schlesinger's work: one inscribed "dessiné sur nature par Schlesinger" indicating he was in Istanbul although there is no document yet found related to this commission.[25]

There aren't many remaining of the portraits that were hung on the walls of official buildings but those that have remained are mostly copies of the Schlesinger type depicting the sultan standing with his head slightly turned right holding a sword and often a pulled curtain behind. Sometimes in the distance his soldiers or some of the buildings he built were represented. This new iconography introducing a heroic image of the sultan on a galloping horse or standing or sitting with attributes symbolizing his reforms suggests a strong relationship with royal portraiture in Europe in the early nineteenth century, very close to the heroic pose usually adopted in the portraits of the European rulers at the time. The popularity of this format can easily be explained as several engravings depicting Napoleon reached the Topkapı Palace in the early nineteenth century.[26]

Mahmud II's successors continued to commission portraits of a monumental size as well as portrait medallions. Sultan Abdülmecid (1839–1861), although sixteen years old when enthroned, was determined to continue his father's reforms. Right after his enthronement the Gülhane Noble Script (*Tanzimat*) was proclaimed demonstrating to Europe that a modern and liberal regime was adopted following which there was an influx of foreign artists into the Ottoman capital. Many European artists took commissions from the sultan and the iconographic models introduced by Mahmud II continued. Early in his reign in 1840, he seems to have been portrayed by Johann Hermann Kretzschmer, who came to Istanbul, and according to sources a copy of the portrait was made for the Berlin palace at the request of Frederich Wilhelm IV the King of Prussia.[27]

It is known that Abdülmecid sat for the British artist Sir David Wilkie (d. 1841) during his visit to Istanbul in 1840. Wilkie was planning to paint a portrait of the sultan for Queen Victoria but he was also commissioned to paint another portrait for the sultan himself and was given special rights to enter the palace whenever he wished. This portrait differs in iconography from the sultan's other official portraits (Fig. 15.5). He is shown leisurely seated on a European type armchair wearing his uniform and white gloves holding his sword. The sultan must have chosen this pose to reflect his life style in the European manner as he was at the time planning to build a new palace in European style with European type of decoration and furniture. Wilkie seems to have painted two versions of this portrait with slight differences in detail, as the original is kept in the Royal Collection.[28] There is a charcoal study[29] and engravings of the two versions.[30]

Some years after in 1845, the French artist Charles Doussault worked for the sultan. He portrayed the sultan standing in the old Çırağan Palace, which had been a preferred pose for Mahmud II's portraits by other local artists as well. Italian artist Luigi Rubio came to Istanbul in 1847 and also painted the sultan.[31] The work of the French artist Jean Portet (d. 1862) was more extensive. As a well-known miniaturist in France, he not only produced portrait medals and single portraits of the sultan but was commissioned to paint the portraits of all the sultans to the time of the reigning sultan.[32] These portraits are all the same size (83 x 67 cm), they are in bust form and have the names of each sultan inscribed in Latin letters above. Abdülmecid's portraits were extensively printed in Europe: bust, full-length or equestrian. Although he had never traveled in Europe, the sultan was portrayed with the leading kings of Europe indicating the sultan's significance in the European political sphere especially in the dispute over the Holy Places and the following Crimean War in 1853.[33]

The new iconography in sultanic portraiture introduced by foreign artists working in Istanbul for sultans Mahmud and Abdülmecid was adopted by local artists, such as the Sebuh and Rupen Manas brothers, a family of Armenian artists working for the Ottoman court. Both brothers were sent as translators to the Turkish embassy in Paris, had art education there and were commissioned to paint the sultan's portraits to be hung in the other Ottoman embassies in Europe.[34] Nevertheless a large oil portrait showing the sultan standing on a porch signed Rubens Manasie and dated 1857, was presented to the Swedish queen and is now at the Drottingholm Palace in Sweden.[35] A similar portrait shows the sultan standing in the old Çırağan palace, next to a table on which there is a map of Turkey, undoubtedly symbolizing his sovereignty. In the background there is a view of the Bosporus and the Seraglio Point. The portrait must be the work of Rupen Manas

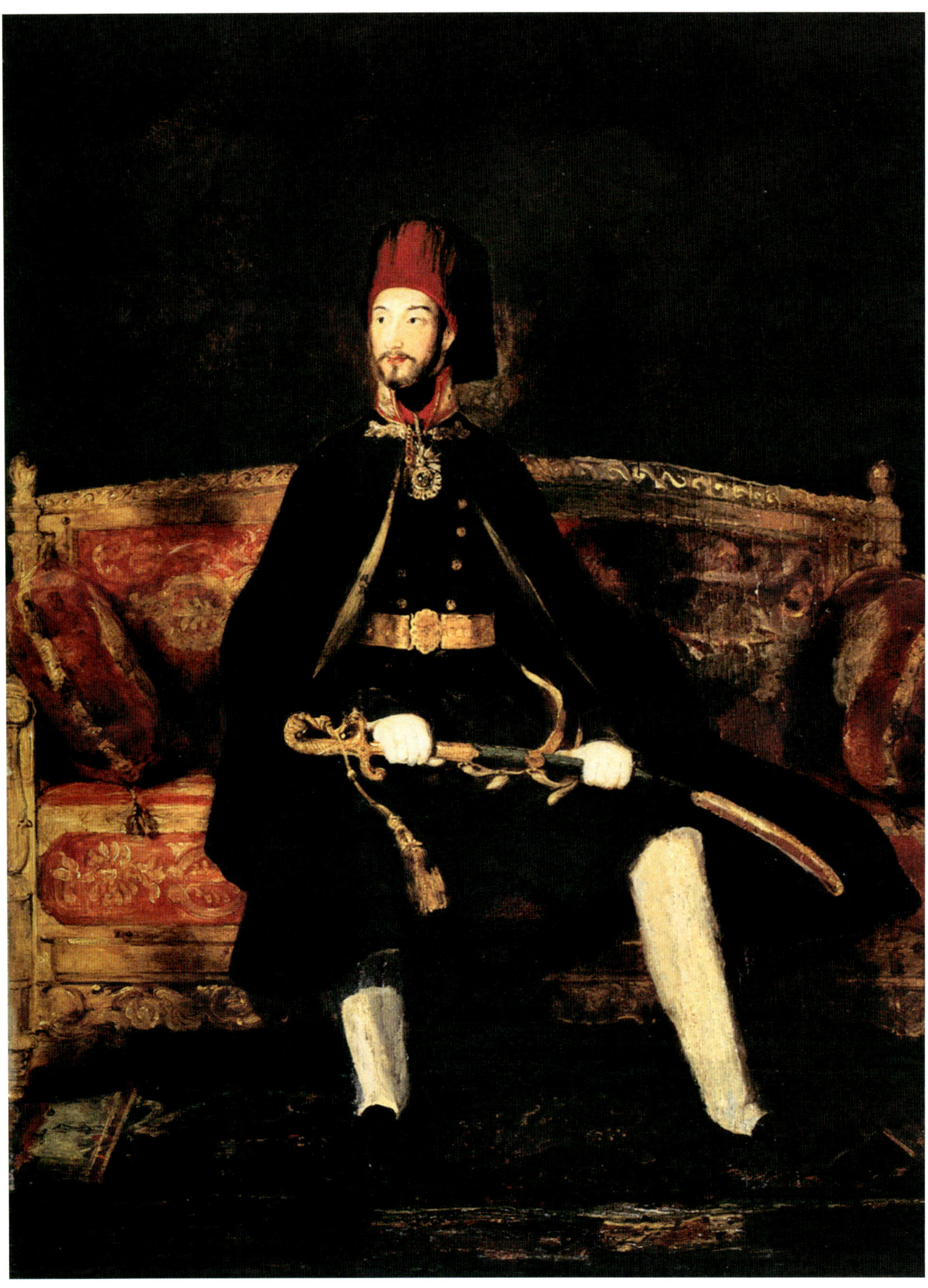

Figure 15.5 *Sultan Abdülmecid*, David Wilkie, 1840, oil on wood, 70 x 54 cm, Topkapı Palace Museum 17/120

as well.[36] These portraits indicate the impact of the European artists working for the Ottoman court on local artists.

The legacy of monumental portraiture continued in the second half of the nineteenth century displaying an even greater variety in technique and iconography. Sultan Abdülaziz (1861–76) was the first sultan to visit the European capitals in 1867 and having attended the Paris Exposition, widened the scope of reforms and extended artistic activity in the empire. Many European artists took commissions from him like the French artist Pierre D. Guillemet (d. 1878) and Stanislas Chlebowski (d. 1884) of Poland, and the Russian Ivan Aivazovsky (d. 1900) who painted the sultan following more or less the same iconography of the standing sultan or the equestrian portrait. Guillemet painted several portraits of the sultan, including one depicting him at the Çırağan Palace and one other, an equestrian portrait of the sultan riding with his troops (Fig. 15.6).[37] Chlebowski made a bust portrait of the sultan in 1866 and a large portrait depicting him standing in the gardens of the Beylerbeyi Palace in 1867.[38] He was also commissioned to paint scenes of historical battles. One such painting depicts Sultan Süleyman on horseback leading his troops.[39] More significant for this period are the sculpted portraits of the sultan. Abdülaziz commissioned the British sculptor Charles Fuller (d. 1875) for his portrait statue. The sultan had seen a number of public monuments and statues during his visit to the European capitals and also during his visit to Egypt in 1863. Khedive Ismail Paşa in Egypt had commissioned equestrian portraits of his father and grandfather. Fuller made an equestrian statue of the sultan in 1871 which was cast in bronze in Munich in 1871 (Fig. 15.7). Although it was not intended to be erected in the city, it is very significant as the first official statue in the Ottoman Empire. Although there had been commissions made by Sultan Abdülmecid for monuments to commemorate the decree of *Tanzimat* in 1839, they were never realized.[40] Sultan Abdülaziz's commissions are very significant as the first examples of official sculpture in the Ottoman Empire. A marble bust of the sultan was also made by Fuller in 1871 following the iconography of the sultan's bust portraits.[41]

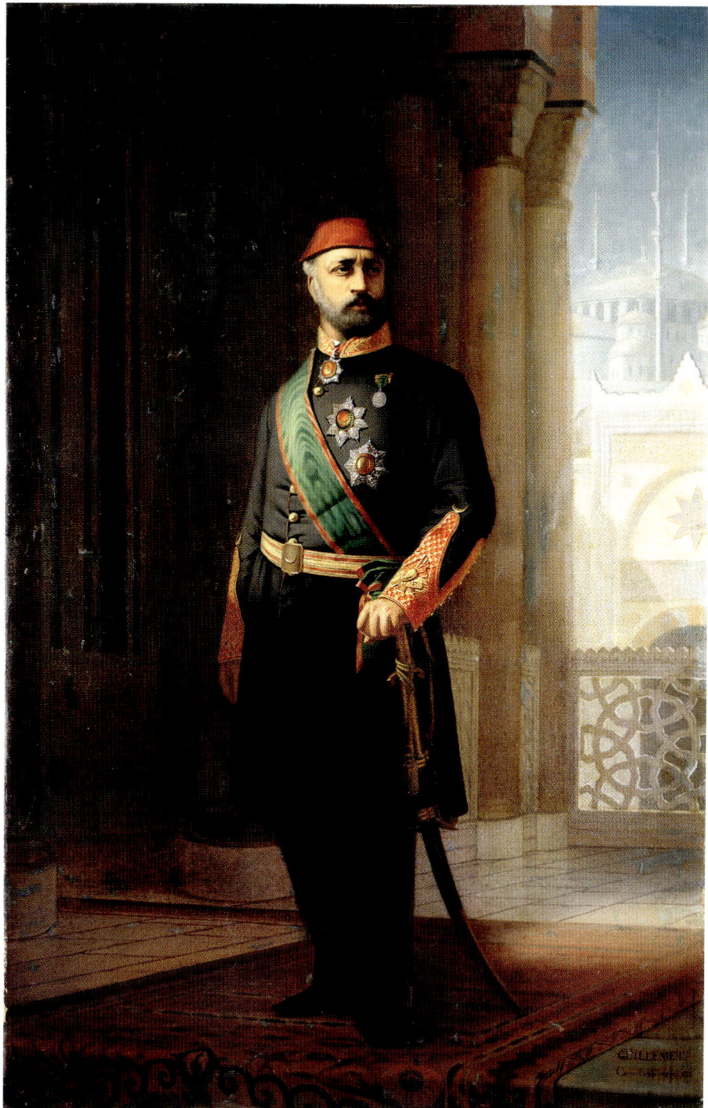

Figure 15.6 *Sultan Abdülaziz*, Pierre Desiré Guillemet, 1873, oil, 140 x 93 cm, Topkapı Palace Museum 17/943.

The legacy of monumental portraiture ended with Sultan Abdülhamid II (1876–1909) who reigned at the end of the nineteenth century as photography became widely spread in the empire. However, his reign is of great significance because he invited foreign and Turkish artists to paint oil portraits of the former sultans to be placed in a museum he was planning to establish at the Yıldız Palace. Hippolyte Bertaux (d. 1928) was a French artist who came after 1885 and painted the earlier sultans Selim III and Mahmud II on horseback.[42] The German artist William Reuter (b. 1859) who was in Istanbul in 1895–96 also painted portraits of former sultans.[43] The Italian artist Fausto Zonaro (d. 1929) was appointed as court painter to Abdülhamid in 1897 and he was commissioned to paint a copy of Bellini's portrait of Sultan Mehmed II who had reigned in the fifteenth century.[44] Sultan Abdülhamid must have planned to display them in his palace. Whether they were placed in Yıldız Palace is not very clear although inventory documents at the Topkapı Palace indicate that some of these portraits were brought to Topkapı Museum from the Dolmabahçe Palace. Some of the portraits in the Yıldız Palace might have been moved to other palaces in the later years. Nevertheless, all these oil portraits show that the sultan wished to have the Ottoman dynasty portrayed in the European manner.

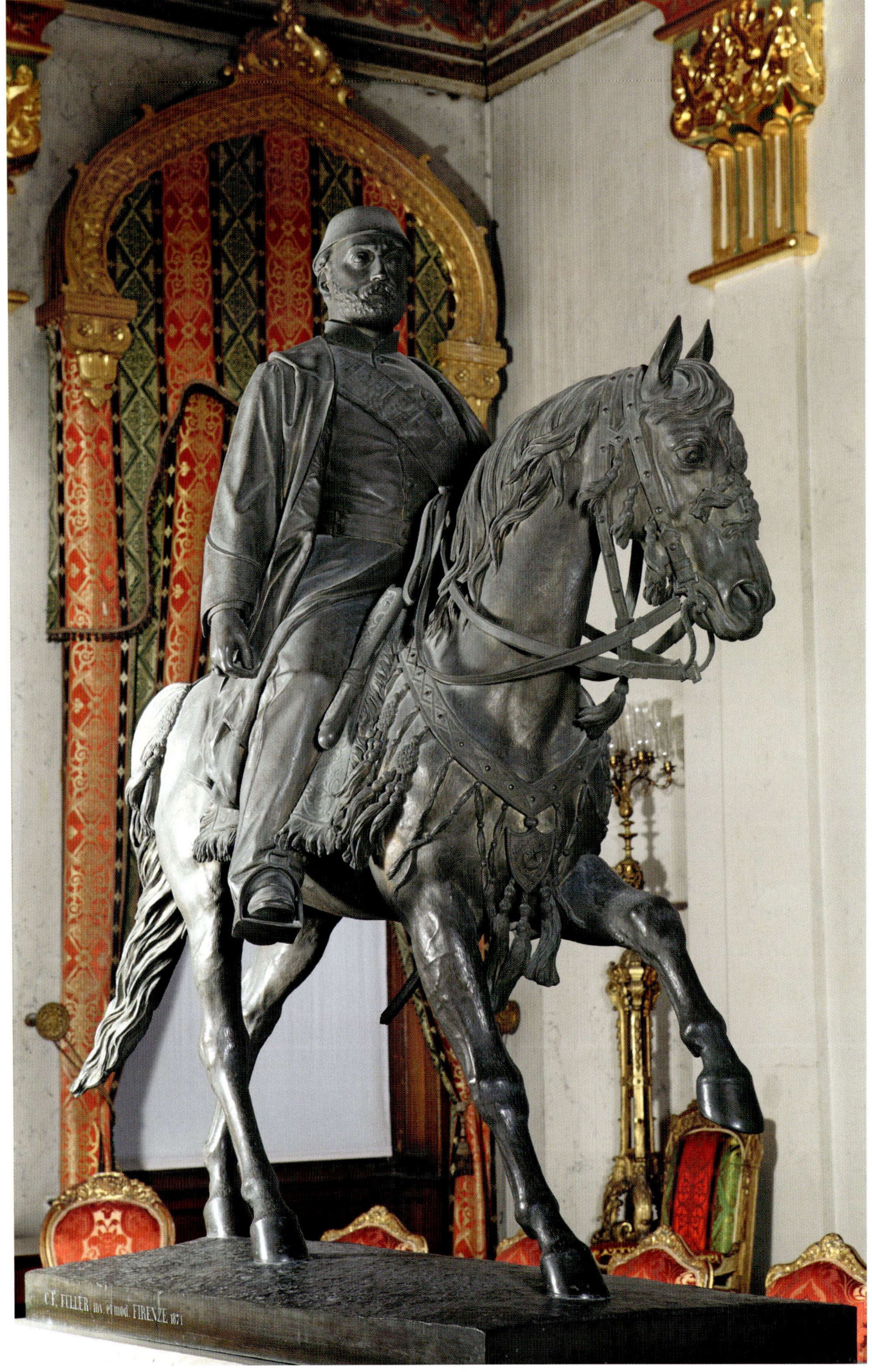

Figure 15.7 *Sultan Abdülaziz*, Charles Fuller, c. 1872, bronze, Beylerbeyi Palace, Istanbul.

A look at the imperial portraiture in the nineteenth century shows that the sultans wished to propagate the dynastic image through various media shifting away from the Eastern concept of the enthroned or the seated sultan to a new iconography of the single image of the ruler dressed in the contemporary European manner posed like the European kings emphasizing the image of a reformist in administration and the image of the modernizing state. In other words, realizing the significance of visual culture and the secular symbolism implicit in portraits for political image making, the sultans commissioned European artists to produce imperial portraiture in the Western sense for propagating a new dynastic image.

Notes

1 For more detailed information about Ottoman sultanic portraiture before the nineteenth century see *The Sultan's Portrait. Picturing the House of Osman*, comp. G. Necipoğlu, J. Raby, F. Çağman, S. Bağcı, B. Mahir, G. Irepoğlu, and G. Renda (Istanbul: İşbank, 2000). Published on the occasion of the exhibition held at the Topkapı Palace Museum in Istanbul between June 6 and September 6, 2000.

2 Musée National du Chateau de Versailles, inv. 8990, b2600. This small sized portrait (36 x 26 cm) painted in 1788 was in the collection of Choiseul-Gouffier, ambassador of France in Istanbul. Boppe, Auguste, *Les peintres du Bosphore au dix-huitième siècle*, 2nd edn (Paris: ACR Édition Internationale, 1997).

3 Choiseul-Gouffier came as the ambassador of France to Turkey in 1784–1792. His book *Voyage pittoresque de la Grèce* with Hilair's engravings was published in two volumes in Paris, 1787–1822.

4 Boppe, *Les peintres du Bosphore au dix-huitième siècle*, 233; Günsel Renda, "Europe and the Ottomans: Interaction in Art," in *Ottoman Civilization*, vol. 2, ed. Halil İnalcık and Günsel Renda (Istanbul: Ministry of Culture and Tourism, 2002), 1113.

5 *The Sultan's Portrait*, 398, 516, 518.

6 The original publication: Ignatius Mouradgea d'Ohsson, *Tableau Général de l'Empire Othoman, divisé en deux parties, dont l'une comprend la législation mohamétane, l'autre l'histoire de l'Empire Othoman* (Paris, 1787–89). A third volume was published in 1820 by Mouradgea's son.

7 Günsel Renda, "Illustrating the *Tableau Général de l'Empire Othoman*," in *The Torch of the Empire: Ignatius Mouradgea d'Ohsson and the Tableau Général of the Ottoman Empire in the Eighteenth Century/İmparatorluğun Meşalesi. XVIII. Yüzyılda Osmanlı İmparatorluğu'nun Genel Görünümü: Ignatius Mouradgea d'Ohsson* (Istanbul: Yapı Kredi Kültür Yayıncılık, 2002), 23–58.

8 *The Sultan's Portrait*, cat. no. 162, 163.

9 (Drawn by Constantin Capoudaghlé, Ottoman subject, engraved by Schiavonetti in London); *The Sultan's Portrait*, cat. no. 137; Günsel Renda, "Selim III's Portraits and the European Connection" (paper presented at the 10th International Congress of Turkish Art, Geneva, September 17–23, 1995), in *Art Turc/Turkish Art*, ed. F. Déroche, C. Genequand, G. Renda and M. Rogers, Geneva: Max van Berchem Foundation, 1999, 577–673.

10 The artist and his works in Istanbul have been studied by Atanasias Papas, "Der Maler Konstantinos Kyzikenos und einige seiner Werke," *Orthodoxes Forum*, Zeitschrift des Instituts für Orthodoxe Theologie der Universität München, 1 (1987): 71–81.

11 Günsel Renda, "Searching for New Media in 18th Century Ottoman Painting," *Festschrift Hans Georg Majer, Frauen, Bilder und Gelehrte/Arts, Women and Scholars, Studien zu Gesellschaft und Künsten im Osmanischen Reich*, ed. S. Prator and C. K. Neumann, 2 vols (Istanbul: Simurg, 2002): 451–79.

12 *The Sultan's Portrait*, 448, 449, cat. no. 132, 145.

13 Catherine Boppe-Vigne, "L'iconographie des dragomans au XVIIe siècle," in *Istanbul et les langues orientales. Actes du colloque*, ed. F. Hitzel, *Varia Turca*, XXXI (Paris: Harmattan, 1997): 267–68.

14 Cabinet des Estampes N20007. *The Sultan's Portrait*, cat. no. 144.

15 For more information on Sultan Selim's portraits in European collections see Renda, "Selim III's Portraits."

16 Julia Pardoe, *The City of the Sultans and the Domestic Manners of the Turks in 1836* (London: Henry Colburn, 1837), vol. 2, 298. Robert Walsh, *A Residence at Constantinople* (London, 1838), 298.

17 Tuncer Baykara, "II. Mahmud ve Resim," *Bedrettin Cömert'e Armağan*, Hacettepe Üniversitesi Sosyal ve İdari Bilimler Fakültesi, Beşeri Bilimler Dergisi, özel sayı, Ankara, 1980: 509–17.

18 Topkapı Palace Museum 17/208. Tradition of portrait medallions continued through the nineteenth century. See Günsel Renda, "Osmanlılarda Portreli Nişanlar," *Uluslararası Sanat Tarihi Sempozyumu. Prof. Dr. Gönül Öney'e Armağan, 10–13 Ekim 2001. Bildiriler*, Ege Üniversitesi Edebiyat Fakültesi Sanat Tarihi Bölümü, İzmir, 2002: 491–502, pl. CXXV-CXXVII, 1–12.

19 W. Dunlap, *History of Arts and Design in the United States* (New York, 1934), 142.

20 Pardoe, *The City of the Sultan*, 2, 104–5.

21 This is indicated in a document in the Ottoman imperial archives BOA. 23410.

22 Topkapı Palace Museum 17/110.

23 Musée National de Chateau de Versailles. MV 4842; *Musée National de Château de Versailles: Les Peintures*, 3 vols (Paris: Réunion des Musées Nationaux, 1995), vol. 2, 823, no. 4653.

24 *La Grèce en revolté. Delacroix et les peintres français 1815–1848* (Paris: Réunion des Musées Nationaux, 1997), 204, cat. no 81. Published in conjunction with the exhibition shown at the Musée national Eugène Delacroix from October 10, 1996 to January 13, 1997.

25 A copy of the engraving made after Schlesinger is found in the Bibliothèque Nationale N28989.

26 Topkapı Palace Museum H. 2074, 2075.

27 Semra Germaner and Zeynep İnankur, *Constantinople and the Orientalists* (Istanbul: Türkiye İş Bankası Kültür Yayınları, 2002), 89.

28 It is registered in the Royal Collection Trust. See *The Lure of the East: British Orientalist Painting*, ed. Nicholas Tromans (London: Tate Publishing, 2008), 127, f.45. Published in conjunction with the exhibition *The Lure of the East: British Orientalist Painting* shown at the Yale Center for British Art, Tate Britain, Suna and İnan Kıraç Pera Museum and the Sharjah Art Museum. See also Topkapı Palace Museum 17/120; *The Sultan's Portrait*, cat no. 161.

29 Deniz Müzesi (Naval Museum) in Istanbul, no. 2359.

30 Topkapı Palace Museum 17/851–10. For a lithography by Joseph Nash of Wilkie's portrait see Sarah Searight, *The British in the Middle East* (London and the Hague: East-West Publication, 1979), 106, fig. 2.

31 *Journal de Constantinople* of December 1, 1845 reports that the Sultan commissioned Doussault for the portrait. Fréderic Hitzel, *Couleurs de la corné d'or. Peintres voyageurs à la Sublime Porte* (Paris: ACR Edition, 2002), 270.

32 Topkapı Palace Museum 17/33-17/52

33 A printed portrait of Sultan Abdülmecid with King Nicolas I and a group portrait with Napoleon III, Queen Victoria, Nicholas I are in Bibliothèque Nationale in Paris, N2.54.3, N2.54.10; *The Sultan's Portrait*, 456–57, figs. 96, 97.

34 For information on Manas brothers see Nurdan S. Küçükhasköylü, "Dolmabahçe Sarayında Bir Ressam: Josef Manas," *150. Yılında Dolmabahçe Sarayı Uluslararası Sempozyumu*, 23–26 Kasım 2006. Bildiriler, I, TBMM, Milli Saraylar, Istanbul, 2007, 377–92.

35 *The Sultan's Portrait*, fig. 95.

36 Topkapı Palace Museum 17/118; *The Sultan's Portrait*, cat. no. 160.

37 Topkapı Palace Museum 17/943, 17/109; *The Sultan's Portrait*, 520.

38 Topkapı Palace Museum 17/968, 17/104.

39 Renda, "Europe and the Ottomans," fig. 735.

40 Klaus Kreiser, "Public Monuments in Turkey and Egypt. 1840–1916," *Muqarnas* 14 (1997): 103–17.

41 *The Sultan's Portrait*, cat. no. 172.

42 Topkapı Palace Museum 17/59.

43 TSM 17/59–17/61.

44 TSM 17/65.

Bibliography

Tuncer Baykara. "II. Mahmud ve Resim." *Bedrettin Cömert'e Armağan*, Hacettepe Üniversitesi Sosyal ve İdari Bilimler Fakültesi, Beşeri Bilimler Dergisi, özel sayı, Ankara, 1980, 509–29.

Boppe, Auguste. *Les peintres du Bosphore au dix-huitième siècle*, 2nd edn. Paris: ACR Édition Internationale, 1997.

Boppe-Vigne, Catherine. "L'iconographie des dragomans au XVIIe siècle," in *Istanbul et les langues orientales. Actes du colloque*, edited by F. Hitzel, 267–68. *Varia Turca*, XXXI. Paris: Harmattan, 1997.

Choiseul-Gouffier, Marie Gabriel Florent Auguste de. *Voyage pittoresque de la Grèce* 2 vols. Paris, 1787–1822.

Dunlap, W. *History of Arts and Design in the United States*, New York, 1934.

Germaner Semra, and Zeynep İnankur. *Constantinople and the Orientalists,* Istanbul: Türkiye İş Bankası Kültür Yayınları, 2002.

Hitzel, Fréderic. *Couleurs de la corné d'or. Peintres voyageurs à la Sublime Porte*. Paris: ACR Edition, 2002.

Kreiser, Klaus. "Public Monuments in Turkey and Egypt. 1840–1916." *Muqarnas* 14 (1997): 103–17.

Küçükhasköylü, Nurdan S. "Dolmabahçe Sarayında bir ressam: Josef Manas," *150. Yılında Dolmabahçe Sarayı Uluslararası Sempozyumu*. 23–26 Kasım 2006. Bildiriler, I, TBMM, Milli Saraylar, Istanbul, 2007, 377–92.

La Grèce en revolté. Delacroix et les peintres français 1815–1848. Paris: Réunion des Musées Nationaux, 1997. Published in conjunction with the exhibition *La Grèce en revolté. Delacroix et les peintres français 1815–1848* shown at the Musée national Eugène Delacroix from October 10, 1996 to January 13, 1997.

Musée National de Château de Versailles: Les Peintures, 3 vols. Paris: Réunion des Musées Nationaux, 1995.

The Lure of the East: British Orientalist Painting. Edited by Nicholas Tromans. London: Tate Publishing, 2008. Published in conjunction with the exhibition *The Lure of the East: British Orientalist Painting* shown at the Yale Center for British Art, Tate Britain, Suna and İnan Kıraç Pera Museum and the Sharjah Art Museum.

d'Ohsson, Ignatius Mouradgea. *Tableau Général de l'Empire Othoman, divisé en deux parties, dont l'une comprend la législation mohamétane, l'autre l'histoire de l'Empire Othoman*. Paris, 1787–89.

Papas, Atanasias. "Der Maler Konstantinos Kyzikenos und einige seiner Werke." *Orthodoxes Forum*, Zeitschrift des Instituts für Orthodoxe Theologie der Universität München, 1 (1987): 71–81.

Pardoe, Julia. *The City of the Sultans and the Domestic Manners of the Turks in 1836*. London: Henry Colburn, 1837.

Renda, Günsel. "Selim III's Portraits and the European Connection." Paper presented at the 10th International Congress of Turkish Art, Geneva, September 17–23, 1995. Published in *Art Turc/Turkish Art*, edited by F. Déroche, C. Genequand, G. Renda and M. Rogers, 577–673. Geneva: Max van Berchem Foundation, 1999.

Renda, Günsel. "Osmanlılarda Portreli Nişanlar." *Uluslararası Sanat Tarihi Sempozyumu. Prof. Dr. Gönül Öney'e Armağan*, 10–13 Ekim 2001. Bildiriler, Ege Üniversitesi Edebiyat Fakültesi Sanat Tarihi Bölümü, İzmir, 2002.

Renda, Günsel. "Europe and the Ottomans: Interaction in Art." In *Ottoman Civilization*, vol. 2, edited by Halil İnalcık and Renda Günsel, 1091–1121. Istanbul: Ministry of Culture and Tourism, 2002.

Renda, Günsel. "Searching for New Media in 18th Century Ottoman Painting." *Festschrift Hans Georg Majer, Frauen, Bilder und Gelehrte/Arts, Women and Scholars, Studien zu Gesellschaft und Künsten im Osmanischen Reich*, edited by S. Prator and C. K. Neumann, 2 vols., 451–79. Istanbul: Simurg, 2002.

Renda, Günsel. "Illustrating the *Tableau Général de l'Empire Othoman*." In *The Torch of the Empire: Ignatius Mouradgea d'Ohsson and the Tableau Général of the Ottoman Empire in the Eighteenth Century/İmparatorluğun Meşalesi. XVIII. Yüzyılda Osmanlı İmparatorluğu'nun Genel Görünümü ve Ignatius Mouradgea d'Ohsson*, 23–58. Istanbul: Yapı Kredi Kültür Yayıncılık, 2002.

Searight, Sarah. *The British in the Middle East*. London and the Hague: East-West Publication, 1979.

The Sultan's Portrait. Picturing the House of Osman. Compiled by G. Necipoğlu, J. Raby, F. Çağman, S. Bağcı, B. Mahir, G. Irepoğlu, and G. Renda. Istanbul: İşbank, 2000. Published on the occasion of the exhibition held at the Topkapı Palace Museum in Istanbul between June 6 and September 6, 2000.

Topkapi à Versailles. Trésors de la cour ottomane. Musée national des château de Versailles et de Trianon. Exhibition Catalog. Paris: Réunion des Musées Nationaux, 1999.

Walsh, R. *A Residence at Constantinople*. London, 1838.

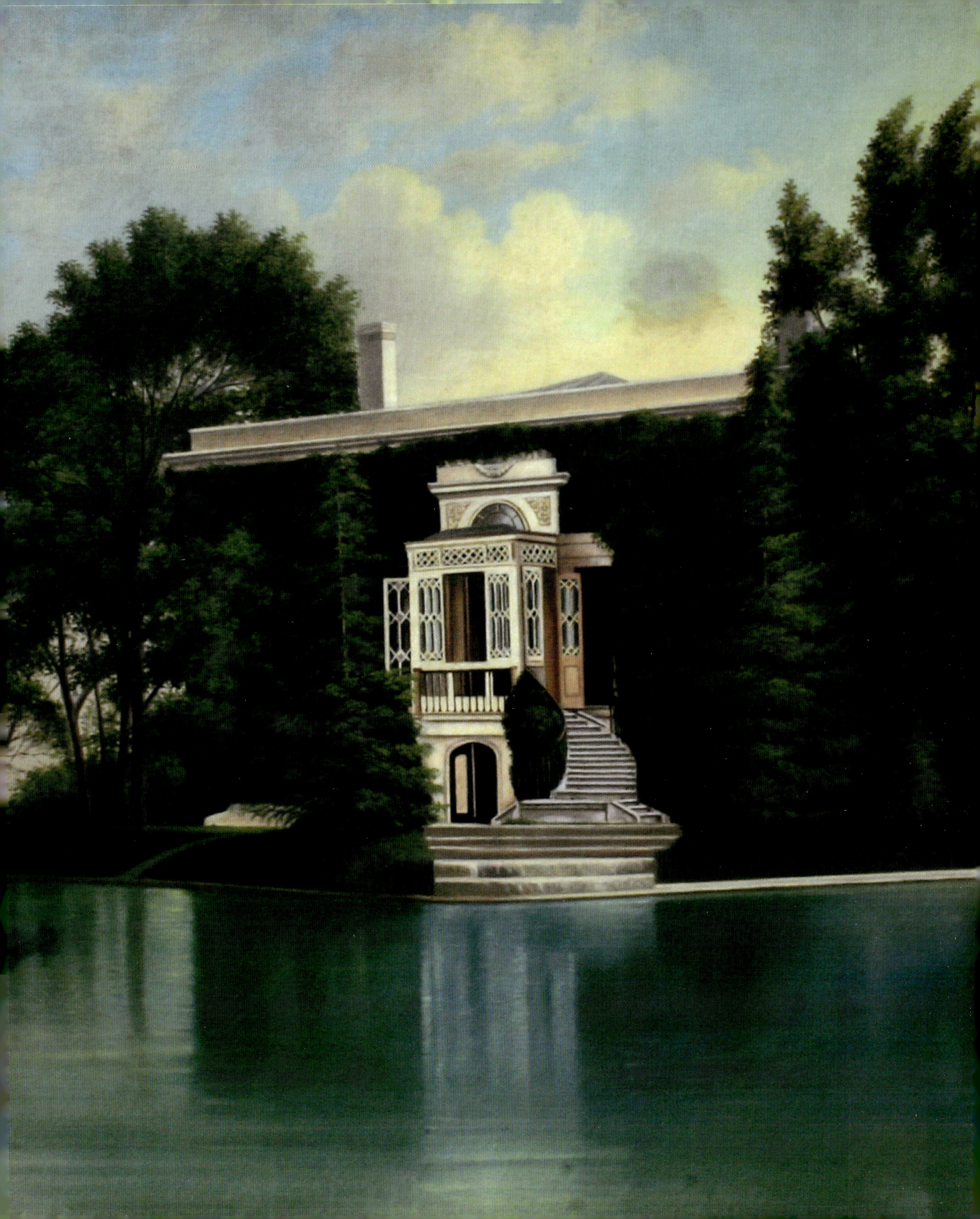

XVI

The Interpretation of Pictorial Space in Nineteenth-Century Ottoman Landscape Painting

Semra Germaner

Traveling European landscape artists who visited Istanbul during the nineteenth century depicted exotic views of the city and its picturesque corners. The life and ethnic richness which is rendered in these paintings underlies the Orientalist nature of the works. It was their pictorial skills and extensive knowledge of coloring techniques that made it possible for these professional artists to sucessfully recreate the atmosphere of the city on their canvases. Starting in the second half of the nineteenth century, Ottoman painters also began to paint Istanbul landscapes. They began to learn the rules of perspective in both the military and civilian schools. Painting courses were introduced in the Engineering School seven years after David Wilkie painted Sultan Abdülmecid's portrait in 1840. Thus this date marks the beginning of the tradition of "military artists," who contributed greatly to the introduction of perspectival painting.

The creative impulse of Ottoman artists at that time originated not only from within their own society, but also from the dilemmas concerning the Ottoman Empire's relationship with the West. Pictorial space in painting was a new concept for the Ottoman artist and they tried to restructure their visual memories by learning perspective—the first word of the vocabulary of Western painting—and applying it in their paintings. To what extent was it possible for these artists to be a part of the Western tradition of painting with this newly acquired knowledge of perspective? The examples included in this chapter are some of the first landscapes that emerged from within this context. Teaching this new tradition of painting continued in the military schools even after the establishment of the School of Fine Arts (*Sanayi-i Nefise Mektebi*), in 1883, for training professional artists. To be able to understand this change one must be familiar with teaching methods practiced in military schools as explained below.

Ottoman modernization began with the army, and one of the first institutions to advocate these changes was the Ottoman Imperial Army Engineering School (*Mühendishane-i Berrî-i Hümâyun*).[1] This was also the first school to introduce painting into its curriculum. For many years, this school was the place where Ottoman artillery and engineers' corps officers, civilian and military engineers, architects and even painters were trained.[2]

The educational principles in this institution, which was established for training officers, architects and engineers, has parallels with the contemporaneous Western education system. Subjects such as topography, mapping, artillery and painting were taught by engineers and officers who were invited from Europe.[3]

In 1847, the upper level courses were shifted from the Engineering School to the Military Academy (*Harbiye*) that had been established in 1834. Prior to 1847 this institution trained only artillery officers. These upper level students studied mechanics, physics, geometric drawing, perspective, French and painting.[4] Many so-called "painters" were trained at the Engineering School and the Military Academy in these early years.[5] The graduates of 1852–65 were classified according to the fields in which they trained, such as "engineer," "artilleryman" and "painter". This Military Academy, which was established according to Western models, was a new and important step in Ottoman modernization. As in the case of European military schools,[6] great importance was given to painting classes at the Military Academy, throughout its history. In order to be able to pursue the new curriculum, which was primarily in French, teachers were brought from France and Prussia; these foreigner teachers also contributed to restructuring that curriculum.[7]

Englishman Charles MacFarlane provides important information about the teaching methods in the Academy in his book, *Kismet or The Doom of Turkey,* published in 1853.[8] The author recounts that when touring the school, he saw approximately thirty students studying French, and some student drawings exhibited in a small library, in which all the books were in French. He also notes that all of these drawings were copies of French or German prints, mostly lithographs, that the technical drawings, maps and city wall plans were carefully executed by hand. MacFarlane, who also made several visits to the military high school at *Maçka Barracks*,[9] writes that most of the time he saw the school director and teachers sitting and smoking pipes under the trees in front of the school. He also recounts that there were around 200 or 300 students in the school, that they enrolled at the age of 12, studied for five years, before moving on to a higher level for three or four years, or being given a position in the government. MacFarlane states:

> Some become engineers; some go into the artillery, some into the cavalry, and others become infantry officers; but they all pursue the same line of study. From the day of their entrance they are lodged, fed, and clothed at the expense of the Sultan, receiving also a small monthly gratuity, which is increased as they advance in age. In spite of all the encouragements, a good many of them get heart-sick of study and confinement, and abscond. I was told the same thing at the Galata Serai, or Medical school. As at that school, the students were drawn from poor Turkish families: they were sons of boatmen, porters, papoush-makers, &c. One of the masters, a Perote Frank, told me that out of the whole number (here and the upper school) there were not above six or seven that could be considered as the sons of gentlemen; and that these few were the children of effendies who had been utterly ruined in their fortunes. Others told me that the reforming government preferred the rawest materials; and found the children of the uninformed, dependent poor more submissive and ductile than the children of the superior classes.[10]

MacFarlane met the drawing teacher, Pierre Guès, whose father was French and who lived in the Pera district of Istanbul. He also taught at the Military Academy. Guès praised the docility and the general intelligence of the students, but added that even though their capacity to imitate was highly developed and they were good at executing both music and drawing, they had absolutely no creative talent.[11] The writer also provides specific information about the drawing techniques taught at the school. He stated:

> Here, above Dolma Baghchi, the favourite pursuit seemed to be drawing; I never saw the boys doing anything else. They were copying, with charcoal or black French chalk, Parisian prints-landscapes, architectural pieces, ruins ornaments, scrolls, flowers, fruit, and, in bold defiance of the Koran, wild beasts, and fancy portraits of women as well as of men. A few of the elder pupils were working in *acquarella*, copying coloured prints in French water colours.
>
> The pupils were allowed to draw nothing from the round or the real, the Ulema having decided that the faithful must not draw from objects with cast shadows. As artists, the youths must thus remain mere mechanical copyists.[12]

The military schools' need for teachers who were able to teach Western-style painting was met not only by teachers who came from Europe, but also by the Levantines who were living in Istanbul and had talent for painting. Pierre Guès (d. 1887), who was mentioned by MacFarlane in his book, is a good example. He was one of the first painting instructors appointed to the Military Academy in 1846. In his third year, he organized an exhibition of graduate works in 1849, that contained between sixty and eighty drawings, water-colors, and lithographs, and sixteen paintings.[13] Guès worked for 40 years in this institution.[14] Another key figure was Joseph Schranz (1803 to c. 1866). He had a Spanish father, who had settled in Malta, and an Anglo-Spanish mother. He arrived in Istanbul in 1832, and in 1838 was appointed as an instructor both to the Military Academy and to the Military High School.[15] Guès taught drawing and oil painting, while Joseph Schranz taught water-color. Pierre Guès and Joseph Schranz contributed greatly to the training of a generation of military painters in the Ottoman Empire. Apart from teaching, they also painted urban scenes and landscapes.

As the number of the military schools increased there was more need for vocational teachers. To meet the demand, a teachers' college (*Menşe-i Muallimin*) was established in 1875. The Menşe-i Muallimin, which was structured in a way that also made it possible for medresse (high-school) students to attend, was a progressive institution in its day, that included painting classes in its curriculum.[16] Courses in perspective (*menazır*) and chiaroscuro, charcoal and ink drawing, sepia painting, copying, painting from wooden geometric models and various objects, examination of the human anatomy and photography were a sign of a sophisticated curriculum, as far as teaching materials and methods were concerned.

During the nineteenth century among the civilian high schools in Istanbul painting was taught only in Darüşşafaka High School (1873) and *Mekteb-i Sultani* (1868), the present day Galatasaray High School. Painting courses in these schools followed a curriculum parallel to that of the technical drawing and drawing courses held in the military schools. The children of the Ottoman elite and the non-Muslim families generally attended Mekteb-i Sultani. On the other hand, Darüşşafaka as a modern institute was established mainly to educate the children of Muslim families with a lower income and orphans. It is interesting that these two civil institutions could bring together the children of both wealthy and poor families and introduce them to European art simultaneously and foster an appreciation for European-style painting.

Landscape painting occupies an important place in this period of modern Ottoman painting. The use of perspective, marks the initial stage of this modern period. However examples show us that during this stage it was more important to paint various buildings according to the rules of perspective, than the landscape itself. The most popular genres of the last quarter of the nineteenth century were cityscapes and monumental buildings that were painted not from nature, but from photographs. Ahmet Ziya Akbulut (1869–1938), known as *Menazırcı Ziya* (Ziya the Master of Perspective), who graduated from the military school in 1887, and also taught there, is typical of Ottoman landscape painters of the time.[17] His *Mosque of Mihrimah Sultan in Üsküdar* is a good example of what these artists understood of the urban landscape (Fig. 16.1). Since these painters learnt to paint from photographs, rather than from nature, they could only perceive the pictorial space through photographs (Fig. 16.2).

The palaces and palace parks were photographed during the reign of Sultan Abdülhamid II by the court photographers' studios such as Abdullah Frères and Sébah & Joaillier. These photographs were published in the *Yıldız Albums* (Fig. 16.3). Some of these photographs were first enlarged by skillful Darrüşşafaka and military school graduates, then colored with oils and glazes. Some of these pictures depicting palaces, palace parks, and monumental buildings were commissioned for the various pavillions of the Yıldız Palace (Fig. 16.4). These paintings are the reflections of a new world as they were conceived in the minds of Ottoman artists. The most characteristic aspects of these paintings are the strange and the still, almost

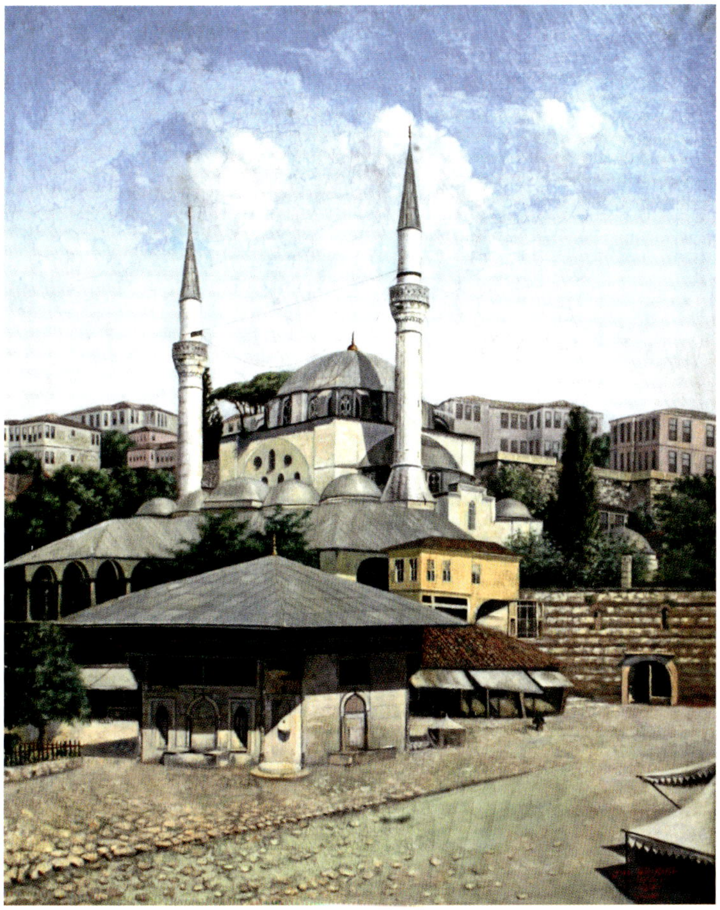

Figure 16.1 *Mosque of Mihrimah Sultan in Üsküdar*, Ahmet Ziya Akbulut, (1869–1938), oil on canvas, 100 x 80.5 cm, Mimar Sinan Fine Arts University Museum of Painting and Sculpture.

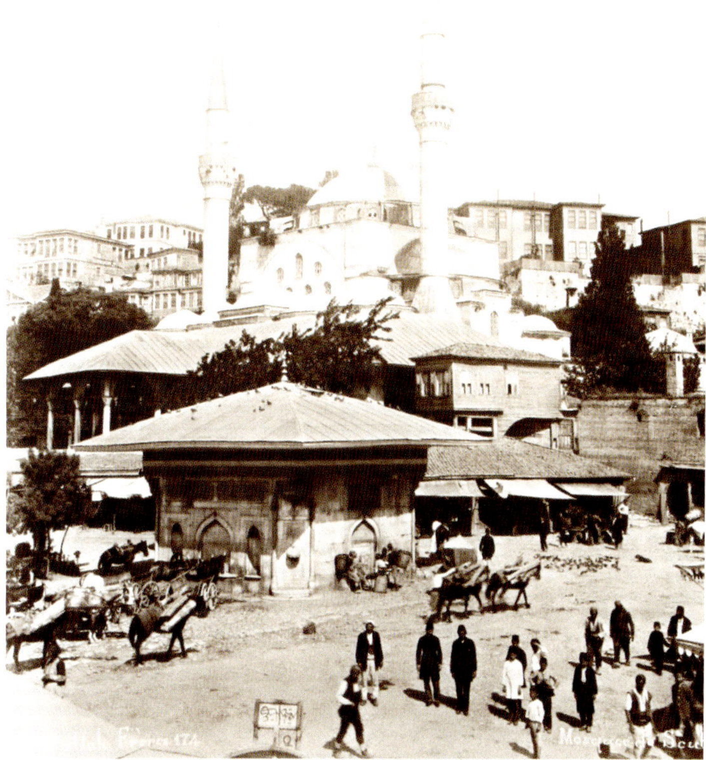

Figure 16.2 *Mosque of Mihrimah Sultan in Üsküdar*, Abdullah Frères, end of nineteenth century, photograph, II. Abdülhamid Yıldız Palace Album no. 90819. İ.Ü. Kütüphane ve Dokümantasyon Daire Başkanlığı.

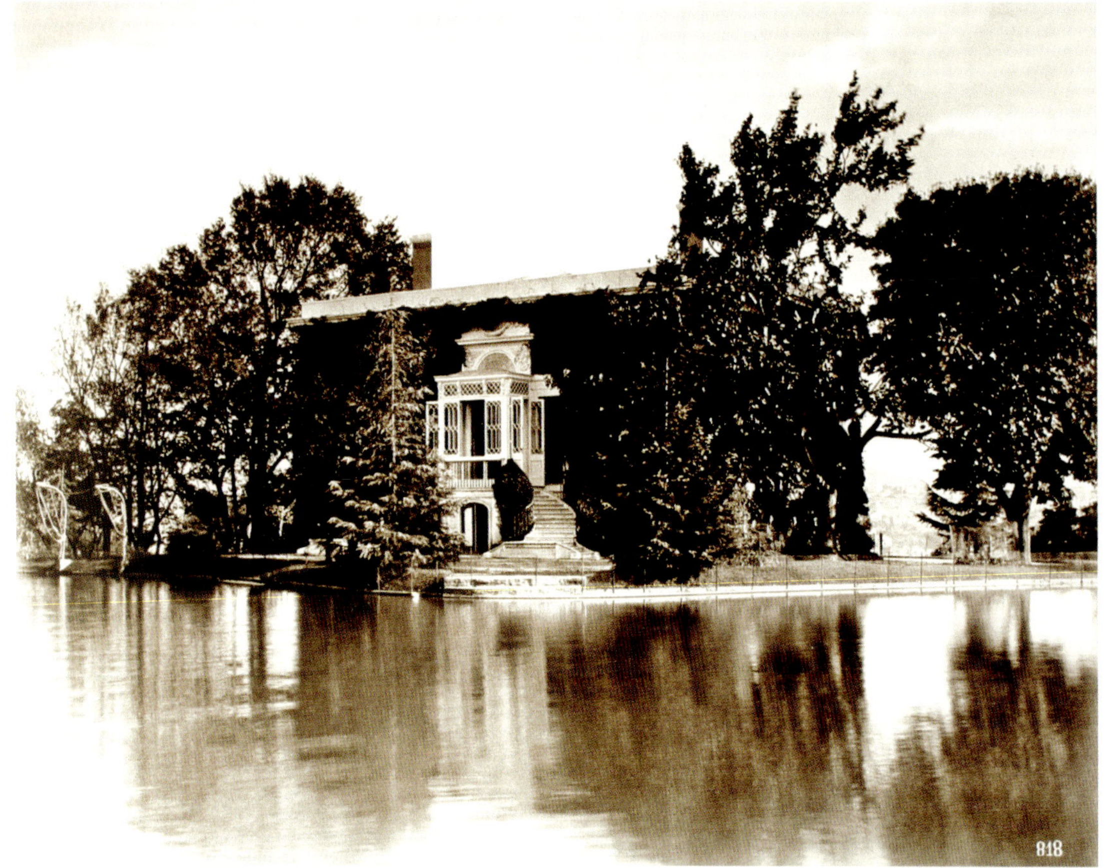

Figure 16.3 *Çadır Pavilion in the Yıldız Palace Gardens*, Abdullah Frères, end of nineteenth century, photograph, II. Abdülhamid Yıldız Palace Album no. 90815. İ.Ü. Kütüphane ve Dokümantasyon Daire Başkanlığı

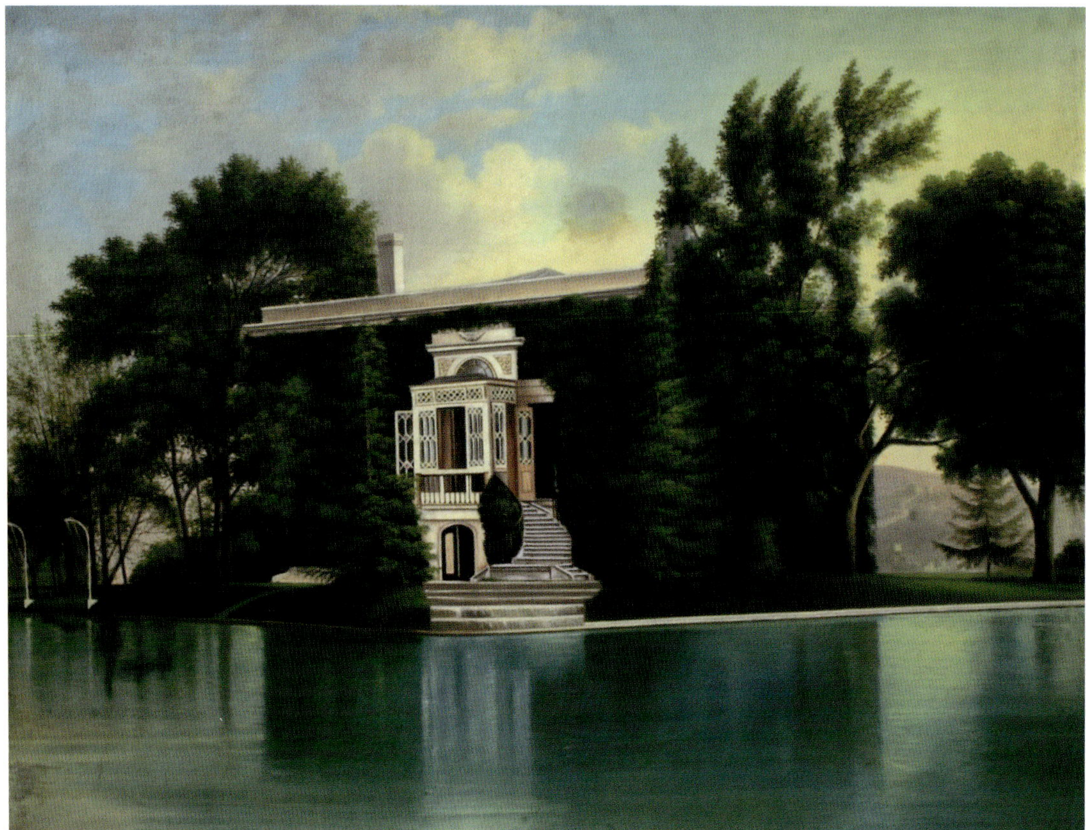

Figure 16.4 *Çadır Pavilion in the Yıldız Palace Gardens*, Şevki, 1891, oil on canvas, 73 x 92 cm, Mimar Sinan Fine Arts University Museum of Painting and Sculpture.

lifeless atmosphere created by a monotonous and diffuse light, and by the juxtaposition of different spatial impressions that are produced by photography and painting. It is always the eye of the camera that dominates in these paintings. Most of these painters who were active during this period did not later pursue an artistic career.

If the use of perspective is one common characteristic in the paintings of the military school artists, the other is the lack of figures. Rules of perspective were taught to the students within a scientific context for them to use in technical drawing. However figural representation as such was not included within the curriculum, or rather, training in how to draw the human figure was not a priority until the establishment of the Academy of Fine Arts in the early 1880s. What is more, these artists training in these earlier schools were the children of traditional Muslim families, who remained removed from the Empire's modernization project. So, for example, we see that when an artist named Ahmet painted *Impressions from Şehzadebaşı* (Fig. 16.5), after a photograph with figures (Fig. 16.6), he removed all the figures. In these paintings, situated at the intersection between modernity and

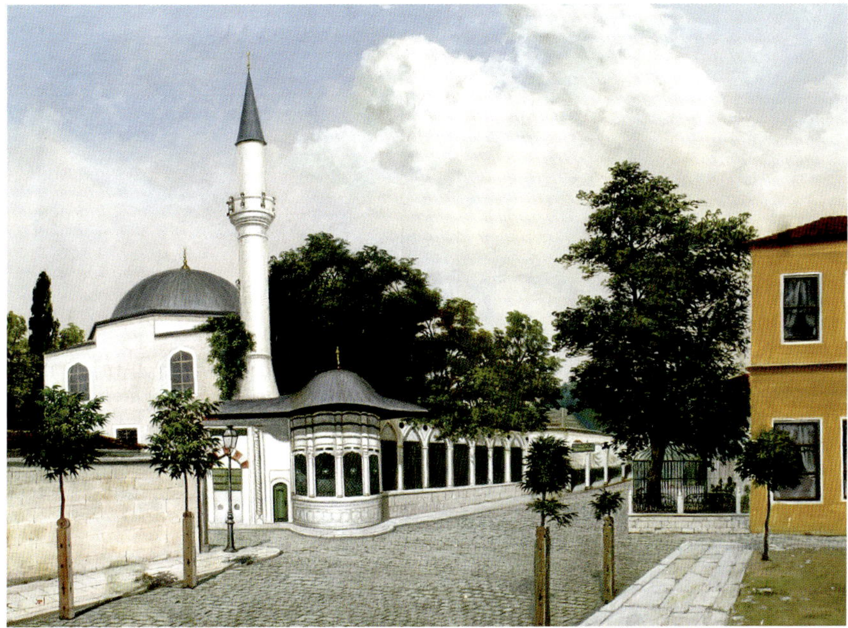

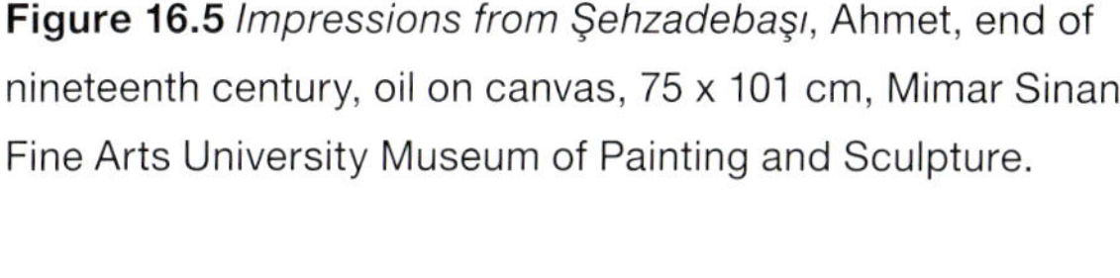

Figure 16.5 *Impressions from Şehzadebaşı*, Ahmet, end of nineteenth century, oil on canvas, 75 x 101 cm, Mimar Sinan Fine Arts University Museum of Painting and Sculpture.

Figure 16.6 *Street at Şehzadebaşı*, Abdullah Frères, end of nineteenth century, photograph, II. Abdülhamid Yıldız Palace Album no. 90819. İ.Ü. Kütüphane ve Dokümantasyon Daire Başkanlığı

tradition, perspective creates the impression of real space, however as seen in Ahmet's painting, this impression is disrupted by the complete absence of figures. These paintings done by careful, patient, neat and skillful practitioners convey a silent and unreal world.

When in 1883, the Academy of Fine Arts (*Sanayi-i Nefise Mektebi*) was opened the students started to study from the live model, and began to be trained in a more sophisticated manner in the handling of oil paint to create effects of light and of color modulation. From then on the drawing-based paintings of the military schools seemed quite amateurish. However, up to the early 1900s, or in other words up to the declaration of a constitutional monarchy (*Meşrutiyet*), the court continued to support these institutions that it had established within the context of modernization, and paintings purchased from school exhibitions continued to be hung on the walls of the Ottoman palaces.

Throughout this period some local artists from non-Muslim communities continued to work with traditional techniques. Mıgırdıç Melkonyan was one of them. He practiced the cut out (*kat'ı*) technique using wood and silk and with oils on canvas. Melkonyan, who painted both a panoramic view and figures to depict the vibrant life along the Bosporus, was an artist outside the scope of art training in military schools (Fig. 16.7).

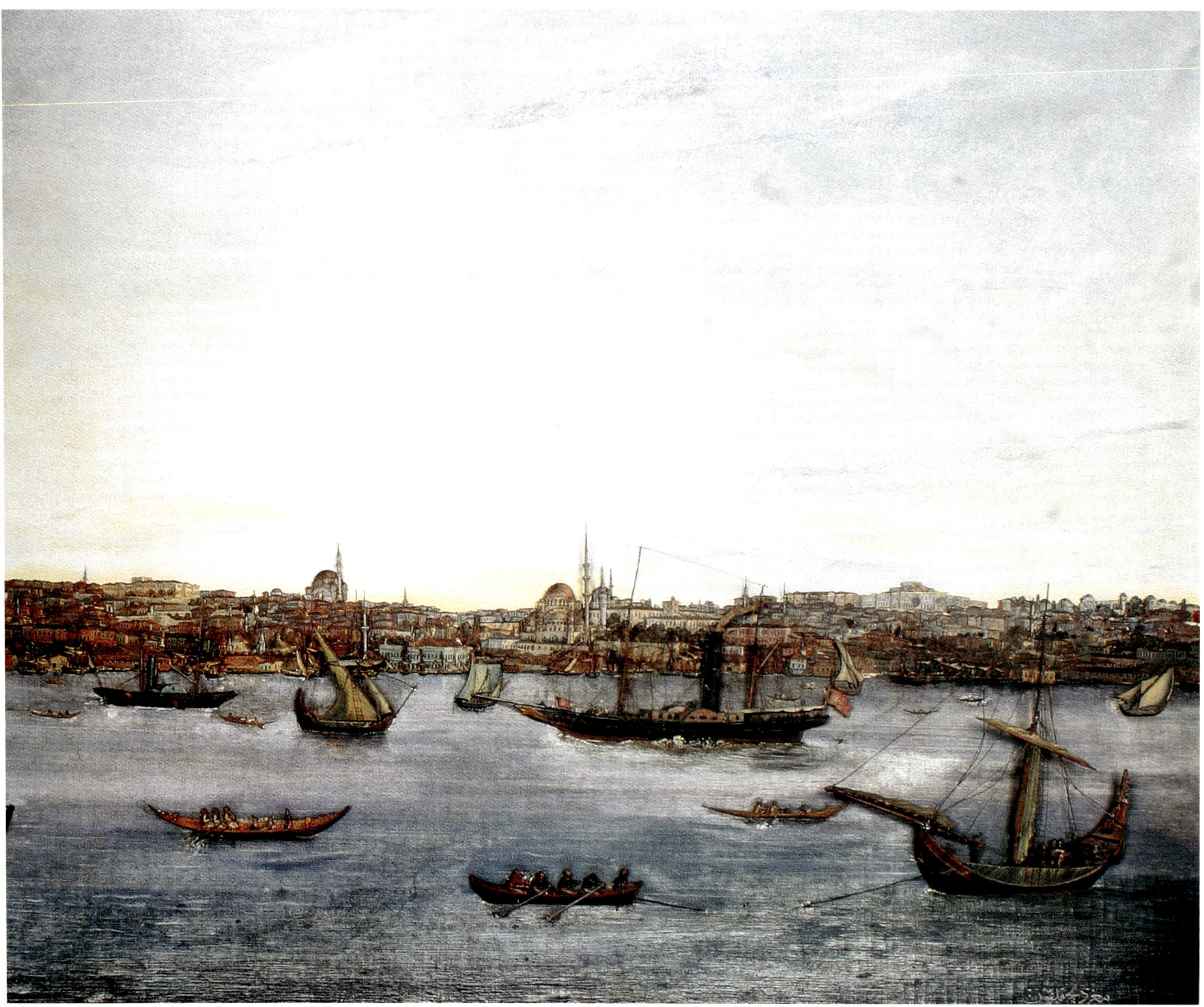

Figure 16.7 *Marmara Bosphorus*, (detail), Mıgırdıç Melkonyan, 1844, oil on wood, silk and canvas, 60 x 90 cm, Naval Museum Istanbul.

The difficulties of changing from one culture to another and from one visual language to another are quite obvious in the landscapes by the Ottoman military school painters, however they still manage to reflect the process of recreating a visual memory and the Ottomans' efforts to modernize.

Notes

1 The Mühendishane-i Berrî-i Hümâyun was established in 1795 and, from a report dated 1833, we know that the first year students were taught painting. Mustafa Cezar, *Sanatta Batıya Açılış ve Osman Hamdi*, (Istanbul: Erol Kerim Aksoy Kültür, Eğitim, Spor ve Sağlık Vakfı Yayınları, 1995), 377.

2 The graduate's profile gives a good idea about the training provided in this school. After 1853, and from then on, artillerymen; after 1855, engineering corps officers; in 1853–60 and then in 1863, military engineers; after 1888 civilian engineers', after 1881 general staff officers; at 1857–58 and 1864 painters. Mustafa Ergün and Tayyip Duman, "19. Yüzyılda Osmanlı Askerî Okullarının Ders Programları ve Ders Kitapları," *Yeni Türkiye*, 7 (1996): 494–511; Mehmed Es'ad, *Mir'ât-ı Mühendis-Hâne-i Berrî-i Hümâyûn,* ed. Sadık Erdem (Istanbul: İstanbul Teknik Üniversitesi Bilim ve Teknoloji Tarihi Araştırma Merkezi no. 3, 1986), 142–227.

3 It was Sultan Mahmud II who decided that it was better to send the students to Europe to be educated in science and technology.

4 By the third year, students would split into the artillery and architecture sections. Even though there were no painting classes in the artillery section, architecture students were obliged to take painting classes for two years.

5 The number of the students increased especially during the decades following the reforms introduced after 1848 by Bekir Pasha, director of the *Mühendishane*.

6 It is said that the curriculum at the *Mühendishane-i Berrî-i Hümâyun* was a mixture of the curricula of the Austrian *Akademie Militär* and of the *Akademie Ingenieur*. Kemal Beydilli, *Türk Bilim ve Matbaacılık Tarihinde Mühendishane, Mühendishane Matbaası ve Kütüphanesi, 1776–1826* (Istanbul: Eren Yayıncılık, 1995), 59.

7 The teachers who came from Europe were supposed to learn Turkish in a very short time in order to be able to teach in Turkish. However, this was not possible, so the teachers started using interpreters. Since these interpreters were often not experts in the fields taught, they could not do proper translations, and with their best intentions they summarized the teacher's one hour course in a few minutes. Ergün and Duman, "19. Yüzyılda Osmanlı Askerî Okullarının Ders Programları ve Ders Kitapları," 494.

8 Charles MacFarlane, *Kısmet or The Doom of Turkey*, (London: Thomas Bosworth, 1853)

9 Charles MacFarlane mentions a military school not far from the *Harbiye*, on the hills overlooking the sultan's new Dolmabahçe Palace, in an airy and pleasant spot. This school was the Maçka Military High School. Cezar, *Sanatta Batıya Açılış ve Osman Hamdi,* 391–92.

10 MacFarlane, *Kismet or The Doom of Turkey*, 50–51.

11 Ibid., 51.

12 Ibid., 53.

13 Seza Sinanlar, "Pera'da Resim Üretim Ortamı 1844–1916," (PhD diss., İstanbul Teknik Üniversitesi, 2008), 56.

14 Pierre Guès worked as a designer at the technical office of the Sixth District (Municipality) of Beyoğlu (Beyoğlu VI. Daire), and according to records, in 1881 he had a studio in Sümbül Street, number 12. Semra Germaner and Zeynep İnankur, *Constantinople and the Orientalists* (Istanbul: Türkiye İş Bankası Kültür Yayınları, 2008), 70.

Pierre Guès taught painting at the university at Çemberlitaş in 1870 and at the school for state employees (*Mahrec-i Aklam).* Halil Edhem, *Elvah-ı Nakşiye Koleksiyonu*, (Istanbul: Milliyet Yayınları, 1970), 32.

15 Ibid., 32.

16 Second Class Painting (2 years): geometric drawing and perspective and shading, calligraphy, charcoal drawing, sepia painting, ink drawing, colored drawing, copying, painting from a model, shading and tinting, drafting.

First Class Painting (4 years): geometric drawing and perspective and shading, calligraphy, charcoal drawing, sepia painting, ink drawing, colored drawing, copying, painting from a model, painting from nature, realistic and imaginary painting, oil painting, mechanical drawing, examination of the human anatomy, photography. Ergün and Duman, "19. Yüzyılda Osmanlı Askerî Okullarının Ders Programları ve Ders Kitapları," 494.

17 He taught at the painting studio of the military school in 1891–94. Of his two painting manuals, *Amel-i Menazır* was published in 1896, and *Usul-ü Ameliye-i Fenn-i Menazır* in 1922. Pertev Boyar, *Türk Ressamları* (Ankara: Jandarma Basımevi, 1948), 92–94.

Bibliography

Beydili, Kemal. Türk Bilim ve Matbaacılık Tarihinde Mühendishane, Mühendishane Matbaası ve Kütüphanesi, 1776-1826, Istanbul:

Eren Yayıncılık, 1995

Boyar, Pertev. *Türk Ressamları*. Ankara: Jandarma Basımevi, 1948.

Cezar, Mustafa. *Sanatta Batıya Açılış ve Osman Hamdi*. Istanbul: Erol Kerim Aksoy Kültür, Eğitim, Spor ve Sağlık Vakfı Yayınları, 1995.

Edhem, Halil. *Elvah-ı Nakşiye Koleksiyonu*. Istanbul: Milliyet Yayınları, 1970.

Ergün, Mustafa and Tayyip Duman. "19. Yüzyılda Osmanlı Askerî Okullarının Ders Programları ve Ders Kitapları." *Yeni Türkiye* 7 (1996): 494–511.

Germaner, Semra, and Zeynep İnankur. *Constantinople and the Orientalists*. Istanbul: Türkiye İş Bankası Kültür Yayınları, 2008.

MacFarlane, Charles. *Kismet or The Doom of Turkey*. London: Thomas Bosworth, 1853.

Mehmed Es'ad. *Mir'ât-ı Mühendis-Hâne-i Berrî-i Hümâyûn*. Edited by Sadık Erdem. Istanbul: İstanbul Teknik Üniversitesi Bilim ve Teknoloji Tarihi Araştırma Merkezi, 1986.

Sinanlar, Seza. "Pera'da Resim Üretim Ortamı 1844–1916." PhD diss., İstanbul Teknik Universitesi, Istanbul, 2008.

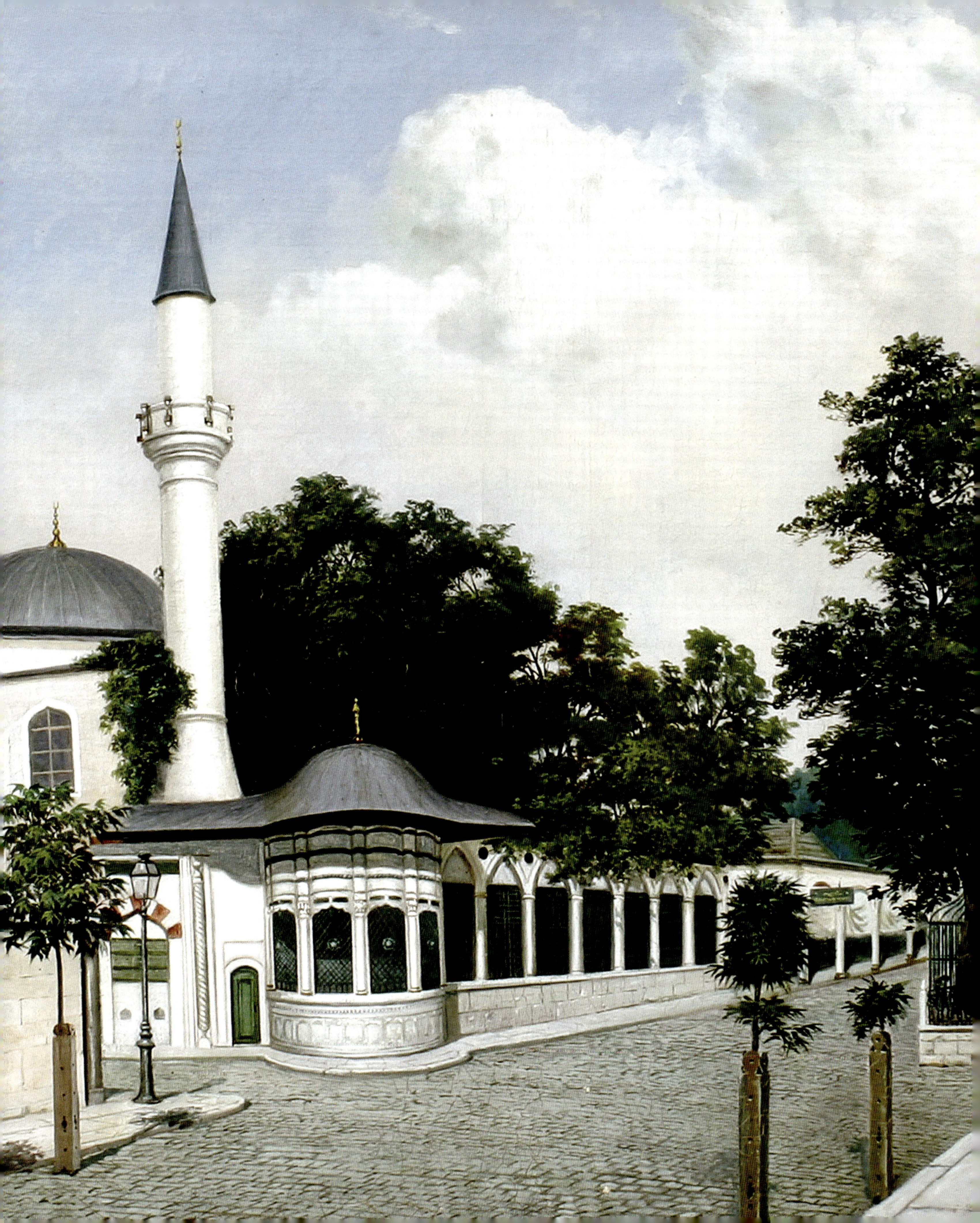

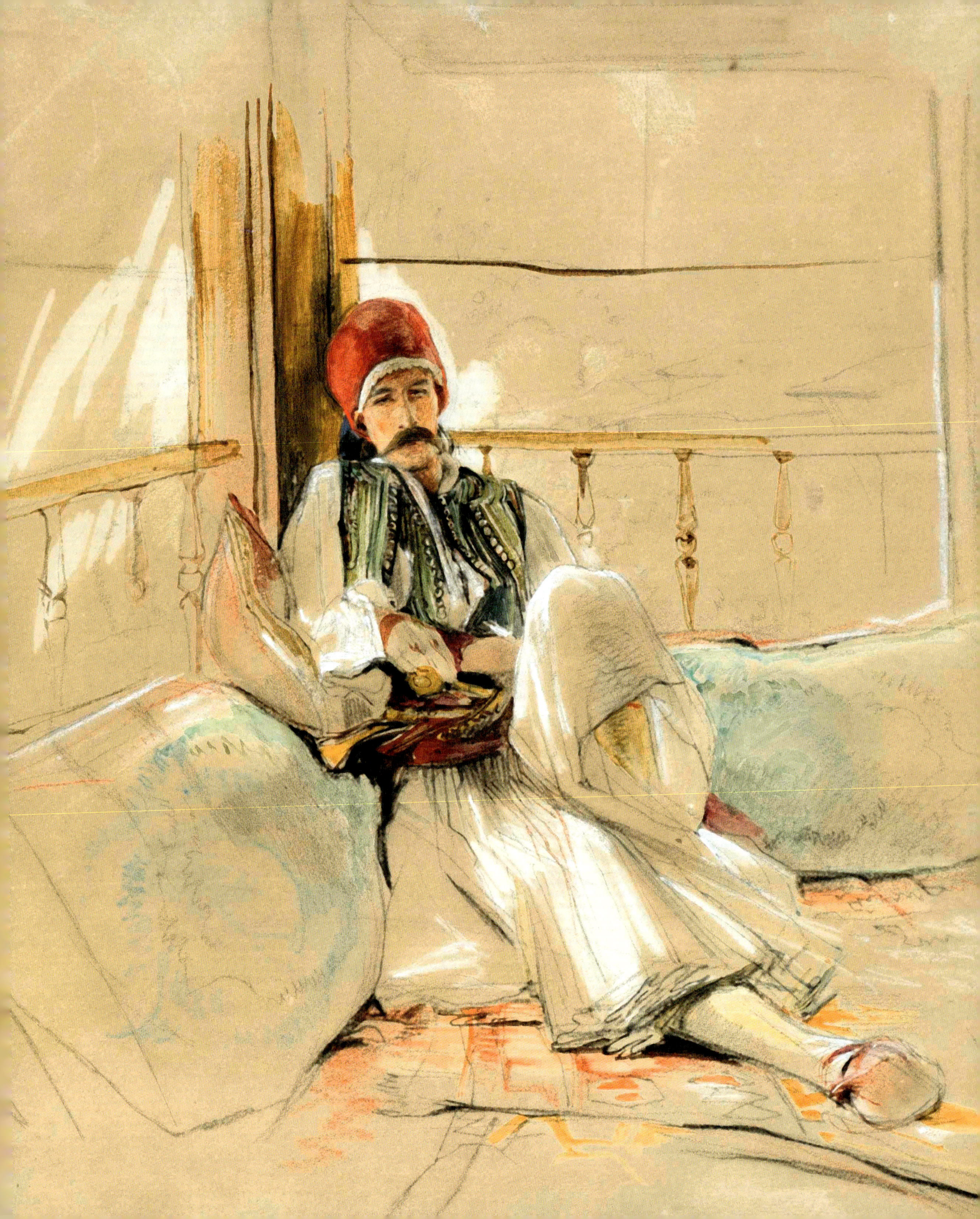

XVII

Orientalism and Aestheticism[1]

Tim Barringer

In this chapter I draw attention to a web of links between two aspects of British nineteenth-century painting that art history has tended, until recently, to consider in isolation from each other. Both Orientalism and Aestheticism in nineteenth-century British art have been the subject of intensive and sophisticated scholarly interest in recent years.[2] Yet these two literatures have remained largely separate. The category of Orientalist painting, unlike that of Aestheticism, is defined, ultimately, by its subject matter, which must refer in some direct or indirect way to that amorphous geographical, cultural or imaginary entity, "the East." Aestheticism, by contrast, has been considered mainly as a stylistic movement in the decorative arts and interior design, as well, more recently, a formative avant-garde intervention in the development of modern art.

Orientalist painting has in recent years taken its place among a range of writings and cultural practices defined as "Orientalism" in the pioneering scholarship of Edward Said.[3] Said's work, as well as the Orientalist texts and positions he identified, have been critiqued from a range of viewpoints, feminist and post-colonial principal among them. While the visual featured only minimally in Said's work, since the mid-1980s art historians have played a lively role in debates about Orientalism.[4] Within this lively international, even global, debate about Orientalism, the character of British Orientalist art was long regarded as being that of a hard-won realism, whose precision of representation was based on periods of travel and close study, in specific contrast to the more extravagantly inventive work of continental painters of Eastern subjects. This characterization has its roots in the nineteenth century. As Nicholas Tromans writes in the introduction to *The Lure of the East* (2008), an exhibition which focused on the artist as eye-witness, "British Orientalist imagery ... was accepted in its own day as a particularly truthful form of art, and, inasmuch as it disavowed flagrant fantasy, differed from some of the most well-known examples of the French variety of Orientalist painting."[5] Recent scholarship has begun to trouble this easy identification of British painters with an ethnographic and topographical realism, drawing attention to the contrivance implicit in various forms of "reality effect" employed, and exploring the sophisticated "visual experiments" and elements of fantasy and construction enshrined in Orientalist work.[6] Mary Roberts has evidenced a shift from "the ethnographic to the aestheticist" in the work of a major British Orientalist painter,[7] while Ruth Yeazell insists that, despite the "intensity of observation" experienced by the critic John Ruskin who admired the precision of detail in a harem scene of this period, the work "remains in a fundamental sense a harem of the mind."[8] However, by focusing the work of British painters who traveled in the Middle East, in relation to texts such as Edward William Lane's *An Account of the Manners and Customs of the Modern Egyptians*,[9] the curators of the 2008 exhibition *The Lure of the East* ultimately reinstated the realist paradigm of Orientalism. The argument of the exhibition became enmeshed in paradox when discussing artists like David Roberts, David Wilkie and William Holman Hunt who "headed to the Orient, a place which as we have suggested existed primarily as an artistic category, to redeem the value of their own art as the potential communicator of absolute truth."[10] Orientalist painting has become a field in which any clear distinction drawn between the real and the imaginary, between scientific observation and artistic interpretation has been revealed to be chimerical.

While any simple identification of Orientalism as a form of realism is under threat, the art of the Aesthetic Movement rests more securely under a completely different rubric. Aestheticism is almost invariably—and, I think, correctly—characterized by its pursuit of "Art for Art's Sake." Style trumps substance, and beauty outweighs meaning as the most desirable character of a work of art. Paintings—or works in any other visual medium, from wallpaper to photography—should aim, so Aestheticism insists, to affect the viewer in the same way that music affects the listener—speaking to the senses through abstract and formal means, rather than through narrative or descriptive content. There could hardly be a stronger contrast to Orientalism's assemblage of ethnographic materials collected through fieldwork to allow the creation of a visually credible—if not necessarily a true—picture of the "East."

Unlike Orientalism, Aestheticist art, as currently understood, seems to stand apart from the worlds of politics and ideology[11]—fields which are, however, routinely invoked in discussions of the work of contemporary painters such as William Powell Frith or the Pre-Raphaelite works of the 1850s.[12] As Elizabeth Prettejohn explains at the opening of her magisterial study *Art for Art's Sake: Aestheticism in Victorian Painting*, the Aesthete confronted "the problem of what art might be, if it is not for the sake of anything else."[13] For the Aesthetic painter, the solution to this problem lay in the creation of beautiful works in the studio—a practice which ostensibly stands in strong contrast to the years of fieldwork and a close study of the latest anthropological handbooks and treatises which characterized the work of prominent British Orientalist painters such as William Holman Hunt.[14]

In this chapter, by comparing two artists—nominally an "Orientalist" and an "Aesthete"—I explore areas of overlap and interpenetration of these two categories. I examine the particular codings of masculine artistic identity associated with each of these formulations and the forms of self-fashioning and self-portrayal employed by each. And I move on, finally, to suggest that the two genres are so imbricated in each other, that no clear distinction can be drawn between them.[15]

* * *

Let us, then, imagine two Victorian painters, both of them successful men whose work is widely known and exhibited. One is an Orientalist—let's for the moment call him "J.," renowned among his contemporaries for the detail and veracity of his portrayals of the Islamic world, based on years of study in Cairo; the other, an Aestheticist, one of the paramount followers of "Art for Art's Sake" in the Kensington art scene of the 1860s—let us call him "F.," famed for his lyric and luscious evocations of the classical world, of Greek maidens at play in the pristine light of the dawn of civilization and of beautiful women sensuously posed in works completely free of narrative content. J's compositions are filled with detail, insistent upon their origins in observations; F.'s are pure contrivances of the studio; classical references, draperies, lighting and all, artworks born of art.

Having worked his way up from relatively humble circumstances as the son of an engraver, J. soon turns to elaborate figure subjects in watercolor, traveling to Spain and then Italy in search of picturesque types and characteristic scenes, especially, of Catholic life. In *Easter Day at Rome: Pilgrims and Peasants,* 1840, he expressed an ethnographic fascination for the chaotic scene in which Neapolitan *lazzaroni* and pious Catholics awaited the blessing of the Pope, seen as if with the disinterested fascination of a colonial official watching some inexplicable gathering of the natives, a corroboree or palaver.[16] In 1840, J. traveled to Corfu, where he made a watercolor study of *A Corfiot Warrior Reclining* (Fig. 17.1; the pose will be significant for us shortly),[17] then to Athens and Smyrna, and finally alighted in Constantinople, where he remained for a year, making careful studies of the interior of Ayasofia and of figures in the markets and streets during 1840–41. After a year, J. moved to Egypt and took up residence in Cairo, effectively disappearing from sight in Britain. Having entered Egypt as a tourist, he remained there under cover, shedding his old identity. He did not exhibit a single work between 1841 and 1850, when *The Hareem* was shown at the Old Watercolour Society.[18] In the meantime, he attained considerable fame in Egypt. The two worlds came together in a celebrated account published in William Makepeace Thackeray's humorous travel essay, *Notes of a Journey from Cornhill to Grand Cairo*, published in 1846. Begun as five short contributions to *Punch*, in book form this became one of Thackeray's most popular literary works. In its final pages, Thackeray provided an account of a visit with his friend, the very artist I have been describing, which took place in Cairo in 1844, whom he refers to only as "J–." To his great surprise, the author found the artist living "like a languid Lotus-eater, a dreamy, hazy, tobaccofied life." J– lived "far away from the haunts of European civilization" and there the two partook of delicious cucumbers and "yellow smoking pilaffs" made by an Egyptian cook. Thackeray's description, as Mary Roberts has noted, employs a tactic of "slippage between fantasy and realist observation" which "ensures that contemporary Cairo becomes synonymous with the Arabian Nights fantasy"—a similar rhetorical strategy to that employed visually in Lewis's paintings.[19] Most memorable, however, was Thackeray's mystified description of J– himself:

> A man—in a long yellow gown, with a long beard somewhat tinged with gray, with his head shaved, and wearing on it first a white wadded cotton nightcap, second, a red tarboosh—made his appearance and welcomed me cordially. It was some time, as the Americans say, before I could "realise" the semillant J–of old times. He shuffled off his outer slippers before he curled up on the divan

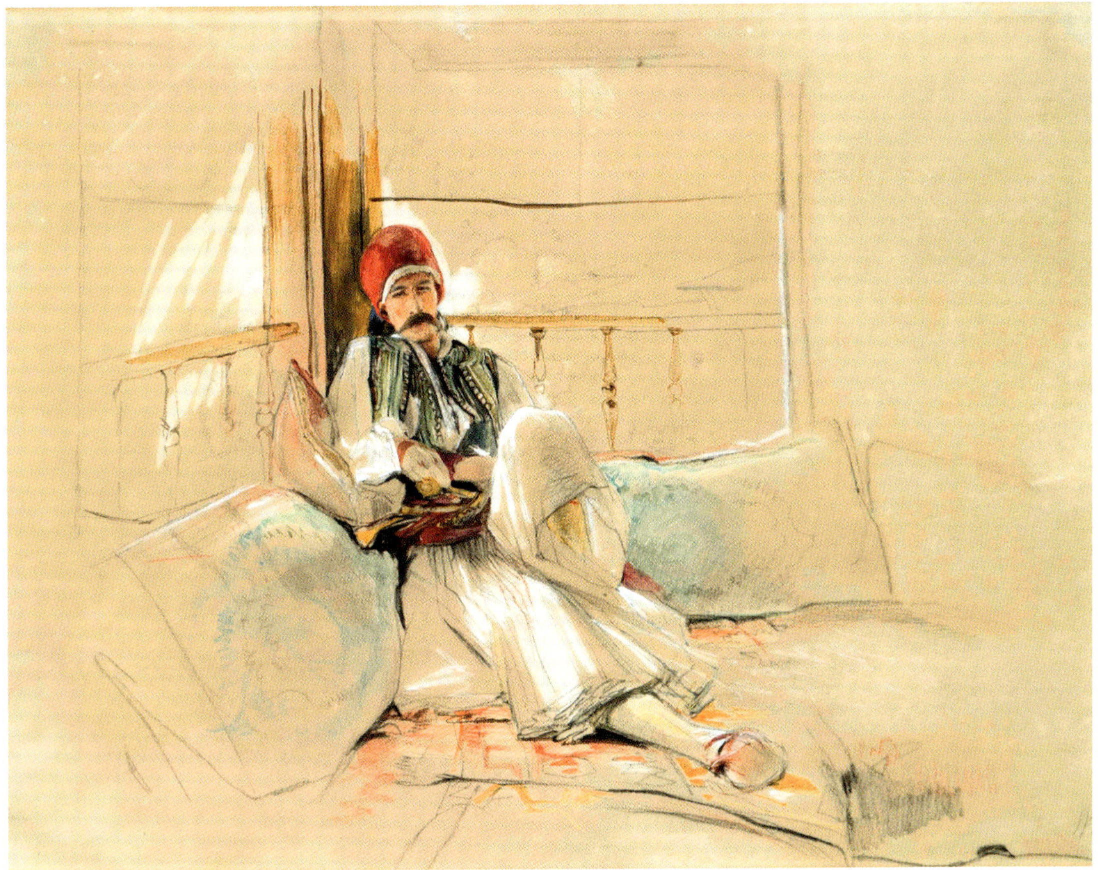

Figure 17.1 *A Corfiot Warrior Reclining*, John Frederick Lewis (1804–1876), 1840, watercolor, Photographic permission courtesy of Yanni Petsopoulos.

beside me. He clapped his hands, and languidly called "Mustapha". Mustapha came with more lights, pipes, and coffee; and then we fell to talking about London, and I gave him the last news of the comrades in that dear city. As we talked, his Oriental coolness and languor gave way to British cordiality; he was the most amusing companion of the –– club once more. He has adopted himself outwardly, however, to the Oriental life. When he goes abroad he rides a gray horse with red housings, and has two servants to walk beside him. He wears a very handsome, grave costume of dark blue, consisting of an embroidered jacket and gaiters, and a pair of trousers, which would make a set of dresses for an English family. His beard curls nobly over his chest, his Damascus scimitar on his thigh. His red cap gives him a venerable and Bey-like appearance .... We ... sat smoking in solemn divan.[20]

Recent scholarship has suggested that this deceptive persona—a facade of "Oriental" coolness and languor—can be discerned in a painting now revealed as hidden self-portrait of J. *In the Bezestein, El Khan Kalil, Cairo (The Carpet Seller)* (Fig. 17.2) offers up a masquerade in which J. appears as a Cairene tradesman, staring inscrutably from among the materials of his trade, in a tour-de-force of illusionistic realism.[21] It was this kind of work which won J. the compliment from his fellow Orientalist painter Edward Lear "perfect as representations of real scenes & people".[22] Thackeray's description of his friend reveals two layers; the surface of "Oriental" languor, luxury and inaction—a body swathed in enough cloth to make a set of dresses for a family of English women; and underneath it, the real clubman, the essence of "British cordiality." It is as if Edward Said's East and West were mapped on to the same body, a palimpsest of cultural tropes, a case-study in cultural cross-dressing. Was J., then, a hearty undercover agent of British imperialism, or had he truly abandoned his heritage and—in the argot of the day—"gone native"? Was he an Aesthete, living for the exquisite sensation of the moment, the beauty of his yellow and blue-grey gowns, the taste of "delicate cucumbers;" or did he retain the ironic detachment of the Orientalist scholar and literary clubman? And what are the implications of these choices about artistic identity, self-fashioning and masculinity for our understanding of his art? What is J. himself, the fabricator of pictures—like his avatar, the carpet seller—offering us? Does he proffer the unvarnished truth about life in Egypt, or a luxurious fabrication, a luminous canvas woven together from the choicest cloth to deceive us, but delight our senses?

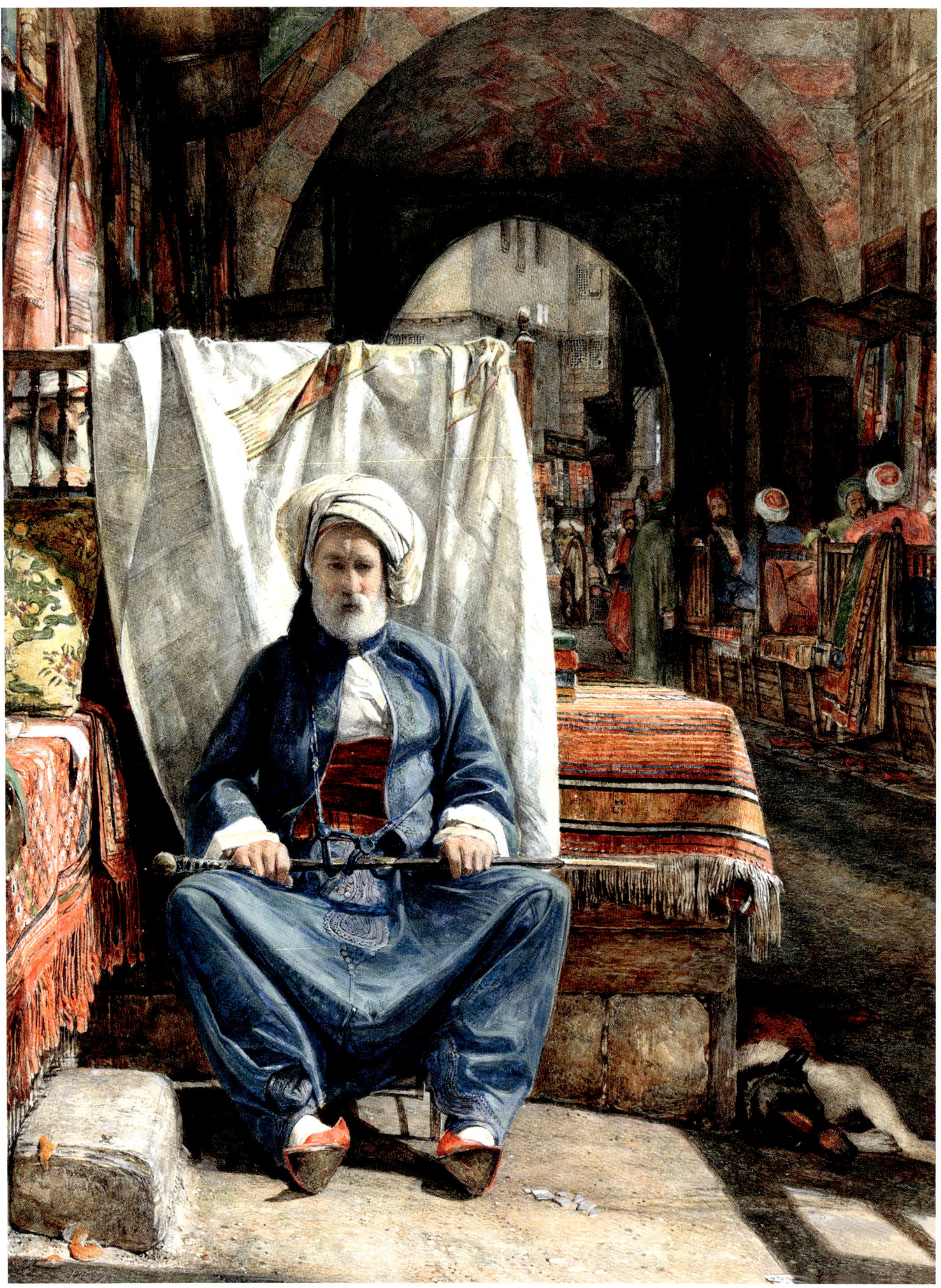

Figure 17.2 *In the Bezestein, El Khan Kalil, Cairo (The Carpet Seller)*, John Frederick Lewis (1804–1876), 1860, watercolor and bodycolor on paper, Blackburn Museum and Art Gallery, Blackburn.

Let's turn now to "F." The son of a wealthy doctor, F.'s childhood was marked by frequent travels throughout Europe. His precocious talent for art, in addition to a literary sensibility and a gift for music, marked him out from early days as an exceptional individual. His artistic training was cosmopolitan, in Munich, Frankfurt, Rome and Paris. From the start, F. seems to have projected his artistic identity in a different direction to that chosen by J., but his was no less a constructed persona. By the time he arrived in London in 1859, F. was (like J.) a dandy, a cosmopolitan Aesthete who was invited to every party. Wealthy, handsome and brilliantly successful as a painter he was accomplished in every possible regard. A caricature by J. J. Tissot presents his willowy Aesthetic body leaning on a doorframe, unable to bear the weight of the lily in his buttonhole, and seemingly unrelated to the physical task of manipulating paint on canvas.[23] Artfully composed, as if itself already a representation, F.'s body can be placed in a constellation of masculine Aesthetic types that includes the enervated knights in the work of Edward Burne-Jones; James McNeill Whistler with his cane and flash of white hair; Oscar Wilde, clad in his trademark velvet suit, and George du Maurier's fictional character de Tomkyns, of whom is written: "Steeped in Aesthetic culture, surrounded by artistic wall-papers, blue and white china, Japanese fans, medieval snuffboxes and his favourite periodicals of the 18th century, the dilettante de Tomkyns complacently boasts that he never reads a newspaper, and that the events of the outer world possess no interest for him whatsoever."[24] Here the distinction between the Aesthete and Orientalist is most finely drawn, for the Orientalist must be interested in the outer world. In some of his most personal works, F., on the other hand, sought out beauty without meaning. Bewitched by the handsome features of the Roman model Nanna Risi, he painted a series of Aesthetic paintings with meaningless titles like *A Roman Lady*, luscious studies in art for art's sake.[25] He imagined a melancholy girl somewhere in the ancient world, lost in her thoughts by the well, accompanied by the song of a bird and the plashing of the water. "I have endeavoured," wrote F., "both by colour and by flowing delicate forms, to translate to the eye something of the pleasure which the child receives through her ears."[26] His artful title, *Lieder ohne Worte*, referenced piano miniatures by Felix Mendelssohn-Bartholdy well known to the cognoscenti.[27] The past, was, at least in his early career, F.'s Orient, his space of fantasy. Where the Orientalist J. masqueraded as a carpet seller in the bazaar, rendered with scrupulous fidelity, F. imagined himself as Cimabue, in a pristine and colorful pageant of the Renaissance, in a decorative panel for the South Kensington Museum, later replicated in Salviati's glass mosaic, which bears F.'s own leonine features (Fig. 17.3).[28] In the masterly

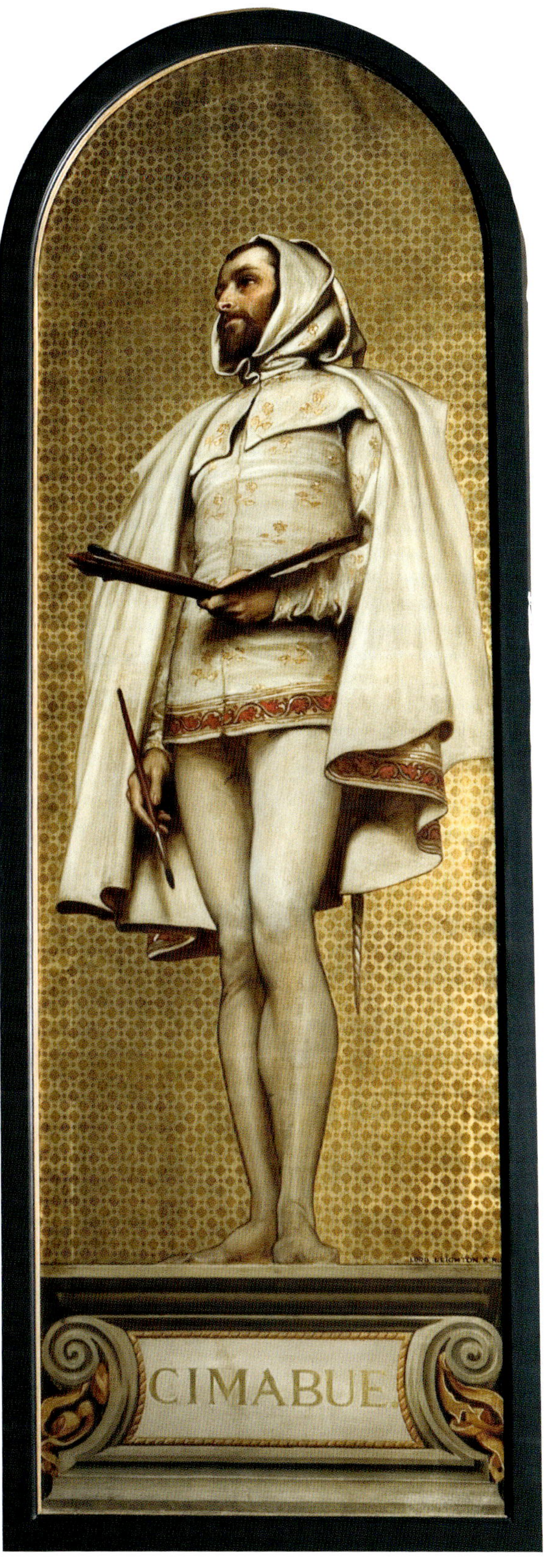

Figure 17.3 *Cimabue*, Frederic Leighton (1830–1896), 1868, oil on canvas, 264.8 x 87.6 cm. Photo © Victoria and Albert Museum, London.

processional painting *Cimabue's Celebrated Madonna is Carried through the Streets of Florence*, it is F. himself as the finely attired Cimabue who leads the boy Giotto through the streets, the Aesthete as hero.[29] We can hardly see the painting of the Madonna, although it is displayed in the illusionistic perspectival space which Cimabue and Giotto are credited with developing. Rather it is the artist's body, gloriously bedecked in white and gold, which stands at the apex of the composition. F. himself enjoyed dressing up in Renaissance costume (just as J. rejoiced in his Cairene apparel) and was photographed in this guise by David Wilkie Wynfield, creating an Aesthetic object from his own body (here, too, paralleling J.'s disguise self-portraiture in painted and photographic media).[30] This in turn he transformed back into art, offering a veiled self-portrait in *The Honeymoon*, in which figures clad in Renaissance garb play a modern piano (one of those artful games which both J. and F. enjoyed playing with their audience).[31] Yet F., the Aesthete, had no time for the reality effects that preoccupied J. the Orientalist; he felt no need to evoke with crystal clarity the details of the world evoked in his paintings, nor to ensure even a superficial coherence of historical period or geographical setting. Even when he turned his attention to the present day, as in his *Portrait of May Sartoris* of 1860, F. produced elaborately decorative works in which the artifice of picture-making overwhelmed any illusionistic quality.[32] Here, the landscape background, with its eccentrically high horizon, rears up as bands of color, breaking down into mere exquisite strokes of paint, even as it suggests a fallen tree and distant meadow. The flattened form of May Sartoris is merely a decorative black mandorla startlingly interrupted by a bolt of red.

It is time to reveal the identity of my two artists—an identity that is, in each case, as artfully constructed as it is "real." "F." is, of course Frederic Leighton, Aesthete, and later President of the Royal Academy, scholar, administrator and lion of Victorian society. Even in later years his melancholy visage can be seen only behind yet another disguise—this time the robes of the president of the Royal Academy and a self-portrait that gestures, through the inclusion of the Parthenon frieze, towards Phidias, and, through the use of the red drapery, towards his predecessor Sir Reynolds and through him to Rembrandt and to Michelangelo. His self-portrait is a palimpsest of art-historical references, but remains bereft of personal revelation.[33] This later Leighton was described by Vernon Lee as "a mixture of the Olympian Jove and a head waiter, a superb decorator and a superb piece of decoration. He paints poor pictures of the correctest idealism, of orange tawny naked women against indigo skies."[34]

Leighton's official self-portrait, made for the Uffizi Gallery in Florence, is hardly more revealing of his interior life than the carpet seller, whom I can finally reveal to be John Frederick Lewis, the "J." of Thackeray's story and the hero of any study of British Orientalist painters. For all their differences, Leighton and Lewis have much in common; both posed for photographs in fancy dress which speak to their imagined identification with their subject matter which, as I have suggested, in turn informs their paintings. Both were dandies, who embraced masquerade as a key forum for self-fashioning.[35]

When we turn to a comparison of their work, close similarities become apparent. In Lewis's *Bouquet* of 1857, as in Leighton's *Odalisque* of 1862, a single female figure, richly clad in textiles, is juxtaposed with opulent products of the natural world to form a highly decorative upright composition.[36] Leighton flirts with history painting, suggesting Zeus's encounter with Leda, but sometimes a swan is just a swan. Both women are lost in Aesthetic contemplation, passive and lacking in agency; they are both, in Said's sense, Orientalized, even though both are painted from English models. In each case, the play of light on fabric, and the beauty of the model, count for more than any fragment of narrative. This is art for art's sake.

Most revealing is a comparison of two images, each of which enshrines an elaborate act of self-fashioning. Lewis exhibited at the Royal Academy in 1873 *A Lady Receiving Visitors: The Apartment is the Mandarah, the Lower Floor of the House, Cairo* (Fig. 17.4).[37] The interior is described in painstaking detail; tiling and woodwork screens, textiles and postures, all are registered by the artist's unerring eye. A critic was so impressed with Lewis's vivid realism as to claim that "the force of effect here is so great that the picture looks stereoscopic."[38] The painting is, however, anything but a simple act of documentation. It may deliberately refer to Thackeray's by then famous description of the meeting with J– in *Cornhill to Grand Cairo*; it seems a representation of Lewis's home in Cairo, peopled with an unlikely, indeed impossible cast of characters. As Emily Weeks has noted, the room shown, a *mandarah*, was considered to be a masculine space, and was recognized as such by Lewis's friend the early Victorian authority on modern Egypt, Edward William Lane, in *An Account of the Manners and Customs of the Modern Egyptians*, published in 1836 and released in a new edition in 1871. Lewis, however, portrays it here as an explicitly *feminine* domain in which the lady of the house presides.[39] Lewis offers a startling verisimilitude of observed detail, while simultaneously—and subversively—undermining any simple sense of equivalence between the "East" and the painted image.

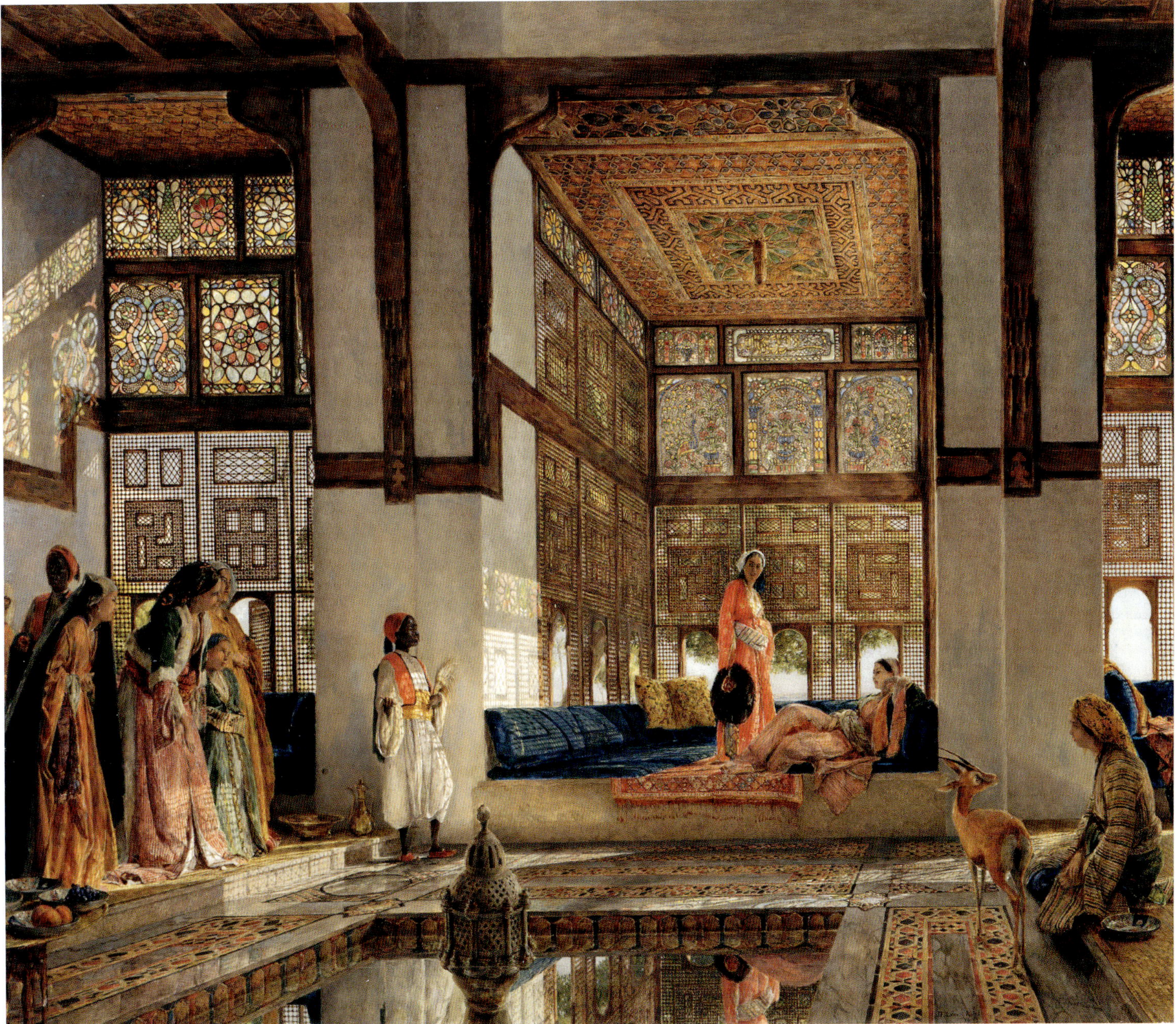

Figure 17.4 *A Lady Receiving Visitors: The Apartment is the Mandarah, the Lower Floor of the House, Cairo*, John Frederick Lewis (1804–1876), 1873, oil on panel, Yale Center for British Art, New Haven CT.

Balancing Lewis's fantastical representation of his own domestic circumstances is an actual room, the Arab Hall, which is not an imaginary structure, but a two-storey extension to his house in Kensington and still survives (Fig. 17.5).[40] The building reflects Leighton's fascination, like Lewis's, with turned-wood screens and with the play of light on blue ceramic tiles. And at this point I have to acknowledge that Leighton can be described as an Orientalist as well as an Aesthete, since after 1857 he traveled to Algiers, Constantinople, Aswan and Damascus—considerable journeys in the nineteenth century—in search of pictorial materials. Partly, he was searching for the Orient of the classical past which his work had already so vividly evoked—his photographs suggest an archeological approach—but he was also ethnographically fascinated, and evidently erotically gripped, by the range of human bodies he encountered on these travels. His sketchbooks include studies of virtually anyone who would sit for him, but it is in his letters that the fascination of the East is clearest: writing from Algiers to his mother in 1857 he waxed lyrical:

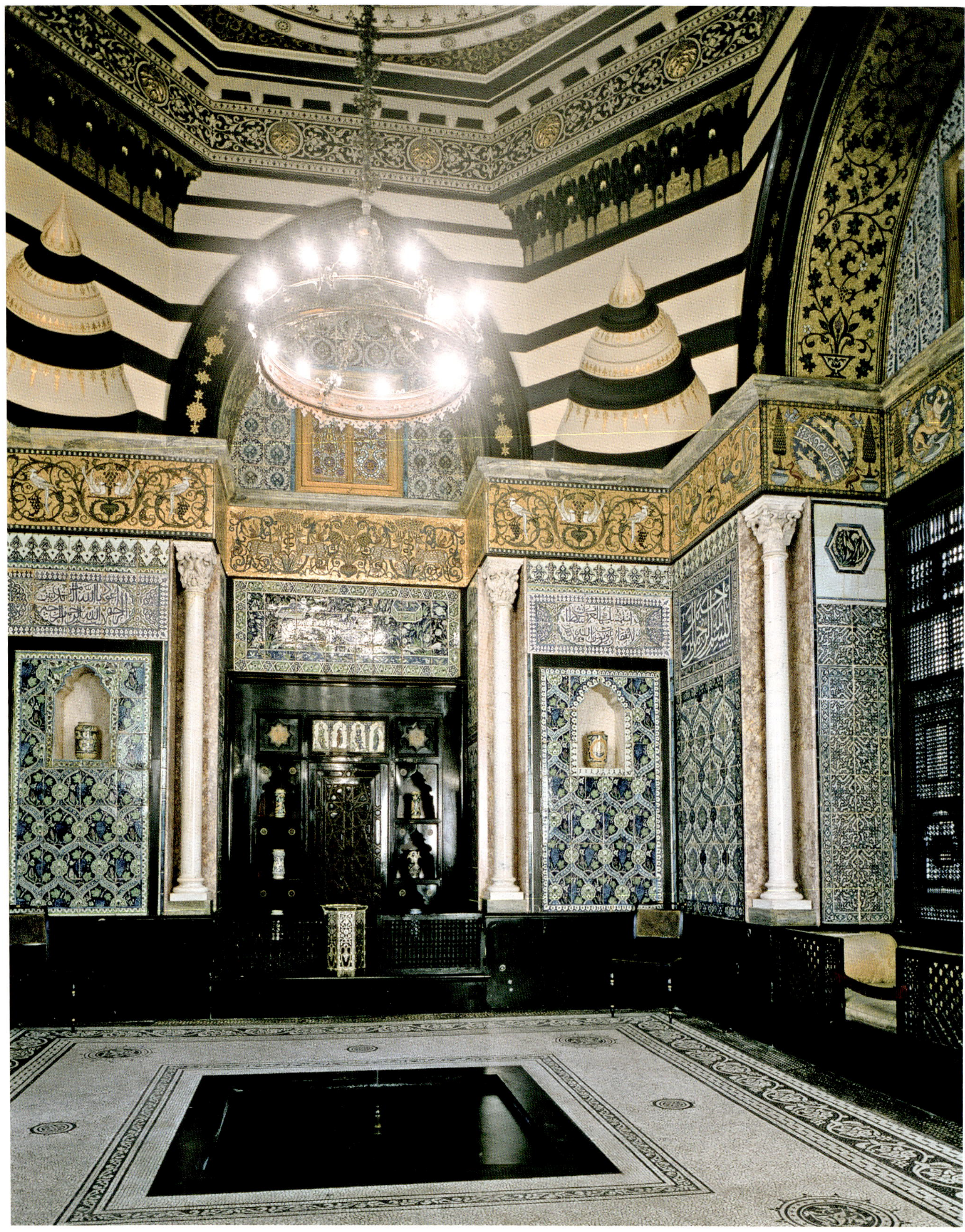

Figure 17.5 View of the Arab Hall with tiles by William de Morgan (1839–1917) and frieze by Walter Crane (1845–1915). Leighton House Museum, Kensington & Chelsea, London, UK.

> Fancy, in the midst of all this gleaming white, the gorgeous effect produced by the varied colours of oriental costumes and complexion: the copper-coloured Arabs, the sallow Jews, the ebony negroes, and the frequent display of every kind of fruit—crimson tomatoes and purple aubergines, emerald and golden melons, glowing oranges, luminous green grapes, and to relieve the blaze of ardent colour, the tender ivory tones of the tube rose and the soft milk-white jasmine.[41]

Encoded within this description are the ethnological and racial assumptions and hierarchies of the era. But Leighton turns all the world into art; and whether he is looking at an aubergine or what he calls a "negro," it is the formal and Aesthetic values rather than the political and ethnographic which come to the fore. It may be this that accounts for his lack of concern with even the most basic tenets of Islamic religious practices in his exquisite essay in tonality, *Interior of the Grand Mosque of Damascus* of 1873–75.[42] Leighton was happy to absorb aspects of Orientalism into his Aestheticist practice. Like Whistler's Japanese fans and plates, Leighton vaguely suggested the East with studio props such as musical instruments. In *Study: At a Reading Desk*, Leighton depicts an Ottoman Qur'an stand, upon which an English girl—modeled by the child actress Connie Gilchrist—has placed what is surely a secular illustrated book, and reads from it attentively.[43]

A more significant fusion occurred while Leighton was at work on the largest and most ambitious of his later paintings, the two thirty-three foot lunettes for the South Kensington Museum, *The Arts of Industry as Applied to War and to Peace*. Intended as his contribution to the morally uplifting genre of history painting, these works, hymns to the commodity in Henry Cole's great temple to industry (which would later be renamed the V&A), the frescoes perhaps inevitably became Aestheticist meditations on physical beauty. *The Arts of Industry as applied to Peace* is ostensibly set in Leighton's other Orient, classical Greece, but at its center is a group of women trying on clothes and jewelry, the wealthy but powerless consumers of the ancient world. What Leighton really shows us, however, is Orientalism's version of the feminine sphere, the harem, the epitome of luxury and lazy, eroticized physical pleasure, as explored so brilliantly by John Frederick Lewis. Leighton made a large number of sketches for this work, and it seems hardly surprising that, returning to these sketches in 1881, he paraphrased the central group, in which a woman (as Mary Roberts puts it) is "frozen in a moment of self-absorbed contemplation," in one of his finest Orientalist paintings, *The Light of the Harem*.[44] History painting, Aestheticism and Orientalism are fused into a single work, simultaneously public and private, moralistic and amoral, sanitized and eroticized. It is amusing, perhaps, to reflect that there is "a masculine fantasy of the harem" only feet from the director's office at the V&A.

Leighton's Arab Hall, designed by George Aitchison, was built in the late 1870s as a means to display the superb collection of ceramic tiles, mainly from Damascus, amassed by Leighton through the 1860s and 1870s. Leighton prized a thirteenth-century Star Tile from Iran and sixteenth-century Iznik tiles, some of them purchased for him by that textbook exemplar of the Saidian Orientalist, Sir Richard Burton, whose portrait—with the prominent scar—Leighton painted between 1872 and 1875.[45] Based on a banqueting room at the Moorish palace of La Zisa in Palermo, Sicily, though also clearly influenced by mosque architecture, the Arab Hall's interior is a unique meeting of Orientalism and Aestheticism. The room is Orientalist in the sources of its design and in the collections it displays; yet it is Aestheticist in function, since it has no function. It was intended as a thing of beauty. Leighton seems to have had no qualms about mixing sacred and secular, or about incorporating this panel of verses from the Qur'an, in a purely secular decorative scheme.[46] Leighton, reclining on a divan in the silk room upstairs, could peer through a *mashrabiya* he had purchased from a mosque in Cairo, to the Arab Hall beyond, and feast on the exquisite visual sensations it produced. Sometimes the sensory banquet was spiced even further by the sound of Joseph Joachim, positioned in the studio beyond, playing Bach's solo partitas on the violin.

Languishing in this position, Leighton had, of course, achieved a perfect fusion of Aestheticism and Orientalism. He had not adopted the viewpoint of the principled Western observer, the Archimedean figure of judgment wielding colonial anthropology or Christian theology as potential instruments of oppression, in the manner of William Holman Hunt. Rather, he, like Lewis, had assumed the position of the "languid Lotos-eater,"—a figure from Lewis's repertoire, indeed, but not the hyper-masculine, but temporarily idle, soldier in Corfu, nor the passive carpet seller of Cairo who is in reality a hardworking Orientalist painter in disguise. No: Leighton's true double can be found in *A Frank Encampment*, 1856 (Fig. 17.6), which depicts an encounter between Frederick William Robert Stewart, Viscount Castlereagh, later fourth Marquess of Londonderry and Sheikh Hussein of "Gebel Tor" (Mount Sinai). Reversing the usual Orientalist tropes, Lewis's masterpiece sets the supine, spent force of the British aristocrat against the monumental presence of the

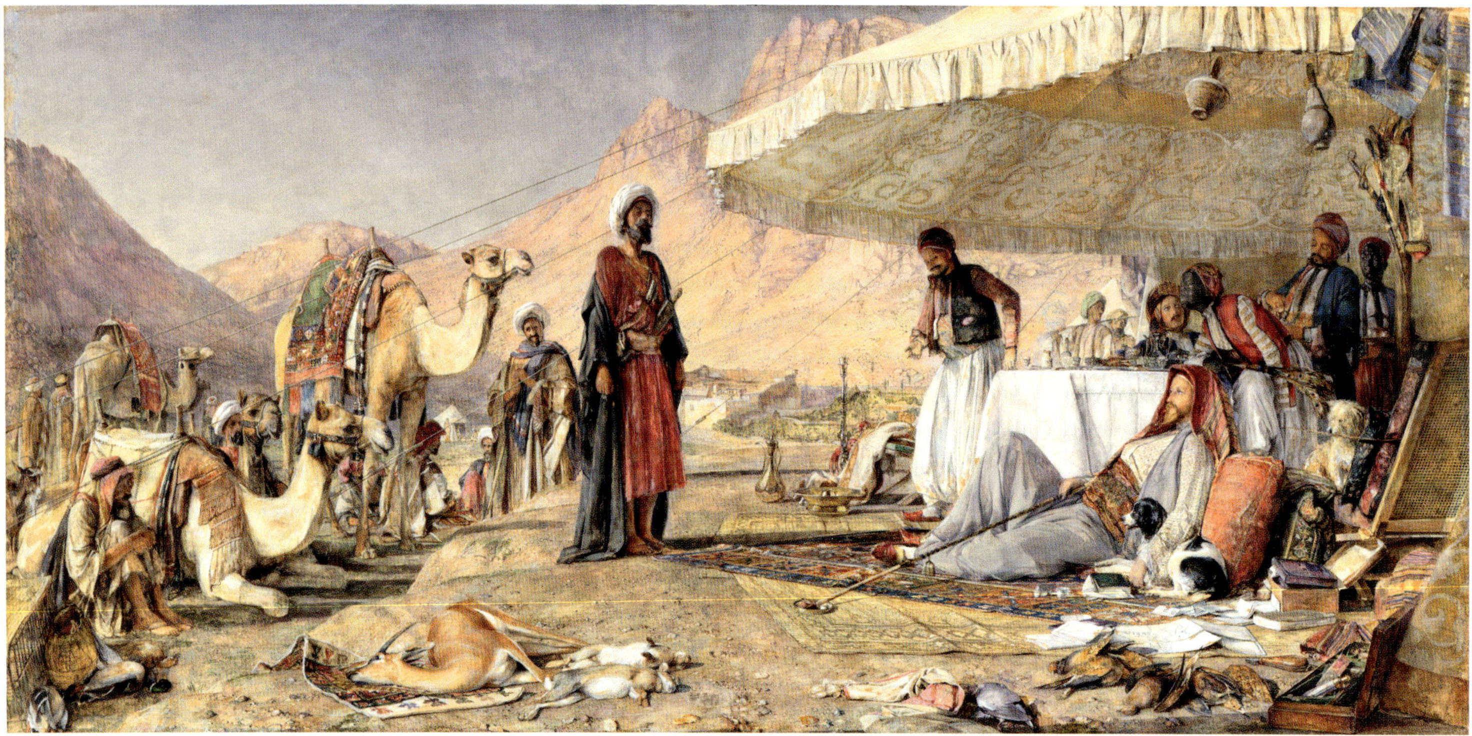

Figure 17.6 *A Frank Encampment in the Desert of Mount Sinai, 1842*, John Frederick Lewis (1804–1876), 1856, watercolor and body color on paper, Yale Center for British Art, New Haven CT.

Sheikh. In the figure of Castlereagh—his hookah lit and all the impedimenta of leisure strewn around him—we have finally an image of Aesthete and Orientalist in a single decadent body. Apparently uninterested in the fate of those around him, Castlereagh's feminized figure as presented here may be taken as an emblem of the dangers of art for art's sake—of the epicurean's pursuit of pleasures at all costs. John Frederick Lewis's refusal to offer simple commentaries, or to proffer oversimplified binaries of East and West is very clearly seen in this painting, in which the imperialist is Orientalized and Aestheticized, while the "East" is embodied in statuesque, dominant form. Lewis, the greatest British Orientalist painter, offered up Orientalist art as a possible site of resistance against empire and its cultural assumptions. The Aesthete Frederic Leighton, by contrast, casually ignored the cultural and political implications of his own work, mining (a verb worthy of Cecil Rhodes) the East as he did the West for luxurious sensations whatever the cost. By failing to notice the malignant operations of empire, Aesthetes became complicit in its ideologies.

Notes

1 This text was written for verbal delivery and has resisted attempts to transform it into a more respectable scholarly form. Intended as a commentary or provocation, it relies nonetheless on the work of my former doctoral student Emily Weeks, who, I gratefully acknowledge, has taught me much about John Frederick Lewis. Echoes of the cadence of Emily's writing, as well as her sharp analytical mind, can be discerned in this essay. Her dissertation, published articles and forthcoming book constitute a major revision of our thinking on this artist, and a significant intervention in the study of Orientalism. See Emily M. Weeks, "The 'Reality Effect': The Orientalist Paintings of John Frederick Lewis (1805–1876)," (PhD diss., Yale University, 2005), and her other works listed below. Keenly awaited is her forthcoming book *Cultures Crossed: John Frederick Lewis and the Art of Orientalist Painting* (Yale University Press).

2 Significant recent contributions to the study of British Orientalist painting include, *inter alia*, John Sweetman, *The Oriental Obsession: Islamic Inspiration in British and American Arts an Architecture, 1500–1920* (Cambridge: Cambridge University Press, 1988); Joan del Plato, *From Slave Market to Paradise: The Harem Pictures of John Frederick Lewis and their Tradition* (Ann Arbor: University Microfilms International, 1987); Reina Lewis, *Gendering Orientalism: Race, Femininity and Representation* (London: Routledge, 1996); Ruth Bernard Yeazell, *Harems of the Mind: Passages of Western Art and Literature* (New Haven: Yale University Press, 2000); Joan del Plato, *Multiple Wives, Multiple Pleasures: Representing the Harem, 1800–1875* (Cranbury, Ontario: Associated University Presses, 2002); Reina Lewis, *Rethinking Orientalism: Women, Travel and the Ottoman Harem* (London: I. B. Tauris, 2004); Briony Llewellyn and

Charles Newton, "John Frederick Lewis: 'In Knowledge of the Orientals Quite One of Themselves,'" in *Interpreting the Orient: Travellers in Egypt and the Near East*, ed. Paul and Janet Starkey (Reading UK: Ithaca Press, 2001), 35–50; Mary Roberts, *Intimate Outsiders: The Harem in Ottoman and Orientalist Art and Travel Literature* (Durham NC: Duke University Press, 2007); Nicholas Tromans, ed., *The Lure of the East: British Orientalist Painting* (London: Tate, 2008).

On Aestheticism, see Robin Spencer, *The Aesthetic Movement: Theory and Practice* (London: Studio Vista, 1972); Elizabeth Prettejohn, ed., *After the Pre-Raphaelites: Art and Aestheticism in Victorian England* (New Brunswick, NJ: Rutgers University Press, 1999); Elizabeth Prettejohn, *Art for Art's Sake: Aestheticism in Victorian Painting* (New Haven and London: Yale University Press for The Paul Mellon Centre for Studies in British Art, 2007).

3 Edward Said, *Orientalism* (New York: Pantheon, 1978); Edward Said, *Culture and Imperialism* (New York: Knopf, 1993).

4 Only a small selection can be noted here: Linda Nochlin, "The Imaginary Orient" (1983) reprinted in L. Nochlin, *The Politics of Vision* (London: Thames and Hudson, 1991), 33–59; John M. Mackenzie, *Orientalism: History: Theory and the Arts* (Manchester: Manchester University Press, 1995); Julie F. Codell and Dianne Sachko Macleod, eds., *Orientalism Transposed: The Impact of the Colonies on British Culture* (Aldershot: Ashgate, 1998); Todd Porterfield, *The Allure of Empire: Art in the Service of French Imperialism, 1798–1836* (Princeton, NJ: Princeton University Press, 1998); Jill Beaulieu and Mary Roberts, eds., *Orientalism's Interlocutors: Painting, Architecture, Photography* (Durham: Duke University Press, 2002); Roger Benjamin, *Orientalist Aesthetics: Art, Colonialism, and French North Africa, 1880–1930* (Berkeley: University of California Press, 2003); Jocelyn Hackforth-Jones and Mary Roberts, eds., *Edges of Empire: Orientalism and Visual Culture* (Oxford: Blackwell, 2005); Holly Edwards, ed., *Noble Dreams, Wicked Pleasures: Orientalism in America, 1870–1930* (Princeton: Princeton University Press in association with the Sterling and Francine Clark Art Institute, 2000); Tim Barringer, Geoff Quilley and Douglas Fordham, eds., *Art and the British Empire* (Manchester: Manchester University Press, 2007), in addition to the works cited in note 2 above.

5 Nicholas Tromans, "Introduction: British Orientalist Painting" in Nicholas Tromans, ed., *The Lure of the East: British Orientalist Painting* (London: Tate, 2008), 10.

6 See Weeks, "The 'Reality Effect'"; Roberts, *Intimate Outsiders*, 39. See also Joan del Plato's comments on "Lewis and the Aesthetic Movement, 1860–76," in del Plato *From Slave Market to Paradise*, 348–50, though del Plato's characterization of the Muslim world as a "primitive culture" (349) seriously misunderstands Lewis's relationship to his surroundings in Cairo.

7 Roberts, *Intimate Outsiders*, 39.

8 Yeazell, *Harems of the Mind*, 225.

9 Edward William Lane, *An Account of the Manners and Customs of the Modern Egyptians*, written in Egypt during the years 1833–34 and 35 (2 vols, London: Charles Knight, 1836).

10 Tromans, "Introduction," *Lure of the East*, 14.

11 A significant rejoinder to this assumption can be found in Diana Maltz, *British Aestheticism and the Urban Working Classes, 1870–1900: Beauty for the People* (Basingstoke: Palgrave Macmillan, 2006).

12 See for example Mary Cowling, *The Artist as Anthropologist: the Representation of Type and Character in Victorian Art* (Cambridge: Cambridge University Press, 1989): Mark Bills and Vivien Knight, *William Powell Frith: Painting the Victorian Age* (New Haven: Yale University Press, 2006); Tim Barringer, *Men at Work: Art and Labour in Victorian Britain* (New Haven and London: Yale University Press, 2005).

13 Prettejohn, *Art for Art's Sake*, 2.

14 On Hunt and Orientalism see Marcia Pointon, "Holman Hunt and the Holy Land: The Artist as Ethnographer," in *Pre-Raphaelites Re-Viewed*, ed. M. Pointon (Manchester: Manchester University Press, 1989), 22–44; Tim Barringer, *Reading the Pre-Raphaelites* (New Haven: Yale University Press, 1999), 118–33; Francesca Vanke Altman, "William Holman Hunt, Race and Orientalism," in *Worldwide Pre-Raphaelitism*, ed. Thomas J. Tobin (Albany: State University of New York Press, 2004), 45–68.

15 An important early exploration of this topic can be found in Kenneth Bendiner, "Albert Moore and John Frederick Lewis," *Arts Magazine* (February 5, 1980): 76–79.

16 John Frederick Lewis, *Easter Day at Rome: Pilgrims and Peasants*, 1840, watercolor and bodycolor on paper, Northampton, England: Northampton Central Museum and Art Gallery.

17 John Frederick Lewis, *A Corfiot Warrior Reclining*, 1840, pencil, color chalk, watercolor with body color on paper. Private Collection. My thanks to Emily Weeks for sharing her catalog entry on this drawing.

18 John Frederick Lewis, *The Hhareem*, 1850, watercolor, Private Collection. See Tromans, *The Lure of the East*, 132.

19 Roberts, *Intimate Outsiders*, 22.

20 William Makepeace Thackeray, *Notes of a Journey from Cornhill to Grand Cairo* [1846] (London: Smith Elder, 1869), 506–7.

21 John Frederick Lewis, *In the Bezestein, El Khan Kalil, Cairo (The Carpet Seller)*, 1860, watercolor, Blackburn, Lancashire: Blackburn Museum and Art Gallery. See Tromans, *The Lure of the East*, 68.

22 Edward Lear to J. F. Lewis, June 22, 1875, quoted in Richard Green and Michael Lewis, *John Frederick Lewis R.A.: Painter of Desert and Harem* (Guildford: Guildford House Gallery, 1977), 10. See also Yeazell, *Harems of the Mind*, 225.

23 J. J. Tissot, *Mr Frederic Leighton, A.R.A.*, 1872, watercolor and bodycolor on paper, London: Museum of London. Published as a lithograph, titled "A Sacrifice to the Graces," *Vanity Fair*, June 29, 1872.

24 George du Maurier, "Intellectual Epicures," *Punch* 60 (1876): 33.

25 Frederic Leighton, *A Roman Lady*, 1858–59, oil on canvas, Philadelphia: Philadelphia Museum of Art.

26 Frederic Leighton to Edward von Steinle, April 30, 1861, quoted in Stephen Jones, et al., *Frederic Leighton 1830–1896* (London: Royal Academy of Arts, 1996), 122.

27 Frederic Leighton, *Lieder ohne Worte*, 1860–61, oil on canvas, London: Tate.

28 Frederic Leighton, *Cimabue*, 1863–64, oil on canvas, London: Victoria and Albert Museum. See Tim Barringer, "The Leighton Gallery at the V&A," *Apollo* (February 1996): 59.

29 Frederic Leighton, *Cimabue's Celebrated Madonna is Carried in Procession through the Streets of Florence*; in front of the Madonna, and crowned with laurels, walks Cimabue himself; with his pupil Giotto; behind it Arnolfo di Lapo, Gaddo Gaddi, Andrea Tafi, Niccola Pisano, Buffalmacco, and Simone Memmi; in the corner Dante, 1854–55, oil on canvas, London: Royal Collection (on loan to the National Gallery).

30 See Juliet Hacking, *Princes of Victorian Bohemia: Photographs by David Wilkie Wynfield* (London: National Portrait Gallery, 2000), 77, 79.

31 Frederic Leighton, *The Honeymoon*, 1864, Private Collection.

32 Frederic Leighton, *Portrait of May Sartoris*, c. 1860, oil on canvas, Fort Worth: Kimbell Art Gallery.

33 Frederic Leighton, *Self-Portrait*, c. 1880, oil on canvas, Florence: Uffizi Gallery.

34 Vernon Lee [pseudonym of Violet Paget], letter to her mother, July 2, 1883, in *Vernon Lee's Letters* (London: published privately, 1937), 123, quoted in Andrew Stephenson, "Leighton and Shifting Repertoires of 'Masculine' Artistic Identity in the Late Victorian Period," in *Frederic Leighton: Antiquity, Renaissance, Modernity*, ed. Tim Barringer and Elizabeth Prettejohn, (New Haven and London: Yale University Press, 1999), 224.

35 On Lewis and masquerade, see especially Roberts, *Intimate Outsiders*, 25.

36 Frederic Leighton, *Odalisque*, 1862, Private Collection; see Jones et al., *Frederic Leighton*, 126; John Frederick Lewis, *The Bouquet*, 1857, oil on wood, Dunedin, New Zealand: Dunedin Public Art Gallery.

37 John Frederic Lewis, *A Lady Receiving Visitors: The Apartment is the Mandarah, the Lower Floor of the House, Cairo*, 1873, New Haven: Yale Center for British Art. See also Emily M. Weeks, "A Veil of Truth and the Details of Empire: John Frederick Lewis's *The Reception*, 1873," in *Art and the British Empire* ed. Tim Barringer, Douglas Fordham and Geoff Quilley (Manchester: Manchester University Press, 2007), 237–53.

38 *Athenaeum* (May 30, 1874): 740, quoted Roberts, *Intimate Outsiders*, 49.

39 See here Emily M. Weeks, "Cultures Crossed: John Frederick Lewis and the Art of Orientalist Painting," in Tromans, *Lure of the East*, 22–32.

40 See Louise Campbell, "Decoration, Display, Disguise: Leighton House Reconsidered," in *Frederic Leighton*, ed. Barringer and Prettejohn (New Haven and London: Yale University Press, 1999), 267–94; and, most recently, Daniel Robbins, Reena Suleman and Margot T. Brandlhuber, "Leighton House: Building, History and Interiors," in *Frederic Lord Leighton: Painter and Sculptor of the Victorian Age*, ed. Margot T. Brandlhuber and Michael Burs (Munich, Berlin, London and New York: Prestel, 2009), 144–89.

41 Mrs. Russell Barrington, *The Life, Letters and Work of Frederic Leighton* (2 vols, New York: Macmillan, 1906), 1: 299.

42 Frederic Leighton, *Interior of the Grand Mosque of Damascus*, 1873–75, oil on canvas, Preston: Harris Museum and Art Gallery.

43 Frederic Leighton, *Study: At a Reading Desk*, 1877, oil on canvas, Liverpool: Sudley House.

44 Frederic Leighton, *The Light of the Harem*, 1881, oil on canvas, private collection. Roberts, *Intimate Outsiders*, 90.

45 Frederic Leighton, *Sir Richard Burton*, 1872–75, oil on canvas, London: National Portrait Gallery.

46 The text is from Sura 55. It reads: "In the name of the merciful and long-suffering God, The Merciful hath taught the Koran. He has created man and taught him speech. [He has set] the sun and the moon in a certain course. Both the moon and the stars are in subjection [unto him]." See George C. Williamson, *Frederic, Lord Leighton* (London: Bell and Sons, 1902), 41–42.

Bibliography

Altman, Francesca Vanke. "William Holman Hunt, Race and Orientalism." In *Worldwide Pre-Raphaelitism*, edited by Thomas J. Tobin, 45–68. Albany: State University of New York Press, 2004.

Barringer, Tim. "The Leighton Gallery at the V&A." *Apollo* (February 1996): 56–64.

Barringer, Tim. *Reading the Pre-Raphaelites*. New Haven: Yale University Press, 1999.

Barringer, Tim. *Men at Work: Art and Labour in Victorian Britain*. New Haven and London: Yale University Press, 2005.

Barringer, Tim, and Elizabeth Prettejohn, eds. *Frederic Leighton: Antiquity, Renaissance, Modernity*. New Haven and London: Yale University Press, 1999.

Barringer, Tim, Geoff Quilley and Douglas Fordham, eds. *Art and the British Empire*. Manchester: Manchester University Press, 2007.

Barrington, Mrs. Emilie Isabel Russell. *The Life, Letters and Work of Frederic Leighton*, 2 vols. New York: Macmillan, 1906.

Beaulieu, Jill, and Mary Roberts, eds. *Orientalism's Interlocutors: Painting, Architecture, Photography*. Durham: Duke University Press, 2002.

Bendiner, Kenneth. "Albert Moore and John Frederick Lewis." *Arts Magazine* (February 5, 1980): 76–79.

Benjamin, Roger. *Orientalist Aesthetics: Art, Colonialism, and French North Africa, 1880–1930*. Berkeley: University of California Press, 2003.

Bills, Mark, and Vivien Knight. *William Powell Frith: Painting the Victorian Age*. New Haven: Yale University Press, 2006.

Campbell, Louise. "Decoration, Display, Disguise: Leighton House Reconsidered." In *Frederic Leighton: Antiquity, Renaissance, Modernity*, edited by Tim Barringer and Elizabeth Prettejohn, 267–94. New Haven and London: Yale University Press, 1999.

Codell, Julie F., and Dianne Sachko Macleod, eds. *Orientalism Transposed: The Impact of the Colonies on British Culture*. Aldershot: Ashgate, 1998.

Cowling, Mary. *The Artist as Anthropologist: The Representation of Type and Character in Victorian Art*. Cambridge: Cambridge University Press, 1989.

del Plato, Joan. "Lewis and the Aesthetic Movement, 1860–76." In del Plato *From Slave Market to Paradise: The Harem Pictures of John Frederick Lewis and their Tradition*, 348–50. Ann Arbor: University Microfilms International, 1987.

del Plato, Joan. *From Slave Market to Paradise: The Harem Pictures of John Frederick Lewis and their Tradition*. Ann Arbor: University Microfilms International, 1987.

del Plato, Joan. *Multiple Wives, Multiple Pleasures: Representing the Harem, 1800–1875*. Cranbury, Ontario: Associated University Presses, 2002.

du Maurier, George. "Intellectual Epicures," *Punch* 60 (1876): 33.

Edwards, Holly, ed. *Noble Dreams, Wicked Pleasures: Orientalism in America, 1870–1930*. Princeton: Princeton University Press in association with the Sterling and Francine Clark Art Institute, 2000.

Green, Richard, and Michael Lewis. *John Frederick Lewis R.A.: Painter of Desert and Harem*. Guildford: Guildford House Gallery, 1977.

Hackforth-Jones, Jocelyn, and Mary Roberts, eds. *Edges of Empire: Orientalism and Visual Culture*. Oxford: Blackwell, 2005.

Hacking, Juliet. *Princes of Victorian Bohemia: Photographs by David Wilkie Wynfield*. London: National Portrait Gallery, 2000.

Jones, Stephen, Christopher Newall, Leonée Ormond, Richard Ormond and Benedict Read. *Frederic Leighton 1830–1896*. London: Royal Academy of Arts, 1996.

Lane, Edward William. *An Account of the Manners and Customs of the Modern Egyptians*, 2 vols. London: Charles Knight, 1836.

Lewis, Reina. *Gendering Orientalism: Race, Femininity and Representation*. London: Routledge, 1996.

Lewis, Reina. *Rethinking Orientalism: Women, Travel and the Ottoman Harem*. London: I. B. Tauris, 2004.

Llewellyn, Briony, and Charles Newton. "John Frederick Lewis: 'In Knowledge of the Orientals Quite One of Themselves.'" In *Interpreting the Orient: Travellers in Egypt and the Near East*, edited by Paul and Janet Starkey, 35–50. Reading UK: Ithaca Press, 2001.

Mackenzie, John M. *Orientalism: History: Theory and the Arts*. Manchester: Manchester University Press, 1995.

Maltz, Diana. *British Aestheticism and the Urban Working Classes, 1870–1900: Beauty for the People*. Basingstoke: Palgrave Macmillan, 2006.

Nochlin, Linda. "The Imaginary Orient" (1983). Reprinted in L. Nochlin, *The Politics of Vision*, 33–59. London: Thames and Hudson, 1991.

Pointon, Marcia. "Holman Hunt and the Holy Land: The Artist as Ethnographer." In *Pre-Raphaelites Re-Viewed*, edited by M. Pointon, 22–44. Manchester: Manchester University Press, 1989.

Porterfield, Todd. *The Allure of Empire: Art in the Service of French Imperialism, 1798–1836*. Princeton, NJ: Princeton University Press, 1998.

Prettejohn, Elizabeth. *Art for Art's Sake: Aestheticism in Victorian Painting*. New Haven and London: Yale University Press for The Paul Mellon Centre for Studies in British Art, 2007.

Prettejohn, Elizabeth, ed. *After the Pre-Raphaelites: Art and Aestheticism in Victorian England*. New Brunswick, NJ: Rutgers University Press, 1999.

Robbins, Daniel, Reena Suleman and Margot T. Brandlhuber. "Leighton House: Building, History and Interiors." In *Frederic Lord Leighton: Painter and Sculptor of the Victorian Age*, edited by Margot T. Brandlhuber and Michael Burs, 144–89. Munich, Berlin, London and New York: Prestel, 2009.

Roberts, Mary. *Intimate Outsiders: The Harem in Ottoman and Orientalist Art and Travel Literature*. Durham NC: Duke University Press, 2007.

Said, Edward. *Orientalism*. New York: Pantheon, 1978.

Said, Edward. *Culture and Imperialism*. New York: Knopf, 1993.

Spencer, Robin. *The Aesthetic Movement: Theory and Practice*. London: Studio Vista, 1972.

Stephenson, Andrew. "Leighton and Shifting Repertoires of 'Masculine' Artistic Identity in the Late Victorian Period." In *Frederic Leighton: Antiquity, Renaissance, Modernity*, edited by Tim Barringer and Elizabeth Prettejohn. New Haven and London: Yale University Press, 1999.

Sweetman, John. *The Oriental Obsession: Islamic Inspiration in British and American Arts an Architecture, 1500–1920*. Cambridge: Cambridge University Press, 1988.

Thackeray, William Makepeace. *Notes of a Journey from Cornhill to Grand Cairo* [1846]. London: Smith Elder, 1869.

Tromans, Nicholas. "Introduction: British Orientalist Painting." In *The Lure of the East: British Orientalist Painting*, edited by Nicholas Tromans. London: Tate, 2008.

Tromans, Nicholas, ed. *The Lure of the East: British Orientalist Painting*. London: Tate, 2008.

Weeks, Emily M. "The 'Reality Effect': The Orientalist Paintings of John Frederick Lewis (1805–1876)." PhD diss., Yale University, 2005.

Weeks, Emily M. "A Veil of Truth and the Details of Empire: John Frederick Lewis's *The Reception*, 1873." In *Art and the British Empire*, edited by Tim Barringer, Douglas Fordham and Geoff Quilley, 237–53. Manchester: Manchester University Press, 2007.

Weeks, Emily M. "Cultures Crossed: John Frederick Lewis and the Art of Orientalist Painting." In *Lure of the East: British Orientalist Painting*, edited by Nicholas Tromans, 22–32. London: Tate, 2008.

Weeks, Emily M. *Cultures Crossed: John Frederick Lewis and the Art of Orientalist Painting*. New York: Yale University Press, forthcoming.

Williamson, George C. *Frederic, Lord Leighton*. London: Bell and Sons, 1902.

Yeazell, Ruth Bernard. *Harems of the Mind: Passages of Western Art and Literature*. New Haven: Yale University Press, 2000.

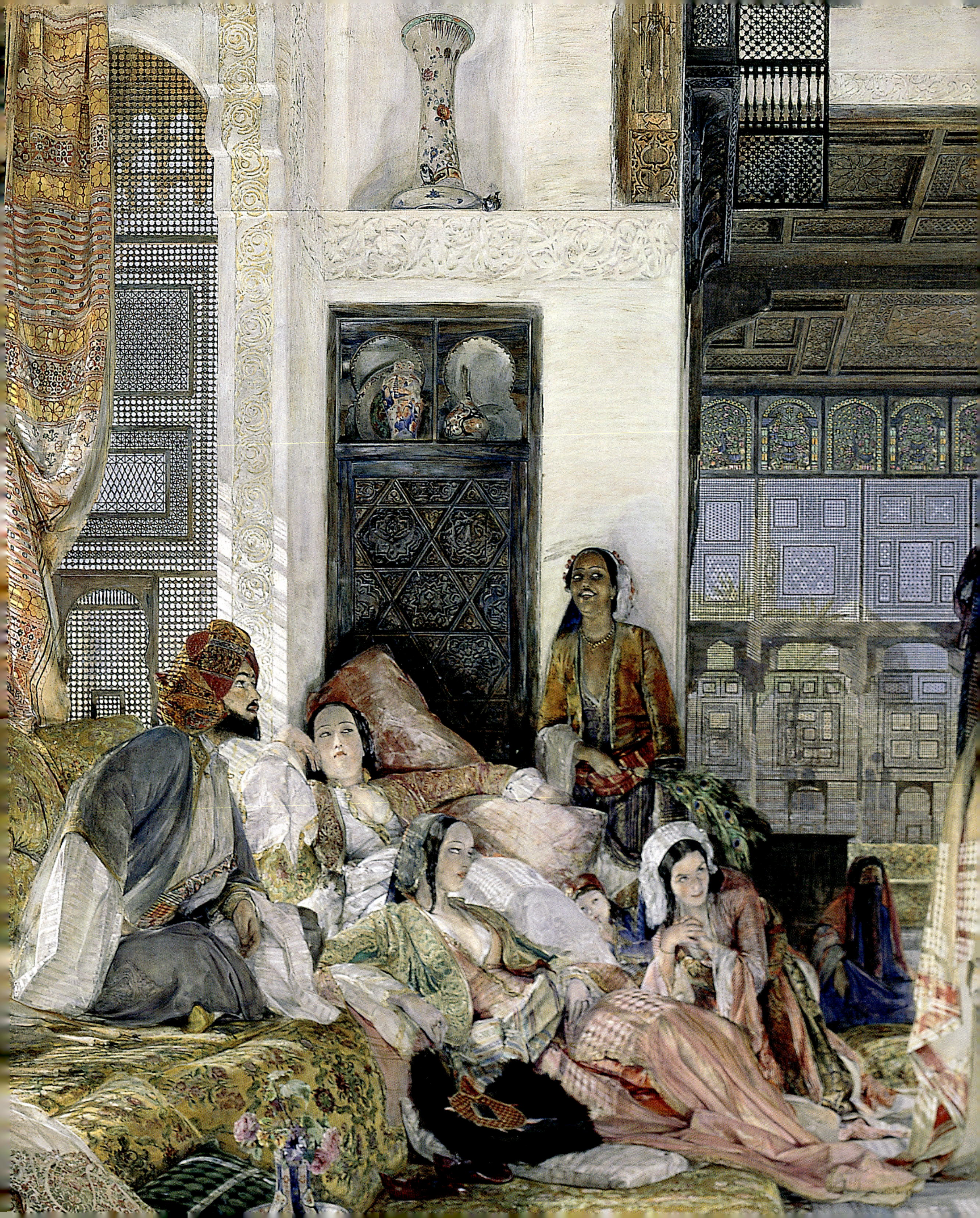

XVIII

The Reception of John Frederick Lewis at the Exposition Universelle in 1855

Peter Benson Miller

While a spirit of free trade and international cooperation between France and England ostensibly underwrote both the 1851 Great Exhibition and the Exposition Universelle in 1855, the critical responses to the Fine Arts displays on the latter occasion were driven almost exclusively by national rivalry.[1] Concerned with defining the hallmarks of national schools, critics isolated mid-nineteenth-century artists from both countries from channels of international exchange. French critics asserted that differences in national character were inscribed in works of art, an interpretive strategy that camouflaged the cross-fertilization of ideas, themes and techniques.[2] This essay revisits their analyses of watercolors by British artists, and those by John Frederick Lewis, in particular, to suggest that, despite the appearance to the contrary, the Exposition Universelle in 1855 was a watershed showcasing a concatenation of productive artistic exchanges. Beneath the veneer of patriotic criticism, these French writers' subtle examinations of the watercolors exhibited by Lewis reveal a great deal about the attitudes and priorities governing the representation of the Orient in the French sphere. Ironically, the very hallmarks of the British watercolor esthetic, the "Englishness" that French critics were at pains to define, reinforced the development of a form of realism by such artists as Jean-Léon Gérôme tailored to Oriental genre painting. The special status of watercolor and ethnological inquiry in 1855 helped distill an esthetic closer in spirit to avant-garde realism than to the Academic verisimilitude with which Gérôme's early ethnographic works are usually associated.

The exhibition catalog that accompanied *The Lure of the East* is an admirable publication that emphasizes for the most part transnational exchange, though it occasionally overstates the differences between national schools. It is asserted, for example, that British Orientalist imagery was "accepted in its own day as a peculiarly truthful form of art and, inasmuch as it disavowed flagrant fantasy, differed from some of the most well-known examples of the French variety of Orientalist painting."[3] As is evident in what follows however, veracity in visual representation of the Orient was as much a priority in France as it was on the other side of the Channel. In 1855, French critics held both French and British artists to account for inaccuracies, whether they concerned the quality of light or the depiction of local customs; they expected pictures to be grounded in fact rather than fantasy. My principal concern here is not whether British or French paintings of the Orient were truthful, a complicated claim under any circumstances, but the way each have been extracted from a series of artistic exchanges to set up the one as the truthful foil to the other.

For too long, it has been reiterated that a fantasy quotient overwhelmed more "truthful" naturalistic tendencies in paintings of exotic subjects by French artists. While this notion is fiercely lodged as a cornerstone of nineteenth-century art, it originates in the highly partisan writings of a single person. The accusation of inauthenticity leveled at French Orientalist painting—as well as the moniker Orientalist—dates to radical realist critic Jules-Antoine Castagnary's sustained attack, initiated in 1857, upon artists who chose to paint exotic landscapes instead of studying first-hand the natural surroundings of the French countryside. To Castagnary, the difference between an Egyptian desert and a French pasture, figured, respectively, as fantasy and reality, could be measured by the geographical distance that separated them. The further an artist traveled away from mainland France, the more foreign the destination, the more flagrant the fantasy appeared in the canvases resulting from the voyage. Castagnary deplored artists for seeking to lose themselves in unfamiliar surroundings, for abandoning the known and visibly concrete for what was far-off and unknown. Misleadingly, the realm of the imaginary has been regarded as the special province of French Orientalist painting ever since. Castagnary's virulent xenophobia and radical political agenda opposed to colonial expansion effectively divorced Oriental genre from its realist roots.[4] Breaking down some of the national boundaries that have structured critical responses to the subject will help reformulate the relationship of Castagnary's own brand of avant-garde realism to Oriental genre in the 1850s, which was considerably less alien to positivist inquiry than Castagnary would have us believe.

Even a cursory look at images by Lewis and Gérôme underscores several areas where their formal preoccupations and subject matter intersect. Both artists were attracted to Eastern bazaar scenes with their riots of bodies, gestures and rich displays of merchandise. They often created atmospheric interiors with single figures or groups set off against or illuminated by the light filtering through *mashrabiyya* screens. Careful itemization of the contents of these interiors and the clarity of visual fact assert strong, if sometimes questionable claims to authenticity. Virile male warriors, Bashibazuks armed to the hilt, Mamluks and mercenaries of varying ethnic origin, alone or in groups, appear frequently in major works by both painters. At times, they explored these figures in indoor-outdoor social spaces in which human activity spilled from cafés or boutiques out into the street. They were equally attracted to the private sphere of the harem and its feminine rituals. Their paintings were the fruit of long, successful careers punctuated in each case by lengthy sojourns in the East. As is now well known, both painters were intrepid travelers, and their respective studies executed abroad yielded and authorized many of the subjects and accessories populating their paintings. Donald Rosenthal underlined these affinities almost thirty years ago, but it is worth looking anew at what brought them about.[5] The reception of Lewis's work at the Exposition Universelle in 1855 is very revealing about prevailing attitudes about the capacities of watercolor and its links to realism in Oriental genre scenes. The entangled fortunes of these categories of artistic practice owe a great deal to a constellation of artists on both sides of the Channel, who found in watercolor an effective medium for the truthful representation of the Orient. It was they who paved the way for a variation upon Lewis's vision of the Orient—what French critic Théophile Gautier called "an infinite world of details"—to become the default mode of European painting on this theme.[6] Concomitant with that broader development, Gérôme's shift to ethnographic realism was helped along by critical reactions to Lewis's watercolors at the 1855 Exposition Universelle. In this way, we might shake up some of the received wisdom about avant-garde versus Academic realism, and which country, if any, had a claim on truthfulness in the representation of the Orient.

The lesson that Gérôme learned from Lewis—and the way that the strengths and shortcomings of Lewis's project, as they appeared to French critics, spelled out the parameters of a viable Oriental genre painting—must be understood in the context of important changes in the French artistic sphere, including a new openness to developments across the Channel. In the preface to his remarks about the 1857 Salon, prominent critic Théophile Gautier, a Gérôme stalwart since 1847, acknowledged a fundamental change in focus in French art from the exalted realms of history painting to the more prosaic matter of factness of genre. Even as he insisted on a profound engagement with concrete fact, Gautier perceived, too, a pervasive international spirit governing European art, which he traced to the build up to and the result of the Exposition Universelle in 1855. On that occasion, Gautier acknowledged a competitive spirit, but one conducive rather than inimical to productive dialogue. He writes:

> the nationalities of art became acquainted, and after the initial surprise, they studied each other silently. Each one sought to surpass the methods of its neighbour, and we find in more than one eminent work the traces of foreign influence. These cosmopolitan exchanges have produced combinations and results that are difficult to classify according to old categories.[7]

Reconsidering the links between the work of Lewis and Gérôme in light of Gautier's comments suggests that Lewis's brand of genre and the nature of watercolor, as they were discussed by critics in 1855, offered an alternative to French artists like Gérôme caught in an impasse between the classical tradition and the growing realist imperative. Albert Boime has argued that Gérôme's embrace of what he sees as an Academic, watered-down realism in the 1850s was chiefly encouraged by state sponsorship of an "official" realism consistent with the policies of Napoléon III's regime.[8] Factoring in the reception of Lewis's watercolors in 1855 offers another avenue through which to explore the development of ethnographic genre in France. For reasons that will be clarified below, the form of realism adapted to this format in the 1850s was perhaps, for a time at least, closer in spirit to the one proposed by the avant-garde than it was to the Academic formulas discussed by Boime.[9]

Lewis was part of the British contingent that took Paris by storm in 1855. His submission included four watercolors: *The Hhareem* (Fig. 18.1), *The Arab Scribe, Cairo* (Fig. 18.2), *Camels in the Desert* and *The Halt in the Desert*, complex pictorial essays linked to an extended sojourn in Egypt in the 1840s.[10] We will return to the critical responses to these works below. At the same venue, Gérôme was a key player in the negotiations of an Anglo-French détente and the author of one of its concrete artistic symbols. In 1852, he had been commissioned

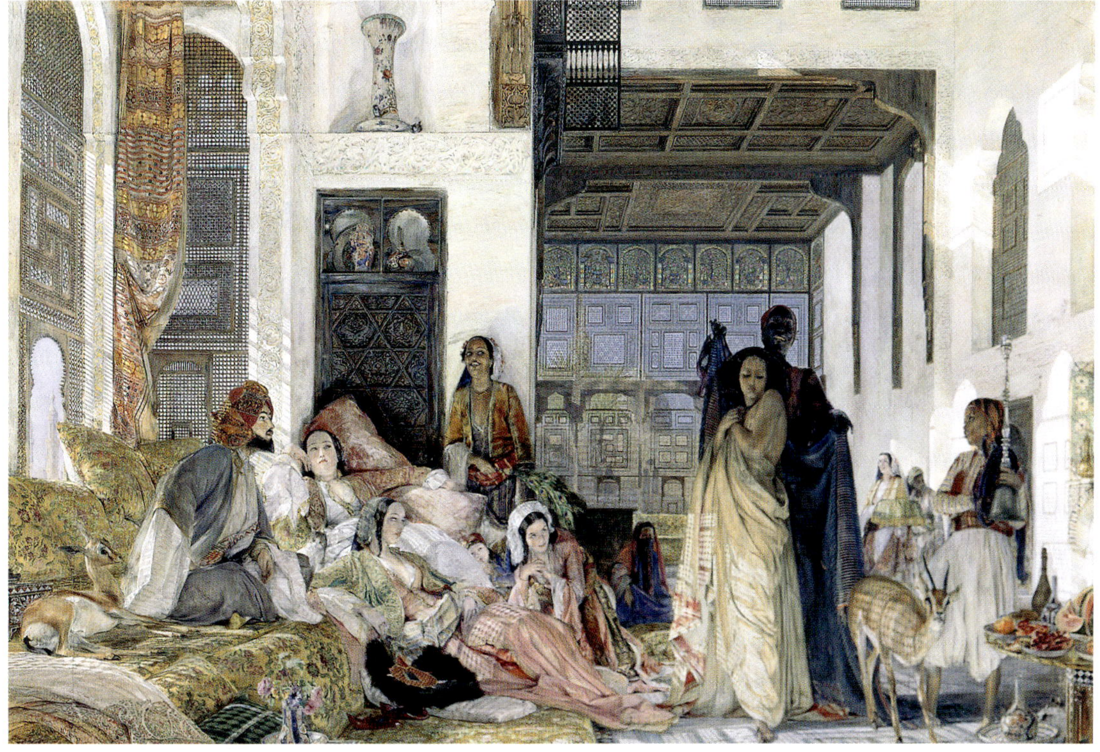

Figure 18.1 *The Hhareem*, John Frederick Lewis (1804–1876), 1853, watercolor, 88.6 x 133 cm, Private Collection.

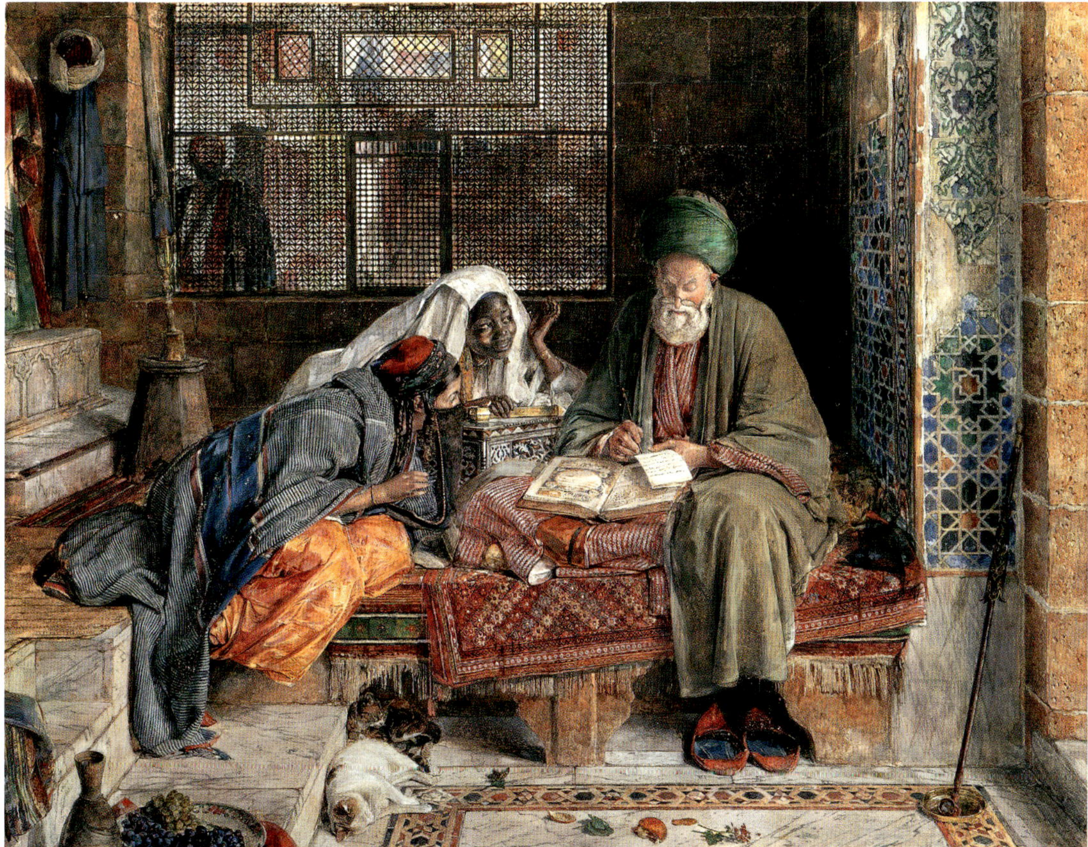

Figure 18.2 *The Arab Scribe, Cairo*, John Frederick Lewis (1804–1876), 1852, watercolor, 47.1 x 60 cm, Private Collection. Courtesy of Christie's.

to design a frieze commemorating the London exhibition of 1851 (Fig. 18.3), which was then applied to a vase offered to Prince Albert by Napoléon III at the ceremonies in Paris in 1855. Allegorical figures representing Concord, Abundance, and Justice, seated on a raised dais, are flanked by processions of national delegations from France, Belgium, Austria, Prussia, Spain, Portugal and the Ottoman Empire, on the right, and England, Russia, the United States of America and China, on the left. As a history painter, albeit an unorthodox one, Gérôme was still trying to live up to the early promise of his *Young Greeks Making a Cockfight (Combat de Coqs)*, which garnered effusive praise at the Salon of 1847. Gérôme exhibited an ambitious canvas in 1855 entitled *The Age of Augustus*, the result of a lucrative state commission. Despite lively depictions of ethnically diverse figures in the foreground, its unconvincing classicism disappointed even the artist's fans. Critics were more taken with Gérôme's painting of a group of Slavic soldiers in *Recreation in the Camp: Souvenir of Moldavia*. Not surprisingly, the composition of *The Age of Augustus*, with its throngs of diverse peoples from the various corners of the Roman Empire, is also marked by the burgeoning interest in ethnography, military exercises and national uniforms manifest in *Recreation in the Camp*. Amplifying to a monumental scale the configuration of the earlier frieze, Gérôme relaxed the stiff postures of the national groups processing around the contours of Prince Albert's vase, multiplying them into the riotous masses of Imperial subjects in *The Age of Augustus*. In both works, Gérôme nurtured a curiosity for racial and national distinctions, the subject of much of his research during a voyage through the Balkans to the Black Sea coast and Istanbul in 1853. Gautier surely had Gérôme's submissions, as well as his wanderlust, in mind in 1855 when he claimed that the expanding horizons of painting and international relations were dissolving the formerly sacrosanct distinctions between French history painting and genre, between the ideal and the real.

According to French critics, especially those whose sense of France's artistic pre-eminence in 1855 was suffused with nostalgia for the hey-day of Davidian classicism, reality was the special province of British artists. Their work was found to be original, but lacking the style and poetic beauty of the best French history painting. As Eugène Loudun put it: "the genius of England is the genius of material strength; this sort of genius is incompatible with the ideal."[11] Thus, the general shift that Gautier detected in the art of his time was closely aligned with the division many critics made between French idealizing tendencies and the purported British preoccupation with the material world. At the same time, English watercolor was held up for special praise. Of the English exhibition in 1855, Nadar wrote, for example: "its real force is in the watercolors, and I asked myself why and how the English artist found in the less profound and more inadequate resources of the wash (*lavis*), the color that escapes him in his oil paintings."[12] Ferdinand de Lasteyrie insisted: "Even as watercolor in England affects strength and power, painting in oil becomes more diminished, impoverished and wilted. Next to admirable watercolors that one would take for genuine painting, one sees oil paintings that one has difficulty in not mistaking for watercolors."[13] While the British contingent was portrayed overall as anchored in material matter-of-factness, their watercolors were celebrated for their rivalry with oil painting, their ambitious dimensions, vibrant color and boldness of execution. Maxime Du Camp conceded that "it is an art in which [the English] are absolutely our masters." "The majority of the English watercolors," Du Camp continued, "are veritable canvases, due as much to their dimensions as to the often bold and vigorous fashion with which they are treated."[14] Influential conservative critic Etienne-Jean Delécluze discussed Lewis's *The Hhareem* in these terms, remarking upon the size of its figures in a work whose dimensions were exceptional for a watercolor.[15] These comments, as well as the prominence accorded to Lewis in many reviews, may have alerted Gérôme—who, by 1855, was already sensitive enough to the hybridization between genres and techniques—to the lessons offered by British watercolor. It provided a reliable guide for his gradual shift away from Academic tenets to an esthetic grounded in the close observation of material reality.

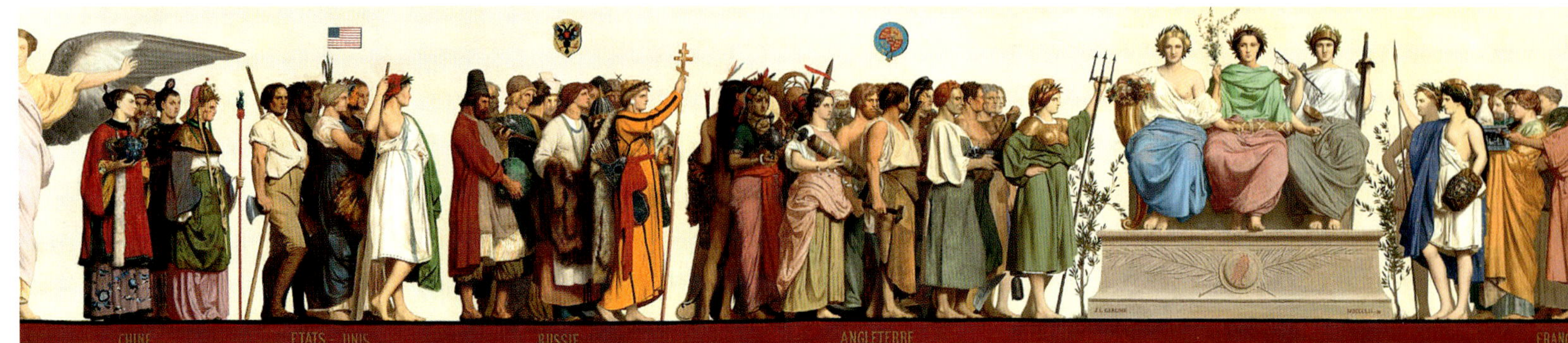

The response to Lewis's watercolors merely brought to the fore the traditional strengths attributed to the medium. A long association with scientific inquiry, which dated to the sixteenth century, enhanced watercolor's innate capacity to transmit documentary information. One of the pioneers of English watercolor, John White, depicted the indigenous populations of Florida and Virginia for an ethnological study undertaken during expeditions to North America in the 1580s.[16] In geological and archeological surveys sponsored by the Society of Dilettanti, which was founded in 1733, topographical studies and the records of the picturesque mountain views and monuments of the Grand Tour, watercolor captured precise detail in an economical fashion. With the support of such institutions as the Society of Painters of Watercolours, constituted in 1804 (now the Royal Watercolour Society), English artists remained at the forefront of the discipline. In the 1820s, Richard Parkes Bonington, an assiduous Channel-crosser, launched an international fad for watercolor, which had important repercussions for French art of the Romantic period and its interest in the Orient. Eugène Delacroix employed watercolor to stunning effect in his Moroccan journals, documenting his observations during the course of an extended sojourn in North Africa. In his unfinished *Dictionnaire des beaux-arts*, there is no entry for watercolor, but under the heading "National taste [Goût des Nations]," Delacroix makes an oblique reference to it, emphasizing "the English love of details [L'amour des détails chez les Anglais]."[17] As we've seen, the close scrutiny of details was one of the chief capacities of watercolor recognized by French critics in 1855.

Following the example of Bonington and Delacroix, French artists by the 1850s had begun to explore the peoples, customs and rituals of the various locales in the Austrian and Ottoman Empires as well as Egypt. They did so with the meticulous precision for which English watercolor was celebrated. But, whereas he freely admitted that English technique was superior to that of French artists, Du Camp held Lewis to a strict standard of veracity set by French draughtsman Alexandre Bida. The latter's *Souvenirs de l'Egypte* (1851) cataloged local types, classifying them by costume and ethnological criteria. Indicative of Bida's prominence in 1855, his drawing *The Ceremony of the Dosseh* was purchased by the State at the culmination of the Exposition Universelle. Questioning the notion that English artists were necessarily more truthful than their French counterparts, Du Camp argued that between Lewis's watercolors and the drawings by Bida, he saw "the difference between a false medal and a real one."[18] Thus, it is not surprising that Gérôme, evidently aware of Du Camp's chastening of Lewis on this count, consulted Bida's compositions as he developed his own brand of ethnographic genre. In his comments about Gérôme's Egyptian scenes at the 1857 Salon, Du Camp asserts that one of these, *Egyptian Recruits Crossing the Desert*, revisited aspects of "an admirable drawing exhibited in 1853 by M. Bida."[19] This observation was seconded by Alphonse de Calonne: "[M. Gérôme] has reproduced the group of Egyptian recruits by M. Bida without making any significant changes to it."[20] Gautier, too, acknowledged Gérôme's debt to Bida, but invoked the comparison to underline Gérôme's commitment to an even more uncompromising realism. Whereas Bida chose the moment of the prisoners' departure, emphasizing "pathetic effects," Gérôme pictured the dreary trudge through a desert wasteland. For Gautier the recruits "were victims caught between the impassiveness of nature and the impassiveness of despotism."[21]

Ethnographic studies in watercolor by two other artists may also have conditioned readings of Lewis's work and shaped Gérôme's subsequent shift to a harder edged realism more in line with avant-garde strategies than Academic prescriptions. These include studies done in the Levant and Egypt in the 1830s by Gérôme's teacher, the Swiss artist Charles Gleyre, who studied watercolor technique with Bonington in Paris in 1825. It is impossible to verify however whether Gérôme, or any one else for that matter, had the opportunity to see Gleyre's Egyptian watercolors, which the artist kept hidden in his studio until his death. Be that as it

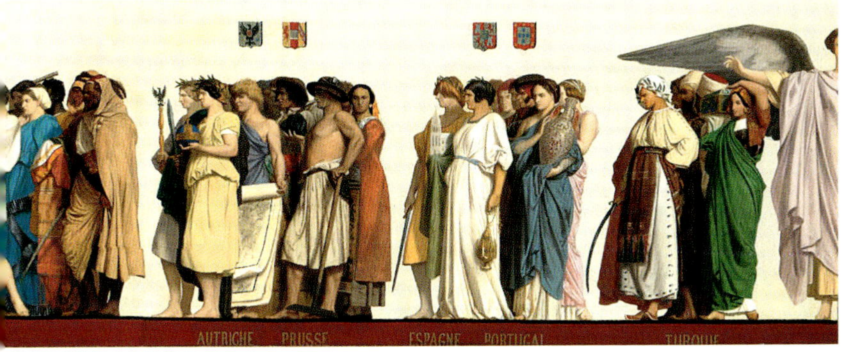

Figure 18.3 *Frieze for a Vase Commemorating the London Exposition in 1851*, Jean-Léon Gérôme (1824–1904), 1852, oil on canvas, 55 x 310 cm, Musée d'Orsay, Paris.

may, those studies done from life are consistent with the paradigm espoused by Du Camp. Gleyre's watercolor technique and its unvarnished documentary style were very different from the Academic manner he employed in Salon paintings after his return to Paris.[22] In part, this was because the former conformed to the scientific interests of the artist's traveling companion and patron, the American industrialist John Lowell, Jr. In their precise recording of data, Gleyre's watercolors done in the Orient presaged avant-garde realist developments in France by at least a decade.[23] In the same spirit, Théodore Valerio's exhaustive inventory of ethnic types from the Balkans, which he executed in watercolor, was shown at the Exposition Universelle in 1855 to great acclaim. Gautier discussed the importance of the series to anthropological inquiry, pointing out that, on the advice of German naturalist Alexander von Humboldt, Valerio had been engaged to document all the diverse peoples inhabiting the Austrian Empire. The artist "attempted to study each race from an ethnographic point of view, marrying the color of the painter to the exactitude of the naturalist."[24] To Gautier, watercolor as a medium was particularly adapted to capturing the variety of physical features necessary for such scientific studies.[25] As an accomplished watercolorist, Valerio managed to fulfill the demands imposed both by an esthetic standard and the requirements of science:

> although his watercolors are expressed with great skill and the wash is applied with a vigorous tone that only [Alexandre Gabriel] Decamps could surpass, M. Valerio has not sought exclusively a picturesque aspect. Without sacrificing effect, he has rendered heads with such exactitude of resemblance that they have anthropological value. The scholar busy with research in this domain will find in these heads the anatomical details and the particularities of conformation that distinguish one race from another and permit him to track the filiations between them.[26]

In retracing the centrality of watercolor to the development of realism in Oriental genre painting, and French esthetics in general as they were nourished by developments *outre-manche* in the 1850s, one must factor in another key figure, the French artist Constantin Guys. His career as a correspondent providing images for *The Illustrated London News* epitomizes the artistic context for which the English Channel was more of a conduit than a boundary. Guys was the subject of an early essay by William Makepeace Thackeray, who later turned his pen to describing Lewis's expatriate existence in Egypt in the final chapter of *From Cornhill to Grand Cairo*.[27] Guys is perhaps best known as "M. G.," the model for Charles Baudelaire's dandified artist-flâneur and urban chronicler in *The Painter of Modern Life*, published in 1863. While he dwells chiefly on Guys' treatment of the public spectacles and social rituals of Second Empire Paris, the hotbed of modernity, Baudelaire nonetheless devotes considerable attention to Guys' watercolors executed in the Balkans, Istanbul and the Crimea. Confronting every day life in a war zone with the sense of immediacy conveyed by watercolor, Guys' Oriental motifs play an important, if largely overlooked, role in Baudelaire's definition of him as an avant-garde hero. It is the unique capacities of watercolor that closes the gap that has opened between Guys' two artistic personas, the consummate Parisian, on the one hand, and the foreign correspondent in Ottoman Istanbul, on the other. Whether it was employed to describe the boulevards of Paris or the alien customs of the Orient, watercolor was a medium to which Baudelaire attributed special powers of communicating on-the-spot observations. Even as Lewis's watercolors were on display in Paris in 1855, Guys sent back images from the various theaters of the Crimean war for reproduction in *The Illustrated London News*. Just as watercolor derived much of its authority from its historical association with scientific inquiry, the medium offered opportunities to the aspiring realist artist because of the facility with which it could narrate current events. To be sure, Guys' wash drawings, much freer in handling than the painstaking technique employed by Lewis, were not published as such, but translated by engravers into the illustrations seen by the readers of *The Illustrated London News*, including one of whirling dervishes (Fig. 18.4). Nonetheless, Guys' watercolors—dispatches from the front alternating with distractions from the main event aimed at the armchair tourist—were credited as documents conveying essential facts of front-page importance.

As a war correspondent, Guys produced views of military encampments, solemn rituals and landscapes peopled with soldiers and local color. In addition to his reportage, Guys published pictures portraying types drawn from the ranks of the indigenous population, including scenes of Turkish hospitality and men smoking in a café (Fig. 18.5), an atmospheric composition with figures set off against a wooden lattice screen remarkably close in spirit, if not in execution, to those painted by Lewis and Gérôme.[28] Baudelaire described Guys' depiction of exotic soldiers, such as Kurds at Scutari as "weird-looking troops whose appearance puts one in mind of some barbarian invasion or, if you prefer, the Bashibazuks, no less extraordinary."[29] Guys also illustrated Muslim festivals, including Baïram, which marks the end of Ramadan, veiled women and "the frenzied dances of the tumblers of the 'third sex.'" The latter may be Baudelaire's reference to the watercolor source for the engraving of the whirling dervishes

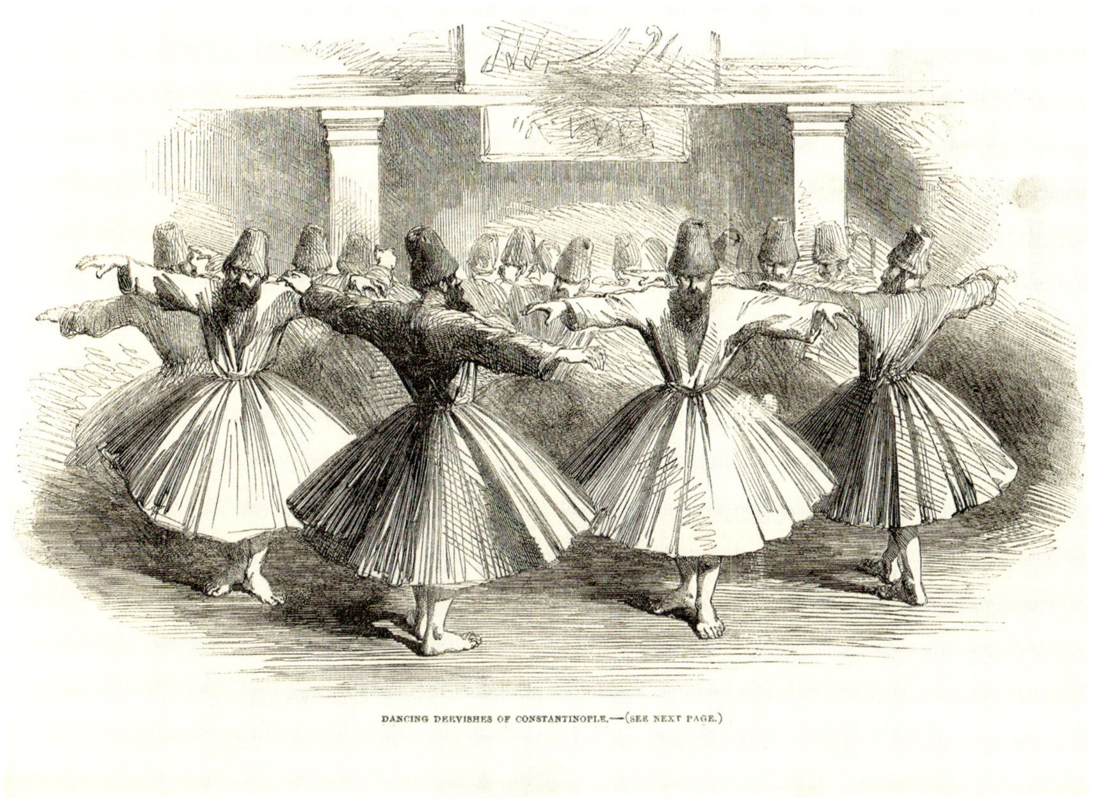

Figure 18.4 *Dancing Dervishes of Constantinople*, After Constantin Guys, from the *Illustrated London News* 23, no. 649 (October 15, 1853): 321. Wood engraving, Bibliothèque Nationale de France, Paris.

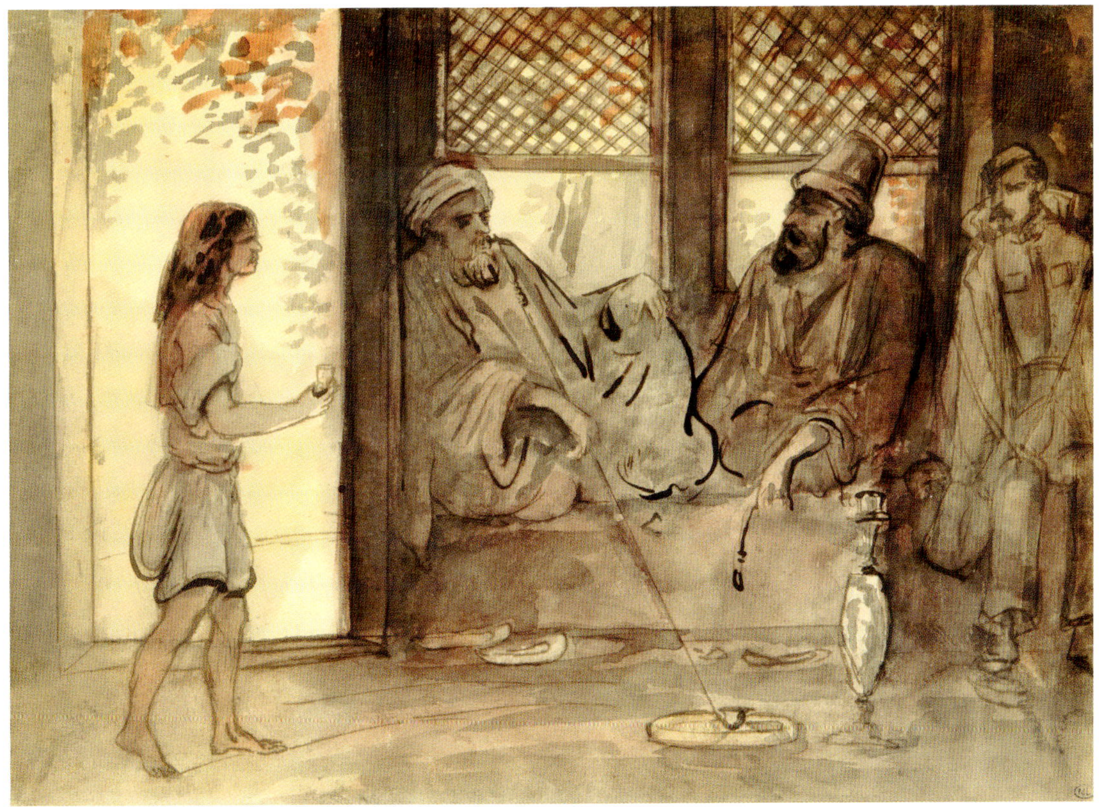

Figure 18.5 *Fumeurs en Orient (Smokers in the Orient)*, Constantin Guys (1802–1892), c. 1853–55, watercolor, brown ink and pencil, 21 x 30.5 cm, Musée du Louvre, Département des arts graphiques, Paris.

illustrated here. Guys documented women who "have kept their national costume, embroidered jackets with short sleeves, flowing sashes, enormous trousers, turned up slippers, striped or spangled muslins."[30] Although dashed off with romantic élan, Baudelaire's heated prose itemizes these elements of costume with an attention to detail not unlike the abundance of information in pictures by Bida, Gleyre, Valerio and Lewis. Well before Gérôme became the most fastidious purveyor of sartorial minutiae, the details of "national costume" and the vestimentary indicators of ethnic identity were cataloged by these artists in watercolor and praised for their scientific value.

As watercolor had assumed this clout in the depiction of concrete fact, especially in the description of the Orient, it is not surprising that Lewis's pictures became the fulcrum for discussions about the accuracy of racial markers and the nature of truth in the portrayal of Oriental customs. Lewis himself, in the description he wrote to accompany *The Hhareem* when it was exhibited in Edinburgh in 1853, emphasized the ethnic diversity of the various wives of the seated bey. The care with which Lewis delineated the features of the Georgian, Circassian and Greek women, as well as those of the Abyssinian slave, suggests that the picture was read as a racial taxonomy.[31] In 1855, French critics, too, carefully itemized racial markers. While Delécluze detected worried tension, jealousy and frivolity, respectively, in the expressions of the bey's female companions, underlining the rivalries that many commentators expected were commonplace in the harem, he also praises Lewis's use of reflected light to highlight the variety of their physiognomies.[32] A.-J. Du Pays saw disdain on their faces; but he, too, dwells on the copper-colored skin and "savage beauty" of the presented slave.[33] In an extended passage, Gautier—an inveterate traveler and a champion of exotic genre painting since the 1840s—described in detail the scene represented in *The Hhareem*. Enveloped in a litany of the sumptuous objects in the interior, Gautier's text ticks off the signs of race distinguishing the various protagonists. The new slave is, according to Gautier, "a Nubian with bronzed skin, […] tattooed with blue markings on her forehead and her breasts."[34] One of the seated wives, either "Circassian or Georgian," "offers an example of the purest type of the Caucasian race: perfect oval-shaped face, slightly aquiline nose, small mouth and large eyes tinted with kh'ol."[35] Gautier found these details so convincing that he asserts "we have described the *Harem d'un bey*—more from the point of view of a tourist than that of a critic—because the talent of M. Lewis transports us *in medias res*, and he sends those who stop in front of his watercolor directly to Cairo."[36]

There was however a major dissenter, and his comments underline further the centrality of racial markers as guarantors of truthfulness in such depictions. The critic in question, Maxime Du Camp, had, in 1855, recently returned from Egypt, where, along with Gustave Flaubert, he had studied Muslim customs with the aid of Edward Lane's *Modern Egyptians* and an Arab scholar, Khalil Effendi. Du Camp asserted that Lewis's watercolors, "despite their extraordinary dimensions, despite the artist's skillful hand, are far from satisfying to us." He continued: "perhaps we know too well the subjects that they attempt to represent, and that they represent nowhere at all." In a phrase that neatly overturns the purported monopoly enjoyed by British painters over truth in the description of the Orient, Du Camp concluded that *The Hhareem* "is a scene of fantasy without any trace of truth [une scène de fantaisie sans verité]."[37] His complaints centered on the depiction of the ethnic identity of the figures. Whereas Gautier was transported to Cairo, Du Camp remained completely unconvinced.

> The bey looks like a young member of the house of lords who, in order to amuse himself, has dressed up as a Turk; the Khanoun who surround him are English girls, and not Circassians or Arab women; only the Abyssinian has in her hairstyle some resemblance to the slaves from the Gondar plateau; as far as the other details, they might be treated with great skill, I do not deny it, but they have no trace of sincerity.[38]

The question of Lewis's accuracy is considerably less important for our purposes here than the rigorous ethnological standard to which his watercolors were held. It reveals a great deal about the realist impulses disciplining and animating Oriental genre painting in France. Du Camp expected the delineation of racial identity to be factual; he could not forgive Lewis for a "lack of exactness," and the semblance of play-acting and costume drama in *The Hhareem*. Paradoxically, Du Camp employed cutting-edge positivist terms to criticize an English artist for producing images that were less truthful than those by his French colleagues. Despite the renown of English watercolorists for their matter-of-factness, Lewis, in this case, was taken to task for using the medium to indulge a theatrical fantasy. Castagnary, cited earlier as insisting on the fantastical nature of French pictures in this genre, was clearly a lone voice in a chorus of critics who saw realism as perfectly at home in the Orient.

These conflicting reactions to Lewis's watercolors, conditioned as they were by French expectations regarding truth, authenticity and scientific fact in Oriental genre scenes executed in watercolor, surely clarified and reinforced the priorities that accompanied Gérôme on his first voyage to Egypt in 1856. The strengths and failures that critics saw in Lewis's work most likely steered Gérôme as he shifted more emphatically and more exclusively towards ethnographic genre. This is confirmed by the reactions to the painter's Egyptian pictures at the 1857 Salon, which focused on their realism, their truthfulness and the reliance on scientific criteria. Responding to *Prayer in the House of an Arnaut Chieftain* (Fig. 18.6) and *Egyptian Recruits*, critics across the board spoke of their "truthful aspect," "surprising truth," and the "truest, most penetrating, most successful effect."[39] Émile de La Bédollière enthused: "And what truth in the character of the physiognomies and the sites, even in the smallest folds of the garments, the chasing of the weapons, and the embroidery of the slippers."[40] On the basis of these responses, it seems that Gérôme deliberately seized upon Lewis's strengths, his meticulousness, for example, but corrected his shortcomings. He paid close attention to ethnographic details, eliminating however the air of play-acting and costume drama derided by Du Camp. Gautier's account of a visit to Gérôme's studio in 1856 confirms that Gérôme's studies executed in Egypt, like those of Bida, Guys and Valerio, concentrated on aspects of "national costume" and the characteristic physical features of various ethnological types. According to Gautier:

> the artist-traveler has executed many portrait-studies in pencil after different characteristic types; there are Fellahs, Copts, Arabs, Blacks of mixed-blood, men from the Sennaar and the Kordufan, so exactly observed that they could serve as evidence for the anthropological dissertations by M. Serres, so expertly drawn that they will guarantee the success of the painting in which they find a place.[41]

Just as he named Humboldt when endorsing Valerio's watercolors, Gautier here invokes a scholar synonymous with recent developments in the field of racial science. Étienne Serres was professor of Comparative Anatomy and the curator of an anthropological gallery at the Museum of Natural History in Paris. There, Serres coordinated a network of artists and scientists pioneering the discipline of physical anthropology, the classification of racial types according to anatomical criteria. In fact, the anthropological collection that Serres created with objects sent to him by colleagues working in the field opened to the public at the Museum in the Jardin des Plantes in 1855, the same year as the Exposition Universelle.[42]

Once again, in 1857, Gautier underlines Gérôme's "ethnographic exactitude," saying that the painter had "satisfied one of the most demanding instincts of the present epoch: the desire which people have to know more about each other

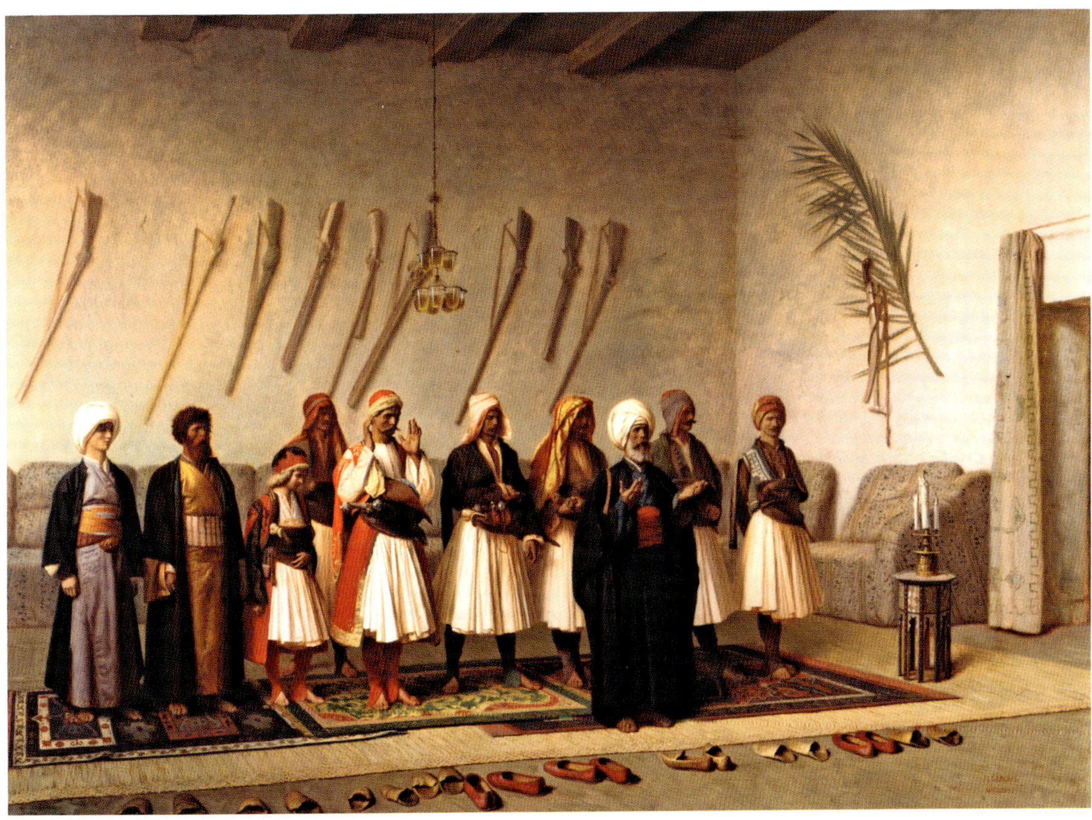

Figure 18.6 *Prayer in the House of an Arnaut Chieftain*, Jean-Léon Gérôme (1824–1904), 1857, oil on canvas, 66 x 95.25 cm, Najd Collection. Courtesy of Mathaf Gallery, London.

than that which is revealed in imaginary portraits." Above all, Gérôme had "a sense for the exotic, for want of a better term," Gautier writes, "that makes him discover straight away the characteristic differences between one race and another."[43] Even Du Camp, whose comments were by no means as unconditionally positive as those of Gautier, conceded that *Egyptian Recruits* demonstrated "remarkable qualities of observation in the diverse types of poor Nubians [...]."[44] In a period in which critics were in thrall to ethnographic inquiry as the key to the truth of human origins and racial filiations, what were understood as the concrete, factual tools of science were far more useful to an ambitious realist painter than boundless creativity or an undisciplined imagination.

By foregrounding the affinities between Lewis and Gérôme, and the capacities attributed to watercolor in the 1850s, we rediscover the productive cosmopolitan exchanges between Britain and France that were invigorating European art and the formulation of realism at mid-century. The realism bred of this cross-Channel interaction between artistic media does not however correspond to the de-Orientalized, Paris-centered avant-garde esthetic in either the canonical analyses of Baudelaire's *The Painter of Modern Life* or Castagnary's xenophobic denunciations of Orientalism. Fruit of a sustained international dialog, watercolor, a medium understood as qualified to document truthfully the myriad aspects of the Orient, its colorful figures and customs, served as an important catalyst in the development of this short-lived cosmopolitan experiment. In 1855, Du Camp testified to the impact of English painting on French artists as a result of the Exposition Universelle and cautions us against looking through too narrow a lens: "The English Exposition is important and ought to be beneficial for us as it proves, one more time, that the field of art is unlimited, for they have been able to discover some effects, often remarkable, outside the realm to which our artists confine themselves."[45] Two years later, Paul Mantz, confronted with Gérôme's paintings at the Salon—which, in addition to the Egyptian scenes, included the popular favorite, *The Duel After the Masked Ball*, set in contemporary Paris—marveled in mock astonishment at the extent to which the formerly confining realms had been redrawn. "But what! As of yesterday, the drama of modern life has yet another historian."[46] Unwittingly or not, Mantz here aligns Gérôme with the moniker Baudelaire later used for his portrait of Constantin Guys, the "painter of modern life," a realist watercolorist equally at ease traveling back and forth between London, Paris and the Orient.

Notes

I am grateful to Mary Roberts, Reina Lewis and Zeynep İnankur for inviting me to participate in the conference where I presented an earlier version of this essay. Their perceptive comments helped immensely as I revised it to its present form. All translations from the French are my own, unless otherwise indicated. Thanks to: Stéphane Guégan, David Lewis, Sebastien de Courtois, Etienne Hellman, Emily Weeks, and, as ever, Giovanni Panebianco. I would like to dedicate this essay to the memory of Robert Rosenblum, who first introduced me to the art of Channel crossing.

1 See Paul Greenhalgh, *Ephemeral Vistas: The Expositions Universelles, Great Exhibitions, and World's Fairs* (Manchester: Manchester University Press, 1988).

2 See Edmund Morris, *French Art in Nineteenth-Century Britain* (New Haven: Yale University Press, 2005), 120; Patricia Mainardi, *Art and Politics of the Second Empire: The Universal Exposition of 1855 and 1867* (New Haven: Yale University Press, 1986); Marcia Pointon, "From the Midst of Warfare and its Incidents to the Peaceful Scenes of Home: The Exposition Universelle of 1855," *Journal of European Studies* 11 (1981): 246–57; and Howard Rodée, "France and England: Some Mid-Victorian Views of One Another's Painting," *Gazette des Beaux-Arts* 91 (1978): 44–46.

3 Nicholas Tromans, "Introduction: British Orientalist Painting," in *The Lure of the East: British Orientalist Painting*, ed. Tromans (New Haven and London: Tate Publishing, 2008), 10.

4 Roger Benjamin, *Orientalist Aesthetics: Art, Colonialism, and French North Africa* (Berkeley: University of California Press, 2003), 23–31.

5 Donald A. Rosenthal, *Orientalism: The Near East in French Painting 1800–1880*, exhibition catalog (Rochester: Memorial Art Gallery of the University of Rochester, 1982), 140.

6 Théophile Gautier, *Les beaux-arts en Europe, 1855* (Paris: Michel Lévy Frères, 1855), 1, 95–96.

7 Théophile Gautier, "Salon de 1857 (1)," *L'Artiste* (June 14, 1857): 190–91.

8 Albert Boime, "The Second Empire's Official Realism," in *The European Realist Tradition*, ed. Gabriel P. Weisberg (Bloomington: Indiana University Press, 1982), 85–86.

9 For a reassessment of Gérôme's realism in the 1850s, see Peter Benson Miller, "Jean-Léon Gerome and Ethnographic Realism at the Salon of 1857," in *Reconsidering Gérôme*, ed. Scott Allan and Mary Morton (Los Angeles: Getty Publications, 2010).

10 On Lewis in Cairo, see Emily Weeks, "Cultures Crossed: John

Frederick Lewis and the Art of Orientalist Painting," in Tromans, *The Lure of the East,* 22–32.

11 Eugène Loudun, *Le Salon de 1855* (Paris: Ledoyen, 1855), 3.

12 Nadar [Tournachon, Gaspard-Félix, dit], "Salon de 1855," *Figaro* 2, no. 73 (August 19, 1855): 3.

13 Ferdinand de Lasteyrie, *La peinture à l'Exposition universelle. Étude sur l'art contemporain* (Paris: Castel, 1863), 34.

14 Maxime Du Camp, *Les beaux-arts à l'Exposition universelle de 1855* (Paris: Librairie Nouvelle, 1855), 314–15.

15 Etienne-Jean Delécluze, *Les beaux-arts dans les deux mondes en 1855* (Paris: Charpentier, 1856), 129.

16 Martin Hardie, *Watercolour Painting in Britain*, ed. Dudley Snelgrove with Jonathan Mayne and Basil Taylor, 3 vols (London: B. T. Batsford, 1966), 1, 53–54.

17 Eugène Delacroix, *Dictionnaire des beaux-arts*, ed. Anne Larue (Paris: Hermann, 1996), 105.

18 Du Camp, *Les beaux-arts à l'Exposition universelle de 1855*, 317.

19 Maxime Du Camp, *Le Salon de 1857* (Paris: Librairie Nouvelle, 1857), 61.

20 Alphonse de Calonne, "Exposition des beaux-arts de 1857," *Revue contemporaine* 32 (1857): 611.

21 Théophile Gautier, "Salon de 1857. IV. MM. Gérôme, Mottez" *L'Artiste* (July 5, 1857): 247.

22 Michel Thévoz, *L'académisme et ses fantasmes: le réalisme imaginaire de Charles Gleyre* (Paris: Les Éditions de Minuit, 1980), 89–91.

23 Nancy Scott Newhouse, "From Rome to Khartoum: Gleyre, Lowell, and the Evidence of the Boston Watercolors and Drawings," *Charles Gleyre, 1806–1874*, exhibition catalog (New York: Grey Art Gallery, 1980), 103–4.

24 Théophile Gautier, "Aquarelles ethnographiques," *Les beaux-arts en Europe, 1855* (Paris: Michel Lévy Frères, 1855), 2, 289. On Valerio, see Christine Peltre, "Les 'géographies' de l'art: physiognomies, races et mythes dans la peinture 'ethnographique,'" *Romantisme* 130 (2005): 67–79.

25 Gautier, *Les beaux-arts en Europe, 1855*, 2, 292.

26 Ibid., 312.

27 Charles Baudelaire, *The Painter of Modern Life and Other Essays*, trans. and ed. Jonathan Mayne (London: Phaidon, 1964), 5. Thackeray's essay on Guys in the "columns of a London review" has not been traced. On Lewis in Cairo, see Thackeray, *Notes of a Journey from Cornhill to Grand Cairo* (London, 1846).

28 See, for example, Gérôme, *Arnaute fumant*, 1865, Private Collection, reproduced in Gerald M. Ackerman, *Jean-Léon Gérôme*, rev. edn (Paris: A.C.R., 2000), 258, cat. 158.

29 Baudelaire, *The Painter of Modern Life and Other Essays*, 19.

30 Ibid., 22.

31 See Mary Roberts's discussion of *The Hhareem* in *Orientalism: Delacroix to Klee*, ed. Roger Benjamin, exhibition catalog, The Art Gallery of New South Wales, 2001 (orig. published 1997), 79–80. Roberts cites Lewis's description of the painting in the *Royal Scottish Academy Catalogue of the 27th Exhibition*, 1853, no. 494.

32 Delécluze, *Les beaux-arts dans les deux mondes en 1855*, 29.

33 A.-J. Du Pays, "Exposition universelle des beaux-arts. École Anglaise," *L'Illustration* 26, 653 (September 1, 1855): 151.

34 Gautier, *Les beaux-arts en Europe, 1855*, 1, 97.

35 Ibid., 98.

36 Ibid., 99–100.

37 Du Camp, *Les beaux-arts à l'Exposition universelle de 1855*, 317–18.

38 Ibid., 317–18.

39 "This Oriental page has a truthful aspect, an appearance of good faith, that imposes itself on the viewer's attention" (A.-J. Du Pays, "Salon de 1857," *L'Illustration* 30, 755 [August 15, 1857]: 1089); "Serene seriousness, brilliant light and the infinite horizons [of the Orient], with a breadth, a precision, a surprising truth" (Victor Fournel, "Mélanges. Salon de 1857," *Le Correspondant* 5 [August 1857]: 744; "It is by the most absolute simplicity that M. Gérôme has arrived at the truest, most penetrating, most successful effect" (Jules Verne, "Salon de 1857," *Revue des Beaux-Arts* 8 [1857]: 273).

40 Émile de La Bédollière, "Exposition de 1857," *Le Siècle* (August 23, 1857), n.p.

41 Gautier, "Gérôme. Tableaux, études et croquis de voyage." *L'Artiste* 6, 3 (December 28, 1856): 34.

42 *Guide des étrangers dans le Musée d'Histoire naturelle, publié avec l'autorisation de l'administration* (Paris, 1855).

43 Gautier, "Salon de 1857. IV. MM. Gérôme, Mottez," 246.

44 Du Camp, *Le Salon de 1857*, 64.

45 Du Camp, *Les beaux-arts à l'Exposition universelle de 1855*, 320.

46 Paul Mantz, "Salon de 1857," *Revue française* 10 (1857): 54.

Bibliography

About, Edmond. *Voyage à travers l'Exposition des beaux-arts (peinture et sculpture)*. Paris: Hachette, 1855.

Ackerman, Gerald M. *Jean-Léon Gérôme*, rev. edn. Paris: A.C.R., 2000.

Baudelaire, Charles. *The Painter of Modern Life and Other Essays*. Translated and edited by Jonathan Mayne. London: Phaidon, 1964.

Benjamin, Roger, ed. *Orientalism: Delacroix to Klee*, exhibition catalog. The Art Gallery of New South Wales, 2001 (orig. published 1997).

Benjamin, Roger. *Orientalist Aesthetics: Art, Colonialism, and French North Africa*. Berkeley: University of California Press, 2003.

Benson Miller, Peter. "Jean-Léon Gérome and Ethnographic Realism at the Salon of 1857." In *Reconsidering Gérôme*, edited by Scott Allan and Mary Morton. Los Angeles: Getty Publications, 2010.

Bida, Alexandre, and E. Barbot. *Souvenirs de l'Egypte*. Paris: Lemercier, 1851.

Boime, Albert. "The Second Empire's Official Realism." In *The European Realist Tradition* edited by Gabriel P. Weisberg, 31–123. Bloomington: Indiana University Press, 1982.

Calonne, Alphonse de. "Exposition des beaux-arts de 1857." *Revue contemporaine* 32 (1857): 609–11.

Delécluze, Etienne-Jean. *Les beaux-arts dans les deux mondes en 1855*. Paris: Charpentier, 1856.

Du Camp, Maxime, *Les beaux-arts à l'Exposition universelle de 1855*. Paris: Librairie Nouvelle, 1855.

Du Camp, Maxime, *Le Salon de 1857*. Paris: Librairie Nouvelle, 1857.

Du Pays, A.- J. "Exposition universelle des beaux-arts. École Anglaise." *L'Illustration* 26, no. 653 (September 1, 1855): 150–51.

Du Pays, A.- J. "Salon de 1857," *L'Illustration* 30, no. 755 [August 15, 1857]: 1089.

Fournel, Victor. "Mélanges. Salon de 1857." *Le Correspondant* 5 (August 1857): 744.

Galichon, Émile. "M. Gérôme: peintre ethnographe." *Gazette des Beaux-Arts* (1868): 147–51.

Gautier, Théophile. *Les beaux-arts en Europe, 1855.* Paris: Michel Lévy Frères, 1855.

Gautier, Théophile. "Gérôme. Tableaux, études et croquis de voyage." *L'Artiste* (December 28, 1856): 33–35.

Gautier, Théophile. "Salon de 1857 (I)." *L'Artiste* (June 14, 1857): 189–92.

Gautier, Théophile. "Salon de 1857 (IV). MM. Gérôme, Mottez," *L'Artiste* (July 5, 1857): 245–49.

Gray Art Gallery. *Charles Gleyre, 1806–1874*, exhibition catalog. New York, 1980.

Greenhalgh, Paul. *Ephemeral Vistas: The Expositions Universelles, Great Exhibitions, and World's Fairs*. Manchester: Manchester University Press, 1988.

Hardie, Martin. *Watercolour Painting in Britain.* Edited by Dudley Snelgrove with Jonathan Mayne and Basil Taylor, 3 vols. London: B. T. Batsford, 1966.

La Bédollière, Émile de. "Exposition de 1857." *Le Siècle* (August 23, 1857), n.p.

Lasteyrie, Ferdinand de. *La peinture à l'Exposition universelle. Étude sur l'art contemporain*. Paris: Castel, 1863.

Lavergne, Claudius. *Exposition universelle de 1855: beaux-arts*. Paris: De Bailly, Divry et Cie, 1855.

Lewis, Michael. *John Frederick Lewis, R.A. 1805–1876*. Leigh-on-Sea, 1978.

Loudun, Eugène. *Le Salon de 1855*. Paris: Ledoyen, 1855.

Mainardi, Patricia. *Art and Politics of the Second Empire: The Universal Exposition of 1855 and 1867.* New Haven: Yale University Press, 1986.

Mantz, Paul. "Salon de 1857." *Revue française* 10 (1857): 54–55.

Morris, Edmund. *French Art in Nineteenth-Century Britain*. New Haven: Yale University Press, 2005.

Nadar [Tournachon, Gaspard-Félix, dit]. "Salon de 1855." *Figaro* 2, no. 73 (August 19, 1855): 2–3.

Nadar [Tournachon, Gaspard-Félix, dit]. "Salon de 1855," *Figaro* 2, no. 76 (September 9, 1855): 6–7.

Nochlin, Linda. "The Imaginary Orient." *Art in America* (May 1986): 118–31, 187–91; reprinted in *The Politics of Vision: Essays on Nineteenth-Century Art and Society*, 33–59. New York: Harper & Row, 1989.

Peltre, Christine. "Les 'géographies' de l'art: physiognomies, races et mythes dans la peinture 'ethnographique.'" *Romantisme*, no. 130 (2005): 67–79.

Perrier, Charles. *Étude sur les beaux-arts en France et à l'étranger*. Paris: Hachette, 1863.

Pointon, Marcia. "From the Midst of Warfare and its Incidents to the Peaceful Scenes of Home: The Exposition Universelle of 1855." *Journal of European Studies* 11 (1981): 246–57.

Rodée, Howard. "France and England: Some Mid-Victorian Views of One Another's Painting." *Gazette des Beaux-Arts* 91 (1978): 44–46.

Rosenthal, Donald A. *Orientalism: The Near East in French Painting 1800–1880*, exhibition catalog. Rochester: Memorial Art Gallery of the University of Rochester, 1982.

Smith, Karen W. *Constantin Guys: Crimean War Drawings, 1854–1856*, exhibition catalog. The Cleveland Museum of Art, 1978.

Stevens, MaryAnne, ed. *The Orientalists: Delacroix to Matisse. European Painters in North Africa and the Near East*, exhibition catalog. Royal Academy of Arts, London, 1984.

Thackeray, William Makepeace. *Notes of a Journey from Cornhill to Grand Cairo*. London, 1846.

Nancy Scott Newhouse, "From Rome to Khartoum: Gleyre, Lowell, and the Evidence of the Boston Watercolors and Drawings." *Charles Gleyre, 1806–1874*, exhibition catalog. New York, Grey Art Gallery, 1980, 103–4.

Thévoz, Michel. *L'académisme et ses fantasmes: le réalisme imaginaire de Charles Gleyre.* Paris: Les Éditions de Minuit, 1980.

Tromans, Nicholas. *The Lure of the East: British Orientalist Painting*, New Haven and London: Tate Publishing, 2008. Published in conjunction with the exhibition *The Lure of the East: British Orientalist Painting* shown at the Yale Center for British Art, Tate Britain, Suna and İnan Kıraç Pera Museum and the Sharjah Art Museum.

Verne, Jules. "Salon de 1857." *Revue des Beaux-Arts* 8 (1857): 273.

Weeks, Emily. "Cultures Crossed: John Frederick Lewis and the Art of Orientalist Painting." In *The Lure of the East: British Orientalist Painting* edited by Nicholas Tromans, 22–32. New Haven and London: Tate Publishing, 2008.

Notes on Contributors

Tim Barringer

Tim Barringer is Paul Mellon Professor in the Department of the History of Art at Yale University and was Slade Professor of Fine Art at the University of Cambridge in 2009. His books include *Reading the Pre-Raphaelites* (New Haven: Yale University Press, 1998); *Men at Work: Art and Labour in Victorian Britain* (London and New Haven: Yale University Press, 2005); and *Broken Pastoral: Art and Music in Britain* (forthcoming). He is co-editor of *Colonialism and the Object* (London: Routledge, 1998) and *Frederic Leighton: Antiquity, Renaissance, Modernity* (New Haven: Yale University Press, 1999). Co-edited exhibition catalogs include *American Sublime: Landscape Painting in the United States 1820-1880* (Princeton: Princeton University Press, 2002); *Art and Emancipation in Jamaica: Isaac Mendes Belisario and His Worlds* (Yale Center for British Art, 2007); and *Opulence and Anxiety: Landscape Paintings from the Royal Academy of Arts*. He is co-curator of *Pre-Raphaelites: Victorian Avant-Garde*, Tate, Washington and Moscow, 2012–13.

Edhem Eldem

Edhem Eldem is Professor at the Department of History of Boğaziçi University, Istanbul. His interests include foreign trade in the Levant in the eighteenth century, the development of an urban bourgeoisie in late-nineteenth-century Istanbul, the history of the Imperial Ottoman Bank, and late-nineteenth-century Ottoman first-person narratives and biographies. He is the author of *Doğu'yu Tüketmek* [*Consuming the Orient*] (Istanbul, 2007); *İstanbul'da Ölüm: Osmanlı İslam Kültüründe Ölüm ve Ritüelleri* [*Death in Istanbul. Death and its Rituals in Ottoman-Islamic Culture*] (Istanbul, 2005); *French Trade in Istanbul in the Eighteenth Century* (Leiden, 1999); *Osmanlı Bankası Tarihi* [*A History of the Ottoman Bank*] (Istanbul, 1999); *Un Ottoman en Orient. Osman Hamdi Bey en Irak, 1869–1871* (2010) and is co-author with Daniel Goffman and Bruce Masters of *The Ottoman City between East and West: Aleppo, Izmir and Istanbul* (Cambridge, 1999).

Ahmet Ersoy

Ahmet Ersoy is Assistant Professor at the Department of History at Boğaziçi University, Istanbul. His work deals with nineteenth-century cultural transformations in the Ottoman realm. His publications include: "Architecture and the Search for Ottoman Origins in the Tanzimat Period," *Muqarnas* 24 (2007): 79–102; "A Sartorial Tribute to Tanzimat Ottomanism: the Elbise-i Osmaniyye Album," *Muqarnas* 20 (2003): 187–207; and, with Maciej Gorny and Vangelis Kechriotis (eds.), *Discourses of Collective Identity in Central and Southeastern Europe (1775–1945): Texts and Commentaries*, vol. 3 (Budapest: Central European University Press, 2010).

Semra Germaner

Semra Germaner is Professor at the Art History Department of Mimar Sinan Fine Arts University, Istanbul. Her specialist fields are Ottoman and Turkish art and Orientalist painting. She is the author of *Son Osmanlı Dönemi İstanbul Ahşap Konutlarında Cephe Bezemeleri* [*Façade Decoration of Wooden Houses in Istanbul during the Late Ottoman Period*] (I.T.U. Faculty of Architecture Publications, 1982); *XVIII.Yüzyıl Avrupa Resmi, Anlatımı Biçimlendiren Etmenler* [*Eighteenth-Century European Painting*] (Kabalcı Yayınevi, 1996); *1960 Sonrası Sanat: Akımlar, Eğilimler, Gruplar, Sanatçılar* [*Art after 1960: Movements, Groups, Artists*] (Kabalcı Yayınevi, 1997). Germaner is the co-author with Zeynep İnankur of *Orientalism and Turkey* (Turkish Cultural Foundation, 1989) and *Constantinople and the Orientalists* (Türkiye İş Bankası Kültür Yayınları, 2008).

Aykut Gürçağlar

Aykut Gürçağlar is Associate Professor at the History of Art Department of Mimar Sinan Fine Arts University, Istanbul. His fields of interest are: Ottoman and Japanese Westernization movements in art, dragoman depictions in the Ottoman Empire, Orientalism and contemporary art. His publications include: "Representation of Ottoman Interpreters by Western

Painters," *Acta Oriantalia Academiae Sciantiarum Hungaricae*, S. 57, Budapest, 2004 (2); "The Diplomatic Trinity: Ambassadors, Dragomans and The Porte," *Çeviribilim ve Uygulamaları Dergisi*, S. 13, Ankara, 2003; "Thoughts on Caliph Abdülmecid Efendi and His Painting Titled *Beethoven in the Harem*," *"Interactions in Art" Symposium* Hacettepe University, Faculty of Letters Department of Art History, *Proceedings*, Ankara, 136–141; Türkiye İş Bankası, Ankara, 2000; "19. Yüzyıl Batı Resim Sanatına Biçim Veren Kaynaklar Avrupa Sanatında Japon Resminin Etkisi", ["The Influence of Japanese Painting in European Art"], *Toplumsal Tarih*, 117, İstanbul; *Hayali İstanbul Manzaraları*, [*Imaginary Views of Istanbul*] (Istanbul: Yapı Kredi, 2005).

Teresa Heffernan

Teresa Heffernan is Associate Professor of English at Saint Mary's University, Halifax, Nova Scotia. She is author of *Post-Apocalyptic Culture: Modernism, Postmodernism, and the Twentieth-Century Novel* (University of Toronto Press, 2008); and is currently working on a new book entitled *Across the East/West Divide: Feminism, Orientalism, and Women's Travel Narratives*. Her articles have appeared in journals such as *Eighteenth-Century Studies*, *Twentieth Century Literature, Arab Journal in the Humanities*, and *Canadian Literature*. Her editing work includes special issues of *Cultural Studies* ("Revisiting the Subaltern in the New Empire" with Jill Didur) and *Cultural Critique* ("Critical Post Humanism" with Jill Didur and Bart Simon). She is co-editor, with Reina Lewis, of *Cultures in Dialogue*, a multi-volume project that brings back into circulation travel works by Ottoman, British, and American writers.

Zeynep İnankur

Zeynep İnankur is Professor at the Art History Department of Mimar Sinan Fine Arts University, Istanbul. She is the author of *19. Yüzyıl Avrupasında Heykel ve Resim Sanatı*, [*Painting and Sculpture in Nineteenth-Century European Art*] (Kabalcı Publishing, 1997); "The Official Painters of the Ottoman Court," *Art Turc, 10e Congrès Internationale d'art turc* (Fondation Max van Berchem, 1999) and "Orientalisti Italiani" ["Italian Orientalists"] *Gli Italiani di İstanbul: Figure, Comunita e Istituzioni dalle Riforme alla Repubblica1839–1923* (Edizioni della Fondazione Giovanni Agnelli, 2007). İnankur, whose area of interest is nineteenth-century European and Ottoman art and Orientalist painting, is the co-author with Semra Germaner of *Orientalism and Turkey* (Istanbul: Turkish Cultural Foundation, 1989) and *Constantinople and the Orientalists* (Istanbul: Türkiye İş Bankası Kültür Yayınları, 2008). İnankur and Germaner are currently working on a project on the cultural exchanges between nineteenth-century Istanbul and Cairo.

Reina Lewis

Reina Lewis is Artscom Centenary Professor of Cultural Studies, at the London College of Fashion, University of the Arts London. She is author of *Rethinking Orientalism: Women, Travel, and the Ottoman Harem* (London and New York: I.B. Tauris, 2004) and *Gendering Orientalism: Race, Femininity and Representation* (London: Routledge, 1996). Reina is co-editor with Nancy Micklewright of *Gender, Modernity and Liberty: Middle Eastern and Western Women's Writings: A Critical Reader*, (I.B. Tauris, 2006), and with Sara Mills of *Feminist Postcolonial Theory: A Reader* (Edinburgh University Press, 2003). She is also co-editor, with Teresa Heffernan, of the book series *Cultures in Dialogue: Women's Travel Writing* (Gorgias Press). Her current project on *Re-Fashioning Orientalism* contextualizes contemporary veiling debates in relation to new trends in Muslim style and the emergence of Muslim lifestyle media and markets.

Briony Llewellyn

Briony Llewellyn is an independent scholar specializing in British artists' depictions of the Near and Middle East. She worked on the catalog of the Searight Collection at the Victoria and Albert Museum, 1985–88. She has contributed to numerous catalogs and publications including exhibitions of Edward Lear (Royal Academy of Arts, 1985), Amadeo Preziosi (Victoria and Albert Museum, 1985), David Roberts (Barbican Art Gallery, 1986), and Black Victorians (Manchester City Art Gallery, 2005). In 2008 she was loans consultant for Tate Britain's exhibition, *The Lure of the East*. She has published several articles on John Frederick Lewis and is currently working on a full-length study of his life and work, as well as continuing her research for the Eastern paintings and drawings section of a *catalogue raisonné* of David Roberts.

Nancy Micklewright

Nancy Micklewright is Head of Scholarly Programming and Publications at the Freer and Sackler Galleries in Washington, DC. Before joining the Freer and Sackler, she was Senior Program Officer in the Getty Foundation in Los Angeles and Professor of the history of Islamic art and architecture and the history of photography at the University of Victoria in British Columbia, Canada. She is the author of *A Victorian Traveler in the Middle East: The Photography and Travel Writing of Annie Lady Brassey* (Aldershot and Burlington: Ashgate, 2003), and with Reina Lewis, *Gender, Modernity and Liberty, Middle Eastern and Western Women's Writings: A Critical Sourcebook* (London and New York: I. B. Tauris, 2006), as well as numerous articles.

Peter Benson Miller

Peter Benson Miller is an art historian and curator of nineteenth- and twentieth-century European and American art. He co-curated the exhibition *De Delacroix à Renoir: L'Algérie des peintres* at the Institut du monde arabe in Paris in 2003. His essays appear in retrospective exhibition catalogs dedicated to Ingres (Paris, 2007) and Chassériau (Paris, Strasbourg, New York, 2003), as well as *Reconsidering Gérôme*, published by the Getty in 2010. He has published articles in the *Art Bulletin*, *Visual Resources* and *48/14: La Révue du Musée d'Orsay*. Recently, he curated and edited the catalog for Philip Guston's Roma series for the Museo Carlo Bilotti in Rome, an exhibition traveling to the Phillips Collection in Washington, DC in 2011. He is currently finishing a book about French art and anthropology in colonial Algeria, forthcoming from Penn State University Press.

Donald Preziosi

Donald Preziosi is Emeritus Professor of Art History at UCLA and former Slade Professor of Fine Art at Oxford. He was born in New York City and educated at Harvard, where he received a PhD in art history, and has taught at Yale, MIT, SUNY and UCLA. The author of twelve books on art history, critical theory, and the historiography of cultural institutions, his book *The Art of Art History* (Oxford: Oxford University Press, 1998; 2nd edn, 2009) is the most widely used introduction to the field in English. He is co-author and co-editor with Claire Farago of *Grasping the World: The Idea of the Museum* (Aldershot: Ashgate, 2004). His newest book, *Enchanted Credulities: Art, Religion, and Amnesia*, is forthcoming from Routledge in 2011.

Günsel Renda

Günsel Renda was for many years Professor of Art History at Haceteppe University, and currently teaches at Koç University. She specializes in Ottoman Art, Ottoman Painting and Interactions of European and Ottoman Culture and is the co-author of *A History of Turkish Painting* (Geneva and Istanbul, 1988); *The Sultan's Portrait. Picturing the House of Osman*, (Istanbul, 2000); *Minnet av Konstantinople. Den osmansk-turkiska 1700-talssamlingen pa Biby* [The Memory of Constantinople. The Ottoman Turkish Collection at Biby] (Stockholm, 2003); *Image of the Turks in Seventeenth-Century Europe*, (Istanbul, 2005); *Osmanlı Resim Sanatı* [Ottoman Painting] (Serpil Bağcı, Filiz Çağman, Zeren Tanındı). She is also Editor of *Woman in Anatolia. 9000 Years of the Anatolian Woman* (Istanbul, 1994) and *The Ottoman Civilization*, with Halil Inalcık (Istanbul, 2002) and the *Book of Felicity* (Barcelona, 2007).

Christine Riding

Christine Riding was the Tate curator and project leader of *The Lure of the East: British Orientalist Painting*. She has been the curator of eighteenth and nineteenth-century British Art at Tate Britain since June 1999 and Deputy Editor of *Art History* (*Journal of the Association of Art Historians*) since June 2007. Her publications include *John Everett Millais* (London: Tate, 2006) and, as co-author, *Hogarth* (London: Tate, 2006). Christine Riding's co-curation at Tate includes *William Blake* (2000), *Constable to Delacroix: British Art and the French Romantics, 1820–1840* (2003), *A Picture of Britain* (2005), *William Hogarth* (2006–7) and the forthcoming *Gauguin: Maker of Myth* at Tate Modern (2010) and *Turner and Marine Painting: Imagining the Sea* in collaboration with the National Maritime Museum, Greenwich (2013).

Mary Roberts

Mary Roberts is the John Schaeffer Associate Professor of British Art at the University of Sydney. She is the author of *Intimate Outsiders. The Harem in Ottoman and Orientalist Art and Travel Literature* (Durham and London: Duke University Press, 2007) and has co-edited three books: *Edges of Empire. Orientalism and Visual Culture* (Oxford and Victoria: Blackwells, 2005), *Orientalism's Interlocutors. Painting, Architecture, Photography* (Durham and London: Duke University Press, 2002) and *Refracting Vision. Essays on the Writings of Michael Fried* (Sydney: Power, 2000). She has been a visiting fellow at the Yale Center for British Art, the Getty Research Institute (2008–9) and the Clark Art Institute/ Oakley Center for the Humanities (2009–10). She is currently writing a book on cultural exchanges between Ottoman and Orientalist artists in nineteenth-century Istanbul.

Sarah Searight

Sarah Searight has written extensively on cultural relations between Britain and the Ottoman Empire, starting with *The British in the Middle East* first published in 1969 (London: Weidenfeld & Nicolson) and again in 1980 (London and the Hague: East-West). Through the 1970s and 1980s she worked as a freelance historian and journalist, continuing her interest in European involvement in the Middle East, focusing on economic development in the Persian Gulf. In 1991 she published *Steaming East* (London: Bodley Head). In 1997 she helped to found the Association for the Study of Travel in the Near East (ASTENE) and has edited two of its volumes of papers: *Travellers in the Levant* and *Women Travellers in the Near East*. She lectures all over the country on the art and architecture of the Islamic world. Her latest publication is in the category of art history: *Lapis Lazuli: In Pursuit of a Celestial Stone* (East and West: forthcoming) which follows the travels of lapis between East and West.

Wendy M. K. Shaw

Wendy M. K. Shaw is Professor of Art History in the Department of Art History and the Center for Cultural Studies Program in World Arts at the University of Bern, Switzerland. She is the author of *Possessors and Possessed: Museums, Archaeology, and the Visualization of History in the Ottoman Empire* (Berkeley: University of California Press, 2003) and *Modernity Reflected: the Translation of Western Painting in the Ottoman Empire* (London: I. B. Tauris, 2010). Her many articles include, “Museums and Narratives of Display from the Late Ottoman Empire to the Turkish Republic,” *Muqarnas* 24 (2007), and “Modernism’s Innocent Eye and Nineteenth-Century Ottoman Photography,” *History of Photography* 33, no. 1 (2009). She is interested in museum studies, modern art history, colonial studies, history of archeology, and history of photography in relation to the Ottoman Empire and the Republic of Turkey.

Nicholas Tromans

Nicholas Tromans is Senior Lecturer at Kingston University in London. He was the curator of *The Lure of the East: British Orientalist Painting* and editor of the accompanying book. Among his other publications are *David Wilkie: The People’s Painter* (Edinburgh University Press 2007) and a forthcoming book on the Victorian asylum painter Richard Dadd (Tate Publishing 2011). His current research is on the reception of Old Master painting in Radical political circles in London in the early nineteenth century.

Index

A

ABC Club *see* Artists of the Bosphorus and Constantinople 128, 132, 202, 204
Abdülaziz, Sultan 128, 130, 205, 207
Abdülhamid I, Sultan 221
Abdülhamid II, Sultan 162, 227, 235
Abdullah Frères 105, 132, 235
Abdülmecid, Sultan 203, 225–227
  Fatma Sultan 131, 202
  David Wilkie's portrait of… 26, 34, 51, 52, 70, 233
Aboukir Bay 80
Abrahamic faiths 34, 35
Abu Dhabi 67, 70
Abu Simbel 81
Academy of Fine Arts (Istanbul) 238
Ackerman, James 123
Ackley, Brian 70
Aestheticism (British) 133, 243–252
Ainslie, Sir Robert 79
Aitchison, George 251
Aivazovsky, Ivan 227
Aleppo 78, 85 n. 5
Alexandria 78, 80, 103
  bombardment of… (1882) 103
Alibi Brown, Yasmin 54
Allom, Thomas 82, 115–123
  Character and Costume in Turkey and Italy 82
Alloula, Malek *The Colonial Harem* 104
Anderson, Benedict 158
aquatints 79, 115
Arab nationalism 58
Arabian cultural identities 68
Arabian Nights 43, 172, 173, 244
Art Journal 169
Artists of the Bosphorus and Constantinople 128, 132, 202, 204
artifacts 36, 89–92, 94, 149
  cultural 20, 22
  Ottoman 24, 49
  traditional 150–152
Asia Minor 78, 79, 115ff, 200
authenticity 51–53, 70, 148, 259, 260, 266

B

Baghdad 25, 37, 77, 184–193
Baltalimanı, Palace of… 203
Balyan, Sarkis 146 (Fig. 9.1), 203
Bann, Stephen 146
Barker, Robert 116
Bartlett, William 82
Bashibazuks 260, 264
Baudelaire, Charles 176, 264–266, 268
Bauernfeind, Gustav 34, 65
  Entrance to Temple Mount, Jerusalem 34
de La Bédollière, Émile 267
Bedouin Arab 115, 173, 185–187, 190, 192
Belzoni, Giovanni Battista 81
Benjamin, Roger 68, 137
Berggren, Guillaume 100
Bermingham, Ann 120
Bertaux, Hippolyte 227
Beylerbeyi Palace 221, 227
Bida, Alexandre 263, 266, 267
  The Ceremony of the Dosseh 263
  Souvenirs de l'Egypte 263
Boime, Albert 260
Bomberg, David 33
Bonhams 69, 72 n. 26
Bonomi, Joseph 82
Borra, Giovanni 79
Bosporus 83, 121, 135, 238
  Mary Walker's sketches of… 204

Bossoli, Carlo 82
Bowman Dodd, Anna 161–162
In the Palaces of the Sultan 161
Boxall, William 172
Bracebridge, Selina 81
Brassey, Lady Annie 161–162
Braun, Georg *Civitas Orbis Terrarum* 78
British Empire 102
see also imperialism
British Mechanics and Literary Institute (Istanbul) 204
British Society of Dilettanti 79, 263
British travelers 37, 120, 121, 158
Browne, Henriette 34, 49, 51, 52, 203
A Visit: Harem Interior, Constantinople 34, 49
A Flute Player 51
le Bruyn, Cornelius *A Voyage in the Levant or, Travels in the Principal Parts of Asia Minor* 78
Burton, Sir Richard 251

C

Cairo 34, 82–83, 103–104, 251, 266
Lewis, John Frederick 169, 170–173, 244–248, 264
Searight, Rodney 77
calligraphy 130, 204, 239 n. 16
Capoudaghlé, Constantin 222
Cassas, Louis Francois 80
Castagnary, Jules-Antoine 259–260, 266, 268
Casteras, Susan 202
catalogs *see* exhibition catalogs
Ceylan, Taner *Spiritual* 69
Cezar, Mustafa 128
Chandler, Richard 79
Chlebowski, Stanislas 227
Choiseul-Gouffier, Comte de 79, 221
Christie's 69
Çırağan Palace 221, 225, 227
Clark Art Institute 33
classification 106, 127, 158, 185, 267
Clausen, George 77
Cleeve, Colonel S. D. 103
Coleridge, Edward 173
collecting 55, 67, 68–70, 83, 90, 91, 92, 95, 104, 105
see also Searight Collection 77–85
collective memory 91
colonialism 92
see also imperialism
Constantinople 115–123, 135, 158, 160
British Ambassador 79
Constantinople Messenger 127–129, 205
European artists in… 82, 83
John Frederick Lewis in… 244, 249
Mary Walker in… 199–205
see also Istanbul
Cope, Charles West *Council of the Royal Academy Selecting Pictures for the Exhibition, 1875* 167
Coste, Pascal Xavier 173
costume albums 146, 151, 211–212, 216–217
Character and Costume in Turkey and Italy 82
Elbise-i ʻOsmaniyye 146, 148
Mecmuʻa-i Tesavir 146
Crimean War 82, 199, 202, 205, 206, 225, 264
Crutta, Antoni Łukasz 215
Crystal, Joshua 116
curating 33–43, 68
Curtis, Charles George 128, 200–202, 204
Curtis, Clara Fanny Montrose 202, 205

D

Dadd, Richard 33
Dagbladet 132
Daguerrotype 123
Damascus 56, 249, 251
Damascus (Edward Lear) 34
Daniell, Thomas *Picturesque Voyage to India* 120
Darby, Michael 78, 85
Darülmuallimat (Teacher Training College for Women) 130, 204
Darüşşafaka High School 234
Delacroix, Eugène 33, 34, 42, 263
Dictionnaire des beaux-arts 263
Delécluze, Etienne-Jean 262, 266
Denon, Dominique *Vivant Voyage dans la Basse et la Haute Égypte* 81
Deringil, Selim 145, 152 n. 1, 183
Dersaadet Darülmuallimat (Women's Teacher Training College of Istanbul) 204
dervishes 103, 147, 187, 264
Dicksee, Frank *Leila* 38, 40, 57
Dinet, Etienne 42
Disraeli, Benjamin *Tancred; or the New Crusade* 161
Dolmabahçe Palace 105, 221, 227
Dome of the Rock 67, 82
Dorment, Richard 66
Dorset Regiment, 1st 103
Doussault, Charles 225
dragoman (role of…) 211–217
draughtsmanship 78, 80, 81, 173
draughtsmen (French) 263

draughtsmen (Victorian) 77
draughtswoman (Selina Bracebridge) 81
Du Camp, Maxime 123, 262–264, 266–268
Du Pays, A.-J. 266
Dubai 70
Duchateau, Jean-François 215, 223

E

Edhem, İbrahim 151
Edib, Halide 51, 158–159
Edirne 161
Egee, Dale 68
Egypt 82, 83, 159, 223, 227, 263
  An Account of the Manners and Customs of the Modern Egyptians 172, 243, 248, 266
  ancient 80, 81, 160
  British soldiers in… 102–104
  Jean-Léon Gérôme 267
  John Frederick Lewis 172–175, 244–245, 260, 264
  monuments 123
  Napoleon's invasion of… 80
  photographs of… 102–103
  slave trade 173
Eldem, Edhem 36, 148
Ellison, Grace 51
ethnicity 53, 116, 157, 159
ethnographic study 160, 263
European artists 67, 78, 82, 221–229
European nationalism 157–162
exhibition advertising 37–42, 57
  catalog 39, 42–43, 69, 101, 104, 259
  making *see* curating
  marketing strategies 37–38, 54, 58, 69
exhibitions
  audio accompaniment 53
  A Grand Tour in the Ottoman Empire 84
  Babylon: Myth and Reality 36
  Consuming the Orient 36
  Eastern Encounters: Orientalist Painters of the Nineteenth Century 84
  Exposed: The Victorian Nude 38
  Looking East 85
  On the Banks of the Jordan 83
  Romantic Lebanon: the European View 1700–1900 83
  Sketches in the Holy Land 1839 84
  Sacred: Discover What We Share 35
  The Orient Observed 85
  The People and Places of Constantinople 83
  The Travels of Edward Lear 84
  Travellers beyond the Grand Tour 84
  Voyages and Visions 85
exoticism 104, 118, 123, 137, 187, 191
expatriate artistic communities 128
  see also Mary Walker; John Frederick Lewis
Exposition Universelle in 1855 259–268

F

Faed, John *Bedouin Exchanging a Slave for Armour* 34
fashion, Western 52, 56, 203
Fatma Sultan 52, 131, 139 n.26, 202–204
de Favray, Antoine 217
female gaze 50, 52
Fenerci Mehmet Efendi 212, 216
Festival of Muslim Cultures 35
Fethi Paşa, Ahmed 225
Fisk, Robert 53
Flaubert, Gustave 266
Fleig, Alan *Rêves de papier. La photographie orientaliste 1860–1914* 104
Frith, William Powell 171, 244
Fuller, Charles 227

G

Galata 135, 162, 200, 202, 234
Garnett, Lucy *Turkey of the Ottomans* 160
Gautier, Théophile 51, 135, 260, 262–264, 266–268
genealogical tree 221–223
Gérôme, Jean-Léon 34, 65, 67, 128, 259–262, 263, 264, 267–268
  Egyptian Recruits Crossing the Desert 263
  Napoleon in Egypt 34
  Prayer in the House of an Arnaut Chieftain 267
  Recreation in the Camp: Souvenir of Moldavia 262
  The Age of Augustus 262
  The Duel After the Masked Ball 268
  Young Greeks Making a Cockfight (Combat de Coqs) 262
Getty Research Institute 104
Gilchrist, Connie 251
Gillray, James 81
Gilpin, William 117, 120
Gilroy, Paul 161
Gleyre, Charles 263, 264, 266
Gobineau, Joseph Arthur *The Inequality of Races* 159
Goldberg, David Theo 158
Goodwin, Albert 77
Goodwin, Paul 54
Graham, John 169

Grant, Sir Francis 167, 175
Great Exhibition (1851) 259
Guès, Pierre 234, 239 n. 14
Guillemet, Pierre D. 227
Gustav III, King 222
Guys, Constantin 264, 265, 266, 267, 268

H

Halil Şerif Paşa 132
Halim, Princess Vijdane 205
Hamilton, Gavin 79
Hammer-Purgstall, Joseph von 145, 152 n. 1
Hanioğlu, Şükrü 127
Harbison, Robert 90
Hardt, Michael and Antonio Negri 158
harem 57, 70, 100, 105, 118, 157, 161–162, 203–204, 221, 243, 251, 260, 266
  A Visit 34, 49, 51
  cliché 42
  eroticized images of… 55
  Harem and Home Gallery 34, 43
  images of… 57, 100, 115
  literature 51
  The Colonial Harem 104
  The Light of the Harem 251
  Thirty Years in the Harem 159
  women 99, 161, 202–204
  Walker's portraits of… 130, 202, 204
Harman, Harriet 157
Harvey, Annie Jane 52
Herzog, Christoph 183
hijab 54
historical genre painting 132, 135, 137, 148
historical record (photographs as…) 99–105
Hobart-Hampden, Edith Katherine 128
Hoca Ali Rıza 152
Hoefer, Ferdinand 184
Hogenberg, Franz *Civitas Orbis Terrarum* 78
Holman Hunt, William 33, 37, 38, 243, 244, 251
  The Lantern Maker's Courtship 38
Holy Land 103, 104, 123
  John Frederick Lewis 171
homoeroticism 52, 69
hooks, bell 56
Hornby, Lady Emelia 205, 206
Humboldt, Alexander von 264, 267
Hunter, William 157

I

Ibn Warraq *Defending the West* 42, 66
iconography 65, 221–227
idolatry 91, 92
Illustrated London News 135, 167, 264
imperialism 51, 102, 121, 135, 161–162, 245
  European 115, 137
  itinerant 121
  see also travelers
  Western/non-Western 24, 52, 162
  see also Ottoman Empire
indexicality 100
Ingres, Jean Auguste Dominique *Odalisque with a Slave* 35
  Turkish Bath 42
Iran 67, 77, 82, 83, 185–186, 251
  Osman Hamdi Bey in… 183–186
  see also Persia
Iraq 36, 53, 77, 83, 183
Islam
  and nationalism 158
  architecture 82, 104
  decorative art 43, 82
  images of 37, 52–54, 58, 66–67, 146–147, 244
  religious practice 104, 157, 251
Ismail Paşa, Khedive 227
Istanbul *see also* Constantinople
  Cağaloğlu Hamamı 38
  images of… see John Frederick Lewis; Osman Hamdi Bey; Mary Walker
  military schools 233–234
  nineteenth-century 90, 100, 127–137, 159, 161
  Ottoman Istanbul 19, 23–24, 51, 56, 115ff., 127, 211ff., 233ff., 264
  press 127ff.
  representations of 24, 135–137
  School of Fine Arts (Istanbul) 148, 233
  twentieth-century 152

J

Jacobson, Ken 103–106
  Odalisques and Arabesques, Orientalist Photography 1839–1935 104
Jazzar Pasha 80
Jerichau-Baumann, Elisabeth 52, 132
Jerusalem 34, 36, 65, 67, 78, 82, 103
Jewish Museum of Greece in Athens 93, 95
John, Augustus 34, 58
Jones, Owen *Grammar of Ornament* 82

K

Kabbani, Rana 67
Kâmil, Abdullah 127, 132, 135, 137, 204
Kauffman, Michael 78, 85
Kaye, Lieut. D. S. 103
Kerr, Martin
Khan, Aaffreen 35
Khan, Yasmin 35
Klee, Paul 33
Klein, Naomi *No Logo* 37
Knight, Richard Payne 120
Knox, Robert *The Races of Man* 159
Köçeoğlu, Krikor 129–130
Köprülü Fazıl Ahmet Paşa 211
Kretzschmer, Johann Hermann 225
Kufic script 130
Kurdistan 186ff.
Kurds 159, 160, 187–190, 264
Kütahya tile workshops 151

L

landscape painting 115–123, 202, 223, 233–238
landscape photography 123
Lane, Edward William *Manners and Customs of the Modern Egyptians* 172, 243, 248
Lane-Poole, Stanley 157
de Lasteyrie, Ferdinand 262
Latham, John *God is Great (no.2)* 35
Lauder, Robert Scott *David Roberts Esq. in the Dress he wore in Palestine* 171
Lawrence, Colonel T. E. 34, 58
Layard, Lady Enid 204
Layard, Sir Henry 128, 202, 205
Lear, Edward 67, 78, 82, 245
  Mount Sinai 80
  Beirut 53
  Travels of Edward Lear 84
Lee, Vernon 248, 254 n. 34
Leighton, Frederic 33, 167, 244–252
  A Roman Lady 247
  The Arts of Industry as Applied to War and to Peace 251
  Bath of Psyche 38
  Cimabue's Celebrated Madonna is Carried through the Streets of Florence 248
  Interior of the Grand Mosque of Damascus 251
  Lieder ohne Worte 247
  Odalisque 248
Leighton House 77
  Arab Hall 249, 250, 251
Levant Herald 159, 200
Lewis, John Frederick 33, 43, 67, 82, 167–176, 244–252, 259–268
  A Corfiot Warrior Reclining 244, 245
  A Frank Encampment in the Desert of Mt. Sinai, 1842 169, 251, 252
  A Lady Receiving Visitors 248–249
  A Syrian Scheik, Egypt 173
  An Armenian Lady, Cairo 34
  The Arab Scribe, Cairo 261
  Bouquet 248
  Easter Day at Rome: Pilgrims and Peasants 244
  Camels in the Desert 260
  In the Bezestein, El Khan Kalil, Cairo (The Carpet Seller) 169, 170, 245, 246
  The Doubtful Coin 175
  The Halt in the Desert 260, 261
  The Hhareem 34, 260, 261, 262, 266
  The Mid-Day Meal 34, 42
Lewis, John Hardwicke 169
Lindau, Rudolf 190–193
lithographs 82, 92, 93, 171, 234
London bombings of July 7 25
looting, museum 36
Loudun, Eugène 262
Louvre 81
Lowell, John Jr 264

M

MacDermot, Brian 68
MacFarlane, Charles 160
  Kismet or The Doom of Turkey 233–234
Mackenzie, Sir Donald 206
Madra, Beral 70
Maghrib 78, 106
Mahmud I 117
Mahmud II, Sultan 116, 118, 224–225, 227
Makdisi, Ussama 55, 145, 183–185, 193
Mamluk
  architecture 82
  Egypt 78, 148
  tombs 82
Manas, Rupen 225
Manasie, Rubens 225
Mantz, Paul 268
marketing strategy 37ff.
Mathaf Gallery 68, 170, 267
Maundrell, Reverend Henry 78

Mayer, Luigi 79, 84
medieval past 115, 148
Mehemet Ali 67
Melek Hanım *Thirty Years in the Harem* 159
Melkonyan, Mıgırdıç 238
Melling, Antoine Ignace *Voyage pittoresque de Constantinople et des rives du Bosphore* 122
Melville, Arthur *The Arab Interior* 38, 41, 42, 43, 44
Memorial Art Gallery (Rochester NY) 33
Mesopotamia 36
Midhat Pasha (Midhat Paşa) 151, 184, 186, 191, 193
Milet, Éric *Orientalist Photographs 1870–1950* 105–106
Miletus, theatre at… (William Pars) 80
Military Academy (Istanbul) 233
military
  artists 233–238
  life, images of… 103–104, 233–234
  schools 233–238
miscegenation 158–161
Mokkatam Hills (Cairo) 103
monogenesis 160
Morocco, sketches of… 128
Moss, Kate 38
Motika, Raoul 183
Mount Lebanon 82
Mount Nemrud (Nemrud Dağı) 186, 193
Mour, Jean-Baptiste van 216, 217
Muhammad ‘Ali, Pasha of Egypt 34
Muller, William 173
museology 90–93, 137
Museum of Islamic Art (Doha) 67
museum stagings 90
Muslim
  community 35
  Council of Great Britain 35
  cultures 52–54, 58, 127, 145, 148, 185, 264, 266
  Public Affairs Committee 35
  women 129, 157
Mustafa Reshid Pasha 202–203

N

Najd Collection 68, 267
Napoleon I 80–81, 222, 223
Napoleon III 260, 262
narrative style 184
narratives 89, 101, 104, 137, 157
  museum 90–93
  Orientalist 69, 191
  travel 157, 159, 161
  Western 67
narratologies 91
National Army Museum (London) 102
National Gallery of Scotland 38, 41, 43
Nazlı Hanım, Princess 52, 129, 131–132
Neuberger, Rabbi Julia 53
Newton, Charles 78, 83, 85, 176
Nightingale, Florence 81
Nikosios, Panayoti 211–212
Nile 81–82, 103, 104, 173
noble savage 185–186
Nochlin, Linda 36, 42

O

d’Ohsson, Mouradgea 221, 222
Old Watercolour Society 244
Omar, Rageh 53
Orientalism (Edward Said) 55, 67, 68, 99, 123
Orientalism 33ff., 49ff., 65ff., 99–106, 145–147, 243–252
  alla turca 183–184
  American 35
  British 19–28, 49, 51, 54, 65, 127, 128, 137, 243
  European 68, 69, 145, 147
  exhibitions of… 33
  genre 147, 150, 115
  Ottoman 20, 24, 55, 183–185, 193
  paradigm 49, 99, 147
  romantic 115
Orientalist painting 20, 49, 55, 65–70
  British 33, 42, 65, 243, 248, 252
  French 36, 259–268
Ortiz, Oscar 118
Osgan Efendi 186–190
Osman Hamdi Bey 72 n. 27, 129, 131–135, 145–152, 183–193
Osmanlı 127ff.
Osmanlis 160
Other, the 55, 117, 121, 122
Ottoman Empire 77–84, 115–117, 127–128, 135–136, 160–161, 211–217, 221–222
  architecture 82, 146, 148, 152 n. 6
  antiquities 79
  artifacts 49, 68, 78, 221–229
  dress 148, 170, 172, 178 n. 50, 51, 216
  Egypt 78
  navy 128
  State education reform 129, 130
  sultanate 105
  traditional arts and crafts 151

travelers 49, 78–79
Ottoman-Armenian painters 127, 129–130
Ottomanism 127, 130, 132, 137

P

Page, William 82
Paget, Violet
see Lee, Vernon 248, 254 n. 34
Palestine 34, 77, 93
Pardoe, Julia 27, 52, 159, 224
Parkes Bonington, Richard 263
Pars, William 79, 80
patronage 23, 26, 28, 51, 52, 131, 132, 222
Pears, Edwin 128, 135, 204, 205
Peirce, Leslie 161
Pera Museum 20, 22, 37, 49, 56, 58, 65, 90, 91, 129
Persia 117, 185, 188
see also Iran
Persians 117, 185, 188, 212
Phanariot 78, 212
Phillips, Thomas *Portrait of a Nobleman in the Dress of an Albanian* 171
photograph albums 101, 102, 104
photographic realism 150
photographic record 101–102
photographs 51, 52, 53, 65
Middle East 99, 104–106
nineteenth-century 100–102
photography 99–106, 122, 123, 234, 237, 243
physical anthropology 267
Pichelstein, Stanisław Kotska 213
picturesque 115–123
pleasure, esthetic 49–59, 133–135, 151
pleasure, politics of… 49–59
politics of display 127
polygenesis 160
Poniatowski, King August 213, 215
Portet, Jean 225
portrait medallions 225
portraiture 33, 34, 211–216, 221–223
postcolonial studies 49
Prettejohn, Elizabeth *Art for Art's Sake: Aestheticism in Victorian Painting* 244
Preziosi, Amadeo 83, 93, 202, 205
Price, David 169
Price, Uvedale 120
Prinsep, Val Ayesha 35
Prisse d'Avennes, Achille Constant Théodore Émile 81, 173
Puchstein, Otto 186

Q

Qatar 67, 69, 85
Qatar Museums Authority 34, 67

R

race 53, 89, 157–62, 264, 266, 268
racialized nationalism 157–158, 160
representation, nature of… 89–90
Repton, Humphrey 120
Reuter, William 227
Revett, Nicholas 79
Richardson, Alan 34, 36
Rifa'a al-Tahtawi 67
Risi, Nanna 247
Roberts, David 33, 37, 77, 171, 173, 243
Robertson, James 128, 135, 138 n. 9
Rochard, Simon Jacques 172
Rogier, Camille 82
Rose, Andrea 36
Rosenthal, Donald 36, 260
Rosewarne, Lauren 38
Royal Academy 33, 167
Royal Geographical Society 84
Rubio, Luigi 225
Ruskin, John 122, 169, 243

S

Saadiyat ("Happiness") Island 70
Said, Edward 35, 36, 42, 54, 55, 59, 66–67, 69, 157, 243
Covering Islam 67
Orientalism 55, 67, 68, 99, 123
Salamandra, Christa 56, 68, 71 n. 19
Salt, Henry 81
Sandby, Paul 80
Sandwith, Thomas 205
Sargent, John Singer 33
Şaşiyan, Boğos 129–130
Saz, Leyla 203
Schlesinger, Henri-Guillaume 224–225
School of Fine Arts (Istanbul) 148, 233
Schranz, Joseph 234
Searight Collection 77–85
Searight, Rodney 77–85
Searight, Sarah *The British in the Middle East* 77
Sebah, P. 103
Seddon, Thomas *Jerusalem and the Valley of Jehoshaphat from the Hill of Evil Counsel* 53

Şeker Ahmed Paşa 128, 132
Selim III, Sultan 223–224, 227
Serres, Étienne 267
Serviçen, Verjin 129–130
Shafik Gabr Collection 69, 72 n. 24, 175
Sharjah Art Museum 49, 65, 70
Silk Road 78
Sinai Desert 251
Smith, Spencer 223
Society of Dilettanti 79, 263
Society of Painters in Water Colours 169, 263
Sontag, Susan 121
Sotheby's 69
Spanton, William Silas 169
Spencer, Stanley 33
Spilsbury, Francis 80
Straw, Jack 38, 157
Süleyman (the Magnificent) 58, 78, 147, 227
sultanic portraiture 221–229

T

Tanzimat 116, 118, 130, 145, 146, 185, 204, 246, 221, 225, 227
Tarabya 127, 128, 129, 132, 204
Tarsia, Jacobus 213–215
Tate Britain 33ff., 52ff., 65, 70
  East West: Objects Between Cultures 35
  The Lure of the East 33ff., 49ff., 65ff., 82, 85, 90, 95, 99, 137, 243, 259
Tenniel, Sir John 82
Tepebaşı Municipal Gardens 129
Thackeray, William Makepeace 172–173, 248, 264
  Notes of a Journey from Cornhill to Grand Cairo 170, 244–245
Thevenot, Jean de *Travels in the Levant* 157
Thornton, Lynne *The Orientalists* 77
Thornton, Thomas 159
Tophane 82, 117, 118, 202
Topkapı Palace (Topkapı Sarayı) 70, 78, 105, 118, 223, 224, 225, 227
trading routes 78, 81, 212
travel diary 187, 215
travel literature 115, 121, 123, 159, 187
travelers 52, 82, 159, 224
travelogs 50, 79, 116, 120, 135, 186, 187, 191
tropes 69, 115, 145, 245, 251
  East/West 117, 157
  picturesque 120, 123
  visual 23,115, 123
Turkey
  and modern art market 69
  contemporary 56–58, 123, 158
  military schools in… 233–234
  of the Ottomans 160–161
Turks 117, 157, 160, 162, 183, 200, 202, 212

V

Vaka Brown, Demetra 51
Valerio, Théodore 264, 266, 267
Varisco, Daniel Martin 42
Vefik Paşa, Ahmed 136, 140 n. 42, 151
veil 51, 157–162, 264
Viardot, Louis 145, 152 n. 1
Victoria and Albert Museum 77ff.

W

Walker, Mary Adelaide 26, 128, 130–131, 135–136, 199–206
  and Fatma Sultan 52, 131, 203–204
Warren, Henry 82
Washington, Reverend George 128, 204
watercolors
  at the Exposition Universelle 27, 259–268
  costume book 217
  in Searight Collection 77–85
  John Frederick Lewis 169–170, 173, 244
  Mary Walker 130, 204, 205
Watkins, John 167
Weeks, Emily 248, 252 n. 1
White, John 263
Wilkie, David 82, 216, 243
  Abdülmecid's portrait 34, 51–52, 70, 225–226, 233
Willyams, Cooper 80
women patrons 131
women, agency of… 50, 157, 248
women's art networks 130
women's education
  Association of Women in Favour of Education 204
  Greek School for Girls (Tarabya) 129
women's history, research in… 49
Woolner, Thomas 169, 173

Y

Yale Center for British Art 36, 49, 52, 65
Yıldız Palace 221, 227, 235
Young Turk Revolution 148

Z

Zangaki 103
Zeyneb Hanım 51
Ziya Akbulut, Ahmet 235
Zonaro, Fausto 227
Zorn, Anders 100